BeingGazza

Also by Paul Gascoigne

Gazza: My Story (with Hunter Davies)

BeingGazza

My Journey to Hell and Back

Paul Gascoigne

with John McKeown and Hunter Davies

headline

Copyright © 2006 Paul Gascoigne

Appendices © 2006 John McKeown

The right of Paul Gascoigne to be identified as the Author of
the Work has been asserted by him in accordance with
the Copyright, Designs and Patents Act 1988.

First published in 2006
by HEADLINE BOOK PUBLISHING

1

Apart from any use permitted under UK copyright law, this publication
may only be reproduced, stored, or transmitted, in any form, or by any
means, with prior permission in writing of the publishers or, in the
case of reprographic production, in accordance with the terms
of licences issued by the Copyright Licensing Agency.

Every effort has been made to fulfil requirements with regard to
reproducing copyright material. The author and publisher will be
glad to rectify any omissions at the earliest opportunity.

A CIP catalogue record for this title is available from the British Library

Hardback ISBN 0 7553 1542 1
Trade paperback ISBN 0 7553 1561 8

Text design: Ben Cracknell Studios
Typeset by Avon DataSet Ltd, Bidford on Avon, Warwickshire
Printed and bound in Great Britain by Clays Ltd St Ives plc

Headline's policy is to use papers that are natural, renewable and
recyclable products and made from wood grown in sustainable forests.
The logging and manufacturing processes are expected to conform to
the environmental regulations of the country of origin.

HEADLINE BOOK PUBLISHING
A division of Hodder Headline
338 Euston Road
London NW1 3BH

www.headline.co.uk
www.hodderheadline.com

www.paulgascoigne.biz

For George Best
1946–2005

Contents

Preface

I was signing copies of my life story in Manchester when I got the idea to write this book. Someone came up to us at the book signing, and just quietly told us how much that book helped them. They thanked us for doing it. I was surprised, and really pleased.

It happened at book signings up and down the UK – people telling me it was a relief reading the story of my problems, because they thought, 'I can't believe it – Gazza's got the same problem as me!' I was playing pool the other day with my sister, and the manager of the pool house came up and said he wanted to thank me because, after reading my story, his wife's panic attacks had got less. I was amazed that that book could mean so much to people.

I wanted to do *this* book even though I knew doing the sessions for it, and going back through everything, would be hard. I hadn't seen my therapist – Johnny Mac as I call him – for about a year and I knew I'd have to go back over all that stuff again – my childhood and all the way up to today. I knew I'd be digging things up, going over and over things in my head. But I needed help – I'd got into bad times again – and I knew I needed to face places in the past I'd rather not face. So I've faced it, and it has been hard – really hard. I've had an unbelievably difficult year but, with the help of my therapist, I've kept fighting. And the fight's not over yet. I'll always have these illnesses, but I'm learning all the time how to do the right things to stay on top of them and to have a good life.

In that first book I didn't go into the details of these different illnesses I've got. It was later the idea came to write this book to show what it's really been like, and to talk about all the therapy I've done, so that maybe it would help people with the same problems. I hope it does.

March 2006

Acknowledgements

My thanks go to Mum and Dad, Anna, Carl and Lindsay, Jimmy Five Bellies Gardner, Bill Kenwright, Dr Neil Brener and Dr Fran Moore for all their support. Also, for their help in writing this book, I'd like to thank Johnny McKeown, Hunter Davies and Emma Littlewood for all their hard work, and Jochen Encke, Tim Leighton and Mark Dunn for their feedback and advice. Thanks also to Jane and Kat at JMM Management, to David Wilson at Headline, and to Calum Best. And, finally, thanks to all the other crazy people 'in the rooms' for listening.

Paul John (Gazza) Gascoigne

Chronology of his life, including some dramatis personae who will appear in this book ...

Personal

Born: 27 May 1967, Gateshead, County Durham

Father: John, hodcarrier

Mother: Carol

Siblings: two sisters, Anna and Lindsay; brother, Carl

Education: left school at sixteen, two CSE passes

Marriage: to Sheryl (Shel) 1996, divorced 1998

Children: one son, Regan, born 1996, plus two stepchildren, Bianca born 1986, Mason born 1989

Meets Jimmy ('Five Bellies') Gardner, best friend, 1983

Meets John McKeown (Johnny Mac), his therapist, at the Priory Hospital, London, 1998

Awards

Young Player of the Year, 1988

BBC Sports Personality of the Year, 1990

Scottish Football Writers' Association and Scottish Professional Football Players' Player of the Year, 1996

Gazza: My Story published by Headline 2004, winner of Sports Book of the Year, 2004

Football career

1983   apprentice at Newcastle United (schoolboy from 1980)

1985   turns professional at Newcastle United

1988   transferred to Tottenham Hotspur for £2.3 million

1992   transferred to Lazio, Italy, for £5.5 million

1995   transferred to Glasgow Rangers for £4.3 million

1998   transferred to Middlesbrough for £3.45 million

2000   free transfer to Everton

2002   free transfer to Burnley

2003   player-coach, Gansu Tianma, China

2003   Wolverhampton Wanderers reserves

2004   player-coach, Boston United

2005   player-coach, Algarve United

2005   manager, Kettering Town

England appearances

57 caps, 10 goals, between 1988 and 1998, including

World Cup semi-final, 1990, and European Championship semi-

final, 1996

Paul goes to see his therapist

Paul

It's late summer 2005 and today I'm on my way to see Johnny Mac. His office is in a posh street, posh address, in London, but Johnny's far from posh. In fact, in some ways I think his background is similar to mine. I've picked up bits, just when it comes out, in relation to me, and what's happened to me, but he doesn't talk about himself much. They're not supposed to, are they? Bloody hell, I hope not. I'm doing the paying, so he can listen to me – I mean, help me. That's the idea.

He's a real Scouser, which I suppose is why I get on with him so well. He's an Evertonian, though I hadn't yet played for Everton when I first met him. I was still with Middlesbrough. It was in, let me see, must have been 1998 when I first met Johnny. It was at a stage in my life when I was still in denial so, afterwards, I sort of pretended it had never happened, that I hadn't seen him, that there was nothing wrong with me. Well, nothing that a few drinks couldn't cure. That's what I imagined then.

I'm not far from Harley Street. I saw the sign. That's the famous street for doctors and medical help. I've always wondered if there was a Doctor Harley. S'pose there must have been. Was he related to John Harley, that little kid who played for Chelsea a few years ago? I did play against him. I think he went to Fulham. I wonder where he is now? Not heard of him recently. That happens with lots of players. Once they retire, or move down the divisions, they sort of seem to sink out of sight, slip away. I wish I could.

Or it could have been the bloke who invented Harley Davidsons. Funnily enough, I used to come and visit Johnny on my Harley Davidson. This was when I was staying at Shel's (my ex-wife), at a time when I had shitloads of Harley Davidson bikes. About nine at one time. Only one now. I've just bought it. A Hot Rod. Built from scratch.

This area of London is pretty handy for me actually. Although I wish it wasn't. It's very near the Princess Grace Hospital, just round the corner. I have a season ticket for that, ha ha. I've taken all my best injuries there, over the years. I first went in 1991, playing for Spurs, after the Cup final when I did my leg in, my own stupid fault. It looked as if my career was over. I went in an ambulance, while the game was still on. I managed to catch the last bit of the game from my hospital bed. I saw poor old Des Walker head the ball into his own net from a corner. We'd won the Cup, the biggest achievement in my football life so far. I ended up with a winner's medal – but I felt I didn't deserve it. I'd acted like a mad bastard. Typical.

I've just come down to London from Newcastle for the day to catch up on a few things. I've got a rented flat in the Jesmond area of Newcastle. It's a smart new block, but I don't really like it. I hate living on my own. If I get a new job, then I might buy somewhere to live nearby, to be handy for it. I haven't owned a house for, must be the last seven years. I've either been in hotels, flats or hospitals. Don't remind me.

I'm seeing Johnny to go over stuff. It's been a while since I saw him. I was abroad for a fair whack of the summer, in Portugal. I do need to talk about what's recently happened but, in other ways, I feel I don't need him.

I've managed to conquer quite a few things in the last couple of years.

I don't have as many compulsive obsessions as I used to, such as having to have things neat and tidy, all in a certain order. That used to drive me mad — and everyone else.

I remember when I was at Glasgow Rangers I bought this house not far from Ally McCoist's. He was in a panic, thinking I was actually moving next door. I was in fact exactly 1.8 miles from his house. Coisty measured it out.

There was a pub near his house that I used to go to and, one night, I was there till about two in the morning, pretty pissed. I suddenly felt really hungry. I couldn't get a taxi so I thought, 'I know what, I'll break into Coisty's.' I'd been to his house many times so I knew which window was left open.

I get in, as quietly as possible, and make myself a huge sandwich, opening all the tins I can find and taking stuff from his fridge. Coisty is upstairs in bed and he suddenly hears this noise in his kitchen. He gets out this baseball bat that he keeps under the bed to arm himself against burglars — not to practise his swing with (I don't think, anyway). He comes down the stairs, rattling it along the banister, making as much noise as possible to frighten away the intruder.

In the kitchen, he doesn't see it's me at first because I'm on a chair. I've cleaned up all the mess I'd made and I'm now arranging all the tins on his shelf. I was upset that he didn't keep them very tidily.

'It's you, Gazza!' shouts Coisty. 'What a fucking relief!'

I told him I was just tidying his kitchen for him, which of course he couldn't understand. He went back to bed. I was a bit more sober by then so, when I'd tidied everything, I managed to walk home.

Today that story makes me smile, as do all the other times in my life I became obsessed by having things tidy. But I've other things to worry about now, God knows. Probably always will.

I've been through lots of therapists, and therapies, in my life — all sorts, all over the place. I often think some of them have just been watching the clock, not really bothered. Others talk a lot of shite and I've no idea what they're on about. Johnny's been good for me. The best I've ever had. In bad times, I have gone to see him every week for months at a time. At other times I might miss a few months, but we usually still talk on the phone.

I have known Johnny since I was admitted into the Priory Hospital. As I've already said, I don't know too much about him but what I do know suggests that he has had his own personal battles in the past. That comes across when we speak, at times, say, when I am struggling with an issue and he shares one or two examples from his own life. I think he is about four or five years older than me – looks more, ha ha – only kidding, Johnny. He's from a working-class background and grew up in Birkenhead, Merseyside, and is a true Evertonian. He has worked in the counselling field for a long time, I think at other football clubs, and I know he worked in prisons for a good few years. All that stuff helps me to get on with him. I can relate to him easily. He doesn't judge. That's one of the reasons I keep going back to him.

I'm going to start seeing him again, after a gap of about a year, and I know what will happen – I'll have to go over all the same old stuff, to revisit the past, the recent past as well as my childhood. I don't know if I can face that. And since I've decided to do this book, I'll have to think about it and talk about it afterwards – about what it's like, before and after therapy, and about what else is happening in my life, all the other things that are going wrong. I'll be doing my own head in. I'll be awake all night and every night, going over things. So I thought, 'Bugger it, nice idea, but I'm not up to it.'

Then I thought, 'Now that I do need help again, and am going to re-start therapy, that's what you have to do anyway – to open up, you need to go back, visit places you might not want to visit, and contemplate possibilities and causes you've been too scared to think about or admit . . .'

Johnny's place is in this big, seven-storey house. It looks like a house where people live, not like offices or a medical building. In fact, it's two big houses knocked together. It still has two entrances. When I first went to see him there, I didn't know which fucking door to go into.

Inside, it's like a sort of old-fashioned posh hotel. It's got two reception rooms with antiques and classy magazines. They also have stuff like notices and leaflets offering to help you: 'STOP SMOKING IN ONE HOUR – 95% Success Rate.' I never read them as they're all bollocks. Yeah, of course, I still smoke, though I lie about how many, but I'm not bothered. If smoking was my biggest problem in life, I'd be laughing, ha ha ha.

In this building, where Johnny has his rooms, there are about twenty different therapists, specialists, doctors and consultants. I could probably keep them all occupied, if I put my mind to it. Spread my custom around. Give them all a bit of work.

Johnny's room has a white sofa, two white chairs and off-white carpet and walls. The only bit of colour comes from some framed theatre posters on a wall. I find myself looking at them if I get bored. Sometimes I just go for a walk about the room.

I always start my sessions the same way. I throw myself on his couch and say to Johnny, 'Can I smoke?' He then says, 'No you can't.' I say, 'Fucking hell!' Then we get on with it . . .

―――――――

Dear Paul

I'm taking the honor of writing in your book first. You're such an amazing guy. You light up the room with humor and laughter. Stay true to yourself. I hope we keep in touch.

Love

Patty

Paul's first session: Getting back on track

John

I hope this book will benefit Paul and benefit his readers and fans. I've known him since 1998, and we've worked together on and off since then. He's wanted to make some of his counselling and therapy into a book for a couple of years, to get across to the readers a realistic picture of what it's like managing and struggling with his illnesses, and hopefully to help anyone with similar problems. It's difficult to put something as private as therapy into the public domain, so he's selected excerpts from some of his sessions that he felt comfortable sharing with the public. Of course there were other sessions and conversations that weren't included, but I think what's here will be revealing in an interesting and helpful way.

It's been some months since Paul and I have had a properly structured one-to-one session. He's keen to get back on track, telling me he's fully committed to doing some more work on himself. Paul had a good stretch of time – over two years – of managing his illnesses very effectively and feeling healthy and balanced. Then things started to go wrong again. So, before we start, I remind him that as we haven't met for a while he should begin by talking about the time from when he feels that everything started to go wrong, and to take his time doing so. He's visibly shaky but keen to get going straight away.

When a client comes to therapy for the first time, or returns after a long break, the therapist usually spends the first one or two sessions gathering as much information as possible. As the therapist, I don't interrupt the client's flow unless it's necessary. It's crucial that the client shares where they are at, what got them there and how it feels to be there. Paul needs to talk.

Paul

Can I smoke? Fucking hell!

I had a really good two-plus years when I wasn't drinking, I was sober, and the other parts of my illness were under control. I was on top of things and my recovery was going great. I was the same person I'd always been, I still had fun, but I was clean. People said to me, 'Why did you ever drink – you're such a great person when you're sober?' I always thought I was just as nice when I was drinking, I couldn't tell the difference myself, but people tell me I'm a pain when I'm drinking.

Anyway, things had been going pretty well for me, the best since I'd given up playing football four years ago. Then I signed up for the TV show *Strictly Ice Dancing* and got injured; it was a terrible injury and it wasn't even through football. I'm used to that at least. At the time, I'd been training really hard. My OCD (obsessive compulsive disorder) had just started to kick in a bit, I'd be training all day every day – and I wasn't eating properly, I was eating just a sandwich and wine gums. The dance programme was a one-off to go out on Boxing Day 2004, but I never actually took part in it in the end. During the rehearsals I fell on my back and injured myself. I was in terrible pain, but still danced one more time.

I then headed to the airport with my dad – I was on the way to Madrid for a charity match – but I never got on the plane. I went to pick up my bag and something went in my neck. The pain was so bad my dad took me straight back into London, to the Princess Grace Hospital where I was given an epidural. That's how excruciating the pain in my back and neck was. I couldn't move my arm. Dave Seaman took my place on *Strictly Ice Dancing* in the end, and won it! I was in the hospital for eight days, and while I was there I was given morphine-based painkillers. That's where the trouble started.

I came out of the hospital and went home to my family for Christmas, but I couldn't really join in with it all or enjoy it. I felt fluey, had a pain in my chest, and was absolutely freezing – I was shivering all the time. I rang Dave Seaman and the physio Gary Lewin at Arsenal who told me to go for an X-ray. After that, I was rushed into hospital – I had pneumonia, and was given injections for the pain.

I just couldn't believe what was going on. It was hard to accept – that I'd got injured through doing something that wasn't playing football, and had then caught pneumonia in the hospital. It's something that happens – people catch infections in hospitals and it's difficult to prevent it from happening. I also got a blood clot while I was in there. Because of all this, I was on *so* many different pills. I had warfarin for the blood clot, strong antibiotics for the pneumonia and morphine-based painkillers for all the pain. I remember thinking I was going to die from that pneumonia, feeling like I couldn't breathe. Now I understand how people can die from that illness.

When I came out of hospital I said I couldn't stay on morphine-based painkillers, because of my addictive personality, but it was difficult because the medical staff didn't really know my background and also I was in terrible pain, and those, of course, are the tablets that help. So they had to give them to me. So I started taking one tablet four times a day, and then it went up to two tablets four times a day, and so on. The OCD came back then. I was constantly checking and re-checking doors and windows, and cleaning and tidying up. All the obsessions came flooding back after I'd been more or less in control for such a good long period of time. The old voice was back in charge again.

At Christmas, when I'd been so ill, I'd taken some of that flu medicine
. . . you know . . . Benylin. What I hadn't realised was that there are two
types of Benylin – one containing alcohol and one without. Anyway, when
I realised I'd been taking the one with alcohol in it I thought, 'That's it, I've
just thrown away two years of sobriety. I've had a drink!' So when I was
recovering from the injury, I decided I may as well have a drink seeing as I
wasn't clean any more anyway. But it was crazy because I started training
again, while still taking the painkillers, so I couldn't really tell whether or not
I was damaging my body with the training. And then for three weeks, every
night after training I'd have just one drink in the evening. Then I began to
think, 'I've had one drink, I may as well have another.'

Soon after that I really tried to get it all back under control, knock the
drinking on the head, but the old voices were back and it wasn't long before
I started drinking Red Bull again – one of my addictive problems I'd
managed to get to grips with over that past year. To some people Red Bull
sounds like a really harmless soft drink, but it's actually banned in some
countries. It contains a lot of caffeine, and I was drinking fifteen cans a
day, which is like at least fifteen cups of coffee a day. Way too much, I
know. I was on a high all the time, with the shakes. Sometimes I couldn't
stop shaking, and I couldn't sleep. I was in my flat in Jesmond at the time.
I'd sleep for around two hours, and go for a run at two o'clock in the
morning, then go to the gym at 6 a.m. I'd train until about 10 a.m., then
go back on the Red Bull. My OCD went off the scale then. I was constantly
checking the door, the bed, the light switches, tidying everything away,
shutting all the cupboard doors, turning the TV off, turning the stereo off.
I have to have everything perfect, and if it's not perfect I can't concentrate.
I was absolutely exhausted, I can't tell you how exhausting it was. I'd leave
the lights off in the house and I'd be going around in the dark so as not to
have to worry about turning the lights off and checking them. Then I'd
want a drink or a painkiller to calm me down. People don't understand
why you can't stop, but there's always this voice in my head saying, 'Have
another, have another.' And I think, 'Fuck it, I've had one, I may as well have
another.'

As I've said, I'd had trouble with Red Bull before then. Overdoing it. In fact, when I was in Cottonwood (the clinic in America) in 2004, just for a couple of weeks, to get me straight before all the promotional work for my autobiography started off, the American psychiatrist reckoned the Red Bull that I'd been drinking at that time could have been one of the triggers that helped set off one of my bipolar episodes. What she said was that, as long as I was taking the right medication and not messing around with any other mood-altering substances, the bipolar would be under control, but hitting the Red Bull might have helped trigger another episode. It was she who first diagnosed me as bipolar, back in 2003.

I was in a bit of a state round about then. When I was on the Red Bull for the first time, I got myself into some dangerous situations. One time, before that visit to Cottonwood in spring 2004, when I was out in the car, I suddenly swerved to avoid a big lorry coming at me that I hadn't seen. The car skidded and I went into the back of an Asda van, and the air bag blew up in my face. I was breathalysed at the scene but of course it came up clear as I hadn't been drinking. The paramedics wanted me to go to the hospital with them. I said I was okay but I wasn't, I was in a state so me dad took me to the hospital where they gave me some Valium to calm me down. I wasn't actually injured, and I hadn't thought much about it all, but the next morning when I looked out and saw the car I thought, 'My God, I could have died.' It hadn't hit me at the time, but it hit me really hard the next morning.

Not long after that accident I found a mole on my head and panicked. I phoned Bryan Robson, the Boro manager, about it, who got me to see a doctor in Manchester. I had to go to a lunch, and I came away feeling really full up and like I couldn't breathe, worrying about this mole. When I saw the doctor he laughed, and said that I'd got myself so stressed out I'd burst a blood vessel. It wasn't a mole at all.

Then, later that spring, I tried to come off the Red Bull. But I needed something, I had to have something, so I went gambling. I've never really been a proper gambler, it's not really me, although I did have a phase of gambling years before when I was seventeen. But this time I won on the very first race, and I thought, 'I'm going to keep on winning.' It got to the point with the gambling where I once took £5,000 out in the casino at one time. I was in tears, knowing I was going to lose the whole £5,000. But that time I won £11,000. I got in my car to drive home, drove around the car park and came back. I thought, 'I've won all this money, I may as well have another go at it.' I bet £3,000, lost it, then another £3,000, lost it. All in all I lost £9,000 in two hours.

At that stage I didn't want to go into a clinic because I thought the press would say I was going in for drink. I didn't want to carry on with the gambling because I knew it would get worse – and I knew I'd hit the bottle. I wrote a note at the bookies and signed it, saying I wasn't allowed to go in and place bets there. I did it at the casino as well, banned myself from gambling – but it didn't work because there was another casino I could go to and there are bookies everywhere.

I went to London and went to AA and talked about the Red Bull. Then I did go to the clinic in America, Cottonwood, for two weeks, and told them about the gambling. They got me to go to GA (Gamblers Anonymous). I went to one meeting and knew straight away that it was exactly the same as with the booze: I have an addictive personality. The painkillers, the drink, the Red Bull, the gambling, the food. It's all the same thing.

I've got a battle on my hands every day of my life. My friend Paul Davis, who used to play for Arsenal, asked me, 'What would it be like to have a normal life?' I actually don't know. I don't have a normal life. Every day I get up and I have to deal with booze, food, my OCD, medication for panic attacks, the whole lot. No matter how well I face the battle, I still have to start again from scratch the next day. It's exhausting. I can't take it or leave it like other people. While I was getting drunk it was great, but once I *was* drunk it was a nightmare.

From that time in Cottonwood in 2004 until the *Strictly Ice Dancing* injury I was sober – I had been for a while anyway, since I got back from Cottonwood in 2003, after China where things had been going wrong for me – and on top of things generally. Now here we are in 2005 and since the painkillers, the Red Bull again and then drinking in Portugal over the summer, it's started going wrong again. I've got a little bit of knowledge about how to get back on the right track. Early in the morning, as soon as I wake up, I write my problems down to get them out of the way, and then I shut the door behind me. I can't conquer my fears until I face them. I know I have a chemical imbalance and I have to take medication to address the imbalance, and for two to three years while I was getting clean I'd have massive panic attacks. They think that was originally triggered by cocaine, which I took a couple of months after leaving Everton, in summer 2002. People think it's fun to take cocaine but it's dangerous. I found that out the hard way.

I sometimes wake up at night and lie there worrying about dying. I worry about what I've achieved and what I haven't achieved, and whether or not I've got time to get it all done. The thought of dying will make me jump out of bed. I watched *The Running Man*, a film with Arnold Schwarzenegger, set in the future. It's about a deadly reality TV show for criminals, and I hated it; I couldn't stand watching it, but I still watched it. He has to battle to survive. I've got this battle on my hands for the rest of my life. But I know, if I keep on fighting it and fighting it, I'll win in the end.

John

Paul had a lot to get off his chest, and I noticed how much calmer he became as he shared. For the first ten minutes of the session he talked as if he were being interviewed on Radio Five Live, which shows how out of practice he is with the counselling. It *is* a peculiar process after all.

I'm pleased that Paul's as aware as he is of what's currently going on in his life. In the session, he was able to track back to where he felt everything had started going wrong, and how he eventually relapsed back to drink. He knew exactly why he did this and, despite all the awful things that he had to deal with, he was still able to be conscious of picking up that first drink. However, drink he did, and that relapse was the start of a pattern that has lasted for the past nine months. Several issues came out of the session that concern me and they will need to be addressed urgently over the next few weeks. Firstly, Paul is now in a regular pattern of drinking that will only progress and get worse. Secondly, since damaging his neck in the skating accident he has been abusing his prescribed morphine-based medication. Thirdly, as a result of the drinking and pills, Paul has been unable to eat properly and this has triggered his food disorder. Meanwhile, the medication that he normally takes for his bipolar disorder, which also helps with anxiety management, has stopped working because of the alcohol and codeine intake, so he has been suffering from panic attacks, and this has also meant the return of his obsessive compulsive disorder.

With alcoholism, once the balance goes and a pattern of drinking is set up, other conditions that co-exist, such as anxiety and mood disorders, are triggered. Also, for an alcoholic, or any kind of addict, swapping one substance for another doesn't work because it keeps the addiction alive, or re-starts it, as in the case of Paul and the painkillers he took for his neck. This is why many treatment models for addiction are founded on abstinence from all mood-altering chemicals and behaviours – once you get into altering your mood the whole cycle of addiction is jump-started into action.

At the end of the session I advised Paul that, over the next week, he should really try to prioritise his time, put his recovery first and practise better self-care. He should knock out his alcohol intake with the help of a home detox regime, which he could get from his psychiatrist, and return to AA meetings to get some extra support with staying sober. This would also help with his anxiety and, in turn, with the OCD. It would give his normal medication a chance to work. We would have to do some specific work on his eating, but for now he should try and have three regular meals a day. He agreed to try this plan.

The primary focus of our sessions together has to be Paul's alcoholism. Until he stops drinking he won't be able to tackle his other underlying problems. So the focus of our next session will be specifically alcohol, looking at whether Paul has been able to achieve the aim of stopping, and focusing on his drinking history: looking at where and when he started drinking and when it became problematic.

Cheers Paul!

It's been so great having you in our group. You always have such smart and sensitive things to say and I know you won't relapse which you are worried about.

You are always so kind and funny. I hope we can keep in touch. I'm excited to read the book you told us about. It's got to be more interesting than the crap books they give you in here.

Kiss,

Stacey 'the lovely lass'

Paul's road to therapy

Paul

I had my first therapy session when I was ten. Lots of shit had started to happen. The worst was about a little kid I was supposed to be looking after, Steven. We were in this shop, mucking around, when Steven ran out into the road. An oncoming car went right into him. I ran out and stood over his crumpled little body screaming, 'Please move, please move!' It was the first dead body I had seen – and I blamed myself for it.

Then my dad, who had been away a lot, for months on end, in Germany and elsewhere, came home at last – and started having seizures. I was with him once, on my own. I tried to pull his tongue out to stop him swallowing it, thinking he was going to die.

It was around this time I started having twitches, and making lots of stupid noises. I also developed obsessions. I became fixated on the number five, everything had to be touched five times. I'd put the light on and off five times, or close the door five times.

My mam got worried about all these twitches and took me to a doctor. He said I had to see a psychiatrist at Queen Elizabeth Hospital in Gateshead. My mam was working that day, so my dad took me. This psychiatrist made me play with a load of sand which I thought was fucking stupid. I refused to go again. My dad thought it was silly as well. So all the twitches and stuff just carried on.

Looking back, I don't regret stopping going, but I'm not saying I still think it was all rubbish. The thing about therapy is that the timing has to be right, and you have to be right. It can be right for you at seventeen or thirty-seven or fifty-seven, or never.

At seventeen, the signs of various obsessions were getting worse, but I don't think therapy would have helped me. Not at that time. I wasn't ready for it. I would not have accepted it. It wasn't for me.

Yet I've never been one of those who were cynical about therapy, who said it was all stupid or just for rich, daft people to indulge themselves. I remember going to see *One Flew Over the Cuckoo's Nest* – and it terrified me. I thought, 'That could be me, I could end up in an institution like that.'

When I was playing for Rangers, I was in a terrible depressed state at one time, feeling suicidal. I asked the Rangers doctor if I could have a word with him. 'These people,' I said to him, 'who want to top themselves, why do they want to do it? What makes them flip?'

'People who flip,' he said, 'don't know they've flipped.' In a way, that reassured me. The fact that I knew I was feeling crazy suggested I might get through it. It's people who don't know who end it. I don't know whether this is true or not, but it helped at the time. I'll have to ask Johnny.

When I was with Sheryl, and everything was going wrong with me and the marriage, Shel insisted we went to see a marriage-guidance counsellor. I agreed to go once – but never again. I thought it was useless. I didn't listen to a word he said and denied everything. But Shel went a few times and seemed to think it helped her, for a bit anyway.

It was landing up in the Priory, in 1998, that's what started me off on the therapy road. I was playing for Middlesbrough at the time and had been on the piss for days. In Dublin, on a break, I had drunk thirty-two whiskies.

Didn't know where I was or what I was doing. One of my best mates, Davey, had just died suddenly, and I was blaming myself, again.

Late in the evening, having flown back to Newcastle, I somehow got myself on a train to visit Shel in Hertfordshire and got off at Stevenage. I was in such an emotional state that I wanted to throw myself in front of a train – but the last train had gone. So I just sat there, on an empty station, crying.

Finally, I somehow managed to ring Shel – but she refused to let me come to her place, not in the state I was in. She'd been through all that before. But she did ring Bryan Robson and he drove down overnight and picked me up. By that time, I was out of it, had no idea where I was or what had happened.

When I woke up, there appeared to be metal bars keeping me in so I said, 'Where am I?' They said it was the Priory. I said, 'Why am I here?' – and they said, 'For alcoholism.' I said, 'I'm not a fucking alcoholic, get me out of here!' But they wouldn't let me go. I had a guy coming into my room, staring at me all the time for the first twenty-four hours, in case I did anything stupid.

One day I heard this bloke banging on my door, asking to be let in. I said, 'Fuck off, go away, I don't want to see or talk to anyone.' He kept on banging and eventually I let him in – and it was Eric Clapton. He said he had been through all this, and it had helped him, so I should make an effort just to try it. So I agreed, but not really. I was touched by him bothering to come and see me, but I still thought it was all rubbish, that I wasn't an alcoholic and didn't need treatment. I'd be okay once I sobered up.

I agreed to answer fifty questions, about my life and drinking and that – but decided just to tell lies, say the first stupid thing that came into my head. 'Do you drink in the mornings?' was one question. I said 'No' to that, which was a lie. They asked if I liked the taste of drink and I said 'Yes, love it', which was another lie. I've never actually liked the taste of drink. When I used to go out boozing with people like Chris Evans, I'd often be pouring away my drink in plant pots. I just like the effect, not the taste. Anyway, I scored thirty-five points on this survey, despite telling lies. I thought that, after all, it might prove I needed help. Don't ask me how.

I got put into a psycho-drama session which, at the time, I thought was really daft. I don't think that any more. I've since seen the benefits. But I did think it daft then. We all had to pretend to be trains, and go 'choo choo choo'. 'I'm Paul Gascoigne and I'm a fucking choo choo train.' I refused to take it seriously. I didn't understand the point. In another group session I had to join everyone was having a go at each other. Most of the people there knew who I was, which made it harder.

In one session, I wanted to throw a chair through the window. I threatened I was going to, so they all laughed and clapped and said, 'Go on, Gazza, you can pay for it.' I stormed out shouting at them, 'You're all mental!' Not very nice, I know; but remember, I was pretty messed up. That's my only excuse.

This was when Johnny appeared. I thought at first, 'Who the fuck are you to tell me things? You don't know fuck all about my life, or about football.' Football had got me into this, so I thought. I would not have been in the Priory, but for football. But when Johnny started one-to-one sessions, it got a bit better and I began to realise more. The point is that we are all trying to help each other, to expose the anger and pain.

As I started to settle down in sessions with Johnny, they began to allow me a few concessions, letting me out, for example, on country runs to keep fit. I went on one long run, not knowing where I was going – and found I had run into Fulham's training ground. That was funny. They all shouted at me, 'You can do it Gazza, keep going Gazza!' I think by then most people had heard what had happened to me, and where I was.

After seventeen days, I pleaded with them to let me out. I promised and promised that I would never have another drink, which of course is what all drunks say.

I'd found Johnny not so bad, not a bad bloke, but I still hated being there.

You are meant to have a full twenty-eight days, that's the minimum first treatment if, like me, you have been brought in paralytic. The average number of times someone needs to go for treatment, before it really hits home, is three.

After twenty days, I was ready to run away. And I was serious. So they agreed I could leave, on condition I came back two days a week for the next four weeks, to get me up to the twenty-eight days.

But when I came out, I was still angry. So I didn't give that first visit to the Priory a proper chance. I was still too busy denying I was an alcoholic.

John

When I first met Paul in the flesh he was just as I'd expected: down-to-earth, funny, one of the lads. On hearing my accent he immediately asked where I was from. When I told him I was a fellow northerner he seemed to relax in my presence. I was to be his counsellor in treatment for the next four weeks, so this was a good start. On the surface, Paul was like most people who have ended up in rehab. He had been drinking far too much over a fairly short period and it had all come to a head after one particular bender, resulting in his being brought in to treatment. He, like most, had hit 'rock bottom'.

When you enter a place like the Priory Hospital as a patient, all sorts of things happen to you. First, when you wake up on the day after being admitted you usually don't know where you are. Paul thought he was in the Southampton Priory because that's what was reported on the news. He was actually in London. The Priory is a chain of psychiatric hospitals with addiction clinics attached.

During the first few days most patients are on medical detoxification which increases the sense of disorientation. At some point you are then taken to the unit that specialises in addiction treatment and introduced to your primary group. This is the bunch of people, usually around eight men and women, who will get to know you inside and out over the following weeks. And of course you will get to know them just as thoroughly. So it's a lot to take in.

As Paul began to settle in, he slowly started to take risks both with his group and in our one-to-one sessions. After some initial resistance he settled in to the idea that he could not control his drinking, and began to talk openly about his alcoholism. This was an important breakthrough as it is a convention that all patients begin group therapy by introducing themselves with their first name and identifying themselves as an alcoholic or addict, or sometimes both: 'I'm Jimmy and I'm an alcoholic.' It's important to remind yourself that you are in hospital because of *your* addiction.

During Paul's early treatment I was surprised to observe how supportive he was towards others in group-therapy sessions. He would be the first to give feedback when a fellow patient had shared a painful life story. He would get angry on their behalf and even offer to confront relatives on 'family day'. His insights were important and genuinely helpful.

As time went on it became clear why Paul had so much insight into others' painful lives. This was because of his own painful life, which included early traumas such as the death of a childhood friend and the illness of his father.

Paul had witnessed a lot as he grew up. It's important to add that Paul's family's social life, like that of all their friends and extended family, revolved around alcohol and the pub. It was where people would meet, have a good time, get drunk and sometimes fight. So it wouldn't be unusual for Paul to witness physical violence every now and then.

Early in life Paul began to develop some tics and stammers due partly to the traumatic events experienced at such a young age. He did the best he could to deal with his lot but developed anxiety disorders. For him this developed into various obsessive compulsive disorders, such as counting in certain ways, checking doors, and obsessively cleaning. Paul began to see the world in a certain way, and to be programmed to think and feel in a certain pattern. Once programmed, it's extremely difficult to change a person's mental and emotional blueprint. Every one of us has a programme, but whereas some of us have a way that gets us through life well enough, for others nothing seems to work. It's as if the world is against us – everything we touch turns to dust. Relationships, jobs, friends – whatever it is, something seems to go wrong. We feel victimised, and sure enough we become victims. This is a lifelong pattern for many people. The really unfair thing about this pattern is that it's unconscious. In other words we cannot see it ourselves;

we are not programmed to review our own behaviour. The only time we get to see ourselves is when someone at home or at work points something out to us and by then it's out of hand and we take the comments as criticism or a put-down. So we react defensively, give them a piece of our minds and, guess what, we become victims all over again, crying: 'It's not fair!'

I was going to hear that statement from Paul time and again throughout his treatment at the Priory. The main focus in any addiction treatment centre is on the illness of addiction. I call it an illness because that's precisely what it is. Not everyone who drinks heavily has it; however, some individuals who only drink moderately *do* have it. You either have it or you don't. Paul was admitted to hospital because he could no longer control his drinking. Everyone around him would tell him this, especially those who were close to him. Friends and family would be on edge every time they were in a social situation with him because they wouldn't know how he would behave. He is a classic 'Dr Jekyll and Mr Hyde': when sober, he's a lovely man, kind and considerate and very generous; however, when drinking alcohol he is unpredictable.

He would sometimes be fine. He'd have a few drinks, tell a few jokes and be the popular figure we all love. Other times he would have one too many, get loud, start to say inappropriate things to friends and become aggressive. Everyone around him would be on eggshells – wondering what they should do next, how they would get him home in one piece, avoiding the press and trying to prevent him getting into a fight. Family and friends would cover for him and even tell lies on his behalf. Why do such people, who usually behave honestly and professionally in their lives, suddenly start to cover things up? It's because they don't know what to do; they feel over-responsible for their loved one and this leads to personal compromise. Suddenly the alcoholic is more important than oneself. This issue is very common in families in which alcoholism is present, and it's got its own name: codependency. Codependency is about relationships, and its main feature is that we say or do what we think will control or fix the other person, rather than what is true or good for ourselves.

Paul began to recover physically and mentally and, by the second week, when his detox was completed, he began to focus on what we describe in the treatment field as 'outside issues'. He was, after all, still playing football in the Premiership and was keen to get back on the pitch. His relationship with his ex-wife was stable, and after three weeks he couldn't understand why he shouldn't return to Middlesbrough. His psychiatrist, the treatment team and I all disagreed with his thinking, as it was too early for him to leave.

The suggested minimum stay is twenty-eight days. We called a meeting and invited in his then current manager, Bryan Robson, to thrash out the issue. The result was that Paul would be discharged that weekend but that he would return for two days a week for the next month to complete treatment. The only person happy with this was Paul. But true to his word he came back the following Monday and stuck to the agreed regime.

Alcoholism is described as a three-fold illness that affects the physical, mental and spiritual parts of our being. Physically, people become addicted and start to suffer withdrawal and other harmful symptoms. Alcohol is a depressant. It impedes the functioning of the brain's physiology, which in turn messes up the whole body's rhythm. Mentally, there is an immediate effect on the thinking during drinking and a long-term corrosive effect on decision-making and other cognitive processes. Spiritually, there is a 'loss of the self'. In other words, our natural personality, the person we have been all of our lives, our 'real nature', starts to disappear.

During the last few days of Paul's stay at the Priory, we began to put together an aftercare plan. This was to remind him that the job he'd started was by no means complete. He would need to abstain from alcohol and other mood-altering drugs and, for a short time, stay out of social situations that involve drinking. He should ideally attend one of the many self-help support groups each day for the first ninety days. I would aim to meet with him every fortnight for one-to-one sessions.

The other issue to be dealt with was his depression. Would he need to be on medication for this? Was he actually clinically depressed or was the depression caused by his drinking pattern and subsequent lifestyle? Paul has suffered from many other conditions besides alcoholism, but for now they have taken a back seat. After meeting with his psychiatrist in the Priory it was agreed that he should take a mild antidepressant. Paul felt okay about this, and agreed to try it.

Around a quarter of people entering treatment for alcoholism or drug dependency will have a co-occurring illness, such as an anxiety disorder, a mood disorder, a major depressive disorder or bipolar disorder. And according to studies, an alcoholic is six times more likely to have bipolar disorder than a non-alcoholic. Making an accurate diagnosis in primary treatment is very difficult. There are many issues to take into account before prescribing any psychotropic medication. Depression and bipolar disorder are particularly hard to spot in the early stages of recovery. That is because, by the time most people arrive for treatment, they are extremely low – or occasionally extremely high – as a result of their alcohol and drug intake.

There is a suggested abstinence of four to six weeks to allow each individual to come out of their addictive cycle and return to normal before any other diagnoses are made. It is essential that a thorough family history be taken to see if there have ever been any psychiatric illnesses in the family. This assessment should also cover a drink and drug history.

The main focus on Paul's treatment at the Priory was his alcoholism. It was not until much later that he would also be diagnosed with bipolar disorder.

After that first meeting in 1998, I was to see Paul roughly five or six times over the next nine months. He didn't attend many meetings and dropped his aftercare plan fairly quickly after leaving London. He eventually relapsed.

Paul

That was just the first of several visits to the Priory over the last eight years or so. I've lost count of how much money I've spent, which is just as well.

After that first twenty-day session in the Priory, I later did two other shorter ones, of ten days and three days. They were for different sorts of problems, not always drink, but for depression, anxiety and addiction to painkillers. That sort of thing. I don't do things by halves, do I?

I've also been a regular at AA meetings, but they're a bit hard if you're well known. I could understand why George Best didn't attend them very often. One of my fears is that you never know who is there, maybe planted by the press, or whether someone who looks and seems okay will then ring up a paper and flog a story for money.

I always kept in touch with Johnny throughout this period, looking upon him as a friend as much as a counsellor, going to see him for regular sessions. Well, to be honest, it was more like now and again, with a few longish gaps, but I still talked to him on the phone. And then I went to see him properly recently.

When I realised I was coming to the end of my football career, I began to dread it, thinking I would have nothing left to live for. That was all I had known, all I could do. And at football, I was a sort of genius. I had a talent, but with talent, so I'm told, there's a fine line between living normally and flipping. I think Robbie Williams is a massive talent, and he's had his share of problems in the past. Yes, I know there are people with talent who don't flip, but it does often go together.

I suppose, really, you are born with it, whether you are a so-called genius or not. It's there inside you, then slowly it sort of creeps up and takes over as you go through life.

I've also been to a clinic in Arizona called Cottonwood, three times so far. I've found it easier to go off to America to get away from everything, the press and other people, to a country where I'm not known.

The first time was when I was at Everton, in June 2001, and the second time after China in 2003, where I was trying to coach. At Everton, I'd got myself in a terrible state, partly because of lots of injuries, worrying about my career ending. I was getting hooked on diazepam as well as drinking heavily. So that didn't help. I also went in 2004. Just for two weeks. Not because I was drinking. I wasn't. I was totally sober then. Had been for a while. It was to do with Red Bull and a bit of gambling. I just needed to get myself sorted.

John

One day in 2001, about twelve months after I'd last seen Paul, I'd just come out of a training seminar at Guy's Hospital when I received a phone call from Bill Kenwright, the chairman of Everton Football Club. He had asked a mutual friend, Paul Roberts, for help concerning Paul Gascoigne, and my name came up. Bill wondered whether I was available to meet with him and Paul the following day to discuss how we could best help him to stop drinking. I agreed.

Bill was sticking his neck out because he didn't want Paul to be sacked from the club, and because he cared about him. He was very concerned, and shared with me that he was shocked at Paul's state of health and felt powerless to help. After meeting with Paul, I too was worried. It was agreed that we needed to talk to Walter Smith, the team manager, and discuss when would be a good time to refer Paul back into residential treatment. Walter agreed it had to be as soon as possible. Sheryl was also very supportive at this stage, and ten days later Paul was off to the Cottonwood de Tucson treatment centre in Arizona.

Paul returned to England on great form. He had spent a month in the desert focusing on getting better. He had learnt a lot from his stay and had been diagnosed with bipolar disorder as well as alcoholism. At the time Paul was very worried about this, but he was also relieved as it helped explain some of his past behaviour and vicious mood swings. Despite Paul being comfortable with this diagnosis, others were not so comfortable. He had been prescribed medication that would influence the way he trained and played, therefore affecting his standing in the first team.

The dilemmas that arise for friends and family and colleagues in such situations are commonplace. First of all, it is very difficult for a friend or colleague to accept that you're ill in the first place. They see you a lot and know you have been run-down, but think all you need is a rest and you'll be 'right as rain'. Furthermore, most friends, family and colleagues have never suffered from a psychiatric illness and therefore have no idea what it's like for you. So they don't help, because they say things like, 'Stop taking that medication, you don't need it!' How do they know? They're not trained to give out that type of advice, only a psychiatrist can.

This is what happened to Paul. Subsequently, over a period of time and with the help of his psychiatrist back in England, he came off his medication. It was a risk, but only time would tell.

His first team appearances were regular, but over the season Paul began to be disillusioned. He stayed focused on his recovery for a while but did not attend enough self-help meetings. He and I would meet on average once every three weeks to start with, but this also fell away again. Over the course of a nine-month period, Paul made a decision to try and drink only socially. He moved from Everton to Burnley. He eventually slipped back into his old pattern and we lost touch.

Then, in 2003, Paul went to China as a player-coach, preparing himself for when he would no longer actually be playing football. When Paul had been at Everton he'd had a great bunch of people around him on the staff. One of those was John Murtagh, who is now the head of Fulham's youth academy. He phoned me to say that Jimmy Gardner, Paul's oldest friend, nicknamed 'Jimmy Five Bellies', had called him as he was concerned that Paul was really struggling in China, and asked for John's help.

John gave me Paul's number. I called him in China and he told me he was in a terrible state. He'd been doing well for a while but was starting to encounter difficulties with the language, air quality, heat and the standard of football. He didn't want to quit but resented being there, and had started drinking. Once again his drinking got out of control very quickly and, as well as that, he was beginning to suffer regular panic attacks.

He was alone most of the time and this increased his need for a drink. I called his psychiatrist at the North London Priory, who suggested that as Paul wasn't able to get home, we send him a detoxification regime that would help with managing the alcohol intake and panic attacks. This helped Paul but in the end there was only ever going to be one conclusion – he would have to come back for help in order to get sober. Paul did return home during a break in the football season and, after some carefully planned tactics (such as not trying to stop drinking until he got to the clinic and could receive medical help), he flew back out to Cottonwood de Tucson for treatment.

Paul, despite the previous few months, felt more positive about his rehabilitation. He completed thirty-two days of treatment and returned on excellent form. He was back with Sheryl and this was going well. He attended regular meetings and would come for counselling every week. He wasn't playing football, but was working on his autobiography.

As time went by he became, in his own words, 'bored'. Life at home was also difficult and he and Sheryl decided that Paul would move out for a period and return to Newcastle. As far as I was concerned, Paul was in a stage of grieving. He was no longer doing the only thing he'd known for the previous twenty years – playing football. The game that he loved. For most of my life I'd played amateur football and if I ever had to miss it, because of injury or holiday, for more than a couple of weeks I would 'crack up'. So what was *he* going through?

At that time – unlike now – he wasn't interested in coaching full time. He still wanted to play but his body would no longer allow for the rigorous, punishing training regimes. He'd suffered many injuries and they had taken their toll. As well as this, Paul was starting to miss the spotlight. Would the fans still shout his name as he walked down the street? Would the football world miss him? This was, and still is, a massive issue for Paul, and I know many other famous people have experienced it too. And it is not just those in the limelight. I remembered reading some research that talked about the effects of redundancy on working-class men in the shipbuilding and coal-mining communities. I'd been shocked at the high proportion of workers who died within a few years of being made redundant, and at the high proportion turning to alcohol in order to cope with the loss of routine and identity. Paul could see that he needed to 'let go' of the idea of playing but couldn't do it. He was feeling unsure about the rest of his life. He shared with me in one session that he had bumped into Barry McGuigan, the former boxing champion of the world, and he'd told Paul about how he'd been struggling with the issue of not being in the limelight any more and that he'd had to seek help to get over the loss of his boxing career. It really helped Paul to hear that someone like Barry had experienced similar issues to himself.

As Paul was in Newcastle I wouldn't see him very regularly. He had split from Sheryl but was busy working on his book among other things.

But he hadn't really let go of football, and went off to train with Dave Jones at Wolverhampton Wanderers to work on his fitness and to see if perhaps he could still play at a high level. After about six weeks he decided it wasn't working out at Wolves, partly due to picking up an injury and partly because his depression had returned. He felt lonely and cut off. He was back living in a hotel environment.

Paul maintained his sobriety until unfortunately he got that injury through the *Strictly Ice Dancing* programme. Then he was back to the same situation – feeling ill and depressed, not knowing what to do with the rest of his life. Eventually he came to see me.

———————

Dear Paul

I hope that this has been a positive experience for you in Cottonwood and that you continue to use the tools you have learned here in your life back home. Best of luck – and we hope not to see you back here.

Best wishes

Greg

Paul goes from the Algarve to Kettering

Paul

I played in the Premiership till 2002, when I left Everton, by which time I was thirty-five. So I'd had a good career at the very top, whatever some people might think. And I got 57 caps for England. I don't know whether football kept me going – helping me to overcome all my other problems because I was so obsessed by football – or not. I think but for football I would probably have been far worse.

I also don't know whether therapy and all the help I began to get towards the end of my career kept me going and able to play longer than I would otherwise have done. I'm sure it did, but who the fuck knows. You only go one way in life and never know which way the other road would have taken you.

In 2004, I joined Boston United, as a player-coach. I thought I'd be able to do some proper coaching, but that didn't quite work out, and I only stayed a few months.

Then, in the summer of 2005, I went out to Portugal to be coach of Algarve United. They'd just come up into the Portuguese league so it looked as if they were going places. I worked with them for two months. I tried very hard, but the proposed contract never appeared. It was all just verbal, or a shake of hands. I could see it wasn't getting anywhere.

Until around that time, I'd had two years not drinking. All the therapy and treatment and AA and stuff had worked, plus my own willpower. In my book, I suppose I did talk at the end, did boast I guess, about that, about being dry at last, but it was true. I'd stuck to it up to that point.

The book finished with me appearing to have got my life in order, that I was a success, which made some people think, 'Oh yeah, Gazza – he's sorted now. His life is rosy now, all right for him. He's got no probs.'

Which of course wasn't true. I was still getting myself in a state all the time for various reasons.

Anyway, it was in the Algarve I went back on the drink again. After I'd previously slipped at Christmas, as I've already told yous. I was stuck in a hotel, all on my own, with things not going well. Very like what happened in China, thousands of miles from home.

The Algarve was not quite as bad. For a start I was in a lovely place, Vilamoura, with all mod cons and luxuries and nice people but, all the same, I was on my own.

I decided to have a glass of wine. I took it for the same old reasons – I was depressed, anxious, desperate to change the way I was feeling. I still don't like the taste much, not even the best, most expensive wine. I take it to numb my pain.

Obviously I felt guilty. I was letting myself down, and other people. Once you're an alcoholic, always an alcoholic. You are never cured. And you always think, once you have one glass, you might as well go and get pissed. So I got pissed, twice. I hadn't talked to Johnny or been to the AA for ages. Hard to do all that, in the Algarve.

Chris Evans tried to help me escape from the press by letting me go to his villa, but I had a few drinks there as well. I admitted it to him, that

I'd had a relapse. I used to go for a ten-mile run, on my own, then I'd come back to the house and just sit there – and then I'd decide to have a drink.

I played golf a few times with Andy Townsend and Gary McAllister. They'd have a couple of drinks after we'd played. I'd pretend I wasn't drinking and say I would just have a Diet Coke, but behind their backs, I'd pour a couple of vodkas into the Diet Coke.

My dad and Carl, my brother, were planning on coming out for a bit of a holiday. I'd gone back to England to go see some tennis at Wimbledon and to do some filming for a DVD I was doing on my career. Well, I had a bit of a problem at the tennis. Had a few drinks. Then my dad, Carl and me were planning on flying out to Portugal together. Just a few days after the tennis final. Waiting at Gatwick Airport for the flight with the both of them, I again had a bit to drink. I caused a scene. I got into an argument with two cops who were called, fighting with them when they tried to restrain me. And giving them a bit of an earful. I know, I know, it was fucking stupid. I'm supposed to have shouted, 'Take your guns off and I'll have you as well!' I'm sure I didn't. I don't remember.

The upshot was that BA banned me from the flight, because of the state I was in. My dad was absolutely furious, shouting and screaming at me for being so stupid.

No, I didn't hit him, which one paper said I did, but I did have a row with him. He would have knocked me out if I'd hit him. I would never hit him anyway, even when drunk. I have too much respect for him. Anyway, he and Carl didn't go to Portugal. How could they? I wasn't going to be there. They went back on their own to Newcastle and I was left, crying my eyes out.

I rang Johnny and told him I'd had a relapse. He tried to talk me through what to do and I went off to the Priory for a few days. When I'd sobered up, things were a bit better. And the police in the end decided not to press any charges. That was good of them. Not that much had really happened. But even still.

Carl and me dad did eventually come out for a holiday, mind. But I was still drinking a bit. Behind my dad's back, I'd get Carl to get me a drink on the beach, but not to let me dad know. But he found out, of course. It is a difficult thing to hide.

He went mad at me. 'Look at the state you're in – go to fucking bed and sleep it off.' Which I did. Craving for a drink is like craving for a cigarette, only a hundred times worse. When I woke up, they'd both gone. Got an early flight home.

My battle with the bottle will be with me for the rest of my life. I know that. Every day when I wake up, I realise it's going to be a battle, just to get through the day without a drink.

The only people who understand these feelings are all the alcoholics. There are four million in Britain who admit it, who have come out, and another four million who have not admitted it – yet. But all of us have got to talk about it, face up to it. It's the only way.

During those two years not drinking, I wasn't sickened by other people getting drunk, spewing up in the streets in Newcastle. It didn't worry me. I've been there. Most of them won't turn into alcoholics. I know that. They won't get addicted. Lucky them.

The real alcoholics, I can easily spot them – by their faces, their shakes, the bulge of a bottle in their coat pocket. I often see them on the street and feel sorry for them.

I feel I can have two glasses of wine, then I'm shitting myself, wondering if I'll be able to stop. I know what I'm supposed to do – go for a walk, read a book, watch TV, or ring Johnny and talk it through. I can do all those things, but it's so hard.

I know I'll start playing the same old tricks. I might be with someone, having a chat, when I'll jump up and say I've got to make a phone call, or do something. But it won't be true. I'll be lying. Instead I'll jump in the car and go to the off-licence. After a quick swig, I'll brush my teeth, have some chewing gum, come back and pretend nothing has happened.

It might sound mad, but at the moment, now that the disappointment and loneliness of Portugal is behind me, I do feel I can control it, that two glasses will be enough for me. I don't see what's wrong with that, as long as I'm not hooked. But, of course, I'd rather not drink for the rest of my life, if I could.

Living in Britain, it's so hard. Everyone drinks. People are drinking, all around, wherever you go. I see people in pubs or at parties cradling a glass of wine – and then they leave it. You can see clearly that they've left half their glass. Only drinking half of their wine! Fucking hell. I wish I could do that. I wish I could leave half a glass. Even better, I wish I could just stick to Diet Coke.

So I went back to seeing Johnny, after that relapse in the Algarve – and then something even better than therapy came along to occupy my mind. I got a job.

Over the last couple of years, I've had various approaches from people saying they were going to buy so-and-so club and would put me in as manager. Some were quite good clubs, in the English First and Second Divisions, but nothing came of them. Usually when we looked into their finances, they were far worse than they'd led us to believe, with millions of debts we didn't know about.

While I was in the Algarve, I got a call one day from a friend, Ian Elliott, to say there was this guy wanting to meet me about buying a club, with me as manager. Sounded the usual fantasy stuff, but I agreed to go and see him.

He turned out to be a twenty-seven-year-old lad, Imraan Ladak, who had made a lot of money. He's a Spurs fan, basically, but he knew he was never going to be able to buy Spurs.

I had a three-hour meeting with him. It was strange, being interviewed by someone of twenty-seven, more than ten years younger than me. That hasn't happened to me before. I suppose it will happen more in the future, now I'm becoming an old fart.

I was struck by his enthusiasm and knowledge of football, so I agreed to go in with him, if he found a suitable place. That's when he came up with Kettering Town. I watched some videos, went to see them play, talked to some of their players, and I thought, 'Yeah, I could work with this lot.'

They are well down the non-league ratings — not even in the Conference, but the one below that, Conference North. That means they are six leagues below the Premiership. So yeah, they've got a long way to go. But they're an old club, 133 years old, who have so far never got into the Football League. So that's our challenge.

The news is now out and people have been quite surprised, asking me why I haven't started a bit higher up, then there would be less far to go to get to the Premiership. But you have to start somewhere. José Mourinho wasn't even a coach when he began, just working as a translator. I think it took him about six years to join a big club. So it can be done.

Kettering over the years has had some good people playing with them or managing them, such as Tommy Lawton and Derek Dougan. Ron Atkinson was with them at one time. So they're not a total backwater. The town is quite big in fact, about, I dunno, about 50,000, but their average gates were only around 500 when we arrived.

I have agreed to put some of my own money in, to show I am committed. I will own about a third of the club.

I'm letting Imraan do all the financial dealing, and the legal work. I'm just putting my mind to the football side. All the players are part time at the moment, doing ordinary jobs during the day, but my ambition is to get them full time — by the end of the season, if I can manage it.

To do this, I need to get in sponsors, which I've been working on, using my name and contacts, speaking to firms or people to sponsor our kit and get us some new balls. The balls we have are rubbish. I've approached about forty sponsors so far and most of them are really interested.

The players train on Mondays and Tuesdays, after their ordinary work. The reserves train on Wednesday evening. Yeah, there is a reserve team, so that's something.

Paul Davis, my friend who used to play for Arsenal and England, is a brilliant coach, with all the qualifications. He's my right-hand man. He takes the training sessions. I just watch, suggest things, keep an eye on progress. I'll be picking the team and deciding tactics, who comes off, who comes on as sub, but I rely on Paul's help.

There was a manager here, Kevin Wilson, who's done a good job with them, got them fifth in the league last season. Obviously he can't be the manager now I've arrived, as part owner as well, but he's agreed to become director of football. He's looking at players we can buy, when we get the money, and to scout the opposition. He's a good lad. He's taken it well. Of course at this stage, I don't know how it will work out.

So that's the position, as of now, at the end of October. We'll have to see how it goes, how I will cope.

I'm serious about it, in it for the long haul, whatever the cynics might think. I agree my track record as a coach hasn't been exactly brilliant so far. Two months has been my longest stint, but I promise you I'll be here for a long time, oh yes. The fucking bookies are taking bets that I'll be gone by Christmas, but what do they know? Fuck them, that's what I say.

I've been lost without football. I haven't found anything yet I love as much. That's been part of my problem. Whatever happens, it will be better than sitting around doing nothing, getting depressed. I suppose you could say football for me has always been a sort of therapy. Well it is now . . .

———————

Hey Freak

I know that it is going to be hard to recover from the devastation of losing to a girl in chess and battleships, but think of it as a learning experience.

I am not going to write anything cheesy in your book, so I am just going to mention that I am excited to receive and give the best. I am sure I can think of new things even for you! Heh heh heh. Also remember that you made two promises. It is bad luck to break them.

So see you in Cali. A chest of a man. Ready to have fun. Going to miss you, even your annoying tendencies. Loads of love. No explanation necessary . . .

Thank you

Tracey

Paul managing to be a manager

Paul

It's now a month since I started at Kettering. After the first couple of weeks, finding my way around, I saw that I was doing far too much. I realised I had to set up certain ground rules. I didn't want people wandering around the club, into the directors' lounge, talking to players or whatever, without me knowing who they were and what they were doing.

I knew I couldn't do it all, although I've done most things apart from make the tea, but I wanted to know who were the people doing the various jobs. I had to know who the kit man was, the club secretary, the security man – then I could concentrate on being the manager.

I haven't seen Johnny for a while, as I've been so busy, and I've also taken on some outside commercial work, such as the DVD, and then gone on *Richard and Judy* to promote it.

I've been working eight days a week and now I'm unable to sleep. I was lying awake all last night thinking about what we'll do in training today, or who I'll pick for Saturday, or how am I going to get more money into the club to pay for things. Me and Paul are really up against it.

We started off quite well, won our first game, but got knocked out of the Cup. That didn't matter too much. I want to concentrate on getting out of this league. But since then we've only got five points out of a possible twelve in the league, which isn't quite good enough – especially as the last three games (all away) were against struggling teams. We should have got more than two draws and a loss.

I now feel for every manager I've worked for – which of course I didn't at the time, when I messed them around, went out on the piss, or got bloated and overweight. I want to apologise to them all for what I did. A bit late now, of course. At least I know the worst things players can do, the tricks they get up to. I did them all.

Almost all the sponsors I approached came on board, so that's been good. We've got new balls, new track suits. I've got the players drinking high-energy drinks and I make them eat pasta and also pizzas. Pizzas are good for carbohydrates. If the Italians eat pasta and pizza all the time, they can't be bad for you. They've won three World Cups after all.

A lot of pressure comes with being a manager, that's for sure. Especially if the results aren't going as well as you'd hoped. I've found myself getting uptight and frustrated, and I don't want to take that out on the players. That isn't good management. Probably time I saw Johnny again, even if I am busy. I can take it out on him. Sorry, Johnny.

One of the things about therapy is using it before it's too late. I have a rough idea of how to cope when things get on top of me, but Johnny always helps me to remember exactly what I need to do. I do try to take on board what he says.

When I feel a panic attack coming on, I have learned to do some deep breathing. Or I might read a book. I'm reading a book of poems, as it happens, propped up by my bedside. It's a collection of modern ones. One even mentions me in it. Ha.

And where is that bed? Good question. It's never easy pinning me down. Knowing where I am staying. As you know, I don't have a house or anything of my own. I'm staying at Champneys at the moment, at Henlow Grange, which isn't too far from Kettering, so that's good, but I've got Jimmy house-hunting in Kettering for me, either a flat or a house.

It's just a small room, here at Champneys, so I haven't got much stuff with me. It's all in Newcastle, or at me mam's. But it's all I need. The grounds are big. I can go for a walk. Use the gym and pool and all the health stuff.

When I'm here, in my room, I try to switch off my mobile phones, give me heed a rest. I have three mobiles, each with different ring tones. One's for Hunter, who's helping me with this book, one's for the club and football things, one's for family and friends and any girlfriends, hopefully. But if I'm in a state, I switch them all off and just listen to music.

Being a manager I've found it very hard to have time for myself. I'm thinking about others all the time, and their problems, or the team's problems, and, if I'm not careful, I let their problems take me over. So I need someone to listen to me – and that's where Johnny comes in.

In theory, I've got my heart's desire, with coming to Kettering. I'm back in football again, as a manager this time, not a coach, and with a stake in the club. I'm not liable, this time, to be messed around or carved up. I'm in charge of my own destiny for a change. I've got what I'd wanted in life, well, apart from the obvious.

I haven't got a relationship, not had one for years, not a proper one. Obviously, I'd like that, everyone would. There is one girl I took to the tennis at Wimbledon, to the women's final, in the summer, and that got in the papers, probably because I had had a few drinks – champagne – on the way there and at the tennis. I was gutted I did that. But I was nervous, even though she is just a girl I know. It's nothing serious. But it was a sort of date. And it had been a long time since I'd done that. So yeah, I was a bit uptight. Nervous like. But I shouldn't have had the champagne.

I don't have anybody. I have no love life. I still hope I will find a partner. I'd like to find someone and live with them, in an apartment or whatever, then buy a big house and start a family. That would be my fantasy. But of course it's harder now, with being a manager. I'm so preoccupied with that I haven't time for anything else, or any proper relationship.

But well, apart from that, I've got all I ever wanted. The trouble is, what I wanted is now causing me stress because of my relationship with the chairman, who I feel is stopping me from doing my job.

There's been something preying on my mind recently. Perhaps because of the stress of this manager job. And the other stuff that's going on behind the scenes. I don't know. Anyway, I keep thinking about a story that was run in the *Sun*, back in August. I'm upset about it again and I was then. Very. At the time I heard there was a story, supposedly by Bianca, that was accusing me of hitting Mason, Shel's son. When I heard it was going to appear in the *Sun*, I went to court to stop it.

I had to hire barristers and all that shit, which you have to do, to beat something like the *Sun*. I lost and it cost me thousands in legal fees. As I've said, the *Sun* ran it with the horrible headline 'Gazza Beat Up Family'. You can see why I was so upset, and still am. That's why I then told my version to the *Mirror*.

The truth is that I once did give Mason a smack – but just on his bottom, fully clothed, with my hand, and there was no injury as far as I was concerned.

I'd got drunk that evening and had gone to bed. Bad, I know, when you are a parent. I woke up when Shel hit me over the head with a shoe. She was trying to wake me up. I woke up, thinking 'Which fucker has been hitting me with a shoe?' and it was Shel.

She said Mason was out of control, she couldn't do anything with him, so why should I be lying in bed asleep leaving her to cope? Not unfair. It was my turn to go down and discipline him.

So I went down and told Mason to go to bed. He wouldn't, so I smacked his arse. That was all. I didn't touch Bianca, or anyone else, just Mason, cos he wouldn't go to bed.

I've smacked Regan, my son, as well, when he was playing up, speaking to us in a way he shouldn't have been. Mind you, Regan has always had me by the bollocks and can pretty much do anything with me.

We did have some good times, some great family outings and holidays. They used to say, 'Dad, I love you so much,' both Bianca and Mason often did. I bought Bianca a new car, and paid her insurance, which cost £12,000. I bought Mason about £10,000 worth of bling, which is what he wanted. Once they got that, it felt to me as though they turned. As if they hated me. I've even had a text saying, 'Wish you were dead.'

I haven't seen them for a while and I miss Regan so much. On the other hand, if I don't see them, they've got nothing to write about me. They can't sell any more stories about me.

In my mind, I've disowned them now, but of course I can't do that with Regan. I don't ever want to do that. He is my son. But whenever I do get to see him, Shel is on the phone to him twice a day.

Shel and I have moved on now, since I've paid her off. I don't know what will happen in the future. Anyway, I've got enough to worry about at present, without starting to think about Shel again. I remember I said, at the end of the paperback edition of my first book, that 'that was that'. I wasn't going to talk about Shel any more. And here I am again . . .

It's going brilliantly still. I couldn't ask for more, despite some of my misgivings about the chairman. I'm so happy being the manager. The lads have been excellent, couldn't have done more. I did get rid of three players and have brought in another three. Just had my seventh game – a win in the FA Trophy – and we've only been beaten once in the league and once in the Cup. I think we're nicely placed. Not a million miles behind the leaders. On Saturday we're playing Barrow at home. They're behind us, about middle of the table. So fingers crossed.

Before I took over, I spoke to various managers I respect, such as Terry Venables and Walter Smith. They all said go for it. Walter said it would be three times as hard as anything I might expect, but not to get downhearted. There will be bad days, sad days, but then good days and good results. I just had to try and treat them all the same and keep working hard.

Coaching badges? I haven't had time to worry about them at present. Anyway, you don't need them in non-league. You only need them in the Premiership. When that time comes, I'll have finished off my B badge. That's all you need anyway and I'm halfway through that.

All the players call me gaffer. Even the chairman calls me that. I didn't ask. They just did it. I feel a responsibility to them all. There are thirty at the club, including coaches and staff. Then I have my own family to look after – and Mason and Regan. I'm still paying money to support them. But not towards Bianca's upbringing any more. So all in all it means I have about forty-five people for whom I feel responsible.

I really want to make something of the job at Kettering. I'm giving it everything I've got. I'm committed to the team and I believe in the players. But I find it hard when we lose. As soon as we get one bad result, the superstition kicks in. I start having to change things around, things like furniture, towels, my wardrobe. Then I have to change them again. I worry that if things aren't arranged right we'll get another bad result. It's stressful and exhausting.

All right then, I have to admit I've started a bit of drinking again. But just the odd glass of wine, now and again, sometimes not for one or two weeks.

I like to think I am in control of it. It's not like when I would take cocaine and then get through four bottles of whisky. Cocaine always seemed to help me drink more. Don't know why. Now I'm not going out to the pub every night, just to get drunk, as I once did.

It's only now and again I have the odd glass to relax. I know I shouldn't. I'm tempting fate. We'll just have to see if I can cope. I have responsibilities, now, to the club and the players. So I have to try and not let them down, not just myself.

But, it has happened again, so I'll have to tell Johnny on my next session . . .

———————

For Paul 'Ginger' Gascoigne

Your book is for a Transsexual! Madame Butterfly aka.

I enjoyed spending time with you at Cottonwood. Stay sober and let's get together soon.

Best wishes

Stefan

Paul's second session: A look back at alcohol

John

In this session, we concentrate on looking at Paul's relationship with alcohol, both in the present and over his life up to now.

Paul talks to me about the various problems he's facing at Kettering, and how he's attempting to deal with them. Most of the issues he has revolve around relationships with personnel at the club. This is pertinent to our work together, because so often what triggers Paul to act out is his struggle with personal and professional relationships.

We then discuss Paul's cravings for alcohol during the week since we last met.

Paul

It's been a tough week, and I've had some cravings for a drink. After the game on Saturday the referee said to us I didn't seem in quite the right state to be on the line. I'm glad he said it because I'd just done a long counselling session, and my good friend George Best had just died, and then I rushed off to the game, *and* I was on medication. I'd taken Librium, the detox medication. So I was tired. I wasn't woozy or anything, and I was paying attention. We won that game, in the FA Trophy, but I wasn't quite on top of things the way I normally am. After that I was with one of the backroom staff at the club, and the cravings were driving us nuts, so I had a pint and a game of snooker.

On Sunday the cravings were driving me mad again, and I had to sign 1,700 photos. My dad picked us up, with Jimmy, and I went training. Later on, about 8 p.m., I was with Dad and Jimmy and they ordered wine. I knew if I started drinking with them I wouldn't stop. And I'd had a glass of wine already. Perhaps two, but no more. So I thought, 'Fuck, I need to get away.' I was upset about George and what was happening at Kettering. I got myself into a bit of a state. And I knew I needed to get away from the drink.

So I went out to the front door and ordered a minicab. I told him to drive. He said, 'Where?' and I said, 'Leeds.' It was the first place that came into my head. I did think about Newcastle, but decided that was too far. I just needed to get away, that was the first thing, then I needed to talk to someone who didn't know me.

I'd left two of my mobiles behind, just taking one, which had a low battery, but I managed to ring Jimmy in case they got worried – wondering where I'd gone, if I'd thrown myself under a train or been abducted by aliens. All I said was that I was in a cab, going to Leeds. Then I hung up.

I could have stayed and talked to them all night, but they know my problems. They know all my stories. They've heard it all before. I needed a stranger to talk to. With a stranger you can unburden yourself. They have no preconceptions, no idea if you're telling the truth. And you and they know you'll never meet again. So I talked to this poor fucking driver, all the way to Leeds.

To get away from the drink, I had to take that taxi. I paid him the £300 fare in cash, and then gave him a tip. I asked him to drop me at the railway station in Leeds. I then found the first B&B place and booked in for the night. I was shattered. I just collapsed. But at least I got away from the drink. That was the whole point. I woke up next morning, felt better and caught a train back again. All the way on the train I talked to a bloke I'd just met who asked me what I'd been doing in Leeds. I just said I'd had a meeting.

John

So Paul has suffered from cravings on and off all week, and each day he has had to take steps to get through them. We're going to look back over his drinking history, so that he can remind himself of what his relationship with alcohol has been over the years. Taking an honest look at this will help him build up a picture of what alcohol means to him, and what effect it has on his life.

Paul

I had my first drink aged fourteen. All the lads in the town were skinheads and all that, but not me, I was totally focused on my football. I was always out training. But that time they were all saying, 'Go on, have a drink!' So I had a triple vodka and I remember it hitting us straight away. CB radios had just come out, and we were going round all the houses talking to each other. I was paralytic. I went home and me mam cracked us over the back of the head and sent us up to bed. She threatened to tell me dad and I was terrified of him finding out. Anyway, next morning I had a stomping headache but me mam made me go to school like that to teach us a lesson.

The effect on me was massive. I didn't have another drink for four years. The next time was when I was playing for Newcastle in a tournament. I was eighteen, we were flying on to Fiji from New Zealand when the plane suddenly dropped 800 feet. I was terrified of flying after that. On the way back I was with Brian Clough, and I thought there was steam coming into the plane through the windows. It was just condensation on the inside, of course, but I panicked at the time. I knew we then had to fly another two hours on to Baltimore and then had a further ten-hour flight home and I was absolutely petrified, so I thought, 'Shit, I'm going to have a whisky.'

Only it wasn't just one. I had twelve, slept the whole way, and woke up twenty minutes before we landed. The lads carried me off through the airport. I don't remember much, but I remember being sick over one of them. Odd the things that stick in your mind. Mind you, I bet he remembers as well.

Anyway, the next day I had no headache, I remember that. I didn't touch whisky again though. But I *did* start drinking at that age – eighteen. I realised there was a buzz to it. I had a laugh, a *craic*. I was the centre of attention. I was already a joker, but I was that bit more confident with the drink.

Then for a couple of years I'd train and not drink all week because I had a game on Saturday. Then Saturday night I'd drink with the lads after the game, and Sundays I'd drink with me dad at working-men's clubs. I liked sweet drinks like piña colada cocktails; I didn't really drink pints. I didn't see drink as a problem back then, I took it in my stride.

Did I know anyone who had a drink problem? No. No one in particular. My brother sometimes got quite drunk. But it was just weekends. He didn't drink much – he wasn't that bothered. Me mam would hardly go out, and if she had anything back at home it would just be a Mackie stout which is a nothing drink – nothing else, she didn't have the money or the time. Me dad would have a beer now and then on a Saturday with the lads, but he also didn't have the money for anything more than that. So yeah, in the family it was only weekends. There weren't any problems in our house with regards to drinking.

But it wasn't that stable a period of my life. When I was seventeen I went through a phase of gambling. I'd bet all my money on slot machines. I was addicted. I remember one Saturday I'd lost all my money and I needed more to keep at it – so I stole money from my sister's purse and lost it. She cried her eyes out.

I love my sister and I didn't want to see her cry, so I didn't gamble for a long time after that. That's probably why I'm not a gambling man.

John

Over his life, Paul has dabbled with gambling on a handful of occasions, but it has never been his primary addiction. That's why he says he's not a 'gambling man'. It shows us, though, that even at seventeen the tendency to addictive behaviour was there.

I asked Paul when it was that his drinking became regular.

Paul

Drinking first became more regular when I moved to London. I was just twenty-one years old, and I went from earning £120 a week to around £2,500 a week. I'd train hard, then go to a big pub down the road with my mates Terry, Jed and Keith. I'd split up with my first girlfriend, Gail, so that was it, I was on my own in the bright lights of London, getting followed everywhere. For the first six months I stayed in a hotel – well, actually three I think. Got thrown out of two of them. I normally drank champagne – or a couple of pints and then moved on to champagne – because it was less fattening. Chris Waddle used to come round and we'd have a bottle of Asti Spumanti, which is another nothing drink, and then we'd drink champagne. I did eventually buy a house though.

It was a massive change for me, coming to London at that age. I didn't like living on my own, I really didn't like it. Jimmy came down now and then. But then my sister and her boyfriend came to live with me, and I'd sit in the house and have a drink with him. He could drink more than me.

I'd have a drink Saturday after the game, and Sunday, and if I had the day off on the Wednesday I'd have a drink Tuesday after training. I didn't have a problem with the drink then, or I never *seen* I had a problem with the drink. Then one time I was cleaning up the house and I came across some cans and bottles of drink around the place. I realised I didn't want to be around a whole load of alcohol in my own home. It didn't feel good to me. So I moved out. Back to a hotel.

All of a sudden I was living in the centre of London, and looking out of the window it looked like a party on every street corner. I had a lovely big suite with a nice big fridge and I started having a couple of beers after training – and I went back to drinking champagne. On Sundays I always seemed to get paralytic, because I'd get Monday off. I'd go without drinking Monday, Tuesday, Wednesday, and maybe have a little drink Thursday, nothing Friday and then drink Saturday after the game.

I'm not a big drinker. I can't drink a bottle of champagne and be sober. Ask any of me mates, they say, 'Gazza, I can't understand it because you're a shit drinker – a couple of drinks and you're pissed.' But I seem to stay that way for a while and then the next one really knocks us out.

No one was making complaints about my drinking or anything. I was getting followed by the press and getting caught having a drink or doing this or doing that, but it wasn't a problem because I'd say, 'See what he writes about me on Saturday after the game!' On the pitch I was scoring goals, getting Man of the Match, banging in hat-tricks and doing everything, so really there was no problem. In the two-and-a-half years at Tottenham I couldn't put a foot wrong on the football pitch, so I thought, 'If I can drink like that and play like that the drinking isn't a problem.'

The drinking started to be a bit less controlled from the time of the World Cup in 1990. The only way I could relax was to have a couple of drinks on the sly. I had a cocktail once, which Bobby Robson thought was a milkshake, and I had a triple Baileys and put the froth from a cappuccino on the top so they thought it was a cappuccino.

The other times I'd drink were when we were given a couple of days off.

Then, when I came back home from Italy, I suddenly got masses of media attention. I was getting followed everywhere. I thought, '*Fuck*'. They were outside my mam and dad's house, outside the hotel, outside my house. They were everywhere. That was when I went to a wine bar and got pissed, and met Sheryl. I fell for her straight away. All of a sudden I'd gone from being a single guy to a family man with Sheryl and her two kids, one aged one and one aged three.

Did I feel ready for that responsibility? No, probably not. But I loved Sheryl, and I decided to take it upon myself to take the kids on as mine, I didn't have a problem with that at all. My family didn't like it, and told me to be careful, and I ended up rowing with my family over Shel. I never wanted anything to come between me and my family. I stopped seeing my family, stopped seeing Jimmy, and was just with Sheryl. Then she split up with me. I'd got injured in the Cup final, making that daft challenge, and couldn't train, and I started drinking every night, getting pissed.

I wanted to get back with her, but it was Catch-22. She found photos of girls in a bag of mine, though I ripped them up to show I wanted to be with her. Then I went round her house and said I wanted to get back together. We got back together, but a few weeks later she said, 'I can't believe what I did. I've let you get so close to the kids they now think you're their dad.'

I was scared, but I didn't have a problem with looking after the kids. I don't know if that was emotional blackmail or what.

Then I was due to move to Italy, so I asked her to come with me. In Italy, I was trying to train really hard, get properly fit, get over the ligament injury and broken kneecap, and also be a family man and understand that role, and learn the Italian language. I was just under so much pressure. Shel always wanted to see more and more of me. I'd be training and I'd panic and have to rush home quickly for her, so I couldn't enjoy training. When I'd get home I'd be so wound up I'd have a few drinks to relax, and then we'd argue. Then she wanted to go back to the UK, but had nowhere to live, so I bought a house and she went back and lived in it. But then I was flying back and forth and all that and we still argued. Then we split up.

It all felt too much: the football, trying to learn the language, 100° heat, never having any peace, never having time off, just busy, busy, training, training, trying to fit in seeing Sheryl and the kids. The only way I could chill out was to have a drink. I'd have a couple of grappas, 100° proof.

At that point, I'd train first but drink afterwards with me mates. I always trained hard. It was on with Sheryl, off with Sheryl. Every time I got back with her I calmed down and trained hard and every time we split up I was back drinking again. For the first year and a half. The drink was an easy way out. Then Shel and my family came over, and my family didn't get on well with her so the atmosphere was unbelievable. Me mam was saying Sheryl wasn't right for me, and Sheryl was going on at me about me mam, and you could have cut the atmosphere with a knife. I was so angry, I went to training, and I just weighed in to a tackle and broke my leg straight through.

I moved my leg but my foot and ankle stayed on the ground, and I knew straight away I'd smashed it. I was screaming as they carried me off the pitch, but I wasn't bothered because all I wanted to do was get out of that atmosphere. I thought, 'Fuck me, I'm going to hospital, I'm going to be cared for, I'll get some morphine.' I'd first been given morphine after I broke my leg during the Cup final in 1991. I knew what it was like.

I thought, 'I'll be in hospital for a few weeks and I won't have to deal with anyone.' I flew back to England. To the Princess Grace. The doctor did a great job fixing it back together and I was given some morphine for the pain. But then the press came and sent flowers and all that, and Sheryl came and stayed in hospital with me for two weeks. Even then I was arguing with her and it was hard for her because she'd come to support us, but I just wanted to be alone. I felt like if it wasn't for all that pressure I may not have exploded into that tackle and broken my leg. I felt stressed again when she was there. I was trapped in the hospital with a broken leg still trying to sort out all these problems: money for the family, money for Sheryl. That was the first time I got a panic attack.

How did it feel? I remember losing my breath, I couldn't breathe. I tried to explain to Sheryl and the nurses that I couldn't get my breath, and I started panicking, but the more I was panicking the more I was losing my breath, and they thought I was joking. I calmed down and screamed at them to get out of my room right now. When they came back in they asked me, 'What was all that about?' It felt like all those flowers had taken all the oxygen, that's what I thought at the time because I just didn't know what had happened. I just couldn't breathe. It must have been my first anxiety attack – panic attack – but I never saw that at the time.

John

Getting that injury was actually a relief for Paul. The only way out of a quagmire of family responsibilities and emotions was for Paul to take out his anger on the football pitch in such a way that he got that terrible injury. Once again, it was easier to injure himself, this time physically, than honestly to confront the people in his life. Things had become so intense, and he felt so trapped by his intimate relationships, that a spell in hospital seemed like a break. For Paul, the awful irony was that even in hospital he didn't get any peace and, trapped in that bed, he couldn't run on to the pitch, he couldn't drink. There was no release. The result was his first panic attack. He was then faced with months of recovery time to get through – the legacy of a moment's passionate anger.

Paul

It is great to become famous but it's a nightmare once you *are* famous, and it all just got right on top of us. When I flew back with a broken leg the press were on the flight trying to take photos of us, and I thought, 'What the fuck is all this about? All I wanted to do was play football, what happened to my life?' I sat in a hospital in London. Then I lived with Shel with a broken leg for six months, and it was quite tough; I was frustrated and angry. I went on holiday with her and was drunk every day. She just thought that was a normal thing. While I was getting drunk I was a good, happy lad, but when I was pissed I was sometimes angry. So they would enjoy being with me, and then all of a sudden they'd be scared, and I knew they were but there was nothing I could do about it. I just wanted to get back to playing football because football was my life and I was frustrated. And we'd argue a lot.

John

Paul and Sheryl argued a lot during that time. I ask him what they argued about, whether any of it was jealousy on his part, and about how he balanced the relationship with Sheryl and the children against his other family and his friends.

Paul

I was jealous at times, yeah. Although I didn't really think there was anything to be jealous of, at the time. But that wasn't really the problem.

After a few weeks with Sheryl and the kids I wanted to be with my mates. Then after a few weeks with my mates I wanted to go back with Sheryl. I lived like that for about six years. Because Sheryl didn't get on with my family, the only way I could see my family was to have a row with Sheryl, split up, and then go and see my family.

John

This is an important pattern for Paul in his relationships – finding it difficult to state his needs.

JM: You felt having a row with Sheryl and splitting up was the only way you could see your own family?

PG: Yeah. Then after a couple of weeks I'd say to Sheryl, 'Let's get back together,' and I always did it drunk. And she'd take us back, we'd go on holiday, there'd be an argument and I'd think, 'I can't argue any more,' and go and see my mates.

JM: How did you eventually break out of that pattern?

PG: I went back to Italy, and split up with Sheryl for seven months. It took three months to get over it, drinking every day, but then I trained so hard and while I was training she was out of my head.

JM: So you dived right back into the football?

PG: Yeah, I quit drink for nine months. Trained five times a day, fit as fuck, enjoying life; my mates and Jimmy drank but I never did. Everything was fine. One day the manager called us in and said they had something to tell me, but they didn't want to tell me because I was doing so well. They said they'd seen a change and I was completely different, I was playing really well. I said, 'Please tell me, put me out of my misery.' So they told me Sheryl had called and wanted to speak to me, and asked me to get in touch with her. She'd called the club because she didn't have my new number.

JM: So even the club were worried about the effect your relationship with Sheryl had on you?

PG: Yes. So I called her and she was crying and wanted to get back together, but it wasn't what I wanted, so I said, 'No – but,' I said, 'if you stop crying I'll come home for a visit.' I remember going back to England, and I thought, 'No, getting back with Sheryl isn't what I want.' But eventually, I decided it was time to leave Italy and start afresh with Sheryl.

JM: Had that became more important to you than Lazio?

PG: Yeah.

JM: Was the drinking continuous throughout this period?

PG: Yes. Then Walter Smith came to see us, asked if I wanted to play for Glasgow Rangers, and I said straight away, 'Yes,' and I moved to Glasgow and saw it was a fresh start. Up there it was good, I was enjoying my football, back with Sheryl, it was great. But there was still the same situation between Sheryl and my family.

JM: Were you always stuck in the middle?

PG: Yes, I was. And then Sheryl got pregnant. I thought, '*Fuck me!*'

JM: So you didn't feel ready for the whole process of fatherhood?

PG: Right. No way I felt ready. But I asked Sheryl to live with me in Scotland and she refused unless we got married. She said I wouldn't see my child unless we were married. During that time Walter Smith was very supportive. Alan McLaren was great as well.

Then came Euro 96. Before that I'd split up with Sheryl. Regan had been born and I'd taken a couple of weeks before I'd gone to see him. I'd been drunk the night he was born and I was embarrassed and guilty about that. No excuse, mind. When I did see him for the first time, held him, I cried my eyes out. He was amazing. Then, before the Championships, we went on a warm-up tour to Hong Kong and China. I did that daft dentist's chair thing. You know, when you sit in a chair with your head tilted back and the barman pours booze down your throat. I was smashed out me head . Next day it was my birthday. I got roses and a card saying 'Happy Birthday Daddy, love Regan'. I cried my eyes out, Dennis Wise put his arms round me, and I got smashed out me head again. I came back and went to the health farm to sort myself out.

I then decided to get well, and that I was going to do well in the tournament, and I was buzzing. I asked Sheryl to marry me. So we started sorting out the wedding. And I thought, 'Am I doing the right thing?' But I'd made me decision and I stood by it. After the tournament she went mad with us and said, 'I just can't believe that *I* had to ask *you* to marry me!' She meant because of what she'd said before, that I wouldn't get to see my son unless we got married.

So I was distraught. Because in spite of what she said, I was getting married for the right reasons. I thought I should be a married man and settle down and look after the kids, and stuff like that. I had a great wedding, didn't really get drunk but had my first go on a joint which knocked us for six.

On honeymoon we argued all the time. We moved up to Scotland and bought a big house. It was just the same situation. Training; couldn't relax; racing to get back home; making sure she was okay; didn't want to argue; constant arguing. I said, 'Let's have a break,' so we went to Gleneagles with Bianca and the nanny. Went down for a meal and me and Sheryl had a row over family, and that was it. I was having champagne and I mixed it with whisky. I grabbed her and said, 'What are you doing this for?' She struggled to get free and I threw her on the floor and that's when she banged her face and her finger. I shit myself. I said, 'Sorry.' I didn't know what to say, I pulled her finger back in, got the doctor. We stayed together that night but the next day she'd gone. I couldn't tell Walter Smith, and went and played a couple of nights later. My head wasn't in it. At the Champions League game against Ajax I got sent off in the first half an hour. Then I said, 'I've fucking beat up my wife.' The next day, there was Sheryl, she'd rung up the *Daily Mirror* – or someone had for her – and got the paper to photograph her bandaged face.

I did beat her up and I was disgusted with myself. I'd behaved badly. Obviously I felt shit about what I'd done. Of course. She said she wasn't coming back and we needed to live separately for a while. In the end I felt massive relief that we'd split up. If we'd been together it would have just been the arguments all the same.

Walter was brilliant. I was always there at his place, playing snooker with his kids. I called her and begged to get back together. We both did that. It was fifty-fifty. I more or less lived with Walter Smith's kids for a year. I bought a speedboat, played the best two-and-a-half years in soccer. But the whole thing with Sheryl was off and on, off and on. And it went on to divorce.

John

Looking back over Paul's life, since a really early age he's had an enormous amount to deal with, and drink became a part of how he coped with that. To begin with it was just at weekends, and then slowly but surely it became more problematic. He didn't see it sneaking up on him.

In this session, I first asked Paul about his cravings and drinking at the current time. Although he did get the prescription for a seven-day home Librium detox that I had suggested in the first session, he still wasn't able to see the week through without a drink – though he did cut down on the intake of previous weeks. He was finding the balance between looking after himself and looking after other responsibilities difficult. This is, and has been, a huge issue in Paul's life. He's never been very good at looking after himself and has mastered the art of 'going with the flow'. Some may be surprised at that and even think of him as a selfish man, but that isn't the case.

Early on in this session we talked about the many aspects of running a football club. For the first time in his life Paul has a lot of responsibility: he's now part of management. He's gone from being picked to being the picker – a massive progression and one that brings with it many challenges. Together, we're now beginning to see a pattern that has contributed to Paul's relapse: his over-responsibility for others. This is one aspect of codependency.

In the rest of the session, I was trying to help Paul identify when it was that he started drinking, who and what influenced his drinking and how it progressed to being addictive. It is usual for clients who come to me for counselling to ask, 'Why *me*, how come *I* am an alcoholic and not my friends? Was I born like this, with this addictive personality?' It seems that Paul has always been an addict of one sort or another. Football was his first drug. He dedicated his whole life to it. It made him feel safe and it gave him everything he needed from an early age. A daily structure, a uniform, status, money, travel, a purpose in life and, I think most important of all, positive feedback. He belonged to something that he loved and that loved him. What more does anyone want? As he reports, he wasn't that interested in what the other kids did: he had found his niche and his surrogate family.

At the age of eighteen, there were expectations on Paul to perform at a very high level and, although most of the time he was able to deliver, he internalised this pressure. His career propelled him from Newcastle United's youth set-up, to the first team, to a move to the bright lights of London and Tottenham Hotspur, all within a relatively short time. A huge move for any young person to undertake. You can't compare that move to others that most young people make. For instance, if you go to university you know months in advance that you are leaving home, you're given time to settle in, you're amongst hundreds of others in the same boat, and there are many social choices available to you.

When any of us finds ourselves in a new situation, we rely on our past experiences to get us through. We can only call on what we've already experienced – the stuff that's in our database. We all have a kind of 'sat nav' system that gets us from one situation to another, which has been programmed over our lifetime from thousands of different situations. It also includes some of our parents' experiences – how they would navigate certain situations, both practically and emotionally. Most of these pre-programmed responses are subconscious, and because they're often effective we don't stop to question them.

Paul did what he knew best. He'd never learned how to live alone, and living with others brought its own difficulties: he'd moved out of his own house, making himself effectively homeless, rather than confront the situation that was unfolding – or upset anyone – which is one of his patterns. So he ended up a young lad living in a London hotel, playing top-class football with men mostly much older than him. It all started to get too much, and his drinking, which had progressed only slowly up to this point, became more regular. On the pitch he was faultless and as long as this continued he could do what he liked off it. In his words, 'I would let my football do the talking.'

The big problem was when he wasn't actually playing. Paul, like most young footballers, put training and practice before his education. Therefore he lacked some of the interpersonal skills needed to manage such a life-changing career. He learned from an early age to be a 'people-pleaser', and his pleasing other people has often been at the expense of his own needs or desires. When people put pressure on him he has bowed to it, so that at times he ended up in situations he didn't want to be in, and therefore became angry or resentful. One way of getting away from this pressure and relieving the resulting anger has been to drink.

When Paul moved to Lazio this pattern continued. As the pressure mounted, so did the need for an outlet. He had met his wife-to-be and, of course, that was a lovely change for him, and an escape. But it brought along many other pressures including children: two stepchildren and later his son, Regan. As Paul admits, he struggled to cope with this at times. Everyone wanted a bit of him: friends, family, the media, the clubs and the fans. To cap it all, his wife and family constantly argued. This contributed to one of his very serious injuries.

Then, while in hospital, Paul rediscovered morphine. He liked the calming feeling it gave him, and found it enabled him temporarily to switch off from the world. The morphine would soon lead him back to the drink.

Paul returned to the UK to play football at Rangers. He was relieved to be home and for a short period his first love, football, kept him on track. He was happy. But by this time his relationship with his best friend – alcohol – was well established. Each time Paul had a good run of sobriety and football, some big life-event – an injury, marriage, bad press – came along that he wasn't able to handle without drink. Alcohol interferes with blood-sugar levels and the balance of chemicals in the brain. Moods swing wildly, and a sudden attack of rage can lead to violence. Paul's drinking was now having catastrophic consequences on his life which were proving harder and harder to recover from.

Paul's pattern of drinking increases in parallel with his responsibilities. It's important that, as well as looking at Paul's life as it is today, we also cover the past. My job is to help Paul see the link between his past and his present: at the moment, history is repeating itself. This feeling of powerlessness links in with his childhood experiences.

When Paul drinks alcohol, instead of standing up for himself he loses control – the opposite of what he wants to happen. He's hoping to feel relaxed, less overwhelmed and more in control. Instead, he relinquishes his personal power and ends up becoming a victim. When this happens all sorts of feelings arise – anger, resentment and even a desire to self-sabotage. He presses the 'fuck it' switch: a self-destruct button. Some in my field would describe this phenomenon as a 'death wish'. This is the most dangerous aspect of addiction and can lead to death through many routes such as alcohol poisoning, drink-driving accidents and violence.

As a manager, Paul's in a new situation which any footballer would initially struggle with, and he needs the key skills of patience and negotiation for the job. He needs to stop drinking before anything else can change. Once Paul starts drinking, even if it's initially moderately, his alcoholism takes over. Rational thought goes out of the window, and denial kicks in. If he doesn't stop, it will eventually get the better of him and bring him to 'rock bottom'. He cannot use alcohol to cope with pressure, no matter how big the pressures are.

Hey Gazza

A true honor, not only to have met you, but to experience the romantic gifts you left us all with your sugar-free 'tablets'. Bring some back from Jimmy for me will ya. Hell . . . fuckin hell . . . bear with me a while.

I get serious for a minute a'rite Gazza . . . you are an absolutely amazing individual Paul and I'm sure you've heard it all before. I just want you to know that I truly respect you . . . and look up to you, for your character and your attitude and the strength you have shown to beat the demons of alcoholism.

Don't just tell the little bastard on your shoulder to fuck off . . . give him a swift kick to the clems and make him wish he was born a woman, a'rite . . . fucking hell . . . a'rite man . . .

Cheers ya wanker. Ha! All my love – keep in touch, stay funny.

Jim

Paul's personal problems

Paul

I never discuss football with Johnny and I never discuss my personal problems with Paul Davis. I keep them separate.

There was one thing, though, I don't think I mentioned to Johnny in that last session. It just didn't come out. It's to do with my weight which I've always been obsessed about. When I was playing, it always ballooned up in the close season when I'd binge on ice cream and sweet drinks or cocktails. It wasn't really junk food like burgers and kebabs that did it, but drink and ice cream, that's what put the weight on.

I can't remember when I first started bringing it all up – and by that I don't mean talking about it – or when I first heard about bulimia, and how you did it. It must have been when I was about seventeen. Funnily enough, my sister Anna was in a TV series at the time, acting the part of a bulimic. So that's when I might have first learned about it.

I've done it regularly over the years, but then I might not do it for a year or two. The last time was two weeks ago. Yeah, here at Champneys. I did it three days running. That's what I haven't told Johnny.

I haven't been going to the dining room since I moved in here, which was before I got the Kettering job. I usually just have room service, snacks and stuff. I love their toasted bagels. This evening I kept on eating them, ordering more and more, plus I had chocolate and milkshakes and cakes from the shop. I was bored, stuck in my room on my own after training, worrying about the team, worrying about Imraan, full of nerves, so I just kept on bingeing, knowing what I was going to do.

When I'd really had enough, I went to the bathroom, put my fingers down my throat, and up it all came, straight away, down into the toilet pan.

I don't do it because I like doing it. I hate the feeling. But if I know I'm going to go on an eating binge, I keep on eating, knowing I can sick it up. That way I won't put on weight. It is a proper eating disorder, I know that. And I know it's bad for you. It brings up the acid and can burn a hole in your stomach.

It's an addiction, like all the others I have. Like drink and drugs. But right now, I feel in control. All right, I'm drinking again, but I feel a couple of glasses of wine a few times a week is okay. What harm can it do?

I've been here at Champneys for two months, thanks to the owner, Steve Perdew, who's a friend of mine. He's let me stay for free. But now I have to get out, as they are filling up for the Christmas season. Anyway, I want to move into somewhere handier for the ground and training.

What I'm going to do is move into the Kettering Park Hotel for two weeks, then I'm going into an apartment near the ground. Jimmy saw a big five-bedroom house he thought I'd like, but I looked at it and didn't fancy it. Too big. I just need a two- or three-bedroom apartment at this stage, as handy for the club as possible.

I've been living out of a suitcase for years, so I'm used to it. I'm not bothered, not really. If I did meet a woman, and bought a house and moved into it with her, she'd take it from me if we split. I lost about £4 million, all down the drain, being married to Shel. I'm afraid of that happening again.

Lots of my stuff is in storage. The clothes will be out of date I guess. And I like to be fashionable. Ha! You've seen some of my haircuts. That proves it.

As you know, I did tell Johnny about going to Leeds. One of my obsessions has always been talking to strangers, telling them about myself. Like that taxi driver. He had to listen. He couldn't escape. And that bloke on the train on the way back. I love it on trains when I get talking to someone who doesn't know me. I can just rabbit.

A few months ago I went up to Newcastle on the train and I found myself beside this old woman, must have been about seventy, and we chatted all the way. She was a brilliant listener, listened to all my problems. After talking to her for two hours, I felt so much better. When we got to Newcastle, I got out some paper and wrote a little thank-you letter: 'With much love, Paul Gazza Gascoigne.' As I walked away down the platform, I could see her looking at it, a bit puzzled. But I think, watching her from afar, it did begin to dawn on her who I might be. I travel a lot on trains. I don't like to fly if I can help it. That's another one of the things that mess me up.

When I started having therapy, I never hid it from anyone. I wasn't ashamed. After that first trip to the Priory, I'd tell all the lads in the Boro dressing room about all the things I had to do, making them laugh. But I also told them about the serious therapy, that I had a therapist, Johnny. And also about going to AA meetings.

I've always talked about what's on my mind, holding very little back. All the teams I played with knew about me. I wasn't ashamed. They never took the piss out of me because I'd revealed something. I think they just felt sorry, or perhaps they just thought that was me, daft Gazza. They probably got fed up with me in the end, when I was hyperactive or was endlessly talking, rabbiting on.

I don't think in my football career I ever heard about any other players having therapy. Not that they told me. But most players are a mass of superstitions – about putting their boots on a certain way, or their shorts, being last out on the pitch, eating certain things, driving a certain way to the ground – and they believe these things. They worry they'll play badly or get beat if they don't do it. With me, I never went in for those sorts of superstitions and lucky charms. I had enough other things going on inside me heed.

I always had obsessions, for as long as I can remember, which I suppose are a sort of superstition. As a kid, I had to tie the right lace on my right shoe last. I always had to have my knife and fork laid out the right way, all my drawers had to be arranged just so, socks in a certain place. I would go mad if anyone ever mixed them up. It scared me. What would happen if I didn't have things always in the right way? It would take me twenty minutes to leave the house, because I always had to go back and close all the doors, over and over again.

Before an important game at Spurs, once, I got in a state because I thought I hadn't locked my front door. I'd just moved into this new house, still getting used to it. It went round and round in my mind as I tried to think back, go over what I'd done. In the end, I rang the next-door neighbour and persuaded him to go round and check the front door. He rang me back to say I had locked it. Only then could I concentrate on the game.

When I was in that house, I had a gas fire, a big one with pretend logs, really good, really hot, but I would often sit in front of it freezing because I worried that, when I went out, I might forget to turn it off. I knew when I did go out, whether I had turned it off or not, that it would dwell on my mind. I'd be wondering all the time. So, I thought, best not to turn it on at all.

For years, I had numbers which I considered as bad or evil, such as 13. Even a combination, like a 6 and 7 equals 13, or 9 and 4, would make me panic, convinced something bad was going to happen. I would change my hotel room number, if I didn't like the number, or my mobile phone. The wrong number would absolutely throw me.

Even now, if I'm doing a text message, and it says I have 13 letters left, I will add something, saying goodbye instead of bye, just to make the text longer, not leave a gap of 13 letters.

In hotels and hospitals, where I've spent half my adult life, if my coat hangers got messed up and were hanging at a different angle from how I left them, I'd go mad. I felt sure something bad would happen. Still do to some extent. But nowhere near as bad. I think David Beckham has a little bit of this. He believes certain signs are bad ones. I saw somewhere, recently, that he's admitted to being a bit compulsive in his behaviour. Like having to have everything in a straight line or in pairs, wanting everything to match, all his cans of soft drinks to be in a certain formation, no untidy magazines or leaflets or books mucking up his room. Some of the lads at Manchester United, apparently, used to deliberately rearrange his stuff in his hotel room, just to annoy him, knowing that it would. It would have upset me.

I remember seeing that Jack Nicholson film, *As Good as It Gets*, and I thought to myself, 'Jack Nicholson, you fucker, you've been watching me.' I understood exactly all the little rituals he had to do each day, otherwise he panicked.

They have tried to treat me for this when I've been in the Priory or Cottonwood. They teach you to blank it out, to divert yourself by going for a walk. I didn't find that sort of thing helped much. What has helped me has been medication they prescribed at Cottonwood. I take Depakote for panic attacks and Seroquel for anxiety attacks. And I do think they have helped. I've been on both of them for two years. I have improved. I could come off them now, so the doctors say, but I'd rather stick with them. I don't want to go back to where I was before.

I don't have the twitches I used to have as a lad. When I was playing football, people did comment on it, how my neck used to twitch, or my mouth. For many years I used to twitch my right shoulder, sort of stretching it out and twitching it. I didn't know I was doing any of these things. They didn't bother me personally, till people pointed them out or wrote about them. When I was at Newcastle, I had this habit of kicking my toe in the ground when I ran. That was just a nervous habit, which I did under pressure. Now, I seem to have grown out of most of my twitches, which is good. Age, perhaps.

Pill popping – I started that when I was at Boro. When I couldn't sleep, I used to get some sleeping pills prescribed but I never had enough, so I would buy them from people, people who had them on prescription, or mates of mine got them for me. It was things like Zimovane and diazepam. I'd take one and find it didn't work, so I'd then take seven or eight. Daft and dangerous, I know.

It was also to lose weight. By 8 p.m. I'd be starving. I'd take all these sleeping pills so I'd fall asleep without having eaten and I'd wake up two pounds lighter. At Rangers, I used to break into the medical room and steal sleeping tablets, just to knock me out, stop the depressions.

I'm still on lots of pills these days, three a day, which the doctors prescribe and Johnny knows about.

Look at the table in front of me now, at my three mobile phones, all lined up in the same way, at the exact angle. I'm not even aware of arranging them like that, till now, looking at them. Now, it doesn't worry me as much if they get messed up. I no longer believe it's a sign something bad will happen. But I still find I have to have all my things in a certain order.

Hold on, there's a text message coming through from Chris Waddle. I'd better read it . . . 'I don't want you to get upset,' it reads, 'but I thought I'd better tell you something. I know you won't like it and you'll only get depressed, but I thought I should let you know about it before anyone else . . .'

What the fuck is he on about? Now he's really got me scared. If the fucking *Sun* has got another story about me I'll go . . .

'Don't ring me back, when you've read what I'm going to tell you, as I know you'll want to. I just feel this is the best way to inform you . . . THERE IS NO FUCKING SANTA CLAUS!'

The bastard! Very funny.

He's got me at a bad moment. Scrolling through his text, I really was shaking. I was thinking something awful was about to come out in the papers, just when I'm getting myself in a state about other things. I was sure it was the press. I do live in fear of them all the time.

That bastard Waddler. I'll get my own back on him some time . . .

Heh Man, what's up

It's been great having you in primary group and getting to know you. You are such an awesome funny guy. Thanks for always listening to me in the group and supporting me.

Good luck staying sober. I know you can do it!

Lil

Paul KO'd at Kettering

Paul

I'm a bit worried about Imraan. I hadn't realised he was going to be so involved. He's there all the time, at all the training sessions as well as games. The other day he came into my little office, the one I share with Paul Davis, to do his paperwork, working on contracts for new players. Me and Paul were trying to get on with our own paperwork, so I didn't want him to be there. I asked if he'd leave, but he didn't. I wasn't happy.

Paul Davis told me that Imraan asked him to help get him through his FA coaching badge. 'Are you serious?', I said to Paul. I couldn't believe it. He can't even do keepy-uppies, so what's he thinking about, wanting to take his coaching badge. Then he told Paul his ambition is to be a manager. Fucking hell.

He's also been playing cards with the players on the team coach, which I'm not happy about. All football players do this on the team coach, always have done, but most managers have an absolute ban on players playing for money. They know what can happen – you lose £1,000, or £10,000, on the way to a game, and it preys on your mind. With us, it would only be £20 or £50 max. But it's the same thing. Playing for money causes problems. So I told him to stop. I wasn't happy with it. He is the chairman after all. I've never heard of chairmen playing cards with the team. Have you?

When he is around he's not always in what I'd call appropriate gear. It's got me thinking, mind. When we have a bit of money, or the right sort of sponsorship, what about having special suits, or perhaps just blazers, for the whole team, and the coaches? I might even pay for them myself. I met someone on a train the other day who was in the clothing business. He said he'd do me a deal. I'll even buy a suit for the chairman.

Apart from that, we're all getting on okay. I love being the manager, every minute of it.

We got beaten by Barrow, 3–1 at home on 3 December. It was only our second league defeat since I became the manager. But we're sixth in the league, so still in a good position to go up.

Imraan gets me afterwards and asks me why I played so and so, why I had done this, done that.

He said, 'Forget about our friendship Paul, I just want to know why you played so and so in that position?' I said, 'I'm the manager, I pick the team, that's my job.' He went on and on about it, really pissing me off.

If we'd lost *nine* games in a row, I could have understood the chairman asking questions, getting worried.

We'd already had words about the reserve team. He'd signed two new players and wanted them played, but I'd got two new players on trial who I wanted to play, one of them an Under-19 England player. He told the reserve-team manager to play his players. I told him not to, but to play my two – one in the first half, one in the second. I wanted to test one of them as soon as possible, because I knew other clubs were after him.

So after the Barrow game, and those words with Imraan, I came back to my hotel in Kettering, and yes, I did have some wine. I then sent him a text saying I thought he'd become a control freak. I'm the manager and I pick the team. If he doesn't like what I'm doing, he can sack me.

I just didn't think it was right, the way he was going on. He'd also said the gates had recently dropped down to 1,400. Fucking hell. They were only about 600 when I joined.

I didn't hear anything, till Andy Billingham, who was also at Kettering, rang me. He said Imraan had asked him to tell me I'd been sacked. He never told me personally, not face to face, not even on the phone.

So I texted him, told him what I really thought. I said I thought it was a disgrace, treating me like that. After everything I'd done for the club. And how could he sack me anyway? I'd never had a contract. So I resigned.

At the very beginning, I said I'd never walk away from the club, whatever happened. And I meant it. But fucking hell, I didn't know I'd have a chairman like that, did I?

The next day, the Sunday, I went up to Birmingham, to stay over with Andy. I was due in Liverpool on Monday to go to a do, for a charity that Johnny's involved with which is opening a day centre for drug and alcohol treatment. It was a fund-raising thing and I'd agreed to be there as the chief guest, do a question-and-answer session, auction some stuff.

After I got the sack on the Saturday night, I told Johnny my head wasn't right and I might not make the do. But then I thought, 'No, I won't back out, I don't want to let them down. I'll go all the same. I've got to stay strong.'

So on the Monday I went on to Liverpool and booked into a hotel in Hope Street, near where the charity do was taking place.

I sneaked a couple of glasses of wine at the event, but that was all. Of course there was drink there. Don't be daft. The fact that it's an alcohol charity is beside the point. If you go to a do which is to help disabled children, you don't have to be disabled to be there, do you? So of course they provide wine for all the guests. And I sneaked a couple of glasses. That was all.

I spent two hours at the do, did all they wanted, did the question-

and-answer thing. I put on an England shirt then I took it off and signed it for the auction. I couldn't have done all that, if I'd been drunk, could I?

I realised I'd left my mobile in the hotel so, during the do, I nipped out to my hotel to pick it up – and there were two paparazzi who insisted on following me. They took dozens of photos. I put up with them at first, wasn't too bothered. Then they followed me all the way back to the event, which was in this restaurant. Later I popped out again to buy some cigarettes, and they followed me down the street again.

I then made a bad mistake. I had agreed to be interviewed by Sky TV about Johnny's charity but then it ended up being about getting the sack at Kettering. Everyone knew about it by then. Jane, my agent, had advised me to say nothing. I don't know why I got sucked into it. I suppose I was still all wound up and emotional and angry about what happened.

But I wasn't drunk. People later said that I was drunk during the interview, they could tell it by the way I was shaky and slurring, but I tell you, that's just not true. I'd only had two or three glasses of wine. The reason I was in an emotional state and shaking was because I was on lots of medication and just one drink on top of it can make you shot. And it was made worse by having had the sack, unfairly, so I think.

I know when I'm drunk. I'm an alcoholic. And I wasn't drunk, whatever people might think. But I was in a state, which might have looked to some people as if I had been drinking.

After the do was over and I was walking back to my hotel, there they were again, snapping away. This time I said, 'That's it guys, you've got more than enough pictures, now just leave me alone.'

One of them was really winding me up, sticking his camera right in my face. I was with a friend from Everton who couldn't believe it, what I was having to put up with. I told him I'd had to put up with this sort of shit for twenty years.

Anyway, I gave this pap a shove. I can't believe I hurt him. I just pushed him away. Perhaps he fell, or bashed himself on his own camera. Anyway, I didn't look. I just walked on, and then into my hotel.

Not long afterwards, two cops, a man and woman, arrive and tell me

I'm under arrest. They put me in their police car and drove me away. The police were fine. No problems with them, no complaints. They knew who I was, right enough, but they explained they had to treat everyone the same, which they did.

At the police station, one of the things they asked me was had I ever been up for assault before. I said, 'Yes, many years ago.' This was in Newcastle, when this bloke attacked my sister and I gave him a punch. They asked me when it had happened. I knew it was 1991, but I wasn't sure when. They looked up my records – and, fucking hell, I couldn't believe it. It was on 5 December! The same date as that day. Incredible coincidence.

I said, 'That's it then. For the rest of my life, I'll never be going out anywhere on 5 December.'

At the police station, they said I could make a phone call, so I tried to ring Robin, my lawyer, in Newcastle. But this was late at night and I failed to get him. I couldn't think who else to ring for help. I needed a solicitor. I knew enough not to make any statements about what had happened until I had a proper lawyer. So I rang my financial advisor, Dave McGhee. I don't know why. Just couldn't think of anyone else. I got his wife out of bed and then Dave comes on the line. I said, 'I'm in a police cell for the night.' He said he'd try to get some help.

I also rang Jimmy, to tell him what happened, and also my brother Carl. I told them to tell me mam and dad that I was okay. I knew it would be in the papers and on TV in the morning – that I was in a police cell. I told them not to worry. It would all be sorted out. I was fine. And I was *not* drunk.

Round about 11.30 at night, I was put in a police cell. Just a little cell, with a bed on the floor and a potty. They took my clothes away for forensic testing. I dunno why. Because of any blood stains, I suppose. They gave me paper pyjamas. I looked like Wurzel Gummidge.

I couldn't sleep. I never do anyway, wherever I am, but this time I was also getting claustrophobia, stuck in that titchy little cell. In the morning, they offered me some breakfast. I said no. I ate nothing.

That's going to be my new phone number – 80 80 80 – eight nothing, eight nothing, eight nothing. Gerrit? Yeah, I can joke about it now, a week later, but it wasn't funny, not then.

In the morning, I pleaded with them not to put me back in the cell, cos of my claustrophobia. They were very good about it. So while I waited for a lawyer to come, they put me in an ordinary little room and left the door open. I then felt a bit better.

Jimmy had eventually got through to Robin at his home about 7.30 that morning, the Tuesday. He then managed to contact a lawyer friend in Liverpool who eventually appeared. I left the police station about 1.30 p.m. The police had to smuggle me out and take me to a meeting place where Andy and Johnny picked me up.

Imraan came out with his twopence worth and was reported as saying that I'd been drunk for thirty-seven days out of the thirty-nine I was at Kettering. What bollocks. He only saw me three times a week for six weeks, which comes to eighteen times max – so how could he have seen me drunk thirty-seven times?

The only time I got near it was after George Best died, my old friend. I rang his son Calum to sympathise. Then I had a couple of brandies with Paul Davis. This was before our Cup game – which we won. That's the only time I had a drink before a game. And I repeat, I wasn't drunk then. I just might have looked it.

I met the sponsors, met the directors from the other club, talked to their chairman. I couldn't have been drunk to do all that. The trouble with me is that, because of all the medication I take all the time, I can appear drunk when I'm not. And also when you've been dry for two years, as I had been, then a couple of brandies can go straight to your head.

But drunk thirty-seven times in six weeks, that's a fucking joke.

I was furious and bitter at the time but now, as I'm sitting here, a few days after it all and looking back, I'm just sad. No, I don't regret getting involved with Kettering. I loved the lads and the team and every moment of being manager. I loved watching Paul Davis do the coaching.

I've learned from it – and what I've learned is not to get involved with a chairman who it seems really wants to be a manager. Next time I want a chairman who takes a back seat with the team and lets the manager and coaches get on with it.

I never got paid, during those six weeks, not a penny, not even my expenses or petrol. I'm going to get my lawyer on to that.

I've spoken since to a few managers about what went on. I mentioned to some of them how I hadn't been paid and how I thought the chairman was a control freak. They said I should have walked away. They said you should never work for no money, not even for one week.

I never did become part owner. The plan was to put £50,000 of my own money into Kettering. That was the deal. It was to show I was serious and had no intention of walking away.

I was always asking Imraan, over and over, 'Where's the contract?' I saw one once, but then he took it back. Said it needed to be changed, but it never reappeared. He always said he was so busy. So I paid out nothing in the end. In that sense, I haven't lost any money. But I wanted to invest.

I don't know whatever happened to that contract.

I feel used, stitched up. I never said a bad word about him to anybody, all the time I was there, never criticised him or said in public how he was interfering. Though I knew he was. I just kept quiet.

Then he sacks me and comes out with this bollocks about being drunk for thirty-seven days. Two players also said a few things about me afterwards – but they were two players I had to drop because *he* wanted them dropped. They don't know that, but it was all his doing, not mine. I took the can. I won't make the same mistake again. Don't say it. I'll probably make different mistakes next time . . .

But honestly, I don't regret it. I'll bounce back. It's made me more determined to succeed next time.

I know I've had a series of jobs that have led nowhere, but there's always been a reason, like China or Boston. People want me involved for my name, for the publicity, to get attention for themselves, to put the gates up, all those sorts of reasons. Then, when they've had all that, they change, lose interest.

I could just try to be a junior coach, with a youth team, perhaps in a higher league, where I wouldn't have the worries and responsibilities of managing a first team. I'd be able to get home at a decent time of night and sleep well – but I don't want that. I want to be a manager. That's the only thing in life I want to be.

The size of the club doesn't matter, though I don't intend to go any further down in the divisions than Kettering. I'm already getting one or two approaches. We'll have to see. But I'm not giving up. I know I'm going to try even harder next time, but first I'll check out the chairman properly.

As for the court case, the photographer has now dropped the charges. In his statement he denies harassing me – but at the same time he says he'd only taken seventy-five photos of me. Seventy-five! Bloody hell. If that isn't harassment I don't know what is. So, no charges will be issued. It's all been dropped, but I have to report back to the Liverpool police station on 15 Feb. I dunno why. That's just what I was told.

The press reaction to me getting the sack, and supposedly being drunk on thirty-seven occasions, was phenomenal, well over the top.

They believed all that Imraan had said, so they all had a go at me. I did think about going away straight afterwards, somewhere abroad, but they'd still find me and hound me. There's no escape. The press want to crucify me.

I really believe they won't be happy till I'm dead. One of the posh papers, the *Independent*, had a headline, 'We won't be happy until Gazza is dead.' It was written by Janet Street-Porter. She repeated all the stuff about being drunk for thirty-seven days without knowing the truth, knowing my version. But what she was also saying was that it was time all those journalists stopped doing to me what they did to George. She said the press should leave me in peace. That was good of her. To understand that.

They didn't, of course. Leave me in peace that is. And they don't get things right either.

The Times is supposed to be a decent paper, isn't it? Yet they had a big piece about me after I got the sack. They used it as an excuse to go over my life. In it, they said, 'his father died of a brain haemorrhage when Paul was 11.' I have the cutting here, 7 December 2005. How could they have got that so wrong? I didn't correct it. I'd spend the rest of my life correcting things, once I started. But it will go in the cuttings and other papers will repeat it, just because it was in *The Times*. To be fair, the journalist did send me an apology.

Then David Mellor in the *Evening Standard* said I was back living with my dad in his 'two up, two down'. Wrong on both counts. I'm not living with him and, anyway, my dad lives in a very nice semi-detached house in a nice area. I know, cos I bought it for him.

I'll bet Mellor just lifted something from another paper and used it. I felt it was a bit sneery. Not a very important mistake, not as bad as saying my dad was dead, but it's typical of what they do. Lots of these columnists don't bother to check things. They believe everything they've read, then add a bit of their own. And so it goes on. And if they can make up stuff like someone's dead, of course they make up that you've been seen out drinking, getting up to this or that.

I'm now back at Champneys. After the police let me go, I decided to come here. No point in staying in that hotel in Kettering any more, when I'd had the sack. Steve, the owner of Champneys, rang and said I could come back.

Some people have said I'll now be going into rehab, to the Priory or to Cottonwood to dry out, after being drunk for thirty-seven days. But I'm not. Why should I, I wasn't drunk. So I don't need to go away and hide.

Yes, I'm an alcoholic, but I still feel in control at the moment. I'm still just drinking the odd glass of wine, that's all. It would mean Imraan had won, if I had to go away and be dried out.

I know what it's like to be drunk, and I wasn't. And I'm not now. I'm just going to chill out, keep my head down for a bit.

One thing I am planning on is to go and see Johnny. Talk to him about what's been happening, then perhaps have a bit of a holiday, go home to Gateshead for Christmas to be with the family . . .

Me Clems!

Hello Mr Gazza. It's been a pleasure getting to know you. You are a genuine person I will never forget. Take care.

Love

Cath

At fifteen I decided I was going to support my family for the rest of my life. Breaking into the Newcastle first team helped me fulfil that promise.

I loved my time at Spurs. I sometimes wonder why I didn't stay longer. I'm celebrating a goal against Sunderland here, by the way, not the fact that I'd eventually got that damn fat pigeon ... I never managed that.

1990 World Cup semi-final. Taking on Augenthaler with the final still in our grasp ...

... and then it was all over. Tears again. Because we weren't winners. And I have always wanted to be the winner. At everything.

Playing for Lazio was great, but the coaches really came down heavy, ha, if I put on any weight.

At Heathrow after smashing my leg at Lazio. I was frustrated and angry cos I wasn't playing football. And the press followed me everywhere. Mind you, maybe it was the fashion photographers, looking for some tips.

THE Sun

Friday, May 31, 1996   27p   Thought: Wasted talent

GAME CARD INSIDE

WIN £1M Keno TODAY

Plus £40,000 Lucky NUMBERS

SEE PAGE 15

2 FREE GOES ON £10M LOTTO IN YOUR Sun TOMORROW SYNDICATES

DISGRACEFOOL

Look at Gazza.. a drunk oaf with no pride

WORLD PICTURE EXCLUSIVE

By EUGENE HENDERSON

THIS is the photo that shows shamed Paul Gascoigne "in training" for the biggest soccer tournament in England since the 1966 World Cup.

Grinning drunkenly, his shirt torn to shreds and a beer bottle in his hand, Gazza looks more like a soccer yob than a £20,000-a-week superstar.

The oaf knocked back cocktail after cocktail in a Hong Kong club as he led a huge binge with England teammates including Teddy Sheringham and Steve McManaman.

Early today it was reported that on the flight home Gascoigne tried to force his way into the cockpit of the Cathay

Continued on Page Two

YOU THE JURY

DO you think Gazza should play for England in Euro 96?

YES: 0891 400699
NO: 0891 400699

Calls cost an extra than 50p

Guzzla . . . Gascoigne, his shirt torn to shreds, sinks another beer with Steve McManaman (left) and Teddy Sheringham

The night of the dentist's chair.

Euro '96. Another semi-final against the Germans. I scored my penalty, but again we were out.

Champions League against Ajax. October 1996. A red mist came over me and I kicked out at Winston Bogarde. And was off. I hadn't told Walter Smith what had happened at Gleneagles a couple of days earlier.

Happier times at Rangers. Coisty is keeping tight hold of the Coca-Cola Cup. Probably worried I'll go off with it and rearrange all the Rangers trophies in a nice, neat order. Just like I did to the tin cans in his kitchen.

Bryan Robson has been amazing to me. It was Bryan who first took me to the Priory when I was in a terrible state. Not that I was admitting it then. This is my first public appearance after I came out. I promised, promised, promised Bryan I would never touch drink again...

Paul's third session: Crisis

Paul

I can't believe that last Friday I was a manager, and by this Monday I'd been sacked and was locked up in a cell. I just can't believe it. On Saturday we lost, and I had it out with Imraan, and he wasn't happy. By Monday I'd been to three cities in three days. Got beaten, got sacked, then the next minute I'm locked up in the cells.

It wasn't very nice in there. I was banged up for nearly ten hours without my medication and, as you know, suffering from claustrophobia. They took all my belongings away from me. It was quite scary. Since it happened I've been trying to get myself back on track again, but the papers have been disgusting. It was Kate Moss's turn not so long ago, now it's my turn . . . But I'm not happy with myself.

I think, 'Right, I won't drink,' and then I get bored and I eat too much. Then I look in the mirror and think, 'Fuck me, I'm putting on weight!' I've got a battle on me hands. I want to stop drinking, but I just want to enjoy

Christmas and New Year and give up afterwards, on 2nd January. But if it gets bad, really bad, I know I'll have to fuck off to the clinic and get a fresh start because, when I get back from the clinic, I'm happy, the sparkle is back in my eyes. But why should I do it just because the press are saying it?

John

I'm keen to explore with Paul this statement he made about not being happy with himself.

For the moment, we need to concentrate on what is blocking Paul from doing the right thing for his health. Paul's stuck because the press are saying he needs to get his drinking sorted out, and he doesn't like being told what to do.

Paul

All my life I've been told what to do: at school by teachers, by me parents, as a player by the coach, the managers, as a coach by other coaches. Now the press.

The press say this and that and I think, 'No.' I can go five days without a drink. But then I get cravings. It's boring *with* a drink, fuck knows what it's going to be like *without* a drink!

I do think I've been depressed. When I'm sober, all the things come back to me that I have to battle with. Obsessions with food, the gym, Red Bull . . . And it's like the press just won't let go.

Do I feel persecuted by them? Yes, but I know I can't ever get rid of the press – it's all about how I deal with them.

But I just think, 'Why should I let them dictate to me what I should do and what I shouldn't do with my life?' You've seen what they've done to Princess Diana and you've seen what they've done to George Best. He wasn't left alone to sort out his own problems. But I *have* to do it, I have to get sober. I can *get* sober, it's *staying* sober that's hard.

John

Paul's very concerned about being told what to do by the press, so I'm interested in how we can get him out of that thought cycle – knowing that he needs to get help with the drink but not wanting to get help because then the press will have won. I wonder if he could look at it another way: if he does get help he'll get himself back, and then *he'll* have 'won'.

We talk about what worked for him last time he got sober and stayed sober for over two years. Paul needs to take responsibility for getting himself back on track. I want to support him in reaching a place psychologically where he's able to say to himself, 'I'm going to get sober, and I'm going to do it for me.'

Paul

I've got this thing focused in my head, get Christmas over and knuckle down to getting myself sorted out after that. I know a lot of friends are worried for me. I'm worried for myself. I'm feeling sorry for myself.

Yes, when I get sober it's going to have to be for me, but at the moment I feel it's for everybody else. After Christmas I'll start afresh. It'll be a bigger battle after Christmas even than it would be now, because I'll want to have a great Christmas. Christmas Day, Boxing Day, New Year's Eve – I know I'm going to drink those three days anyway, so why stay sober now?

John

Another part of Paul's resistance right now is the idea that Christmas is around the corner and he doesn't want to spend it having a miserable time, trying to give up alcohol, or in a clinic. He's more or less made the decision that he's going to drink until after Christmas and New Year. What worries me is what he said about wanting a good Christmas. I ask him to watch out for thinking, 'This is my last party before I get sober,' and going out with a bang.

We go back to this feeling Paul has of being controlled. One of the first times we met, he was feeling trapped and controlled by the football club. I suggest that what seems to happen is that he has a good run, even getting away with drinking for a while, but then one way or another alcohol seems to get in the way of his life. Then when he loses control because of the alcohol, people around him rush in and try to control him, telling him what to do, and he feels manipulated and controlled again.

Paul

It's been that way my whole life. Everybody's trying to tell me what I should do. And I've had a drink problem, cocaine problem, food problem, so many problems to deal with. I'm not forty yet, I'm going to live a long time, I've got to battle these problems every day. What sort of life is this? So then I just want a glass of wine.

But the drinking doesn't even bring me relief, because as soon as I have one glass I think, 'Fuck me, what have I done that for?' I'm even regretting it as it enters my mouth.

It's a battle I find hard to fight. If I can see sense again, or light at the end of the tunnel . . . But at the moment I feel like I've just entered the tunnel and it's very dark and dull, and there's a long way to go.

I thought there was hope when I took the Kettering job. But I've had that man Imraan breathing down my neck every single day for six weeks: trying to pick the team, trying to pick the reserve team, trying to sack the reserve-team manager, getting rid of players, making *me* get rid of players and then the papers having a go at me for getting rid of them and not reporting when they were injured. My two top strikers were out injured and no one said anything about it in the papers when the results didn't go our way.

John

The analogy of the tunnel is a good way of describing the feeling of powerlessness. Everything that's happened has led to Paul starting to lose hope. The whole job experience has been really hard, and he's still feeling it.

I think it's important that Paul tries not to sabotage himself. He got the job he wanted at Kettering, the drink sneaked in and that was okay for a while, but then it turned. I ask him for a minute to forget about Imraan's behaviour. Here was something he really wanted, and yet the drinking crept in almost unknowingly. Then it increased to the point where he'd given his power away, because when Paul's boss felt he couldn't control him he was able to blame the drinking, and he was able to list issues and events, whether there were thirty-seven of them or not. Looking at Paul's process, it's as if he gives his good things away – things are going well, then something in him says, 'I'm going to fuck this up.'

Paul

I don't know where he got those thirty-seven incidents from. I wouldn't drink for six days, then I'd be feeling pissed off and want a drink. I'd have a couple of glasses of wine, then not drink again for two days. I can't remember the last time I was drunk. You know what it's like, Johnny, I have to hide my drinking. So it's not easy, fun. I think, 'Why am I doing this? Why can't I just sit there and relax and enjoy it?'

But I know what the problem is. I'm an alcoholic so I can't be like others, social drinkers. I have to do it myself. I rang Eric Clapton up the other day, to ask him about his clinic. But the thought of two hours of group therapy every day ... And they take everything off you, mobiles, everything. And I have to spend a fortune. How many times have I got to keep on going to clinics?

There's no way I'm going into a clinic over Christmas. But that doesn't mean I'm going to get drunk every day until New Year. No way am I going to do that.

I'm so fucked off about the job. Now I've got nothing to look forward to when I wake up in the morning, nothing to get up for. I do want to get back into management, I enjoy it. If I prepare myself properly I'm hopeful I can crack it once I get myself sorted out. That job was a mad rush. I had the players ringing me up distraught. I was still trying to help the players even though I'd been sacked and there was no one to help and support me. Just Paul Davis and Andy.

John

A lot of people have to go to treatment for alcoholism and addiction a lot of times. People even have to go nine or ten times before they get it. I know Paul resists that idea. Most importantly we need to do what's right for Paul, and never mind what other people think. But at the moment he's angry and hurt by his boss and by the media, and the injuries to Kettering players he feels haven't been made public, and being made to drop players he didn't want to drop. In public he's been blamed for the whole thing, so he doesn't want to be proved wrong by going to a clinic so that everything can be blamed on his alcoholism, and no one else has to take responsibility for their own behaviour. When we drink we set ourselves up to be blamed for everything, whether it's all our fault or not.

We talk about how he'll get sober in January. I've suggested going to a clinic, but if he doesn't want to go he'll need a lot of support at home, going to AA meetings and arranging his life so that it supports not drinking.

Paul

I'm not good at getting support. I've got Jimmy, and in the past I've belonged to football clubs. But apart from them I've always managed alone.

I hate being an alcoholic. People don't understand the illness. And you can't get away from alcohol — adverts, billboards, mates at the pub, off-licences — everywhere you look, alcohol is there.

John

On the football field, fighting to win is everything. When it comes to our health and well-being, trying to 'win' can be our downfall.

JM: I want to go back to one thing. The way you were brought up was to fight and to win. You've won so much but, with this, you can't win, you can't beat it.

PG: This is one battle I can't win.

JM: I think that's where your pride comes in because, really, the only way to beat it is to give in — to stop, isn't it?

PG: Yeah.

JM: We need to put a plan in place. We've tried different strategies. We talked last time about cravings: how to ignore the thoughts. And it's important to talk about it and that's the good thing about AA, hearing people talking about being angry about having to stop. Why are you an alcoholic and someone else isn't? It's not fair is it?

PG: No, it's not fair. I have to face the fucking fact that I can't drink. I wish there was an injection for it.

JM: Is that how painful it is for you right now?

PG: I just can't believe it; one minute manager, the next minute in the cells. If I thought I deserved it I'd hold my hands up, but I don't think I deserved it.

JM: You know now and then when something reminds you of your own life? A friend of mine broke his neck playing football. I was injured that week so I wasn't at the game. He went up for a ball and fell awkwardly and he's been in a wheelchair ever since. He was a good footballer, but he's had to accept he can never get out of that chair. Remembering that helps me put things in perspective: it could have been me. This is not to take anything away from your feelings at the moment, they're valid, but maybe you need, finally, to have that acceptance that you can't drink. Whatever your desires and dreams, you can't drink, and you have to accept it.

PG: I understand. I can't win. It brings out the child in me. The fact that I can stay sober for six months, then have just one drink and that's it, I'm away again.

JM: Maybe you have to accept this is the battle you'll never win. You can't be too stubborn, it'll kill you, like George, your friend.

PG: I don't want it to end that way. It's going to take time. I'm slowly slipping into this depression. I've got to get through these two-and-a-half weeks. I wish it was 2nd January now, I really do.

JM: I know you've said you won't get sober before 2nd January, but I want you to reserve the right to change your mind. I want you to get to that point where you say, 'I'm ready to put down the drink.'

PG: I will be, 2nd January.

John

I found this session difficult. I'm very concerned for Paul and don't know what will happen over the next few weeks. He's in a corner and knows he has a fight on his hands. It's an either-or situation: either he surrenders and asks for help, but then feels weak – not strong enough to cope on his own – and gets judged by the media for going back into rehab; or he continues to drink and takes the risk that he won't get through to January without losing control and inviting further condemnation from the press as a 'no-good alky'. He knows how powerful his illness is. By drinking, he ended up giving control to others, something that he hates doing. He is, and has been, a victim of his own success and he needs to take some control back before he can feel okay about himself; the only way to do that is to get the help he needs.

Paul is in denial. I want him to explore other situations in which the old pattern of feeling controlled and helpless has led to sabotage. Paul's refusal to see his part in the self-sabotage is obvious, yet there are valid grievances against people who want to control and dominate him. Taking responsibility is all that Paul or anyone can ever do – he can only look at his own part in what's happened, and see how the drinking has set him up to be caught out by anyone who might want him out of the way.

The paradox of the addictive personality is that the illness leads the addict on into battle with the disease – they try to 'beat' it, by proving that they can control it. But to beat it they need to accept that *it* has beaten *them*. By pitting their will against the object of their desire they come crashing down again and again: every time they set foot in a bar with the intention of having 'just one', they end up drinking all night. Small successes further encourage the addicted person to believe in their own willpower. Paul talks about how long he can go without a drink, or the times when he only had 'a couple of glasses of wine'. Alcoholics talk about these occasions as proof of their ability to control their intake. And at times and for a while they can. But while you might not drink anything for a week, or even a month, you're safe in the knowledge that you'll be having a drink on Friday night, or at the end of January, and some part of you is looking forward or holding on to that, even if it's subconsciously.

Accepting that they need to abstain is a massive leap for most people, and they'll look for every other way around the problem before coming exhaustedly to that point.

Over the last few days I have been in regular contact with Paul and his close friend Jimmy. Paul's moods are at an all-time low and he hasn't managed to stop drinking. The good news is, he's now considering entering treatment before Christmas.

My role as an addictions counsellor is very different from my role as a psychotherapist. One aspect of the addictions role is to make clinical interventions outside of the consulting room. This can include planning the best way to get someone into treatment, if that's what they need. It involves talking to family members, friends and colleagues: anyone who'll help.

I was in daily contact with Jimmy, discussing how we could get Paul back into treatment and getting a report on how Paul was. He was looking after Paul, ensuring that he didn't get too drunk and would get home okay after going out drinking. Jimmy acted as liaison officer, talking to John, Paul's father, and the rest of the family. My main aim was to persuade Paul that now was the right time to go and get help. The longer he left it, the worse he would get.

This stage is probably the most frightening for the family and friends of alcoholics because it's so unpredictable. There's just no way of knowing what will happen. I could not tell you how many times I have heard, 'Will he get drunk tonight and not come home?'; 'Will he crash his car?'; 'I think she's sleeping with other men!' I have worked with many family members who need counselling in order to cope with this stress. Research says that for every alcoholic drinking, there are at least four family members or friends suffering as a direct effect, whether that be emotionally, physically or financially.

In the run-up to Christmas I was on stand-by, not knowing what would happen from one day to the next, hoping that Paul would make that call for help. Then, out of the blue, Jimmy called me and asked if I could get Paul on a flight to the USA. I thought it would be better if he could get Paul to fly to London so that I could meet him at Heathrow for a time before he flew out to Arizona. Paul then called me and said that he had had enough. He was sick and tired of being sick and tired, and was ready to ask for help. He arrived at Heathrow the next day. We talked about the treatment and I told him I thought he was showing great courage in going for help. He felt shame and guilt about the last few weeks but had enough courage and humility to admit defeat. The ability to do that can mean the difference between life and death.

I suggested that Paul concentrate all his energy at the clinic on getting better, staying in touch with me only now and then as the need arose. I would catch up with him again in around a month's time.

––––––––––

Dear Paul

Ya cheeky Bastard. Wishing you the best in this new chapter of your life. Thanks for the Psycho Drama and the advice. I am going to attach myself to winners and stay on this like you said. I appreciate your wit, sense of humor but not your colon. Take care. Rock out with your c..k out. I hear voices in my head . . .

Vince

Paul's connections and responsibilities

John

I always worry, before a session with Paul, that I might make him feel worse. This does happen with some clients. When you get deep into stuff, they can become furious and angry. I have had to stop certain people coming to see me at nine in the morning – because I know they'll leave angry, go to work, sack people, do things they regret.

Sometimes you have to allow them to get angry. Jokes and being matey are all right, but don't actually get you very far or uncover stuff.

In that first session with him, back in the early autumn, when I let him do all the talking, I didn't want to engage on too deep a level and be disruptive. That wouldn't be helpful. At that point, I wasn't trying to get in touch with his core pain – to use the jargon.

He talked a lot about his accidents and injuries – and there's no doubt they spark off his mental problems. He was in hospital for his neck, then he got a blood clot and had to be on warfarin. Then he developed pneumonia while in hospital. So he was in a mentally as well as physically bad state for weeks.

He managed to work out for himself what the accident he had while skating, which hurt his neck and gave him such agony, had led to. He was prescribed morphine for the pain, even though he knew that in the past he had been addicted to morphine. The doctor had to give him this sort of painkiller because the other sort might have affected his stomach – and he has had a history of stomach ulcers.

I think going back on painkillers, and the fact that he was cut off from support, did trigger the relapse he had into alcoholism over the summer and into the Kettering period.

I encourage people to make the links between what has happened to them and how they felt and behaved, so they can understand the causes. He gets addicted to painkillers: he knows he's having to take them to relieve the pain, but worries about being addicted to painkillers, so has a drink to escape it all . . .

The big thing about Paul these days is that he knows where he is going, where it might lead. That's progress. When he had the major relapse in China back in 2003, and went on an alcohol binge, the fact that he was able to take himself off to Cottonwood showed he is able to check himself. It is always good when I hear him being so honest.

One of the things I was trying to get across to Paul when he was at Kettering was that he was now like a father – he had a responsibility to his players. He's not a kid any more. Which is hard, when he's had years of acting and being treated like a kid.

But I could see he was soon aware that he wouldn't get love and caring as a manager. He had to give all of the time, not take. He must have been thinking, 'What about Paul Gascoigne?'

There is a lot of shame in the way people like Paul think. They feel weak, yet they know they have been indulged.

I know Paul has always found it hard in the past to ask for help, so we have to work on what blocks him.

As a child, I think he didn't get much help. He looked after the family when he was still quite young, assuming financial responsibility for them when he started earning money – for his parents, and his sisters and brother. He assumed the financial load – and it's stuck. He sees himself as a provider.

He has also always seen himself as an entertainer. He puts his tongue out at a serious moment and we all laugh. He wants to make people feel better. It's part of being a provider. He is providing light relief, entertainment, although I'm not sure he's always realised it, not in those terms.

So what happens when he's depressed? Who is providing for him? He has, of course, not got a relationship of his own, where someone is caring and providing for him. He is totally on his own, physically and emotionally.

I know a lot of people rubbish therapists when they start on about the influence of parents, but in my experience it's very hard to avoid a link between how you yourself relate to and attract people, and how your parents related.

Paul's parents had rows, lived apart, his dad worked away from home, then they eventually got divorced. His two sisters are both divorced. The same has happened to Paul.

I'm not saying his ex-wife Sheryl was anything like his mother, but nevertheless there is a pattern. For whatever reason, she would appear not able to give Paul the love he needed – and he probably didn't give it to her.

That sort of love was not there to go around when he was growing up either. He didn't receive it, and was thus unable to give it out.

We rarely, of course, receive the kind of love we would like in life, but coming from Paul's sort of background makes it even more difficult.

The more people talk consciously, the more it disturbs the unconscious. By talking, you can make connections you might not have made before.

With Paul, I think he has been able to look back at events and perhaps now make connections he has not made before. I have tried to get him to talk about his brother Carl's drinking and I think he has thought about that and sees it in relation to his parents. Some things pop into your mind immediately. Others take time.

I think he can now see the stages he went through in his drinking, how he was emotionally going up and down till he crossed a line, which all alcoholics cross, where it doesn't alter whether you feel happy or sad – you just want to drink anyway.

At Newcastle, he was contained by the club, having been with them from a young boy. At Spurs, he didn't feel part of a family. Then there was a lot of stress when Sheryl came along because she didn't like his family, and vice versa. That was a very revealing moment when he said that he deliberately had a row with Sheryl in order that he could leave and therefore go home and see his family.

In the early days, he was pleased that Sheryl's children saw him as a father, and called him Dad, but of course that gave him more commitments. Don't forget, he was very young.

It takes time to build a picture, to track things back, but I think he is aware of the stresses and strains he has had in his life, and how ill-prepared he was to cope with them. But I hope eventually to get him to look at his own part in his problems.

I haven't been particularly tough on him so far. With all addicts, you have to make it safe for them. From the first minute they come into your room, the therapy is starting, even if you appear to be doing nothing. You are settling them down, putting them at ease.

Because we missed a few months, I had to get Paul used to sessions again, so I might not have appeared earlier on to have been pushing him very much. I tend to say. 'Yeah, that must have been hard,' rather than criticise or suggest, just to encourage him to come out with it all.

With someone like Paul, you have to nurture them so space opens up and you can get beneath what they are saying. Most of the addicts I deal with are much more stable than Paul, despite all their problems. Paul has got few internal foundations to fall back on. He's been without a home of his own for five years and has no partner in his life – but you could say he's been like that for *all* of his life.

It is amazing, with alcoholics, how some of them do find a way round to asking or crying out for help. It's often not obvious or straightforward, and they don't know themselves why they are doing it. I have had clients coming to see me drunk — as a sort of statement, a defiance, to let me see what's happened, but in reality they are asking for help. Getting drunk was a way of saying what they couldn't put in words.

It was hard to get across the notion of self-sabotage. I'm not sure Paul accepted it. But in his career, it's noticeable how often things go wrong — just when they are going well. He did love being at Kettering, and there was no real need to start drinking again, so why did he do it? It's as if he can't cope with success. There are people like that. They don't believe they deserve success. It's not always happened with Paul, but often enough to suggest an underlying pattern.

I did vaguely try to suggest it but I don't think he quite grasped it. It's a form of masochism which all goes back to his lack of an internal structure. If he was more comfortable with himself, had secure foundations in his life, he would be able to step back and analyse what happened when things go wrong, rather than immediately see himself as a victim, which is what he often does. There's an old joke they use at AA meetings. 'Poor me, poor me, pour me another drink . . .'

At the same time, there were specific causes for his recent problems, which led him to start drinking again in the summer. That accident during the ice dancing did trigger off certain events which have had a bad effect on him.

When people relapse, there are real causes, proper triggers, but of course the main thing which has to be done is get the person to face up to them, to accept that ultimately they are responsible.

I'm very pleased he did agree in the end to get away and get treatment and is now at Cottonwood.

———————

Dear Paul

'I'd do anything, for you dear, anything, for you mean everything, to me.

You know that I'd go anywhere for your smile, anywhere, for your smile everywhere I see'

Ha Ha Ha

Wow am I going to miss you pal. I never thought I would laugh my ass off so much in rehab.

I would love to see you in California. You are a great guy with a great heart. Your stories are truly amazing and I love listening to every one of them.

I don't have a cell yet but I'll make sure I get it to you as soon as I do.

Love

Daz

PS Every time I eat sugar-free Mentoes I'll think of you and fart. Ha ha!

Paul gets help in the desert

Paul

Well I'm back from Cottonwood now. It's mid-January. Getting there was a nightmare. I flew first class to Phoenix where a driver from the clinic was supposed to pick me up but I somehow missed him. So I hired a taxi at the airport and told him I wanted to go to Arizona Cottonwood. Took four hours, before we both realised I should have asked for Cottonwood de Tucson. There's more than one Cottonwood clinic, just as there's more than one Priory or more than one Champneys. We had to drive back two hours. He charged me $860 – then asked for an extra $50 for petrol, cheeky bastard.

I should have arrived at the clinic at seven in the evening but didn't get there till one in the morning – after a ten-hour flight, plus six hours in a car. Fucking hell. What a state I was in.

And all the way there I was thinking, 'I don't want to be here, it's a waste of time, I'm only going because I've been talked into it' – by Jimmy,

Johnny, and my agent Jane. But most of all, I blamed the press. They'd been going on that I was gonna die unless I got treatment. After the Kettering shambles and all the allegations about being drunk, some of the tabloids were putting out a warning under my photo: 'Don't serve this man a drink.' I knew that even if I went to a pub with Jimmy and stuck to water it would appear in the papers that I'd been drinking champagne.

But I honestly didn't think I needed help anyway, not all that much. I know when I've been on a bender. In the past I've been on binges that have lasted three months – that's when you definitely need detoxing. This time, okay I'd been drinking again, but just three days on, three days off, nothing that five days going to AA meetings every day wouldn't have sorted. That's all I thought I needed – one week detox, max. But, what the hell, just to keep the peace, make everyone happy, keep the press at bay, I agreed to go. And then I ended up with this fucking nightmare journey.

Cottonwood is in the desert, miles from anywhere. It's all fairly new, not in an old building like the Priory. There's a group of single-storey buildings, round a sort of square. A bit like a prison, really, with all the different units – but that might give the wrong impression. It's an attractive building, in a wild but really beautiful area.

The first thing they do is take your photo. They want a record of how you looked when you arrived – in other words, like shit. Then they take another photo when you leave. You get to keep both of them – as a warning.

They test your blood for alcohol, drugs, all sorts. They do a body search the moment you get there, and they take away things like your mobile phone and any credit cards. Not because there's any way you can use a card to buy things – but in case you slash your arms with it. It has happened.

They also take away your aftershave and any mouthwash, anything with the slightest hint of alcohol, any stuff you might start drinking if you get desperate.

On the first full day I had an AIDS test, tests for hepatitis C, liver and kidney tests. They were all okay – even my liver – no problems. That proved what I thought – that I had not been on a right binge, not like the old days.

I suppose the real reason I agreed to go was that I was depressed. I just felt fed up. My head was taking a beating after that mess at Kettering. I'd had enough. I couldn't trust myself not to do something really stupid.

For the first five days I was in the detox unit. This is a sort of big ward divided into little single rooms. You have privacy in each room, but each one is very small, with one window, just really a bed and bathroom.

The bed has plastic sheets, which is part of the treatment, to keep you sweating, night and day. They give you tablets to stop your shakes – yeah, the shakes had started before I left England. I admit it. They also give you vitamin B tablets and tablets to help you sweat.

At any one time there's up to fifty people staying at Cottonwood – people come and go so for a few days it can go down to nearer thirty, but it's normally about fifty. There was also a small unit for adolescent girls, aged from fourteen to seventeen, but they were kept separate. I never saw them. They used the same pool, but on different days.

Over the weeks, I got to know all of the fifty. You mix with them, though basically you are put into groups of eight. You stay with this group, and the same therapist, all the time you are there.

I got put into my eight after my five days of detox. We had a woman therapist looking after us, Elaine. She was quite young, probably just over thirty.

Almost all therapists have had first-hand experience of some sort of addiction – either suffering it themselves or they've been brought up in homes where one or both of the parents have been addicted. I don't know her background, but she was good. I liked her.

Once I joined my group, I moved out of the detox ward and shared a room with three other blokes. All of them like me – alcoholics. In each group of eight, there are both women and men, and they can be suffering from all sorts of addictions, such as drugs and gambling. There were two sex addicts while I was there, but not in my group.

I suppose the average age of all the fifty patients was about my age – mid to late thirties. But there were a couple much younger, about nineteen.

You don't know who they are, what they do. That only comes out in passing, if you've made a particular friend and get talking to them. Otherwise you don't know any personal details. It doesn't matter. You are all equal, trying to struggle together.

They were all American in my group, which is how I wanted it. I didn't want to be with any English people. There were a few Brits when I was there, in other groups, and a couple did recognise me eventually and told some of the Americans. But I didn't get bothered cos I still didn't mean anything to them . . . That's really why I prefer Cottonwood to the Priory. I can be really anonymous.

I didn't mind sharing the bedroom with three others – except for one thing. All my life I've slept with the light on, since I was a kid. I can't go to sleep otherwise. This time, I had to have the light off, because the others wanted it off. But I managed. When we got to bed, we were all so tired. You're on the go all day long.

Once at least during the night someone comes round and shines a torch on your bed – to make sure you haven't scarpered or topped yourself, I suppose.

I'd get off okay, but then didn't actually sleep much. Three hours max. I was always up by four o'clock. I'd just wander around or go outside into the desert and watch the sun rise, or listen to the coyotes. I liked sitting in the sun for that first hour after it rises. It was hot, up to 90°, even early in the morning.

I never had breakfast. I couldn't be bothered. I didn't feel hungry. Perhaps later in the morning, I might grab a handful of cereal, but that was about all. I'd just have a coffee and wait for the medications to come round. They started at seven in the morning, along with various medical tests.

After my first five days of detox had finished, I felt much better – and I wanted to come home. The shakes had gone. I didn't fancy starting all the rehab stuff and the therapy sessions. This was my third time here, after all.

I did think of booking myself out, but I remembered that Jane – my agent – had warned me not to. She said the papers would find out and it would be held against me again. I had to do it – to show the world I could, that I could stick to it.

So I started all the therapies. You have to do them, really. The place is full of doctors and psychiatrists and specialists and they have you down for shitloads, doing things all day long, while there's usually someone sitting monitoring you, writing endless notes.

I specially didn't want to go to anger management. I'd done that twice already. I don't consider I get angry any more, not in the old way. First time I was there, I did cause a few scenes in the anger-management sessions.

This bloke was telling us to count to ten when we feel anger coming on. So I says to him, 'Someone smacks you in the fucking face so you then count to ten? Fuck off.' He said, 'Yes, that's what you must try to do.' 'By that time,' I told him, 'you're on the ground and he's kicking your fucking heed in . . .'

But they said I had to go. At the first session, the bloke told us how he used to lose his temper when driving, now he thinks to himself, 'Why am I in a hurry? Do I need to get there at a certain time? Who is being harmed most by me losing my temper?'

I know, I know. All very sensible. But I know all that. I haven't actually lost my temper for some years. So after two sessions, I didn't bother to turn up to anger management any more.

All the same, I was still on the go all the time, with other sessions. You start with your own group every morning, from 9 to 11. You have to begin your bit by saying, 'My name is Paul, I'm an alcoholic and OCD.' Everyone starts off like that. 'My name is Jake, I'm a drug addict,' or whatever . . .

Then you have to tell the group how you are feeling today. There are big signs on the wall with the words written in large letters, like ANGRY HAPPY DEPRESSED SAD UPSET GRATEFUL GRIEVING etc. It's to help you describe how you feel, which one applies to you that day. If you stand up and say right away that you are sad or grieving, then the others know not to take the piss or joke with you. If you are happy, then they know it'll be okay to tease you.

You then try to explain *exactly* how you feel – and they all listen. Perhaps some might ask you questions. Then the next person describes how they feel. The therapist is mainly taking notes, watching how everyone behaves and reacts. It's being with the others, hearing them, that's the main point and, yeah, I think it does help. By listening to others, you do identify with a lot of what they are saying and going through.

One of the sessions was psycho-drama. You play out dramas or little scenes from your life, incidents and events which matter to you. I didn't do any scenes from my life, not this time. Instead I helped others.

What happens is that you tell everyone about this real drama from your life, then the other patients take the parts. You explain what was said, how you felt, the rows and shouts and arguments or whatever, and they have to act it out.

I took one part as a bloke when he was aged two. Yeah, not exactly a hard role. I didn't have much to do. I just had to sit in a corner and shake. That was his memory of his childhood.

In previous sessions at Cottonwood, I had played out bits from my own life. I had someone sitting in a chair as Steven, aged eight, the little boy who got killed. I apologised to him, said how sorry I was, blaming myself, saying I was responsible for his death, and would he ever forgive me. And in the psycho-drama, he did forgive me.

Another time I described some of the scenes with Shel, how I used to shout at her, how she shouted back, what we argued about and why. The person who acted Shel did it so well I felt battered afterwards. She'd won, once again.

They do have family-therapy groups as well, real ones, where your wife or husband or children are invited to come along. When I went out there while I was at Everton it was arranged that Shel would come over to Arizona, and join in a family-therapy group. She'd agreed. And it was all fixed for her to travel. Then I changed my mind. I cancelled it. I just couldn't face it.

No, I've never thought of inviting my parents to any family-therapy sessions, either here or America. Why should I? I am responsible for my drinking. Not them. And I never will. I don't see any point.

Dinner at Cottonwood was early, about five o'clock. For lunch and dinner, for the whole five weeks, I ate the same thing – bagel salad. Cos I liked it, that's why. At seven o'clock in the morning and evening, you have the medications coming round.

On Friday and Saturday, we had a movie show. We would be given a list of movies and we'd each have a vote, then one would be chosen. You're not allowed anything violent, or about drugs, drink or sex. Bit of a limited choice then. They were rather soft, but I went to them all. Something to do. They give you popcorn as well.

One Saturday we saw *Finding Nemo*, which is a cartoon. We also saw *Seabiscuit*, which is about horses. Strictly speaking, we shouldn't have seen that, as there's some gambling in it and one of our group was a gambling addict.

In the evenings, I just rested or read or wrote. I wrote about how I felt, moaning on really, saying to myself, 'What the fuck am I doing here? What is the point?' The thing I wrote most was 'I hate myself for being here again.' I kept going over how I'd put myself in the situation of needing to be there.

One of the things I did was fill in a Body Map. Yous'll see it in this book. Bit scary, eh? What you do is you have to lie down on the floor on a big sheet of brown paper. Someone then draws round the shape of your body. Then you slowly fill in all the parts of your body that you have damaged through your drinking or drugs or whatever – not just the liver and stuff, but injuries and brain damage and obsessions. One time I was in there, I did that Life Line, the Path to Recovery, which was used in my autobiography.

When you've finished your Body Map, you hold it up and talk to the group about it, talk them through it, explain what damage you have done to yourself over the years.

About three times a week, there's a Community Meeting. That was when all the patients, all fifty of us, met together.

When you first arrive, you're known as one of the 'peers', that's the name they use when you're a newcomer who's just checked in. As the weeks go on, you become a senior peer. At the beginning of every Community Meeting, you elect from the senior peers, by a vote of hands, who will be the chairman and secretary for that meeting.

I made it to senior peer quite early. I'd been acting like one from almost the beginning, as I'd been there before, helping new people to acclimatise. I would take people round, show them the building, explain what would happen, make them feel at home.

I always said to them, 'Cry if you want to, say anything you like to anyone. You'll never see me again, or any of them. So don't be scared or embarrassed. Just show your feelings.'

I explained to them that feedback from the other people would help them. It had helped me. I told them to have faith, that they would feel better when they left. They had to give it a proper chance.

At the meeting, jobs would be given out, such as cleaning out the ash-trays in the smoking areas, which were outside. Or you might have the job of raising and lowering the Stars and Stripes flag, in the morning and evening. One job I got was bell-ringing. You had to go round ringing a bell to tell them it's five minutes to go to the next session. I quite enjoyed that.

In the third week, I got made chairman for one meeting. Fucking hell. There was a lump in my throat, having to address all of them. But I think I managed okay.

One of the things the chairman has to do is go round the room and ask everyone if they have any problems. They might, for example, have a problem with one of the therapists, or a doctor or psychiatrist. As chairman, you encourage them to speak out, if they want to, and name the person they have a problem with, if they want to.

In the first week or so I was there, many of them did have trouble with my accent. Mind you, I have had the same problem in England, especially when I came to London for Spurs. But as the weeks went on, they did get used to it. By the time I was chairman, I think most of them could manage to work out what I was saying. Just about anyway.

If you didn't want to speak out, you could write out something and put it in the God Box. This was just a wooden box, where you shoved any notes. They can be good or bad. It's called the God Box because the idea is you are addressing God, up in the sky, and only He can hear or read what you've written. At the end of every week, the contents of the box are burned, so no one ever knows what it was you wrote. It got things off your chest. The note I put most in the God Box was: 'God, please get rid of my OCD.'

But you still can stand up and say it aloud, to everyone, even if you have already written it in the God Box. This way the other patients get a chance to react — meanwhile the therapists are all making frantic notes.

When I was acting as chairman, this woman stood up and said she had put a note in the God Box, but now she wanted to share it. I asked her what it was she had written.

'Thank you God, for getting me through all this.' That was what she said.

'You're welcome,' I replied.

They all laughed. In fact it brought the house down . . .

Every week we had an outing, such as to a church. You could join in the service, if you wanted to. I made friends with a Jewish bloke. He took me to a Jewish synagogue and I wore the skull cap at the service.

I also made friends with a girl there. She challenged me to play chess. I pretended I'd only just learned to play since coming to Cottonwood. That wasn't true. I learned years ago. Anyway, I hammered her 3–0 and she was furious. I went round telling everyone, of course, that I'd only just learned and yet I'd beaten her. She did eventually beat me — and of course she went round telling everyone this time.

I did play quite a bit of chess and draughts, as well as a game called battleships. They also had some horses and you could go and wander amongst them, and do a bit of riding if you wanted.

After twenty-nine days, I did feel better. It had helped me to be healthier and cleaner but, really, I still felt I need never have bothered. Five days detoxing at the Priory, who use the same sort of methods, would have done me as much good. I wasn't in desperate need of all the therapies and group sessions. But I suppose they helped. I was glad to be away, out of England. I felt secure, which I never feel in England.

I was thinking of George Best a lot. He never stuck at such things. Then I'd think, 'But it's my fucking life. If I want to drink, I'll drink. Fuck them all.'

Then I'd think, 'No, I don't want to drink. I have no wish to start drinking again, ever.'

One of the things we all did at the end of Cottonwood was get people to sign your book. You could buy a book in the Cottonwood shop, just a simple little notebook, or a more elaborate, expensive one if you wanted. I bought a fancy one, with thick leather binding and a clasp thing. That's just cos I'm flash, I guess.

You ask all the patients who've been there with you to write in it, anything they like. And you do the same in their books. It's like the class books or year books they have at American high schools.

You just leave it out when you're about to leave, on a table, with all the other books. People sign if they want. You can write anything, good or bad, you'll be gone very soon and you'll probably never see any of them again.

A lot of people wrote in my book. That's what those messages are at the end of all the chapters. I thought you'd like to see them. See what other people thought of me. Not as Gazza. As Paul. They were all American, so they didn't use words like 'wanker', which was one of the words I taught them. I also introduced them to 'clems', which means balls. I think it's a Geordie phrase, one my father uses. They've got no fucking idea what a Geordie is of course. A lot of them used my words when writing in my book, just as a joke, or wrote about things we'd laughed at during my stay.

One or two of the people who wrote in my book were staff members, but mainly they were my fellow patients – alcoholics, drug addicts, manic depressives, sex addicts, all sorts.

The reference to the Mentoes mints was because I loved them. I'd never come across sugar-free ones before. They were on sale in the

Cottonwood shop. I bought the whole lot – a carton containing something like fifteen packets. I got through about two packets a day, until I finished them. What I didn't know was that they made you fart. So that's why people were writing remarks about farting. I gave some to a girl, and she started farting as well. It was a running joke.

I don't understand why some of them went on about me being rude and obscene. They didn't see nothing, not like the old days, when I was playing football. I'd get drunk, then go around flashing my arse. I never do that sort of thing these days, and I'm sure I didn't do anything rude at Cottonwood. I never showed my cock or my bum. You wouldn't dare anyway, not with sex addicts around!

Did you read that one from the girl, who wrote out the *Oliver* song, 'I'd do anything . . .'? She had arrived very depressed and wouldn't talk to anyone. Instead of talking to her, I sang that song to her – and she immediately started smiling. From then on, every time I met her, she sang the song to me.

The reference to being a transsexual, that was because of my fancy book, 'decorated like a tart's diary', so this bloke said. It was his little joke.

They all gave their addresses or emails, asked me to look them up if I ever get to America again. I have texted a few of them.

I sometimes open the book and read their remarks again. They saw me as a winner and someone who was trying to make them winners. So I have to try not to let myself down, for their sake as well as my own . . .

On the other hand, when I read their comments, I think, 'Who was helping me?' I needed help as well, but all I seemed to do at Cottonwood was give. But then that often seems to be the case with me . . .

––––––––––

Dear Paul

I've loved our chats and sidebar conversations. I have appreciated your insight and humor. I may not have lasted as long here without you . . .

Jen

Paul's fourth session: Back from Cottonwood

John

It's been just over five weeks since I've seen Paul, although he called me a few times while he was away in Arizona, and he seemed to be engaging well with the treatment process and working hard to get better. Today we started by discussing his three-month 'aftercare plan', which details the support Paul needs in order to continue the process begun in the clinic. This includes self-help meetings, counselling, healthy eating and keeping a balance in his work life.

One of the big issues for Paul is that of codependency. There's a link between when he's feeling manipulated or controlled by people and his finding it hard to tell people when to back off, i.e. laying down a healthy boundary. When we suffer from codependency we put other people before ourselves more often and to a greater extent than is balanced – or 'healthy'. At some stage we then feel angry about this – we feel taken advantage of – and this anger may be swallowed down as resentment; it may be acted out in a row or a fight; or it may lead us to use an addictive substance or behaviour. Codependency is therefore a cycle of behaviour that is very destructive.

We began the session by talking about this, and how things had gone generally at Cottonwood.

Paul

The treatment at Cottonwood was good. The first ten days in the clinic, I didn't do much. I did the meetings, the groups, spending two hours with the same eight or nine people each day – that was enough. I felt quite comfortable. It was nice. I could be relaxed and get some of my shit off. I talked about when I got worried when George died. Oh, yeah – I've been asked to say a little bit about George at a memorial dinner. It's nice to be asked to do that. Anyway, so I talked about George, and about being harassed by that photographer, and about the sacking, and feeling harassed by the chairman at Kettering. And, of course, about the drinking.

They said in the clinic I was codependent. Codependency is like not setting rules, not having boundaries.

I like to be a happy and fun person. Easy-going. I've enjoyed my life. I've done things and I hate saying 'No' to anybody. They were laughing in the clinic: I can't say 'No' without saying 'Fuck off'. If someone asks me to do something and I can't do it, instead of saying 'No, I'm really sorry, can I do it another day?', I'll say 'Yeah', and try and squeeze the two things in the one day. Then I'll be tired and then I'll be angry and end up saying 'Fuck off' to someone. They were laughing at us when I talked about it, and kept asking why so many people asked us to do things for them. They couldn't understand it until some English person told them I played professional soccer.

How do I get myself some peace back here? It's difficult. When I wake up I've got to deal with bipolar, alcoholism, OCD, food – all these things before I even walk out of the house. I take a mood stabiliser every morning. My OCD's more under control. I'm not touching things, I'm walking away from them. I'm enjoying myself again. I enjoy sobriety. I try and live for the moment and, if it's a good moment, then great. I've got AA. I'm not going to think to myself that I'm missing football on TV because I'm stuck in a room full of alcoholics, which I have thought in the past. I'm not going to think like that. What I get from AA is, not just to stay sober, but to get confidence back. I realise I'm not the only one with this problem. I'm lucky: I've got football – I mean going to matches – I can write this book about my problems, I can get counselling. But there are people who live on the streets and have to go through what I go through without any money or anywhere to live or anything, and I feel sorry for them. I hope this book will help some of them.

You know, it was a relief being away for Christmas and New Year. I didn't have to be round people who were drinking. Anyone who's an alcoholic and says it's easy being around drinkers at Christmas and New Year – I don't know! But I've got no wish ever to drink. I'm tired of being tired. Never say never, but if I relapsed again I'd have to find a different clinic. It's embarrassing when you get a discount at the clinic! I've been four times.

John

Paul showed me some of his Cottonwood book the previous night, and people had written lovely messages of appreciation for him. He touched people in a deep way – there's something in him that comes alive in those environments, and he gives good feedback to people. Paul doesn't see that side of his character himself. I'd like to stay with this point, so I suggest to Paul he doesn't recognise this caring and insightful person. I ask him if he can appreciate that people mean it when they say these good things about him.

Paul

When people say anything nice to me I push it away because I think there's something nasty round the corner. Maybe because of what the press say about me. The press never give me a chance to start enjoying sobriety. Most people believe what they read. I get scared of taking too much praise. When I played football and I scored a hat-trick or got Man of the Match it was nice, but I got worried that then I'd get followed for the next few days so they could see what I was up to. I got hammered by the press and it's not nice.

So it's true that, for me, it feels like to do well will bring trouble. Every time I had a good tournament or went on holiday to relax, I was getting cameras up my arse. It's a nightmare. It doesn't matter how strong a person you are, mentally and physically, these people do get to you and you can't escape it.

I've been back from the clinic a week. I'm feeling good. But there is pressure. Off-licences, cameras – you know. If you walk into a pub with a friend to get a soft drink, because of what's happened in the past you get paranoid about what might be said, and think some guy in there's a reporter, when in fact he's a really nice guy just minding his own business.

It's sad that the media don't recognise this illness, considering there are so many people dying on the streets in this country because they haven't got any support with it. If I see an alcoholic on the street, I give him a drink and some money. I know some of them haven't got long to live. There's no help for them, so I buy them a drink.

John

I'd like us to think about how Paul can maintain his health in order to work towards his aims for the future.

JM: I think any therapy has to look at trying to find happiness. Keeping in mind what we've discussed about what you want to do – go back into management – the next few months need to be about stability, sobriety, self-care and self-management in order to prepare for that.

PG: I know what I want and I know what I have to do to be happy. I've done it before for two years. I've got to change the people and places around me. I can do that – it's no problem. I'm taking up fishing again. Going to meetings. I don't want to go every day – I'll go every other day. Until I feel secure in myself. The good thing is, if I'm somewhere and I'm not happy I can leave, but when I was drinking I couldn't leave because I had to stay for one more.

JM: It's also crucial that when you're not happy with something, you express it and set boundaries. Talk honestly to me, talk to your friends, family and the people you work with. In the past, because you didn't like letting people down, you ended up in situations that made you angry and resentful and thinking, 'What about me?' I'm worried that if you can't say 'No' to people, that pattern will establish itself again.

PG: It's boundaries, I've got to set boundaries for myself instead of changing my mind at the last second. I've got to stick with my decision. I've said 'Yes' for so long that people aren't used to 'No', and they keep pushing and pushing and then I think, 'Fuck it, I'll do it.'

JM: I know you've done it with me. It's important to say 'No, I can't', and if people are offended, then they'll have to deal with it. There are so many charities and good causes, but together they'll all suck you dry.

PG: I need to have a structure each morning and stick to it and not change it, and if I do that I'll be okay. That's what I've got from the clinic, apart from sobering up. Sometimes I get worried hearing stuff in these clinics, about the effects of drugs and stuff. I remember when I was thirty-five, after I left Burnley, I thought, 'I won't drink but I'll take cocaine.' Now I think, 'But how much damage did that do to me?' And I was only on it for six weeks. What about these people who've been on it for years? They don't realise the damage they've done to themselves.

You have to look at Danniella Westbrook and how courageous she was, she's come forward and told her story. She took cocaine as a social drug and look what happened to her. In the clinic someone spoke about the damage opium can do, and I thought, 'What the fuck's opium? Opium's a perfume for women!' It's good to go to a clinic and find out the facts about addictive drugs. That wasn't the first time I've been a bit naive about drugs. I remember one time, when I was on tour with Newcastle in Holland. Must have been about seventeen or eighteen. A kid comes up to us and says, 'Do you fancy some grass?' I looked at him and I said, 'Are you fucking daft? I'm playing on a field of it, aren't I?' That's how green I was back then!

Every day I say, 'Fuck me, I've put on weight.' I eat more, and then I start training. I love training. But it's like with the fishing. Once I go fishing on a Monday, I'll go Tuesday, Wednesday, Thursday. Same with golf. And once I go to the gym, I'll go every single day. Same with my diet. Having an addictive personality is terrible. Once I put my mind to something, I just stick to that one thing for weeks. That's why people said I was a great trainer, because once I start training I put everything into it. But it gets out of hand. I train every day. I mustn't do that, but I wish I could.

John

Part of Paul's life now is finding a balance. Working the recovery programme and being aware of himself, but not feeling like a victim of it either, and balancing that with having fun, relaxing and training. These are issues that over the last few years have pulled him back towards drinking. It's about setting up a structure that works for him, that he can maintain. And it's tough to have the acceptance to learn to say, 'Yes, I'd like a drink, but no, I know I can't.' I remind Paul that he's managed to do it before.

Paul

I have done it before. Sometimes I did go out and enjoy myself without having a drink. I'd get myself ready, be prepared. Then if the thought came: 'I don't want a Diet Coke, fuck this!', I'd know temptation was coming on. I'd get ready for it. So I got quite comfortable doing it. My structure is, if I'm going out, I'll go to an early AA meeting first or speak to you, Johnny, if I'm feeling I need to.

John

Putting together the right structure and training the mind can be done, and Paul has shown that he can do it.

That 'fuck it' voice has to be watched, because addiction is like a split personality. There are two voices. One says, 'I can have a drink tonight,' and the other says, 'Hang on, no I can't, I'm an alcoholic and I know what having a drink could lead to.' If you don't look after yourself properly and keep balanced, the addictive voice wins – and that's what being an alcoholic is.

Paul

That voice is murder, saying, 'Have a drink, have a drink.' It creeps up on you and won't go away unless you give in to it. But if you have a good habit, a way of working round it, you can fuck it off in a few minutes. If I've relapsed in the past, it's because for three or four days I've had that voice in my head and it wouldn't fuck off because it knew it would have us in the end. Somehow I had lost whatever good habit I had got into before – that managed to get rid of the voice. We were laughing in the clinic about some bloke whose friend got addicted, but they wouldn't give him money or serve him. He just went out on to this airfield and started a jet, flew it until it got to Mexico and ran out of gas, sold it to the mafia for $10,000 when it was worth, like, $10 million, spent the $10,000 in two days and got a boat back. Mad.

I did three or four lines of cocaine one night – during that six-week session – and then bought nine Harley Davidsons. The bloke who delivered them to us checked the house to see if I had loads of mates! I spent over £100,000. Then the next night there I am taking more cocaine.

People ask why you do that mad thing a second time. It's because you're powerless. It's got a grip of you. And I was thirty-five and coming to the end of my career. I really wanted to get fit and have one more season. Not take more cocaine.

John

Paul has mentioned coming to the end of his playing career. Letting go of the past is an important aspect of Paul's life at the moment. We talk about how much letting go he's had to do over the last couple of years. Alcohol, Sheryl and, of course, football – twenty years of his life. That was his identity – that was what he did. He lost the family he had for a while with Sheryl. And he talks about giving up booze as another loss.

Paul

I've got to deal with it the rest of my life. I can't keep battling for the rest of my life. I'll just give in and stop drinking.

The reason I'm doing this book is because I want people to see where I'm coming from, with all these illnesses. I'm actually coming forward and saying, 'Yes, I'm eating too much, I'm codependent . . .' With the co-dependency, this is the first time I've worked on it in the clinic because I've always blanked it, because I knew what it meant – I can't tell people 'No'. I cried my eyes out with it, and I explained to them I'd rather relapse than tell somebody 'No'.

Going to the clinic and getting away from all that is kind of like a holiday. Like a man said in the clinic, 'Taking heroin or cocaine is like a holiday from that voice in your head.'

John

People know that Paul's an extremely generous person, with his time and energy as well as his money. But if he's saying 'Yes' all the time there's no space for himself. That's one reason why he likes being away: the demands on him aren't there in the same way. Practising laying down healthy boundaries and being honest with people is one of the key ways we've been working on Paul's codependency.

We talk again about that 'voice in the head' his friend in the clinic mentioned. It's important to make sure it doesn't get listened to. Paul tells me that voice has gone away for the time being. We end the session by talking about being in the right environment for recovery, where the voice is less likely to pipe up.

PG: That voice has gone out for the time being. I won't go clubbing, I won't put myself in dangerous situations. If there's a match on TV I'll go out and watch it, but that's it.

JM: As you said, it's important to be in the right environment for recovery.

PG: I think for the next few months I've got to be selfish.

JM: That is music to my ears, because of the need to use your time well for yourself. Self-care is so important for you, you don't have to justify it. People will move their arrangements if you're not up to something that day. You can say 'No'.

I can see now, you're thinking about it, the idea of saying 'No' feels difficult, doesn't it?

PG: Yes. I've said 'Yes' all my life. People will think I'm being a bit of a prick.

JM: Well, they might not be used to it, but they will get used to it.

John

It's good seeing Paul back and looking well. He clearly worked hard when he was away and, as well as breaking the very important cycle of drinking, he was able to look at the issue of codependency. He recognises the need to set a structure for himself that works for him. This includes attending self-help support groups and getting regular but moderate exercise.

It's imperative that he has control of his agenda. I've always known how difficult he found setting boundaries with people. This has to change if he's to be happy. We'll be going on to explore where this codependent behaviour originated. It usually stems from our very early relationships with our parents and siblings.

As well as seeing how well Paul has done, I've also been reminded of how delicate he is at the moment. In fact it's normal for anyone returning from treatment to be like this: sensitive, raw and vulnerable. Spending time in a recovery treatment centre can't be compared with anything else. You're turned inside-out – you *have* to be in order for the programme to be beneficial. Therefore it's important that at the moment Paul should be surrounded by people who understand 'where he is at' – those who know what a tough job it is to combat alcoholism and his other, related, conditions.

I don't like to say this but it needs to be said: not everyone makes it. Rehab is a very important stage but it does not guarantee anything – nothing can. As Paul said in the session, many people die of these conditions. We can't count on a happy-ever-after ending. What Paul is dealing with is massive. I was fortunate enough to receive the right support in order to deal with my problems early on in life. There is alcoholism and bipolar disorder in my family and it has caused much pain and anguish. It doesn't go away; all we can do is continue to treat it. Self-awareness, a supportive lifestyle and, for some, the right medication will help. But it takes maintenance and hard work.

Paul will need to work really hard on all of his issues and, as he said, understand that this has to come first. The next few weeks are paramount as he needs to consolidate what he's taken from his time in rehab. We'll be focusing on this over the next few weeks: helping Paul to help himself, helping him understand that now he has more information he needs to put it into practice and to watch out for that old cry of, 'It's not fair.'

With Paul now back from Cottonwood, and having heard what he felt about the treatment he received, it's interesting to look at what they're trying to achieve there, and how they go about it. There are many different types of rehabilitation programme. Most aim to help the addict build a life away from drinking and taking drugs. Behavioural modification programmes examine the underlying reasons for the addicted person leaning towards a life involving dependency on drink and drugs, and aim to change that learned behaviour. The most popular programmes use the 'disease model', which classifies addiction as an illness. The majority of private-treatment programmes in the UK and the USA are based on the Minnesota model of treatment, which is a version of the disease model. This method of treatment was formulated in Minnesota in the 1950s and incorporates the 'Twelve Steps' of Alcoholics Anonymous. The first step says: 'We admitted we were powerless over alcohol, that our lives had become unmanageable.' Minnesota is a very successful model of treatment and has helped millions of people to overcome addiction.

Paul has been in two treatment centres (sometimes referred to as clinics): the Priory Hospital in London, and Cottonwood de Tucson, in the USA; both use the disease concept as the model of treatment.

It's a pretty busy schedule – you may be surprised by how much there is to do. While one or two groups are optional, it's strongly suggested that you attend all sessions. When you arrive you're assigned a focal counsellor, the person who will be working with you in many of the groups and with whom you will be having one-to-one counselling. You will be part of that primary group of around eight to ten people who will be in treatment for many different reasons, ranging from drug addiction, alcoholism, depression and bipolar disorder, to food disorders and codependency. The treatment team decide which group is appropriate for you, taking into consideration many factors.

Cottonwood, like many treatment centres, has a policy of room-sharing. This can be a shock for some people initially, but most actually prefer it as time goes on. The reason for the sharing is to promote interaction and communication at all times. It's easy to isolate yourself, especially during the first few days when you're feeling nervous and unsure of yourself, and sharing helps you to settle in and make contact with others at the centre. Another benefit of sharing is that it's a leveller – no one is more special than anyone else: there is only one class of room. Recovery in treatment centres depends on unity and identification. It doesn't matter what you do or don't do for a job, where you're from, how much money you do or don't have, or what your race or sexuality is. These are important issues in everyday life, but they're not why you are ill, and this will be brought home to you.

During the first few days you'll see several specialists, from psychiatrists to nutritionists. You'll be weighed and have blood taken for many tests. Your physical, mental and emotional states will be assessed and you'll also be treated on all three levels. Most patients need a medical detoxification and this can last up to fourteen days, depending on your addiction. But this doesn't mean that you lie around all day in bed. You're expected to get to work straight away on your first assignment, which is usually a written life story. You will be expected to complete various assignments throughout your stay including drawing out a 'timeline' (see Paul's Path to Recovery in his first book).

The Cottonwood day starts early, with a brief meditation at around 8 a.m., and ends with a look back over the day at 8.30 p.m. There are group therapy sessions that give you the chance to open up and explore some of the issues that have been bothering you throughout life. It's also a time when you can exchange feedback with your peers about everyday events, and find out how they perceive you and you them. This can be invaluable since such opportunities don't normally occur in our day-to-day lives.

There are assignment groups, for which specific time is set aside in a structured way to allow you to share your written work. Each assignment is designed to help you go deeply into a certain area, such as the consequences of your alcoholism on you and your family. As there is a focus on the 'Twelve Step' programme of Alcoholics Anonymous, a typical assignment might be to look at the first three steps and complete some written work about them. There may well be a need to focus on past traumas, such as grief and loss or physical or sexual abuse.

There are also educational lectures and the psycho-dramas that Paul mentioned. It's a non-stop programme: if you're not sharing your own life experiences in a group or a one-to-one session, you'll be listening to someone else's.

Cottonwood has an excellent five-day family programme for the families of all patients. As you come to the end of your stay it's strongly recommended that you invite your loved ones in for the family programme since it's not only helpful for you but extremely educational and supportive for them. However, not all families will be in a position to attend or engage with this process.

Your one-to-one counsellor will help you focus on what you need to work on. Most counselling staff have themselves battled with addiction problems or have experienced some of the traumas you have been through. They are trained to a high level and can spot denial at fifty paces. The relationship between patient and counsellor is key to a successful outcome.

The minimum stay is twenty-eight days, but it's usually suggested that you stay for longer to give yourself the best chance you can. About 25 per cent of patients leaving primary treatment will move on to secondary care for another three to six months. This is what we call 'half-way house'. It's less structured than primary care but allows you to develop your recovery in a safe and supportive environment. The other 75 per cent or so return home, and for these a comprehensive aftercare plan is put together by their counsellors so that when they wake up back in their own beds, they have a plan for how to get on with their new lives.

———————

Dear Paul

Just remember to strip away all that exterior shit. You still are a fucking great guy. I haven't got much to offer but what I have is yours. Call me if you need anything. Much love. Keep it real.

Peter

Paul takes a break

Paul

After I'd been to Cottonwood, and had a session with Johnny, I decided to have a holiday. I went to Dubai, with Jimmy and my younger sister Lindsay. She's divorced – in fact both my sisters are divorced – and has a little boy called Cameron who came with us. He's great at football. I thought she needed a break. I felt I needed one as well. And of course Jimmy is my best friend, who has always stood by me, so I had to take him too, didn't I?

I enjoyed it, the sun and swimming, but I've come back a bit depressed. It was fucking hard, during those two weeks away. Jimmy and Lindsay were drinking, naturally enough, as it was their holiday. But I couldn't. It got so bad I could hardly talk to them, as I was so down.

Then, when we left, I realised I had put on ten pounds in the two weeks, with sitting around eating all the time, no training or going to the gym. So that made me more depressed.

On the way home, on the plane, I hardly dare say it, I had a drink. For the same old reason. I'm shit scared of flying.

I thought, I can't cut myself off totally for the rest of my life from drinking, not be able to go into bars when Jimmy goes or any of my other friends. What will I do with myself?

Then when I got home, I got a text from Jimmy saying that Bianca (my stepdaughter) had been on TV, a week or so before I got back, slagging me off again – the old so-called abuse story that I'd hit them as kids. I asked him if anything bad had been said and it had, it was nasty. I just wish she and Shel could stop using the name Gascoigne. If they hate me so much, why doesn't she go back to her old surname, or her maiden name? Bianca's real name is Bianca Failes. The way they all keep on using my name I think I'll have to be the one to change. I'll no longer be Gascoigne. That might be the only way round it. I just don't understand it. I was never nasty to the children. I wish they'd move on – why don't they move on? I wouldn't mind if what they were saying was actually true.

I'm fed up anyway being Gazza. I can't keep that up seven days a week. I want to be Paul John Gascoigne.

I know people think I'm a nutcase, but I'm not. I just have violent mood swings, and the rest. And I'm getting better all the time.

The therapy sessions *do* do me good, even if I may relapse and have the odd drink, like on that plane. I might hate the session at the time, but I feel better afterwards. I know I have to get rid of all the shit in my head, get it all off my chest.

For the five days after I got back from Dubai, I didn't answer my phones at all, even though I knew my friends had been ringing and texting me. I was just too depressed. I knew I would just moan at them, give them all the shit in my head. They don't want that. No one wants that.

But now that I've gone and done some gym work and had another session with Johnny, I feel I can talk to my friends, be normal, like. My head feels cleared. I can have jokes and laughs, not make them as depressed as I am.

There's no real cure for alcoholism of course – AA is the best thing. I have this little book I read – *A Day at a Time* – which has little sayings and stories for every day of the year. They're meant to make you feel positive. And they do, for a few moments at least.

I'm bipolar. That's what Johnny calls it. It's called that because you go between two extremes, two opposite poles, all the time. In one state, you're manic, your speech gets all speeded up, you rush around, can't sleep, are full of ideas and excitement. Then you go to the other extreme when you are down and depressed. When you are up, on a high, you have so much energy and ideas, you feel on great form – even if other people don't think so. The flip side is when you go down and get depressed.

They used to call it manic depression. I dunno why they changed it. Bipolar is the new term, that's the one Johnny uses all the time. I suppose it sounds better than manic depression. Being a manic-depressive makes you sound really mad. Being bipolar doesn't sound as bad, does it?

Too much coffee and caffeine can get me on a high, or drinking all those Red Bulls I used to drink. And cocaine could cause it, of course.

I've now given up Red Bull and I know not to have more than two cups of coffee a day and none at all in the evening. I'm also still taking my medication, which has helped. I don't think I'm as bad as I was. Just as I don't think my OCD is as bad, thanks to all the therapy and medications. So, really, alcohol is my biggest problem.

My other problems are a bit easier, so I like to think. Being in that police cell, forced to stay all night in that fucking little cell, did help ease my claustrophobia. I managed to calm myself and got through it. It sounds mad, I know, but thank you, cops.

When I went to a clinic for the very first time, it was a revelation. I had never heard addicts talk before about their addictions. I hadn't realised that people were going through what I was going through. It does help, to hear others. You find out you are not quite as bad as some people. Mind you, it does scare me a bit – when I see the trouble some people are in, the damage they have done to themselves. That does affect me.

A lot of the people at Cottonwood were in a far worse state than me because they had no friends at all, no family, no money. I'm lucky that I have all those things.

They weren't all rich people. A lot of them were on health insurance, taken out a long time ago, perhaps through their work. They didn't have much money themselves. My stay there cost me, let's see, I did get 10 per cent discount as it was my fourth visit. All in all, with flights, the cost probably came to £23,000, which I paid for myself. Good job I'm a best-selling author, ha ha.

When I'm in a clinic, I do find myself not thinking so much about my own problems, because I'm so busy cheering up others. But you do learn to be a bit ruthless. You want to stick with the winners.

On my first visit to Cottonwood, there was an English guy there who greeted me and took me around. 'You'll really love this place,' he said. 'I've been here nine times . . .'

I thought, 'Fucking hell. What chance have I got? I'm not coming back here, again. Once will be enough.'

What you need is willpower. You need the willpower to win and, even more important, the willpower to want to win. I think I read that somewhere, in one of my little books . . .

I don't know about God. If he's so fantastic, why did he let little Steven die? That thought bugged me for years.

A lot of people who go to clinics do end up finding God, and good luck to them, but it hasn't happened to me. I can't see myself as a Bible-basher.

But I do believe in God. I know I'm shit scared of dying, because I'm probably frightened of hell. He is probably up there, somewhere, watching us all. He must exist. For me to be still alive, it proves there is a God . . .

But nah, I've never had any spiritual awakenings. At Cottonwood, that last time, I did have about three hours once when I felt sort of light-headed. I was sitting on this rock, at the edge of the desert, and I suddenly felt at peace. It was actually a bit scary. Then it passed and I forgot about it. Don't know if that was some sort of religious experience. Might just have been the sun . . .

About a year ago, up in Newcastle, I had a panic attack one day when I felt really suicidal. At the time I was in Dunston, near Gateshead, where I come from, visiting me mam and dad.

I suddenly felt I needed help – at once – so I knocked on the door of a local vicar's house. I knew a vicar lived there, though I'd never met him or been to his church. When he opened the door, I said, 'I know it's a bit stupid, but can I come in for a chat?' I stayed for an hour. He made me a cup of tea and I told him how I'd felt suicidal. I was much better afterwards.

I do pray, now and again. Just the Lord's Prayer, Our Father and all that. But I don't go searching for him. I don't want to. I don't feel I have to. But you never know, he might search me out one day . . .

Yeah, I do seem to have this nurturing side. I do like helping others, in clinics and elsewhere. That's why I was always an entertainer. I liked to cheer people up, make them laugh.

But at the same time, I know I am a spoiled, selfish, arrogant bastard. All alcoholics are like that. We drink because we are self-centred. We believe we are the centre of our universe. We believe we are God.

I made them laugh once at Cottonwood – I said that God thinks he's Gazza.

It's strange, though. While I know I'm selfish and self-centred, I do have a genuine need to help others. I believe I am a caring person.

'There's no rules for loving and sharing,

But hearts beat faster when someone is caring . . .'

Don't know where I got that from either. A pity I haven't got someone to share things with and to love. I know that's a huge lack in my life and filling it would help me a lot.

But I'd never like to do any proper caring work. I couldn't go from being an addict to being a therapist, the way so many have done. I only like doing it when it's fun, when it just sort of happens, not when it's all planned. When people come my way, I try to do what I can for them.

Hold on, just got a text from my old friend, Archie Knox. He was the assistant manager when I was at Rangers, under Walter Smith. He's always stayed a close friend, helped me and given me advice when I needed it. Oh, he seems to want some help from me now, according to his text . . .

'Dear Gazza, I want to know if you can do me a big favour. I know people are always on at you for favours, but this is important. I am in London at the moment so could you ring me on . . .'

I'd better do it now, see if I can help him. I'll just dial that number.

Oh fucking hell, just listen to this message . . .

'This is Buckingham Palace. You could have received a hoax message asking you to ring this number, in which case hang up. But if you have a valid reason for ringing Buckingham Palace, then please hold on for an operator . . .'

Bloody hell, Archie, bastard. I'll get him back . . . Just like Waddler.

Dear Paulie

I loved beating you time and time again in sokky. You are one funny son of a bitch. You made my stay here so much easier and I am thankful I met you. I will never forget your dirty mind.

I hope you continue with your sobriety and good luck in all you do.

I love you ME CLEMS!!!

Claire – one third of Paulie's Angels

Paul's fifth session: Making links – food, exercise and having to be happy

John

Talking about ourselves in a counselling session is a process. We don't usually get to the crux of the matter straight away. We talk around the subject, test out the sound of what we're saying, then move on to talk about something else for a while. A lot of the issues we talk about link up with each other in some way, but at first we're not conscious of how. We might dart all over the place from topic to topic but we are, in fact, gradually homing in on what's really eating us. The counsellor hopes that, as we talk, both during an individual session and over a number of sessions, we'll begin to recognise the links and get braver about looking into ourselves. And we'll come back to issues we've brought up early on in the session, or in previous sessions, and perhaps look at them in a different light.

It's towards the end of February and Paul came back from his two-week holiday a few days ago. Now he's come in to see me. We spend a long time going over what happened to him while he was away, how it feels for him at the moment, post-holiday and post-clinic, his depression, his food and exercise, and especially his relationships with people and his tendency to isolate. Paul manages to recognise some links between his current behaviour and thought patterns and his early experiences as a child and young adult.

Paul tells me, and I can see, how low he is at the moment. We discuss Paul's medication, and we decide to contact his psychiatrist to talk about reducing the amount he takes so that his mood isn't so depressed. Getting the right kind of medication at the right level can be an on-going process.

Paul tells me about his holiday. After all that work in the clinic, he wanted a break, but he found it much more difficult than he thought he would. He was still raw, having just spent thirty-three days getting himself sober and back together in a safe setting, with daily support. Out there in Dubai, he had no structure and no support at all. He tells me about two occasions on which he drank.

Paul

While I was on holiday with my sister, Cameron and Jimmy, it was tough. Going out there, I was frightened of flying, so I took a brandy. There were rumours in the papers that I was back drinking and I thought, 'I'm never going to win. Every time I go out they're going to say I'm drinking whether I am or not, so I may as well have a drink.' But I didn't drink while I was out there.

It was tough, because in the evenings people were hanging out, chilling out, drinking, and I didn't want to be in that situation. There was a forty-day music ban because one of the princes had died, so I couldn't listen to music to switch off, and that made not drinking harder. I was eating and eating, and then I panicked and started obsessing about putting on too much weight. I really wanted to drink, but I didn't. You said it wasn't a good time to go on holiday, right after coming out of the clinic, and maybe it's true, maybe it wasn't the right time. Sometimes it was okay, and I kept myself busy during the day. I took a boat out with Cameron and we went fishing, and I played around with him in the pool. But then I hurt my neck in the pool, and I panicked and after that I stopped going in the water. I've had so many injuries, I can't get injured again.

I thought if I went there on holiday I'd lose weight quickly. I'd put some pounds on in the clinic. I knew it would be easier to lose weight in the heat, and in England it was -2°C. But it didn't work. While I was there it was a matter of just eating so as not to drink. I didn't drink out there but, on the flight back, I had fear of flying again, and someone said there were going to be bad storms, so I took a tablet and had a couple of drinks to get through it.

When I got back from Dubai, I thought I needed to get properly fit so I went to Champneys. I just wanted to lose weight and feel good. The place is stuck out a little bit in the middle of nowhere and I haven't got my friends around or meetings to go to. But it's good because, when I train, that's when I'm at my happiest. Before I went there I was really depressed and worried.

I was worried about work – not the money, but what I'm going to do with the rest of my life, to keep myself busy. There's stuff I can do at the moment, but there are also certain things I feel uncomfortable doing, such as talks, dinners and travelling. I get embarrassed being paid for doing after-dinner talks as a footballer. You should be doing that in your fifties not in your thirties. But I'm forced to do them in order to pay Sheryl the maintenance for the kids. But something will come up, some football job. In the meantime, I'm just concentrating on doing my counselling and the book. It's nice to do a follow-up to my last book.

I have lost weight. I've lost half a stone in four or five days, but I'm still feeling down. There's a chance of meeting up with Chris Evans. I'd like to, but I don't feel up to seeing people, anyone. I don't know why I'm feeling down.

José Mourinho kindly invited me to Chelsea for a couple of months, to watch the lads training; it's a great opportunity. I could watch the way he works. But I'd be no good like this – feeling low. I could learn a lot from José Mourinho, I know that, but I don't know if I want to come to London or go to Newcastle. I feel lonely. I just feel like I'm battling all the time. Others seem to me to be enjoying themselves, seem happy.

I do feel alone, it doesn't matter how many people I talk to, I still feel it inside. Everyone thinks I'm a happy-go-lucky lad. I come off holiday and try to cheer myself up and then get stepped all over. I was fine until that business with Sheryl's daughter being on telly.

I'm really pushing myself with the training. I wake up, do my training. I'm happy when I've finished it, then after an hour I'm bored and lonely. I have a salad for lunch. I lie there and worry about what I'm going to do in a month's time when I'm fit. I worry about the future. So I look forward to six o'clock when I start training again. Then if there's no football on TV I'm fucked.

When I'm down like this there's nothing I want to do. I just want to lock myself in a room. When the football on the TV finishes, then what am I going to do? I can't go and train again because I'm already killing myself. My moods are terrible at the moment.

Right now, I'm hardly taking any phone calls, I can't be bothered to text anybody. People think I'm blanking them. I'm not, I've just got fuck all to say to them at the moment. And I can't be honest with them, so I say I'm feeling great. If I said to me mates, 'I'm really down at the moment. I need a bit of company, a bit of help,' I know they'd come, but then I think I'd be shit company.

If I started telling people what I'm really feeling they would stop calling me because they'd think, 'He's always down.' I do think they'd care for me – but what could they say?

John

How many times have any of us hidden away at home when we've been feeling down? The thing is, we feel pressure to be on good form when we see people:

JM: I think you've got this view of yourself that people will only accept you if you're on good form or behaving a certain way, and I think you think they won't like you as much or they'll reject you if you're not those things. Is that what you think?

PG: Yeah, of course it is.

JM: I think we've got to challenge that thinking. People will care for you no matter what mood you're in. Everyone suffers from time to time.

PG: Trouble is, I was brought up as a fighter. They get upset when they see us upset because they're not used to seeing us upset.

JM: You hide your feelings a lot. What do you think that does to you – hiding them?

PG: It makes me want to just give in. Thing is, everyone shakes my hand and says they want an autograph, and it's great for me to do things like that, but it's hard. You walk out on Chelsea or Everton football ground, and both sets of fans are cheering, it's great. But two hours later I think, 'I used to have that every week, but I don't have that any more.' I feel like I'm training to get back playing again. But I'm not. I've got depression and mood swings.

JM: Some of your friends, perhaps only a few, do understand what you go through. But a lot of people just know the happy-go-lucky, funny, generous Gazza. Few people know who Paul Gascoigne is.

PG: People haven't ever seen Paul Gascoigne.

JM: I really want to help you with that because that's the next stage in your life.

Paul

Something that's affecting me a lot is not seeing my son. I want to see my son, and I miss him. It hurts. I've got my own family, but I haven't got my son. They say, if you want to speak to him call the house. So I call the house to speak to him, and the next thing I get the lawyer on the phone saying I'm getting done for harassment. I send him cards, texts. I suspect he's not got them. So I sort of give in and think, 'Well, I'll have to wait till he's older.' I'm happy then I'm sad and then I'm all right – my mood swings.

I've been invited to a football club to start learning with the coach, but I'm not ready for that yet. It feels like laziness, but it isn't. I don't like having to be patient. Having to wait for the right time to get on with my life. It's a nightmare. I start thinking negative. I get bored. Sometimes I think positive – come May things will pick up for me – but February, March, April, I have to get through them first.

Thanks to the health farm I keep myself busy. I've got company. There are people there I know. There's lots happening all the time. That's good. I want to get myself fit.

I have had these problems for eighteen years. Some days I deal with them really well and some days it's hard.

The thing with this book, the people that read it are going to be the ones with the same sorts of problems, and they're the ones who are my friends. They understand my illnesses. But only I can pull it round. If I can come through after all of thirty-odd operations, I've got the determination to pull this one round. If I break my leg I've got to get my leg fixed and that's it. This time I feel like I've got to fix about six things. What woman is going to want to be with a guy who's had all these problems?

It's true, I do judge myself for being ill. I can be my own worst enemy. I feel like I'm forced to train really hard. I've only just been back training since Monday. It's Thursday now and I've done seven sessions in three days – and I'm in agony. I have to tell myself to rest – rest tonight and train tomorrow morning, but I feel like I've got to train tonight. I feel like I have to do it because if I don't then I'm going to put on weight. My hips are sore, my calves are sore, my arms are going into cramp all the time because I've started doing weights on them.

John

I've seen Paul punishing himself through rigorous exercise. I ask him about that.

JM: Why are you so hard on yourself?

PG: Fuck knows.

JM: What might it be?

PG: I feel I have to prove to people all the time – I can do this, I can do that. But I've got nothing to prove.

JM: Can you say that again?

PG: I've got nothing to prove.

JM: They're so important, those words. You've proved your abilities beyond the ordinary. People know what you've been capable of. But of course none of us can sustain that level throughout our lives – partly because of our physical bodies. And yet there's that voice somewhere in your head that says, 'I've got to keep proving that I'm okay.' Most people who know you say, 'I wish he'd just relax a bit more, we love him as he is.'

PG: I have to keep proving to the outside world that I'm fine. While really, I *am* fine.

JM: You are fine.

PG: But I have to keep on proving it. You know Archie called me and said, 'What are you doing in the gym? Don't go killing yourself!' Too late Archie – I've already fucking done it!

JM: What would help you slow down a bit? What would help you believe what other people say – 'We love you as you are, you don't have to prove anything any more, you're good enough?'

PG: I wish I could answer that.

JM: We need to work on that, because it's a massive issue for you.

PG: Chris Evans has been in contact with me. I do want to meet up with him – and Danny Baker – but I said I'd see them when I come out of the health farm. It's a shame because I think the world of Chris and Danny. They're great people to be around, but I don't think I am at the moment. I said I'd look after myself this year. I thought last year was a tough battle but I've got another tough battle this year. It's too easy for me to relapse and go back to drinking. They made me look at things other than alcohol in the clinic. Being myself without a drink. The other thing that was worrying me was it was too easy to relapse and go back to drinking.

JM: Treatment gets harder. It's never the same as it was the first time.

PG: You do the detox, then you've got another twenty-four days to get through. I do now have a good support system back here: yourself, my sponsor (a sponsor is a friend in AA who is like a big brother – a mentor and guide), AA meetings. But I don't like other people seeing me upset.

JM: I want you to keep reminding yourself that you judge yourself too harshly. If you're seeing Chris he doesn't have to see Gazza, he wants to see Paul. Danny can be a comedian, but he's not like that all the time, is he?

PG: No, and they'll tell you when *they're* pissed off as well. Chris knows me well enough to know when I'm down. When I've got a miserable face.

JM: So what if you've got a sulk on your face? So what if you're not happy? People will have to deal with it, won't they? How many people do you see who are happy all the time? Can you tell me any?

PG: None.

John

There's a link between Paul's punishing exercise regime coupled with not allowing himself to eat properly, and feeling that he has to prove himself: that he's not good enough as he is. During the remainder of the session we also have a look at where some of his beliefs might have originated. I ask him about his exercise routine now, and whether he got the feeling of always having to fight and battle from his family background.

Paul

I can enjoy half an hour's run but I push myself until I'm exhausted. I do push myself because I've done it all my life, I really don't know any different.

Mum and dad worked really hard to make ends meet, and of course argued a lot because things were so difficult – we had an outside toilet, and a tin bath, you know. I've said it before but that does affect you. I think it's just something that doesn't go away until you let go and I never seem to let go. I carried it on into my football career. I know things will get better, I know they will, I'm confident of that, but I do need to let go.

I was always up to mischief, mucking about – me and my sisters. It's true that that was when I first learned to cheer people up. I just wanted to be in a happy family and we did have great times. Even now I still go back to that accident when I was ten. It still affects me, that young boy dying, seeing his lips move . . . I was looking after him, we only had a quarter of a mile to go to the boys' club, but that happened.

John

I suggest to Paul that the accident and that whole period of his life could be where his problems started. To deal with that kind of trauma at that age takes a lot of help and support.

A lot of us have had difficult childhoods. Things can go wrong in life, and they do. But it's learning how to deal with the situations and accompanying feelings that's key to how we develop as adults. Paul believes he had enough support after that accident, and after the other deaths and situations that occurred while he was growing up.

I suggest to Paul that if such an accident happened to a child of ten today, there would be a lot more awareness about trauma, and the support to go with it. And I ask him if it's right that, because there wasn't the right support, back then when he was ten, he buried something. It was no one's fault, it's not about that, but that was the effect on him.

Paul

I guess there would be much more support nowadays if something like the accident happened to a kid. The support nowadays is fantastic, the number of people in America who see psychiatrists and therapists is phenomenal, whereas we tend more to blank it. Even when I mentioned the OCD in the first book, the amount of letters I got was encouraging. It helped me. And it helped me that a lot of people also had OCD when I went in the clinic.

After the accident I got nervous twitches, made nervous noises, and got kicked out of the classroom for it, because I was making noises and the other kids couldn't concentrate on their work. Noises like clicking or gulping.

Sometimes when I played for Tottenham I got twitches – until I actually watched myself on TV doing it, and then I stopped. Even the smoking is like a nervous thing. I started smoking when I was twenty-nine, and I've thought, maybe I should give that up, but it actually feels like one of the things that calms me down.

I buried loads of stuff when I was young. Had to. My dad was working away in Germany trying to make money to make ends meet, and my mum was left with us four kids, and she had masses of other things on her mind so she couldn't just concentrate on my needs and my support. She had to work, feed us all, keep the house going, look after the other children. So I kept loads of stuff hidden.

And she had to look after my brother when he got into some trouble. He ended up in a care home for a bit. So she had him, me with nervous twitches, and we nearly lost my sister three times. My sister Lindsay got run over by a car and we nearly lost her, she got clipped on her head. Then she got stung by a wasp and the poison nearly went to her heart. Then when she was on a swing in the woods a huge branch snapped and fractured her skull. My mum had all that, and then my sister was leaving school, looking for work, my brother would come home and we'd be arguing, and I had an obsession with the slot machines, and I stole that money from my sister's purse. All stuff like that.

Yeah, it was tough. And I said I was going to support my family for the rest of my life.

John

I ask Paul to say again what he's just told us: that he decided to support his family from then onwards. That was a huge decision to make. He actually made that conscious decision and determined to stick to it. He took responsibility for his family upon his shoulders. I ask him what age he was at that time.

Paul

I was fifteen when I decided I was going to be the one to support my family for the rest of my life. My mum had three jobs: cleaning cars in the morning, cleaning offices in the afternoon, working in the fish shop at night. My dad was in hospital, it was fifty-fifty whether he was going to live or not; my sister was looking for work; and it must have been really hard for my younger sister seeing all of that because she was only seven. Getting into a tin bath in front of the fire, finding wood and newspapers to burn to keep us warm; I saw football as a way of helping them all for the rest of their lives. When I packed in football, it felt like suddenly everyone hated me.

John

Before we move on from this topic, I recap this moment at which Paul made such a big commitment. At fifteen, there were all the stresses he mentioned – the deaths, then soon after that his father's brain tumour, and all of his mother's anxieties about the children. And so he made the decision, at that age, that he wasn't going to let that struggle go on for his family; he was going to become a professional footballer and look after everybody. He seemed to feel that he had to hold it all together. As if he thinks to himself, 'I can't afford to break down, I can't afford to have depression, I can't afford to be myself. I've got to look after this one, look after that one.' That's a pattern that's continued all throughout his life right up until today, and he now has another family to support financially as well.

So, he has massive responsibilities, which contribute to him thinking he's got to keep it all together. And yet what happens sometimes is that he does fall apart because, if he's drinking, he gets anxious and he gets ill and he can't look after everything. It will destroy any of us, this stuff, not because we're not brave or because we don't care or try hard, but because that's what having this illness means.

Paul feels how hard that truth is, and how hard it is to keep going. I think one of the powerful things for Paul about doing this book is that it's given him a chance to go back over everything again, and remind himself about how much he's taken upon himself. And I suggest to him that now it's time for him to concentrate on sorting himself out – that now it's time for Paul to be Paul.

Paul

I need to just drill that into my head.

Sometimes when I played football and played well and got Man of the Match and there were 50,000 people applauding, I still went home sad. It was job done, now back to the real world again. Pleasing others.

It felt like all that applause wasn't really for me. It was me making others happy, but I was still sad. I'd go home and sit in the house and wouldn't go out. Jimmy's a witness to that. He'd say to me, 'Why don't you go out?' It's weird, I know. I felt like all those cheers and everything weren't real, for me anyway. And yet I miss football more than anything because I still love it. There's a massive cloud above my head, and it's just not clearing.

That's the way I am at the moment. The other day I had a workout, and a lovely steam afterwards, and I ended up with this massive headache. What's all that about? It's not normal.

John

The headaches could possibly be linked to the balance of food and exercise. Over-exercising can cause headaches. If you push yourself working out, and then steam, you sweat a lot and sweating takes salt out of the body and can dehydrate you. If you're not drinking enough water and not eating, you're not putting the salts back, and that can cause headaches. I suggest Paul needs to drink lots more water and needs to eat properly, especially while he's training.

Part of the solution at the moment is to say, 'I'm not going to punish myself.' Even Archie – and Paul's mentioned how tough a trainer Archie is – asked Paul what on earth he was up to doing so much in the gym. I ask Paul where he thinks the punishing voice comes from.

Paul

I think it comes from all the operations, saying to myself afterwards, 'I've got to get fit, I've got to get fit.' In 1991 I had a year to get fit at Lazio otherwise I'd be off, so I pushed myself hard. Ever since then, every time I've had an operation I've pushed myself. That's stuck with me for fifteen years.

John

An important thing for us to do is practising and strengthening that voice that says, 'I'm all right at the moment. I don't need to abuse myself or punish myself. I don't have to be together.'

Paul

I don't like being overweight, it takes away my confidence and self-esteem. There's a negative voice that says, 'I'm not good enough, I'm overweight, I'm not confident with people.' If I feel I've let someone down I get depressed. It's when I say to someone I'm going to talk to them tomorrow and I don't, and I leave it a couple of weeks, and by then I'm too embarrassed to contact them. I hate it.

But I can't always be in a good mood, or contact people straight away when they need something. I've got to find a balance. I've done it before, so I know I can do it.

JM: Yes you can. And I'd like to go back to the way you made a decision to support your family financially, as you still do today, and suggest it's your turn now to have some peace. When you train so hard and push yourself so much, are you on some level still trying to please your parents?

PG: They don't expect it.

JM: They don't expect it, exactly.

PG: They don't put us under pressure.

JM: They love you as you are, don't they? They don't want to see you getting stressed and anxious. They both told me that. They just want you to be happy. So can you say to yourself, 'Who am I trying to please? I'm not trying to please my parents and family any more.' And try bringing it back to Paul. Can I get comfortable with Paul, feel all right about Paul? Does that makes sense?

PG: Definitely, yes.

JM: Because you deserve it.

PG: I've done it before so I can do it again, I know I can. I don't feel like it at the moment. I know I'm depressed, and my mood swings are all over the place at the moment, and I need to knock the food and the exercise on the head again.

JM: And obviously keep talking. If you meet up with Chris, can you be yourself? Because the people who care about you, they don't mind what mood you're in.

PG: Hmmm.

JM: They don't. They'd rather see the real you, than see someone pretending that he's fine when they know you're not.

Paul

People have been so good, and I'm lucky like that. Richard and Judy texted me, the amount of help offered is unbelievable, José Mourinho, Alex Ferguson, David Moyes, Paul Jewell, they've all phoned me. Terry Venables. Bobby Robson even called us: 'How are you doing, what are you up to, do you want to come round?' Dave Seaman texted me. Shearer's been fantastic. The help I've got is amazing. Maybe taking some of the help is what's hard.

John

I tell Paul that this is genuine care, these are genuine offers. These are people who don't want anything from him other than just to see him. They have problems too, everybody does. It's all right to be himself with them, he doesn't have to be entertaining.

Of course he doesn't want to see people all the time, and feel overwhelmed, but I think it's important that he just allows a bit more care into his life. And he says he'll take that step, and try it.

We've reached the end of talking for today, and we've looked at his early life. It's as if he felt he couldn't afford to fall apart, he couldn't afford to show his mum and dad that he wasn't well because they couldn't take that pressure at the time. And so he decided he was going to push it down and suppress it, and those noises or tics or the OCD came out. I myself know those noises he talked about, because it's something I used to do, funnily enough. If stresses are stuffed down, the anxiety has to come out, and that's how it sometimes does it.

So he's had to hide that pressure all his life, while he's achieved amazing things on the football pitch. But off it he's an ordinary man who needs the same love and care we all need.

Dear Paul

It has been such a special time getting to know you. You brighten my day every time I see you. Be strong and stay sober. I'm gonna read your book and if I'm ever on your side of the world, I will visit. Much love

Kerry

Paul receives some good news

Paul

I've just had some good news from the doc, from my surgeon. He's the one who operated on my neck, after I buggered it practising for that BBC ice-skating show. He now says I can start football training again. I've done ten sessions in the last five days in the gym at Champneys, which is too much really, one a day at this stage would be enough, but that's me. I take everything to excess.

I'm just doing fitness work at the moment, on my body and legs. I can't start actually football training till 15 March, because of my neck. But if all goes well, I can do full football training from 1 May, including heading the ball. I've been very touched because I know that both Alex Ferguson and José Mourinho would let me go and train at their place, if I wanted.

The reason for wanting to get football fit is that I've agreed to play some six-a-sides and some charity games and a testimonial. The testimonial is for Ted McMinn, at Derby. He used to play for them, and Rangers. He got some sort of infection – and lost part of his leg. Terrible. The charity match is on 27 May. A sort of World Cup warm-up – England against Rest of the World, which will have celebs as well as football legends playing. Ha, I wonder which one of those I'm meant to be playing in! It will be at Old Trafford and will be live on ITV. All profits go to UNICEF.

So, I've taken on quite a lot, considering I haven't played for about a year, but I'm looking forward to all the games. It will get me fit again, concentrate my mind and body.

After all that, who knows? I might have another job as a manager or coach lined up by then. But I don't see myself playing football professionally again. Those days are finished. I'll just do it for testimonials or charity. You do get offered expenses but, if it's for a testimonial, I never take any. I pay all my own expenses. If of course it's an event with a TV deal, then you get a fee for that.

After all that, I will have the Big Decision to make – where am I going to live?

I'm still at Champneys, this time at Tring, and it suits me champion, but I know I should start looking for something permanent for myself. Johnny has been on at me, saying I need some stability in my life.

I suppose I should buy something, but I can't decide whether to find something down here, near London, which will be handy for most things, or back up in Newcastle, where I feel at home.

I don't mind living in one small room, where I am now, and having all my stuff shoved in storage. I'm used to it.

If you're in a hotel or health farm, you don't feel lonely, at least I never do. You can walk into the corridor and there will be people to talk to, round the hotel, in the gym or the restaurant.

The thing about hotels and health farms is that if you have to, you can hide inside all the time, yet still be with other people – but the paparazzi can't stake you out. If you have your own house, they get to know it. If there's some stupid story in the papers about you, they'll sit outside your front door all day long, waiting for you to go the pub and get smashed.

David Beckham has gangs of them outside his house in Madrid, all the time.

In hotels, I might go to the bar, and have a Coke, and just talk to anyone who happens to be there. In Dubai on holiday, in our hotel, I went to the bar one afternoon and there was this woman sitting there – reading my book.

'Do you like it?' I says to the woman.

'He's a fucking idiot,' she replies.

'Do you know him?'

'No,' she says.

'Well you do now . . .'

I got up off the bar stool and walked out of the bar.

As I left, I could hear her screaming, 'Ohmygod, Ohmygod . . .'

Another time, one evening when the bar was quite crowded, a bloke nearby had heard my accent and he leans over and asks where I'm from. I told him I was from Newcastle.

'Oh aye,' he says, 'that's Gazzaland, where that fat bastard comes from . . .'

I didn't say who I was, but wound him up for ages. Talking about Gazza and Newcastle and all that stuff. Then another bloke comes over to me and says, 'Hiya Gazza, will you sign an autograph for me?' 'Certainly,' I said, 'no problem.'

The first bloke then turns and stares at me. 'You bastard. You didn't tell me who you was . . .'

My gym work is still going well, in fact I've now just done twenty sessions in the last ten days. I know I said before that was too much – and stupid. It still is, but I'm so desperate to get in shape to play football again. My day revolves round getting fit, that's all I seem to do.

Here at Champneys, I usually get out of bed about 7 a.m. I don't have any breakfast, except a couple of cups of coffee, with no sugar, plus usually two ciggies. Then I'm in the gym from 8.30 till 10. I usually do forty-five minutes on the bike and fifteen minutes on the running machine, or the other way round. I also do 1,000 sit-ups and I lift 400 light weights.

I don't usually have any lunch or dinner, perhaps a bagel salad in the evening if I haven't had one at lunch time. So no, I'm not eating much. Just one bagel salad a day.

In the old days when I woke up I would say to myself, 'I want a drink. I want a drink.' Now when I wake up, my mind is racing all the time with the words, 'What shall I eat today, what shall I eat today?'

It's become my major obsession, just when I thought I was getting to grips with all the others. It's worse than thinking about the alcohol. Since Cottonwood, that's been under control. Now I seem to be in the grip of this eating disorder. I've been doing my best to eat sensibly but I can't eat three meals a day, as Johnny suggested I do when we first got together again, this time round.

What's happened is that I'm scared to put on weight and so, in order to be fit for the football games, I don't eat, and yet I know I'm losing too much weight – but I can't help myself. And I want to lose more while I'm here.

I've had eating disorders since I was seventeen. I remember when Jack Charlton arrived as manager at Newcastle he could see I was overweight, with all the junk food I was eating.

He calls me into his office and asks me, 'How long's your contract?'

'I've got another two years, boss.'

'Two weeks,' he says. 'You've got only two weeks to get that weight off, or you're out . . .'

I was in a panic. Went running all the time, wearing plastic bags, trying to sweat it off. I did some training with Brendan Foster which helped.

That was about when I first learned to stick my fingers down my throat, after I'd stuffed my face with burgers and sweets and stuff.

That's how it all began. Since then, for the last twenty years, I've usually had some sort of fight with eating.

I've told Johnny all about it and he's trying to train my mind to fight it. I managed it for quite long spells, but now I'm back on it again.

I've battled against OCD and now I don't really worry about that as much, but I can't conquer the food problem. There was a girl at Cottonwood with the same problem. She was in tears all the time. I suppose it's a bit like anorexia. You get it into your mind that you're getting fat and you're scared to eat.

After my first lot of training in the morning, I come back and sit in my room, watch TV, do nothing really. At the moment I'm not answering the phone or texts from my friends. I feel too depressed, too obsessed. I don't want to moan on to them.

Yesterday I did think of having a salt beef bagel at lunch time. I really fancied one, then I decided not to. I do have some salted popcorn in my room. I eat a bit of that, now and again. It's fat free, so that's something. I always check the fat content before I eat anything.

Of course people still think I'm a fat bastard, stuffing my face with burgers all the time. I was in this minicab the other day and picked up the driver's paper, the *Daily Star* I think it was. The headline said 'Kebabs can kill you'.

Before I'd read the first paragraph, I turned to the driver.

'I bet I'm in this story,' I said to him. And I was.

They dragged out that 1998 story when I got photographed having a late-night kebab with Chris Evans and then later I got chucked out of the England squad by Glenn Hoddle. Eight years later, and that story is still following me around. And it's balls. I haven't eaten that sort of stuff for years. I wish I could.

I do my second training session between about 5 and 7 p.m., and then just go to my room again, watch TV, do nothing really, perhaps read one of my therapy books, thought for the day, that sort of stuff.

Two days a week I come to London. I see Johnny at his place.

I've been reading all these stories in the newspapers about obesity, about these overweight kids we're now breeding. I do feel sorry for them. They're in a far worse state than I am – as they're getting no help. I'd love to try and help them, to work with some of these obese kids, try and get them to eat fat-free stuff, as I do. But of course I wouldn't want them to go the other way and get obsessed.

I keep telling myself I can't eat, because if I eat, I'll get fat and won't be able to train. I just can't break that cycle of thought. Then I tell myself it will just be till the end of this summer. Once the various testimonial and charity games are over, I'll sit down and look at the rest of my life. I'll try to work out a different routine, not worrying about being fit to play football. I'll get involved in other things and try to have some stability in my life. But in the meantime, that's all I think about – not putting on weight and getting fit.

During those two years not drinking, I would often have a glass of wine sitting on the table in front of me. It was to prove to myself I was strong enough not to touch it.

Now that I'm obsessed by food, I'm doing a similar thing. I've just been to Tesco and bought some tomato ketchup and some bags of sweets, six packets of jelly babies and other stuff. I have them in my room, here at Champneys.

I know they're here, in the room, tempting me, but chances are that when I leave, they'll still be here, lying in the wardrobe. I've done that sort of thing for years – been in hotels or apartments and, when I've gone, there's loads of stuff left behind. I feel good, leaving them behind. I've risen to the challenge and won. Of course sometimes I don't – then I stick my fingers down me throat.

I know what I should be doing. No need to tell me. I should not be worried about my weight at all. I know I'm not remotely fat. I'm probably at least a stone underweight. I should be striking the right balance between a decent healthy diet, with three meals a day, while keeping fit. I know all fucking that. But I can't do it. I wake up each day and my head is going round, 'What shall I eat today, what shall I eat today?'

I wish I could jump out of bed every day and shout, 'I'm really happy, I'm really happy today.' That's what I'd like to do. But I'm so down at the moment. There's no fucking chance.

Then I tell myself how well I've done. My OCD is under control. I'm not drinking. I just have to hang on in there and, after this summer, I'll have beaten the eating problems. I'm sure I will. I'll then have started a new life, I dunno what or where, but things will be much better. That's what keeps me going . . .

Who can say what causes all this shit? Search me. I dunno. But I don't blame it on my parents, or my family.

Me mam and dad, they were never alcoholics, nor my sisters, so I didn't get it from them. None of my family has OCD. None of them had twitches or the sort of mood swings I have. You can't blame it on them and say that was the way I was born, inheriting stuff through their genes or whatever.

It was events that did it, that's what caused it all, like when Steven got killed. That still hangs over me, all these years later. It's always coming out when I'm talking to Johnny. I know I've mentioned it a few times already in this book. That was what led to the twitches. No question. I never had them till he got killed. That's a fact.

Then I became a crowd pleaser, always acting the fool, being the joker. I don't know why. I just did. I wanted to amuse people.

When I started football, that's when my real obsessions took over. I was obsessed by football, just as for a time I was obsessed by tennis. I loved tennis. I did think I might like to be a professional tennis player, till football took over.

I often think what would have happened if I'd played pro tennis not pro football. In tennis, you are on your own, one against one, you don't rely on anyone else. In football, you have to be part of the team. In tennis, I might not have become the team joker. I would just have been playing on my own, not in a group.

But for football, would I be in a worse state today? Who knows? My stealing might have got worse and I could have ended up in jail – but then again I did anyway, if just for one night.

I might not have become an alcoholic because I wouldn't have had the money I earned in football to pay for drink. I would have been like most of my mates from Newcastle, not able to go out for a drink till the weekend. By the time I was drinking heavily, when I was at Rangers, I had the money to drink every evening, and all afternoon after training, which for a time I did.

Playing football gave me a lot of money, so I've been able to pay for a lot of help with my problems – for clinics and therapy that I couldn't have afforded otherwise. On the other hand, I might not have needed all that help. I do think the pressures of football made things worse.

I often think it would have been nice to have had an ordinary job, been an ordinary person, unknown, able to go anywhere without being pestered.

God knows what my ordinary job would have been. A carpenter, perhaps. I quite liked woodwork at school. But perhaps I might not have managed a trade. I'd have been like my dad, a hodman, a labourer. Yeah, perhaps that's it – I would have ended up like me dad, doing odd jobs. Nothing wrong with that. He's a good lad. And he's not an alcoholic or a manic-depressive and he's certainly not got an eating disorder.

But, all things considered, I am glad I became a footballer. I did enjoy it. I might be more relaxed today, as a person, if I'd done something ordinary, but no, I don't regret what I did. I'm glad what happened to me happened to me.

———————

Paul my love

Oh Paul. If I wasn't single I'd marry you! No but seriously you have meant and will always mean so much to me and I wish I could have shown you that. Unfortunately I'm terrible when it comes to that kind of stuff.

You made me laugh when I could think of nothing but crying – and there have been few in my life who could do that.

I wish you would stick around forever, then life would never go wrong again. You were the first person here that asked me how I was doing and made me stop dead in my tracks because I just know that you were genuine and you actually wanted to know. You have changed so many lives here for the better.

Now I know what kind of guy I need to marry. Hee hee. Enough of this mushy crap. I wish you all the love and best of luck in your recovery. You deserve it . . .

Rachel

Paul's sixth session: Where to go next?

John

Paul and I start by following up on the previous session, when we talked about his daily structure, and about what it was like for him when he first arrived back in the UK after Cottonwood. Paul had said that he probably shouldn't have gone on holiday at the time he did, given the stage he was at, and in some ways against the advice he was given, bearing in mind how vulnerable he was.

Paul looked at the treatment options available after the thirty-three-day stay in Cottonwood. One of these being to go into three months of aftercare in California. This would form a transition stage, involving support and a period of adjustment to ease people back into a more normal routine. But this wasn't really an option for Paul: he felt he needed to get back home.

We need to talk about what's going to help Paul, first of all in the short term, to continue moving in the right direction – to keep his feet on the ground, keep talking about how he's feeling rather than reacting to it, carry on taking the right steps to keep himself on track, and continue to monitor himself. A key factor is to maintain balance – not to overdo anything: not caffeine, sugar, exercise, isolating himself, obsessive thinking, or anything that can tip him off balance.

One of the suggestions I keep making is that Paul goes back to AA meetings again. These are good for support, for being with people who totally understand without having to have anything explained to them. Attending such self-help groups is good for discipline, routine and for building up a strong inner reserve so that, when temptation strikes, you're ready for it. They're also a very powerful way of dealing with the 'addict' inside, which will so often emerge in a different way, like food or gambling, if the feelings aren't dealt with. When he's in Newcastle, there are a lot of the old temptations around such as Paul's old drinking friends and haunts. Although there are AA meetings in Newcastle, it's not so likely that he'll go to them because he's got so many other distractions.

Paul

When I've been in a clinic just a week, I know exactly what I need to do to live well and be happy; and then, when I come out of the clinic, for the first month I'm really down. When I'm in the clinic I'm away from everybody who's part of my everyday life. Instead I'm with people who understand. Unfortunately, there aren't many people in this country who do understand.

I want to do the training. I've trained for the last twenty years. I don't want to stop now and I don't want to be uncomfortable in my body and in my clothes. I want a good level of fitness, because that's when I feel good; I don't want to turn forty and be out of shape.

I could go and join a football club for training any time I want, and that's a nice feeling. To feel still wanted. I'm in two minds: I don't know whether to live in London or stay in Newcastle.

I hate the traffic in London, and I can't go fly fishing, though there are some lakes outside London, but you have to travel. I think, 'What else is there in London apart from meetings?' There are great meetings, but I don't want to live my life somewhere just because there are great AA meetings!

I know living in London would only be a short-term thing; you've suggested I move to London for three to six months because of the support here, but I'm in a situation where, when I wake up, I must take my medication, and if I forget, it ruins my training in the gym. Instead of enjoying it, I'm thinking, 'I've got to take my meds' and if I've got to go to a meeting, then as well as remembering the meds, I've got to remember to go to a meeting. I have to keep saying to myself, 'Don't forget the meds, don't forget the meeting', and that's what's really pissing me off. Having to remember all this stuff.

I do hate feeling trapped and being told what to do. I know I've said it before, but it really gets to me. I started off getting told what to do by my mum and dad, then my teachers, then captains and coaches, then managers, and now you, my counsellor, are telling me what to do, to come to live in London, and it's pissing me off.

I know the meetings are important. It's true I have got good friends in London, and I could live with them. I like the people in London, but it's an expensive place to live. I haven't got a job at the moment. I could bring my stuff down, and if I hate it I could go back. If a job comes up, a manager's job up north, then I'll go up there. I can head Gateshead Football Club, I've been offered it, but owning a football club doesn't appeal to me.

John

I tell Paul the reason I recommend meetings is that in a group environment where people do understand him, and identify with his problems, he thrives, he can be honest. There's something dangerous for him about not being free to say how he's really feeling. In meetings he's more free to talk about his 'demons'.

One of the problems for Paul is that he's so popular with people, and of course there's a tradition in self-help groups for people to be friendly and give you their phone numbers. With Paul, he might get overwhelmed by this and, as we've discussed before, he can have problems saying 'No' to people. In the past, he's taken too many phone numbers and felt obliged to ring them all. He felt he was constantly on the phone, which of course isn't the idea – those people are there to call only if and when you really need to, there's no pressure. It's another area of learning for Paul about his recovery.

Paul talks a lot about getting his body into shape through training. The work of recovering is about training the mind, just like training the body. This is something Paul resists. He really needs to make the decision to train his mind, just as he trains his body, because his mind can work against him. That part of his mind that is associated with 'the addict' works against him. It might say, for example: 'I have to be a stone lighter than this in order to feel okay about myself, so I have to train three times a day, once isn't good enough; I have to lose x stone in y days; why shouldn't I have a drink, just one – everyone else is having one.'

In order to guard against this 'addict head', I suggest Paul builds into his structure one or two meetings a week, a counselling session, regular nutritious meals and a meeting with a nutritionist to get expert advice. There are also many other things that can be built into his routine to strengthen his mind, that build up that good feeling and resistance. In order to overcome that 'addict thinking', when it comes, we need to have built up a store of good beliefs about ourselves, and a strong sense of identity that's separate from the addict side of our natures. If Paul doesn't feel good about himself, he's more likely to work extra hard physically and push himself so that he gets out of balance, and possibly even gets injured.

I want to get over to Paul the concept of detaching from the thoughts and feelings that are not going to benefit him. He can have the thought but he doesn't have to act on it. It takes a lot of work, but it's possible to observe the thought, and feel the feeling and acknowledge it, but at the same time to have a strong self that doesn't attach to the thought and doesn't act on it. For example, you might feel terrible because someone has rejected you, and it sends you back into a kind of depressed thinking. You might then get some other bad news, and just feel you can't take any more and your life's unbearable. You feel lonely, rejected, angry and you can't see a way out. At that moment you might feel like the pressure in your head is too much, and you want some relief. You want to act on this feeling by going to the gym/pub/cake shop/bookies so that you're feeling something completely different. You might be thinking of sabotaging everything – resigning from your job, walking out on your partner, getting the next bus home and never speaking to your friend again.

Alternatively, you might take a deep breath, phone someone or arrange to meet someone, and talk it all through. You might have a walk or run in the fresh air, do a yoga class, even some meditation – all of these things will put the actual problems you have into perspective. Getting someone else's take on a situation can be of invaluable help. If you have these good habits already in place, they come naturally at a time of crisis, and you have that store to draw on.

At the moment Paul runs with the feeling that he's not going to be satisfied until he gets to a certain weight, and that he won't be satisfied until he's achieved various external goals. I wonder if he could now prioritise his mind health over what he believes his body ought to be.

Paul

I've proved that saying, that an addict alone is in bad company, because that's when I relapse. I'm definitely an alcoholic, no doubt there.

An addict always wants something right now. What I'm worried about is putting on weight. I put on weight in Dubai, and at the clinic before then. And now I want to lose it all. I've done nine sessions in four days and I'm still worried about my weight. It's got me down again. I looked at myself this morning and I thought I'd lost a little bit more weight. I did two sessions yesterday, I ate last night, I drank two bottles of water, some Diet Coke and ate some popcorn. I think to myself, 'Good, I've lost weight.' I went to the gym, then I looked in the mirror again. It's an absolutely stupid thing I'm doing. I think to myself, 'What am I doing this for?' If I gave it time the weight would drop off me. I am getting into good condition, but it's really stability I need.

Once I get into the routine of going to meetings I'll be fine. I won't go to meetings until I've got the weight down. Another two weeks and I'll have done it. I've been on a crash diet and I want it straight away – that's me.

I feel like if I come to London I'm keeping other people happy, but what about me? If I knew there was work in London I'd move down here straight away. I don't fancy sitting on the train all the time commuting back and forth. People might think that I'm mad to put anything else before my health and my life. If London's going to help me get well, then why don't I move here now? Once I get my weight back to the way I want it, I'll speak to Chris, and maybe stay with him for a month in London and go to meetings.

I should have carried on with my coaching badges. Some people say the badges are so hard, but I didn't find it that hard, so maybe I should go back to that. I want to go back to football when I come out of the health farm. I'm really looking forward to the games in May.

It's true that the training is partly me trying to alter my mood. Training changes the way I feel, it lifts my mood. But I've got to the stage where I've gone past that, and now if I don't train, my mood that day will be shit. Look what happened last time I pushed myself after I'd damaged my neck skating. Once I'd been given the okay to train I went at it too hard. And I ended up in hospital. I'm a little bit worried about that, but it's still not stopping me.

It's true about starving yourself being like a withdrawal. I went from eating everything in the clinic and on holiday to now eating almost nothing, so it's like a withdrawal.

John

We need to keep finding ways for Paul to approach his obsession with weight, food and training. We talk a lot about structure, meaning the structure of how we use our time, both daily and weekly. I ask Paul about structure, how it's worked for him, and to take us back over some of the progress he's made with alcohol, OCD, bipolar and panic attacks, and to look at how it could help with food and exercise.

Paul

I know that a daily structure will help. A meal plan for each day, how many meals I'll have, roughly what time, when I'm going to train and for how long, and when I'm going to do a meeting. That's what's suggested. A food disorder needs structure to overcome it.

I've proved that structure works because I've done a plan with my OCD. You practise shutting doors and just walking away, and I have managed it. It's funny, as soon as I mention 'OCD' I look at the door. I just did it then. I can actually shut the door and walk away now. I don't touch light switches five times, I just turn the light off. I also used to have to switch off sockets in the wall. Say in a hotel corridor. I'd walk all the way up and down the corridors, checking to see if the socket was switched to 'on' but with no plug in. I had to have them all switched off. At Champneys I practised walking up and down the corridor there. Not switching off the sockets.

What's helped with the OCD is being distracted by other things, the medication a bit, and just practising good habits and structure. The thing with OCD is you think if you don't touch something three times or whatever, or if you don't do something or other, something bad will happen. I used to think it would mean I'd get run over.

I now think, 'Fuck it, if it happens, it happens.' I tried it – not switching lights off, or whatever. After a few days of nothing bad happening, I learned. I used to have to sleep with the light on. Now I sleep with it off. Being at Cottonwood helped with that. Having to share a room. So I've trained myself. It's like smoking. You can ask for help, and take stuff for it, but only you can conquer it. I've taught myself with the OCD.

When I hurt my neck I asked, 'Will I be paralysed?' The doctor said, 'Today you could walk across the road and get run over or you could have an operation and get better, you just don't know what's going to happen' – and that's true. I don't know what's going to happen and I can't control what happens, so I try to deal with things in that way now.

One thing, though. I'm okay on the arranging things in the right order, or light switches, opening and closing doors or switching off wall sockets – all that stuff. It doesn't get to me any more. Well, not much anyway. Not as much as it used to. But I don't know if I'll ever conquer OCD as regards numbers. Bad numbers and numbers that can protect me. It started when I was young. It was number five. Everything had to have five in it. I'd look at things five times. I'd touch things five times. I tried to get off five, and then it was thirteen. That was the bad number. And now it's number nine. And if I have loads of caffeine it really starts to get on top of us. If I let it. It doesn't take much caffeine – coffee, Coke, Red Bull – to trigger my anxiety. And that's when the superstitions about bad things happening if I don't do the numbers thing gets worse. I am trying to cut the coffee and other stuff down.

Doing all the right things and following the right habits does work to keep the OCD at bay. It's my own fault when I do the wrong things.

And compared to two years ago, I've managed to sort out the panic attacks as well. The more I talked about them the more I got conscious of them and I knew what was going on. When I came out of the clinic two years ago and got one of my first panic attacks I didn't know what was going on, so I spoke to someone else who suffered from them, and asked them how their panic attacks came on. And I realised that this was what it was, and I dealt with it. The very first time I had one was when I was in hospital, back when I had that injury at Lazio, and I didn't have a clue what it was. But now I take a few deep breaths, switch myself off, calm myself down. At first they lasted fifteen minutes but now they would only last about two minutes because I know how to deal with them.

Now, about the mood swings. Bipolar was diagnosed officially by the psychiatrist in Arizona. It's another condition that co-exists with my alcoholism. I say in the groups, 'I'm Paul, I'm an alcoholic.' When people ask how I am, I try not to say the word 'fine' – Fucked-up Insecure Neurotic and Emotional. In the clinic someone would be fine one minute and then saying nothing the next minute. One night there, I was lying in bed reading the *Big Book* (the main AA book, written by its founders Bill W and Dr Bob), and I got scared, thinking if Bill hadn't met Bob and set up AA, I think I'd be dead.

The programme's simple. Very simple. Being an alcoholic messes with my brain chemistry and sets up mood swings. I'm not the only one with bipolar and I'm not the only one who's an alcoholic. Thing is, I've got the bottle to tell everyone. Maybe I think my life would be a lot better if I could tell people when I'm sad. Best thing is to get on the phone to someone who cares for you.

I used to walk to the streets and stop and say hello to people, even when I was down, and stop for a photo, when I wasn't in the mood. I need to control the mood swings and learn to say 'No' in a nice way instead of saying, 'Yeah I'll do it,' and then getting fucked up. I need to say, 'No, sorry I can't do it – can I do it next week?' But I don't want people to not ask us to do things – I'll always do something that I'm asked to do, always. I've always done that. I can control mood swings if I use the right methods but, if I don't, my mood's shit and the only thing that'll cheer us up – instead of speaking to someone and telling them how I feel – is if I just go and have a few drinks, and then the next day I'm in a worse mood.

With bipolar, when I get a high or manic mood, I just want to spend money. I don't spend that much now, but I've got that beautiful Harley Davidson stuck in a garage in Jesmond. I can only use it in this country two months of the year because of the weather, and I'm sitting here with a spanking new Hot Rod.

I was on Red Bull once and I'd started to go into a high. It wasn't funny at the time because it was like being on cocaine. I ran outside – I was meeting a girl – but someone must have polished up the glass door, and I smashed straight into it. I was going so fast I just didn't see it. I went out to meet this girl with a tissue on my bleeding nose, and an ice pack on my eye, and said, 'Hello, nice to meet you.' The date didn't go that well.

It sounds daft now, but at the time it felt horrible.

It's hard not to have regrets. I regret so much what happened to young Steven, I regret that I didn't see as much of my son, Regan, as I'd like to, as I'd love to. Sometimes I think about the transfers I made. Also, if only I'd invested some money.

I have loads of regrets. The only great times I've had have been playing football. Or times with my mates. And now I don't have the football. All these thoughts are going through my head all the time.

John

I believe it's important for Paul to be occupied, when he's up to it and when he's ready to do something, because the nature of the addictive personality is that, when left idle or turned inward, it goes into self-destruct. Only the alcoholic can take responsibility for his condition. No one else can do it for us, for when we close that door at night, we have to be able to be the one who says, 'I'm all right, and I'm going to be all right.' We have to be the one who can deal with the negative thoughts.

Paul

I try my best to deal with those negative thoughts. I do need to start doing something soon, some kind of work or training. This Chelsea thing: I told Archie about the offer, and he said, 'You can't turn that down.' I'll get back in touch with José Mourinho when I come out of the health farm. I've had a fantastic offer from Alex Ferguson as well. I'm lucky. But the way I feel at the moment, I can't do anything until I get fit. I've just got to keep searching. I've searched before and found what I wanted. It's a case of digging deep. Maybe I have to get through the next couple of months to find what I want.

I couldn't have been more honest than I was in my last book, but this new book is more detailed and more me. This is what's really going on in my life. In me heed. The first one was more football and career. I've come to terms with everything I've got, I'm facing things and I'm a hell of a lot better person than I was ten years ago and a hell of a lot better person than I was three years ago. I've been told I've got this problem and that problem, and I've had to deal with all of that.

The only problem I haven't really conquered to the best of my ability is the drink, and that's me being honest. It's hard when you get invited to parties and premieres. How am I going to sit there for three hours? I'm not always the best at making conversation, unless I talk about football.

I'm always caring about somebody else – that's one of my problems. I don't really care about myself as much as I really should do.

I mustn't cut myself off from people. I can't wait for this book to come out. I might be a bit embarrassed, I don't want people thinking I'm a fruit cake – because I'm not – but I have to deal with all these things I talked about in our last session, and the life I've had. And I want people to know the truth, not just rubbish they read in the papers.

It is stressful being followed everywhere, dealing with my ex-family, the press, photographers, just totally watched 24/7. That's the type of world I live in. I have to be careful about everything I say and everything I do. Even now, three years after packing in football.

I went to watch a movie – this happened twice – and, when I came out of the cinema to get some popcorn, my sister called us up saying it said in the press I was staggering all over the place, in and out of the cinema. All I was doing was getting popcorn, and it said in the press I was getting drunk. I sometimes think I just can't live in this country. Maybe I could go off to Australia for a year or something. I don't like living like this.

John

As we go on with the sessions in this book, we see it is like a jigsaw, and we're putting together all the pieces, and seeing how they fit. There are different aspects of Paul's illness, and they're connected with each other, and we're gradually piecing together what those connections are.

One of the things that's so difficult for Paul at the moment is beginning this new chapter in his life, and not knowing where it'll take him. Everything he's known since being a very young adult has changed. He's got to get used to still having the pressure from the media, but without drinking, and without the fans singing his name every week. He is missing aspects of his old life, the 'good times' in the Premiership, but those have come to an end. Paul needs to grieve for this and then move on. Of course this is easier said than done. He is letting go of so much at the moment, and sometimes when I sit in a session with him, my feelings, or what we call in the field my counter-transference, swing from frustration to admiration. But I'm very aware that he's clearly doing the best he can with what he has at the moment, and one of the main ingredients of success is patience, on the part of the counsellor as well as the client.

We've gone back over where he's up to with various aspects of his illnesses: he's made good progress with managing his anxiety in terms of the OCD and the panic attacks. He even used his own version of cognitive therapy on himself to deal with claustrophobia, and realised that he could get himself through the experience of being locked up alone in a tiny space.

Paul knows what to do about alcohol, but he's struggling with accepting that meetings or some kind of regular support group needs to be part of his life. He's also grappling with the exercise and food. His self-esteem is dependent on his fitness and weight, and he doesn't want to lose control of that. That's good, but it's important for anyone that they lose weight slowly and with the advice of a qualified nutritionist. Dieting can deplete vital nutrients from the body, for example zinc. Deficiencies in these nutrients can in turn affect appetite and help contribute to food disorders. Balance is what we're aiming for, and that is achieved through hard work and discipline. There's still plenty of work for us to do.

Dear Pauly

As you have been told many times, you are the most humorous son of a bitch I have ever met – not to mention rude, crude, obnoxious and insane individual I have ever met. Yet your honest, humble way of dealing with the issues of not only yourself but of others makes you one of the most sincere kind-hearted blokes I have known. You befriended me as I did you, knowing not a thing about each other or our pasts – that to me was the foundation of one hell of a good time during a very difficult time (at least for me).

Julie

Paul's seventh session: Letter to Paul

John

It's now the beginning of March. What I'd like to do in the session today is summarise the issues Paul and I have covered over the past few months, and look at a range of solutions. I'm going to read Paul a letter that I've put together, outlining some of the events of the past, linking them up with behaviour patterns, and looking at some steps he can take to keep well. This is loosely based on the Cognitive Analytical Therapy (CAT) tool called a 'reformulation letter'. Although we haven't had the opportunity to do a full sixteen-week CAT course, I use CAT in my approach with Paul, and this letter should help us concentrate on behaviour patterns, or what CAT calls 'procedures'.

Dear Paul

I'm writing this letter to acknowledge the main issues we have covered in our sessions together. This is in order to help you recognise your problematic areas and to help you take more control of your life.

It has now been several months since you came back to see me for help. This time there was an added aspect to our relationship – 'to write a book'. It was clear that in order for us to do that, you needed to get back to basics again if you were to give yourself any chance of tackling the many issues that have been getting in the way of your happiness. These things have been affecting you for most of your life. These are the issues I have outlined below, and over the next few weeks we will be working on them specifically.

Ever since you were a young child there has been pressure on you to perform. You were a sensitive boy and seemed to 'tune in' to what others were feeling. You are the second eldest of four children. You grew up in a stressful home environment where money was hard to come by, and this meant that your parents were under great pressure to work, in order to feed and clothe you. Your father would have to travel abroad to find work and this meant that your mother was left to look after the four of you and go out to work. You shared with me that she had three jobs at one stage. She, like you, is sensitive and, I feel, has an anxious nature. You related well to your brother and sisters but, because of the many pressures, your brother Carl was put in a care home because he misbehaved. That was difficult for you to cope with.

You liked school and always wanted to be first in everything you did, especially sport. Outside of school you were always on the move and would attend a boys' club most days of the week. The joining age for that club was nine, but your father pretended you were older than you were and got you in from the age of seven. Despite the age difference you were able to compete with and often beat the other children at most sports. It was as if the club was a safe place for you and gave you an outlet – a channel for your stress and anxieties. It soon became clear that you had a natural talent for football.

Aged ten, you and the younger brother of a friend were out at the shops when he ran on to a road and was killed by a car. You held him as he died. That trauma heightened the already sensitive side of your character and you began to stammer and have physical tics. It was at this stage you began to be superstitious about certain numbers.

Your mother did what she could to help with these problems and your father took you to see a psychiatrist but you report this did not work, because he just made you play with sand. After one visit your father felt that it was a waste of time, so you never returned to those sessions. Clearly, there was not enough support to help you through that difficult period and you were left to deal with it as best you could – even today you feel responsible for that accident.

When you were about fourteen, your father was very unwell, and had a series of operations to deal with a brain tumour. One time he had an attack and you thought he was going to die right in front of you – another trauma, another time alone. His operations also meant that he could no longer go out to work, and this meant more stress at home. Sometimes this stress would boil over and your parents would argue and occasionally have physical fights, especially when alcohol was consumed. They would frequently separate.

It is no wonder that as you got older you took on the role of provider. This combined with the existing role of the 'funny guy': the one that made everyone else happy and okay. Aged fourteen, you knew you would become a successful footballer, and started practising your autograph. The praise and attention that you had always received from football increased, you were now achieving great things in your home town, and became a 'local hero'. What a relief – a way out of that old lifestyle – freedom! But not for you. You have shared with me over the past few months that instead of feeling better you felt worse. You loved playing football, but the rest of it got to you. There were lots of conditions attached. As well as the pressure to perform you had to lose weight. You had always been a little overweight but this was no longer acceptable. You were threatened with the sack if you did not lose weight. This was the start of another dysfunctional pattern, bingeing, purging and not eating. A pattern that would last till today.

It seemed that the external expectations of others, i.e. your family, friends, supporters and the media, were affecting you internally and you were struggling to cope. You did not have the right type of psychology to keep up with the changes. Football, the very thing that had supported and helped you, now seemed to be adding more problems. It's likely this is when your depression started.

Over the next few years, these pressures were magnified as you became more successful. You met your wife and had your son Regan. You were happy for a time but, due to arguments and pressure on you to perform, you would regularly separate. Yet more disruption.

Over a four-year period you progressed from local to national hero. The whole football world now knew of you. Your obsessive compulsive disorder went up and down depending on your anxiety level. So too did the food disorder. And there was now another problematic pattern emerging: your drinking pattern. Alcohol helped you relax and, to a degree, cope with the many stresses. But you could not drink like others did. You would lose control and this eventually brought you to your knees and you ended up in a clinic. You were told that you had the physiology (brain chemistry) of an alcoholic and that you had to abstain from alcohol.

Despite not liking that advice, you stayed sober for six months, but then started drinking again. On the football pitch you would still perform well but you were getting frustrated. You had been dropped from the England squad, your marriage was over and you were now in the newspapers for more negative things than positive. It was as if the adoration you had received for years was now turning into criticism: you were being portrayed as a failure. You felt betrayed, angry and misunderstood.

From that time to now you have been determined to carry on, to go forward and show that you are still that winner, that hero. You have been back into treatment for your alcoholism and bipolar disorder, but you still won't give up. It is no surprise that you now struggle to look after yourself – you were never shown how to.

I feel that in order for you to move forward in your life we should concentrate on the following areas:

1. To stay focused on your sobriety by attending AA meetings and following the programme as suggested. Never mind what you read in the papers – AA is a safe place. There are many people in your position who attend. This consistency will give you more control over your life and help you stay in touch with your sober friends.

2. Pay daily attention to your eating habits and stick to a food plan. We can do this plan together, but I suggest you sit down with a nutritionist and get that expert advice. Your food disorder needs special attention at the moment, and by not addressing it you are abusing your body. It may help to re-read some of the books that you have found helpful in the past.

3. Exercise is good for you – in moderation. I am going to suggest that you swap one gym session every other day for a meditation session. Being still and learning to relax will help you concentrate and feel better, and help you detach from your thoughts.

4. Write a daily journal at the end of the day, focusing on your moods. How you have felt that day, what things have affected your moods and what you might be worried about. This will help you focus on any signs of depression, or spot early signs of becoming manic. You should also note if there have been any panic attacks or signs of OCD.

5. Remember to say 'No'. It is your life, and people will only listen when you are clear with them. Don't blame anyone else and don't become a victim. You are a powerful man who is kind and considerate but who has needs, gets tired and needs rest – so stand up for yourself. Stop looking for other people to tell you that you are okay. You have proved that you are a success. You are good enough as you are. Learn to be yourself, Paul John Gascoigne.

You are already achieving some of the above but I believe you need to do it all. Over our next sessions we will be looking at how well you were able to achieve these goals. It is important that you ask your friends or me for help in achieving these aims. You are not responsible for your illness but you are responsible for your recovery.

Johnny

Paul

I think that letter gives a quick overview of my life, from being born to now. It sums it up quite well really. How it all actually did creep up on us.

In my village there were a lot of homes like mine. It wasn't unusual. It was quite normal, my home. But, like it said in the letter, the other boys were left alone to get on with it at the age of seventeen. I wasn't, I went to play for Newcastle. So I had to deal with the press and I wasn't ready for it. They really hammer you and put you down. I'd had quite a tough upbringing, and I just really couldn't understand why they wanted to put me down.

Unless you've got these problems, you're not going to understand what I'm going through. When people ask questions, as an outsider looking in, it's complicated for them because they don't get it. People think, 'He's been into treatment a few times now, what's up?' But it's not resetting a broken leg. People think, 'Why isn't he fixed now – he's been to hospital, what's the matter?'

No, there's people who've been to rehab nine times – more. I don't want to be in and out of clinics, but I'm not going to promise I'll never go back again, because I said that last time. I promised Bryan Robson. I said, 'I promise, I promise, I'll never touch drink again.' But I did. At the clinic they showed the damage drugs do to your brain, and that put the shits up me, it really did.

People say, 'How are you Paul?' 'Yeah, I'm all right at the moment,' I say, 'I'm writing a new book.' And I tell them the truth about my problems, and that it's not a problem if I stay on top of everything. Of course I'm always going to have the pressure on us, things are going to come down hard on us, my ex-wife and the kids, all of it. I'll have the worries I've always had. I'd like to see my son. That's sad. That is sad.

But I think, 'I'm lucky.' Gary McAllister's wife's just passed away with cancer and I just think, 'How lucky am I?' I've been thinking about him, and wanting to text him. They were a lovely couple, and she passed away at such a young age. I really want to go to the funeral. For me going to a funeral – it brings back a lot of sad, bad memories.

A letter like this makes you look back a bit at your life. I've been asked this question since I was nineteen: 'If you weren't a footballer, what would you be?' Thing is, I was a footballer, and that's it. I don't think, 'I could have been this or done that.' People say, 'Do you have any regrets?' Yeah, course I have fucking regrets. Why I make the most of the good times is because I know there are always going to be bad times round the corner. Whenever I had a good time I probably went over the top. But I wouldn't change me life. Yeah, I'd love to change all the fucking things I've got – these problems – but the fact is I have them and that's it. I've got to get over them. And challenge them on a daily basis, a day at a time.

Last week I was really down and I didn't want to do the counselling session. Unfortunately I have got these problems, and sometimes it's embarrassing for us talking about them. Last week I was really fed up, but this week's better. And I'm not far off the weight I want to be.

I've had a decent week. I hope it continues. These sessions are hard. It takes some time to recover from one. Sometimes I go to the gym and run it off. If there's traffic, it takes almost two hours to get back, and my thoughts are going round me head while I sit in the traffic. I don't want to talk to anyone or see anyone. I just have to be alone with it. I won't make arrangements to meet anyone for two days afterwards. In some ways I was looking for a fix, doing this book, but there isn't a quick fix. I thought, 'I'm going to come out of this really, really well, and I won't have any more panic attacks, no more alcohol, no more this or that.' But I'm taking it seriously. If I fuck about with these illnesses then they'll come back.

I remember getting a cry for help when I was doing me last book signing. I hardly put any of this stuff about my problems in me last book, but I still got people coming up to us and asking us stuff. I remember even ringing you, Johnny, about someone who asked me to call his house that night, who was depressed.

I had a phone call today from someone who started laughing, and he said, 'I've just been diagnosed with bipolar,' and he was on lithium. We both just laughed, because we knew. And that's a way forward for me a bit, being able to laugh about it.

My emotions are up and down. I'll tell you something, and this is absolutely ridiculous. I was watching football on TV, this guy scored a goal, and he was totally over the moon. The light on his face, his whole expression and everything, was just amazing, he was that happy. And I had a lump in me throat seeing it. I couldn't believe it, it wasn't even a team I particularly like. Any happiness I see at the moment, I get a lump in me throat. And I think, 'Where's that coming from? What the fuck's all that about?' I think it's getting in touch with my emotions again, that's the way I look at it.

I think a lot about what I'm going to do. There's loads of stuff I can do for charity. Stuff all over the world. But I have to wait till I've put me own house in order, then I can get into doing stuff like that again.

I loved being a manager and I loved working with Paul Davis. I thoroughly enjoyed it. The week before it was all over we won 4–1 in the Cup. Then, at the end, I had the most disastrous three days. We talk in the sessions about saying 'No'. And I said 'No' to that chairman. He wanted to do things at the club I didn't agree with. I said 'No', and it didn't work, he didn't like it. So for me, saying 'No' backfired on us. But I don't regret holding my own, because he doesn't know football like I do. I wouldn't say anything more about him, because I wouldn't do that. But I'm still glad I said 'No'.

What I've been thinking is, if I want to be a manager I can't just keep talking about it, I've got to do something about it. I've got to finish me badges, and get me next manager's job and take it by the scruff of the neck. I really think football's the only thing for me. I've got to start ringing people and listening to their advice. All these managers, they worked their nuts off to get where they are. They watch eight matches every weekend, searching for players. They work really hard, never stop. I really want to give management a go, grab it by the horns.

I think, 'Fucking hell, why did I pack in football?' When I was at Rangers I used to stay behind and train on me own, so I wouldn't go out drinking with me mates, and Walter Smith spotted it and he knew why I stayed in the gym till 4 p.m. And Walter helped us, as lots of other managers would or the PFA. If a player asks for the help.

There isn't enough knowledge about drink for kids. I don't like the taste of alcohol, but I drank it for the feeling. Now what chance have our kids got if we're bringing out alco-pops, which taste sweet, so you haven't got even the taste to put you off when you're a kid?

I saw a friend who goes to meetings this week, and she was really nice and invited me for a coffee, and I appreciated that. She's absolutely living evidence and proof that the programme of meetings can work. And she's got lots of work, she's extremely successful. She's famous, and she tells people she's an alcoholic. I can see that can happen for me, it's a possibility, if I can put the amount of effort into it that I put into the gym.

I have got to stay on top of things. I try and look at the things I can do. I do keep a journal and write things down. Well, I try to. I've been a bit slack recently. These things will come when I'm ready. Diving into stuff's not good. I dived into the training when I got back from holiday in Dubai. And the Boston thing, China, Kettering, I dived into them. It wasn't to be. It's a learning process for me.

I'd like to go to a men's group, where you see it's okay to vent your feelings in front of other blokes. They told me there's a good AA and a good NA (Narcotics Anonymous) men's meeting near where I live. A lot of people go to both fellowships because NA covers all drugs – and alcohol counts as a drug. And so do painkillers. I know if I take any type of painkillers, sleepers, or drink, it does not help. I know that for a fact now, it makes it worse and worse and worse.

I'll take it easier with the gym, go in at 9.30 and again at 5.30, and have a steam and try and relax. Not getting up so early. I need to give meself time out, and relax. I was going to come to London earlier, have a nice cup of coffee and just relax. But what stopped us was the gym. It's a shame because I'm in a beautiful health farm, but I can't relax because of doing the gym. Steve and his girlfriend invited us for dinner, and I said, 'Oh, I'll be all right, thanks,' because I can't relax. Steve's a good guy and he loves his football. Arsenal fan. Really nice guy to be with. If you can't relax in a health farm, where the fuck can you relax?

Last week I was in therapy on Wednesday and Thursday, and after it took two days to chill out. And then here I am back in the session again. It's hard, but now that I'm coming here I'm glad I'm coming. I look forward to the sessions now.

That was a good letter for me to look at, and for other people to see what happened to me. From where I was very early on in my life, to where I am now. What I've had to try and cope with, to the best of me knowledge. But the skills I had weren't fantastic apart from football. I'll never play in the Premiership again, the FA Cup again, the World Cup again, but I will be able to play football. I know, I've had my time in the spotlight, but you can still play football. I can get over these illnesses if I stay doing the right thing and stay on top of it, and I can have a good life. There's proof out there, there are people who've done it and gone on to achieve things. I've met them, I've mixed with them, I've drunk with them – tea and coffee of course. I have seen living proof that it does work, and that's not just with the alcohol, it's everything that I've got. You can get out of it. I want to put that letter in the book.

The thing that matters more than everything is self-belief, confidence. Getting that back. I've got to remember about codependency. And letting go. Letting go's a big one. What helps me with letting go is Step One – like, I'm powerless over saying 'Yes'. I'm not going to be like Alan Sugar, saying 'NO!' But I need to be able to be who I am. And accept who I am. This is my personality. This is my personality sober. This is me having the balls to come out and say this stuff; if I can do it then I hope that it'll help others.

I've had a decent week, I don't know what it's going to be like next week, I really don't, but I'm staying in the moment. I looked forward to coming to this session. I'm happier with everything that's going on. I'm enjoying the day, I'm enjoying the session. I hope, now I'm nearing forty, I can have some time to enjoy some of my life.

John

Paul's speaking with so much clarity. It sounds like he knows what he wants, and he knows he can achieve it. He also knows it's going to be tough and there'll be days when he wants to throw in the towel.

He's taking responsibility for his part in things, which is all any of us can do. He's learning from the past, but trying not to regret it. He's been doing a lot of intense therapy, and a lot of thinking in between, and facing things.

We've talked about separating ourselves from the punishing thoughts. Paul mentioned applying the principles of the AA Step One – powerlessness – to his codependency, and we can do the same with the 'addict' when we say, 'I'm powerless over these thoughts.' So we stop trying to argue with them and engage with them – what we do is detach from them. We can learn to ignore thoughts that aren't real; for example, we might think that before we can relax we've got to do something by a certain time. These thoughts happen so often that we believe them, and the only thing we can do is to give into them. Like the alcohol craving that goes on so long that in the end we think, 'Fuck it, I'll just have a drink to get it out of the way.' Our own thinking tells us to do something that's actually bad for us. What on earth is that about? Put like that, doesn't it sound incredible? Why would my own head tell me I've got to do something that's bad for me, and dress it up in such a way that I think it'll be good for me? That's addiction.

A film that brilliantly portrays the concept of separating from a part of one's mind is Ron Howard's *A Beautiful Mind*, based on the book by Sylvia Nasar. The problem's obviously different, in that John Nash hallucinates, but the principle's the same. He learns that his mind sometimes tells him things and shows him things that aren't real. He teaches himself how to separate from that part of his mind, to recognise it, acknowledge it – even make friends with it – but not to believe it.

Dear Paul

You've been a true fuckin' mate. Stay true and stay honest to yourself. Keep letting the gas out. Farting keeps you sober. Thanks for all the laughs and wisdom. Keep in touch and stay sober.

Tony

Paul looks back on pigeon shooting and Jimmy shaving

Paul

Johnny's letter was good, full of stuff going over my life. I know it all, of course, as I've lived it, but it was interesting to read. In fact it was quite powerful. It was as if I'd written the letter myself, to myself. It reminds me where I've come from, what I've been through.

Then there's the five areas I have to concentrate on. That first one, about going to AA meetings, I know all that, been told it all before. I have gone to them over many years, but now and again, when I relapse, I don't go to them for a long time, when I know I should.

When I wake up in the morning, I hate the idea of my first thought being, 'Now, should I go to an AA meeting today?' What sort of fucking life is that? When I'm lying in bed, thinking about that, wondering how can I fit it in, I'll then think, 'What the fuck, I might as well buy a bottle of whisky today and get drunk.'

His remark about it being a 'safe' place. Yeah, it is. It's rare for people to stitch you up at AA meetings and sell a story to the papers. So that doesn't worry me – it's just waking up and realising I should go to AA. That's what I hate. Wake up, go to an AA meeting – if I'm doing that every fucking day I'll be like a robot.

His second point, about sticking to a food plan, I know all that as well. The trouble is I feel bloated all the time, when I know I'm not. It's just how I feel, in my head as well as my body. I often feel like eating a bar of chocolate, then I think, 'If I do that, I'll have to eat nothing for two days.'

I've seen a nutritionist before. I know what's what, what I should eat and not eat, but I think I've got a different metabolism to other people. I do watch what I eat, keep fatty stuff under control, but I hate doing it. It makes me depressed, the fact that I have to think about what I eat.

I know I should eat little and often, that makes sense. Johnny has given me a diet programme I should follow. I know it's all down to me. I've been given all the help and advice, but what happens is that I don't feel right with my body. I can feel this stomach now, and it feels bloated. I've got too much flesh round there. I want to get it off, because I want to be fit and thin for these games coming up.

It's another obsession I've got myself into. Most of the old ones are gone, but I seem stuck with this eating disorder. I just hope after this summer it will be all gone.

In his third point, he suggests I exercise in moderation – but I never do anything in moderation. When I was playing, I was the hardest and longest trainer – because I took it to extremes.

In theory, this should be a perfect place for relaxing, where I still am now, at Champneys, in a health farm. Steve, the owner, said to me the other day that I should really be relaxed, living here, but I'm not. It's not the environment, the place, because that's brilliant. It's me. Living with me, that's what makes me not relaxed. I still have all these demons running around in my head, battering at my brain to get out.

For twenty years, since I first became a footballer, people have been telling me to relax. It hasn't worked yet.

Point four is about keeping a journal. I did do one in Cottonwood, but

I haven't written anything for over a month. I'm in this cycle of training all day. I don't have time or the energy to write things down. When I'm not in the gym, I'm resting, waiting to go for the next session.

He's been on at me for some time about saying 'No' to people, which is his fifth point. I do try to say 'No', quickly, in a nice way, which I know is the best thing to do. But I find it so hard.

It's just happened again. Someone has asked me to play in a charity five-a-side. I know I can't play on the date they want, as my neck won't be ready in time, according to my surgeon. But instead of saying that, I didn't want to let them down. So I said, 'Yeah I'd love to, but we'll have to wait and see how my neck goes.' Yet I know it won't be right in time. Now they'll come back. It's all going round in my head now, festering away, wondering why I didn't say 'No' straight out. Stupid, or what?

So, all Johnny's suggestions are good. Can't argue with any of them. The hard bit is doing them. I'm so impatient, that's another of my problems. I can't wait. I'm rushing things now, to get fit, overdoing it, instead of slowly, patiently building myself up.

If I did do all these suggested things, it would be like starting a new life. I'd have to break the pattern of this life, the one I'm now in.

I think I'd find that just too hard. I certainly couldn't do it in a month.

Anyway, I will try. At least I'll bear them in mind and try eventually to work my way through them . . .

One of the things Johnny agrees with in that letter is that I haven't had an easy life. What has always pissed me off is people, even good friends of mine, who will say, 'Gazza you're looking well,' when I know I'm not. Then, if they realise I'm down, they say, 'You'll get over it,' which pisses me off even more.

They don't seem to understand or appreciate my situation. They just try to cheer me up, as if that will help, as if that will solve things. So it's nice when a therapist who is properly trained, and has had some of the personal problems I have had, tells you, 'Yeah, it hasn't been easy for you.' He's been there. And come through it. Those are the sorts of people I can relate to.

It's funny how I have the willpower to go to the gym twice a day but I don't seem to have it for other things. I don't understand it myself. I feel mentally drained at the moment. It's been a hard two weeks. I've done twenty gym sessions in twelve days. Yeah, I'm counting. I've been doing my first one at seven in the morning, instead of nearer ten, which means I'm hanging around, waiting for my next one, so I then I think I'll just fit another in.

I'm still speaking to nobody who calls me, except Jimmy or me dad.

Today I'm feeling a bit better. No I haven't started on any of Johnny's suggestions, but I feel quite cheerful, well almost cheerful. I've been concentrating my mind on this summer, when this cycle of fixation on training will be over, wondering what I should do next. It will be a chance to start a new life, so that could be exciting, well, at least interesting, if only I can think what this new life will be. The trouble is, I left school with no qualifications. I wasn't stupid, and could easily have passed more exams. I just couldn't be bothered. Once football seemed a possibility, I couldn't be arsed with anything else.

Now, twenty years later, it's as if I'm leaving school today, this moment, and I have to decide what I'm going to do, not just for a few weeks or years, but the rest of my life.

I've got to find something I enjoy, then I can put everything into it. So I sit and think of the things I enjoy, and football always comes out top.

But I do honestly think I'm getting better, so that makes me feel a bit cheerful. I can cope with my depressions more than I could.

One of the things they teach you in the clinics is what they call the tools – and I do believe I have enough tools now. Whether I use them or not, that's up to me.

I haven't had a panic attack for a while. I see them coming on, recognise the signs, mainly thanks to Johnny, and I can deflect them. You just have to do the obvious things, going for a walk, reading my *Day to Day* book for a few pages, or I put a film on the telly and watch it.

It was wonderful when I first spoke to Johnny about the attacks – he knew exactly what I meant. When I'd told other people, like Jimmy or my dad, they didn't understand. When I said to Johnny that I had a pain here, or I feel dizzy, that I was worried a panic attack was coming on, Johnny knew at once what I was going through. Jimmy or my dad would say, 'Don't worry, you'll be all right,' and that just made me more anxious, speeded up the panic attack.

It was such a relief to know it wasn't just me, that I wasn't imagining, that it wasn't unique to me. He let me see I wasn't alone. These things happen to people. That was so comforting.

So I am trying to relax and clear my head of negative thoughts, which is what I'm always being told is best.

When all this training is over, I will take up some of the hobbies I used to have, like fishing. I love fishing. I used to do it a lot. It was perfect for taking my mind off football. At most clubs I've been at, I've always managed to find a place to go fishing – even if it was catching the goldfish in the hotel's ornamental pond! Yeah, done that. At the moment, though, it's too cold, and I haven't got the time, with the training.

I also like shooting and hope to take that up again. When I first came to London and moved out into the country (firstly in a hotel and then in my own house for a while, in Essex), I always had a gun, just a 2.2 rifle which I kept in the boot of the car and shot at things, even if it was just Jimmy's fat arse.

One day the groundsman at Spurs was moaning on because of the pigeons on the pitch, eating all the seeds. I said I'd sort them. I got out my gun and fired a few shots so that frightened them. But there was one big fat pigeon I just couldn't scare away. Every time I got within shooting range, it flew off. It was taking the piss, this pigeon, so I thought I've just got to have it.

It seemed to disappear for a while then I noticed it had got up on top of the East Stand, where they have the golden cockerel on top. This was the old East Stand, before they rebuilt it. At the very top there was a TV platform with an open window. The pigeon was sitting on the open window, looking down and laughing at me, the bastard.

I climbed all the way up the stairs in the East Stand and eventually reached the entrance to the TV gantry. It was boarded up, as it was derelict and no one was supposed to enter.

The pigeon was still there, looking down on the pitch, wondering where I was. I was just fifteen feet away. I thought I'll just move one pace nearer, then I won't miss it. I took one more step – and I went right through the floor. I hadn't realised the floorboards were rotted.

I must have fallen about fifteen feet, bruising all my side and my legs. It was a Tuesday and I wondered if I'd be fit for Saturday. Venables did see the bruises next day at training. He asked what happened. 'A fucking pigeon did it,' I told him. But I was okay in time. Never did get that bastard pigeon though.

I was very close to Terry Venables's dad, Fred, a great character, who lived near the hotel I was living in, in Essex. There was a pub right next to his house that I used to go to, then pop round to see Fred.

I was with him one day, in his back garden, and I heard a noise which I thought was a pheasant in the field behind his house. He said, 'Yeah, it is a pheasant, but don't bloody touch it.' He looked upon it as his pet pheasant, which he'd been watching for about ten years. I said, 'Don't worry, I won't.'

I love pheasants, shooting them and eating them, and this looked a really juicy one. I thought if I get it, then in three days' time, when it's been hung, I'll get the hotel chef to cook it for me.

Next day, I checked Fred was not at home and got into the field. I chased this pheasant for about an hour – and eventually I shot it. I shoved it in my game bag and was just jumping back into Fred's garden – when he reappeared.

'What's in that bag?' he says.

'Nothing,' I said.

Now Fred was as crafty as his son Terry.

'I can see a feather sticking out.'

I don't think he had seen a feather, but he had guessed what I'd done and caught me out, so I admitted it.

'I'm telling Terry,' he said. I took him to the pub and we had a few pints and some games of darts. The pheasant tasted brilliant, but I wish I hadn't done it. Fred had liked his pet so much. Don't know why I did it. Selfish. Fred was a great bloke. I did miss him when he passed away.

I don't do such daft things any more, which makes me worry if perhaps I'll become boring, that people will find me boring, no longer the entertainer, the daft lad, daft as a brush.

One thing about my drinking days was that I did have some laughs. And not always when I was drunk. I generally did have some funny times. These days I don't do stupid, silly things. Haven't done so for at least three years. The laughs seems to have disappeared from my life.

I remember once with Jimmy, when we were up in Scotland, staying in this hotel, and a friend gave me some morphine tablets. They were in sachets, sort of like sherbet dabs.

Me and Jimmy went to the bar and I said, 'Let's have a drink and we'll each put a sherbet in our drinks, see what happens.' We ordered a couple of Bacardi Breezers and put a sherbet in each. After fifteen minutes, we both felt so nice, so relaxed.

I said to Jimmy, 'Do you think it's working?' and, as I said it, he suddenly slumps over the bar. But he comes to, looks around, and I say let's have an Aftershock. That's another drink. When he's not looking, I put another sherbet in his, but not mine. We ended up having about five Bacardi Breezers each. By this time, he's out of it, but feeling great. The morphine had made him feel happy, numbed his senses.

I managed to get him up to his room – which wasn't easy, he's a big lad you know – and he just collapsed on a couch. He's not much fun, so I was thinking, 'What am I gonna do now? I know, I'll do some shaving.'

I got out a razor and shaved half his hair off. Then I shaved off his eyebrows. I did his chest hairs as well. I found a black pen, the sort you use for signing photographs for fans. It's like a marker pen. Very hard to wipe off. On his forehead I wrote NUFC and then on his naked, hairless chest I wrote FAT BASTARD. Just for good measure, I found a coloured pen and coloured in his ears and nose.

I was pissing myself laughing, he looked so fucking funny. He was dead to the world of course, with no idea what I'd been doing to him.

I went to my room and fell asleep. First thing in the morning, I rang Jimmy. He was still asleep, so I woke him up. I could imagine him grunting and swearing, trying to find the phone. I'd stationed a mirror near the phone, so I knew when he answered he'd see himself.

I asked him how he was and he started to say, 'Eee that was a good night . . .' and then he goes 'NOOOOOOOO! You Bastard! . . .'

I could hear him screaming and swearing from further down the corridor.

When he got back to Newcastle, he sat for three days in a bath before the writing on his chest began to fade. But of course his head and eyebrows were still bare.

A delivery man arrived at his door with a parcel. He took one look at Jimmy and burst out laughing. 'Can I go and get my mate in the van and let him see you . . .?'

'Go on then,' says Jimmy. In the end, half the street was coming knocking at Jimmy's door, asking to see him. They all stood there, pissing themselves.

The first time I did that trick was to a hotel manager, very responsible man, always wore a suit. He was manager of a Swallow Hotel I stayed at when I first moved to Spurs and we became good friends.

When I moved to Rome, with Lazio, I had this big villa, so I invited him to come and stay with me. He was a great guy, good fun. I took him out on the town and got him well pissed.

When we got back to my place, he slumped on a couch and began singing some soppy song about 'I'm in love.' Then he fell asleep. While he slept, I shaved his head, leaving just a little bit at the back.

Next morning when he woke up, he went mad and I could hear him shouting as he ran round the house. 'Gascoigne, I'm going to kill you. How can I go back to work now?' I was hiding in his bedroom wardrobe at the time, waiting for him to wake up and see himself.

He stayed on another three days, but his hair hadn't grown at all. So

I said, 'Tell you what, I'll shave all your head this time, leave nothing at the back. It'll then just look as if you'd had a skinhead.' So I shaved it all off – but unbeknown to him, with the razor, I made a little cross on the top of his head. When he left to go home, he looked from the back like a hot cross bun . . .

Those tricks still make me smile, but I never do anything like that now.

Johnny's diet sheet that he gave me, strangely enough, does not contain pheasant. Here's what Johnny suggests, which of course I will try to follow, eventually . . .

John's food guide for Paul

Seeing a qualified nutritionist, and having a hair analysis done, is the best approach to getting the right nutritional advice. They'll recommend what you eat, and prescribe supplements based on what you're lacking.

Until then, here's a guide loosely based on the very healthy eating programme they follow at Champneys, Paul's regular haunt. There, the correct types of food – wholefoods, slow-burn carbohydrates, pulses and seeds, fresh fish and plenty of fruit and vegetables – are readily available with fantastic choices.

For food disorders, it is recommended to avoid sugar, processed foods, white flour, and fast-burn carbohydrates. So that means no white bread or pasta, potatoes or white rice – choose brown bread, wholewheat pasta and brown rice instead. Here's a list of the 'good' foods versus the 'trigger' foods that are more likely to make you want to binge.

Breakfast
Fresh fruit, natural yoghurt
Gluten-free muesli with unsweetened soya milk and pumpkin, sunflower and sesame seeds
Lightly boiled egg or a kipper

Avoid:

• White bread/toast, pastries

• Jam

• Fried foods

Lunch/Dinner

The lentil dishes, the short-grain brown rice, tofu, fish dishes, salads and stews are all excellent.

Fruit – give yourself a good selection, and natural live yoghurt (live yoghurt contains the 'good' bacteria which will need replacing after illness or dieting).

Avoid:

• Fried products (except fried fish)

• Vinegar/salt/sugar/ketchup added to food

• White pasta or other refined wheat products such as pizza

• Crisps/sweets/cakes/biscuits

Drinks: Stick to water. If you want tea or coffee, limit it to one or two cups a day, without sugar, and replace the others with herb tea such as peppermint. Avoid at all costs fizzy and diet drinks containing added colour, sugar, caffeine, aspartame or saccharine.

Sugar and processed starch are 'trigger' foods, which set off a craving for more. These foods are empty calories, not satisfactory to the body, so we eat and eat them trying to fill up that need for goodness which our body is telling us about.

However, if you eat enough fish and secondary proteins (beans/pulses/nuts/seeds/tofu), you will not feel hungry – you will feel satisfied but your stomach will not feel full or bloated. You will feel *good* – full of energy but still light and not full up.

Dear Paul

You're so real, so kind, so full of energy - a real pleasure.

You've added real joy to my stay here, laughs by the sack full (no, not your sacks . . .).

May your journey continue to be as successful and safe as it's been so far. Loads of love.

Col

XXXX

Paul's eighth session: The punishing voice

John

We all have internal voices, which we don't always notice. Individuals with addiction problems, depression and low self-esteem often have a louder than usual critical voice. This is programmed in at an early age and can often lead to approval-seeking and negative thinking. By the time we reach adulthood, we don't really know whose approval we're striving for, since the original task masters (parents or guardians) are long forgotten, left behind in childhood. We might look for someone to please – our boss, our partner, the public – but the real critic is inside ourselves. Although this punishing voice may now only be inside the mind, it's incredibly powerful, and has huge expectations of the addicted person. Even perfection isn't good enough, so that we push and push ourselves to succeed at work, or at sport, in the gym, with a diet, or whatever else it might be, striving for that approval we never got.

Today I aim to encourage Paul to recognise this voice, where it comes from, what it's saying to him at the moment — and that he doesn't have to listen to it. Paul starts the session by telling me what his state of mind is at this time.

Paul

I'm nearly at the end of my three weeks here at Champneys and I've been averaging two training sessions a day. That's what I'm aiming at. For my time here. Forty-two sessions in total. And I've nearly lost the stone I was hoping to when I arrived. I feel a bit better that way. My fitness is coming back.

John

We now track back to when Paul was a child at home. I ask what he remembers about his anxiety in those days, and what was driving it.

Paul

I was anxious as a kid, but only anxious about wanting to win everything. I wasn't worried about money or anything like that. The anxiety was about winning. When I played with me brother and sisters, we'd argue and fight over a game of monopoly — over everything we played.

Part of it was my embarrassment at losing. I always wanted to be the winner. Everyone knows I cried at the World Cup when I got booked and couldn't play in the final. But I also cried at the end when we got beat. When we weren't winners. We were out and I felt my life was over. It was also because of the fans. They had been so great and deserved the final. So did the players.

When I was younger, it was fear of losing that drove me. At school I wanted to be the best player in the park all the time.

Even when I won I sometimes cried tears of joy, and that was stupid really. I never really enjoyed my sport because I put myself under that much fear to win. I enjoyed playing it, but I couldn't wait to see the end result.

It was while signing copies of my first book that I got the idea to write this one. So many people came up to me and said it had helped. And I hadn't even scratched the surface of my problems.

Leaving the Princess Grace Hospital – with Jimmy's help – in January 2005 after recovering from pneumonia.

October 2005. A dream come true. Announcing my appointment as manager of Kettering Town. L-r: Kevin Wilson, Imraan Ladak, me, Paul Davis.

In the dugout with high hopes of being the gaffer for a long time.

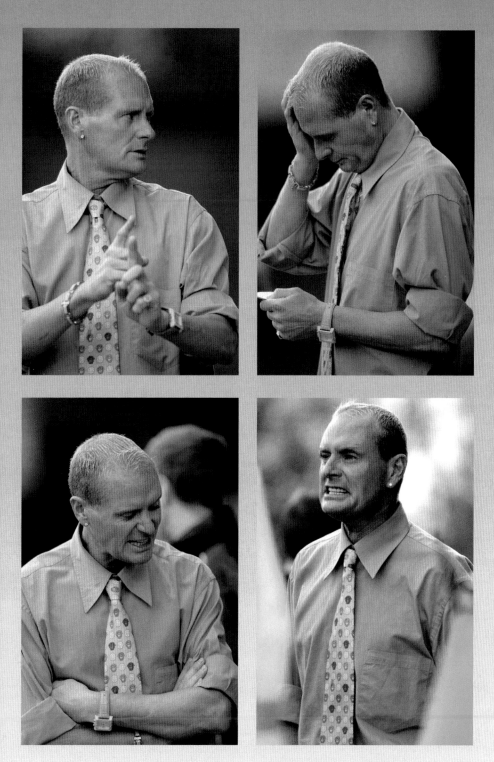

There's a lot of pressure, but I loved being a manager.

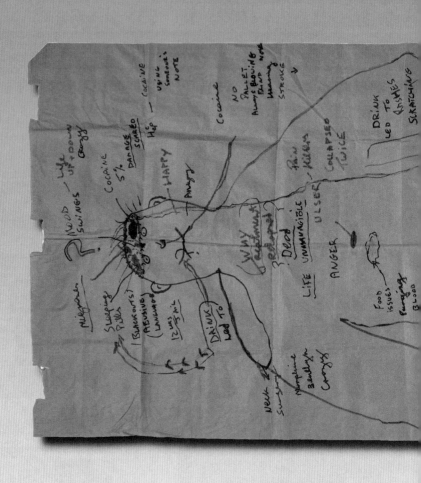

My Body Map. Cottonwood 2006.

At the charity do in Liverpool. December 2005. Relaxed and not drunk. I couldn't have imagined at this stage in the evening where I was going to spend the night.

Sir Bobby Robson has always been there for me with guidance and has supported my ambition to be a manager. He said, 'I know he has it in him.' Thanks Bobby.

Jimmy. My best friend. He always makes me laugh and helps me feel better.

The Dubai Masters. April 2006. Back playing for Newcastle with a ball at my feet after all my injuries. It felt great to reconnect with football again.

Would we win? And that was every sport, not just football: I was in the rounders team, I even played for the girls' netball team – goal shooter – also basketball, tennis, ping-pong, badminton, everything. I played in all the teams at school. I just never stopped playing. I played pool at the boys' club twice a week when I was seven. I went as often as possible, competing against older boys.

I was younger than the rest of the boys at the club – and I was little as well – but the other kids were brilliant. All the other boys had football strips on, and I had this yellow vest, because I couldn't afford a football strip. But it never bothered us, so long as I was playing football I didn't care. We often didn't have money for the kit and stuff but I still played football.

Me mam would buy new shoes and a new outfit for the school term, and we had to make them last the whole year. I remember once, on the first day of the new term, virtually taking the sole off my new shoe playing football. I couldn't wait for PE so I played in the school yard before lessons started. Me mam went mad. She couldn't afford to buy me new shoes so I went to school with a hole in me sole every day. It was embarrassing sometimes, so I tried to glue it. And it was like that in PE once as well. I'd done the same with my trainers – ruined them scraping along the ground and playing football. So I had no trainers for PE. I remember one PE session when my sister was doing PE before us, and I had to wait for her to finish and then go in the girls' dressing room and borrow her shoes so I could play football. It used to drive me mam crazy with me playing football. Ruining all the shoes. From then on, and even to now, I just thought, 'Me mam and dad must never want for nothing.'

I've carried them thoughts with me all this time, for years. I never forget my roots. I never forget where I come from: I'll always stay the same guy I was when I was seven.

Newcastle's my home. I've been away eighteen years. But I've always been in and out of the city, I'm always going back there.

I hate being on my own though. Even in Newcastle. When I'm on my own I start thinking about the career I've had, the great times, all that. I never watch myself playing football or anything because them times have gone, I'm never going to have them times again. But I remember all that. Then I think, 'What can I do next that's going to make me happy for the next twenty years?' That's why I go to the gym twice a day, because it takes my mind off things.

John

There's an anxiety, a drive, a restlessness, a need to get up, play something, join in with something, avoid our feelings. It's unease. Some people simply label it part of the addictive personality. That unease makes us act on how we feel, whether it's food disorders, drinking, or other habits. And Paul describes not just feeling lonely, but this energy inside him that stops him being able to relax, or just be.

It's hard for him to accept this stage of life that he's at. He's not alone with it, though people don't usually talk about this stuff. It's hard just to look back over your life and say, 'Yes, that was fantastic, but it's different now.' I ask Paul about whether there's a part of him that isn't yet ready to feel that, and to move on.

Paul

There's this arrogant side of us that says, 'Why should I have to move on? Why don't I get fit, have a good pre-season and play for a football club, even at the age of thirty-nine?' Okay, so some days doing this training, my knee's sore, and some days my hip's sore. But I still have the desire, even now. I look at Teddy Sheringham, he's forty and apparently they're offering him another year at West Ham. And Paul Merson and Dennis Wise, I see they're still playing football. And I think, 'Why don't I have another year just to see what it's like?' I've had a good career at the top level, and you might wonder why I'd go and play in front of a couple of thousand people. But I'm not bothered about that, just having that thrill again would be it.

But at the moment I'm putting myself under extreme pressure all the time. I'm always anxious to get back to that gym. I'll always try to squeeze in another session. What drives it? Thirty years of it, that's what drives it.

Since I was seven I've been pushing myself with the training.

I'm not eating right at the moment, as I've said. When I played, the managers were okay with me. They liked us a bit overweight, and I think I've played some of my best football when I've been, say, four or five pounds over. But I wouldn't feel good within myself. I felt I wasn't quick, sharp. Then I'd lose weight and I'd feel great and feel sharp. But then when I was lighter I didn't have the strength. So I'd put some weight back on – but then I wouldn't feel good within myself, I'd feel sluggish and all that, and I'd be back down to not eating and go through it all again.

There might be two spells of about a month in a season where I'd go to the gym at 8 o'clock in the morning, train at lunch time, train with the guys in the afternoon, and then train by myself later on. Sometimes I'd train five times a day and have one meal. No wonder I got injured. I just didn't know any different. I trained myself to do that. It's the obsessive side of it.

John

An important thing to recognise is that, in spite of being harmful, those eating and exercising patterns that Paul had did use to work for him at one time. Paul achieved an incredible amount. But now he's got to a different stage of life, and it's much harder to get away with such extreme regimes.

We look more at how this pattern with the food has affected Paul, and how it affects him now.

Paul

Since I was twenty-one, I've had injuries and operations. Some of that's because of not having the right stuff inside my belly when I trained, and tearing muscles, and not being strong enough.

I'm still in that pattern now. I'm not yet forty and I'm already thinking, 'I don't want to be buying bigger clothes when I'm fifty!'

As soon as I wake up, I start obsessing about food. I think, 'I can't have breakfast, because if I do I'll think, "Well, I may as well have lunch" – and so on.' The other pattern is that I'll have breakfast and then I'll be so pissed off

I'll have loads of lunch, etc. Food's going through my mind all day. But if I train, I can enjoy my food and just have salad with a bit of chicken or fish perhaps.

So how does that affect my mood? When I don't eat I feel down. Like today. I didn't train this morning and because of that I think I can't really eat anything at breakfast. And I'll miss lunch as well.

John

With this type of food disorder, we swing from saying, 'I'm fat or I'm overweight and I don't like myself' to 'I'm wafer-thin which I like.' Either way, we're abusing our bodies which has consequences. There's a constant inner dialogue.

Again we need to bring Paul's focus back to looking at where that punishing voice comes from, why it's not accurate, and what strategies work for Paul in contradicting it and not listening to it. That's where counselling comes in, and people and meetings and structure. And learning to let go of the control and get help from a nutritionist to work out your own diet plan that you stick to for a number of weeks. Then, when you wake up in the morning, you already know what you're going to eat so there are no decisions to obsess about. You're free from having to think about food. And, meanwhile, you get support from other people who understand the problem. Paul thinks it's stupid that he can't just sit and have an ordinary meal in a restaurant at the moment. But that's the food disorder, and thousands of people will identify with it – there's nothing stupid about it.

That's the voice that I want to challenge, the one that says, 'I can't eat now.'

Paul

The voice says I can't eat because I'll put on weight. Then if I do eat I'll think, 'It's not worth training today because I've eaten,' which is ridiculous.

It started when I've had coaches saying I'm fat. In Italy I got weighed four times every week. I remember being told off for being half an ounce overweight. That's not even a spoon of sugar. And I had to do thirty-five kilometres on a bike and an eight-mile run afterwards when I wasn't even half a pound over. You have to be an athlete, when you're a footballer.

I loved it at Glasgow, I could eat normally and enjoy my football. And I loved my football at Lazio, but that coach he was a tough coach, with regards to the weight anyway. He wouldn't let us join in training. He'd make us go with another coach – the fitness coach. All the lads were laughing, looking at us. I was overweight. He said Casiraghi had a bad game just because he was one pound overweight, but I was six pounds overweight sometimes. If you want to keep up with their standards you have to match them and stick to that lifestyle. If you haven't got as much skill you have to be even more physically strong and very fit.

John

If the power of the punishing external opinion is more powerful than your internal opinion of yourself, this form of criticism is a big problem. If in a newspaper someone says you're an idiot, somewhere in your head you think, 'No I'm not, he doesn't know what he's talking about.' But that comment has the power to make you behave in a way you don't want to behave, and to feel hurt or angry in a way you don't want to feel.

To shelter ourselves from the external critical voice and from the internalised critical voice we need to learn to 'parent' ourselves – to look after and encourage ourselves, to forgive ourselves and teach ourselves good habits.

Paul

With the food, I could parent my own son, I would never force my kid to eat, but I'd ask him if he was hungry, and I'd get him something good and healthy to eat. I'd make sure he eats properly and regular. Of course.

But with the press, it's hard. In some ways I wish I was like Chris Evans. He just doesn't let anything bother him. I wish I could be like that with the press. How does he do it? Well, one, he doesn't get the newspapers. And two, he just does whatever he likes. It's his life. And when he had a rough time in the press he didn't really let it get on top of him. He's got a place abroad where he could shoot off to, and he had good support round him. It's good to see Chris back and doing well again. He's got a job for life, and he's very talented. With football, it's a short life-span.

Not listening to that punishing voice is hard. I think, 'I've got to do two sessions, I've got to get back to the gym.' I just don't want to do anything but training at the moment.

John

There's a point I want to raise about Paul working hard all his life to train his body, learning different techniques to achieve different types of fitness. In a similar way, he's already learned mind techniques through counselling and other methods. But it's an ongoing process. Perhaps Paul needs media-skills training, for example. And to learn how to switch off, how to relax. A lot of people who are successful get help and training of all kinds. Paul's taught himself how not to listen to the anxious voice of the OCD. I ask if he can use that technique with the food – not to listen to his 'addict voice'.

Paul

It's like with the alcohol, the addict voice won't go away. The food is like alcohol, which is like OCD.

People reading this are probably thinking, 'How fucking daft is he?' I know it's daft, but by talking about it and letting people know, and letting myself know how stupid it is – like how stupid it was to turn light switches off all the time – I hope it helps. The food one *is* stupid, really, because in the health farm everything that's served is healthy, there's no fat in it whatsoever, it's all healthy stuff. Steve's been good and keeping an eye on us, and he's been telling us: 'Make sure you eat properly,' and 'This is good for you.' When I've been going down the gym he's been coming down and saying, 'Get this down you, eat this.' He's been a different class.

It's probably a good thing I'm in the health farm and training the way I am – I think if I was back home and training like this I'd be injured by now, because I wouldn't have eaten anything at all. At least there's food there. Talking about this is quite embarrassing really, because someone reading this is going to think, 'Imagine having that for the rest of your life. But I'm not going to have it for the rest of my life, because I've got most of it under control, and this is just the battle I'm going through at the moment. I can't all of a sudden turn it around in one session of talking about it. I have to get it under control and enjoy food again.

There was a programme on TV about these fat kids and some of them won't live longer than their parents because they're so overweight, and I felt so sorry for them. I went to the shops last night, and there were two tramps sitting outside on the step. I gave them a tenner because I knew they wanted some beer – they just had one can between them. I knew what it felt like because I've been in that position myself. I know what those fat kids feel like as well.

Seeing other people's pain gets me. I sometimes think about going to another part of the world. This last year, I've been thinking our country is mad, as regards everything that's been happening. You hear about kids overweight, kids getting abused, deaths, robberies – all that's been affecting me. I don't think I've listened to the news so much in my life. One of my favourite programmes – you won't believe it – is watching the debates in the House of Commons, seeing what Tony Blair's got to say about our country – never mind what's happening in Iraq. Everything in our country's bothering us.

I feel selfish at the moment, because I'm doing a book and I get to talk about my problems, and there are so many people in this country who've got problems and really have to struggle through life. They can't afford to talk to anybody, or they're too embarrassed to talk to anybody, and they think people are going to think they're screwed up. They've got their backs to the wall, they feel there's no hope for them. So I feel guilty in a way. I can honestly tell them not to be afraid to talk to someone about things. You're clearing your head, and especially if it's someone with experience they can talk to you back and help you deal with it. Not a lot of people in this country do that, not enough.

I know there are some people out there who can't leave the house, or it takes them two or three hours to leave the house because they can't shut the fucking door behind them. I had that real bad in China. I know I'm better now – but I only know that because a lot of people say it to me. I wish I could see it, I wish I could relax.

When I have addict thoughts, the normal way I manage them is I just go against them. If my addict says, 'You can't eat,' I just say, 'Fuck, I'm going to eat.' By challenging the thoughts and not believing them, I've conquered some of the problems I've had to go through.

I think, when I go to Newcastle, just at the train station there's a bagel shop, and I can see myself getting two big bagels.

John

Sometimes we need to try saying, 'Hang on, I'm not going to beat myself up. Instead of worrying about food, I'm going to ring up a friend, and meet up.' It's about taking a small risk, trying something different in a small way.

When we've got more time on our hands, that's when we have to watch that addict. The addict puts on a different costume: one minute he's an alcoholic pestering you to have a drink, and you say, 'No'. The next minute he pops up in the kitchen as a chef, asking you to overeat. The addict pops up in different disguises. And that's what we call cross-addiction. When one addiction gets arrested, another one appears.

It's good for Paul to remind himself that he's not at all stupid, that he's suffering an illness which isn't his fault. So he needs to let himself off, but at the same time accept it, and take responsibility for what he can do about it.

Paul

One of the big things is acceptance. The more I accept it the easier it is. If I write down everything – the panic attacks, the mood swings, everything

– it's easier. A girl saw us once writing everything down, and she said, 'Oh my God!' I wanted to laugh. And I said, 'Yeah, I've got all of them.'

I think if I accept it, it really works. Like with OCD: I've accepted I have OCD and now I can walk away from the light switches. Same with the food, if I accept I have the weight and food problems, I can just eat sensible. You can eat stuff that doesn't put weight on you and still enjoy it. If I'm honest though, I don't think I've quite accepted all that with the food yet. I haven't quite conquered that.

Trying to lose this stone in three weeks instead of in three or four months is exhausting me. I think, 'Why have I punished myself like that? Training and not eating. Do I need to do that?' And then when I've done it I'll think, 'Well, what can I do next?' I don't seem to live a day at a time, I don't relax.

I'm still obsessed with football, I absolutely love football, and I get invitations to matches and I don't take them up. Whether that was a good thing, taking the manager's job, I don't know. Because having a taste of it for just such a short time – it's still in me mind now. I'd love to be a manager again. And I've learned from it the last time, from my mistakes. With anything anybody wants to do, they have to learn it.

John

Not eating properly affects our brain chemistry, which in turn affects our mood. Then, feeling low, we won't do the things that could help us, like ringing a friend or taking some first steps to change things. I've suggested to Paul to try having two balanced meals: a healthy breakfast, and lunch. If we don't eat, our bodies start to get eaten into, and vital nutrients are missing.

Not every thought we have is an accurate thought. If we think, 'I mustn't have breakfast today,' that doesn't mean that's healthy for us just because we think it. Learning not to engage with the addict voice can take years of practice.

Paul's in a very difficult stage at the moment. He's dealing successfully with his OCD, his panic attacks, his alcoholism, and tackling the food and exercise. And he's uncovering what lies beneath. What we've done previously together has been mostly counselling rather than psychotherapy. But now we've started doing some therapy – looking at where some of the thought and behaviour patterns originate. People-pleasing, having to rescue people, keeping the peace, having to fix everything, having to be the perfect weight, not being good enough just as he is – the punishing voice. We look at where some of these ingrained beliefs have come from. And of course he's going to feel up and down while we're digging things up.

Paul's body is still recovering, and that's part of why he's been depressed. Also he's not stimulated enough, and hasn't got the job he wants yet. But he talked about acceptance, and he's struggling to accept the way things are at the moment. Some things have gone, and it's no use worrying about them, but there are some things which hopefully he can change. To quote philosopher Reinhold Niebuhr, we need 'The serenity to accept the things we cannot change; courage to change the things we can; and wisdom to know the difference.'

––––––––––––

Dear Paul

You're a top man. People love you just as you are. You don't need alcohol. Please stay sober.

Lots of love mate

Jack

Paul looks forward – to life and the World Cup

Paul

I'm about to have my final session with Johnny. I was scared yesterday morning, though not about the session itself. I woke worried about what I'm going to do next. It's at the back of my mind all the time. I could go round the country giving talks, 'An Evening with Gazza', but I'm too young to do that. I've got bits and pieces of TV and DVD work, but I just have the one goal – to be a manager. Will I achieve that or not? That's what worries me. I do feel I have conquered most of my problems. Well, I've minimised them. They'll always be there, but with a bit of luck and willpower, I'll stay on top of them from now on.

After I've seen Johnny tomorrow I hope I'll have no appointments again, none of that once-a-week, or twice-a-month appointments written in my diary which I've been doing for almost a year. No more will be pencilled in. It'll be the end, for now. I'm hoping to manage without him, now

I have the tools. I have my own GP in Newcastle, and when I need any new medication, he'll prescribe it.

I'm checking out of Champneys tomorrow. I've been in this one, at Tring, for three weeks, then before that I was six weeks at Henlow Grange. Jimmy is coming down to drive me home to Newcastle. I'm moving back into my apartment in Jesmond.

It felt a bit lonely living there earlier on, when I got it two years ago, so I haven't really unpacked. But now I'm looking forward to it. I think I'll cope okay now, as I'm in a much better state. It'll be nice to have a proper place of my own for a change, till I decide whether to buy a house or not.

On Saturday, there's a party for my dad's sixtieth birthday, a big family gathering, so that'll be good. I'm sure I won't get tempted by the drink. Then on Sunday I'm going with Kenneth Shepherd, son of Freddy Shepherd, to watch Newcastle United.

I don't see going back to Newcastle as a danger. Not the game, obviously. I mean moving back there. I survived two years last time, living up there without drinking. I want to be back with my old mates. The press are always describing them as hangers-on, but to me, they're true mates.

I'll keep on training, up in Newcastle. Now the weather has at last got better, I'll do some road running, just around Gateshead. And gym work in a hotel.

A six-a-side tournament in Dubai is coming up, which Sky will televise. I'm playing for a Newcastle veterans team, along with Chris Waddle. I'll be seeing more of him now, when I get back. He is my oldest friend in football. And I still haven't forgotten that Santa Claus text. Careful, Waddler – I might not be as daft as I used to be, but I've still got a few tricks up my sleeve.

I used to say he was in my genes, because I seemed to follow him around. He started at Newcastle, like me. I first met him when I had to clean his boots. One day he said I hadn't cleaned them well enough. 'Boots are the tools of your trade and you have to keep them in top condition,' so he said. 'Fuck off,' I replied.

I was only sixteen and pretty lippy. So he gave me a kick. A dead leg.

I managed not to cry in front of everyone in the dressing room, but after that I didn't give him any more cheek.

Chris moved on to Spurs, and so did I. He went abroad, and so did I. He played for England, and so did I. At the end of his career, he played for a lower league club, as I did. He had a spell at managing, like me. I said to him the other day, 'I hope you win the fucking lottery, cos that means I will as well . . .'

I'm looking forward to being back in the North East, going to watch Newcastle play. And of course I can't wait for the World Cup.

What pissed me off, during the weeks leading up to it, was everyone saying, 'This is the best England team since 1966.' It's bollocks. What has this team won? Nothing so far. A team can only be the best team, or better than another team, if they win something.

They come out with this sort of shite before every World Cup and European Championships. They said it in 1994, 1998, 2002, 2006 and I bet you any money they'll be saying it again in 2010.

When I was in the 1990 World Cup, and Euro '96, we got to the semi-finals each time. This present team has yet to get anywhere near that, so how can they be better? On each occasion, we got knocked out in the semis by Germany on penalties. And you know what Mourinho says – being beaten on penalties doesn't count as losing. So, yeah, it did annoy me, all the talk about this lot being the best England team ever.

There are some good individual players, but it's playing as a team that will matter, how they all perform, on the day.

Obviously I hope England win, or at least do well, and I'm sure they will, but I'm not looking further forward than the semi-finals. I see the four semi-finalists as being England, Brazil, France and Italy. Out of those four, if it happens, I hope England draw Italy. Our football is so different from theirs, with all the pressing we do, working them hard. Italians don't like that, they don't like our style, so we could have a chance against them. If we face Brazil or even France, it will be harder and I wouldn't reckon our chances of making the final itself.

Even as individuals, I don't think they are better than in the past. There is one truly outstanding player, Rooney, but that's about it. Of course Beckham, Lampard and Gerrard are world class as well, and very experienced.

But are they better than individual players in the past? In my day, we had Bryan Robson and Paul Ince in the middle. They were world class, but also grafters. They did all the work, then gave the ball to me. So no, I don't actually think today's individuals can be said to be much better. Joe Cole, he's good. I forgot him. I like him.

I don't worry about the so-called problem of having no one on the left. Good players – which Beckham, Lampard and Gerrard all are – can work anywhere. When I was in the England team, Chris Waddle was officially a winger, but he would be tucked into the midfield when there was a need, and he did a good job. That's what all good players have to do.

Most fans and players in England today have no problem with England's first eleven, and the five subs. There's a solid sixteen players there we all agree on. They pick themselves, when fit and in form.

Some people have gone on in the past about having to choose two from Sol Campbell, John Terry and Rio Ferdinand. I don't see it as a problem. They are all good. I think if I was manager, and they were all fit and in form, I'd think about trying to play all three together. Up front, well, there's no argument, it's Rooney and Owen.

As for the rest of the squad, well, everyone has had their say on that. I probably would have chosen Crouch and also perhaps that boy at Wigan, Jason Roberts. He's done well this season when I've been watching him. In fact I sent a text to Paul Jewell, saying he should be pushing Roberts for the England squad, but I didn't hear anything back.

I wonder at the last moment if anyone will come through, have a late spurt, or take the place of someone who gets injured or loses form? It's still two months to go, so we don't know yet.

For the 1990 World Cup, I was keeping my fingers crossed to be in the squad, but I wasn't sure. My best hope was to get in the squad and sit on the bench, then poor Neil Webb got injured. I took his place, got in the team, and never looked back. That might happen again to someone. You just have to stay on your toes, then jump at any chance that comes up.

I have no problems with Sven. He was ridiculed and criticised by the press, especially when he got stitched up by the fake sheik, but I feel sorry for him. He took the bait, so he made a mistake, but it was all the work of the media.

It's as if the English media don't want England to win. They hounded Sven and tried to get him sacked. They stalk all the England players, or their wives and girlfriends, making their lives hell, putting them under such pressure. They never help England's cause, do they? You would think they would. It's in their interest, if they really are genuine England supporters, as they say they are.

Sven's record is good. All the players I've spoken to privately have no problem with him. They all like him. And so do most managers I've met. It's just the press that's been against him.

I think being the England manager is a harder job than being the Prime Minister. You need the hide of a rhino to survive, or you stay at home and never go out. It will be interesting if England do win. The press will suddenly start shouting 'Don't Go Sven'. That could be funny.

It doesn't bother me that Sven never appears emotional on the bench. Mourinho gets criticised for being too emotional. You can't win.

All the England manager has to do, basically, is keep his nose clean and pick the best twenty-two. Then when he's got his best twenty-two, if each is performing well, he stays in, if not, he's out.

What is a good manager anyway? What is a good player?

I think Wigan's Paul Jewell and Blackburn's Mark Hughes are good managers because they have had little money. Their teams are not flash, they don't have stars, they play simple 4–4–2, and yet they work so hard and get their rewards. To me, that's a mark of a good manager.

A manager who can spot a kid at fourteen and see him through into the first team and then the England squad, that's also a good manager. Fergie and Wenger, they both have good eyes for young players.

A manager with more resources, and a large squad of world-class players, and yet one who can manage a rotation system and keep everyone happy, that to me is also a good manager. Mourinho has that ability. And he also has this quality of being able to change players just at the right time in a match. He reads a game to perfection.

A manager who has a team of stars, who win most games, and yet manages to keep everyone motivated, that's a good manager too. I'm thinking of Walter Smith when I was at Rangers. He had twenty players who were internationals, in a team where we were 3–0 up in many games by half time – but he then had to keep us working and focused to the final whistle. That's good going.

There are lots of ways of defining a good manager, just as with players. A player playing well in a shit team is a good player.

All the millions of pounds swilling about in football today doesn't worry me. I was very well paid, compared with the generation before me, if not quite as well as today. But I'm not bothered they can now get £100,000 a week. I'm not resentful. A star player gets followed all the time, and his family. He gets slaughtered each week in the press by someone. I think they deserve all the money they can get. The clubs are raking it in. So is the television. The press is living on the back of football, selling millions of copies, doing extra supplements for things like the World Cup, without paying. So good luck to the players if they can screw as much as they can for themselves.

All the diving, that does worry me though. I don't blame the players, or the managers. Diving has always gone on. Players will always try to steal an advantage and con the ref – and if it works managers don't care. But now it's got out of hand. And I blame the refs. They should be able to spot it and clamp down on it.

I think what would help would be if refs went and watched some Premiership training sessions. When teams play practice games, they play to win, and play hard – but they don't dive. You wouldn't dare, not against your own players. They'd either just laugh at you, or thump you. In training games, when someone falls down, it's for real. In real games, they do it because they think they can get away with it, that refs won't know the difference. If the refs were to watch training sessions, they'd be able to differentiate between a real fall and a pretend one.

I am sorry that kids don't play football in the streets or the parks any more, as I did, not so long ago. Jumpers for goal posts and all that. You hardly see it now, even up in Newcastle and Gateshead. The streets are full of cars, that's one reason. I think it's also because parents are scared, worried about any weirdos wandering about, or bigger kids. You hear about these fourteen-year-olds beating up eleven-year-olds, stealing their mobiles or trainers, or just knifing them for fun. No wonder responsible parents don't let their young kids out in the street to play.

I often wonder what our football would be like today, without all the foreign players and managers. We seem to be obsessed at the moment by Mourinho, he's in the papers all the time, as if we didn't have any English-born managers. But I think we would be a lot poorer without the foreign guys.

My real worry is the level of coaching being done in our football academies. I don't think they are all as good as they could be. In Europe, they do seem to teach them better, which is why Arsenal is always buying all these good European kids. If the British ones were as good, they'd buy them. I worry more about a talented English kid not getting a decent enough training over here, rather than his way being blocked by some imported foreign player. If you're a shit player, no one will pick you. If you're good enough, someone will pick you.

But if a kid starts thinking he's going to have no chance, because of all the foreigners ahead, then he will have no chance – because his mentality will be wrong. You have to believe you will make it.

There is such pressure on all managers today, so you can understand what happens. If the choice is between a seventeen-year-old English kid, who has come up through the academy but is still learning, and an experienced foreign player of twenty-seven, you can see the manager's dilemma. He tends to think in the short term. He doesn't want the sack if his team gets stuffed. So he has to play safe, unfortunately.

Rooney has come all the way through the English system, and his natural talent has flourished, but he was carefully looked after by David Moyes at Everton. I was there at the time and I remember Colin Harvey, the academy director, telling me to look at this lad. Rooney was a little freckled kid, only fourteen. He came on as sub for the academy Under-17 team and scored two goals. I never talked to him, but I could see he was brilliant for his age.

I do think he's already almost on a par with Ronaldinho, who is of course today's best player in the world. Rooney is usually bracketed with Messi, when people speak of world-class young players. Messi is really a new Chris Waddle. But with a better hairdo. Not hard. Rooney is a different player entirely. He can't be compared with Messi. I think Rooney is better. He can attack, create, defend.

I never get fussed about who should be the next England manager. I'd like, in theory, the England manager always to be English, but it doesn't bother me if he was foreign.

Personally, I would go for any older manager, such as Terry Venables. He's had so much experience and is a brilliant coach and manager. If it has to be someone a bit younger, I'd have Bryan Robson. He's done an amazing job at West Brom, with little money. But I don't expect either of them to get the job. Loads of yous will know, by the time you read this, what happened. I wonder if I am right.

People in the press often say, when writing about Rooney, that me and George Best should be a warning to him. But when I broke into the England team, a few years older than Rooney, mind you, people said the same to me – that I should take heed, and not turn into another George Best.

Okay, we have alcohol in common. Which has been bad. Obviously. And people are right to draw attention to the dangers of alcoholism. But they forget how much I achieved. I didn't throw it all away. But for injuries, I'm sure I would have got near 100 caps, not just 57. And George achieved a lot. He didn't play in World Cups because Northern Ireland didn't qualify. But look what he did achieve at Manchester United. He won the European Cup for fuck's sake.

Anyway, alcoholism is a disease. There's no point in warning people against it. It happens. You get it or not. I don't think Rooney will have that problem. He seems fairly stable. I like the fact that he's still with his childhood sweetheart. That must be a help. I wish it had happened to me.

I often wonder how my son Regan will turn out, if I'll be used as a warning to him. At the moment, he's more interested in being a ballet dancer than a footballer. That's fine by me. I hope he does well. It's what his mother wanted to be when she was young, so perhaps he's inherited her genes. I hope he doesn't inherit OCD from me, but I don't think he will. I just hope he has an enjoyable life, and gets left alone by the media. Perhaps when he's grown up, we might get close again. He might understand more what I have been through, and that I'm not all bad.

There's lots to look forward to football-wise at the moment for me, which is good. And you know what, when I'm doing all this mad training to get ready for these charity games and testimonials, I often have lurking at the back of my mind the thought that, hmm, could it just happen? Could I possibly get one last crack at it?

Ah well, just a thought. I'm sure it is too late now. Or is it . . . ?

———————

Dear Paul

You made me laugh when I thought I could not and seemed always to put me in a better shape. This disease is your worst enemy, don't let it beat you. I will always remember being in my room on my first morning shaking like a leaf and you were the first person in the community I ran into. I saw the fire in your eyes and your disdain for this disease ('fuckin' relapse'). How friendly and at home I immediately felt. Thanks for all your help.

Phil

Chapter Twenty One

Paul's ninth session: The final countdown

John

In this final session I'd like to talk about what helps Paul more than anything with his state of mind, his health and his happiness. Whether it's friends, his parents, meetings, counselling, working — whatever the ingredients are that he needs to feel well.

Paul

The last couple of weeks have been mixed really. I wanted to get fit, to get myself back in trim, look after myself, and I think I've done all that. I'm quite excited because I'm leaving the health farm. I've got the memorial dinner to go to with Calum Best for George. I'll be sad, but being there for Calum's a good thing.

I've been isolating myself from everybody. But now I've got a few matches coming up, so May's going to be a good month. I'm making sure

I'm going to be busy. It's been frustrating not doing stuff, but the fact is I've had to come through a hell of a lot during the last year and a bit, and I had to work on that. I've still got these problems for the rest of me life.

It's time to get myself back into real life, out of the health farm. I've been a bit worried this week about money, how some of the investments I've made in the past have backfired on us. It wasn't a brilliant weekend.

There's lots of things I've got planned that I'd like to do, but the last few days I've been doing some negative thinking. I've lost confidence. I need to get a feel for football again. I haven't done any interviews on the football side of it, just worked on this book.

I feel quite nervous going back home, seeing the family. When I go to Newcastle I'll see homeless kids, and there's nothing worse than seeing a homeless kid. At the traffic lights they're washing cars in the freezing cold and I really feel for them.

My head's gone again on what I'm going to do with the rest of my life. I want a steady job and a decent income. I want to get something that'll really make us happy. I'm not depressed, I've just got mixed feelings at the moment with regards to everything. Why am I thinking this way again, when last week I was really on top of everything?

The big question for me is, what do I want to do after the World Cup? As you know, I'd like to be a good manager, to really work hard on that. It's great saying I want to be a manager, but I'm going to have to put in the work. Bryan Robson came straight into it at a young age, and he's worked himself real hard for it. Obviously I'd love to get another manager job. But I'm not going to set meself big targets yet, only small achievements to aim for, otherwise it'll be too much while I'm still sorting myself out.

John

I'm not surprised he's feeling like this because he's been in the clinic, then came the holiday when he didn't relax at all, then came this intense period of therapy and training. I've said to him before, and I say it now: this is like a growing-up period, going from one phase of his life to another, a transition.

It's quite normal to feel scared, to feel nervous, to worry about financial responsibilities, what you're going to do, where you're going to end up living. I think the most important thing is for him to be really kind to himself at the moment – to look after himself. To allow himself to say, 'I am worried about not drinking, I am worried about situations, I am watching my food, my exercise.' To try to nurture himself over the next few weeks. He's got a very busy couple of months ahead.

I tell Paul I was talking to my supervisor, and he said this is like sitting in the cockpit of our plane. Sometimes what we want to do is get the parachute and bail out. We don't want to take the controls – the responsibilities. Ultimately, Paul's now in control of his plane. No one else is doing the piloting. Previously he's been in the back of the plane, so being the pilot is new, and it feels scary.

Paul

Last night I had cravings for everything. I was worried and scared. And this morning I feel like I'm going mad again. I can't put me finger on it. I'm thinking negative thoughts all the time. I'm thinking, 'What am I going to do in Newcastle? What am I going to do about training?' I can't think of anything positive.

John

I ask Paul whether he's had any breakfast this morning, and how many cups of coffee he's had. We work out he's had about six cups of coffee, and no breakfast. Caffeine is a powerful drug, and it makes us anxious. On an empty stomach, the effect is magnified. The Chinese see caffeine almost like a Class C drug. To them it's a mood-altering stimulant. You go to an acupuncturist, and the first thing they do is tell you to stop drinking caffeine.

Paul's drinking lots of water, and I also suggest that after this we get some lunch. You can't drink six coffees and get away with it. We've all done it – or something just as extreme that we know at the time we're going to pay a price for – but we go ahead and do it anyway. I can only have one, or maybe two, coffees a day. Any more than that and I get anxious. Paul's got worries, fear is still an issue, but put caffeine into that equation and he's going to feel extremely anxious.

Paul

I've had that much more coffee than usual this morning. I feel tired as well, from all the training. I'm glad I'm talking about it, to be fair. It just hit us last night: I haven't been communicating with anybody. Loads of things have been racing round me head. There are loads of things coming up that I can do. I suddenly felt, like, from doing nothing I have to keep myself busy now. My confidence went out the door.

But I'm looking forward to Newcastle, seeing Jimmy, and my family at home. It will be nice to chill out as well. I'll find a happy medium I think. I'm so pleased I'm talking about this now, because it must have been the coffee – I haven't felt like this for a long time – it's mad having that much coffee.

John

I'd like Paul to try and get to an AA meeting, just to go and listen, to realise he's not alone – because he's alone with this stuff at the moment. It's simple, but if you don't talk about it, and you keep going round and round the same worries, with caffeine on top of it, it feels like the world's going to end.

What I've done is draw three columns on this bit of paper, headed: Morning, Afternoon, Evening. We're going to write down the daily basics of Paul's day. Paul's got some big projects coming up, but I think before he writes lists for those, we should do this simple schedule.

Paul

Let's get started then. Basics. Wake up, take meds. I must admit I will have a coffee. Okay, let's put down ONE cup. And breakfast if you say so. If I'm really starving I'll have half a slice of toast or cereal without much milk.

And I will try soya milk. That nutrition sheet you gave us the other day, tailored to the menu at Champneys, it had soya milk on there. I like soya milk. Then after breakfast I have to have a good workout, so let's put that down there in the morning.

Next thing I need to do in a day is check the diary, or check with Jane, my agent, what's on that day. There might be something on in the afternoon, but if there isn't that's my main worry – the afternoons. I have to try to keep myself busy. At the health farm I was just steaming. Stuff like that. The whole of April I'll probably train in Newcastle, in the mornings. Training and gym work. I'm going to have to start looking at some stuff, like, if it warms up a bit, do some fishing. I love fishing. I've got to get myself into the habit of going to the AA meetings. I know. I enjoy meetings but it's just getting into the habit of going. I don't want it to be so that I've got to go to a meeting every day, but I like being around people who've got the same problems. When I was down, going to meetings cheered us up a little bit.

Anyway, I'll put down doing two or three meetings a week, which I can do. I can go in the evenings as well.

John

We've put down meals as basics. I know I've mentioned it a lot, but Paul's got to put food in the tank at the moment. It's not massive meals we have to have, but what we do eat has to be the right stuff. Fish salad is great.

Paul

I love me fish. I'll always have that. I will eat healthy stuff.

John

I've put here – morning, afternoon and evening – 'Watch thoughts'. That's the cockpit stuff again – you're in charge of your thoughts, they're not in charge of you.

Paul

Over the last couple of days I've been thinking again about what I had and what I fucked up. I've never really had any regrets before, about my career or things I did in my personal life, only they've started to creep in a little bit recently.

Some days I feel depressed and I don't want to go anywhere, don't want to see anyone, don't want to do anything. Then there's some days I feel on top of the world.

John

Paul hasn't any validation from a job at the moment, and that's a key thing he needs to do next – get involved somehow with a club. In the short term, he's going to be in Newcastle for a few weeks, so it would be good to clear it with the staff at Newcastle that he's going in to train, and work out which days and times that's going to be so the lads know what days he's going in. Meanwhile, other longer-term offers will come in.

Paul's doing really well. If I was in his position, would I follow all these suggestions I'm giving him? I'd like to think I would, but I don't know, and I understand why it's hard. It sounds easy and looks easy on paper but, when you're caught up in your own battle, it's a different story.

I ask Paul if he thinks he'll be able to check each day with this basic list we've done, and look after himself, keep to the basics, keep it positive. If he'll be able to say, 'I feel shit, I feel uncomfortable, but I know if I look after myself it will pass.'

Paul

Hopefully I will be able to do that, because I know it's worked in the past. I went into the clinic, had thirty days or so in the clinic, then I came back from the holiday, then the health farm, and I look at myself and I think, 'Am I further down the line, have I took a little step backwards, or have I moved forwards?'

John

When I go to a football match, or when I listen to other people's problems, it can distract me from my own problems. For Paul at the moment, because of the intensity of the book – we're going through every issue he's ever suffered with in one big hit – and because he hasn't got a job or anything big on at the moment, it's full-on. It's eat therapy, sleep therapy, everything therapy. So, although in the previous session he mentioned getting invited to matches, but not being bothered about going, I think going to the games will be a positive distraction.

JM: You are a thinker, you think a lot, don't you? And I wonder sometimes, do you think too much?

PG: Yeah, it never stops.

JM: So at this stage could going out and doing something different help, to give you a rest from the thinking?

PG: Yeah. A friend phoned me a couple of times and said, 'Why don't you come to California for a month? We'd be doing some meetings and some surfing and relax with a load of people.' It sounded quite good. But then I thought, 'No, I'll be the same as I was in Cottonwood, feeling I want to get back home.'

JM: Remember this, you're dealing with a lot. Okay, let's try this, it might sound silly, but what if you're in your room and God suddenly turns up. What do you think He'd say to you at the moment?

PG: I think He'd say, 'Just hang in there. There's things in life you can look forward to, and things will start happening.' You're right, sometimes doing this talking does bring up stuff. It brings back old memories. Like memories of the OCD. That feeling that if you don't touch something, something bad is going to happen that day.

JM: It's a control thing, but we don't have that control. OCD relies on an illusion of control, stemming sometimes from a trauma – you felt unsafe, out of control, so you're then trying to re-establish control. When I had that it was really bad. I'd think I was safe walking down this street, but not down that one – all sorts of things about staying safe. I've still got the odd little routines I do now and then, to ward off bad things.

So, what about taking up some offers while you're in Newcastle, going to some games?

PG: I love being up there in Newcastle, I must admit. I will treat myself to a few games. I went through this feeling, where I got myself really excited and I went to watch football one night, thinking about managing. It's hard work. Some of these managers really struggle if they haven't got money to spend on players, and they face relegation, and it's a lot of pressure. But I suppose if someone can do it, then I could do it as well.

JM: Maybe, in the short term, you could do your badges and your coaching, like Stuart Pearce did, learning the skills. The invitations are there, and you can learn from the best people, without having to carry the can. I want to pick up on this issue of looking after yourself. It's an inside job. I think what God would say to you is, 'Look after yourself.' So you could start planning your next move a bit more – okay, you might not even get paid to start with, but you'll be learning, managing. Clubs will see you're serious. And if you're also serious about training they'll see you're having a good pre-season. And say to yourself, 'If I can prepare a plan for where I want to be next year, move slowly towards it, do my badges, be a coach – it's a guide, a direction to move in.' Does that make sense?

Paul

Yeah. I do want to put the effort in first, for free, and then in the future things will start to pick up again.

I'm obsessed with football, because I've been doing it all my life. With the managing side of it, where do I start? I need to be positive about myself.

John

I'd like Paul to try and remind himself each morning about the structure, and remind himself, 'Today I'm going to be okay, I might have a shit day, but I'll be okay.'

I'd like to suggest that he sits down over the next couple of weeks, and lists the top five or six clubs he'd like to go to in order to learn from the manager, or maybe as a coach. Then, perhaps in July, with someone he feels comfortable with, go round each of the clubs and see what they've got to say. Just to get five or six options.

Paul

That's what I've been thinking about doing meself anyway. The other thing is, there are players around getting on a bit like us, with good fitness. I want to see how I am, see if I am fit, what I'm capable of. See if I could have another year or two of playing. It would be brilliant if I still felt fit enough to play. Then, I don't know why I keep thinking of Australia, but I keep thinking of fucking off to Australia for three months. There's loads of things going through my mind. But the most important thing is that I want to get back to football training. To see how I feel with a ball at my feet – and to get my confidence back with football in general.

John

I hand Paul the beginning of the list of clubs. Where would he like to be? What work would he need to do to get there? I know he can work hard and train hard. My only worry is him pushing himself *too* hard.

Paul

I heard Andy Gray said, 'Has anyone seen Gazza? We don't know where he is.' I've been away doing the clinic and the training and therapy for that long. But you're right, Johnny, football's where I belong. I know it's gonna be hard work, and I'm working on the hard work. I'm going to get back out there and see what happens.

John

I hope Paul can be himself. He's been going through a transitional stage of his life and he's trying to turn it round. He's done a lot of intense sessions in a short period of time, and he needs a break. He's leaving for Newcastle. But I hope he'll still come and see me whenever he can, get to some meetings and, most of all, look after himself.

—————————

Dear Paul

I'll stop using your words like clems and fuck and wanker and I'll just leave a few of my own. You've been an amazingly kind, caring, generous, loving friend to so many people here Paul. I hope you don't forget to leave some for yourself. But if you do man, I'll give you whatever I got. It's like that. Bros for life.

Jed

Paul sums up Paul

Paul

I don't know what will happen to me. People ask me that all the time. They also keep asking my friends what they think I'll end up doing. Fuck knows. The press, they know of course, being fucking experts. They're convinced I'll end up in the gutter, wasted, a dead loss and skint. That's what it feels like they wish for me, sometimes.

But the country as a whole is on my side I reckon. The sales and the reaction to my book showed that. They sympathise and understand that I have problems I'm trying to deal with. And I still am, if not very well. But I did manage two years without a drink. For ten years I have not hurt anyone, not since that awful moment with Sheryl. Even that photographer, I didn't really hurt him. I think he sympathised with me in the end.

I've given the press acres and acres of free stories over the last twenty years. They've fed on me. Okay, they often paid me for stuff as well. That's because I often felt I had to defend myself against what other papers have said. They make up all these lies about me. Then others repeat the lies. I'd much prefer never to appear in the papers at all.

The press can ruin your life. They can make a sick person much sicker. I really believe they helped to kill off George Best. I really do. They're certainly making me sicker than I am already . . .

My number one ambition, in my fantasy world, is still to be a manager in the Football League. It doesn't have to be the Premiership, not at first. Any club out of the ninety-two in the Football League, that would do me. I'd be happy then. And just to finish off that particular fantasy, I'd like a three-year contract, so it becomes a steady job where I can work away slowly and quietly. I know that doesn't happen in football. That's why it's fantasy.

My second desire in life is to settle down with someone. I'd like to be with a woman I love and have kids together. It would need to be a woman I can trust. She would be my best friend and partner. I have quite a few married mates who often tell me about their wives and they say, 'She's my best pal.' I'm dead jealous when they say it. I wish it could happen to me. Must be wonderful.

It wouldn't matter where we lived. And I wouldn't worry where she was from, English or Russian, Asian or American or whatever. I just want a woman I can trust.

Funnily enough, I've just heard from that American girl I met at Cottonwood. She rang me up to ask me why I haven't been in touch. We had a good laugh on the phone, talking about when she was singing the ABC song in a funny childish voice. We were in hysterics. I teased her about being educated and all that, yet she sang the ABC song in that silly girlish voice.

She asked me how my book was getting on and I told her she gets a mention, in one of the messages to me at Cottonwood. She laughed, but doesn't object. She's a nice lass.

At the end of our conversation, when she was laughing at things I was telling her, she said we should meet up again. I should come out to California and see her. Perhaps we could arrange to be locked up inside again, on a bipolar session.

She's just a friend, that's all. I've yet to meet my soul mate. It might be in the chip shop, or at a bar, or a coffee shop. It can happen anywhere, but let's hope it does, some time soon.

If I had to choose between these two fantasies, getting my ideal job, or meeting my ideal woman, and I could only have one, well, thinking about it seriously, I'd have to say the job. That would have to come first. That's how I feel.

If neither of those things happen, I won't go around regretting things. I think I've had a brilliant career and a brilliant life. I got to a World Cup semi-final, and a European Championship semi-final, played 57 times for England, won cups in England and Scotland. I've travelled the world, done loads of TV shows, all the things I would never have done if I hadn't been a footballer. I have been married, have a lovely son, so I've had that experience, even if it didn't work out, the marriage part. I've done everything, really, I ever wanted to do. So far. Managing a Football League club, that's my remaining ambition.

When I look back, even though I don't regret things, I often find myself thinking, 'Why did I do that, why did I go there?'

I loved Spurs. I went as England's most expensive ever transfer. I loved it there, did well for them, and they all loved me – and yet I willingly left them and went to Lazio. Why? That's what I often ask myself.

I know there were specific reasons, things happening at the time. I got into a sequence of events that landed me there, but now I can't quite remember or understand what happened. Why was I so keen to go? I had a world-class manager in Terry Venables. Why didn't I stay another two years at least?

I'm not saying I didn't like it at Lazio. I did, apart from all the injuries. I'm not knocking Lazio. Something that must have been clear in my mind at the time has gone hazy. It seems a bit of a mystery now, what my motivation was for leaving. I suppose that happens to lots of people, looking back at their life.

Then at Rangers. I just seemed to find myself there, wake up one day and there I was. But I settled in and loved it. Next thing, I'm at Boro. Nothing wrong with Boro, but why did I leave Rangers? I can't quite remember now. Then at Everton, I was playing well in the Premiership. I was fit and well, got myself a nice apartment – but I then left for Burnley. Sometimes I'm a mystery to myself.

Yes, it's true that Everton ended after I had made my first visit to Cottonwood, but the year before that, I was sober and doing well.

I think I must get bored, that could be it. Or, as Johnny suggests, I self-sabotage. It's a pattern I must get out of.

I said earlier I was worried about becoming boring as a person. Now that I think about it, what I worry about is being bored. Being sober is pretty boring. Doing all this training is pretty boring. Going back to therapy sessions or AA meetings, that won't exactly be exciting or good fun.

Often when I was in a minicab, coming to London to see Johnny, I looked out at people bustling along the pavements. I looked into their faces and wondered what they were thinking, where they were going. Were they excited because they knew they were going to do something good? Or worried about something bad. Or were they just generally depressed and stressed out . . .?

One way I try to cheer myself, when I get into this cycle of feeling depressed, is to think about how I succeeded in the past. In my career, I had thirty-one operations – yet I recovered from each of them, and was able to to play again, even though some experts said I never would. I got over them all and returned to the first team, playing at the top till I was thirty-five. I did it then. I can do it again. I can recover.

Okay, I also keep relapsing. I've been four times to Cottonwood, which isn't good, but I did manage to take myself there each time, to face up to what I was doing and get help.

Of all those things – all the operations, going to the clinics – doing this book has been the hardest thing in my life. Honestly. I've found it so tough, going to all these therapy sessions, and then trying to describe how I feel.

All week I worried about the session, and then I worried about what I'm revealing. I worry that people will think I'm mad, that no one will ever employ me again, or go out with me.

Then I think, 'It takes balls to do what I'm doing. I'm proud to have done it openly, and to have done it properly, putting all my effort into it.' Because that's what I do if I decide to do something. And I do hope it will help other people, who might have some similar problems. Let them see what it's been like for me. When I meet people in future, after they've read the book, I'll willingly talk to them, listen to their problems.

I'm not looking for sympathy. I hate sympathy anyway, friends trying to cheer you up, feeling sorry for you. I'm just describing what happened to me. How I tried to cope – or not, as the case may be.

It's been harder than being in a clinic because in a clinic you can say, 'Sod it,' then walk out, sit in the sun, watch the birds, and never go back. With all these sessions, and then talking about them, I've been stuck inside four walls, trapped with myself. I could of course have packed it in, early doors, which I did at one time want to do. But I decided to carry on – and that's when I felt trapped, that's why it's been so hard.

Has it all helped? That's the Big Question.

Well, I regret I've done it so intensely, packing so many sessions into such a short time. That's me, that's how I do it, taking things to extremes. At times I've felt I'm going to explode.

But, given all that, it's still helped me. No question. I wouldn't have continued with all this, if I didn't think it was helping me, or would help me.

First of all, through therapy and stuff, you get given the tools. That's the phrase they always use in clinics. Things to do, how to distract yourself, re-focus your mind when you have a problem.

Then it gives you understanding. I mentioned those panic attacks. Talking to Johnny about them, and him explaining them to me, I could see he understood what I was going through. That was a huge help. You feel you are not alone, you are not some sort of one-off nutter experiencing something no one else has ever experienced.

You also learn, from understanding something about your problem, when an attack is coming on. You can recognise the signs and symptoms better. You can get ready, or try to. That all helps.

I'm also grateful for the medications that clinics and doctors have prescribed for me. They have helped calm me down, reduced the chance of panic attacks or my OCD coming back. With OCD, I'm definitely improved, compared with how I was, thanks partly to the various pills I still take.

Medication can also help with depression – but the trouble is, your GP might just be ramming you full of tablets without really knowing the root of the problem. He probably hasn't got time to talk it through with you.

And finally, just talking to someone, letting all the shit come out of your head, that's definitely helpful. You might not at the time feel you've come away with anything positive, with a plan of attack, far less a cure, but talking is like a safety valve that gets released.

I know a lot of people will think, 'That Gazza, he's not a good example of therapy working, hasn't done him much fucking good, has it? He's confessed he's had a few drinks over the past few months when he's meant to be on the wagon, and he's still putting his stupid finger down his stupid throat.' Perhaps I shouldn't have admitted that. On the other hand, it's only happened once in the last year. Okay, three times then. But it was far worse in the past. I am getting better, all the time. Honestly. I do believe it.

And things will continue to get better, as long as I don't try to rush things. I have to be patient.

Already, I find people asking me for advice. Me of all people, as if I know fuck all.

Friends who have been worried about their drinking, thinking they're becoming an alcoholic, have often spoken to me, asked for any help. I usually do the obvious and easy thing – give them Johnny's number. I ring him first like, to see if he minds.

I did recommend one friend who has OCD, who was checking doors all the time, going mental because he couldn't stop. He had one session with Johnny and, bingo, his OCD was finished.

It does happen, that in one session you can be sorted, first time out. But other people need lots of sessions. You just don't know when you start how long it might take.

If a therapist doesn't help you with OCD, there is one specialist OCD clinic in Philadelphia. I haven't been there, but I'm told it's good.

With some friends who are alcoholics or addicts and are trying to cure themselves, I always tell them – don't do cold turkey, not on your own. Say you've been drinking solid for four months, then suddenly you force yourself to stop and have four days without drinking – the withdrawal symptoms will be far worse than the addiction. In fact, it's pure hell. That's when you could top yourself, or do something really stupid. If you are trying to withdraw, you must do it with a friend, in company, or with your doctor's help. Doctors can also give you special tablets to cope with withdrawal.

The other advice I would give to anyone is – don't be afraid to talk, to admit your problems. It has to be someone you can trust, of course, and who will understand. You don't want someone who'll just dismiss it, or just tell you to get a grip – that you'll soon get over it.

One thing I will say to other footballers with problems is, 'Don't keep it to yourself.' I wish I had revealed more to my various managers about what was really happening to me. I didn't tell them early enough, when I knew what was happening, what I was doing.

I know there are footballers who take cocaine. It gets out of your system after three days, and if they're given from Saturday to Tuesday off they can go and drink water and sweat it out of their system before they next play. If there are any players reading this book who are taking it, it will affect your football. You can tell your manager and the manager will keep everything discreet.

Things eventually will get into the papers, about bad habits and behaviour, but the papers will get it wrong, so that won't help. It's best to confess as soon as you can to your manager. They'll then keep it quiet, help keep it out of the papers. I wish I'd done that.

If you feel you can't approach your manager, for any reason, ring the Professional Footballers Association, speak to Gordon Taylor. I've found him helpful. He was always there for us. If you say, 'I'm struggling with this, I don't want anyone to know,' I know Gordon and the PFA will help. And keep it very discreet. After all, as a pro footballer, you pay them a fortune in subs, so they are there to help you. I wish I'd done that more often. But I didn't have the knowledge.

These days, the PFA is better equipped and more understanding when dealing with personal problems than in the old days. And these days, the personal problems are more personal, brought on by all the stress, all the temptations and distractions. There's always been stress, but not to the same extent as today. Not many people, even in football – except a few of the old style, old sweat coaches – honestly think that the solution is a cold shower, and that you'll snap out of it.

My therapy sessions have now come to an end. That's what I hope. For now, anyway. I expect to need Johnny less and less in the future. He has given me the areas I have to work on, which I will, once this summer is over.

But he'll still be a friend. I will still ring him up, perhaps go and watch Everton with him. I'll contact him again, professionally, if I get into a panic or fear I'm relapsing.

What you have to realise, when you have problems like mine, is that there's not likely to be a miracle, sudden cure. I have to live with me. But there are ways of coping. And I think I have coped pretty well, during my career, all things considered. I *will* do even better in the future. I know it won't affect any management job I get next, because I know what to do now. And I'm sure it won't affect any relationship I might get into. I am improving, all the time.

I know much better than I ever did how to cope. And I suppose, when you think about it, that's what life is all about, for everyone. How to cope.

And just before I go, I want to tell you all something amazing. Something that has made me cry. Not surprising you might say. When you are talking about Gazza. But these were tears of happiness.

It happened just last night. I was in Dunston, where I used to live. In the Dun Cow pub to be exact, with my brother. I was watching him play darts and playing some pool with other mates. I was having a good time, drinking Diet Coke, enjoying everyone's company. That made me feel good. But that's not the amazing thing.

My phone went off. I didn't recognise the number, but I answered it anyway. Don't know what made me. I don't usually if I don't know who it is. But I did this time – and it was the most important call I've ever had in my life.

I heard a small voice. It was Regan, saying how much he missed his dad. It was the best news I'd had in years. I hadn't seen him in months. I could tell he was emotional and I spoke to him for ages. I was crying my eyes out. Half the pub came out to see if I was okay. Bringing me my Coke and ciggies. They were brilliant. They could see I was overcome with it all, but happy.

I am going to see him tomorrow. When he's out of school. I'll drive down. I spoke to Sheryl and she was fine about it. Saying I could come down any time I was ready. I'm ready now. I can't wait to see him. This is the start of the next stage of my life. I know it. I'm feeling really positive for the first time in a long, long time.

That's it from me. Now fuck off. I'm going training. And tomorrow I'm going to see my boy . . .

———————

Hey Paul

My stomach still hurts from laughing with you. I know your life is busy as is mine, but let's keep in touch. My experience here was made easier because of you. If there is something in the future you think I have to offer, it's yours.

Fond memories to you mate - stay fucking clean!

Yours

Christie

PS Send me a copy of your new book you door knob . . .

John's summing up

John

Over the past few months Paul's had a lot to deal with. We've seen through the session notes that he has shown courage and commitment, and despite the recent relapses and being rejected from his first job as manager he was determined to bounce back. He has put a lot into our sessions and I hope has gained a lot too. Paul is more aware of his addictions and aware of the reasons why he behaves as he does in certain situations.

He has wanted the world to know what it's really like being Paul Gascoigne, and as you can see it's not easy. I hope as he moves into this next stage of his life he has the courage to be himself. For now we've finished our sessions together, but his work is by no means complete. As we've seen, Paul has substituted one addiction for another and at the moment his obsession with his weight has triggered his food and exercise disorders. This is still a tricky time for him since full recovery cannot be properly established until all addictive behaviours are arrested. Paul will always need to keep an eye on his addictions and his bipolar disorder, like many millions of sufferers around the world. He has learned some more techniques, ways he can help himself, but he needs to put them into practice on a daily basis to get the benefit and be truly free.

He has lived life in a fish bowl for us all to see and I think he always will. I hope as he develops ways of being comfortable in his own skin, he will stop looking for attention from harmful things and people (including the press) to tell him that he is okay. He's been honest in this book but has fears that people may misinterpret why he is doing so. That is a risk, but he has been determined to go ahead. He genuinely feels for others who have similar stories and by sharing about his treatment he hopes to share a message of hope – that help is available.

I too have struggled at times writing this with Paul. It has thrown up all sorts of dilemmas, which I've spent many hours discussing with my partner, therapist and clinical supervisors. Paul and I have discussed time and again how it should be written and what we want to achieve. But I know that the process we've been through in charting Paul's progress (writing his own personal case study) has helped him to recognise and revise his old patterns of behaviour as he interacted with people around him. These insights gained through counselling are very valuable. For example, when Paul has to assert himself and say 'No' to people he risks hurting their feelings, which he finds difficult even if they have been behaving badly. This pattern goes back to that anxious child who had experienced so much trauma at an early age and who just wanted everybody to be happy. Those unmanageable feelings have contributed to Paul drinking alcohol to change his mood, which eventually triggered his alcoholism.

I hope that he re-reads this book once a year for the rest of his life. I also sincerely hope that there are some readers who, after reading about Paul's journey, will take the brave step to ask for help. I have attended too many funerals due to the illnesses described in this book, and I guess that's where we should end: in the reality of what being ill is really like, the loneliness, the self-hatred and the desperation of addiction and mental illness.

Paul inspires me to continue in this field of work. He won't give up despite the many setbacks he's experienced. Whatever he goes through in his life I'll be there for him no matter what.

Introduction to the appendices

This section provides further information on the various conditions mentioned in Paul's story. Each appendix concentrates on one 'illness', and is a brief outline of what the illness is, what the symptoms are, and what treatments are available. I have also provided some basic advice and a questionnaire to be filled out by anyone who thinks they may need to look into one of these issues. These are not psychometric tests; in other words, they will not replace a professional diagnosis, but should help to indicate whether there is a need to seek help. Should you have any doubts at all about any of these conditions, in relation to yourself, a family member or friend, it's always advisable for the person concerned to have a consultation with their GP and talk the matter through. It may be that you have another, related, condition, or that you need a full health check-up. If, in fact, there's nothing wrong, having that confirmed will put your mind at rest. However, if you do need treatment, it's always better to arrest the illness at as early a stage as possible.

The final appendix, 'Where to get help', gives a list of organisations that can provide information, support and treatment for various conditions, including some of the self-help groups that meet both in the UK and in many other countries of the world.

Alcohol

Alcohol has a massive impact on our society. There are nine million problem drinkers in the UK, and 7% of our adult population have alcohol dependence[1]. Around 33,000[2] die each year because of alcoholism, and many more suffer health problems such as liver disease, pancreatitis, diabetes and heart problems.

The families of problem drinkers also suffer. Most domestic violence and death at home is caused through drinking too much. Of men who hit their partners 60% to 70% do so under the influence of alcohol. 800,000 children are living with parents experiencing serious drink problems.

Alcohol is a factor in 60% to 70% of homicides in the UK[3], and almost half of all violent crime is committed while the offender is under the influence of alcohol[4].

What's an alcoholic?

Alcoholism is the excessive and repeated use of alcohol in a compulsive and addictive way. According to some experts, the electrical brain-waves in people suffering from alcoholism are different from those who are non-alcoholics, meaning that alcoholism is a physical as well as a psychological disease.

So how do you know if you're one of these 'problem drinkers'? Try this basic questionnaire as a first step to finding out.

1. Do you ever drink to relieve emotional stress?
No ❑　Occasionally ❑　Always ❑

2. Do you ever drink alone?
No ❑　Rarely ❑　Once a week or more ❑

3. During the past year, have you ever felt remorse after drinking?
No ❑　Once or twice ❑　More than twice ❑

4. How many times in the past year have you tried to cut down or stop drinking?
Never ❑　Once or twice ❑　More than twice ❑

5. How many times in the past year have you missed work because of a hangover or drinking?
Never ❑　Once or twice ❑　More than twice ❑

6. On a typical drinking day, how many drinks do you have?
1 or 2 ❑　3 to 5 ❑　6 to 8 ❑　9 or more ❑

7. In an average week, how many days do you drink?
None ❑　1 to 2 ❑　3 or 4 ❑　Every day ❑

8. How often do you have more than six drinks in one go?

Never ❑   Less than monthly ❑   Weekly ❑   More or less daily ❑

Scoring

In each question, give yourself a score of 0 for the first answer; 1 for the second answer; 2 for the third answer, and so on. For example, in question 1, if you ticked 'occasionally', that's answer number 2, so you get 1 point.

If you scored —

- 0 to 3: It's unlikely that your drinking is harmful to you.
- 4 to 7: It's unlikely that your drinking is hazardous, but you should check and remain within the recommended safe limits of alcohol, to be sure your drinking does not cause you health problems.
- 8 to 10: It's possible that your drinking is becoming harmful to your health, and you should ensure that your alcohol intake is within the recommended safe limits, and seek further professional evaluation.
- 10 to 14: It's likely that your drinking is harmful to your health, and you should seek further professional evaluation.
- 15 to 19: Your score is believed to indicate a problem with drinking, it's likely to be harming your health and well-being, and you should seek further professional evaluation.

This questionnaire is only a basic first guide, and cannot replace a professional consultation; if you are in any doubt about your drinking you should always contact your GP.

Recommended safe limits of alcohol

- Men should drink no more than **21** units per week, and **4** units in any one day
- Women should drink no more than **14** units per week, and **3** units in any one day

What's a unit?

- Half a pint of ordinary beer, lager or cider
- A small pub measure of spirits
- $^2/_3$ of a small glass of wine

How do you work out your units?

- 2 small glasses of wine = 3 units, the daily limit for women
- 2 pints of beer = 4 units, the daily limit for men
- 1 bottle of wine = 9 units, so a maximum of $1^1/_2$ bottles per week for women and $2^1/_3$ bottles per week for men
- 1 litre of strong beer = 6 units, so the maximum for women is 2 litres per week, for men $3^1/_2$ litres per week

If you think you have a problem with your drinking, talk to your GP or use the information at the back of the book and contact someone who could give you confidential and accurate information. The longer you put it off the worse it will get.

Food disorders

The Eating Disorders Association estimates that about 165,000 people in the UK have eating disorders with 10% dying as a result, but experts believe it could be higher. Most sufferers are women, but one in ten are now men.

If you have an eating (or food) disorder, you use food to alter your mood – rather than for nutrition. You might do this by:

- starving
- overeating
- bingeing
- purging

– or a mixture of all of these. The behaviour brings short-term relief from depression, stress or intense anxiety, until it builds up again and the action is repeated. The desire for control is a big factor. People with eating disorders often have a distorted view of the size of their bodies (body dysmorphia); they often have an exercise addiction as well; and use nicotine and caffeine to help stop hunger pangs. Two types of common food disorder have been given their own names:

Anorexia nervosa – this is a self-starvation syndrome involving body dysmorphia and intense fear of weight gain, in which the sufferer typically loses 20% or more of their original body weight, leading to muscle wasting. Sufferers usually have low self-esteem and intense feelings of shame and guilt, but are in strong denial about having a problem.

Bulimia nervosa – this is characterised by secret 'binge' episodes involving eating large amounts of very high-calorie foods, often followed by 'purging' either by vomiting, swallowing of laxatives and diuretics, or obsessive exercise to rid the body of the calories consumed. Sufferers have the same low self-esteem as anorexics, but are usually more aware that they have a problem.

This pattern of seeking relief from negative feelings is typical of any addiction – e.g. to drugs or alcohol. People often don't know or deny to themselves that they have a problem. Sufferers can recover using the same model of addiction as any other type of addict – although, instead of abstaining completely from food, they abstain from the addictive foods (foods like refined flour and sugar are known to alter mood), and eat three nutritious meals a day and nothing else. Thus, this model of treatment involves:

- admitting the problem
- medical assessment – some sufferers may be dangerously ill
- supported abstinence from the addictive procedure
- getting ongoing support with the feelings that prompted the behaviour in the first place – possibly including medication for depression

If you know someone with a food disorder, it's pointless getting bossy or frustrated with them and trying to get them to eat more, or less. They're in an addictive process and they're powerless over the behaviour. If you try to stop that behaviour, the person's underlying negative feelings will escalate until they're unbearable, and they'll be forced to react. So the sufferer has to be shown that there's another way to deal with those terrifying feelings, at the same time as quitting the addictive cycle.

However, if you do know someone with food problems, do ring the Eating Disorders helpline and ask how to best get them help. It's important to say that food disorders are potentially very damaging to physical and mental health, and can be fatal. Anorexia nervosa can result in sudden death, believed to be due to heart failure, and other organs are adversely affected by the malnutrition accompanying this disease. Anorexia also causes amenorrhoea, low blood pressure, decreased heart size, dry skin, hair loss and cold intolerance (leading to increase in body hair). The self-induced vomiting of bulimics can lead to swelling of salivary glands, erosion of tooth enamel, electrolyte and mineral deficiencies, oesophagus tearing and irregular heart rhythm, while laxative abuse can cause long-lasting damage to bowel function.

Most food disorder sufferers begin with strict dieting, exercising, or overeating, and the condition escalates from there. Spotting the potential problem in the early stages can prevent years of misery and ill health.

How's my relationship with food?

Try this simple quiz as a first step to finding out:

1. I worry about being overweight.
Yes ❑   No ❑

2. I'm usually on a diet of some sort.
Yes ❑   No ❑

3. Every day I spend a lot of time thinking about what to eat and what not to eat.
Yes ❑   No ❑

4. I quite often feel guilty after eating.
Yes ❑   No ❑

5. If my favourite food's not in the house, I'll hunt around the shops at night to buy some.
Yes ❑   No ❑

6. When I exercise I'm thinking about how many calories I'm burning up.
Yes ❑   No ❑

7. I often eat until I feel bloated.
Yes ❑   No ❑

8. I sometimes use laxatives to help me lose weight.
Yes ❑   No ❑

9. I don't like going out to dinner or eating in company.
Yes ❑   No ❑

10. I feel more in control when I don't eat.
Yes ❑   No ❑

11. The thought of just having normal meals makes me miserable.
Yes ❑   No ❑

12. I'll only be happy when I'm the right size and shape.
True ❑   False ❑

If you've answered 'Yes' to six or more of these questions, it's suggested you seriously think about getting some help:

- talk to your GP and ask for a blood test to make sure you're not anaemic or deficient in any other vital nutrients (such as vitamin B12)

- if your GP agrees you have a food problem, ask their advice; you can ask to be referred for counselling
- if you have dangerously low body weight, you may be admitted to hospital for treatment
- contact the Eating Disorders Association – details in 'Where to get help' in the back of this book
- ring the Overeaters Anonymous helpline and ask for advice
- you can be referred into residential or day treatment programmes, either subsidised or paid privately – some are listed at the back of this book

If you're a yo-yo dieter, a mild overeater, or someone who worries about weight and food but hasn't yet got a serious problem, make an appointment with a qualified nutritionist (try the Institute of Optimum Nutrition at the back of this book for a nutritionist near you) and learn how to feed your body regular nutritious meals in a balanced way that can be maintained for life – no more diets, no more starving yourself, just simple self-care and an end to guilt and worry. Meanwhile, do something about your emotional pain – counselling, self-help, or even a life coach or good friend who can help you put together a plan to get your needs met.

This questionnaire cannot replace an evaluation by a professional, and is only a first guide in the assessment process. If you are at all worried about your relationship to food, please seek a professional diagnosis.

Obsessive compulsive disorder (OCD)

Some 2–3% of people in the UK are thought to suffer with some form of OCD. Some manage it on their own and find ways of coping and negotiating their peculiar habits without drawing too much attention to themselves. Others suffer badly with the condition, and it affects their lives both personally and socially. At its worst the individual can become completely debilitated by it, even housebound, and this could lead to suicide or self-harm. OCD is one type of anxiety disorder, of which there are several different kinds.

What is OCD?

We've all driven up the motorway worrying that we've left the oven on or the front door open, or we avoid a certain unlucky number. It's normal sometimes to have doubts, worries or superstitious beliefs. But with OCD they become so excessive that they control your daily behaviour. OCD involves behaviour, or compulsions, in reaction to a set of obsessive thoughts that are continuous, repetitive, anxious, time-consuming and often out of proportion to reality. In other words, you keep thinking you've got to do something according to a certain rule, or else something bad will happen. The compulsions are ritualistic and repetitive actions – far worse than everyday rituals or habits – that temporarily relieve the obsessive thought. For example, checking door handles several times in order to prevent an accident from happening to a loved one. Or counting an exact number of steps before getting in the car. A common form is anxiety about illness and germs, and the sufferer will repeatedly wash hands and clean themselves and their surroundings.

This need to 'act' on the thought and obey certain rules is powerful and convincing. It usually alleviates the anxiety for a short time, but the obsessive thought will return and gradually get worse. The condition often develops in childhood and gets progressively worse in teenagers.

There are many types of OCD: obsessively checking things, washing and cleaning, orderers (constantly placing objects in a certain order) and repeaters (repeating the same action), hoarders and people with scrupulosity – in other words, having to be thorough.

How to get a diagnosis

If you or someone you know is suffering with any of the symptoms described, there is help available. The first thing to do is visit your GP and ask to be referred to a trained clinician for a diagnosis, which is made on the basis of the symptoms you describe.

Related conditions

Common conditions that closely resemble OCD are tic disorders – for example a vocal tic disorder such as snorting. Tic disorders are involuntary behaviours in response to a feeling of discomfort. It's much more common for OCD and tic disorders to occur together when the conditions began in childhood. Many OCD sufferers also have depression, and some have accompanying food disorders.

Treatment

You might be recommended a course of therapy — usually Cognitive Behavioural Therapy (CBT). If you don't have a CBT practitioner in your area, you could try Cognitive Analytic Therapy (CAT).

You might be prescribed medication for the condition. It's believed that decreased serotonin levels in the brain are linked to OCD, and certain antidepressants that increase serotonin levels have been shown to be effective in treating the condition.

Treatment of other anxiety disorders

Most anxiety disorders are treatable through a combination of medication and counselling or psychotherapy. Whether the patient is treated with medication alone, therapy alone or both, and exactly which type of medication and which type of therapy, will depend on the anxiety disorder and the preference of the prescribing doctor and the patient. It's important to be honest and thorough when telling your doctor about your symptoms, because the only information they have to make the diagnosis is what you give them, and it's vital to get the correct diagnosis so that the right treatment can be given. Try not to be embarrassed — your doctor will have heard these symptoms many times before and regard them as part of a medical condition which is not your fault, and nothing to be ashamed of.

Do I have OCD?

A simple questionnaire cannot diagnose you, but you could try answering these questions before you visit your doctor, to get an idea of the kind of information the doctor will need.

1. I have to repeatedly check doors and windows every time I leave the house.
Yes ❑ No ❑

2. I feel anxious if lights are left on, because I'm worried they won't get turned off.
Yes ❑   No ❑

3.There's a special number of times I have to do certain tasks.
Yes ❑   No ❑

4. My hands are sore and dry from constant washing.
Yes ❑   No ❑

5. I have to cancel out every 'bad' thought with a 'good' thought.
Yes ❑   No ❑

6. I keep a lot of items at home that other people would throw away.
Yes ❑   No ❑

7. I always put things like towels, clothes, books or other objects into a special order or pattern that has to be just right.
Yes ❑   No ❑

8. I go over and over in my head events, things I've said, or things I've put in an email or text message.
Yes ❑   No ❑

9. I spend a lot of time each day cleaning objects or the house.
Yes ❑   No ❑

10. I hate using public lavatories and don't touch door handles with my bare skin.
Yes ❑   No ❑

11. I have to repeat tasks until it feels to me that they've been done just right.
Yes ❑   No ❑

12. I feel anxious about certain words and phrases being spoken.
Yes ❑   No ❑

13. I feel worried every time other people leave the house.
Yes ❑   No ❑

14. I avoid driving in case I cause a road accident.
Yes ❑   No ❑

15. I get very worried about illness and don't like being near people who are ill.
Yes ❑   No ❑

16. Tasks have to be done in a strict order and in a certain way, and if it doesn't go perfectly I have to start from the beginning and do them all again.
Yes ❑   No ❑

17. The things I do help to stop disaster from happening.
Yes ❑   No ❑

If you've answered 'Yes' to four or more questions, it's suggested you speak to your GP. Tell your GP about your anxiety and rituals in detail so that they can decide whether you need help. Contact the organisations listed at the back of this book who will talk to you in confidence. If a full assessment concludes that you have OCD, remember, help is available – this condition is treatable.

This questionnaire is only a basic guide, and cannot replace a professional evaluation – if in any doubt always contact your doctor.

What are anxiety disorders?

The most common are:

Generalised anxiety disorder (GAD) involves chronic and constant excessive worry and anticipation of disaster in every area of life. Symptoms include insomnia, headaches, sweatiness, fatigue, trembling, hot flushes and difficulty swallowing.

Panic disorder involves repeated and sudden panic attacks characterised by pounding heart, weakness, dizziness, tingling, chest pain, nausea, choking, terror, fear of loss of control and impending doom.

Post-traumatic stress disorder (PTSD) can develop after a terrifying event such as violent attacks, natural disasters, accidents and experience of war. The symptoms include persistent frightening thoughts and memories of the ordeal, sleep problems and traumatic nightmares, emotional numbness, loss of interest and motivation, and even aggression and violence.

Social phobia involves overwhelming anxiety and self-consciousness about ordinary social situations. Sufferers are so nervous and fearful of being judged by others and are so embarrassed by themselves that the condition affects work, school, and friendships. Symptoms include trembling, nausea, blushing and sweating.

Specific phobias are irrational and extreme fears of a thing that is actually little or no danger, which lead the sufferer to go to extreme lengths to avoid the object of fear. Some examples are fear of flying, tunnels, water, dogs, spiders, heights, rodents, blood.

Obsessive compulsive disorder involves anxious thoughts and rituals that control the sufferer's life and compel them to stave off disaster through acting out certain behaviours according to specific rules. It takes many different forms, but the feelings of intense anxiety and the need to act out rituals to relieve the anxiety are common to each.

Bipolar disorder (manic depression) and depression

Bipolar disorders and depressive disorders are classified as types of mood disorder. Major mood disorders are the leading cause of suicide in the UK. The mortality rate of bipolar disorder is two to three times higher than that of the general population. About 10-20% of individuals with bipolar disorder take their own life, and nearly a third of patients make at least one attempt at suicide.[5]

People with alcoholism are more than six times more likely to suffer from bipolar disorder than the general population, and almost four times more likely to have major depressive disorder[6]. When there is a dual diagnosis of alcoholism occurring together with another psychiatric condition, this is called comorbidity or dual disorder. The alcoholism (or other addictive illness) often makes diagnosis and treatment of the second psychiatric illness more difficult, because the behaviour and symptoms of alcoholism mask the symptoms of the other illness, and also prevent the patient seeking help.

Bipolar disorder, formerly manic depression, is described as a mood disorder, because it severely affects an individual's emotional responses. Moods swing from high to low, from one pole to another – sometimes in a very short period of time, sometimes over days or weeks – but when it does happen it's always severe.

There are two types of bipolar disorder: bipolar 1, the most severe type involving mania, and bipolar 2 disorder, still very serious, involving hypomania. Hypomania is a less severe form of mania not usually requiring hospitalisation. There is also substance-induced mood disorder, which is brought on by the physiological effects of a substance, e.g. cocaine, ecstasy or prescribed medication.

These disorders can be difficult to detect, especially in the early stages. The main points to look out for are:

The highs – mania[7]

Inflated self-esteem or grandiosity – feeling on top of the world, imagined special connections with people in high places or powerful positions, imagine others think very highly of you

Decreased need for sleep – going to bed late and rising very early, surviving on little sleep but still feeling refreshed

Pressure of speech – hurrying, inability to get the words out in time, difficult to interrupt, usually loud and emphatic, continuing to talk even when no one is listening

Flight of ideas – accelerated speech, thinking of one thing then another, speech becoming incoherent

Distractibility – moving from one project to the next, can't sustain attention, easily distracted

Psychotic episodes – paranoia, imaginary friends, delusions, hallucinations, impairment of ordinary everyday activities

Increased involvement in goal-directed activities – workaholism, obsessive behaviour

Psychomotor agitation – cannot sit still, fidgeting, pacing around, inner tension

Excessive involvement in pleasurable activities with a high potential for painful consequences – substance abuse, sexual acting out (several partners in a short period of time), excessive gambling and spending sprees

The lows – depression

What goes up must eventually come down, so on the other end of the bipolar scale the mania will usually at some stage switch into a major depressive episode. Your depression may last for months, weeks or only a few days before you return to mania or hypomania.

Major depressive disorder is major depression only, without the mania. If you feel you're suffering with depression only, then the symptoms listed below will also act as a guide. Dysthymia is a milder form of depression, more subtle than major depressive disorder, and therefore not always easy to recognise. Dysthymia doesn't attract as much sympathy from family and friends because it appears as if sufferers are just feeling sorry for themselves. But it's a diagnosable condition in itself, and needs treating.

Signs of a depressive disorder include:

- strong, consistent feelings of sadness
- change in normal appetite leading to weight loss or gain
- loss of interest in normal activities
- helplessness
- lack of energy
- negative thinking
- low sex drive
- loss of normal sleep pattern
- hopelessness
- crying
- insomnia or hypersomnia
- suicidal thoughts and planning

To meet the criteria for bipolar disorders, most of the high and low symptoms must be persistent and continuous over a sustained period of time (or less if you have needed to be hospitalised).

If you do identify with even a few of the above symptoms from either section and are worried, it's strongly recommended that you visit your GP and describe the problem. Your doctor should refer you to a psychiatrist for evaluation. The important thing to remember is: *if in doubt – check it out.*

If you do have any of the symptoms listed, or can relate to some of the issues Paul described – or if you think a family member or friend is suffering – it doesn't necessarily mean that you or they are suffering with bipolar disorder. There could be many reasons for some of those highs and lows. If you have recently been detoxed for alcohol or drug dependency, you may still be in the early stages of recovery, and mood swings are normal at this stage. If, however, you've been in recovery from addiction for several months, and recognise some of these symptoms described, you may have a dual disorder. Getting a diagnosis for a secondary condition will not interfere with your twelve-step recovery – in fact, you may be in danger of relapse if this goes untreated.

Another cause of highs and lows could be that you're suffering with another type of mood disorder. Or you may have been feeling on a natural high due to something going well at work or in your relationship, and then that has come to an end, and you now feel really low and down.

If you feel you have been suffering with any of the conditions described above, then give yourself a break and get the support you need. Paul did. We live in an age when the science of psychology and pharmacology is beginning to receive the recognition and support it deserves. There have been massive advances in psychotropic medication for mental illness. There are many types of medication that help with mood stabilisation that can make a huge difference to the way you live your life. These types of drugs are non-addictive. It might be that you need a course of counselling or psychotherapy to help you deal with and understand your illness. Most National Health medical centres now have a counsellor on site. If you want to find out more, there is a wealth of information on the internet and in the psychology sections in larger bookshops. For contacts, ring the Bipolar Organisation listed under 'Where to get help'.

Codependency

Codependency is a set of compulsive and maladaptive behaviours learned in order to survive in an emotionally painful and stressful environment, in a family or group set-up. It was at first defined as originating in families where addiction, mental illness or severe physical illness existed, but it's now understood that these behaviours can be passed on from generation to generation whether alcoholism is present or not. The dysfunctional pattern of relating to others is developed during childhood according to family 'rules'.

Those family rules might include:

- other people are more important than you
- it's not okay for someone to have a bad mood – it could lead to disaster
- you have to earn approval
- keep your problems to yourself
- keep your feelings to yourself

- if you're feeling bad, it's your own fault
- be strong
- do everything perfectly
- don't be selfish
- don't rock the boat
- don't speak about anything difficult or painful
- if you don't obey these rules, you won't be loved or liked
- if you don't obey these rules, everything could fall apart

Codependency is especially common when verbal, physical and sexual abuse or violence is present. When children grow up in an environment where there is drunken or abusive behaviour, or neglect, they have to learn to cope with the chaos and unpredictability. One way of coping is to be the family 'fixer' or 'rescuer'. This role usually consists of trying to look after one or both parents, often breaking up family disputes and acting as peace-keeper. The child quickly learns to put their needs second to others in the family, and subsequently when they grow up are attracted to partners who are either addictive in some way, or emotionally unavailable and need looking after.

Most of us have elements of codependency. In fact, it's very important that at times we consider others before ourselves. However, for some codependency sufferers it gets in the way of happiness and can lead to ill health or addiction.

Am I codependent?

Here are some of the main features and characteristics of codependency, presented as questions for you to answer:

1. Do you have an unhealthy dependency on your relationships?
Yes ❏   No ❏

2. Do you say 'Yes' when you should be saying 'No', at a cost to yourself?
Yes ❏   No ❏

3. Does your family have a history of addiction or psychiatric illness?

Yes ❑   No ❑

4. Have you been in previous harmful relationships, putting up with behaviour that you shouldn't?

Yes ❑   No ❑

5. Have there been signs of addiction in your past or present relationships?

Yes ❑   No ❑

6. Have you put up with physical, sexual or verbal violence or bullying?

Yes ❑   No ❑

7. Do you work long hours for no extra reward, or not take your allowed holiday?

Yes ❑   No ❑

8. Have you covered up for others' drunken or intoxicated incidents, lying on their behalf?

Yes ❑   No ❑

9. Have you bailed someone out financially, lending them money, paying gambling or drug debts, or turning a blind eye when they've stolen from you?

Yes ❑   No ❑

10. Do you feel guilty for standing up for yourself?

Yes ❑   No ❑

11. Do you feel anxious if things are not perfect?

Yes ❑   No ❑

12. Do you try to control others' behaviour?
Yes ❏   No ❏

13. Do you find it hard to trust others?
Yes ❏   No ❏

14. Do you take excessive precautions against real or imaginary disasters or accidents?
Yes ❏   No ❏

15. Do you need constant reassurance from your partner/spouse/child?
Yes ❏   No ❏

16. Are you prone to jealousy?
Yes ❏   No ❏

17. Do you feel that if you don't do what your loved one wants, they might leave you?
Yes ❏   No ❏

18. Do you often lie awake watching your loved one sleep?
Yes ❏   No ❏

19. Do you try to anticipate what mood your loved one is going to be in when you next meet?
Yes ❏   No ❏

20. Do you purposely start arguments to get your loved one's attention?
Yes ❏   No ❏

If you've answered 'Yes' to five or more of these questions, you may fit into this category. Don't put off seeking help. On the surface it might not appear as harmful as a chemical or alcohol addiction problem, but being dependent on someone who constantly lets you down is bad for self-esteem and can lead to depression. Ask yourself if you're happy with how you respond to your family, friends and colleagues.

If you're living with an addicted person and you're codependent, not only are you suffering but you might not be helping the person that is ill, if you keep tolerating their lies and excuses. Children copy our behaviour, so if you're a parent it's important to seek help, look after yourself and put appropriate boundaries in place.

How to get help

The understanding and treatment of codependency is still in its infancy in the UK, but there is help available and there are many excellent self-help books. In some parts of the UK the self-help group Codependents Anonymous (CoDA), is available. There is also a twelve-step programme called Adult Children of Alcoholics (ACoA), which addresses some of the issues discussed for those whose parents were addicts or alcoholics. Most major addiction treatment centres now treat codependency.

As the condition stems from childhood it will be important to look back over some of those painful issues with a counsellor, therapist or even a group in which you feel safe. You can find a counsellor or therapist through the UKCP or BACP, both of which are listed in 'Where to get help' at the back of this book.

Some clinics and treatment centres run 'family weekends' which involve the family of the ill person attending a weekend workshop. Additionally, there are weekend workshops held, for anyone who wishes to attend, which concentrate on various aspects of relationships, codependency and boundaries (contact details in 'Where to get help').

Gambling

It's estimated there are currently around 370,000 problem gamblers in the UK. This is an estimate because a lot of problem gamblers do not declare themselves or seek help, and gambling is often not recognised as an addictive illness. However, the behaviour of problem gamblers causes extreme disruption and hardship both in their own lives and in the lives of their families. Debts mount up, homes are lost, families split up and gamblers can acquire criminal convictions.

In just five years, the amount gambled on sports alone in the UK has risen from about £7bn per year to £40bn, according to Professor Leighton Vaughan Williams, a government adviser on gambling[8]. This year, £1bn will be staked on the World Cup. It's now easier than ever to place a bet – through the internet, mobile phones, and television. The 2005 gambling laws and proposed 'super casinos' offer yet more opportunities to gamble. Online gambling in particular has taken off in the last few years. Gamcare, an organisation offering support and information about gambling (listed in 'Where to get help'), says that the average debt reported by people looking for advice is £25,000, but this is likely to be under-reported. Young people are particularly vulnerable to slot machines, internet gambling and scratch cards. And the problem is growing: Gamcare receives 52,000 calls per month.

Because gambling can be seen as glamorous – attending exclusive casinos requiring vast minimum stakes – high-earning, highly pressurised professionals such as Premiership footballers are often attracted to it as a form of relief, relaxation and entertainment. It is, however, deceptively easy to fall prey to the 'habit', and even those with money to burn can literally lose everything.

Why do people gamble?

'At that point I ought to have gone away, but a strange sensation rose up in me, a sort of defiance of fate, a desire to challenge it, to put out my tongue at it. I laid down the largest stake allowed – four thousand guilden – and lost it. Then, getting hot, I pulled out all I had left, staked it on the same number, and lost again, after which I walked away from the table as though I were stunned. I could not even grasp what had happened to me.' – Fyodor Dostoevsky, *The Gambler*.

Gambling creates a high, a rush of adrenalin, which is exciting and, like other addictive behaviours, blocks out all other considerations, concerns and emotional pain. It's not winning that the gambler becomes addicted to – it's taking the risk. That's why the gambler goes back and loses all their winnings – they're not doing it for the money, they're doing it for the feeling.

What is problem gambling?

When your gambling disrupts either your work, family life, social life, psychological or physical well-being, then it's called 'problem gambling'. When problem gambling becomes pathological it qualifies as a progressive addiction. At this point the gambler needs to bet more and more often and larger and larger amounts, and becomes restless and irritable when they try to stop or when they can't gamble. They become preoccupied with gambling, they chase losses (trying to recover losses by gambling more and more) and continue gambling despite increasing negative consequences of their behaviour.

Addictive gambling involves denial about the problem, an inability to stop or control the gambling, mood swings and depression. Like any other addictive disease, pathological gambling has phases. These include chasing the first win (always trying to have again that first wonderful high when winning), experiencing blackouts (periods of gambling of which the gambler has no memory at all) and using gambling to escape emotional pain. Addicted gamblers experience low self-esteem, they use rituals, and are driven to seek immediate gratification. There's also a significantly high suicide rate amongst compulsive gamblers.

Questionnaire

If you think you may be gambling too much, try answering these questions as a first step towards working out if you need help.

1. Have you ever gambled to relieve stress or worry?
Yes ❏   No ❏

2. Have you ever borrowed money to gamble?
Yes ❏   No ❏

3. Have you ever lied to friends or family about your gambling – how often you gambled, or how much you lost?
Yes ❏   No ❏

4. Do you often go gambling to celebrate something – a birthday, or a new job?
Yes ❏   No ❏

5. Have you ever missed work because of your gambling?
Yes ❏   No ❏

6. Have you ever thought about stealing or getting money in other illegal ways to gamble?
Yes ❏   No ❏

7. Do you think about gambling quite often when you're doing other things, like working or socialising, or when lying in bed at night?
Yes ❏   No ❏

8. After you've lost money, do you feel an urge to keep going to try and win it back?
Yes ❏   No ❏

9. Do you feel regret or remorse about gambling?
Yes ❏   No ❏

10. Have you often gambled until every last penny was gone?
Yes ❏   No ❏

11. Have you ever gambled money you needed to pay bills?
Yes ❏   No ❏

12. Do you promise yourself you'll stop after a certain point or after spending a certain amount of money, and then find yourself carrying on, unable to stop?
Yes ❏   No ❏

If you have answered 'Yes' to four or more of these questions, it's possible you have a gambling problem, and it's recommended that you see a professional to get an assessment. (This questionnaire is only a basic guide, and cannot replace a professional evaluation. If in any doubt, always contact your doctor.)

How to get help

Here are a number of steps to take to get help:

- visit your GP
- contact a specialist addiction treatment centre for an assessment and diagnosis (some are listed at the back of this book in 'Where to get help')
- contact Gamblers Anonymous (listed at the back of this book in 'Where to get help') – self-help meetings for people who think they may have a gambling problem
- make an appointment with a counsellor or psychotherapist (via UKCP or BACP, listed at the back of this book)
- contact Gamcare – details in 'Where to get help'

The addictive personality

Addiction is responsible for many deaths, causes devastation to family units and wrecks communities around the world. Addiction often runs in families, and many experts believe that predisposition to addiction is a combination of biological, psychological and environmental factors. A common term for this predisposition to addiction and the progressive alteration of personality during addiction, is the 'addictive personality'.

Addiction is defined as a disease of the mind, body and spirit. When we take or do something that makes us feel good, it's normal to want to do it again. If you have an addictive personality, you will *definitely* do it again. Some describe addiction as having a 'hole in the soul', because of the constant search to find the missing piece – the thing that's going to make you feel complete. But that feeling of completion is elusive – it only ever comes in short bursts, after which its absence is felt all the more keenly.

Addictive behaviour is mood-altering, i.e. changes the way we feel. Messengers are sent to stimulate the pleasure centre in the brain, which then produces dopamine, a chemical that makes us feel good. So we go back for more and more, and this creates dependence – thus begins the addictive cycle.

Types of addiction

Here are some of the more common forms of addiction:

- prescription drugs, e.g. sleeping pills, painkillers
- alcohol
- food
- street drugs, e.g. cannabis, cocaine, ecstasy, amphetamine, heroin
- sex
- shopping
- gambling
- exercise (addiction and bulimia)
- relationships addiction (often called codependency)

Am I an addict?

Diagnosis of addiction requires a thorough examination by a professional. However, below is a short self-assessment questionnaire as a first step to finding out whether you have the disease of addiction. When answering the questions, apply them to your chosen substance or behaviour. For example, if you go shopping to make yourself feel better, apply each question to your shopping habits. If you have more than one habit, apply the questions to the one that affects you most frequently.

1. Do you continuously use the substance or act out the addictive behaviour, despite knowing there are harmful consequences?
Yes ❑   No ❑

2. Do you sneak or hide consumption or behaviour, for example, covering up how much money you have spent/gambled, or sneaking away to purge after a meal?
Yes ❑   No ❑

3. Do you lie to friends, colleagues, family or doctors to disguise the behaviour?

Yes ❑   No ❑

4. Have you had accidents, or been in dangerous situations due to consumption or addictive behaviour?

Yes ❑   No ❑

5. Have you lost a job due to the addictive behaviour/consumption?

Yes ❑   No ❑

6. Have any relationships with friends or loved ones been broken as a result of the behaviour/consumption?

Yes ❑   No ❑

7. Do you minimise your use of the substance or addictive behaviour (i.e. pretend you use/do less than you actually do)?

Yes ❑   No ❑

8. Have you tried to stop and failed?

Yes ❑   No ❑

9. Do you have continuous feelings of shame, guilt or remorse?

Yes ❑   No ❑

10. Are you always thinking about the next high, the next meal or bet?

Yes ❑   No ❑

If you have answered 'Yes' to more than two of these questions, it's likely you have an addictive personality, and it's recommended that you see a professional to get an assessment. (This questionnaire is only a basic guide, and cannot replace a professional evaluation. If in any doubt, always contact your doctor.)

How to get help

Here are a number of steps to take to get help:

- visit your GP
- contact a specialist treatment centre, most of which offer a thorough assessment and diagnosis (some are listed at the back of this book)
- contact a self-help group (listed at the back of this book)
- make an appointment with a counsellor or psychotherapist (via UKCP or BACP, listed at the back of this book)
- get informed – search for charities and organisations on the internet
- be honest with yourself and share it with someone you trust – addiction thrives on secrecy

You might be guilty and ashamed of your behaviour but it's important to be honest – do not minimise or maximise your problem. Addiction is easy to deny, and even the most experienced practitioners don't fully understand its nature.

What treatment?

Statistics show that the most effective treatment is abstinence, where applicable. Experiences in my own life and of working with many clients who suffer with addiction problems suggest that cutting down seldom works, and neither does substituting one addiction for another, e.g. swapping alcohol for cannabis.

Addiction is always progressive, and the consequences become more painful and more dangerous with time. If you have already crossed the line identified by the questionnaire, you'll need support to get you through the difficult process of withdrawal and into some kind of recovery programme. Addiction is a primary rather than a secondary illness, that often requires urgent assistance. There are normally deeper psychological reasons for the use of substances or behaviours to make oneself feel better, but until you address the addiction you won't be able to examine those underlying issues and get better.

Once an addict always an addict? Perhaps, but with the right support you can change – millions have.

Where to get help

Self-help groups

Alcoholics Anonymous – for anyone who thinks they may have a problem
with alcohol
0845 769 7555
www.alcoholics-anonymous.org.uk

Narcotics Anonymous – for people with problems with any kind of drugs
0845 373 3366
www.ukna.org

Gamblers Anonymous – for anyone who thinks they may have a problem
with gambling
08700 50 88 80
www.gamblersanonymous.org.uk

Debtors Anonymous – for people who have problems with spending, debts or finances
020 7644 5070
www.debtorsanonymous.org.uk

Overeaters Anonymous – for overeaters, anorexics, bulimics and people with other food disorders
07000 784985
www.oagb.org.uk

CoDA (Co-dependents Anonymous) – for people with codependency issues
07000 263645 (answer phone)
www.coda-uk.org

Al-Anon – for people whose lives are affected by a problem drinker or addict
Alateen – for children affected by alcoholism in someone they know
020 7403 0888
www.al-anonuk.org.uk

Families Anonymous – for people whose lives are affected by drug addiction in the family
0845 120 0660
www.famanon.org.uk

ACOA – Adult children of alcoholics
USA 310-534-1815
www.adultchildren.org

Organisations

UKCP – UK Council of Psychotherapists – professional body regulating psychotherapists, which can help you to find a therapist in your area
020 7014 9955
www.psychotherapy.org.uk

BACP – British Association of Counsellors and Psychotherapists – to find a counsellor or therapist in your area
0870 443 5252
www.bacp.co.uk

Action on Addiction – addiction research, advice and support
020 7793 1011
www.aona.co.uk

Chemical Dependency Centre – charity helping those with chemical dependency
020 7351 0217
www.thecdc.org.uk
– SHARP London – a day programme for alcoholics and addicts in London
020 7349 5772
– SHARP Liverpool – a day programme for alcoholics and addicts in Liverpool
0151 703 0680

OCD Action – charity offering advice and support for people with OCD
0845 390 6232
www.ocdaction.org.uk

OCD-UK – charity for people with OCD, including list of support groups
www.ocduk.org

The Institute of Optimum Nutrition – nutritional advice and diagnoses
0870 979 1122
www.ion.ac.uk

Eating Disorders Association
01603 621414
www.edauk.com

Gamcare – gambling addiction and problem gambling help, advice and support
020 7378 5200
www.gamcare.org.uk

MDF The Bipolar Organisation – support and information for those with bipolar disorder
08456 340 540
www.mdf.org.uk

SANE – information and support for those with mental health problems
0845 767 8000
www.sane.org.uk

Association for Cognitive Analytic Therapy (ACAT)
020 7188 0692
www.acat.me.uk

John McKeown
www.johnmckeown.org

Treatment centres and hospitals

Cottonwood de Tucson – USA private residential treatment centre for addiction and other psychological disorders
020 7486 6222
1-800-877-4520 (USA)
www.cottonwooddetucson.com

The Priory Hospital – group of private residential psychiatric hospitals (most with addiction unit attached)
020 8882 8191
www.prioryhealthcare.co.uk

Priory Hospital North London – walk-in and residential psychiatric services including addiction unit
020 8882 8191
www.prioryhealthcare.co.uk/Find-a-centre/Facilities/Priory-Hospital-North-London

Priory Hospital Roehampton, South London – walk-in and residential psychiatric services including addiction unit and specialist eating disorders unit
020 8876 8261
www.priory-hospital.co.uk

Clouds House – residential treatment for all addictions – private and health authority funded
01747 830733
www.clouds.org.uk

Promis – treatment centre for all addictions, specialising in food disorders and gambling
020 7581 0222
www.promis.co.uk

Hazelden – USA private residential treatment for all addictions for adults and adolescents
1-800-257-7810 (USA)
www.hazelden.org

Crossroads Centre – Eric Clapton's treatment centre for addiction in Antigua
0800 783 9631
1-888-452-0091 (USA and Canada)
www.crossroadsantigua.org

Broadway Lodge – treatment centre in west of England
01934 815515
www.broadwaylodge.org.uk

Notes to the appendices

[1] Department of Health Strategy Unit Alcohol Harm Reduction Project: Interim analytical report, 2003.

[2] Alcohol Concern (www.alcoholconcern.org.uk).

[3] 'Alcohol and Crime: Breaking the Link', All-party group on alcohol misuse, 1995.

[4] Home Office Statistical Bulletin, 'Violent crime overview, homicide and gun crime 2004/2005', ONS January 2006.

[5] Muller-Oerlinghausen B, Berghofer A, Bauer M., 'Bipolar Disorder', *Lancet* 2002 May 11;359(9318):1702

[6] *Comorbidity of Alcoholism and Psychiatric Disorders – an Overview*, Ismene L. Petrakis, M.D., Gerardo Gonzalez, M.D., Robert Rosenheck, M.D., and John H. Krystal, M.D., National Institute of Alcohol Abuse and Alcoholism, November 2002.

[7] *Diagnostic and Statistical Manual of Mental Disorders – Fourth Edition (DSM-IV-TR)*, American Psychiatric Association, Washington D.C., 2000.

[8] Sean Coughlan, 'Billion pound game', *BBC News Magazine*

Picture credits

GERMANY
IN THE EIGHTEENTH CENTURY:
THE SOCIAL BACKGROUND OF
THE LITERARY REVIVAL

AN EVENING WITH THE DUCHESS ANNA AMALIE OF WEIMAR
From the drawing by G. M. Kraus in the Landesbibliothek, Weimar.

Left to right: Heinrich Meyer (artist), Henriette von Wolfskeel (lady-in-waiting), Goeth
F. H. von Einsiedel (gentleman-in-waiting), the Dowager Duchess, Eliza Gore, Char
Gore, Emily Gore, Luise von Göchhausen (lady-in-waiting), Herder.

GERMANY
IN THE EIGHTEENTH CENTURY:
THE SOCIAL BACKGROUND OF
THE LITERARY REVIVAL

by

W. H. BRUFORD

Schröder Professor of German
Fellow of St John's College, Cambridge

'Sage man sich daher, dass die schöne Literatur einer Nation
nicht erkannt noch empfunden werden kann, ohne dass man den
Komplex ihres ganzen Zustandes sich zugleich vergegenwärtigt'

GOETHE, *Ferneres zur Weltliteratur*

CAMBRIDGE
AT THE UNIVERSITY PRESS

1952

PUBLISHED BY
THE SYNDICS OF THE CAMBRIDGE UNIVERSITY PRESS

London Office: Bentley House, N.W. 1
American Branch: New York

Agents for Canada, India, and Pakistan: Macmillan

First Edition 1935
Reprinted 1939
1952

First printed in Great Britain at the University Press, Cambridge
Reprinted by offset-litho by Lowe and Brydone Ltd., London

CONTENTS

PART III

THE NEW ORDER OF SOCIETY— THE MIDDLE CLASS

PREFACE

This book is intended in the first place, as the sub-title indicates, for the English student of German literature and thought. Its main aim is to provide material for a socio-logical study of eighteenth-century German literature by describing the chief classes of society in that age, and the political and economic conditions under which they lived. In a final chapter some general characteristics of that literature have been discussed, features which seem to have resulted from the reactions of whole groups to political and social con-ditions, rather than from the fortuitous similarity of individual points of view. To study these social influences in detail in particular works is beyond the scope of the present volume. In the absence of suitable presentations in English of the social history of the period, it seemed desirable to concentrate attention to begin with on the historical facts, especially as the German works on this subject, such as those of Bieder-mann, Freytag, Lamprecht, Sombart and Steinhausen, being written for different readers and with different ends in view, fail to answer many questions which arise in the mind of the English student. While gratefully making use of these writings, and many monographs on particular phases of the subject, the author has endeavoured not only to select and present the material in a manner better suited to the present purpose, but also to draw more fully on contemporary memoirs, essays and books of travel, especially on those by English travellers. Imaginative literature, on the other hand, has intentionally not been used as a source, because to do so would have interfered with the author's purpose of studying the influence of the world in which the writers of that day lived upon that which they created, but attention is fre-quently drawn to particular features in literature, to which a knowledge of the social life of the time lends a new significance. The wider conception of Modern Studies which has steadily been gaining ground in this country for the last twenty years, and is paralleled by the growing interest in 'Kulturkunde' in Germany, calls for such attempts at a synthesis of disciplines formerly isolated, in spite of the difficulties and dangers which the specialists in each field affected will necessarily perceive.

To the general reader the present work may be of interest for the light it throws on the evolution of the German national character. It is apparent to any student of eighteenth-century German life that many traits, of which the Englishman only became aware late in the following century, were clearly in evidence in the Germany of the age of Goethe, a land of many other types besides poets and thinkers. It is of some importance to the ordinary citizen to know what this Germany was like, especially at a time when it is the expressed aim of many leading political thinkers in Germany to correct the 'liberal' aberrations of the nineteenth century and undo the work of the French Revolution.

The author gratefully acknowledges his indebtedness to many Cambridge and Zürich teachers and friends, and especially to the late Professor Karl Breul for constant help and encouragement.

W. H. B.

1934

PART I

POLITICAL STRUCTURE AND SYSTEM OF GOVERNMENT

Chapter I

'KLEINSTAATEREI'

'Germany is undoubtedly a very fine country', writes David Hume in 1748, 'full of industrious honest people, and were it united, it would be the greatest power that ever was in the world.' Germany was not at this time, like France and England, a single national state, but, in reality though not in name, a loose confederation of states, the boundaries and authority of which were so ill-defined that it is for many purposes misleading to speak of the 'Germany' of that age without explaining what territories the name is intended to cover. From the earliest period of what may properly be called *German* history (the time of the Saxon emperors) the Empire had shown a tendency to disintegrate into the tribal units which had only been brought together by force to make it, and these units themselves soon began to split up into smaller ones, through the lack of a law of primogeniture and the incapacity of their rulers to distinguish between personal ownership and political authority. 'Particularism (Kleinstaaterei) marks German history', says Professor Haller, 'from the very beginning.' The result was that long before the eighteenth century the Empire was a short name for a collection of virtually independent states.

Many general causes have been suggested for the growth of particularism in Germany. The one least in dispute is the geography of the country. The abundance of barriers in the interior and the absence of clearly marked natural boundaries on its borders made the centralisation of authority much more difficult in Germany than it was in either England or France. If the Hundred Years' War was necessary to teach the English kings in their island the lessons of geography, it is not surprising that Germany should have remained for so long politically amorphous and divided against itself. The Franks might succeed in conquering the other five tribes, but only a series of rulers endowed with the genius and vigour of a Charlemagne could have maintained a hold over clans which, although they spoke dialects of the same language, possessed a marked individual character and were widely scattered over a land merging almost imperceptibly, on two of its boundaries at least, into the adjoining territories. The area was too vast to form a single unit, given only medieval communications, and it was constantly open to invasion. Moreover, it was almost inevitable (as Mr McDougall has suggested) that with boundaries so indefinite the growth of national feeling should be long delayed. Then the facts of geography strongly reinforced other causes in bringing about that endless struggle with the Papacy, which deprived the German kings of the only force making for unity in their lands, for a rich Italy so near at hand was an even more tempting prey to the king of an undeveloped Germany than France was to Edward III. It was its geographical position, finally, which more than anything else put Germany at a disadvantage when the routes of world trade became sea-routes in the age of colonial enterprise, the great epoch of national expansion and unification.

We find no parallels in the history of the Holy Roman Empire to the successive steps by which England achieved a greater and greater measure of unity. No German king was able to establish a system of common law. The maintenance of peace and justice had to be left to the territorial princes from the beginning of the thirteenth century. No effective system of taxation made all parts of the country

conscious of a common authority or drew representatives of
scattered provinces and towns together in one assembly like
the English Parliament, for the Reichstag was not really a
comparable institution. No industry grew up like the
English cloth trade based on national organisation, in spite
of the promising start made by the Hanse. No literature was
produced comparable with that of even pre-Elizabethan
England in continuity of tradition and wideness of appeal,
to reflect the life of the whole country in a language under-
standable by all. It is not surprising then that the same forces
which in many other countries fostered a strong unified
state—the growth of the money-system and the consequent
replacement of feudal organisations by a professional bureaucracy and a standing army, the invention of gunpowder,
which left no baron's castle impregnable, the spread of
education among the laity and the extended application of
reason and experience to secular problems, the Reformation
and Counter-reformation with their innumerable political
repercussions—all these factors, in Germany, strengthened
the hands, not of the emperor, but of the territorial princes.

The history of the separate states that made up the Empire
is a subject of baffling complexity, but there are typical
features common to most of them which may be described.
The oldest princely families can be traced back, it seems, to
the counts appointed by the Carolingians to administer
justice in their name in the various provinces of their realm,
and granted a fief in return for their services. With the
extension of feudalism, from the ninth century onwards, the
offices became hereditary, being now inseparable from the
fiefs, which, owing to testamentary dispositions, marriages,
purchases of land and other purely personal transactions, were
continually changing in extent. By taking advantage of
weak kings, and especially of the strife between Empire and
Papacy, Hohenstaufen and Guelph, these hereditary officials
and landowners gradually acquired various regal rights, first
legally confirmed by the *Statutum in favorem principum* in

1232, when Frederick II, too deeply engaged in Italy to retain much authority at home, gave the princes full rights of jurisdiction in their own lands. From now on they were referred to as 'domini terrae' and definitely supported by the emperor against the towns, the Church and the minor nobility. But their lands were made up of many separate portions and their authority precarious, being founded on a variety of legal titles not necessarily connected with each other. A prince might be landlord here, chief officer of justice there, in a third place he might have a near relative in power and in a fourth he might hold fishing or hunting rights. As his sons had all at first an equally good claim to his rights and estates at his death, it proved very difficult to concentrate power in the hands of the head of the family, but successive generations gradually overcame this difficulty in most states and apart from a temporary set-back round about the fourteenth century the princes continued to increase their power at the expense of the emperor, the lesser nobility and the towns.

The set-back occurred during the transition from the feudal natural economy to the money-system, when the towns, the pioneers of the new system, were at an advantage through the possession of ready money, as well as of skill in organisation and abundance of enterprise. More and more of them secured their independence from their lords, and for a time it seemed that city-states or city-leagues might be able to assert themselves successfully against the princes as in Italy. The princes, to pay for military support and for the services of their new non-feudal officials, had to pledge lands and rights to such an extent that their position was seriously weakened, and their former claims to feudal service made almo.t worthless. The small revenues they enjoyed were still paid mostly in kind, and it proved almost impossible to impose direct taxation. The lesser nobility took advantage of the situation to make themselves almost as independent of their prince as he was of the emperor. Fortunately for the princes however the knights did not join forces with the towns, as in England, for each estate thought only of its own interests, so that in the leading states the princes soon had them under control again.

The princes survived this crisis by the conversion of more and more payments in kind and manual services into money dues, while credit became easier to obtain owing to the great expansion of the metal currency. Their chief rivals, the towns, declined economically and politically owing to the loss of their privileged position at home and abroad, combined with a decay of civic spirit. Most important of all, the dynastic ambitions of the princes were aroused by the success of their more powerful neighbours abroad.

The fate of any individual territory depended above all on the personal qualities of its ruler. In some districts, particularly in the south and south-west of Germany, a number of small independent authorities, Free Towns and Reichsritterschaften, survived in all their medieval variety until the end of the eighteenth century. In all the larger territories, although no two of them developed in the same way, some form of absolute government was gradually established more and more firmly.

But however powerful the German princes might appear to be in their own domains, in European politics they were almost negligible factors until the world was startled by the achievements of Frederick the Great. Though constantly threatened by powerful neighbours they were too jealous of their dynastic rights to seek strength in unity. Accordingly the Empire, never a solid structure, was even in the fifteenth century nothing but a loose league of princes. Its titular head might still be endowed in theory with the power of a Roman emperor, but in practice, as J. J. Moser said, 'he had not a foot of land or a single subject; no country was governed in his name or was a source of revenue to him'.

The German monarchy had been elective from the beginning, but down to the year 1250 the succession had remained for a century or more at a time in the same family. As the princes had by then come to look upon the emperor not as their lawful overlord but as a dangerous rival, they took care that there should be frequent changes of dynasty. At the same time the right of election came to be restricted to seven princes, the Kurfürsten, the rest being at the time indifferent. The hereditary succession of the Hapsburgs (from the year 1437) became possible only because the Kurfürsten had so whittled away the authority of the emperor at successive elections that they did not fear him any longer. The title was an expensive luxury now that few could afford, for the emperor had no dependable revenue in spite of all attempts to make a general levy. A strong personality might perhaps still have brought the princes to heel, but none was produced. The results of the listless rule of Frederick III (1439–86) were not retrieved even by Maximilian I.

From the fifteenth century onwards the Reichstag made frequent attempts to reform the Empire, but their only result was to make the impotence of the emperor a patent fact. Provision was made for maintaining the peace of the realm by the so-called 'Grundgesetze', the Golden Bull, the measures concerning Landfriede and Religionsfriede, the Exekutionsordnung of 1553 and Charles V's Wahlkapitulation. A serious attempt was made to put the administration of justice in the Empire, its military defence, and its finances in order, and in each of these reforms the essentially federal nature of the Empire was clearly reflected. The emperor was allowed no control over the *Reichskammergericht* or Supreme Court of the Empire which was established in 1495. The court was given a permanent meeting-place, not in Vienna but first at Speyer, then from 1684 at Wetzlar, its members were appointed for life and paid not by the German king but by the electoral princes. It was agreed at the Diet of Cologne in 1505 that the new military forces which were meant to replace the feudal levies of earlier days should be provided and maintained by the German princes, each contributing his due share of men and money according to the importance of his territory. The various Estates of the Realm (Kurfürsten, Fürsten, Reichsstädte, Reichsgrafen) agreed to make a regular contribution towards the cost of the Reichskammergericht, and other moneys could be raised for government purposes, if the Reichstag consented, in the form of the so-called *Römermonate*, levied on the various Estates in a fixed proportion.

In justice, military affairs and finance a certain measure of unity had thus apparently been achieved, on the initiative not of the head of the Reich but of the leading princes. There seemed to be the beginnings of a federal constitution here, but further development in the direction of a confederation was prevented, first by the excessive number and variety of political authorities concerned, and secondly by the nature of many of the existing institutions of the Empire, which were still those of a feudal state.

The confederation would have had to include, in the eighteenth century, kings of European importance like those of Austria and Prussia, the electoral princes, 94 spiritual and lay princes, 103 counts, 40 prelates, 51 Free Towns, in all some 300 separate 'Territories', each jealous of its time-honoured privileges and little affected by any memories of a common inheritance. This multiplicity of interests prevented even the modest beginnings of a federal constitution outlined above from working satisfactorily in practice. The *Reichskammergericht* proved ineffective because the territories, unwilling to lose any of their own authority, tried to have the right of appeal to it denied to their subjects, or if they were unable to obtain this concession, refused to contribute towards its upkeep. In 1769, for instance, the territories were half a million Thalers in arrears with their contributions. Consequently the number of judges had to be reduced from 50, the staff first proposed, to 18 or even at times to 12 or 8. The result was the accumulation of business graphically described by Goethe in *Dichtung und Wahrheit*. In 1772,

61,233 cases still awaited trial. Similarly the imperial military force provided for by the Diet of 1505 was in practice of little real value. The troops remained under the control of the territory that provided them. The prince who paid them appointed their officers and was responsible for the commissariat even when they were acting with other contingents. Uniforms and equipment were of the utmost diversity, discipline was lamentable, funds were always inadequate, and the human material pressed into service in this universally despised force was naturally of the poorest.

The features that had survived from the feudal state were the office of king and emperor and the Reichstag. Backed by no army, no revenues, no state Church (for after the Thirty Years' War religious disunity had had to be accepted as permanent), the emperor was now the not undisputed fount of honour and for the rest little more than an occasionally picturesque anachronism. The emperors strove to maintain their authority. Shortly after the establishment of the *Reichskammergericht* the emperor set up, for instance, a rival institution, the *Reichshofrat* in Vienna, and endless disputes followed as to the limits of their respective competency. No decision was ever reached while the Empire lasted and both courts continued to perform similar functions. The *Reichshofrat* had the reputation of being even more slow and inefficient and certainly more corrupt than the other court of appeal.

The *Reichstag* had lost the authority it had once possessed as a feudal council of the realm, at which the emperor's principal vassals appeared in person to confer with him, when it was made a perpetual assembly in 1663. The change was a natural one given the tendency towards a federation. The result of it was that the Diet became an assembly of envoys, who, not having full powers, had to await instructions before expressing an opinion on any important measure. There was no debate. The envoys dictated their instructions to clerks. This not only caused infinite delay but also made it possible for rulers to dissent in cases where they would not have had the heart to do so if they had been present in person. Their decision announced from a distance had an impersonal quality. Since, moreover, for a measure to become law, some hundreds of authorities had to vote on it, and a majority had to be obtained for it in each of the three chambers of the Diet, as well as the emperor's assent, it was almost impossible to put through any far-reaching measure in the public interest. If any measure was agreed on, it had become usual for the constituent states, the real centres of executive power, either to take no notice of the *Reichsschluss* or to look upon their acceptance of it as an act of grace. Like the coronation of the emperor, the meetings of the Diet were a time-honoured but empty show. The Chamber of Electoral Princes, nine in number during most of the eighteenth century, formed a sort of cabinet and dominated proceedings. It was in practice usually sufficient if they obtained the concurrence of the Chamber of Princes, the third Chamber, that of the Free Towns, being in the eighteenth century negligible. Consequently, hardly any but negative measures were passed, all in the interest of the higher nobility, and most of the time was taken up in endless disputes about trifles, questions of precedence, congratulations on happy events in the emperor's family and the like. For the transaction of this kind of business few states were willing to maintain a separate representative. Usually an envoy represented several states, and not more than some score of envoys were ever present at once.

> Das liebe heilige römische Reich
> Wie hängt's nur noch zusammen?

So the boon companions are made to sing in Goethe's *Faust*, and it was a common question. Yet memories of the earlier glories of the Empire were not entirely dead. However much theorists might say in defence of the existing state of things as a guarantee of freedom, the consciousness of belonging to a people that had maintained the Holy Roman Empire saved many Germans from utter dejection and shame in times of political impotence and lent Germany a status among the European nations to which its actual political and economic condition could have given it no claim.[1]

[1] The best account of the constitution of the old Empire is probably still C. T. Perthes, *Das deutsche Staatsleben vor der Revolution*, Hamburg and Gotha, 1845. K. Biedermann, *Deutschland im 18. Jahrhundert*, 1, 185 ff. and L. Häusser, *Deutsche Geschichte*, 1, Berlin, 1854, contain additional details.

Chapter II

BENEVOLENT DESPOTISM

We have seen that the real political authority in eighteenth-century Germany was not concentrated in the hands of the emperor, but distributed among the rulers of the three hundred or more sovereign states, ranging in extent from Austria to the tiny domains of the Reichsritter in Swabia.[1] It is in fact hard to draw the line between these last-named 'sovereigns' and the multitude of other landowners who, though not 'reichsunmittelbar', enjoyed almost all the powers of independent rulers. Their inclusion would bring the number of authorities nearer to three thousand than to three hundred. It is the use of their power made by these authorities that we must examine if we would understand how Germany was governed in this period, and in the present chapter some features which seem typical for the great majority of states will be singled out, and some few examples cited. Leaving the republican Free Towns for a later chapter, we may attempt to give a concrete first impression of the autocratic system which prevailed in all the remaining states by a method favoured by contemporaries, the description of a typical day in the life of some of their rulers.

The day of Ernst August of Weimar, the grandfather of Karl August, and a sufficiently representative ruler of a small state in the first half of the century, is described by Pöllnitz in 1729 as follows. The duke did not rise before midday, after breakfasting in bed and perhaps amusing himself before rising with his violin, or, if he felt disposed towards business, by receiving reports from his architects, gardeners and ministers. (The order in which they are named is instructive.) His first task on rising was to inspect and drill his guard,

[1] See Appendix II.

consisting of thirty-three men. Then came a walk, and at two or three o'clock the chief meal of the day. Dinner might last anything from three to five hours. Ernst August drank freely and talked a great deal, though usually on topics very little to the taste of the cavalier who leaves us this description. After coffee he would play quadrille with his two ladies-in-waiting and a major of his army, or spend the evening in his room, smoking, fiddling or drawing. A few miles away from him lived the more serious-minded Duke Friedrich II of Gotha, who rose every day at seven and spent an hour in prayer and devotional reading before dressing and giving audiences to his ministers and other callers. At midday he dined with the duchess and his children, and other people of distinction, and after this function, which lasted an hour and a half, he would walk in the gardens or read till five. A visit to the assembly of the nobility in the house of one of their number, where he would play hombre, took up an hour or two, and on his return he supped and retired at nine o'clock.[1]

We have a livelier picture of a still smaller potentate, the Prince of Wallerstein, in Lang's memoirs.

The lever of the Prince took place on our lucky days at eleven o'clock, but more often at two. As soon as the groom of the chamber threw open the folding doors of his bedchamber, all who had been waiting for hours in the ante-room entered, the marshall, the equerry, the physician-in-ordinary, we secretaries, the gamekeepers and any strangers who might be there. The Prince, who was now in the hands of his friseur, talked to people in his usual charming way, and anyone whom he addressed would try to produce some witty or amusing reply. As soon as the Prince got up from his chair and gave his further directions to this one or that, all who were not specially commanded to remain would withdraw. Then the Prince usually joined his family for a while, after which he hurried to mass and gave audiences till dinner, which took place at varying times, sometimes late in the afternoon.

[1] C. L. Baron de Pöllnitz, *Mémoires*. Nouv. éd. corr., Liége, 1734, I, 204 ff.

After dinner a ride to a farm or a hunting-seat was followed by individual audiences or conversations. In the evening he played cards, or gave a reception or concert for the court. Supper, never before midnight, did not occupy long, and the Prince would take one of the guests back to his room with him, unless he contented himself with the secretaries, who were still waiting in his ante-chamber at two or three in the morning. Often he would walk past the poor martyrs pretending not to notice them, and begin to read or sign papers in his study, while they fell asleep on their chairs.[1]

Frederick the Great distributed his time rather differently. In his prime he used to devote ten hours a day in peace time to state affairs, four to study and writing, and two to society and music. He dressed immediately on rising, at four in summer and five in winter, usually in the same old blue coat faced with red, yellow waistcoat and breeches and dark brown high boots. His friseur was given a very short time to arrange and powder his hair, and when his toilet was over, every hour in the day was methodically devoted to some particular piece of business or amusement. Instead of re-ceiving those who had business with him in levers and audiences, with their fuss and waste of time, he required them to communicate with him in writing, and indicated to his secretaries what reply was to be made by means of a note in the margin. By using every moment of his time he was able to keep all important affairs of state under his personal control. He dined, usually with eight or nine of his officers and one or two men of letters, precisely at noon, and often remained with the company till three. At table he tried to put everyone at their ease and delighted in witty conversation. Until his old teacher Quantz died in 1773, Frederick used to fill in the intervals he allowed himself between work, and an hour before supper, by playing the flute, either alone or accompanied by one or two other instruments, and he devoted

[1] K. H. von Lang, *Aus der bösen alten Zeit*, 1842. (Reprint Stuttgart, 1910, p. 129.)

much time to perfecting himself in the art of writing—in French. He retired to bed at nine o'clock.[1]

These brief descriptions already indicate that the methods of government varied from state to state in Germany according to the personality of the prince, though all states resembled each other in being dependent on the whims of an absolute ruler. But no state, however small, was governed by the prince without assistance, though in all he was the ultimate authority. An elaborate machinery had everywhere been contrived for translating what was in theory merely the prince's will into action, machinery that for long periods could be left to run itself. Government in the German states was despotic, and it was exercised through a bureaucracy, organised with varying degrees of efficiency in the different states.

The growing complexity of society, reflected in the rise of distinct classes and occupations based on the division of labour and the increasing use of money, had made a professional and non-hereditary civil service necessary from the thirteenth century onwards over wider and wider areas of the Continent. The princes still based their own rights on the hereditary principle, and great landowners continued to inherit powers of patrimonial jurisdiction with their estates, but the great majority of offices ceased to be hereditary because no longer remunerated in land. France and Burgundy led the way in the rational organisation of the state, followed by Austria and more slowly by other German states, particularly after the Renaissance and the reception of Roman law. By the eighteenth century there was an elaborate bureaucracy in every state. Round about 1500 a further great advance in efficient administration had begun in Germany,

---

[1] For descriptions of Frederick's day see Dr J. Moore, *A View of Society and Manners in France, Switzerland and Germany*, London, 1779, II; N. W. Wraxall, *Memoirs of the Courts of Berlin, Dresden, Warsaw and Vienna*, London, 1799, I, 114 f., and H. Prutz, *Preussische Geschichte*, Stuttgart, 1901, III, 41.

the institution of central governing bodies or councils. The medieval chancellor and other high officials had been dismissible, but not whole-time state servants with special offices where they could always be found. They were usually ecclesiastics, they moved about with the court, and their organisation was very amateurish. From the sixteenth century the princes found it necessary to have whole-time officials, drawn partly from the nobility, partly from the middle class, and in this case trained in law and without independent means. The leading officials formed the prince's council or 'Hofrat', with definite duties, forms and traditions, and from this council a number of committees, each the nucleus of a later government department, branched off. In all states the local nobility, mistrustful of this process, strove, with varying success, to maintain at least their old right to the chief offices, or 'Indigenatsrecht'. While the smaller states were busy imitating Brandenburg-Prussia and Austria, these states themselves, Prussia leading, extended the power of the ruler further and further at the expense of the towns and the nobility, until a standing army and an efficient and reliable bureaucracy made the central authority almost irresistible within the state. The result of this single-minded pursuit of order and power was in Prussia the well-policed military state, and in other states various approximations to this ideal.

Though the driving power behind this development came mainly from the princes themselves, their desires were reinforced by the general trend of Protestant opinion, for after the Reformation the idea had gained ground that princely rank was a sacred trust from God, involving responsibilities on the part of the prince but calling for unquestioning obedience on the part of the subject. Rulers were taught now to take their office seriously, for a new moral value was attached to work as such, quite apart from its results. They in their wisdom and under God's guidance were answerable for the physical and spiritual welfare of their ignorant subjects, whose main characteristic was always assumed to be their inability of themselves to help themselves. This doctrine, so repugnant to the sense of corporate self-determination of the early Middle Ages, and that of individual self-determination that ripened later, justified any infringement of individual liberty, from regulations concerning food and clothing to the pressgang methods of Prussian and Austrian recruiting sergeants. In the seventeenth and early eighteenth centuries more stress came to be laid on the duty of the subject to obey than on the prince's responsibility for his welfare. Many rulers came to look upon their office less as a trust than as a sinecure, the fortunate holder of which was justified in exploiting it for his own personal advantage. In no case was very much heed paid to the wishes of the great body of subjects; there were usually no organs to express them. Where the despotic ruler, of his own choice (as in Prussia under Frederick the Great), subordinated his interests and those of his house to what he conceived to be his duty to the 'state' we may speak of 'benevolent despotism'.

After this preliminary survey we must look a little more closely at the aims and methods of German absolutism in their local variety. We have noticed already that after the breakdown of the decentralised medieval state, the central governments had gradually extended the scope of their activities. The prince and his privy council were responsible for foreign policy, for defence, for the administration of the prince's private estates and property and, mainly from this source, for the financing of his expenditure, whether for his court or for what would now be looked upon as public services (for no distinction was yet made between his private and public liabilities). The prince was the fount of justice and his council the supreme instance short of the *Reichskammergericht*. In most states an attempt had been made at some time since the spread of Roman law to codify the law of the land, in particular to define the duties of the subject in a *Landesordnung*, but by the eighteenth century most of these codes were very much out of date. There was nothing in any of these functions that had changed in principle since the Middle Ages. But the Reformation had brought the established church in Protestant lands also under the control of the government, a heavy responsibility as well as a source of power. Even in Catholic states it came to be felt necessary to exercise a similar but less far-reaching control over Church affairs. That the young might be brought up in the pure doctrine, schools had to be looked to, and many princes set up state universities, where only the established religion was taught. The government also frequently attempted to control many things in its subjects' life, in addition to religion, that are now felt to be purely private matters.

What was then called 'police' covered every kind of regulation considered necessary for the health, prosperity and moral welfare of the subject. Under this head were included the first sanitary regulations, concerning water-supply, drainage, the removal of rubbish, etc., as well as the provision of qualified apothecaries and midwives. This was no less a 'police' matter than the patrolling of the streets and the prevention and detection of crime. Any control of industry and trade that was attempted (generally in the interests of the prince's treasury), the regulation of prices, of hours and conditions of labour for apprentices, measures to prevent competition, the prohibition of begging, all came under the same head. In these matters the territorial governments took over and applied to a wider area the control that had been exercised in the Middle Ages by town councils and gilds, whose grip was now weakening. There was a similar precedent for sumptuary edicts, still considered necessary to prevent the spread of luxurious habits, lest the time-honoured external distinctions between various classes of society should be obliterated. They were designed to secure for every one the status due to his rank, just as the economic regulations aimed at a decent living for all in the traditional style of their class. In both matters modern individualism refuses to recognise any norm and finds the older practice tyrannical. There is nothing more characteristic of the old régime than edicts such as the one promulgated in Brunswick in 1758, forbidding servant girls to use silk dress-materials, to wear gold or silver ornaments, or shoes made of anything but plain black leather, or the one in Posen instructing the wives of burghers not to wear capes, or to wear their hair down their back. The German papers naturally noted with interest about that time that in Constantinople the Sultan was prohibiting under pain of death the use of silk jackets and muslin-lined turbans. It was well-meant but misplaced zeal, however, that inspired patriarchal guardianship of this kind. A good 'Landesvater' like Karl Friedrich von Baden really considered it to be the duty of his Hofkammer 'to teach his subjects even against their will how to order their domestic affairs', or, as he expressed the ideal again with unconscious humour, 'to make them, whether they liked it or not, into free, opulent and law-abiding citizens'.

The administrative machinery that had been evolved by the eighteenth century was of considerable complexity even in small states. Everywhere routine business and minor matters were left in the hands of properly constituted authorities, 'Behörden', which generally decided differences of opinion among their members by a vote. But the reins of government were still in the hands of the prince, who received advice from these boards of officials but acted as he thought best, without being effectively controlled, except in a very few states, by assemblies representative of his subjects.

With one exception, these boards or committees of state had branched off from the older council of the prince and his advisers, which in a simpler society had decided all problems alike. The exception was the body created in Protestant lands to carry out the new function of Church government, the *Konsistorium*, on which laymen sat along with clerical members. From the beginning the princes reserved important affairs of state such as foreign policy for their own private control, perhaps making use of a small inner council or *Geheimer Rat* of three or four favourites. Of the committees of the main council, the chief was the one that dealt with finance, and this was naturally the first to become a separate department, the *Treasury* (Hof-, Amts- or Rentenkammer). The council was then left with the administration of justice (sitting as one body it was the court of appeal for the state), of defence and of home affairs, including 'police' in the broad sense indicated above. It had to draft any new legislation that was considered necessary. The working of the whole system depended on the character and business methods of the prince. He might at any time upset the plans of his permanent officials, and against his decision there was in practice no appeal. What was particularly resented in the eighteenth century was the increasing use made by princes of their privilege of Kabinettsjustiz, a summary form of jurisdiction intended as a check on the often cumbrous normal procedure of the courts, but one used more and more irresponsibly by despotic rulers in their own interest. It was, for instance, by the exercise of this power that Karl Eugen of Württemberg was able to imprison the poet Schubart and the publicist J. J. Moser for years without the semblance of a trial.

Lang's description of Prince Wallerstein at work may be a little overdrawn, but it is certainly true in the impression that it gives of the capriciousness inherent in absolutism of this stamp. The prince used to open all reports that came to him from his permanent officials and heap them up on the floor beside his desk, until the pile was as high as he could reach. Then one day, in the midst of walking up and down the room and chatting to his secretary about everything under the sun, he would go to the pile and take out a document at random. He would quickly consider its contents, not neglecting any opportunity of doing the opposite of what was recommended, and finally indicate his wishes in a brief marginal note. It was Lang's business to make a formal draft of the decision. When he brought some thirty of these drafts back to the prince next morning at his lever, they were thrown on to a second pile at the other side of the desk, and there they remained until the prince was going away on a long journey, leaving town for his summer residence, or having the room decorated. Then he would begin to think it was time to clear out his study and would send the signed documents down pell-mell into the chancellery. To counteract his dilatoriness at least in matters of justice, his officials got into the way of sending up the same matter for his consideration once a month, often revising their own recommendations, so that before long several different sentences were hanging over the head of the person concerned. One poor man arrested for stealing was kept in prison for years, it is said, while the courts waited for the prince to choose between the many decisions they had suggested to him, which included hanging, the lash, penal servitude, expulsion from the country, or an immediate pardon in view of his long detention. In the end, according to this well-invented story, he solved the problem for himself by escaping from prison.

This description indicates how true a picture Lessing has given us of a German prince in the first scene of *Emilia Galotti*:

Emilia? (Indem er noch eine von den Bittschriften aufschlägt, und nach dem unterschriebenen Namen sieht.) Eine Emilia?— Aber eine Emilia Bruneschi—nicht Galotti. Nicht Emilia Galotti!—Was will sie, diese Emilia Bruneschi? (er liest). Viel gefordert; sehr viel.—Doch sie heisst Emilia. Gewährt!

Or in scene 8:

CAMILLO ROTA. Ein Todesurteil wäre zu unterschreiben.
Der PRINZ. Recht gern.—Nur her! geschwind.

In fact to understand any work with a political bearing (*Götz, Die Räuber, Fiesko, Kabale und Liebe, Don Karlos, Egmont* are only the most famous of them) as it was understood then, we need always to remember that almost every German state was ruled by an autocrat, often as irresponsible as Prince Wallerstein.

The territorial princes had not always been in a position to govern without troubling to consult their subjects, but after the Thirty Years' War they had not kept up even the forms of the old assemblies representing the 'Estates' of the territories, in particular the country nobility and the towns-people, that had formerly claimed some control over at least the finances of the state. These provincial diets (Landtage) had always met unwillingly and never shown any initiative or political sense, principally, no doubt, because the two Estates had scarcely anything in common, far less than the squires and burghers in the English Commons, who had never formed themselves into closed castes. In England it often happened that the children of merchants married into the gentry, and the younger sons of country gentlemen engaged in commerce, but not in Germany. By the eighteenth century, apart from four or five exceptions that will be discussed separately, the Landtage, if they met at all, were only picturesque survivals.

With the decay of the Landtage the majority of princes had no one to remind them of their responsibilities. Aping the French court in externals without trying to rival the French government in efficiency, they held it to be their chief duty to their people to make a splendid display. The rather unreal magnificence that was then the ambition of so many princes is expressed in the art they inspired and paid for—architecture, opera, literature, painting, above all, in their portraits by court painters. One of the finest of these, Rigaud's picture in Dresden of Augustus III as crown-prince, presents to us the incarnation of refined pomp and power. We read it in the proudly poised head, the over-erect figure, and in every feature of costume and background, the leonine state wig, the incongruous shining armour, the silk and ermine cloak that swells in the breeze against a stormy sky. It would

have been lèse-majesté for a court painter to suggest that a
king was no more than a man. The note is not 'What care
these roarers for the name of King?' The troubled elements
only serve to make more admirable the unruffled majesty of
that royal brow. With one hand on his marshal's staff, the
other on his sword-hilt, Augustus stands there like a baroque
Jupiter. In life, of course, he (and still more his father,
Augustus the Strong) most resembled the god when, like the
Jupiter of Molière's *Amphitryon*, he was assuring his courtiers
and their wives that

> Un partage avec Jupiter
> N'a rien du tout qui déshonore,

but there were strangely few men of the time who ever
looked behind the façade. One of the few was Frederick the
Great, who as crown-prince directed his *Anti-Machiavel*
against such rulers. It is true that his own statecraft later was
nothing if not Machiavellian, but he never made himself
ridiculous, and his chief charge against the petty despots of
Germany was that they were never anything else. 'Most
small princes', he says, 'particularly the German ones, ruin
themselves by reckless extravagance, misled by the illusion
of their imagined greatness.... The youngest son of the
youngest son of an appanaged dynasty imagines he is of the
same stamp as Louis XIV. He builds his Versailles, keeps his
mistresses and has an "army" at his beck and call—perhaps
strong enough to fight an imaginary battle on the stage at
Verona.'

There were, it is true, a few states where more or less
representative assemblies still had some influence. The most
famous of these assemblies (the only one in Europe considered
by Fox to be comparable with the English House of Commons) was the Landtag of Württemberg. It survived
because it was a homogeneous body of burghers only, that
had established its position amidst the anarchy of Herzog
Ulrich's reign in the early sixteenth century. The nobility

in Swabia had made itself independent (reichsfrei) and if undisturbed on their small estates the free knights cared little what happened to the duchy in which their lands formed enclaves. Eberhard Ludwig (1677–1733), Karl Alexander (1733–37) with his unscrupulous financial adviser 'Jud Süss' Oppenheimer, and Karl Eugen (1737–93), Schiller's 'tyrant', defied the Estates and for a long time contrived to raise money enough without them, but in a prolonged struggle with Karl Eugen the Estates proved the stronger. Led by J. J. Moser, who did not shrink even from forming alliances with foreign powers, at the risk of civil war, they not only maintained their constitutional rights but established them more firmly than ever. Similarly in Mecklenburg-Schwerin the Estates persuaded the emperor to depose one duke (1728) and forced his successor to grant their demands (1755). In Hanover, in the absence of the Electors (as kings of England), the nobility maintained an oligarchical rule through the Estates (powerful, as in Württemberg, because one strong party took the lead), but though they ruled in their own interests, there was at least no extravagant court to be maintained, the English connection made for freedom of thought, and the people were comparatively contented. In Saxony too the older nobility predominated and at least succeeded in maintaining Protestantism as the state religion even after the Electors, as kings of Poland, had turned Catholic, but they took no steps against the reckless extravagance of Augustus II and his successor, agreeing to any taxation if they themselves were exempted from it. 'Rabiosus der Jüngere' (Rebmann) described the Saxon Diet in 1795 as 'a farce performed every six years, in which all the actors have to say is "Yes".'

If after the middle of the century there was a change for the better in the government of many German states, it was due (except in Württemberg, and even there in part) to the spread of humane ideas in the Age of Enlightenment and to the example set by Frederick the Great in Prussia, rather than to any pressure from below. It will be of interest then to see how the rulers of Prussia differed in aims and methods, as well as in native ability and energy, from those discussed above. It is difficult to exaggerate the effect of the personal qualities of the Hohenzollerns on the fate of their country. Their lucky inheritances would only have made the already ramshackle state still more unstable if the fragments had not been welded into one whole by this line of capable and ambitious rulers. There is no need here to dwell on the statesmanlike rule of the Great Elector and Frederick William I, or on the military genius of Frederick II—these are matters for the political historian. But to understand why the life of the ordinary man was different in Brandenburg-Prussia from that of similar men in other states we must know what those who ruled him were striving for and how they moulded the institutions of their land.

It was not so much in their general aims that they differed at first from their contemporaries, though they were more determined and consistent in their pursuit of military power, as in their energy and efficiency. Every prince aimed, as we have seen, at absolute autocracy, and a Machiavellian Realpolitik was the order of the day. But the Great Elector and his successors were of tougher fibre than most of the would-be 'princes', and encouraged by the dour nature of their subjects, taught by their experience in defending scattered and backward dominions, they came to believe that all their resources must be systematically exploited by an efficient bureaucracy, and all their energies bent to the building up of a strong army, if their land was to survive as a political unit. Bismarck was expressing an age-old maxim of Prussian policy when he said (1888): 'The pike in the European fish-pond prevent us from becoming carp'. Personal ambition and presently a dynastic tradition made the Hohenzollerns ready to sacrifice even what were elsewhere the most treasured values of civilisation to the pursuit of power.

In their administrative methods their great principle was

unification, concentration, 'rationalisation'. The councils that had existed in every province were replaced in the Great Elector's time by the central Geheimer Rat of Brandenburg when, by various devices, the provincial Estates had been, if not in all cases abolished, at least deprived of their importance. The functions of the Geheimer Rat resembled those of the councils of the other states already discussed, the greater, not the inner councils, for it did not handle foreign affairs, but its main business, and this is characteristic of Prussian developments, was to finance the military power of the state. 'It was the necessity for a standing army that provided a motive for the reform of taxation, etc. and the bureaucracy developed in the main out of the military commissaries' (Schmoller). The 'military commissaries', at first agents appointed by the Kurfürst to negotiate with the colonels, who at that period raised regiments privately as a kind of speculation, became permanent officials when standing armies came in. From about 1660 there were commissaries in every corner of the land to negotiate in matters of excise, taxation, billeting and so forth with the local authorities, the beginnings in fact of an anti-feudal bureaucracy, hated by the Estates, but given ever increasing powers by the Electors. There was a separate set of officials concerned with the management of the crown lands, the collection of rents, regalities and the like. These corresponded to the 'Kammer' or treasury officials of the other states and were at first responsible to the Kammern of the various provinces, but by 1689 these had been brought under a central Hofkammer, and it was possible for the first time to budget for the whole land. By gradual stages the two sets of officials were brought under one control, the Generaldirektorium, which lasted with few changes from 1723 till 1806. The Generaldirektorium had at first four departments, each of which, besides looking after the special affairs of a province, had to take over specialised duties for the whole state ('Grenzsachen', army supplies, post, mint). Frederick the Great added five more to the number of these special departments or embryo ministries (trade and industry, military administration, customs and excise, mines, forests). The Geheimer Rat, deprived of so many functions by special committees, had become by this time merely a department for justice and religion. Frederick William I had already set up another advisory body, the Kabinettsministerium, as a sort of Foreign Office.

It was a complex system, but here as in the other states the monarch was the real mind of the state, because he alone was responsible for the co-ordination of the work of all these special bodies. From the time of Frederick William I all important business was dealt with by the king in his Kabinett or office, where by marginal notes on the departmental reports, letters or petitions submitted to him he indicated his decisions to his Geheimsekretär, who then had to draft them as Lang did Prince Wallerstein's. Frederick the Great simply continued his father's system, avoiding whenever possible the audiences which in smaller states were considered so valuable a means of protecting the individual against bureaucratic tyranny. It was his pithy marginal notes that were imitated, with a difference, by the Emperor William II.

The Generaldirektorium directed the activity of a well-planned system of local organs, which may be more briefly described. The land was divided into circles (Kreise) and these again into districts. In the developed system (from 1723) there was in each circle an intermediate authority between the local organs of the Generaldirektorium (called Kriegs- und Domänenkammern) and the central government, in the person of the 'Landrat'. The Landrat, generally a big landowner, who served rather for the honour than for the small salary he received, had as Landrat no judicial functions like the English Justice of the Peace, whom he might seem to resemble, but exercised a general control over the civil service of the various districts of his circle and was responsible for the maintenance of roads and bridges, for military provisioning and for 'police' in the broad sense defined above. The interests of the state were represented similarly in the towns by 'Steuerräte', each of whom supervised in the king's name some six to fifteen towns, keeping an eye both on civic administration and economic development. The 'Kriegs- und Domänenkammern' finally, with large staffs, managed the royal demesnes, collected taxes and dues, and exercised all the functions included under 'police'; they were even concerned with the fostering of industry, in so far as it increased the royal revenues. To this end they were given considerable powers of jurisdiction in matters affecting the revenue, powers that remained a bone of contention until late in the reign of Frederick the Great.

This was by no means the only objectionable feature in the administration of justice. 'Cabinet justice' was still not unknown in Prussia in Frederick's day, and the patrimonial jurisdiction of aristocratic landowners often proved a source of petty tyranny. Procedure was clumsy and very slow, and equality before the law was far from being a reality, though the ideal was more nearly approached in Prussia than elsewhere in Germany. Many improvements were made in the second half of the century, their general tendency being, in Schmoller's phrase, towards a 'nationalisation of justice' parallel to the nationalisation of the army, taxation, police and administration, through the substitution of whole-time trained officials for amateurs with an inherited (or purchased or transferred) right of jurisdiction and claim to its rewards in the way of fees, fines and authority. Sustained and largely successful efforts were made by Frederick's minister Cocceji and his successor Carmer, helped by the great jurist Suarez, to expedite normal procedure and to codify the law. A 'Prozessordnung' was published in 1781 and the 'Preussisches Landrecht' and its supplements a few years after Frederick's death (from 1794 on). The supreme instance was the Geheimer Rat. Next came the provincial 'governments' (this was now practically their only function) and finally the town councils, the owners of manorial estates (Rittergüter) and the king's agents on the royal demesnes.

The Prussian system of government was still despotism, but under Frederick the Great and his father before him it was efficient and 'benevolent' in the sense that, though the king insisted on holding the reins of power and brooked no interference, he did not use his authority and wealth for his own personal gratification and that of his court. The various territories he had acquired and the people he ruled formed an entity Prussia, that came before the royal house in importance and gradually became conscious of itself as a state. Frederick William called himself 'the field marshal and finance minister of the King of Prussia', Frederick the Great 'the first servant of the state', and their actions proved that they were moved not only by personal and dynastic motives but still more by a feeling of community of interest with a larger whole, a strong *esprit de corps*. So Frederick William would line up with his regiment before his palace at Potsdam every Easter, even if snow was on the ground, to be bled with the rest of them, and for years would have no other doctor than his regimental surgeon. His son was pursuing the same aim when he encouraged his young officers to think of themselves as Prussians, from whatever province they came, and made his officials realise that they were civil servants and not servants of the king. Yet even the philosopher on the throne did not escape the penalties of absolutism. He still had much that reminds us of Schiller's picture of the absolute monarch in *Don Karlos*. Like Philip he could trust no one, he could not believe that any of his servants was animated by a sense of duty and honour like his own. And his sense of duty blinded him often to ordinary considerations of morality, because the narrow interests of his own state came for him before everything, while his determinist philosophy could at a pinch shift the responsibility for his actions from himself to the First Cause, just as Philip's scruples could be overcome by the Grand Inquisitor.

Moreover, Frederician absolutism would have required for continued efficiency a succession of Fredericks, a clear impossibility, while it made continuity of policy from reign to reign difficult and left too little room for the natural expansion of the functions of the government. The Stein-Hardenberg reforms were urgently necessary when they came, as a halfway house between despotism and representative government.

In the second half of the eighteenth century a number of German princes tried, generally somewhat half-heartedly and never with much success, to imitate the benevolent despotism of Frederick the Great. Maria Theresa and her advisers instituted many reforms in the administration of Austria after the War of the Austrian Succession, and paid less respect than Frederick to the rights of the nobility. The most pressing practical problems were solved in a way that allowed for the vast differences between the various parts of the Austrian dominions. Joseph II, however, in his impatience to see results and his doctrinaire idealism, introduced with excellent intentions an immense number of ill-considered reforms that could not easily be put into effect by the bureaucracy at his disposal. In him centralisation and government-guardianship overreached themselves, and most of his good work was later swept away with the bad.

Influenced by the spread of humanitarian ideas as well as by Prussia's example, a number of smaller states attempted to reform their administration, particularly after the Seven Years' War. Saxony did so under Kurfürst Friedrich August III, 'der Gerechte' (1768–1827), Baden under Markgraf Karl Friedrich (1746–1811), Weimar under Karl August (1775–1827), Anhalt-Dessau under Leopold Franz (1758–1817). A number of ecclesiastical states imitated them. These states, however, in their attempts to improve the conditions of trade and industry, to economise at court, to reform justice and education and abolish serfdom, were not aiming at power but at the individual welfare of their subjects. Poor-relief was reorganised, new poor-houses, prisons, hospitals established, and in every way the governments showed themselves conscious of their responsibility for what would now be called social services. The subjects of these true 'Landesväter' certainly did not envy the Prussians their military power, with its concomitants, compulsory service and high taxation. Mirabeau sums up the current view concerning these smaller progressive states well in *De la monarchie prussienne*[1] when he says that though small states cannot prevent invasions of their territory, undertake great public works or remove the hindrances to trade and intercourse that are caused by customs duties and the diversity of weights, measures and coinage, their rulers have on the whole too little power to be tyrannical, they are very close to their subjects, who often look upon them as their father, and they keep each other in check, because dissatisfied subjects can so easily emigrate to a neighbouring state. Each state needs good professional men, they are as it were sold by auction to the highest bidder, and for similar reasons the press tends to be freer than in larger states.

As an example of the smaller enlightened states Weimar under Karl August is particularly interesting, because of Goethe's share in its government. The mature Karl August earned universal praise from his contemporaries. In Goethe's well-known summing up of his character and achievements (Eckermann, 23rd Oct. 1828) and in Alexander von Humboldt's description (quoted there) of a day passed with him just before his death, we see a man of strong and generous character, a good judge of men, who had enriched his native endowment of common sense and vigour of will and intellect by profound cultivation. Goethe himself was of course responsible for evoking not a little of what was most attractive in him. He had shown the sulky headstrong boy whom we see in the early portraits that the real world of nature and men was an inexhaustible source of interest for

[1] 4th edn., London, 1788, III, 677 ff.

one not attracted by the empty pomp of courts and not overmuch by literature and art. When Goethe first knew him, his tastes and habits were those of a country squire. His relationship to his small land was, until well into the nineteenth century, very like that of the squire to his manor. He got to know every inch of it by shooting and hunting over it. Every expedition gave him a fresh opportunity of acquainting himself at first hand with the life of his people, and these interests were stimulated by Goethe, the admirer of Möser (who praised patriarchal government with its close personal contacts) and the frequenter of the craftsmen's workshops in his native Frankfort.

It was Karl August's rural rides that suggested his many attempts to improve agriculture, forestry and mining, most of which were, however, too amateurish and sporadic to have much permanent effect. In agriculture it proved extremely difficult to get rid of the old open-field system. The landlords and even the duke's Kammer did not wish all the fallows to disappear, over which they had valuable grazing rights, the peasants were heavily taxed and had no capital, and no faith in new-fangled ideas, the only result of which was to lower the price of corn. But interesting discoveries were made at the experimental farm (run at a loss) and by Batty, the English bailiff, in his small district up in the Thüringer Wald, while forestry was put on a scientific basis and introduced as a subject of university study at Jena before the end of the century. It proved impossible in the long run to do much for mining (at Ilmenau), stocking-weaving (at Apolda) or any other industry. Industry and trade were both crippled by the protectionist policy and old-established rights of neighbouring states, which prevented for instance until 1804 the diverting through Weimar of the trade-route from Frankfort via Erfurt to Leipzig.

Karl August's reign illustrates in fact admirably both the strong and the weak points of patriarchal government at its best. The duke was in close touch with his subjects and was always ready to help them in any practical difficulty of which his own senses convinced him. He took an active part in fighting village fires, he led rescue parties when Weimar or Jena were in danger from floods, and once at least (unlike the count pilloried in Bürger's *Lied von braven Mann!*) he was nearly the victim of his reckless bravery. His curiosity in practical and scientific affairs was insatiable. 'Now he would be in the conservatories, where he knew every plant and moss and flower, now in the gardens and park, now with the professors of Jena, now at one of his farms, now parleying with artists, now exchanging views with poets, now buying antiques, now viewing pictures'[1]—so Frau von Heygendorf describes his versatility. But wide interests and good intentions were not enough without some of the hardness with himself and others that made Frederick truly Great, without a more methodical attention to detail and a much larger measure of the gifts of fortune. The day for tiny states was over. They could not be self-contained and they could not effectively demand what they needed from outside. The more one knows of them, the more one sympathises with Frederick's Machtpolitik, that at first appears so brutal.

Karl August's comparative ineffectiveness was not, however, altogether due to fate and his good nature. Although he was 'ein Mensch aus dem Ganzen' he was an absolute prince and a man of his time, not a martyr to duty. His personal tastes, it is true, were very simple. On his hunting expeditions he would sleep in the meanest cottage or beside a camp fire; he liked a hard bed and plain fare (see for instance Goethe's instructions to his mother for their reception in Frankfort in 1779). Even at court, though appearances had to be kept up, there was nothing sybaritic about the life at Weimar if, as a former page tells us, four bottles of champagne, on the rare occasions when it was served (perhaps four times a year), had to suffice for 50 or 60 people. But the duke wasted far more money than his little land could afford on

[1] Kar. Jagemann, *Erinnerungen*, p. 139.

field sports, on a merely decorative army, on parks and palaces and on women. In his delight in the chase he did not shrink from causing inconvenience and more to his subjects. Goethe had to protest, diplomatically but firmly, against wild boars being allowed to roam freely on the Ettersberg, to the annoyance of neighbouring squires and peasants and the ruin of agriculture. Before this Karl August had arranged pig-stickings in the riding-school, till the spectacle had proved too much for the nerves of his court. His smart keepers and foresters were as dear to his eye as his little army, and he never lost his passionate love of hunting. His favourite dogs had to accompany him everywhere; they were allowed all sorts of liberties at table; they frequently interrupted court concerts with their howls when the tenor sang. When old citizens of Weimar later called up memories of the duke, it was on horseback that they saw him, riding recklessly surrounded by dogs to the chase, or as in his later years, driving out in his old two-horsed almost springless Droschke.

Another even more expensive hobby (for Parforce and Treibjagden, smart keepers and thoroughbred English horses were expensive) was his 'army'. When he came to the throne he pensioned off the senior officers, took command himself and brought in a Prussian officer to train his hussars. There were only some thirty-six of them, but they were given a new riding-school and new stables and were drilled with all due solemnity, a trumpeter playing the cavalry march every day as Rittmeister von Lichtenberg led his men out to parade. In spite of Goethe's protests against 'militärische Makaronis' (Tagebuch 10 Jan. 1779) Karl August increased the army after his visit to Berlin in 1778, set up a company of grenadiers and dressed his men very much like Prussians. He would often get up at four o'clock to drill his battalion himself. It was now 800 strong, infantry and cavalry. In 1783, however, being 200,000 Th. in debt, he had to promise his Landtag that he would economise. He was left with 38 hussars and an officer, and 136 infantry under six officers, but he soon tired of drilling this handful of men. From 1788 he began to satisfy his military tastes by acting as Major-General of a Prussian regiment of cuirassiers stationed at Aschersleben. It was in this capacity that he served in the campaign in France on which Goethe accompanied him in 1792. He resigned his commission in 1794.

Among the duke's cavaliers many extravagant tales were told about his amours. He was unhappily married, and certainly made no secret of being attracted by Corona Schröter, Emilia Gore, Gräfin Jeanette Luise von Werthern, Kammerrätin Crayen and others. From 1802 he had an official mistress in Karoline Jagemann, the brilliant actress and singer, whom he ennobled, with their children, in 1809, with the title of Frau von Heygendorf. Her memoirs present the lovers in a sympathetic light. Though the neglected duchess put a good face on the matter, the usual consequences of Maîtressenwirtschaft, extravagance and intrigues, were not lacking. It was apparently because of Karoline Jagemann, for instance, that Schiller's *Jungfrau von Orleans* was not, like the rest of his later plays, given its first performance in Weimar (Karoline was the only actress for the title-rôle, and the duke and the court were very well acquainted with Voltaire's *Pucelle*), and that Goethe retired from the management of the theatre, after the dispute about the staging of the *Chien d'Aubry*.

Karl August was not free, then, from the usual defects of absolute monarchs, but his peccadilloes were no more than was expected of a German princeling. At bottom he was a man of good sense. But he was decidedly fortunate in chancing on the greatest German of his day and just the educator he needed. Can anyone but a patriotic German historian believe that without Goethe Karl August's name would have been remembered for more than a generation? He was fortunately not spoiled by too much of the conventional education of a prince before he came under Goethe's influence—one has the impression that Graf von

Goerz and his assistants had found him very intractable—
and possessed by nature a sense for realities and an impatience
with shams to which the genuineness of Goethe, his outstanding moral quality, made an immediate appeal. But
under other influences, one fears, he might have become
something very like another prince who was considered
unusually promising as a young man, Karl Eugen von
Württemberg.

The machinery of government in Weimar was of the type
described above, modified a little by the influence of Prussia.
There was no nonsense about the rights of the people. The
Diet of his Estates, or rather a committee of it, was summoned regularly but at long intervals, about every six years.
It represented only a small minority of his people and was
thoroughly under his thumb, because the nobility were so
dependent on court favours. It scolded him mildly for
extravagance but agreed to the proposed taxation, its only
real function. It never initiated anything. The attitude of the
court towards it is reflected in Karl von Lyncker's description
of the 'comical' sights that were seen when the country
squires and mayors had been well plied with liquor at the
banquet of welcome to the duke's first Diet. The Estates
Treasury (the office that collected the special taxes agreed to
by the Estates) even considered itself a government department and took the duke's part against the Estates. It is not
surprising that the duke did not think highly of such an
elected assembly. When different views prevailed after the
Napoleonic Wars, he was ready as usual to make a fair
bargain, and was the only prince in the Deutscher Bund who
kept his promise to grant a constitution.

The central organs of government were the usual ones.
At the head was a 'Konseil' of three ministers and the duke
(from 1776 it consisted for several years of Herr von Fritsch,
as 'Erster Minister', Schnauss and Goethe), each member of
which made himself responsible for particular departments.
Goethe for instance was entrusted at first with mines, roads,

and waterways and later with recruiting, Herr von Fritsch with 'police'. Then there was the supreme court of justice and chief administrative body, called as usual the 'Regierung', with a Chancellor as its president. There was a 'Kammer' or treasury, presided over by a Kammerpräsident. Goethe was given this office also temporarily from 1782, when Herr von Kalb proved unreliable. Finally, for Church government and education there was the 'Oberkonsistorium', with the Oberkonsistorialpräsident, a layman, at its head and Herder, 'Generalsuperintendent' or chief of the clergy, as vice-chairman. The various parts of the scattered territories of the duke, some 33 Quadratmeilen (c. 700 sq. miles) in extent, had been inherited by the dynasty at different times and were still to some extent separately administered. So the Fürsten-tum Weimar and the Fürstentum Eisenach each had its separate Kammer and Konsistorium, though they shared a Regierung, and even the Landesportion Jena and the 'henne-bergische Ämter' (of which Ilmenau was the chief) were separate for purposes of taxation. The work of these various bodies was co-ordinated only by the duke or his immediate advisers; their decisions needed his approval and could be set aside by him. Every morning he received petitioners in person, a practice that contributed much to his popularity, for in times when there were no real newspapers and no organs of public opinion, direct access to the 'Landesvater' was the subject's one hope of redress. One might briefly describe the system of government in Weimar as patriarchal bureaucracy; patriarchal, by tradition and because of the smallness of the state, and not very efficiently bureaucratic, in imitation of greater states. In both these respects it was an unusually good specimen of the commonest type of German state in the later eighteenth century.[1]

[1] For Karl August's rule consult the studies by F. Hartung named in section B iii of the bibliography, the memoirs of K. von Lyncker and Karoline Jagemann (bibliography, section A), and the letters of Goethe and Karl August.

It would be beyond our scope to consider the efficiency of every department of state under German benevolent despotism, but we must at least enquire how the princes raised their revenue and who bore the chief burden of taxation, for the administration of finance already affected every person in the land.

We are not surprised to find that rational forethought played a much smaller part in this matter then than now, that the courts of those days lived very much from hand to mouth. The problem of finance was constantly increasing in difficulty, not merely because of the extravagant personal claims of the princes and their entourage, but because of the new responsibilities that governments were forced to take upon themselves as the structure of society became more complex, the simple machinery of the Middle Ages broke down and more central control, involving fresh expenditure, became necessary. With the disappearance of feudal services, and the consequent need for paid armies and paid officials, the princes had to imitate the Free Towns and buy the services they needed with the revenues from their crown lands and royal dues, or with money raised for the purpose by taxation or loans.

The revenue from crown lands was still the most important item on the credit side of German state budgets in the eighteenth century. Even under Frederick William I half of the state revenues of Prussia came from this source. Frederick the Great too found it necessary to devote much attention to the development of the royal demesnes. This source of income was only unimportant in states where the prince had been forced through reckless borrowing to mortgage his family possessions.

Regalities ('Regalien') were a second important source of income, one that had grown since the Middle Ages because the territorial princes had concentrated these rights in their own hands, depriving the towns, for instance, where they could, of the customs and currency rights which many had formerly possessed. The customs barriers of the towns were replaced by new ones on the boundaries of the state, on roads, bridges, rivers, that crippled German trade until the establishment of the Zollverein. There were few princes who did not also abuse their currency rights, overcoming crises temporarily at the cost of debasement of the coinage. There were sound economic reasons of course for the action of the governments against the towns, larger economic units being urgently needed. The trouble was that even the states were not large enough, and that the protectionist policy of the greater European states was being imitated by them in entirely different conditions.

The economic theory prevailing in these greater states was what is known as 'Mercantilism'. It advocated self-sufficient national units in which trade and industry were fostered by tariffs and made to give financial support to the state whose protection they enjoyed. It was a policy that could not be successfully pursued, economists think, except by countries owning undeveloped colonies which they could exploit; it may in fact be considered as the extension of the old policy of the medieval towns, which aimed at exploiting the country districts around them. In the same way the new nations used their colonies. It was a policy demanding larger units than any to be found in Germany. Even Prussian mercantilism, as we shall see later, was not a success, still less that of the average small state. It was in pursuance of this theory (particularly as put into practice by Colbert in France) that porcelain, tapestry and cloth manufactures were established in a number of states. They were nearly always worked at a loss, and provided for the most part only luxuries for the court or equipment for largely ornamental armies. They sometimes proved the starting-point for important later developments, and enriched the world with many beautiful things, but they were no more economic than the average amateur gardener's home-grown vegetables.

The only kind of export that brought in a really considerable sum to the German princes was that of men, the troops whose services were lent in return for subsidies to England, France and Holland. By this means the Landgraves of Hesse-Cassel, for instance, maintained a magnificent court for more than a century. They built themselves an elegant capital, and a palace at Wilhelmshöhe, one of their many homes, that astonished all visitors with its artificial cascades and other expensive glories. They formed one of the best collections of pictures in Germany. Sixty persons sat down with the Landgrave to dinner every day.[1] And the first of the Rothschild dynasty, Meyer Amschel, laid the foundations of his fortune by assisting Landgrave William IX.[2] Brunswick, Württemberg, Bavaria, Saxony, the Palatinate, Hanover (in 1776 under our George III), as well as smaller states like Ansbach, Hanau, Waldeck were all concerned in varying degrees in this trade, particularly at the time of the American War of Independence, a struggle watched with enthusiastic sympathy for the colonists by thinking people in Germany, when 30,000 German troops, 12,500 of whom never returned, were 'lent' by their princes to England for over half a million pounds. In Frederick I's time even Prussia lent troops, for subsidies, to the Dutch. There is ample justification for the celebrated scene in Schiller's *Kabale und Liebe* (II, 2).[3]

Taxation, the last resource of the prince's treasury, demanded, in order to be productive, a more equitable distribution of the burden and a more effective system of collection than had yet been devised. It was indirect taxation that was favoured, and in some states (particularly in Prussia under Frederick the Great) it became a serious burden. Taxes of this kind became common from the end of the seventeenth century (in imitation as usual of France). The usual form, the

[1] In 1779, when Dr Moore was there.
[2] Corti, *The Rothschilds*.
[3] Biedermann, I, 205-7, 225; v. Boehn, I, 222 ff. The standard book on the subject is: F. Kapp, *Der Soldatenhandel deutscher Fürsten*.

'Accise', was a levy on all goods offered for sale. Frederick the Great developed the system into the notorious 'Regie', managed by a host of French customs officers, armed with powers of search that extended even to private houses. But even this elaborate system was very ineffective because so much of the proceeds stuck to the Frenchmen's fingers. These indirect taxes were raised almost entirely at the expense of the common citizens of the towns. The direct taxes, where they existed, were provided almost wholly by the peasantry. Conditions varied so much in the different states, and even in different districts of the same state, that it is impossible to summarise accurately the details that are known. The one important fact that emerges is that in the country (and for that matter in the Free Towns too), the people best able to pay, being also best able to resist payment, contributed least. The country nobility were practically exempt from taxation. They paid a so-called 'Donativ' to the prince, a substitute for feudal services, which was in no sort of proportion to the taxes paid by others. Landowners who were not nobles, and peasants, paid a land tax to the prince, at rates which varied in different parts but were usually high (up to 50 per cent. of the income for instance in Bavaria), though not so high as they sound, because they were based on very old land-valuations, since the making of which the land had greatly increased in value.[1] Similarly the rich patricians of Ulm and Nürnberg, whose capital was in land, paid a very low rate in comparison with the ordinary citizens whose capital was in trade and industry; while in Frankfort the tax on capital was a small fixed sum on large fortunes, and a comparatively high rate on those below 15,000 gulden. In some provinces there was a poll tax levied at a uniform rate on every person over 14 years old, which also weighed most heavily of course on the peasant. We hear also, it is true, of special levies graduated according to capacity, in Weimar for example, but these always bore hardest on the peasant, who had so

[1] Details in Biedermann, I, 209 ff.

little ready money. It must be remembered that we are speaking here only of payments to the prince; the peasant had also to satisfy the very high demands of his landlord (Grundherr) for services and dues. There is a striking passage on the exploitation of the peasant in Weimar, a comparatively well-governed state, in one of Goethe's letters. Writing to Knebel (on 17th April 1782) he compares the peasantry, wresting a bare living from the soil, with the plant-lice he has observed in his biological studies, for as soon as these creatures have fed themselves full and green on the rose bushes, they are sucked dry in their turn by ants. 'Things have gone so far now', he adds, 'that more is consumed in a day at the top than can be produced in a day at the bottom.'

A concrete example will give a better idea of the finances of an average German state than necessarily vague general statements. As Weimar is one of the few states of that time whose finances have been competently studied (so far as they can be at this distance in time), we may conveniently take it again as our type,[1] and study the financial policy of Karl August in the first decade of his reign. When Karl August came to the throne the land was at least free from debt. His grandfather, Ernst August, and his father, Ernst August Konstantin, in his brief reign, had been extravagant, while Anna Amalie, during her Regency (1758–75), had only managed to make both ends meet because the Seven Years' War, at first a source of expense and debts for Weimar, which had to furnish a 'Reichskontingent', had proved in the end profitable through providing opportunities for selling the treasury's stocks of inferior wheat, its tenants' tithes, at an exorbitant price. But profiteering of this kind was not a permanent remedy for financial difficulties. Unfortunately there was not much wealth in the country to tax. It was an almost entirely agricultural province, and the backward farming methods practised, the so-called three-field system, kept the peasants moving in a vicious circle of constantly

[1] See for the following the works by F. Hartung referred to above.

diminishing crops and increasing burdens of debts and interest. If there was by chance a good harvest, there was no sale for the surplus, because Weimar was so far from the sea that for its wheat to reach a buyer prohibitive tolls and costs of carriage had first to be paid. When the experiment was made, later, of sending wheat to Bremen, the government lost 8000 Thalers in a very few years. There was, as we have seen, scarcely any industry or trade of which toll could be taken by the government.

The only remedy that the Konseil could suggest, at the beginning of Karl August's reign, was economy. They persuaded the young duke to agree to a fixed allowance for the expenses of court and mews (till now the treasury had been considered, as in most small states, as a glorified Privy Purse for the reigning family); they had to fix the amount at 54,000 Thalers, 10,000 more than had been so far needed, and to provide this additional sum they eventually decided on a personal levy, rejecting the alternative proposed by the treasurer, Kalb, of an indirect tax, or 'Accise', on the Prussian model. Though the poll tax was graded, from 16 Thalers for a Geheimer Rat to 4 Groschen for day labourers and rag gatherers, it bore hard on the poorer country people. By this measure and a stamp tax the situation was temporarily met, but in 1782 the duke was obliged to dismiss his treasurer for incompetence and peculation, and after his flight the treasury was found to be deeply in debt again. Goethe was now temporarily given the additional office of treasurer. He persuaded the Estates to pay off the debt by inducing the duke to accept their suggestion of a reduction of the 'army', involving the curtailing of his allowance to 30,000 Thalers. It was possible to balance the budget now without the poll tax, but the financial position was still precarious and continued to be so. None of the government's attempts to improve the economic state of the country had much effect. The duke's subjects would not or could not themselves make any serious move to improve their condition (by adopting improved methods of agriculture for instance) and the government's half-hearted measures could do little with only indifferent local officials to enforce them. Goethe complains in a report for the year 1786 of the 'pettiness' of conditions in small states. It was impossible even to keep the duke down to his allowance (says Vehse). It was Goethe's pent up disgust at the futility of his uncongenial labours in this atmosphere, as much as anything else, that drove him to Italy in 1786, for an activity that produced no results, as he said, made him furious.

PART II

THE OLD ORDER OF SOCIETY
NOBILITY AND PEASANTRY

Chapter I

THE NOBILITY IN GENERAL

The loose political structure of Germany naturally favoured the utmost variety in its social life. State differed from state, and class from class, and though there were influences here as in other countries tending to level out differences of this kind, the process was slow and frequently interrupted. Goethe speaks more than once of the lack of 'general culture' in Germany, contrasting it unfavourably with France and England. It was one of the difficulties that the writers of his age, with their new ambition to reach a national public, felt most. 'Because no general culture can establish itself in our country, every part keeps to its own ways and prides itself on its oddness', says Goethe. Or again: 'We are a collection of private individuals.... Every one is content with the views of his province, his town or his own mind, and we may have a long time to wait before we attain to a creditable average standard of cultivation'. Knigge, contrasting the task of the German writer or actor with that of a Frenchman, with the taste of Paris to guide him and the confidence that his allusions will be understood in every part of France, asks how it is possible for any writer to appeal at once to 'the good-natured, naïve, sometimes rather materialistic Bavarian, the refined smooth-tongued Saxon, the heavy Westphalian, the polite Frenchified Rhinelander, the blunt North Saxon'. And Justus Möser, in a similar passage in his *Patriotische*

Phantasien, declares that the Germans are even reduced to swearing in French for lack of a national oath.

Local differences were naturally most marked among those classes of society that saw least of the outer world, peasants, country gentlemen and the inhabitants of small towns. They were least noticeable in the nobility of the courts, who were not considered educated unless they travelled, and who were influenced by the arbiters of European taste in Paris. What one might call the horizontal cleavages between the 'estates' of society were far wider in fact than the vertical ones between states. A description of the social condition of the country at this period must almost of necessity follow the social strata in its arrangement rather than geographical regions, and it will be convenient to discuss the old-established classes, nobility and peasantry, the relics of feudalism, before the more recent growth, the middle class.

In each state big or small, there was a similar pyramid of social groups rising tier on tier to the ruler. At the base in each was the peasantry, not an undifferentiated mass, as we shall see, but relatively homogeneous. At the apex was the aristocracy, graded from the prince down to the simple country gentleman, who would often lead a life hardly distinguishable from that of a peasant. In between came the middle class of town-dwellers, again with many subdivisions, overlapping both nobility (in its patricians and higher officials) and peasantry (in its semi-agricultural tradesmen), and forming, at least at the end of the century, the backbone of the people.

It was not the first time that the middle class had played a dominant part in the life of the country. In the later Middle Ages the towns had been politically powerful and culturally highly developed, at the culmination of a long period of growth, the history of which we shall glance at later. Economic changes had gradually made it possible for a middle class to break through the old, purely hereditary stratification of society, as the new class of knights had done at an earlier period. 'Towards the end of the twelfth century the re-shuffling of social classes, in progress since the early Middle Ages, was almost complete. New occupational groups on an essentially economic basis had taken the place of the old hereditary classes. What was important now was similarity of occupation and through it of way of living, while the features formerly decisive lost their prominence. In the thirteenth century it is already quite usual to speak of peasants, burghers, knights and clergy as separate "estates".'[1] The corporate feeling of the towns had on the whole tended to obliterate distinctions between classes; serfs had become free, and first merchants and then craftsmen had entered the ruling class of patricians, originally purely aristocratic. It seemed probable in the age of the Reformation that the lower nobility would coalesce with the richer patricians and learned professions—much as they did in England—but the up-heavals of the sixteenth and seventeenth centuries prevented it.

At the beginning of the eighteenth century then the medieval estates, nobility, burghers, peasants were still sharply distinguished from each other. In spite of, or perhaps because of, the fact that the basis in reason for these class distinctions was fast disappearing, they had hardened in Germany into something very like a caste system. The French Revolution was the next turning point. Germany began to follow England and France. Within the separate states, as in the towns earlier, men began to lose their con-sciousness of differences of rank as they became aware of their membership of one community. The legal distinctions between nobleman and commoner were then gradually abolished, though the distinctions in the law of the Empire between Fürsten, Grafen and Herren, Reichsritter, Reichs-städter and Reichsbauern were jealously maintained till the end of the old Reich in 1806.[2]

[1] L. v. Ebengreuth, *Kultur der Gegenwart*, II, 2. 1, p. 297.
[2] Cf. H. Brunner, *Grundzüge der deutschen Rechtsgeschichte*, 1901, p. 222.

The change of view may be seen in such small things as the use of titles in public documents. In the Durlach church registers, Roller tells us, the Hofprediger divided people in the early part of the century into three grades. Noblemen were always referred to as 'der gnädige Herr, die gnädige Frau', their daughters as 'Fräulein'; the 'Honoratioren', that is, the better-class townspeople, higher officials, professional men with university training, etc., were styled 'Herr' and 'Frau', their daughters 'Jungfer'; the rest, craftsmen, farmers, labourers and so on were not even mistered. At the end of the century, however, the predicate 'gnädig' was reserved for persons of princely rank, others, though of good birth, simply sharing the 'Herr' and 'Frau' of the Honoratioren.

Even after the French Revolution Mme de Staël could write with truth: 'En Allemagne chacun est à son rang, à sa place, comme à son poste, et l'on n'a pas besoin de tournures habiles, de parenthèses, de demi-mots, pour exprimer les avantages de naissance ou de titre que l'on se croit sur son voisin'. It seemed to her that in France one rank had not been definitely marked off from another in this way even at the end of the Ancien Régime, when the distinctions between classes were more marked, we are told, than ever before. 'La bonne compagnie, en Allemagne, c'est la cour; en France, c'étaient tous ceux qui pouvaient se mettre sur un pied d'égalité avec elle, et tous pouvaient l'espérer, et tous aussi pouvaient craindre de n'y jamais parvenir.'[1] Lady Montagu, Lord Chesterfield, Dr Moore and the author of the *Introduction to the knowledge of Germany* all speak in the same strain, but there is evidence enough in the German memoirs and general literature of the time. Knigge speaks of the privileges of the aristocracy, the exclusiveness of the courts, the lack of influence of the merchant class in the national life, von Loen of the absurdity of the view held in Germany that no nobleman may engage in commerce, and there are scores of novels and domestic dramas which take this class conflict as their

---

[1] *De l'Allemagne*, part I, chap. XI.

main theme. Schiller's *Kabale und Liebe* and Grossmann's *Nicht mehr als sechs Schüsseln* were only the most famous.[1] The nobility were taught from their childhood to look upon themselves as a class apart. They differed from the middle class in legal status, standard of living, social customs and moral code, in their education, their taste in art and literature, in the very language they habitually used.

But the Bürger, the more or less educated middle-class citizen of the towns, insisted equally narrowly on every privilege and tradition that marked him off from the peasantry. There were well-marked social divisions among the Bürger themselves, for the 'scholars' who had attended the Grammar School and perhaps a university and taken up a profession, or entered an old-established firm of wholesale merchants, considered themselves superior to the mere retailers (Krämer) and craftsmen, and eligible to enter, by marriage or otherwise, the ranks of the patricians of their town.

Then there were occupational groups that cut across the older caste-like divisions. The clergy and military formed systems for themselves, though family tradition played a big part in their recruitment and in determining the status of their members. Army officers were almost always aristocrats, private soldiers peasants, or the riff-raff of the towns. As to the churches, a distinction must be made between Catholic and Protestant, and in the Catholic Church, between the higher clergy and the simple priests. The higher Catholic clergy and the members of cathedral chapters and most orders, whether of men or women, were always of good family. In the Catholic south and the Rhineland the Church provided ecclesiastical princedoms for many younger sons of ruling houses, and a life of dignified leisure in religious foundations, by no means severe now in their discipline, for a whole multitude of lesser aristocrats. The lower Catholic

---

[1] For some titles see K. Brombacher, *Der deutsche Bürger im Literatur-spiegel von Lessing bis Sternheim*, Munich, 1920.

clergy would usually and the Protestant clergy of all ranks almost invariably be of middle-class or peasant origin. This explains why the Protestant clergy did not enjoy the same social standing as the Catholic. The Protestant theologians were the poorest and most despised students in the universities, for it was almost impossible for a needy student to maintain himself in any other faculty. When after years of private tutoring they obtained a living, they had usually more book knowledge than their Catholic colleagues, but less breeding, having enjoyed fewer social contacts.[1]

By the eighteenth century, the numerous 'Beamten' in the government service formed a group that was in many ways just as truly a separate Stand or estate as church or army. Its upper categories enjoyed high consideration, resembling the nobility in their way of life and possessing even some of its legal privileges. Most of the higher officials were university men, and throughout the century academically trained men in every profession were steadily rising in social esteem and power. If we take away the contributions to intellectual and artistic culture made by the Protestant clergy, professors, teachers, doctors and 'Beamten', that is, by the various categories of the educated middle class, there is very little left. The prestige of this class was so great by the end of the century that the life of the princes themselves was, in Lamprecht's phrase, 'verbürgerlicht', but as the frock-coated middle class approached the aristocracy, they drew away from those who worked with their hands, and the

1 Cf. e.g. J. M. v. Loen, *Der Adel*, p. 57: 'The Roman priesthood is respected because many people of good birth and excellent talent devote themselves to the Church, and the Protestant clergy are despised because they are usually of lower class origin and display little magnanimity and Christian love in their doctrinal wranglings', or *Sophiens Reise nach Sachsen*, by the Protestant minister Hermes, where a minister who speaks French provokes surprised comment. Most Prediger, especially if themselves sons of the manse, looked on French, we are told, as a wicked language, being poor and having had little time or opportunity to become acquainted with people of fashion. They are contrasted in this respect with French abbés, who were men of the world.

unity of the 'folk' was more a thing of the past than ever. All the Romantics could do was to dream about it.

We pass now to a consideration of the various classes of society in turn, first to what was left of the feudal organisation of society on the basis of land-tenure, and then to the class that had made itself an indispensable element in society by skilled personal services, whether of hand or brain.

The status of the aristocracy had been defined in the course of the centuries in law. To understand their way of life in the eighteenth century we must first know something of their legal privileges, which were still numerous and important, though the duties that had originally justified the granting of privileges had almost entirely vanished. A nobleman had no longer to furnish and lead a certain number of men in his prince's army. If he served in it or assumed any court or state office, he did so for a material reward or because it suited his own interests, not because it was looked upon as his duty. The sense of duty was only invoked as a motive for state service by Frederick William I and Frederick II in Prussia, supported by other motives and not always successfully.

It was the obligation of military service that had originally justified the exemption of the aristocracy, which still held good, from nearly all rates and taxes and from excise duties. The principle of taxation followed in the eighteenth century, as we have seen, was to tax those who were powerless to resist. A gentleman was not only freed from the obligation of military service (a privilege that was shared by the better middle class); he was also, unlike the Bürger, relieved of the inconvenience and expense of billeting. His was in fact the only class in the state that was 'free' in the sense that nothing was demanded of it.

This class also enjoyed many prescriptive rights, usually fortified by law. It had an almost exclusive right to the chief offices under the government and at court, only the lower ill-paid posts being normally open to Bürger, though the

attempts of the nobility to preserve this so-called Indigenatsrecht were occasionally frustrated, as we have seen, for
instance by Frederick William I, in Prussia. It was possible
too to give a middle-class man who was desired for high
office the necessary standing by having him ennobled *ad hoc*
—we think of Goethe in Weimar—but this did not happen
very often. The nobleman enjoyed further special privileges
('Schriftsässigkeit') under criminal law; he could generally
claim to be tried by the central courts of the state instead of
by the local 'Ämter', could more easily get off with a fine
or arrest in his own home instead of imprisonment, and was
always in practice more lightly treated than others, even
serious offences often going unpunished.[1] If the worst came
to the worst he could claim to be beheaded instead of being
hanged.

There were many rights of the aristocracy connected with
the ownership of land. They alone could entail their estates.
In most states they alone might own 'adlige Güter' or
manorial estates. So Herder was ennobled for instance by
the Elector of Bavaria in 1801, so that one of his sons might
hold a small estate in Bavaria which he wished to farm.
A right usually possessed by the nobility as landowners and
very important, especially in colonised lands like East Prussia,
was that of patrimonial jurisdiction, with all the power it
conferred. The right to representation in the provincial diet
was another, hardly so important, as we saw, at this period.
Noble landowners could exact dues from merchants or
craftsmen making use of their land. They often had the gift
of a living in the Church.

In western Germany, as in France, it was their game rights
that aroused perhaps the loudest public protest. This is not
the place to go into all their complexity, the right to 'hohe
Jagd' (stag-hunting, etc.), 'mittlere Jagd' (for roe-deer, wild
boar, wolf, etc.), or 'niedere Jagd' (for hares, rabbits,
partridges, etc.) and the struggles for their possession between

---

[1] For examples see von Boehn, *op. cit.* I, p. 541.

prince and squire and peasant. It was the peasantry that
always suffered. J. M. von Loen tells us how they were constantly being requisitioned to act as beaters, as well as forced to
lie out all night in the fields like beasts, to keep the game off
their crops.[1] Literary protests, like this passage and the satire
Die Parforce-Jagd[2] by Freiherr von Gemmingen, were not
entirely due to the excessive humanitarianism of the age.
Complaints occur in almost every state. We saw above how
Goethe for instance had to urge Karl August, in December
1784, to do away with the wild boar that he allowed to roam
freely on the Ettersberg, to the annoyance of the whole
neighbourhood and the hurt of the peasantry, but Karl
August was by no means a bad offender compared with
monomaniacs like the Landgraves of Hesse-Cassel in the
early part of the century.

Not the least prized—and resented—of the privileges of
the gentry were the 'prééminences honorifiques', as the
French called them, the symbolic marks of distinction that
a man of birth could claim. The peerage and gentry had the
'pas', took precedence, before the commoner on all public
occasions. They were constantly squabbling among themselves about questions of precedence, as Lady Montagu
discovered in Ratisbon and Vienna. There is at least one
instance of a 'war' between two tiny states resulting from
such contentions (amusingly described by Gustav Freytag).[3]
The aristocracy could claim, in addition to their titles and
the use of *von*, *zu*, *auf*, *aus* before their surnames, the super-
scriptions *Edelgestrenge*, *Hochwohl-*, *Wohl-*, or *Hochgeborene*,
Ew. Gnaden, *Gnädiger* or *Gestrenger Herr*, and the other
uncouth formulae that had to be mastered by every complete
man of the world. The insistence of the Germans on these
minutiae already provided amusement for their neighbours.
Lord Chesterfield tells his son that he had known many a

---

[1] *Freye Gedanken vom Hof*, 3rd ed. p. 28.
[2] Printed e.g. in *Deutsche Literatur*, Reihe Politische Dichtung. 1.
[3] *Bilder aus der deutschen Vergangenheit*, IV (Der Wasunger Krieg).

letter returned unopened because one title in twenty had been omitted in the direction.

Like the English *Esquire*, many of these appellations later suffered a social decline. A modest visitor to Bavaria may now discover to his surprise that according to the envelopes of his letters he is *Wohlgeboren*. The normal modern use of *Fräulein* is also strictly irregular. It was only beginning to lose its original sense, in which it was applied only to young ladies of good birth, about the middle of the eighteenth century. 'Twenty years ago', says J. M. von Loen in 1752, 'the daughters of Augsburg patricians were addressed as *Jungfer*, but now they are no doubt *Fräulein* like the rest.' 'In Breslau', he adds, exaggerating, no doubt, 'the young women in small shops and at herring stalls are styled *gnädiges Fräulein*.' Even in 1816 one might read in a German newspaper that the post-offices in a north German town had been instructed not to deliver letters to middle-class girls if the writer had called them Fräulein on the envelope.[1] Hence Gretchen's retort to Faust: 'Bin weder *Fräulein*, weder schön' and Marthe's remark: 'Der Herr dich für ein *Fräulein* hält'.

It was impossible in the long run to prevent other classes from imitating the aristocracy in externals by sumptuary laws, however elaborate. Strictly, only the gentry were entitled to wear swords, though well-to-do citizens and anyone who wished to pass as a man of fashion imitated them in this as in the wearing of silk stockings and powdered hair. Even the little sons of better-class townfolk wore them with their Sunday clothes, as we see for instance from Goethe's tale, *Der neue Paris*. They could further distinguish themselves by the use of plumed hats—we hear of many a duel on this point between nobleman and commoner at the universities— by putting their servants into livery, displaying coats of arms, using special seals, wearing pink dominos at masquerades, and a thousand and one such trifles.

Most of these badges of rank were the outward signs of

[1] *Anno Dazumal*, II, p. 318 (? *Vossische Zeitung*).

a special standard and manner of living. It was often impossible to imitate the one without the other. This was true for instance of dress. The fashions for both ladies and gentlemen, extravagant in both senses of the word, were a tolerably effective mark of distinction when rank and wealth still went together and the aristocracy were the only people who lived a life of leisure and could avoid exposing themselves to the elements. No one else could afford these brocades and silks and damasks, the lace and embroidery and jewels, and all the skilled work that went to the making of the lady's hooped skirts, long trains and towering coiffures, or the gentleman's fancy vests, lace cuffs and powdered wig. And no one leading an active life out of doors could have worn them. To be 'natural' in Rousseau's sense was in any case too dull and plebeian. In the absence of other occupations, a game was needed that had complex rules. In classical French tragedy, as in the absolutism of Louis XIV, the pride characteristic of the Renaissance in man's control through reason over what happens to exist finds noble expression, and we may find a remnant of it even in eighteenth-century fashions. Man, as the measure of things, had to improve on nature, whether it was in trimming gardens into formal patterns, or forcing a girl's waist into V-shaped corsets. Native grace and art could turn life even under these conventions into a second nature in conformity with reason, as reason was then conceived.[1] The Revolution reminded the world that it was a reason in blinkers, for the foundations of this life, beautiful as it might sometimes be, had long been insecure.

In Max von Boehn's books on fashion the 'systematic exaggerations that are the essence of women's fashions' can be followed in detail.[2] At the end of the seventeenth century it was the headdress that was inordinately high (the *fontange*),

[1] See for instance Goethe's praise of the countess in her finery, in *Wilhelm Meisters Lehrjahre*, Book 3.
[2] *Die Mode, Menschen und Moden im 17., 18. und 19. Jahrhundert*, 6 vols., Munich, 1913 and later.

then from about 1720 coiffures were low and skirts began to expand, with the return of the hooped skirt in its various forms (it had been common in the sixteenth century, as we see from Velasquez portraits). This remained an item of ceremonial court dress in France till the Revolution and abroad even longer, but for more general use it began to go out in the 60's, and coiffures rose again, rose as high as chandeliers would allow them and higher, to the great profit of ladies' hairdressers, a new necessity in court towns. As visits to the hairdresser were expensive, even great ladies often could not afford to have their hair done more than once a week; others went for as long as a month, we are told, though it is difficult to believe it in view of the practical difficulties, not to speak of the lack of cleanliness this entailed, but cleanliness was not a strong point even with the most refined. The hair was always powdered, and this necessitated the liberal use of rouge, for white hair 'killed' the natural complexion. Of course it was impossible even for the most fashionable to live always in parade dress. More comfortable costumes were invented for everyday occasions. Many forms of négligé are heard of, of which the loose *Adrienne* (originally a maternity robe) and the tight-fitting *Caraco* (imitated from a tail-coat) were perhaps the best-known types. In both of them the lower part of the dress formed one whole with the jacket, whereas in full dress the upper skirt or manteau was separate from the tight-fitting bodice. The manteau was open in front to show the highly ornamented hooped skirt, and it had a train behind. The négligés, being of the nature of long coats, were open in the same way. In England the *Adrienne* came to be closed in front, giving the *robe anglaise* worn by the sitters of Reynolds and Gainsborough, while the *Caraco* developed into the tailor-made costume. The English ladies were the first to give up elaborate coiffures and rouge (from the 60's), but both were still fashionable in Germany in the 80's.

There were few changes in the dress of gentlemen through–

out the period. At first they wore the long, closed, wide-sleeved *justaucorps* over a long vest, with knee breeches and silk stockings. Later, coat-tails were stiffened and coats worn open, then vests, sleeves and coat-tails were reduced, following military fashions, and the prototype of modern evening dress was already recognisable. But the same bright and delicate materials were used as for ladies' dresses, with braid and embroidery on coat and vest and a lavish display of lace at neck and sleeves. For travelling and ordinary occasions 'English suits' became more and more popular. In these, coat and vest were of comfortable cut and heavier material; the colours were more sober, though brighter than what is worn now; leather breeches and top-boots completed the costume for out-door wear, but it was only the 'genius' of the 70's who insisted on wearing them on all occasions, as a sign of the return to nature. Wigs, of various shapes according to the status of the wearer and the particular occasion, held their own until the 80's. Long before this a good many had begun to follow the Prussian army fashion and wear a pig-tail (whence the expression 'Zopfzeit'), and from the 70's the younger men, even in good society, infected by the passion for the natural, began to wear 'their own hair', so that by the time of the French Revolution wigs were already old-fashioned and by 1800 a mere survival. The Protestant clergy, the last class to adopt them at the beginning of the century, were the last to leave them off at the end.

It was impossible of course for the nobility to avoid all intercourse with the vulgar, but they made every effort on public occasions to keep social inferiors at a distance. In the theatre they sat apart from the common man, either in the front seats or in boxes, a device for securing their privacy first thought of in Paris. At public concerts too a space was left between the chairs of the quality and the rest. At ceremonious court concerts, on the analogy of the solar system, the very great were left surrounded by a number of empty chairs in direct proportion to their rank. In the village church, the local nobility would of course have separate pews and a family vault. In the council chamber and in lecture-rooms (like the law lecture-room at Leipzig), where noble and commoner met for a like purpose, each class was assigned its separate benches. Even at the few schools like the Karlsschule in Württemberg, where boys of good birth and others were educated together, the nobles wore distinctive silver epaulettes, dined at different tables, slept in separate dormitories and used bathing places at the river parted by a raised bank.[1] The fashionable world had its separate assemblies and balls, to which the common citizen was not admitted. From the emperor down to the penniless widow of a ruined Reichsritter, the nobility considered themselves in fact, with rare exceptions, to be a different race from the untitled mass. There were even those who thought that in a future life too they would receive differential treatment.[2]

If so much deference was due to any of the gentry, it can be imagined how much was expected by even 'duodecimo' princes. When Karl August visited a village in 1776, the peasants received him, Goethe tells us, 'with music, salutes of mortars, rustic arches of honour, garlands, cakes, dancing, fireworks, serenades and so on', and this kind of welcome was no more than what was expected.[3] Because the Fürst von Wallerstein's secretary, who had been sent ahead to prepare his master's coming, did not have all the bells of a village rung to greet him, but merely arranged a procession of notables, accompanied by the blare of trumpets and the firing of pistols, he was severely reprimanded, and reminded that 'nothing was to be neglected, that might bring home to a subject, through outward signs, the majesty of his lord'.[4] This lord ruled 36,000 people in a province about 320 sq. miles in extent, and the village in question was not even in his own lands.

---

[1] Berger, *Schiller*, 1; Nicolai, *Reisen*, vol. 10.
[2] Freifrau Karoline von Wöllworth Pahl—quoted by v. Boehn, 1, 545.
[3] Letter to Aug. zu Stolberg, 20 May 1776.
[4] K. H. von Lang, *Aus der bösen alten Zeit*, p. 147.

What made these aristocratic privileges particularly galling to those among the middle class who did not accept the position unquestioningly was the fact that the historical justification for them had vanished. Hereditary privileges had not seemed arbitrary when they involved hereditary duties. Institutions had lagged behind the development of the life of society to such a dangerous degree that it was not only Mephistopheles who thought:

> Es erben sich Gesetz' und Rechte
> Wie eine ewige Krankheit fort.

The various ranks of society had never in reality been closed castes made up of a limited number of families, though they all tried to make themselves so in times of declining prestige. No very profound study of the history of the different grades of the aristocracy is required to prove that each grade had been very considerably diluted in the course of time.

It is not necessary for the present purpose to attempt to trace the history of the nobility back to its obscure origins amongst the Germanic tribes, but it is of interest to note the source of the distinction, carefully made in the eighteenth century, between 'hoher Adel' and 'niederer Adel'. The 'hoher Adel' were all those who had the right to a seat and vote in the Reichstag, from the Kurfürsten down to the Reichsgrafen. They claimed descent from those free knights of the Middle Ages, who besides being of noble descent had held fiefs in return for military or administrative services. In the Middle Ages a subordinate class of knights grew up in Germany, recruited from the Ministeriales, men not of noble birth and usually not freemen, who as direct servants of the king or some great lord gained the reward of a fief. As influential associates of the great, resembling them in their way of life and particularly in their tenure of considerable feudal estates, they soon came to be looked upon as a free feudal nobility. Their lands and privileges became hereditary in their families and in a generation or two they succeeded

in closing their ranks to newcomers. A candidate for knighthood had now to be himself the son of a knight. This is the
origin of the 'niederer Adel' of modern times. The 'lower
nobility' in the eighteenth century was further subdivided
into the 'Reichsadel', or 'Reichsunmittelbare Ritterschaft',
mostly to be found in Swabia and the south-west corner of
Germany, acknowledging no lord but the emperor and no
court but the supreme courts of the Empire, and the 'Landes-
adel', who were subject to the prince of the territory in
which their estates lay. As the feudal system decayed, it
became usual from the time of Karl IV on for the emperor
to raise commoners to the nobility even if they possessed no
land and performed no feudal services. The higher nobility
saw to it that the emperor did not abuse his privilege, at least
as far as the higher ranks were concerned, and insisted that
all candidates should be in possession of estates held from the
emperor direct. They could insist that even if the Kaiser
conferred a title, its holder would not be given a seat as a
peer in the Reichstag unless they approved of him, and in
point of fact only half a dozen men were so dignified during
the last century and a half of the Empire.[1]

The lower nobility tried to be equally exclusive, but they
could not so easily prevent the Kaiser from making use of his
power. The Kurfürsten of Saxony and Bavaria, when
Reichsvikare, were particularly generous with letters-patent,
and other princes, for example the kings of Prussia, claimed
and exercised the same right. The Catholic 'Stifte', cathedral
chapters, and any other aristocratic bodies which had the
power in their own hands, retaliated by refusing to admit
anyone to their ranks with less than a certain fixed number
of noble ancestors, generally four, but a claimant for admission to the cathedral chapter of Trier, and even to the
masked balls in Mainz, had to prove the blood of every one
of his ancestors back to his great-great-grandparents to have

---

[1] R. Koser, in *Kultur der Gegenwart*, Teil II, Abt. V, 1, p. 248.

been blue beyond reproach, a pedigree of sixteen quarterings (*Ahnen*) being demanded.

For a time doctors of law were considered to have the rank of noblemen, and there was the possibility of the development of a *noblesse de robe* as in France, but the Jurists did not manage to consolidate their position, and by the eighteenth century a doctorate did not carry this privilege any longer. It was in fact not 'standesgemäss' for a young man of rank, if he had passed the examinations for the doctorate, to make use of the title. The title of Hofrat was far more highly rated at court than any doctorate.

Though educated people in Germany, as in France, were coming to value personal merit more highly than birth, there were rich merchants who were ready to pay large sums to the Imperial treasury for titles, in spite of the knowledge that they would not be recognised by the existing nobility. Joseph II made financiers into noblemen by the dozen; in his time it cost in all about 20,000 Gulden to become a count (5952 Gulden in fees), 6000 to become a baron (3015 Gulden in fees), and 386 Gulden in fees to be a mere Adliger ('von-').[1] J. M. von Loen tells us that in the large Free Towns like Frankfort-on-Main and Nürnberg, the new nobility were not highly esteemed, while in Hamburg, Lübeck, Bremen and Basle, towns with a really active trade, a title of nobility was not esteemed at all and the nobles had been excluded from the council.[2] If this is true, it had not always been so, for in the flourishing days of the Free Towns, in South-west Germany particularly, a great many retired merchants had purchased themselves estates and titles of nobility; the consequent loss of brains and capital is even one of the causes suggested for the decline of the old Free Towns in trade and industry.

The political developments sketched in Part I had removed

---

[1] v. Boehn, I, 544. It cost Schiller, in 1802, 428 Gulden 30 Kr. when through Karl August's recommendation he was raised to the nobility by the Emperor. (Berger, *Schiller*, II, p. 596.)

[2] *Der Adel*, 1752, pp. 128, 129.

most of the rational grounds for the privileges still enjoyed by the aristocracy in the eighteenth century. The lower nobility in particular, as such, had almost ceased to perform any useful military or administrative functions since the breakdown of feudalism and the development of paid standing armies and a paid permanent civil service. Many of their number were to be found in the state service, but for the same material rewards as attracted the middle class too. If they insisted on the local nobility's first claim to high office ('Indigenatsrechte'), it was to maintain their privileges and in the hope of obtaining lucrative posts or sinecures. They became less and less conscious of having any duties in this respect, though it was clear to anyone who looked into the history of the matter that they had been exempted from taxation, for instance, because they served the state in arms, just as their ancestors had been given fiefs for administrative or military services rendered. In both cases the reward had become hereditary, but not the duty. It is true that in Prussia the Great Elector and his successors made excellent use of the nobility, but the severe measures needed to re-establish a tradition of state service are a sufficient indication of the unwillingness of their subjects to serve them. No other rulers attempted anything of the kind. As to the higher nobility, they had become, as we have seen, rulers in their own right, and were as little mindful of any obligations to the emperor as the Landadel was of any to them. They assumed, however, full responsibility for the government of their own states and in so far justified their position.

Those of the country nobility who still managed their own estates had on these grounds a good claim to a privileged position, one almost as good in its way as that of the petty princes, who were often little more than glorified squires themselves. Even if not directly useful in a military or administrative way they were, as landlords, an essential factor in the economic system and had important functions to perform. In the management of their estates, the encouragement of good husbandry, the maintenance of order and dispensing of justice in the squire's court, they could if they liked be princes in small, with a vast power for good— and of course for evil—over the peasants on their land. Moreover, they had as landlords the right to a seat in the Landtag and, if it ever met, they could, in combination with their fellows, bring some pressure to bear on the government of their small state. There were here and there German Sir Roger de Coverleys—we find a similar type described in Eichendorff's reminiscences, and occasional references to patriarchal squires occur in books of travel, and essays in publications like the Moral Weeklies and Möser's *Patriotische Phantasien*, as well as in novels and dramas. On the whole we should perhaps not expect the good squires to be so often mentioned as the bad, who are certainly numerous enough in literature. But there were no village Hampdens amongst the squires of Germany. They never played the same political rôle there as in England. One of the main reasons for this, and for the neglect of their estates by so many absentee landlords, was the attraction of the courts. As in France in the age of absolutism, the courts offered, to those who had the *entrée* to them, political power and wealth, social esteem and display, the society of their fellows and refined luxury. No wonder that so many noble families preferred to spend most of their time at the capital. But though occasionally a source of gain, court life was too extravagant for the resources of most noble families, and necessitated the delegation of their responsibilities as landlords to paid servants. Extortionate demands on the tenantry by the extravagant lord and his often irresponsible bailiff, mismanagement and debts were the result.

Besides the more than occasional inefficiency of the aristocracy as landlords there was another reason that weakened their claims to privileges on economic grounds, namely that there were many other citizens who were just as important in the economy of the country but who enjoyed no such social rewards. J. M. von Loen draws an interesting contrast between the life of a Frankfort merchant's wife and that of a country lady, and asks pertinently which of these is the real 'lady'.[1]

If the merchant of the towns challenged the exclusiveness of the nobles on economic grounds, the cultivated middle classes generally, and particularly those academically trained, could claim that they were the real leaders in many branches of intellectual culture and art. In the age of chivalry, the knights had been the creators and patrons of literature, as well as the indispensable defenders and local governors of the country and owners and controllers of most of its real wealth, the land. The towns and the princes had taken one after the other of these functions from them, until only those concerned with the ownership of land were left. It might at least have happened, as it did to some extent in Italy, France and England, that the privileged and sheltered aristocracy would maintain spiritual, intellectual and artistic values in an increasingly materialistic world.

The nobility as a whole did not, however, contribute very much to intellectual life either creatively or by encouraging the work of others. Over and over again we are told that their badge in the first half of the century was ignorance, and in the second half they only slowly followed in the footsteps of the bourgeoisie. The phrase which Goethe uses in his notes for the continuation of *Dichtung und Wahrheit* about the Weimar court as he found it in 1775 is: 'Gutmütige Beschränktheit, die sich zur wissenschaftlichen und literaren Kultur emporzuheben sucht'.[2] Their peers in England and France

[1] J. M. v. Loen, *Der Adel*, 1752, pp. 134 ff.

[2] *Goethe-Jahrbuch*, 1907, XXVIII, 9. For the earlier period cf. *Wilhelm Meisters Lehrjahre*, VI, where the Schöne Seele is made to say: 'Die Leute, mit denen ich umgeben war, hatten keine Ahnung von Wissenschaften; es waren deutsche Hofleute, und diese Klasse hatte damals nicht die mindeste Kultur'. Cf. also J. M. v. Loen, *Freye Gedanken vom Hof*, 3rd ed. Frankfort and Leipzig, 1768, p. 21: 'Die Unwissenheit ist beinahe das Kennzeichen einer vornehmen Geburt'. See further Knigge, *Umgang mit Menschen*, 3. Teil, 3. Kap., Biedermann, *op. cit.* II, 73, and M. v. Boehn, *op. cit.* I, 543.

looked on them for the most part as ignorant boors, and this judgment seems to be borne out by their poor record in literature and science.[1] The phrase put into the mouth of Olearius in *Götz von Berlichingen*: 'So gelehrt wie ein Deutscher von Adel' hid, like so much else in the play, a contemporary reference. It was fashionable indeed at most German courts to take a mild interest in literature, especially of the lighter kind, and as there was no German literature of general interest to speak of till late in the century, it was natural enough that French should be favoured. But German noblemen really cultivated even in French literature were rare exceptions. The majority were content if they could carry on a conversation in passable French, or at least lard their German with 'French' words,[2] and appear not to be ignorant of popular French writers. Almost all considered it beneath the dignity of a nobleman to desire any genuine scholarship. It was particularly difficult for women to cultivate their minds without losing in esteem. 'Learned women had been made ridiculous', says the Schöne Seele in *Wilhelm Meister*, 'and people could not bear even well read ones, probably because it was thought impolite to put so many ignorant men to shame.' Of course there were brilliant exceptions at Darmstadt, Brunswick, and Weimar, which we shall deal with later, and in encouragement of the fine arts and architecture the nobility had a better record—though

[1] Biedermann (II, i, 133) mentions a few names of aristocratic scholars and writers from the first half of the century, none of them very eminent: Herr v. Tschirnhausen, H. v. Seckendorff, H. v. Bünau-Dahlen, Baron v. Boyneburg, Graf v. Manteuffel, Frh. v. Münchhausen. In the second half there were of course more. In literature one may mention the Stolbergs, M. A. v. Thümmel, the Humboldts, and the less distinguished Weimar wits, H. v. Einsiedel, S. v. Seckendorff. There were many cultivated men of birth in high office: Hardenberg, Stein, Vincke, Schön. A certain number of salons were not without importance, such as those of Graf Stadion at Biberach and Fürstin Gallitzin at Münster.

[2] A young lady in Weimar for instance was capable of saying that she had received a 'grande gronde' from her mother because her 'terrière coiffure' was not 'goûteuse' (v. Lyncker, p. 16).

here again they were no more creative than an American millionaire. The German aristocracy could not therefore have rationally defended their privileges in the eighteenth century on the grounds of their services to culture.

As to their influence on manners, the evidence is almost wholly unfavourable, but it must be remembered that many of our witnesses were scarcely impartial, as bourgeois themselves. Everywhere in these middle-class writings we read of the vices of the courts and their disintegrating influence on the life of the country. The wicked aristocrats were contrasted with the virtuous middle class in one 'bourgeois drama' and novel after another. Courtiers are represented as being, for the most part, selfish, unprincipled, extravagant, licentious, addicted to gambling and drink and every kind of excess. Mephistopheles is made to tell us 'Den Bösen ist man los, die Bösen sind geblieben. Du nennst mich *Herr Baron*, so ist die Sache gut'. But of course the majority of courtiers could not claim to be so distinguished even in iniquity. What is probable is that, through the influence of the Thirty Years' War, the weakening of religious sanctions, the growth of materialistic thought in France and England, and the enjoyment by the aristocracy of power without responsibility, the moral standards of the age of the Reformation (never of course observed by everyone in Germany) had lost most of their meaning for the court classes. Except in pietistic courts, it was decidedly bad form to be 'virtuous'. Most of us would not condemn the life of the eighteenth-century aristocrat quite so strongly to-day as our grandfathers did, as Biedermann does for instance in his *Deutschland im achtzehnten Jahrhundert*, both because the bourgeois values have been rather shaken since then both by thinkers and by events, and because we have learnt to see morals themselves in evolution. Even the bourgeoisie of the time were divided in their attitude towards aristocratic ways of life. What one half of them condemned, not without a hint of concealed envy in some cases—one notes the eagerness with which backstairs scandal was sought after—the other half, particularly in court towns, fostered with all their might if it served their own interests. They had too little independence for their criticism to possess much force. One must in fact realise that it was only in theory that the same ethical ideals held for the whole community. In practice a working balance had to be reached between the very different ideals, different in historical origin and different in social background, of quite distinct classes of society.

We can form some idea of what the German aristocracy in the eighteenth century consciously aimed at in life, from a study of the type of education which was given to their sons in that age. This was the same in all essentials for the higher and the lower nobility, and was imitated by the patricians in the towns. In the course of the seventeenth century the education of the nobleman had come to resemble less and less that which was given to the sons of the better middle class in the town grammar schools. Court circles wanted their sons prepared for life in the here and now. Latin and religion, the main subjects of instruction in the grammar schools, were therefore largely replaced by modern utilitarian subjects or by training in the accomplishments which made a young man welcome in good society. In the official instructions, drafted in French, for the education of Karl Eugen of Württemberg and his brother, for instance, though the traditional phrases are repeated about bringing up the princes in godly and virtuous ways, the main stress is laid on modern languages and the arts of dancing, fencing and riding. The elder prince was to learn a modicum of Latin, 'because he might occasionally need to understand a few sentences in that language'.[1]

The curricula of the special boarding-schools which had been set up for the nobility, the 'Ritterakademien', and those recommended in the numerous handbooks for tutors, follow much the same lines. The indispensable subjects of study are,

---

[1] Quoted in Biedermann, II, i, 75.

first, languages. French and Latin are usually advocated. French was taught conversationally from a very early age, if possible, and Latin was not made a 'pedantic' discipline. Other languages sometimes taught were Italian, English and Spanish. German was not entirely neglected. Next in importance came the study of the modern world, history (modern political history, and the reading of the reviews), geography, genealogy and perhaps some snippets of natural science, the 'curiosities' of botany, anatomy, physics and chemistry. Philosophy was considered pedantic, but time might be found for a little ethics. Law was important for future rulers and officials, and 'politics', in the special sense attached to the word then, was of value to all. It meant the art of self-advancement by 'finesse' and civility, the 'suaviter in modo' praised by Lord Chesterfield. The 'politic' man or 'Politikus' who figures so largely in literature at the beginning of the century, is the master of the 'lesser talents', whose *savoir-vivre* wins him favour with the great.

A more specialised study was mathematics, in which such great advances were being made at this time. It was important for future officers. Rhetoric, the art of persuasive speaking and writing, was chiefly restricted to letter-writing. For many pupils much the most important item in the curriculum was 'Exercitien', which took the place of the older knightly exercises and led up to modern sport. The exercises included dancing, fencing, riding, shooting and 'Ballspiel', an early form of tennis. Among minor accomplishments, the art of carving at table was still taught, drawing was encouraged, and music was thrown in along with card games and chess. Then apart from the formal studies, sports and pastimes there was the 'science' of manners and deportment, 'Conduite', to be mastered, with all its prescribed forms for various occasions—how to pay compliments, how to dress, to pay calls, to behave in company, at table, on travel and so on.[1]

[1] Curricula from Steinhausen, 'Die Idealerziehung im Zeitalter der Perücke', in *Mitteilungen der Gesellschaft für deutsche Erziehungs- und Schulgeschichte*, IV, 1894.

For final polish, the young man went on his grand tour to foreign courts. The Netherlands, England, France and Italy were the countries most commonly visited, but a long stay in Paris was the one indispensable feature of the journey. Elizabeth Charlotte, the German-born Duchess of Orleans and mother of the Regent, whose letters give an entertaining though scarcely edifying picture of life at the French court, sometimes had twenty or thirty Germans of high rank at her parties at once. At foreign courts the young aristocrat was supposed to continue his education by studying the national character and conditions of life, making the acquaintance of leading statesmen, and above all by endeavouring to shed his native rusticity in the company of ladies and gentlemen of refinement. Of course there were many less desirable things he could and often did learn too at pleasure-loving courts, so that in spite of the many advocates of travel as a form of education, from Montaigne onwards, there were never wanting those who saw in it the source of all evil.[1] It was certainly an expensive and often fatiguing and dangerous part of one's education in those days. No young man of birth could go on his travels without a tutor and a man-servant; a young prince of any consequence might have a whole suite of followers. Friedrich III of Gotha for instance (born 1699, reigned 1732–72) made two great tours. On the first, which lasted eighteen months, he took a Hofmeister, two gentlemen-in-waiting, a secretary, a chaplain, a doctor, a treasurer, two pages, a Kammerdiener and lackey, a cook and two other servants. It cost 6500 Thaler.[2]

Naturally an education like this served to deepen the gulf between the lesser aristocracy and the middle class by the stress it laid on the court as the model in all things and a career at court as the goal of all ambition. It was quite openly a 'class-conscious' education, not even modified, as in the English public schools, by friendships between young men of birth and the richer bourgeoisie. Dr Moore noted

[1] See e.g. Biedermann, II, i, 79.   [2] Vehse, vol. 29.

in 1779 the deference paid to boys of rank in the schools of all the countries of Europe, except England, and considered the English public schools 'peculiarly useful to boys of high rank and fortune', because they avoided this 'mean partiality'. In the sixteenth century nobles and bourgeois had attended the same schools, where there were good schools available, the grammar school in a town, for instance, and the 'Fürstenschulen', the new state boarding-schools, in the country. But with the intensification of class distinctions it became usual to educate boys of good birth privately until about the age of eighteen, when many of them (though not, as we have seen, those of the highest rank) would go to the university with a tutor. It was absurd, they said now, to send members of the ruling class to 'scholastic monasteries' to learn Latin and mingle with boors, but they were often sent, especially if destined for the army, to special 'Ritterakademien' reserved for the nobility, small boarding-schools with a score or two of pupils. A few of these had been founded by princes in the sixteenth century,[1] but most had sprung up with the demand for a 'gentleman's education' after the Thirty Years' War.[2] The usual curriculum has been outlined above. These schools were almost all in court towns and provided their pupils with opportunities of mixing in court society and using the prince's stables. Otherwise they seem to have been expensive and inefficient institutions in the eighteenth century, their pupils being too ill-prepared and too proud to learn. By the middle of the century, it may

[1] E.g. the Academy at Selz (Palatinate), 1577, followed by the 'Collegium Illustre', Tübingen, one at Mömpelgard, and the 'Court School' of Moritz von Hessen at Cassel.

[2] In the seventeenth century: Lüneburg, Vienna, Wolfenbüttel, Brandenburg, Berlin, Kolberg, Erlangen. In the eighteenth: Hildburghausen, Kloster Ettal (Bavaria), Liegnitz, Brunswick and a second in Vienna, the 'Collegium Theresianum'. The 'Karlsschule' of Karl Eugen of Württemberg, founded in 1778, may be regarded as the last of these foundations, but it was already more on the lines of a university. See Paulsen, *Gel. Unterricht*, 1, 501 ff., and Steinhausen, *Kulturgeschichte*, p. 495.

be noted, the distrust of schools had spread to the better bourgeoisie. It is in this way that Goethe, in *Dichtung und Wahrheit*, explains why he was educated privately.

In their educational ideals, as in so many other things, the nobility were influenced by the Italian Renaissance, modified by Spanish and French currents of thought. The ideal courtier sketched in Castiglione's *Cortegiano* (1528) was brought down to earth and made a little more middle-class by the court of Louis XIV, and more frivolous and 'arriviste' by the Regency. The proper study of mankind was how to please the great. This is almost the whole theme of the many books on 'Lebensklugheit' (ultimately derived from Gracian) that sold so freely in eighteenth-century Germany. The last one of note, Knigge's *Umgang mit Menschen* (1788), strives valiantly but in vain to introduce a note of middle-class independence. Gottsched, in his manuals, like most scholars until the second half of the century, is still frankly servile. One of his reasons for keeping noblemen out of comedy, for instance, is that it is not fitting to display the great as ridiculous.

It seems impossible to avoid the conclusion that the life of the German aristocracy, considered as a whole, was intellectually and morally at a low ebb in the eighteenth century. Yet the picture must not be made too black, and we must not assume too easily that every cultural feature of which we now approve came from the bourgeoisie. The fact remains that the German classics, Goethe in particular, not only found generous patrons at court, but were profoundly affected in their outlook on life by the court atmosphere. They found something so valuable in the essence of aristocracy based on inherited privilege, however many defects the existing aristocracy might have, that in spite of radical beginnings they desired no imitation in Germany of the French Revolution, and showed themselves in their mature outlook decidedly conservative. We can hardly believe that Goethe would have written with such warmth of the ennobling influence of a court as he did in *Tasso* if his own experience suggested the opposite. *Tasso* then might be cited as evidence in favour of the courts and of the claim of the aristocracy to privileges as guardians of a precious standard, of what Korff calls 'the perfection of courtesy', a necessary corrective to excessive individualism. The spirit of 'noblesse oblige' which is taken for granted in everyone here, and expressed in cultured conversation, perfect manners and social tact, that instinctive deference paid by the individual to the feeling of the group, that moral sensitiveness, on which an action out of keeping with the inherited code jars like a false note—this is the fruit of a long tradition, of which Goethe must have found at least traces in Weimar, in Gräfin von Werthern perhaps, the model for the Countess in *Wilhelm Meister* in her grace and charm, and above all in Frau von Stein. The instinctive feeling for decorum which Goethe praises in Frau von Stein was not an individual quality, but one which she shared with the best type of great lady. Where Goethe probably goes beyond his model, and creates a new ideal of society, Korff thinks—and this view is confirmed by a study of the letters and memoirs of the time —is in giving the society so strictly bound by convention the appearance of perfect freedom, in making 'feinste Gesittung' second nature for its members. One's impression is that it was usually, in Germany and, as may be seen from Lord Chesterfield's *Letters to his Son*, in England too, a very much more external affair, not a convention freely and joyfully accepted but one enforced by social conservatism and above all by a snobbish exclusiveness, of which there is no hint in *Tasso*. Goethe was consciously aiming, as in *Wilhelm Meister*, at the imaginative creation of an ideal aristocracy of mind and heart, for which the old aristocracy of birth could only furnish hints.

Chapter II

COURTS AND COURTIERS

Having considered the position of the German nobility in a general way, we may now look at the way of life of each of the two great categories, court and country nobility, separately. About the life of the eighteenth-century courts whole libraries have been written, and in this outline only a few bare details can be touched upon. A great deal of what has been written recently about this matter is neither true nor edifying, being worked up from the more scandalous memoirs of the time, which are about as reliable, it would seem, as the society news in our modern cheap newspapers. These books are almost wholly concerned with the pleasures of court life. Although pleasures were taken very seriously, there was, as we have seen, another side to the life of princes and their following. They did still perform certain useful functions in society, though not enough to justify their privileged existence. We turn now to their more decorative aspect.

The 'court' meant the ruling family and its immediate entourage, all those, let us say, who were regularly invited to official receptions. They would include, in larger states, some representatives of foreign powers, and in all alike the nobility, with holders of court or government offices and their families, and all those aristocratic families from the country or from other states who had chosen to take up their residence in the capital. For foreigners the rules were often relaxed, but in general much more stress was laid on rank as a prerequisite for the *entrée* to good society in Germany than in France or England, where men of letters at least enjoyed high standing, though here too it was a precarious one if not backed by good birth and powerful connections.

Madame de Staël's impression was that in Germany it was only the court that counted as good society, and that one could only enter it with letters of nobility. Two famous examples may be given in support of her statement. Charlotte Schiller, though herself of good birth, was not invited to court functions in Weimar until her husband had been ennobled, and long before this, elaborate management had been necessary before Goethe, the author of *Götz* and *Werther* and a close personal friend of the duke of Weimar, could be allowed to play cards with the young duchess, who took the rules of etiquette seriously. He had to create a precedent for this high privilege by first playing whist with the duke and duchess of Meiningen, a still smaller state, where manners were easier. Then, one evening when Herr von Stein was playing cards with the Duchess Luise, Stein, by arrangement, was suddenly called away and Goethe asked in to take his place. The dowager duchess, it is true, was far less stiffly ceremonious and regularly invited the literary men to dine with her. It can be understood, however, how indignant the old-fashioned courtiers were when Goethe, an upstart bourgeois, was made a Geheimer Legationsrat. It was for his own comfort that it was necessary to have a title of nobility conferred on him.[1]

The court officers, paid and unpaid, were quite numerous even in small courts. Taking Weimar again as a convenient example, we find that in 1806 the ducal household consisted of four groups of people, those in attendance on the duke, the duchess, the crown prince and the dowager duchess respectively. The court proper included a Hofmarschall, thirteen gentlemen-in-waiting, fifteen gentlemen of junior rank (Kammer-, Hof- and Jagdjunker), five pages and ten teachers for them (!), an equerry with two assistants and some fifty underlings, four valets, one chief huntsman, twenty-eight lackeys, two heiducks, two running footmen (Laufer) and two negroes. Thirty-six musicians were attached

[1] Vehse, XXVIII, 107; Karl v. Lyncker, *Am Weimarischen Hofe*.

to the court. The duchess had her Oberhofmeisterin and three ladies-in-waiting. The crown prince and princess had an Oberhofmeister (Herr von Wolzogen, Schiller's brother-in-law) and Oberhofmeisterin, one gentleman and three ladies-in-waiting. The dowager duchess finally had an Oberhofmeister (Herr von Einsiedel) and two ladies-in-waiting (Fräulein von Göchhausen and another).[1] These were the court offices, as distinguished from government and army.

The majority of these offices, though not all, were paid, and they involved perquisites which were a great source of expense to the duke. They are surprisingly numerous when one considers how simple and 'bürgerlich' so many features of life at this court were. The best reminder of this is the charming sketch by Kraus of an evening with Anna Amalie, where we see the dowager duchess and her three attendants sitting with half a dozen guests at a plain square table littered with paint-boxes and sketch-books. The ladies are painting or embroidering, Goethe seems to be reading aloud to the party, and the painter Heinrich Meyer has evidently been showing them prints. The other guests are Herder and a retired English merchant, Mr Gore, with his two daughters.[2] At the official concerts of the Duchess Luise, on the other hand, there was a good deal of ceremony,[3] and she was far more representative of the usual tone in German courts than her mother-in-law. Though entertaining was on a modest scale, even Weimar needed a kitchen staff of twenty-two. Only one or two people dined with the duke every day, but there was a large 'Marschallstafel' to be maintained for the court staff. In some courts of moderate size, dozens of people had the privilege of dining regularly at court—at Cassel, as we saw, some sixty persons dined with the Landgraf every day. At Munich, von Lang tells us, there was not only a large daily company, but vast quantities of food and drink were taken from the court kitchens to persons outside who

[1] Vehse, xxviii, 308 f.   [2] See frontispiece.
[3] Kar. Jagemann, *Erinnerungen*, p. 93.

made claim to this bounty. This was quite in the old tradition of the courts. The ruler's purse was looked upon as bottomless; if he was the father of his people, he was still more the father of his court, and it was his duty to provide generously for his own. In the older records we find quite astonishing figures. At Brandenburg in 1537, for instance, a decree had to be made that not more than four hundred persons should be fed at court. There were four grades of dinner in the common hall, for noblemen, councillors, clerks, servants. It was as noisy as an inn and the Marschall had all his work cut out to maintain order. In addition to these there were numerous 'Abspeiser' who took food out. The sentry at the gate was more necessary for preventing misuse of this privilege than for keeping out intruders. Vast quantities of beer and wine were regularly allowed to the residents at breakfast, dinner, supper and as a night-cap, some two litres of beer a head for instance at Küstrin.[1] It can be understood that any departure from the customs of the good old days was fiercely resisted and that much survived even in the eighteenth century. It must be remembered of course that the court treasury received vast quantities of consumables from court estates and as dues paid in kind.

The Weimar list of court officers looks very modest when compared with that of other small states, let alone the greater or more extravagant ones, such as Saxony in its palmy days. At the neighbouring court of Gotha for instance in 1767 there were the following higher offices: Oberkammerherr, Oberhofmarschall, Hausmarschall, Hofmarschall, Oberschenk, Oberstallmeister, Stallmeister, Oberlandjägermeister and Landjägermeister, in addition to the duchess's Oberhofmeisterin and an Oberhofmeister for the prince.[2] Even Ernst II, in the following reign (1772–1804), after severe economies, needed seventeen Kammerherren and eleven

---

[1] Kurt Trensch von Buttler: 'Das tägliche Leben an den deutschen Fürstenhöfen des 16ten Jahrhunderts' in *Zeitschrift für Kulturgeschichte*, 1897, an article based on old 'Hofordnungen'.   [2] Vehse, vol. xxix.

Kammerjunker, as well as a Directeur and a Sousdirecteur des plaisirs. As an example of an extremely elaborate court we may take Saxony under Augustus the Strong and his successor. In the order of precedence drawn up in 1716, ninety grades of rank at court were distinguished. In the Saxon State Calendar for 1733 (says Vehse) the list of court offices (Hofétat) takes up fifty-three pages. There was an Oberhofmarschall and ten other 'Obers' (Kammerherr, Stallmeister, Schenk, Küchenmeister, Jägermeister, Hofmeister der Königin, Falkenier, Kämmerer and Generalpostmeister). Then came eighty Kammerjunker, twenty pages (with a tutor and six teachers), a French choir of twenty with a French composer, André, in charge (at a salary of 1300 Thalers), a musical staff of forty-eight led by Hasse (at 6000 Thalers), a separate Polish orchestra of seventeen, a ballet of sixty persons, all French, a court company of eleven (French?) actors and sixteen actresses. The lower servants included about eighty lackeys, the staff of sixteen palaces and sixteen cooks.

This does not represent anything like all that had to be paid for by the Kurfürst's subjects, for his ministers had households of their own like princes' courts. They were in fact, so long as they remained in favour, 'more truly lords of the land than the king himself', as a contemporary tells us. With a recommendation from one of them or some other favourite one could obtain money, offices, estates, or almost anything. It goes without saying that they provided well for themselves. Graf Flemming, for instance, Generalfeldmarschall under Augustus the Strong, the soldier and diplomat who secured for his master the throne of Poland, at first an obscure Pomeranian count, had, according to a description of his 'Hofhaltung' made in 1722,[1] about a hundred domestics

---

[1] K. Biedermann, 'Aus der Glanzzeit des sächsisch-polnischen Hofes', in *Zeitschrift für deutsche Kulturgeschichte*, Neue Folge, I, 1891. Title and salary of every servant are given, together with much precise information about the household equipment.

of different grades. There were twenty-three 'superiores', from an Oberhofmeister, secretaries and tutors down to an equerry responsible for ninety-two horses; and over seventy 'inferiores', from the five pages and a 'Polish gentleman' who played the Bandor and waited at table, the eight musicians and their Italian leader, through various skilled tradesmen and lackeys to the chambermaids and kitchen-maids. The count's salaries and wages bill came to 13,534 Thalers a year (nominally 40,000 M., but in pre-war values at least three times that amount, so about £6000). The appointments of the count's palaces were correspondingly magnificent; he lived on a scale that would make the life of a Hollywood millionaire look tawdry. He could, and did on occasion, entertain a hundred and ninety people to dinner without requiring to borrow any table ware; for state occasions only silver, silver-gilt or fine porcelain services would be used.

It will be understood that the standard of elegance in Dresden was high. Several other notables would rival Flemming in display and the other noblemen would ruin themselves in trying to do the same. Later, under Augustus III, we hear similar tales about Graf Brühl, who was particularly famous for the magnificence of his wardrobe.

It would be a waste of time to accumulate lists of court offices in Germany, but in discussing Germany as a whole, the infinite variety of conditions there must always be remembered. This makes a description of court life in Germany a very different matter from one of contemporary France or England. A full description could only be wearisome, yet no selection of details can do justice to the complexity of the theme. The only method is to indicate the range of variation in each particular, and we have seen now how great it was in the matter of court staffs. We find a corresponding variety in the activities of the various courts, though again there is a similarity in the ground plans which makes a summary description not impossible. We are not dealing now of course with the court as an instrument of government (this concerned a particular set of officials, who would however partly share the social life of the rest), but with the courtiers as the ruler's social companions and friends. This function of the court soon became largely an end in itself, and an elaborate traditional round established itself, constantly influenced by the examples of foreign courts. It is obvious that the existence of such a large number of courts in close proximity enormously strengthened the prestige of the courtier as a type and gave a special character to German society.

The prince was the sun of the court world; everything that happened there was regulated by his actions. Yet he himself was not quite free, he was bound by long established custom and etiquette, in some courts very completely, in others much less. At the imperial court in Vienna, for instance, the court year and the court day were alike regulated by ancient custom, inherited mainly from Spanish sources. On a certain date the emperor regularly went into residence at Schön-brunn, on another fixed day to Laxenburg, on another he returned to the Hofburg. The order of procedure on saints' days and at recurring festivities (such as birthdays), at banquets and receptions, and to a slighter extent, the activities of an ordinary day were all governed by time-honoured custom, just as much as the election and coronation ceremonies. One can well understand that much of this had to be so. Ceremonial functions at the imperial court would have been meaningless if they had not been dignified, and dignity and improvisation are incompatible with one another. On such days the consciousness of continuity with the past and future had to be awakened. For more ordinary occasions, the established routine served a useful function by making thought and new decisions unnecessary. It was as salutary as habit, the 'flywheel of society', is in everyday life. It was particularly necessary for a society that was freer than most from the imperious demands of material conditions. The farmer is bound by the weather and the seasons; he must, if he is to live, do certain things at certain times, and so it is in varying degrees with all engaged in useful work. Experience seems to teach that a society which does not need to work has to invent for itself artificial restraints to replace the pull of external necessity. The ceremonial, even of the imperial court, was probably not felt as a cramping influence but as a welcome support, though custom, like law, could become tyrannical here as everywhere. That the strict rules of etiquette could, however, be relaxed on occasion for strangers is indicated in a letter written by David Hume from Vienna in 1748. The rather corpulent philosopher, in a uniform which he was said to wear as awkwardly as a grocer of the trained-bands, accompanied General St Clair to court and was introduced to the empress dowager.

'You must know', he says, 'that you neither bow nor kneel to emperors and empresses, but curtsy, so that after we had had a little conversation with her Imperial Majesty, we were to walk backwards, through a very long room, curtsying all the way, and there was very great danger of our falling foul of each other, as well as of tumbling topsy-turvy. She saw the difficulty we were in, and immediately called to us: Allez, allez, messieurs, sans cérémonie. Vous n'êtes pas accoutumés à ce mouvement et le plancher est glissant. We esteemed ourselves very much obliged to her for this attention, especially my companions, who were desperately afraid of my falling on them and crushing them.'

The various courts were bound by custom in different degrees, but in all there was some norm, the chief features of which were usually laid down in black and white in a 'Hofordnung'. One important matter that had to be dealt with in such a document was the order of precedence—we saw how elaborate this was in Dresden, with its ninety grades. It was a very important matter everywhere, as foreign visitors like Lady Montagu soon discovered. Freytag's essay on the serio-comic 'War of Wasungen', mentioned earlier, shows how far disputes about precedence could go.

The Hofordnungen also defined the duties and privileges of important court officers and the customary rights of all grades, and laid down rules for the conduct of the court, particularly the immediate household, in the interests of order and dignity. But there was much of course that was governed by unwritten laws.

Regulation and custom lightened the burden of the prince and court officials, but if they took their duties seriously many of them still had plenty to do. The greater number of the residents at courts however had no serious functions. Their duty was pleasure, and their enemy ennui. We have glanced at the day's activities of a few ruling princes above. It may be of interest to describe the activities of the court now more systematically. The great outdoor amusement for men was hunting, especially at the smaller courts in wild country. Innumerable stories are told of the extravagance and excesses of German princes in pursuance of their favourite sport. 'Treibjagden' called for the services of hundreds of beaters, usually peasants for whom this work was part of their 'Frondienst'. Crops were trodden down in 'Parforce-jagden', and game was so jealously protected that the crops and poultry yards were always in danger. Great sums were spent on horses and equipment. From the point of view of the outsider it was all very wasteful and cruel. Protests were naturally not lacking in the humanitarian age. One out-spoken one is L. F. G. von Göckingk's poem *Die Parforcejagd*, written about 1771, a description of a stag-hunt in verse dialogue, in which the physical pain of man and beast and the indifference of court circles to the sufferings their pleasures cause to others is expressed in lines such as the following:

Ein Bauer

Jesus Maria! Was ist das?
Ach weh! mein schön Getreide,
Und meiner Wiese langes Gras!
Da seht mir nun mal beide!

Wer gibt für mich nun Martinshahn,
Zinskorn und Steuer? Keiner!
Der gnäd'ge Fürst hat das getan?
Ach Gott! erbarm dich meiner!

Ein Reitknecht

Hundsfött'scher Bauer, halt das Maul!
Um solchen Quark solch Lärmen anzufangen?
Ihr Lumpenpack seid so so faul:
Wär' ich der Fürst: ich liess euch alle hangen![1]

But the hunting man himself had a different point of view. His unbounded delight was shared by the large staffs of keepers and foresters. Rude energy found an outlet here that had formerly often spent itself in feuds and faction fights, and the health and pleasure it gave were positive goods to be set off against the damage that was done to others. A hunting prince, like a hunting squire in England, was not the worst type of man and ruler. We have seen how Karl August, for instance, was led in his hunting expeditions into every corner of his lands and given a direct acquaintance with the life of his people, and though hunting rights were a jealously guarded privilege of the aristocracy, the enthusiasts had some reason on their side when they claimed that hunting helped to maintain something of the primitive unity of the folk, and to prevent pampered courtiers from losing touch with the roots of things.

Hunting was not usually considered in those days a fit sport for German ladies, though one hears of some Dianas, and ladies might be asked to pig-sticking displays. Their open-air pleasures were drives and walks, usually by prescribed routes and in full dress, and undertaken in the bigger towns rather with a view to meeting other people than to enjoying the charms of nature. Every court town had its promenade, and extensive gardens, at first exclusively formal gardens in the manner of Versailles, an extension of baroque architecture

[1] Reprinted in *Deutsche Literatur*, Reihe Politische Dichtung, Band I, 1930.

into the landscape, extravagantly adorned with artificial
fountains, waterfalls, orangeries, and later, with the spread
of the fashion of the picturesque from England, 'English
parks' with carefully planned prospects, of little hills, woods
and rivulets, curving lawns and artificial ruins. Almost the
only outdoor game we hear of, except some winter sports,
is the 'jeu de paume'. Winter sports, however, were very
popular. In the long continental winters sledging was a great
delight. The court would sally forth to the tinkling of bells
in a long procession of sledges carved and painted to resemble peacocks, dragons, swans, fish, each holding two or
three ladies and driven by a cavalier.[1] In Vienna they would
even cart hundreds of loads of snow into the town to make
this amusement possible.[2] In some places (Weimar for
instance) skating became all the rage and gay parties and
masquerades were held on the ice, but the delights of skiing
remained to be discovered.

But one does not think of German court life as mainly
lived out of doors. So much more is heard in that age of the
theatre and opera, of card parties, concerts, balls and redoubts.
The chief resource of the courtier in his idle hours, which
were many, was cards. If the imperial court drove out in
sledges to Schönbrunn, they played cards there before returning. Even in summer the goal of their drives would
often be a quiet country retreat where card tables had been
set out for the court in tents and arbours. There were few
games that were not played for money, and gambling was
one of the vices most commonly laid to the charge of courtiers
as a class.

Almost every day, in the season, there would be organised
entertainments held at the prince's expense. Amongst these
the opera and the drama took the first place, and they were
as lavishly supported in all courts as the prince's resources
would permit. It had long been customary to invite foreign

[1] See for instance Göckingk's charming poem, *Als der erste Schnee fiel.*
[2] Wraxall, *Memoirs of the Court of Berlin*, etc. I, 316.

6-2

troupes of players to German courts. There had been Italian comedians at various courts in the sixteenth century, even before the English players first began to tour the Continent in 1586. The Thirty Years' War had interrupted these visits, but soon after it was over there were French and Italian troupes to be found again at the courts of the Tirol, Bavaria, Saxony, Austria and elsewhere. From the middle of the seventeenth century opera, already well established in Italy and France, found a footing in the German courts too, some of which soon began to maintain permanent Italian companies of their own and to build theatres to house them. The first specially built theatre in Germany was the wooden one put up by Landgraf Moritz von Hessen at Cassel in 1605. It was followed by many others, especially in the second half of the century, after the war, each bigger and more luxurious than the last. The most spacious of all in the eighteenth century was the Ludwigsburg theatre built in 1750, which had a stage across which squadrons of cavalry could gallop, and was so arranged on the bank of a lake that elaborate nautical spectacles could be displayed.[1]

In Germany, as in France and England at an earlier date, there was a period when the courts were the sole support of opera and almost the only support of the spoken drama. It

---

[1] For details see e.g. Nestriepke, *Das Theater im Wandel der Zeiten*, Berlin, 1928, and *Deutsche Literatur*, Barockdrama Band v, Die Oper, ed. W. Flemming, Leipzig, 1933. Amongst the earliest court theatres are, in the seventeenth century: Vienna (Hofburg), 1626, Innsbruck (2, c.1650), Munich, 1657, Vienna (opera), 1666, Dresden (opera, 1667, holding 2000 people), Brunswick (1691, opera for 2500). Hanover followed in the early eighteenth century (described by Lady Montagu, 1716), Berlin in 1741, and additional theatres were built in Dresden and Vienna. Almost all the smaller courts gradually followed suit. The courts were imitated by Augsburg (1630 and 1665), Ulm (1641), Nürnberg (1667), Hamburg (1678), Leipzig (1693), the *city* of Vienna (1708). Frankfort-on-Main did not possess a theatre till 1782, though a concert hall had been used as a theatre since 1756. Before that time travelling troupes coming to Frankfort put up their own temporary wooden building, as they had to do in most towns.

was the ambition of every court to have an Italian opera and
a French comedy of its own, an ambition seldom realised,
it is true, for lack of means, but the German courts were
slower than the French or English in encouraging a native
drama and opera. Their influence was more beneficial on
the technical side of stage production than on the drama as
literature. The revival of the literary German drama in the
Sturm und Drang and the classical period owed very little
to the courts directly. The smaller courts sometimes accepted
the services of German players when a French troupe was
beyond their means or not easily available, but it was with
the same air of condescension to the second-best that is
displayed by the count and countess in *Wilhelm Meister* when
they engage the German actors to entertain an illustrious
visitor. The half dozen German touring companies that
existed in the first half of the eighteenth century would all
occasionally play in court towns, but they were seldom
engaged for a long stay. It is only in the third quarter of the
century that we hear of German troupes enjoying the
patronage of courts for longer periods (Schönemann in
Mecklenburg-Schwerin, Döbbelin, Koch and Seyler in
Weimar). Gotha was the first court to have a regular court
theatre for German plays directed by a court official. The
experiment did not last long there (1774-7) but Gotha was
imitated in turn by Vienna, Mannheim (under Dalberg,
Schiller's first patron), Munich (for German and French
plays), Berlin (from 1786, with Iffland in control from 1796),
Weimar (from 1791 under Goethe), and by the courts of
Cassel, Mainz and Stuttgart. The first of these 'national'
theatres (i.e. German repertory theatres) had been the one
founded at Hamburg in 1767, the history of which can be
followed in Lessing's *Hamburgische Dramaturgie*. Hamburg,
the greatest commercial centre in Germany, could not support
its repertory theatre for more than a couple of years.
Similarly Frankfort-on-Main, a little later, was glad to share
a troupe with the Elector of Mainz. It was only the courts

that were willing to spend money on these unprofitable enterprises.

The courts then kept alive a taste for acted drama at a time when other classes had lost interest in it, providing models later for private enterprise in the towns, and they accustomed people to the idea that good drama (like opera, and music generally) ought not to have to depend on box-office receipts. They thus prepared the way for those German state and municipal theatres of to-day which are the envy of other countries. In the eighteenth century, there was perhaps too much decentralisation. Material resources and the available talent were too widely scattered to produce notable results, but on the other hand there was a spirit of rivalry that maintained standards, here and there (as in Weimar) a man of genius was given free scope, and a far larger proportion of the people were educated to the more expensive forms of art than in England. The general public was usually admitted to performances at court theatres, though they had to pay for their seats (the court usually did not) and be quiet and unobtrusive. The court theatres had an atmosphere of their own, far from democratic, but none the worse artistically for that, if the taste of the élite was good. At Cassel, Dr Moore says, the front gallery, with a convenient room behind, was reserved for the court. When the prince or princess stood up, between acts or during the performance, all the audience, pit, box and gallery, did so too. Elsewhere we read that if the ruler was present no one might applaud before him, and even in Weimar Goethe would stand up and shout 'Do not laugh' if the audience did not take a poor tragedy (like Schlegel's *Alarcos*) as it was meant, and they would accept the reproof with perfect good humour.[1]

Opera owed everything to court encouragement, as in Italy and in France. It was a form of entertainment that went admirably with baroque palaces and despotic government,

[1] For an interesting impression of the Weimar court theatre see *Crabb Robinson in Germany*, pp. 100 f.

for it expressed better than any other the love of power and
magnificence that filled its patrons, and their exclusive claim
to culture. Nothing could have been less 'of the people'.
It was a great temptation for extravagant princes. In Vienna,
Dresden, Munich, Ludwigsburg and many other capitals vast
sums were spent on it, especially on spectacular staging, for
spectacle was of the essence of opera as then conceived, and
it was for opera that all the tricks of the producer were
devised. Lady Montagu writes to Pope in 1716 from Vienna,
describing an opera performed on a Sunday in the garden
of the Favourite:

Nothing of that kind ever was more magnificent; and I can
easily believe what I am told, that the decoration and habits cost
the emperor thirty thousand pounds sterling. The stage was built
over a very large canal, and, at the beginning of the second act,
divided into two parts, discovering the water, on which there
immediately came, from different parts, two fleets of little gilded
vessels, that gave the representation of a naval fight.... The story
of the opera is the Enchantments of Alcina, which gives opportunity for a great variety of machines, and changes of the scene,
which are performed with a surprising swiftness. The theatre is
so large, that it is hard to carry the eye to the end of it; and the
habits in the utmost magnificence, to the number of one hundred
and eight.

The only drawback was the cold. Later, as we have seen,
covered opera houses were built with stages almost as large,
and they too sometimes made good use, as at Ludwigsburg,
of the natural landscape behind. The spectacles of the na-
turalistic stage and the modern music-hall, with their 'real'
waterfalls and living animals, or, on a higher plane, the
crowd effects at Oberammergau and the enchanting view
of the Niesen through the central stage—all these things were
anticipated in the operas of that time and were no doubt
more important for most of the audience than the music.
One is reminded in this connection of the remark of an
English traveller to Germany in the eighteenth century,
made about the Heidelberg tun, that 'what the Germans seem

chiefly to aim at in their undertakings is the surprising or the prodigious'.[1]

It goes without saying that what the poor courts could offer was only an inferior imitation of all this splendour. Even in the big courts there was little opera outside the carnival season. If the smaller courts could support a professional theatre or opera at all they usually had to combine the two in an unsatisfactory way, using many of the actors as opera-singers. This was so in Weimar under Goethe's management. It was in such conditions that the 'Singspiel', the forerunner of the Operetta, became a popular genre, with its combination of spoken dialogue with songs and instrumental accompaniments. From the memoirs of Karoline Jagemann, the Weimar court singer and actress, one learns with mingled amusement and admiration how limited the resources of the Weimar court theatre were in Goethe's day. In *The Magic Flute* the Genies were three seminarists, awkward country boys in brick-red tights several sizes too large, and soiled tunics not long enough to hide their muddy boots. They wore clumsy rose wreaths round their unruly hair and their cheeks were painted as red as Easter eggs. In the same performance the Queen of Night, being unfit to appear in public, sang her aria from the wings while a substitute performed her actions on the stage. Stage knights were content with cardboard helmets and armour, and the velveteen coronation mantle of the Jungfrau von Orleans, obtained after difficult negotiations, served for many years as the state robe for stage princes or princesses of any time or country.[2]

Though instrumental music and singing naturally benefited enormously through the patronage of the courts, conditions were far from ideal for the great composers whom Germany

---

[1] The anonymous *Introduction to the Knowledge of Germany*, London, 1789, p. 184.

[2] Karoline Jagemann, *Erinnerungen*, 1926, p. 90; Nestriepke, *op. cit.* p. 352.

now produced, as a study of the life of J. S. Bach, Mozart or Beethoven teaches us. We feel it was an ignoble thing for men of genius to be dependent on such crotchety, tyrannical private patrons, but dependence on the general public can hardly be said to have proved better. The courts provided great artists with the indispensable instruments for their training and development. What Mozart learned by his stay in Mannheim almost justifies in itself the huge sums (200,000 Gulden a year or more) that Karl Theodor spent on his opera and theatres. In providing for the fashionable pleasures of the moment the princes were indirectly enriching the world's permanent treasures of art. Even quite small courts engaged a permanent Kammermusiker or two, and any virtuosos who happened to pass through on their tours, to supplement the performances of talented amateurs in the regular concerts which every court expected.

In the second half of the century a perfect craze for amateur theatricals spread from the French to the German courts and all of them soon had their 'théâtres d'occasion', usually for French plays, but occasionally, as in Weimar, for German, though in Weimar too French plays were more popular with the majority of courtiers proper.[1] It was only a step to acting from the masquerades that had been popular since the Renaissance. One elaborate kind of masquerade called a 'Wirtschaft', a kind of picnic in costume, or pastoral in action, centred round an acted scene, written in verse by the court poet. The notables dressed up as peasants at a village wake or wedding, as shepherds, fishermen, millers, game-keepers, waggoners, knife-grinders and all kinds of characters 'of the people'. It was found delightful (though expensive for the cavaliers, who, in Vienna at least, had to provide costumes for their partners) to escape from ceremony and etiquette by such a change of costume. In Bavaria the courtiers in costume would drive in from Nymphenburg and be received at the Residenz in Munich by the Kurfürst

[1] See v. Lyncker for contemporary descriptions of these plays.

and Kurfürstin dressed as village innkeepers (whence the name 'Wirtschaft'). The Georgensaal would be turned into an inn, at the sign of the 'Bavarian Lion', and provided with rough tables, painted chairs, and earthenware beer mugs and plates.

Even Goethe at Weimar did not escape the duties of the Renaissance court poet. He provided original plays and adaptations for amateur performances, some of them rapid improvisations, some the product, in whole or in part, of his best powers. The first version of *Iphigenie* itself was written for a court entertainment, in which Goethe took the part of Orestes. The 'Singspiele' and 'Maskenzüge' are lighter works of the same nature, uneven but full of delightful details, and in his old age Goethe made supreme poetic use of the Masquerade in the second part of *Faust*. All this work would have been inconceivable without the court background. It gives us a vivid idea of what this festive poetry and poetic festivity could be at their best.

Receptions, banquets and balls were the standing form of entertainment apart from plays, operas and concerts. At ordinary receptions cards were played and the ladies often brought their 'work'. Fashions in ladies' work were led by the French court. Under the Regency, it was cutting out scraps for screens and candle-shades; towards the middle of the century 'les nœuds', netting, came into fashion, and from about 1770 the ladies kept their hands busy with 'parfilage', the unravelling of gold braid. That their tongues were not idle is suggested in the neat verses sent by Mme du Deffand to a friend:

> Vive le parfilage!
> Plus de plaisir sans lui!
> Cet important ouvrage
> Chasse partout l'ennui.
> Tandis que l'on déchire
> Et galons et rubans
> L'on peut encore médire
> Et déchirer les gens.

In Germany the more bourgeois sewing and knitting were not despised, either at court or at the assemblies which the gentry arranged among themselves. An assembly held in Hanover in 1769 is described by J. G. Zimmermann as follows:

Last Friday I was at one of these gatherings, one in which about eighty people meet every week, and to which my wife and I have a standing invitation. The company assembles in four fine long rooms that form a suite and are lighted by some hundreds of wax candles. Of these eighty people thirty or forty will play cards. Of the rest some sit and work at their 'entoilage' or 'réseau' while others of us entertain them with our conversation, or they walk hand in hand and arm in arm from sofa to sofa and room to room. At the end of this suite of rooms there is an anteroom where musicians are usually playing. Both ladies and gentlemen are attired in all their finery, the ladies in satin dresses, deeply décolleté and richly trimmed with 'blondes' and lace, and with shawls of Flemish lace over their shoulders. They all wear diamond hair ornaments, earrings and necklaces, their coiffure is in the latest Parisian fashion, their gowns are imitations of the latest models from Paris. Not a word of any language but French is spoken. You flirt and rally and kiss all à la Française.[1]

Dancing was never more important as a social accomplishment than in the eighteenth century, and balls of every degree of magnificence and formality were frequent in all court towns. The usual German ball from the 70's onwards (like the one in *Werther*, 1774, or Mozart's *Don Juan*, 1787) included three types of dance, one French and stately, like the minuet, pavane, coranto or quadrille, one English and less formal, the 'country dances' in which couples arranged themselves face to face in two long lines (whence the name 'contredanse'), and one German and still more individualistic and intimate, consisting almost entirely of waltzing. Even dance programmes mirrored the influence of country on

---

[1] Quoted by E. Buchner, *Das Neueste von Gestern*, II, p. 81. 'Entoilage' is the cutting and mounting of scraps, 'réseau' or 'filet' the making of a net-like lace.

country and class on class, for the minuet was essentially of the court, while the waltz had descended from a vigorous peasant's 'Ländler' and only gradually made its way into good society. When Goethe was in Strassburg he found he must learn to waltz; he makes Werther and Lotte 'revolve round each other like the spheres', but they are the only couple in the party who can waltz well. It was many years before the waltz displaced the older stately dances, especially at court, where it was at first considered vulgar and rather shocking. The queen of Prussia averted her eyes when it was danced at a Berlin court ball for the first time (in 1794) and the young duke of Devonshire, when he saw English girls dance it, vowed he would never marry a girl who waltzed, though he had been charmed with it on the Continent. A similar remark had been put into the mouth of Werther thirty years before. 'Redoubts' were in great favour. At these masks were worn, with either 'dominos' or fancy dress. In many court towns, especially in the Catholic south and west at carnival time, the young people of good society formed exclusive dancing clubs to supplement the regular balls.

Not the least among court entertainments were the pleasures of the table. German cooking had not a good reputation with foreigners (Lord Chesterfield calls it 'execrable') but every effort was made in high circles to temper its grossness with French art. In smaller towns it was abundance that was aimed at rather than subtlety. In Treves, for instance, at big dinners 'the dishes were heaped so full of meat and game that the tables were near to sinking; often ten large fowls, three roast geese, or two huge turkeys in one dish'.[1] Everywhere it was usual to serve several dishes at each course, as much as would suffice now for half-a-dozen meals. To offer 'not more than six dishes' to nobility was a gross insult (see Grossmann's play of 1777, *Nicht mehr als sechs Schüsseln*). The middle-class Viennese, we are told,

[1] Graf Boos von Waldeck, quoted Buchner, II, p. 366.

offered ten or twelve, and at a banquet twenty-four were expected. It was like Schlaraffenland.

In the matter of drink too the Germans had an unenviable reputation. Even in 1789 the writer of the *Introduction to the Knowledge of Germany*[1] says that in some courts a visitor 'is initiated and purchases in a manner his freedom by submitting to drink till he has lost the use of his reason'. This was especially the case now, he added, in ecclesiastical courts, where gallantry was taboo. The account that Baron von Pöllnitz gives of the heavy drinking at Würzburg, Fulda and other ecclesiastical courts is borne out by many other descriptions. In Würzburg Pöllnitz could not avoid being drunk twice a day, so numerous and well-honoured were the toasts.[2] Every contemporary would understand why in Goethe's *Götz* the Bishop of Bamberg and the Abbot of Fulda when we first see them are drinking together after dinner, and why Liebetraut is made to speak of 'Das Weinfass von Fulda'.

At the greater courts there were gourmets as well as gourmands. Vast sums were spent on the elaborate preparation and on the elegant serving of banquets, though to judge by all we read the 'prodigious' had a way of creeping in. Lady Montagu was impressed by the good taste and magnificence of the tables of Viennese people of quality. She was more than once 'entertained with fifty dishes of meat, all served in silver, and well dressed; the dessert proportionable, served in the finest china'. She was particularly surprised at the variety and richness of the wines. A wine list was laid on each guest's plate, often to the number of eighteen exquisite varieties. Vienna was already famous for good living. The Berliner Nicolai could not conceal his astonishment at the variety and excellence of the food even in the restaurants. It was in Vienna that à la carte meals first became usual, and for 45 Kreuzer, Nicolaï says, one had (in 1781) six courses, with a choice of seven soups, five kinds of

---

[1] London, 1789, anon. [2] *Mémoires*, I, 224.

fish and other things in proportion, and this on a fast day. There were cafés, always crowded, resplendent with mirrors, hangings and pictures, and Nicolai considers it worthy of mention that in the Kohlmarkt you could buy ices. It will be remembered that Frau Rat Goethe poured away the ices sent down to her children from Count Thoranc's table (in 1759). Food was a more important matter to the Viennese, Nicolai thought, than it was even to the Bavarians, Swabians or Swiss.[1] Vienna was already the 'Phäakenstadt', but so was every court town in a greater or lesser degree, though they could not all be instinct as Vienna was with the spirit of the warm south.

The serving of meals on special occasions was so elaborate that one could almost speak of a new mixed art, comparable with opera, combining the pleasures of the table with those of the concert-room, the sculpture gallery and the theatre. There was nothing new in dining to sweet music, but the art of the court confectioner was quite a new development. The Konditor at a great court had had the training of a sculptor, and it was his function to produce sugar ornaments for the table that would have put into the shade the most elaborate of modern wedding cakes. The 'Dresden china' figures, debased versions of which are to be found on the humblest mantelshelf in England, were at one time used as ornaments for the tables of the great, but earlier still the rococo shepherds, dairy-maids, huntsmen and so on were made by the court confectioner in sugar. There might be a formal garden the length of the table, with a little fountain of perfumed waters in the centre edged with statues, avenues of trim trees, beds of flowers in natural colours and little sugar ladies and gentlemen promenading on the paths. Or a sugar castle might be shown from which in the course of the evening a miniature firework display would be given. The chef often rivalled the confectioner with his surprise pasties, from which a dancer might emerge to delight the company.

[1] Nicolai, *Reisen*, v.

The 'town' in any little Residenz was an extension of the palace. Several of the German capitals in the eighteenth century were creations of the recent past, and it is easy to follow the process by which a whole town grew up to provide for the needs of a court. There is an instructive example in miniature in the memoirs of the court painter and architect Mannlich. A relative of the mistress of his patron the duke of Pfalz-Zweibrücken (Karl II August) owned a farm near Homburg (Pfalz) that she wished to sell. The duke was accordingly persuaded to visit it one day. It was made to look very attractive. The farmer and his family and all their servants were working in their picturesque Sunday clothes, the finest of cattle were brought there for the visit, delicious cream and butter were served and by good fortune the weather was glorious. The court doctor assured the prince that it would be impossible to be ill in such surroundings, and the ladies and gentlemen-in-waiting could not sufficiently praise the view. The duke easily fell a victim. Next day Mannlich was summoned to him. The stables and byres had to be enlarged, a cottage for the farmer and his family had to be built, the rooms needed structural alterations, decoration, and furnishing. An English garden had to be made of the woods, valleys and meadows near the house. In a few weeks the farm had already grown into quite a village, for the crowds of workmen who were needed had been accommodated, with their families, in specially built huts, where you saw their wives washing their linen out of doors and their children playing and dancing. The 'Luisenhof' had become the 'Karlsberg'. At first the duke just drove over every afternoon, but presently he wanted to dine there. This necessitated further alterations—a new kitchen wing, a large dining room. And so the farm grew and grew until the duke was living there permanently. Soon a regular Schloss had been built, with stables for a thousand horses, kennels for a thousand dogs, an enormous riding-school, with quarters for the equerries, grooms, keepers, cooks and servants; an 'orangerie' with rooms for the gentlemen-in-waiting, pages, officers, doctors, chaplains and gardeners; a picture gallery and library, a theatre, a zoological garden, and barracks for 1400 men. Finally a whole town had to be called into being, to accommodate all those whose services were required by the duke and his court. All this happened in about ten years (1777–86). It is said to have cost the duke fourteen million Gulden—the income of the duchy was 800,000! The new town was burnt by the French in 1793 and now dense woods cover the site of it.

It was in a similar way that bigger capitals like Mannheim (1606), Karlsruhe (1715), and Ludwigsburg (1704–33) had been built at the whim of a prince—that is why their streets are laid out in some clearly planned symmetrical pattern, a chessboard or a cartwheel—and the older established capitals, though not so obviously built to order, were similar to the new ones in the make-up of their population. It consisted, besides the court proper, of officials and personal attendants, a garrison, and craftsmen and shopkeepers catering for the wants of all these. If there were any 'manufactures', they were almost always of luxury articles for the court (ribbons, gold braid, lace, various fine stuffs and hangings, silk stockings, hats, snuff and playing cards are the items which recur most frequently in the lists of manufactures in court towns given in Reichard's *Guide des Voyageurs*), or of fine porcelain, some of which would be made to order for foreign patrons and some sold in the open market, after the requirements of the prince, for court use and for presents, had been met. There were such factories for instance in Meissen, Nymphenburg, Berlin, Vienna, Ludwigsburg, Cassel, Ansbach, Gotha and Fulda. Even in Prussia the chief manufacture subsidised by the state, apart from porcelain, was blue cloth primarily intended for soldiers' uniforms, though for a time the citizens of Berlin were forced to wear it too.

The craftsmen of these towns worked mainly to order for the aristocracy. Nicolai contrasts Stuttgart, with its 250 tailors to 18,000 inhabitants, with the Free Town of Ulm, with only 31 to 13,000. In Munich, he says, there were sixteen goldsmiths and seventeen wigmakers, but only fifteen clothmakers. In all these capitals there was a considerable trade in luxuries imported from France and England, for court circles despised German work. Early in the century Lady Montagu had already been struck with the contrast between the free towns of Germany and the capitals.

'In the first', she said, 'there appears an air of commerce and plenty. The streets are well-built, and full of people, neatly and plainly dressed. The shops are loaded with merchandise, and the commonalty clean and cheerful. In the other, a sort of shabby finery, a number of dirty people of quality tawdered out; narrow, nasty streets out of repair, wretchedly thin of inhabitants, and above half of the common sort asking alms. I cannot help fancying one under the figure of a handsome clean Dutch citizen's wife, and the other like a poor town lady of pleasure, painted and ribboned out in her head-dress, with tarnished silver-laced shoes and a ragged under-petticoat, a miserable mixture of vice and poverty.'[1]

Weimar, tiny as it was, was a typical court town in this respect too. In the market-place, in addition to the apothecary's, the proprietor of which also practised as a doctor, there were only two shops. One of them sold fine cloth, velvet, gold and silver braid for ladies' and gentlemen's clothing, and the other, kept by a Frenchman, perfumery and cosmetics. (Until the eighties, as we saw, ladies at court generally rouged very heavily.) There were butchers and bakers, of course, a shoemaker or two, a smith, and all the other tradesmen required, but they would not have shops with goods displayed in a window. They would either use the front room of the house to receive customers, or sell their goods (particularly consumables like bread) at a counter formed of the shutters to the front window, or at special stalls. The butchers had booths arranged side by side under

[1] Letter of Aug. 22nd 1716.

the arcades of the town-hall, and the smith worked under an old gate arch. In Dresden or Vienna there would be dozens of shops, but there would be the same distinction between luxury and everyday goods, a preponderance of the luxury trades, and consequently an increased dependence of the citizens on the patronage of the court.

It is difficult to obtain statistical information about the proportions of the various elements in the population. Some which are quoted by Reichard for Vienna are instructive so far as they go. Out of a total population of about 260,000 (in 1795) there were 3253 members of the aristocracy, 6000 lackeys and 34,000 other servants. In Berlin in 1783, out of a total of 141,000, the garrison with the men's families made up no fewer than 33,000. Officials and families accounted for 14,000, and personal attendants on these and the court another 10,000, so that 57,000 persons, well over a third of the population, were directly dependent on the king.[1] There were only some 10,000 citizens with full rights. Similarly in Dresden in 1791, out of a total of 58,000, about 20,000 were not subject to the jurisdiction of the town but to that of the electoral prince's agent. They included 6621 officials and soldiers. We get an idea of the figures in small capitals from the very careful statistics compiled by Roller for Durlach. In the first ten years of the century, while it was still a Residenz, the proportion of servants to the whole was over 12 per cent., but in the last ten years, when it was a country town again, only 2 per cent. The number of those following the learned professions declined in the same period from 12 to 6 per cent. There was a correspondingly greater number of persons engaged in agriculture (25 instead of 15 per cent.), while the figure for handicrafts remained fairly constant at about 40 per cent., for the garrison at 8 to 10 per cent., and for trade at 5 per cent.

It was useless to expect civic spirit from the inhabitants of any such town. A very large proportion of the inhabitants

[1] Preuss, *Entwicklung des deutschen Städtewesens*, p. 172.

were 'gefreite Bürger', exempt from the ordinary rates and taxes and often subject to special jurisdiction. They included, in Durlach for instance, all connected in any way with the court, the nobility, the officials down to the lowest, the official court purveyors, the servants of the nobility and officials; and almost all the 'Intelligenz', the ministers of the state religion and their subordinates, teachers, doctors, apothecaries, artists and scholars, rich rentiers, manufacturers and their chief staff, the Bürgermeister and council and in fact all the 'better class' or 'Honoratioren'. The citizens of the court towns were naturally extremely conservative and loyal in their attitude to the court. They would accept the existing order of society as one ordained by God, and would be very chary of criticising even the worst extravagances of their ruler, for they would take a pride in the magnificence of his palace, and have a share even if merely as onlookers in court festivities.

The poet Justinus Kerner, in his reminiscences of his boyhood in Ludwigsburg (*Das Bilderbuch aus meiner Knabenzeit*), gives us a vivid impression of what the pageantry in such a little capital might be.

During my earliest childhood [he says], Duke Karl Eugen was still reigning. He resided in Ludwigsburg during the summer months, and then the broad streets of Ludwigsburg and its avenues of limes and chestnuts, usually so empty, would be thronged by courtiers with silk coats, bagwigs and swords, and by the ducal military in brilliant uniforms and grenadiers' caps, beside whom the townspeople in their modest civilian clothes formed an inconspicuous minority. The splendid palace with its spacious squares and gardens, the neighbouring park with its palace, the 'Favorite', the shady avenues that led to the town and made delightful cool promenades full of blossoms and perfume in the town itself, the great broad market-place with its arcades, often provided the scene for the pleasures of this worldly-minded prince, the scene of festivities which seem like dreams of delight when one looks back on them from the present. In the 'Favorite' opposite the main palace firework displays were given

7-2

that equalled those of Versailles in splendour. Fêtes were held on the lake near the town at which the pretty daughters of citizens had to appear as queens of the sea. In the early years of his reign the Duke, whose birthday was in the winter, often made magic gardens, to celebrate it, like those we read of in the Arabian Nights. In the middle of autumn he had the existing orange gardens, a thousand feet long and a hundred broad, enclosed in a huge framework of glass to protect them from the winter cold.

It was a select company to which concerts and plays were given, in a setting of eternal summer, in these 'winter gardens', but the whole town could witness the 'Venetian Fairs' held in the market-place.

The whole market-place was covered with an awning, buyers and sellers were all in fancy dress. It was a motley throng of gaily costumed figures that moved there in procession and played the maddest pranks. There was one of the Duke's Heiducks, a perfect giant, who was dressed up like an infant, wheeled about in a cradle, and fed with bread and milk by a wet-nurse who was a dwarf, and this was only one strange sight among many.

It was not in the little capitals themselves then that independent critics of the princes were to be found, for these circles were kept loyal by 'bread and circuses'. But they were to be met with in the Free Towns, in proud republicans like Goethe's father, as well as among disgruntled state servants like J. J. Moser or Freiherr von Knigge. To the typical Aufklärer the 'slavish submissiveness' of the inhabitants of towns like Dresden already appears ridiculous. Rebmann in 1795 for instance quotes derisively passages like the following from a Dresden weekly paper:

'*Hofbegebenheiten.*' Dienstag den 31. Januar und Freytag den 3. Februar brachten Seine Kurfürstliche Durchlaucht einige Stunden im Grossen Garten mit Fasanenschiessen zu. Nachmittags fuhr unser Landesvater nebst seiner teuersten Gemahlin einige Stunden aufs Fischhaus.

Montags den 24. May erlustigten sich Seine des Prinzen Anton Hochfürstliche Durchlaucht mit Spazierengehen in der Friedrich-

städter Allee, und geruheten darauf bey des Prinzen Max
Hochfürstlicher Durchlaucht einen Besuch abzustatten.

The Bürger proper are accustomed to subservience, he
says. They look on with equanimity when the carriage of
a nobleman is driven through the streets at such a pace that
the lives of pedestrians are every moment in danger. When
the servant of some bankrupt count strikes out with his
burning torch amongst well-dressed people at a gate, because
the crowd has held up the carriage a little, they wipe the
burning pitch off their clothes and go quietly home. For
anyone who is not a member of one or other of the two
privileged castes, nobility and army, seems to be here merely
on sufferance.[1] Nicolai comments on the pleasure-loving
easy-going way of life of the people in capitals, such as
Vienna, Munich, Stuttgart, but he admits that the citizens
of the Free Towns are far too stiff and ceremonious. In many
of the capitals, especially in the south, one can find something
of the old spirit even to-day. The people are more often in
holiday mood; they cannot live without their theatre and
their music; popular festivals (like the Munich Oktoberfest)
are still celebrated with gusto and the sense of pageantry is
not dead. They are interested in the appearance of their town,
its public buildings and streets and fountains. They are not
absorbed in the making of a living, they still find time to live.
The general level of art and taste in Germany would be much
lower without them.

The multiplicity of little courts certainly favoured the
diffusion of a taste for luxury and certain kinds of art. It is
more doubtful whether court patronage was a benefit to
creative art, especially to that of native artists. Since the
Renaissance the 'artist' in the modern sense had gradually
come to be distinguished from the craftsman, not only in
consequence of increasing specialisation, but still more
because the men whose services were sought after by the

[1] *Wanderungen und Kreuzzüge durch einen Teil Deutschlands*, von
Anselm Rabiosus dem Jüngeren (G. F. Rebmann). Altona, 1795.

condottieri of Italy and their later imitators, to express their personal pride and glory, naturally became 'personalities' themselves, not patient anonymous workmen executing prescribed tasks by a routine method. It is true that they were often exploited by their patrons, and with our modern romantic ideas of the respect due to creative genius, we cannot help being painfully conscious of this fact when we contemplate certain forms of rococo art. Even a Renaissance picture, as Mr Clive Bell says, 'was meant to say just those things that a patron would love to hear', and 'in the eighteenth century painters are, for the most part, upholsterers to the nobility and gentry'. The career of J. C. Mannlich was probably typical of that of the general run of court painters in Germany. His father, descended from a family of Augsburg goldsmiths, was court painter to the duke of Pfalz-Zweibrücken (Christian IV), and as the boy showed talent for painting while still at school, the duke had him trained at Mannheim. Later he accompanied the duke on his annual visits to Paris, had lessons from Boucher and became acquainted with all the young French artists of note. After this education had been completed by four years' residence in Rome he became chief court painter to his patron (1771). Finding that serious and tragic subjects like the sketches he made from Homer and the history of antiquity did not please the duke, he had to turn to Ovid's *Metamorphoses*, Guarini's *Pastor Fido* and similar works for motifs that would. Soon afterwards we find him painting scenery for amateur theatricals at court, and as the taste for them grew and he expressed ideas about theatres, he was asked for plans for a court theatre. It was built, earned loud praise, and to his consternation Mannlich found himself appointed chief architect by the new duke, although he had never studied building-construction in his life. His chief task was the planning of the new 'Karlsberg' (see p. 95) with all its decorations and furnishings. Finding that Mannlich had a good collection of pictures, the duke informed him one day that he would pay him whatever he liked for it, and had already given orders for its removal to the palace. Soon he was entrusted with the supervision and the cataloguing of the duke's growing collection of pictures, though still acting as chief architect and superintendent of the theatre. In his capacity as 'Director of all the Fine Arts', his duties included even such things as the planning of court festivities. He ended up after the French Revolution as Director of the Bavarian Picture Galleries in Munich. What is particularly striking in his well-written autobiography is the absolute dependence of even a highly placed official on the whims of his duke. It also reminds us how much of the artistic energy of the day went into applied art. The artist was not there to express himself, but to give appropriate and agreeable forms to everything that surrounded his patron, from his palace and its gardens to his snuff-boxes and walking-sticks.

This social fact is important if we would understand the character of German baroque and particularly rococo art. Art had become a luxury. Of course great personalities would not have let themselves be suppressed by any patron, but except in architecture Germany did not produce any artists of outstanding genius at this period, and the lesser men were content, like Mannlich, to adapt themselves to the taste of their patrons, who in their turn followed the prevailing fashions of France and Italy. But the glorious use that architects like *Neumann* (Würzburg, Residenzschloss) or *Pöppelmann* (Dresden, Zwinger) made of the opportunities given them by extravagant princes shows that not all the blame for the rather weak and characterless art of the age is to be laid at the door of the patrons. The general run of them had no doubt no more taste or understanding than the count, the patron of the actors in *Wilhelm Meisters Lehrjahre*, but an artist with ideas could usually contrive to express them much as Wilhelm does in his *Vorspiel*. For the true artist, a patron was simply a necessary evil, one element in the situation that he had to master in his art, and one advantage of Germany's separatism was that it offered the man of genius at least a considerable choice of evils, so big a choice, if he was of outstanding merit, that he could hardly fail to be appreciated at something like his true value somewhere, as we see from the lives of the great musicians of the age. They suffered greatly, but perhaps not more than artists in other ages. Of the necessity of the evil there was, however, no doubt, for no art but literature, and that only in part and only late in the century, was able to dispense with the support of the higher aristocracy. Even a theatre with pretensions to art could not, as we have seen, maintain itself without their help. Art inevitably owed much to aristocratic patronage, if only for the reason that the aristocracy controlled such a large share of the resources of the country.

It can be readily understood that at every court the suitors for the favour of the prince were as thick as flies round a honey-pot. 'Antichambrieren' was raised to the level of a fine art by those sufficiently well connected and well dressed to secure entry. It was a subject of instruction at the Ritter-akademien. This was the golden age of adventurers. Casanova and Cagliostro were only the most famous of a host of plausible knights of fortune with assumed titles, unbounded self-confidence and the external appearance and manners of gentlemen, who maintained themselves by making themselves agreeable and by scheming and gambling, while many like Herr von Pöllnitz, with better claims to their titles, were hardly distinguishable from adventurers in their way of life. Knigge's description of the type is perhaps worth quoting:

Wherever there is a rich widow to be married, a pension or office to be had at any court, they are quickly on the scent. They baptise themselves, give themselves titles, re-create themselves, as often as they please, and as the matter in hand requires. What they cannot pull off as a simple nobleman they attempt as Marquis or Abbé or officer. There is no enterprise or state department between heaven and earth which they would not be prepared to take charge of, no branch of knowledge about which they cannot converse with a self-confidence that puts even scholars to confusion. With admirable adroitness, with a *savoir vivre* that better men might learn from them with advantage, they obtain things which honest and capable men have not the courage to desire. Without profound knowledge of human nature they have that quality which, in the world as it is, enables men to gain the mastery over the truly wise, namely *esprit de conduite*.[1]

They are a real danger, he says, in the small German courts, with their pockets full of projects for the good of the land. Memoirs and letters of the time are full of complaints of the impudence of foreign adventurers at the little courts, with their slavish admiration of everything French. In fact, where externals were so important and self-interest the only motive, even the *honnête homme*, as described for instance by Chesterfield, had something of the adventurer about him.

[1] Knigge, *Umgang*, p. 306.

Chapter III

THE AGRARIAN ECONOMY

From the point of view of the economist, court life with all its splendour was an elaborate superstructure raised on the basis of an agrarian economy. The prince usually derived a good half of his income from his own estates, and the rest was raised in taxes, the burden of which lay chiefly, in most states, on the cultivators of the soil and small landowners. The court nobility lived partly on money rents from their estates and partly on the prince's generosity. As Goethe wrote in the letter quoted above, 'more was consumed at the top in one day, than was produced in one day at the bottom', or in another letter, 'It is always the peasant who has to carry the burden'. In turning now to the conditions of life in the country we shall be studying the principal material foundation of German civilisation in that age and shall be concerned with much the most numerous section of the German people, forming at this time almost three-quarters of the whole.

Among the conditions that governed life and labour in the country in those days two sets of facts are particularly important, those concerning the legal rights of landowners and tenants and those concerning the technique of agricultural practice. To understand the legal aspect of country life is a matter of great difficulty because of the extreme complexity of the conditions of land tenure, yet this was a factor of the highest importance, for it determined ultimately by whose hands the necessary labour should be performed and what every individual's share of the produce should be. The system of land tenure went back of course to a time when money was unknown, but it had been very considerably modified by the rise of towns and the increasing use of money.

The whole available land had long since been staked out and every portion of it was the property of some individual or group. The landlord was in the great majority of cases a ruling prince or a nobleman. There were also landed proprietors of middle-class origin, members of families that had grown rich in the towns, but the restrictions placed at various times on the purchase by members of the middle class of old feudal estates kept their number comparatively small. In the east almost the whole of the land was in the hands of the nobility. Round about the towns of the west and south a number of Rittergüter had passed into the hands of townsmen, but many of these had purchased a title to match their estate and had become, or were on the way to becoming, country gentlemen hardly distinguishable from the descendants of the medieval Knighthood, whose estates, as we have seen, were fiefs granted originally in return for services to the former owner of their land, some prince or great nobleman. Very large estates were still owned by the Catholic Church in the west and south. In Protestant states they had of course been seized by the princes after the Reformation. The Free Towns still owned much land round their walls. So the 'lord' spoken of in what follows might be a city corporation, a 'Stift', bishop or abbot, or a retired merchant, but in most cases it would be a member of the nobility or a ruling prince.

It was not enough for any such lord to own land. It brought him in nothing unless it was worked, and it was necessary for him to give or lend land, or the use or produce of land, in return for labour services. After so many centuries of development, the relations between landlords and peasantry were very various. Some peasants were little better than the slaves of their masters, while at the other extreme we find peasants who have almost complete right of ownership over extensive estates and only pay nominal dues to a landlord.

A true slave has no human rights. He is a kind of human domestic animal, who can be forced to work till he drops, and made to live under any conditions that please his master.

He may even be bought or sold. The serfs of Russia at this time had been reduced to a state very like slavery of this kind. In some parts of Germany too there were peasants who were very little better placed than Russian serfs. Their lord could demand labour from them and their families without limit, he allowed them no possessions of their own and could turn them out of their house and land when he wished. They and their children on the other hand could not leave the estate or even marry without his consent. Being bound to the soil they were turned over to the new owner if the estate changed hands. They were subject without effective appeal to the jurisdiction of their lords, and some lords even claimed and exercised the power of life and death over them. Though this sounds to us an utterly wretched state of life, it might not be so if the lord was generous and just. Besides possessing rights over his serf, he was responsible for his welfare and in his own interest could not afford to neglect this responsibility entirely. A serf had to do a great many things against his will, but he was spared some of the dangers of freedom. He was assured at least of a bare sufficiency.

Serfdom of this kind or approximating to it is found in eighteenth-century Germany east of the Elbe, in the regions, that is, colonised in the Middle Ages by settlers from the older German lands west of the Elbe. In this area towns were far less numerous than in the west, the peasantry could not pay dues in money because there was no market near enough for their produce, and the landlords found it therefore to be in their interest to farm as much of their estate as possible themselves and produce corn for export, instead of letting out their land at a money rent. They accumulated large compact estates by selling or exchanging any inconveniently distant portions of their lands, and by dispossessing, whenever they could, peasants with hereditary rights. They then worked this new land along with their old demesne, the labour for both being provided by the tenants who remained. The estates in this colonised area were no doubt less scattered from the beginning than in the west, and the landowners were always given rights of jurisdiction over their tenants, whereas in the west a tenant's landlord and 'Gerichtsherr' were by no means always the same person. It was the combination of 'Gerichtsherrschaft' and 'Grundherrschaft' in the same person that constituted the 'Gutsherrschaft' characteristic of the east. The 'Junker', as we now call them, were noblemen owning and usually farming for themselves large compact estates, who also administered the law and tried the peasants on these estates not only in civil but in criminal cases. Being a kind of sheriff, magistrate and police-chief in one, the landowner in these parts exercised an almost irresistible authority over his tenants and was able to introduce a system which, though not strictly serfdom or true slavery, came very near to it in its practical working. His peasants were bound to the soil, they could not marry or learn a trade without permission; he could demand unlimited services from them and had the first claim on the labour of their children. One even hears occasionally of peasants being bought and sold or gambled for, but these are isolated and usually not strictly legal transactions (whereas in Russia serfs could be openly put up to auction in the days of Catherine II).

The services demanded varied from estate to estate and were seldom definitely fixed. In East Prussia, we hear, the peasant had to work at least three days a week under the whip of the overseer for his lord, and often up to five or six. He had often only the nights left for work on his own plot. Services were in general very heavy east of the Elbe, but payments in money and kind correspondingly light. In the west it was the other way round, but whatever the system might be, the peasant was seldom left with more than the bare minimum necessary for existence.

In the eastern districts a peasant's tenure of his land was on a very insecure basis. He was usually a so-called 'Lassit'. He was allowed the use of some land in return for services and dues, but the term of his tenure was seldom defined. He was simply 'left' in possession until further notice (Lassbesitz) and could seldom dispose of the land freely or even be sure that his son would succeed him. He usually did not even possess his buildings and farming tools. Holdings were of course of various sizes. The peasants with large holdings would usually perform 'Spanndienste', i.e. supply horse and man for ploughing or carting; those with smaller holdings would have no horses and be obliged to work for their lord with their own hands (Handdienste). There were already a large number of workers who had no land of their own, dispossessed peasants and others, whose position was that of farm labourers.

If conditions in the east closely resembled those in Russia, conditions in the west were very like those in France. Feudal services had usually been commuted for money payments, the peasants being able to sell produce in the towns. Restrictions on the peasants' personal freedom had also almost all disappeared. The 'corvées' were usually fixed; in some places they did not amount to more than a few days' work a year, in others they might perhaps come up to about fourteen days. The peasants usually held their land on a hereditary basis, their rights were well protected, they could generally dispose of their land freely and they owned their buildings and implements.

Nearly all these differences between east and west resulted from the fact that in the east there were extensive Rittergüter run by the owner himself, while in the small states of the west and south-west more and more land and rights had been ceded to the peasants, in return for fixed money payments to lords who spent most of their time in the local capital. Except on the estates of the Imperial Knights, in Baden, and in one or two smaller states, the landowner in the west had jurisdiction only in minor cases, the major being reserved for the courts of the prince. Owing to this fact and to the more scattered nature of their holdings they could not use these rights as an instrument for petty tyranny. Some of the

Reichsritter, however, had a very bad reputation for the way in which they treated their peasantry. The state of Bavaria too formed in many ways an exception in the area west of the Elbe, conditions here being on the whole very like those in the east.

The peasant, it will be seen, besides being dependent on the vagaries of the weather and exposed more than any other class to the ravages of war, was less of a free agent than the average townsman, being more closely bound by the routine of the little society into which he was born. On the other hand he was seldom in danger of actual starvation, as a 'free' townsman might be, and although he had to work hard, he never experienced the still more unhappy situation of being out of work. Naturally his personal dependence was looked upon as a great evil by the liberals of the Aufklärung, while agricultural reformers criticised the inefficiency of forced and therefore scamped labour. We meet with many reflections in literature of the movement for the freeing of the serfs. In the strict legal sense there were no actual 'serfs' (Leibeigene) in Germany like those of the early Middle Ages and of classical antiquity. The feudal dues and services still exacted were a burden on the *land*, not on the *person* of the peasant, and had mostly been commuted for money. Most of the restrictions on their freedom had had their origin not in medieval serfdom but in later developments, particularly in the 'Gutsherrschaft', described above, of the lands east of the Elbe. But even if the peasants were at worst only what Knapp has called 'erbuntertänig' (hereditarily subject) it was natural that the reformers should use the familiar word serfdom for a relationship which in practice was very little better than slavery. The movement for the freeing of the serfs made little progress in Germany until the nineteenth century.

It was only from the prince of the territory that the peasant could hope for relief. He did not always look to him in vain, for in Prussia and Austria the state needed a flourishing peasantry, to provide healthy recruits for the growing armies, and billets in their houses and barns for the soldiers. Actuated in the main by these motives the Prussian and Austrian rulers endeavoured by a number of ordinances to prevent the confiscation of peasants' land (Bauernlegung), but they, were not so successful, or perhaps so desirous of success, when they joined in the attempts at the abolition of serfdom that began to be made in Germany in this century. The demesne peasants were freed in Prussia in 1798 and the following years, but the rest did not obtain their freedom until between 1808 and 1816, and then only at the cost of concessions that made the landowners' position even better than before. In Austria, in spite of Joseph II's humane attempts, the peasants were not freed till 1848, but other German-speaking territories were not so backward. In the north and west, where conditions were better to begin with, it was only a small step to release the peasant from feudal dues and give him an independent holding, yet here too it needed the impetus of the French Revolution to induce the peasants to assert their claims.

To pass now from the legal to the technical aspect of country life, we may note that there are two extreme types of agricultural system, the primitive or self-sufficing one and the modern capitalistic type, in which the agricultural unit, a larger and more highly organised one than before, produces mainly for export, and is consequently obliged to purchase many of the commodities it requires, instead of producing them itself. In eighteenth-century Germany the former type prevailed almost exclusively, and it continued to do so till quite the middle of the nineteenth century. The main aim was, both on small holdings and on large estates, to grow what the owners and their families and dependents themselves needed for their upkeep. Any surplus there might be would be sold in whatever market was available, but commercial considerations were not paramount.

There were of course exceptions to this rule, conditions

naturally varying considerably over so large an area. Three zones may be distinguished, one of small independent holdings in the south-west, one of dairy-farms in Hanover and Schleswig-Holstein, and one of large estates in the colonised east. Of these the dairy-farms, under Dutch supervision, early became dependent on trade owing to their specialised nature, but the small farmers of the south-west were for the most part content if they could feed themselves. Even the large estates of the east only exported a small proportion of their produce. Sombart estimates (*op. cit.* II, 630) that the annual export of corn from Danzig in this century was only about as much as could be grown on 100,000 acres, or half one Prussian 'Kreis'; yet Danzig was the main port for the whole of the eastern corn-land. The agricultural population consumed about two-thirds of their total production even in 1850; out of the remaining third came not only the amount exported, but also the supplies of the towns. The smaller towns very often needed little from outside, for they grew a large proportion of their food themselves, and in the larger towns too (in Frankfort, for instance —see *Dichtung und Wahrheit!*) the citizens had large gardens and vineyards outside the gates, while some kept cattle or pigs on the common and in the woods. There had been edicts since the fifteenth and sixteenth centuries forbidding citizens to allow their pigs to run about the streets at all hours of the day and night, but pig-sties were to be seen in front of the houses in Berlin till nearly the end of the seventeenth century,[1] and small places like Weimar still had their 'town herdsman' at the end of the eighteenth century.

When we know that the claims made on the productivity of the land were so modest, we do not expect to find very advanced methods of cultivation in practice, nor indeed had the methods in vogue in Germany at this time progressed very far beyond the standard of the Middle Ages. In this respect, however, Germany differed little from the rest of

[1] Biedermann, *op. cit.* I, 366.

BG   8

Europe. England only began to introduce rational methods on a large scale, following Holland's example, in the second half of the eighteenth century. We know from Arthur Young's writings that a large proportion of the English land under tillage lay in open fields, the same rotation being used on all soils alike. These village farms were run by associations of agricultural partners who occupied intermixed strips, and cultivated the whole under common rules of cropping, or 'field constraint'. The obstinate conservatism of the farmers added to the inherent defects of this system. 'In 1768 turnips and clover were still unknown in many parts of the country; and their full use only appreciated in the eastern counties.' 'Turnips remained, at the close of the eighteenth century, an alien crop in many counties.' 'In Middlesex, in 1796, it was no uncommon sight to see ploughs drawn by six horses, with three men in attendance.' 'Traditional methods were treasured with jealous care as agricultural heirlooms.'[1]

The reforms initiated in England by Young did not spread to Germany till well into the nineteenth century. Cultivation remained extensive instead of becoming intensive; deep ploughing was held to be not merely unimportant—it was generally left to the most incompetent labourers or even children—but harmful and unnatural. The open-field system (Dreifelderwirtschaft) with an unvarying succession of spring-sown corn (barley and oats), autumn-sown corn (wheat and rye) and fallow, was all but universal. Only gardens, where vegetables, fruit and fodder were grown, were exempt from 'Flurzwang' or field constraint, the community routine of cultivation. Age-old tradition, unaided by theoretical knowledge, determined all the methods employed, and there was no room for individual experiments, for the 'natural' methods handed down from antiquity had a greater sanctity in the country than even the traditional arts of the craftsmen in the towns. To attempt with impious hand to improve on nature,

[1] Lord Ernle (R. E. Prothero), *English Farming Past and Present*, 2nd ed. pp. 202–3.

in the manner of manuring the soil, for instance, was a crime against God, said an old steward in Bohemia in the early nineteenth century. Conservatism so deeply rooted could only be overcome by interference from high quarters: 'Your burgher or peasant will do nothing unless he is paid for it or kicked into it', said the officials of those days.[1]

Agriculture proceeded therefore in a vicious circle. The open-field system with its large and neglected permanent pasture provided insufficient fodder, so that the cattle were often so weak in spring that they had to be dragged on sledges to their grazing ground; shortage of cattle involved lack of manure, without which an improvement of the yield was impossible. It is not surprising then that J. C. Schubart (1734–87), who in the latter half of the century made great efforts to extend in northern, south-eastern and central Germany the cultivation for fodder of clover, that had been grown in the Spanish Netherlands for centuries, was hailed as one of the greatest benefactors of the century, and ennobled by the emperor, Joseph II, with the title of 'Edler von dem Kleefelde'. The effects of this revolution were slow to make themselves felt, for throughout the century the productivity of the land remained on the whole extremely low. In Silesia for instance between 1770 and 1780 wheat gave an average crop of 5·6 fold, and rye of 5·2 fold, while in England in Young's time wheat and rye already produced a ten-fold crop, bad as methods were, and other crops were twice as good as the Silesian ones.[2]

In parts of northern Germany and in Austria sheep-rearing was carried on for the export of wool and was considerably improved in this century by the Spanish government's consenting at last to the export of merino sheep. These sheep-farms, and the dairy-farms on Swiss and Dutch models, that produced cheese and later butter beyond home needs, were the most advanced types of farming to be found in Germany then, though in proportion to the rest they were of small

[1] Biedermann, I, 168.   [2] Sombart, op. cit.

account. Before the end of the century attempts were made at the reform of other branches of agriculture, particularly by the above-mentioned clover-Schubart, and by an admirer of Young, Albrecht Thaer (1752–1828), who did much to spread the 'Norfolk System' of rotation in Germany. By this the years of corn-growing were interrupted by the growth of other crops to allow the soil to recover and to supply fodder. With more fodder the stock of cattle could be increased and the land could be more adequately manured. But what was principally lacking was a theoretical understanding of the processes involved, and only the first steps had been made in this direction by Priestley, Lavoisier and others in the last two decades of the century.

The vigorous efforts made by the rulers of Prussia, by some lesser princes (like Karl August) and by a number of individual landowners—for the national importance of agriculture was obvious to all—were not attended by proportionate results. The most useful accomplishment of the Prussian government in this direction was the establishment in the thinly populated eastern districts of religious refugees from France and Holland (from 1685 onwards), and later of emigrants from the southern states like the Palatinate and Württemberg, where agricultural practice was relatively good. It was with the same intention and by the promise of similar privileges that the Russian government attracted South German settlers to the Volga basin, where their descendants still form separate communities to-day. Frederick the Great continued in this respect the policy of the Great Elector and his own father. Frederick William had also gained new land for cultivation by extensive draining operations in the Havel valley, had deepened rivers and improved roads to facilitate the export of produce, and made many efforts to improve methods. Frederick the Great similarly carried out a big drainage scheme in the Oder and Warthe marsh, an area of 300,000 acres. In the matter of methods perhaps his best work was the encouragement of the cultivation of the potato. It was not until the 70's that potatoes were grown in fields, and we hear that severe measures were needed to overcome the apathy and prejudice of the peasants. It was commonly believed for many years that eating potatoes gave rise to scrofula, rickets, consumption, gout and all sorts of diseases. Nettelbeck tells us in his memoirs that when Frederick sent the first cart-load of them to Kolberg in 1744, after a famine, so that citizens might try the crop in their gardens, they could make nothing of them. 'The things have no smell and no taste', they said, 'and not even dogs will eat them (raw!). What is the use of them to us?' But next year a gendarme, a Swabian by birth, was sent with the load to show people how to grow and use them. In the south the potato was better known, though only as a garden plant. Perhaps the greatest single difference between the usual diet of all classes in 1700 and in 1800 was that in 1700 the potato was almost unknown and in 1800 indispensable. For the peasantry the chief consequence was that absolute famine came to be a thing of the past. If the corn crops failed they had potatoes to fall back on, and in time the potato was a more important staple article of diet than bread.

Chapter IV

THE PEASANT

The everyday life and thought of the country dwellers were such as one might expect, given the fundamental conditions of their life outlined above. There were naturally great differences between family and family, both amongst the nobility and the peasantry, according to the economic position and inherited privileges of each. As in France, there were some families of noble extraction whose standard of life was no higher than a peasant's, and there were free peasants here and there, particularly in the south, who were little lords in everything but name.

The average peasant and his family, as we have seen, had never much more than was necessary to keep body and soul together. There could be no question of luxuries in their life. It was necessary for them to buy from the towns only what could not possibly be dispensed with, a few spices perhaps and metal ware. For the rest they depended on what they themselves or their neighbours could grow in their fields and gardens and make with their own hands. Houses and furniture and the clothing of both men and women were the work of members of the household, assisted occasionally perhaps by a neighbour, or more rarely by a travelling craftsman. The following description of English rural life at this period could be applied in almost every detail to German conditions:

The inhabitants had little need of communication with their immediate neighbours, still less with the outside world. The fields and the live-stock provided the necessary food and clothing. Whatever wood might be required for building, fences or fuel, was provided on the wastes. Each village had its mill, generally the property of the lord of the manor; almost every house had its oven and brewing kettle. Women spun wool into coarse cloth; men tanned their own leather. Wealth only existed in its simplest forms, and natural divisions of employment were not made, because only the rudest implements of production were now used. The rough tools required for the cultivation of the soil, and the rude household utensils needed for the comfort of daily life, were made at home. In the long winter evenings farmers, their sons, and their servants carved the wooden spoons, the platters, and the beechen bowls; fitted and rivetted the bottoms into the horn mugs, or closed, in coarse fashion, the holes in the leather jugs. They plaited the wicker baskets; fitted handles to the scythes, rakes and other tools; cut the staves, and fixed the thongs for the flails; made the willow or ashen teeth for rakes and harrows, and hardened them in the fire; fashioned ox yokes and forks, racks and rackstaves; twisted willows into scythe cradles, or into the traces and other harness gear. Travelling carpenters, smiths and tinkers visited farmhouses and remoter villages at rare intervals to perform those parts of the work which needed their professional skill. But every village of any size found employment for such trades as those of the smith and the carpenter. Meanwhile the women plaited the straw for the neck-collars, stitched and stuffed sheepskin bags for the cart saddle, wove the stirrups and halters from hemp or straw, peeled the rushes for and made the candles. Spinning wheels, distaffs, needles were never idle. Coarse, home-made cloth and linen supplied all wants. The very names of spinster, webster, shepster, litster, brewster, and baxter, show that women span, wove, cut out and dyed cloth, as well as brewed and baked for the household.[1]

In the matter of clothing the villagers were almost beyond the reach of fashion. They used their clothes until they were worn out. Styles of dress did, of course, change over long periods. The great variety of peasant costumes worn as best clothes on special occasions all embodied features of the town dress of much earlier periods, perhaps of the sixteenth century or earlier.[2] The peasantry had at some time or other adopted modified versions of town fashions, but these had become stereotyped, because the conditions necessary for

[1] *Social England*, ed. Traill, v, 101 (article by R. E. Prothero).
[2] See K. Spiess, *Die Deutschen Volkstrachten*, Leipzig, 1911.

quick changes of fashion, above all a surplus of means and variety of stimulus, were not present in the country. It was the same with many other features of their material civilisation and even of what higher culture they possessed, as has been pointed out by Hans Naumann and those who like him believe in the 'Sinken des Kulturguts'.[1] But the opponents of this theory are no doubt right in claiming a considerable degree of creativeness for the peasant. It was by no means all the features of his culture that had been passively received by him from 'higher' social classes. Many of the most important went back to a time when there were no other classes—the form of the peasant house and of the chief agricultural implements, as well as innumerable customs and beliefs owed little or nothing to either knighthood or bourgeoisie, for they were older than both. And though admittedly strongly attached to tradition, the peasant was no more incapable than any other man of modifying what he borrowed to serve his own purposes, and of having occasionally good ideas of his own.

What prevented rapid change was the strength of community feeling in the village, and institutions like the three-field system, with its rules of common cropping, which both expressed and fostered this feeling. It is now fashionable in Germany to praise the traditionalism of the peasant, by a reaction against the views expressed when the individualistic middle class led public opinion. For the townsman from the Renaissance age onwards, however, the countryman was 'der dumme Bauer'. He was held to be coarse, stupid, dishonest, drunken and quarrelsome, and it was not until the time of the Romantics, after hints from Rousseau and the 'Sturm und Drang', that it was discovered that the countryman was in his own way a completely civilised person who was even superior to the townsman in much that was now held to be important in life.

In reading eighteenth-century descriptions of peasant life

[1] See H. Naumann, *Grundzüge der deutschen Volkskunde*, Leipzig, 1922.

the change of attitude, by which our present-day views have been affected, must be kept in mind. It was not the townsman's feeling of superiority, however, that inspired the following description of the peasant's life by a man revered by Goethe in his youth, J. M. von Loen:

The peasant is brought up in complete ignorance like a mere animal. He is plagued continually with feudal services, running messages, beating up game, digging trenches and the like. From morning till night he must be digging the fields, whether scorched by the sun or numbed by the cold. At night he lies in the field and becomes little better than a beast of the fields, to keep the beasts from stealing his seed, and what he saves from their jaws is taken soon afterwards by a harsh official for arrears of rent and taxes. The countryman to-day is the most wretched of all creatures. The peasants are slaves and their men are hardly to be distinguished from the cattle they tend. The traveller comes to villages where children run about half-naked and call to every passer-by for alms. Their parents have scarcely a rag on their backs. A few lean cows have to till their fields and give milk as well. Their barns are empty and their cottages threaten to collapse in a heap any moment. They themselves look neglected and wretched; one would have more pity for them, if their wild and brutish appearance did not seem to justify their hard lot.[1]

These general impressions are confirmed by such different writers as Laukhard, *Der reisende Franzose*, Nicolai, Knigge and Crabb Robinson. The references to the peasantry by Crabb Robinson in his *Letters* are particularly interesting because he is able to compare German with English conditions. The condition of the peasantry varied greatly in the provinces he visited. He was never in the eastern and northern states, where the lot of the peasantry was hardest. Of those he saw, the peasantry of the Catholic ecclesiastical states like Bamberg and Würzburg seemed the best placed. Even where the material prosperity of the peasant was equal to that of the English villager, he seemed to Crabb Robinson

[1] J. M. v. Loen, *Freye Gedanken vom Hof,* 3rd ed. Frankfort and Leipzig, 1768, p. 28.

to be more subservient, owing to the feudal burdens he still bore, and it seemed wrong to him that so much field work should be left to women. Howitt, writing forty years later, but before the Industrial Revolution had seriously affected Germany, was inclined to minimise the hardness of the German peasants' lot because he was so pleased to find that the majority of them owned the land they cultivated, whereas the average villager in England was a labourer dependent on a master. Howitt too was only familiar with the south and the Rhineland, where it is true that the peasant proprietor preponderated, and where he had, by this time, commuted his services for money payments. His picture would not have been so favourable if based on conditions in Mecklenburg or Prussia. He was struck by the patient laboriousness of the German peasants, men and women, and by the economy they practised, collecting as they did every scrap that could be used for fodder, manure or firewood. These habits he explained as the result of their working for themselves and not for a master. Aesthetically, however, he preferred the English countryside, with its variety of large and small estates, manor-houses and cottages, and the neatness and cleanliness of even the smallest homesteads. The rarity of gentlemen's seats in the country was a point noted by all English travellers—it was due to the attraction of the nobility to the courts. The cottages were less spick and span than in England because the women worked so much more in the fields, and perhaps also because there was no Hall near by to set a higher standard in these matters.

The chief civilising influences in the village were the minister and the schoolmaster. The power of the minister was so largely a matter of personality, whatever the sect he represented might be, that no brief general statements can be made about it. Some varieties of Protestant ministers will be dealt with later. The power of the village schoolmaster can be more usefully discussed at this point. Generally speaking, it was very slight indeed, for though, in an age that believed so passionately in education, country people were not neglected by the reformers, most of their proposals remained on paper. In Prussia, for instance, the most advanced of the German states in this respect, the village schools seem to have remained wretched in most cases until after the end of the century. From official reports of an inspection made in 1802 and 1803 in Cleve, a Prussian province where conditions were favourable, it appears that Frederick the Great's admirable General-Landschul-Reglement of 1763 had remained a dead letter. Theoretically, attendance at school for six hours a day was compulsory for all children between the ages of five or six and thirteen. For the poor no fee was charged. The qualifications necessary for a teacher were defined, classes were to be duly graded and uniform textbooks to be used. But at their inspection it was found that forty-three teachers out of sixty-seven were incompetent. Hardly any had attended the training school set up for Cleve in 1784, they had usually been appointed without being examined and once in office they had neither the leisure nor the books they required to improve themselves. They were so wretchedly paid that all had some other occupation. Many were organists or vergers or both, some were tailors or exercised some other craft, some sold brandy or collected tolls. The school buildings, where regular buildings existed, were almost always in bad repair. Often a room had to be hired for the purpose in a house, and sometimes the teacher slept in the school-room. There were often no separate classes. Each child came up book in hand and said its lesson. The curriculum was extremely narrow, reading, writing and perhaps a little arithmetic, and a good deal of religion. Little was read beyond the Bible and catechism. Attendance was extremely irregular. In summer the schools were empty.[1] If these were the conditions in an enlightened state, it can be imagined what they were like in

[1] W. Meiners, 'Landschulen und Landschullehrer im Herzogtum Cleve vor hundert Jahren', in *Archiv für Kulturgeschichte*, III, 1905.

the average small state. But in the second half of the century a considerable number of peasants could at least read and write, as is indicated by the large sales of the calendars and so forth that were written for them. Of R. Z. Becker's *Noth- und Hülfsbuch*, for instance, a million copies are said to have been sold in just over twenty years.

Chapter V

THE COUNTRY GENTLEMAN

The everyday life of the average German country gentleman in the eighteenth century would not be very different from that of an English squire. There were perhaps greater differences between rich and poor noble families in Germany than in England. There would be many who, like the Reichsritter of the south-west, ruled as little sovereigns over broad estates and perhaps owed allegiance only to the emperor himself, and other *Junker* who, in Freytag's phrase, 'were only distinguished from other country dwellers by their superciliousness and their scorn for work in the fields'. As in France, many of them would have no estates of their own, but only a house in the village and a few acres of land, of which they might merely be tenants. Some again, though of moderate means, would have good connections with the leading courts, whose protection would ensure for their sons good careers in the army or the diplomatic or civic service, while others, buried in the depths of the country, would have no ambitions exceeding those of an English yeoman. They differed from each other immensely, again, in breeding and in intellectual attainments. There were the Hardenbergs and the Humboldts at one extreme, and, at the other, boorish Junkers such as those who figure in so many German stories, or in the memoirs of K. H. von Lang, Friedrich von der Trenck and many more, worthy descendants of the robber knights of the late Middle Ages and the restless *Krippenreiter* of the seventeenth century. In between came the great mass of the country gentry, who, living in peace and comparative comfort on their estates, could count themselves among the most fortunate of their time. Such a country gentleman 'took no more notice of the great world than was necessary, mixed without ceremony at great family parties with the whole nobility of the neighbourhood, allowed himself an occasional carousal, bred his foals, sold his wool, and disputed with his parson. If he was not too strict he maintained tolerably good relations with his subjects and seldom had any conception of the harm that he himself suffered through his labourers being serfs'.[1]

The country nobility were still often able to maintain their position, even when they did not administer their estates wisely, because of the many privileges their birth conferred on them. In the Catholic south there were few old families who had not relatives in some cathedral chapter, some wealthy order (like that of the Knights of St John or the Teutonic Knights) or some monastery, convent or other religious foundation, on almost all of which the best sinecures were reserved for the nobility. Where this privilege was not available, as in the Protestant north, families when hard pressed had to be content with mortgaging their lands or seeking an alliance by marriage with one of the many wealthy middle-class families who were eager enough for this honour.

The healthiest and most contented families were usually those who remained independent of lay and ecclesiastical courts alike, living a simple patriarchal life, the essential features of which had been much the same in the time of Horace as they were in eighteenth-century Germany or England. The more attractive side of this life has been charmingly described in an essay of Eichendorff's, himself the descendant of such a family in Silesia. On the rare occasions when they read something about the life of the great world in the newspapers, he says, it seemed to them like a fairy-tale. The monotony of their lives was only broken by frequent shooting parties, which ended with much firing of shot-guns and phantastic huntsman's tales, and by ceremonious visits to the annual fair in a neighbouring country town. In the winter each family in turn would give

[1] G. Freytag, *Bilder aus der deutschen Vergangenheit*, III, 9 Kap.

a ball in its own home, a jolly improvised affair, for which a large living-room, emptied of furniture, would serve as ballroom, and the schoolmaster and a few cronies would provide the music. The ball would be opened, as at court, with the traditional minuet, but strenuous and noisy dances would make up most of the programme.

These fortunate folk lived simply but contentedly in houses that were for the most part quite unpretentious even though always dignified with the name of 'Schlösser', houses which, however lovely the country might be, were not constructed to afford the aesthetic delight of a distant prospect, but to allow the family to see from their windows what was going on in their stables and barns. The ambition of the men was to be sound farmers, and the pride of the ladies was a reputation for good housekeeping. They had neither time nor feeling for the beauty of nature, they were still products of nature themselves. The poetry of life, such as it was, was left as a useless luxury to their young daughters, who did not fail in their few idle hours to strum old-fashioned arias and sonatas on a tuneless clavichord and to brighten the kitchen garden behind the house with choice beds of flowers. As soon as day broke there was so much bustling activity in house and farmyard that the startled visitor would hastily take refuge in the garden. Doors would fly open and bang to on every side, and amidst much unnecessary shouting and disputing they would sweep and milk and make butter, while the swallows flitted gaily over the confusion as if they were part of the household, and the morning sun shone brightly all through the house over the faded family portraits and the brass mountings of the old furniture.

Such a country gentleman's estate was necessarily very little dependent on the outside world. When the nearest main road was itself an ill-defined cart track, as it usually was, things could not be otherwise. Once inside the lane leading to the 'Rittergut', the visitor felt himself to be in a little world apart. Here were the houses of the peasants who had lived and worked on this estate all their lives and never travelled further than the nearest market town, here the fields with their intermingled strips, the produce of which was almost all consumed within the estate boundaries. In the manor house and the adjoining farm buildings not only every kind of food required by the squire's family was stored and prepared, but beer was brewed, much of their clothing was made, and all kinds of common articles now bought in shops were produced by the skilled hands of the ladies of the household and their servants.

Such a large estate could not be run successfully without a great deal of skill and knowledge. All those arts were needed which are now the domain of the pioneer rancher. We can form a good idea of the range of knowledge required by the ideal country gentleman from such works as W. H. von Hohberg's *Georgica curiosa oder adeliches Landleben*,[1] the first of a number of 'outlines of knowledge' for the landed gentry. Here we read for instance of the laws that affect the landowner, the precautions to be observed in purchasing estates and building houses, the elements of agriculture, horse-breeding, gardening, brewing and the cultivation of silkworms, as well as of the duties of the father and mother of a family and the arts of riding, hunting and fishing.

It goes without saying that the more bookish type of education was of little importance for a young nobleman from the country unless he aimed at a career at court or in foreign service. The majority would be taught to read and write by the village schoolmaster or parson and continue their education either at a 'Ritterakademie' or at the grammar school of a neighbouring town, or perhaps they would receive all their instruction at home from the local pastor or some young theologian. The ideal presented to them would be much the same as for the young aristocracy in general, but with less insistence on the refinements of the courts and a knowledge of the great world. They would seldom be submitted to a severe discipline and would make no secret of their being more interested in horses and dogs than in languages or history. From the age of sixteen or so they

[1] Nürnberg, 1687, 2 vols. folio, with many interesting plates.

would turn their back on their studies for good and give themselves up to the occupations and particularly the sports of a country gentleman. It is this type that Knigge paints in his picture of the country squire at court, who, appearing in the antechamber in the embroidered dress that is so stiff and so cold after his familiar top-boots, surtout and smoking cap, trips over his sword and evokes the contempt of the Frenchified cavaliers assembled there by his blunt speech and provincial manners.[1]

It was by no means every member of the country nobility who was as unfamiliar with courts as this. It has been mentioned that one thing which struck English travellers in Germany was the comparative scarcity of gentlemen's country seats, for in the south and west, as we have seen, large numbers of the country nobility were attracted to the courts, often residing almost continuously in the capital and leaving the management of their estates to stewards. Many who lived chiefly in the country would contrive long visits to neighbouring capitals, especially if they had a daughter to marry or a son to start on a public career, and a large number would be in touch with the courts through relatives and friends. It was a privilege of the nobility, including the country families, to send their sons to court as pages, a privilege of which those who had the necessary means and good friends at court still made frequent use. But in spite of all these links between the country and the capital, there remained an easily perceptible gap between court nobility and country nobility. On the whole, the cultivated and much travelled country nobleman, who, while not neglecting his estate or his public duties, maintained an interest in the liberal arts and perhaps contributed himself to science or literature, was a very much rarer figure in Germany than in the England of the Augustan Age.

[1] Knigge, *op. cit.* Einleitung.

PART III

THE NEW ORDER OF SOCIETY
THE MIDDLE CLASS

Chapter I

RETROSPECT

The section of society to which we may apply the vague term middle class was already so large in eighteenth-century Germany, and the differences between its various groups were already so marked, that some study of its historical development is necessary before its complex structure can be understood. Each century since the early Middle Ages had left its mark on middle-class life, but the new features as they appeared had never entirely effaced the old, so that life in the eighteenth century is constantly reminding us of one aspect or another of the life of past ages.

The history of the middle class or 'Bürger' is, as the German word itself suggests, the history of the towns. Towns arose at a certain stage in the economic development of Germany with increasing specialisation, as they had arisen earlier elsewhere. The division of labour was carried much further in a town than in the self-sufficing communities which had preceded it. A large proportion of its inhabitants were craftsmen and traders who could give little or no time to agriculture, and for whom food had therefore to be imported from the surrounding country. In the primitive agricultural communities of the early Middle Ages, on the other hand, almost all the material needs even of great land-owners were met by the produce of their own estates and the labour of those living on them. We have seen that many agricultural communities in the eighteenth century still needed very little from outside.

Yet the difference between village and town in this respect, especially in early times, was only one of degree. In medieval towns there were always many citizens following purely agricultural pursuits. Many craftsmen and traders too spent a portion of their time in this way, or at least had gardens, and kept cattle on the common, so that every town in medieval Germany presented a semi-rural aspect, with its cultivated fields within the town boundaries, its barns and pigsties and the cattle straying through its streets. There were hundreds of semi-agricultural small towns of this type still in eighteenth-century Germany, in fact there were few towns which did not produce a fair proportion of their food supplies within the area owned by their citizens. In other respects too there was still much to remind one of the self-sufficient period, for a good deal of work was done in the middle-class home which in England at this period would have been left to a tradesman. Goethe tells us in *Dichtung und Wahrheit* that his father, a well-to-do citizen of Frankfort, chose men-servants who had some skill as tailors, so that clothes could be made for the family at home. In the early nineteenth century all English travellers expressed astonishment at the 'cooking and linen mania of the ladies'. As late as 1842 we read: 'The hoarding of linen and of stockings is a passion with most German ladies. Spinning-wheels abound, and are to be seen in the houses of many people of great pretensions: in still more of the burgher class, and in every house of the common people. Ladies of rank and fortune are still plentiful, who spend their mornings in the kitchen up to the elbows in flour'.[1] Bread, preserves, even soap and candles, were made at home.

Traces of self-sufficiency lingered long, but the medieval town was already a settlement that could not exist without obtaining foodstuffs and raw materials from the surrounding

[1] W. Howitt, *The rural and domestic life of Germany*, p. 233.

countryside, in return for the products of its craftsmanship and for ready money. By the end of the thirteenth century Germany was already honeycombed into economic regions, each one of which had such a town as its centre. These towns dotted over the country would be perhaps three to five hours' journey apart in the south and west, seven or eight in the more thinly populated north and east, so that from almost any village a peasant could go to the nearest market and return in a day. The boundaries of the regions were of course fluid, fixed by convenience and custom, though legal considerations might enter in, because of the rights often acquired by towns to compel the use of certain roads by carriers. In the town market once a week the produce of the country was exchanged for the industrial wares of the town. There was also an active exchange of goods and services between the members of the town population and a certain, usually very limited, amount of trade with other towns.

It is easier to describe the economic function of the fully established town than to account for its origins. Some scholars stress the importance of the market, others that of the castle. Both were essential features of a town. The land on which a town was built belonged to the king or to some feudal lord, lay or ecclesiastical, and all towns began under the protection of some lord. If the legal and political aspects of their history are emphasised, the castle appears more important than the market, but economically it is the market which gives the town its *raison d'être*. Sombart[1] thinks that we must seek the origin of towns in the demand for the services of craftsmen on the part of the only people who could pay for them, lords and bishops living on the revenues of their lands. However this may be, it seems clear that the growth of towns is a phenomenon connected with the development of *Grundherrschaft* and the increasing use of money, as well as with the increasing contacts between peoples and the new standards of life that resulted from the

[1] *Op. cit.* 3rd edition, I, 134 ff.

Crusades. It is clear too that when towns had reached a certain stage their development could not be very rapid, because even apart from the ravages of epidemic diseases three great obstacles limited the range of their trade: unproductive agricultural methods, bad communications and the lack of a sound currency. These checks to the growth of towns had not been removed, in most cases, even in the eighteenth century, so that Germany's towns were still small. They had seldom spread much beyond their medieval walls, and we must remember that even the leading towns of the Middle Ages were very small indeed compared with modern cities. A town with 20,000 or more inhabitants was an exception. There were only ten or twelve of this size in fifteenth-century Germany.

Small as the medieval towns were, they soon became a political force to be reckoned with. In the time of the later Hohenstaufens they came to share the real power with the territorial princes. By the power of combination and by money payments, many of them gained one privilege after another from their original lords. All of them, even if they were under the rule of seignorial officials, were privileged places as compared with villages. They were fortified and comparatively safe to live in. They were sanctuaries invested with the town peace, so that if runaway serfs succeeded in remaining for a year in a town before their lord could establish a claim to them, they became free. They had a monopoly of trade, and held their weekly market under the protection of their lord or bishop. The larger towns held periodic fairs for trade with more distant parts. They aimed at and usually secured the full control of their market and its tolls, and authority to regulate wages, prices, hours and quality of wares in their gild industries. They frequently gained independent jurisdiction, the right to set up a mint, and authority to impose duties and taxes.

It was as a result of this bargaining process that the distinction arose, still a very important one in the eighteenth century, between Free Towns (Reichsstädte) and Territorial Towns (Landstädte). The Free Towns carried the conflict with their feudal superiors one stage further. Instead of owing allegiance to a lord inconveniently near at hand, they succeeded in establishing a communal form of government for themselves and were subject only to the emperor. The Landstädte were not always worse off, for a happy compromise or the weakness of their lord might make conditions very favourable for them.

Both types of town were constantly contending not only with their lord but also with two other forces, the surrounding villages and other towns. The first of these conflicts led to the domination of the organised town over the unorganised country. The town wished to establish a monopoly of industry and trade, and to ensure its supplies of food and raw materials. This policy involved the control of roads, so that all goods in transit should pass through the town market, the prohibition of rival markets within a fixed area, rights of pre-emption (Stapelrecht), the prohibition of industrial activities in the country (Bannrecht), and other similar measures. The second conflict, with other towns, the struggle for monopolies, was carried on partly by the means mentioned above, but mainly by tariffs. All these measures of civic egoism were enforced with greater consistency and success in Germany than anywhere else in Europe except in Italy, because of the lack of a central authority in these two countries. Many effects of these measures persisted down to our period, in innumerable tolls and restrictions on trade—it was owing to an old agreement of this kind that it was impossible, for instance, to divert the main road from Frankfort to Leipzig through Weimar (see above, p. 31)—but many privileges of the towns had been curtailed by the state governments.

The internal organisation of the towns naturally underwent great changes according to the varying success of their policy towards the outside world, and the rate at which their inhabitants grew in numbers and became differentiated in function. The town council of the Free Towns was for long elected from the ranks of the patricians alone, the families of some standing in the town, 'who had exercised no craft and engaged in no petty trading, but had lived on their incomes (from property) or kept themselves honestly by enterprises of some scope, or in some respectable official capacity'. In towns with a large trade, especially in the northern ports, the merchants soon came to be the dominant element in these councils. They generally contrived to maintain their position here against the attacks of the artisans, but in the more industrial towns the craft-gilds successfully claimed a share in the government, or even took it entirely into their own hands, becoming in many cases exclusively political organs. These struggles too had left very clear traces in the constitutions of the German towns of our period, with important results for their social life.

No less important were the effects on everyday life, in the eighteenth and even in the nineteenth century, of the medieval organisation of industry in gilds. Down to the time of Gottfried Keller and later, German literature is full of figures whose life and outlook is still in all essentials that of the medieval gild craftsman, a fact which lends support to those economic historians who hold that the forms of German industry were not fully capitalistic until the second half of the nineteenth century. A brief description of the gild system, in its less controversial aspects, must therefore be attempted.

A gild craftsman was, at least in the early days, one of a small group of people in his town who alone possessed skill in a certain craft, or later, who were officially authorised to practise such a craft. He only needed a few tools which anyone might acquire, but his skill had had to be gained by serving a long apprenticeship. It was handed down from one generation to another. It was very usual for a master's son to succeed him, and a master treated his apprentices, even if they were not his own children, almost as members of the family, for his apprentices and journeymen lived with him in the same house. Though the difficulty of training young craftsmen and the slow growth of the population themselves tended to keep down the number of craftsmen, it was considered necessary that they should be organised in a corporate body. Whether the initiative came originally from the workers themselves or from the lords who employed them, and how much the gilds were influenced by older (Roman) models, are still matters of dispute, but it is clear that the individualistic point of view which comes so naturally to us was then comparatively rare. Men had no desire to stand alone. They instinctively grouped themselves with their relatives in clans, or when that was no longer possible, with fellow-villagers in a village community, or later still, when this tie too was broken, with fellow-workers in a gild. So some see in the gild a kind of artificial family, others the forms of the village community adapted to industrial conditions.[1]

The gilds were therefore nothing if not clannish. Their policy was directed towards maintaining equality and solidarity among the members of the gild, and excluding non-members from the enjoyment of their privileges. Not competition, but co-operation between masters was their aim. All members enjoyed the same rights and advantages. No master might make a corner in raw material; the available resources had to be equally shared. No one might have more than a certain maximum number of apprentices and journeymen, or more than one workshop and stall. The masters fixed prices in common council for all classes of goods, and determined what wages might be paid to journeymen. Uniformity of price was further ensured by their houses being side by side (they had no regular 'shops') and their stalls together in the market. There were no middlemen required in most trades; the craftsman himself sold the

[1] So Sombart, *op. cit.* I, 190.

things he had made. Further, all gilds were exclusive. They were never content unless they had a monopoly of producing their particular kind of wares. No one was allowed to practise the same trade in their town without belonging to the gild. Some gilds had their monopoly recognised in a charter obtained from the town authorities; even when it was not mentioned in their charter, or if the gild had no charter, it was taken for granted by everyone that gild membership was compulsory for all engaged in the craft.[1]

The interests of gild members were maintained not only by active measures against blacklegs (Pfuscher, Störer), but by the various tolls and vexatious restrictions imposed by the town, to protect home industries, on imported goods. It was possible for a long period to prevent competition because of technical conditions, the nature of the demand and the prevailing habits of thought and feeling. However much he might exert himself, a master could only turn out a limited amount of work, because everything had to be done by his own hands or those of his apprentices and journeymen, whose number was strictly limited, both by the possibility (at least in theory) of their setting up for themselves when they had acquired skill, and more effectively, by gild and town regulations. Moreover, one man's wares were usually as good as another's. They were all in a traditional style, and if an individual made any slight improvements they could not be patented. The demand too was steady and conservative, governed by tradition and habit in a society essentially static, arranged in something very like castes.

But the most important factor of all was the mentality of the craftsman in this static society. A man worked to keep himself and his family according to the usual standard of that state of life unto which it had pleased God to call him, to use the phrase that still survives in the English Church Catechism. The characteristically modern desire to 'get on', to be better than one's neighbour, was certainly active in

[1] Kulischer, *Allgemeine Wirtschaftsgeschichte*, I, 194.

some individuals, but it was combated in every way by the 'vis inertiae' of the mass, fortified by the disillusioned wisdom of the Church. Here too the parallel with the village community is striking. As each villager, in the ideal village, had just enough land to be cultivated by a family and to provide food for it, the gildsman was to have enough work to keep him occupied and to furnish him with a maintenance. He made goods for certain regular customers, usually to order, and he was his own salesman.

We have considered the gilds so far only from the point of view of production, as it concerned the masters or independent craftsmen. We must enquire further how the gilds served the interest of the consumer and of the lower grades of workers. The needs of the consumer were satisfied well enough by the gilds so long as he asked for a good solid piece of workmanship in a traditional style. The gildsman wished to live and let live. The danger to the consumer that a monopoly seems to us to bring with it was counteracted by the strong ethical feeling of the gilds, which inspired their efforts to ensure good quality in their wares and to charge a just price, and secondly by the fact that the producers of one class of wares were consumers of others. Living as they did side by side with other craftsmen they were far more vividly conscious of being members one of another than men can be to-day, when the relations between producer and consumer are impersonal and determined only by the 'cash nexus'. The governing body of the town, whether under the control of the lord or not, had not an entirely impossible task in trying to reconcile the views of the various gilds and was usually able to give its authority to their recommendations. Of course there were incessant conflicts between opposed interests, there was corruption and legislation in the interests of a class. In the later days, as we shall see, both gilds and town councils were sometimes instruments of oppression, but in the Middle Ages a good working balance of interests was, it seems, generally attained.

The position of apprentices and journeymen was probably not so ideal, even in the best times of the gilds, as some enthusiasts would have us believe. The gilds were corporations of masters and they seem to have had monopolistic tendencies from a very early date. The older view (of Gierke for instance) that this was the case only in the period of their 'decline' (sixteenth to eighteenth century) is no longer widely held.[1] All the three types of restriction governing full membership of a gild were imposed already in the thirteenth and fourteenth centuries. These restrictions concerned (a) the candidate's parentage. They excluded strangers to the town, sons of serfs, illegitimate children or sons of members of the 'unehrliche Berufe' (a motley list: barbers, shepherds, tanners, millers, watchmen, gravediggers, executioners, etc.). (b) Technical training. The apprentice, once admitted, had to 'serve his time', usually four years in Germany, to work as 'Geselle' or journeyman in different towns (this was called his 'Wanderzeit') and produce a prescribed 'Masterpiece'. (c) Finally he had to be able to pay for his privileges. At the beginning of each of the three stages (as apprentice, journeyman, master) he paid a fee to the gild; before admission as master he had to prove that he was in possession of a certain amount of capital, and had always to provide an expensive 'Meisteressen'. Many of these conditions could be relaxed in favour of masters' sons, or those who married masters' daughters or widows. It is probably not true, even for the best days of the gilds, that every journeyman could hope to become a master in due time. Some remained journeymen for life, and a great many had to work for many years for a master at a wage fixed by the gild before they could attain independence. There were married journeymen, no longer living in their masters' houses. There were unions of Gesellen and strikes in Germany even in the fourteenth century.[2]

[1] Kulischer, *op. cit.* I, 199 ff.
[2] *Ibid.* 210 f.

The gilds were far more than industrial unions. 'They embraced the whole man', in Gierke's phrase, like all the brotherhoods which were so numerous in the Middle Ages, ranging as they did from associations of lawyers to unions of prostitutes. Men could not detach parts of their personality, as it were, in the modern way, and join an association for one limited purpose. The gild had a particular *raison d'être*, but the members formed at the same time a fellowship for all purposes which they could have in common. Those practising the same craft lived as true neighbours in the same street (as old street names still remind us). In addition to its function in industry, a gild might perform that of a modern friendly society, a freemason's lodge, a social club, a company of volunteers, even a political party. The citizens grouped themselves by gilds on ceremonial occasions, and for some religious purposes; the gilds, not individuals, were represented in the town council.

In the early days of the towns there were comparatively few people engaged purely in trade. It has been calculated for instance that in medieval Frankfort, which had more trade with distant parts than most towns, four-fifths of the population were occupied in direct production (including agriculture).[1] The one type of exchange that was absolutely vital for the towns, that of industrial wares for provisions, took place in the open market on market-day, and no intermediaries were needed here between craftsman and peasant. There were often separate markets for cattle, horses, corn, hay, wood, fish, meat, salt, etc., and even here, where wholesale trade must have been permitted, the private citizen was always given the first chance of buying. The number of middlemen was kept down to the minimum and they were closely watched by the town authorities. The craftsmen sold their wares retail, either in their market booths or in their houses. The butchers and bakers had their booths on or near the market, and here stood also the stalls

[1] G. v. Below, *Das ältere dt. Städtewesen und Bürgertum*, p. 106.

of the Krämer, the only real 'shopkeepers', who were usually prohibited from selling articles made in the town. They dealt in small imported articles, such as dried fruit, dyes, perfumes, imported ironmongery and hardware, hats, gloves, ribbons and finer dress materials. Woollen cloth was sold by the cloth merchants (Gewandschneider). Below the Krämer there were street-sellers of local produce, fruit, fish and so on.

This local trade, almost entirely concerned with the produce of the land and labour of the town and of the country a few hours' journey round, would be almost the only trade that mattered in small towns, and much the most important even in large towns. Except for cloth, salt and some spices, the articles brought from a distance were still almost all luxuries, which would scarcely enter the lives of any but the well-to-do. The products of ordinary handicraft were naturally not exported, unless they were a speciality of the town, like Nürnberg ironware and instruments. The same natural principles governed the export of agricultural produce and raw material generally. Every region was normally self-sufficient in food supply. It was possible to maintain the wheat trade of the Hanse, for instance, only because in every year it was necessary somewhere or other in their area to import grain owing to a local bad harvest. Their herrings, on the other hand, were in wide demand, because they could not be obtained elsewhere. Owing to the predominance of local trade, there was no hard and fast distinction in medieval times between wholesale merchants and retailers. The wholesale merchants were retailers who had extended their scope, and they still sold goods retail too. The merchant (or later his agent) accompanied his goods to their distant destination, just as to the local market. The long distance trade was mostly conducted at the periodic fairs, held at fixed times in convenient centres. Only the bigger towns had fairs of any importance. The imported goods were distributed from these centres by pedlars.

How little an eighteenth-century Free Town had changed since the Middle Ages may be seen from Goethe's description of his native Frankfort in the first book of *Dichtung und Wahrheit*:

The great bridge over the Main was my favourite place for walking. Its length, its massiveness, and its fine appearance made it a notable structure, and it was, besides, almost the only memorial left from ancient times of the protective care which civil government owes to its citizens. The beautiful stream above and below the bridge attracted my eye, and it always filled me with delight to see the gilt cock on the old cross over the bridge glitter in the sunshine. Generally I extended my walk through Sachsenhausen, and for a farthing enjoyed the experience of being ferried at my leisure to the other bank. Back once more on the Frankfort side of the river, I would stroll along to the wine-market, and admire the mechanism of the cranes when goods were being unloaded. But it was particularly entertaining to watch the arrival of the market-boats, so varied were their cargoes, and so extraordinary, sometimes, the figures which could be seen disembarking. If I went on into the city, I always paid a respectful greeting to the Saalhof, which at least stood on the spot where the castle of the Emperor Charlemagne and his successors was reported to have been. I liked to lose myself in the old industrial quarters, and, particularly on market-days, to mingle with the crowd surging round the Church of St Bartholomew. From the earliest times, the throng of craftsmen and retailers had jostled each other there, and because of their right of possession, it was not easy in later times to provide for more space and light. The booths of the so-called *Pfarreisen* were very important places for us children, and we took many a copper there to buy coloured sheets printed with animals in gold. Only rarely, however, did we care to force our way through the narrow, tightly packed and dirty market-place. I call to mind also that I always fled with horror from the disgusting butchers' stalls, standing close together and abutting on the market-place. The *Römerberg*, on the other hand, was a delightful place for walking. The way to the new town, through the *Neue Kräm*, was always cheerful and interesting, though we were sorry that there was not a street leading into the *Zeil* past the Church of Our Lady....But what chiefly attracted the child's attention were the many little towns within the town, the fortresses within the fortress. I mean the walled monastic enclosures, and several other buildings dating from earlier times and more or less like castles to look at—the *Nürnberger Hof*, the *Kompostell*, the *Braunfels*, the ancestral home of the family of Stallburg, and several other strongholds, transformed in modern times into dwellings and workshops. Nothing of striking architectural beauty was to be seen in Frankfort at that time. Everything pointed to a period long past and full of disturbances, both for the town and its surroundings. Gates and towers, defining the bounds of the old city—then further off, other gates, towers, walls, bridges, ramparts, moats, with which the new city was encompassed—all indicated only too plainly that the necessity for safeguarding the common weal in times of unrest had called for these arrangements, and that all the squares and streets, even the new ones, broader and better laid out as they were, owed their origin to chance and caprice, and not to any regulating mind.... It was one of our favourite walks, which we endeavoured to take several times a year, to follow the course of the path which ran along the inside of the city walls. Gardens, court-yards and out-buildings extended to the foot of the wall; a glimpse was afforded into the home-life of thousands of little families, each shut off and hidden from its neighbours. Passing from the ornamental pleasure-gardens of the rich to the orchards of the ordinary citizen, kept for the sake of their produce—thence to the factories, bleaching-grounds and similar establishments, and even to the churchyard—for a little world lay within the limits of the city—we saw before us, changing at every step, a most strange and varied spectacle, which our childish curiosity could never sufficiently enjoy.

In this description, as in so many others in *Dichtung und Wahrheit*, Goethe has selected and arranged the details in such a way that his picture of Frankfort, without losing its individuality, has become that of a typical town, of an 'Urform des Lebens'. Our attention is drawn first to Frankfort's geographical position at an important river-crossing, its primary *raison d'être*, and to its water-borne trade, then to the Saalhof, on the site of the castle of the first town lords, under whose protection a market had first been established. The congested Old Town, with its industry, its market, its butchers' stalls side by side, reminds us of the chief activities of the medieval town and its gilds, the *Römer* of its self-governing town-council and its struggles with the emperor, the fortifications of its political independence and power of self-defence. The complexity of the social structure of this community, a state in small, is brought home to us by the mention of the strongholds of the patrician families, the monasteries, and the houses and gardens of citizens rich and poor. Finally the growth of new forms of industry is hinted at in the last sentence.

Frankfort was of course not merely a local market. Its fairs had been famous from an early date, for it was marked out by its geographical position as a convenient meeting-place for traders from northern Germany, southern Germany and France. It is important for our purpose to enquire where the comparatively small number of German towns which were more than local centres were situated, because, although many of them had lost ground by the eighteenth century, they were still the strongholds of the old-fashioned middle class, and usually exhibited many features by which they might be distinguished from the court towns, discussed above, and from the newer centres of trade with which the next chapter will be concerned.

These more important medieval towns were to be found for the most part either in the west and south-west of Germany, on the Rhine and upper Danube and their tributaries, or on the Baltic and North Sea coasts. The opening up of Europe that began with the Crusades, and the shifting of the stream of trade between Constantinople and the West from the Roman overland route to the Mediterranean and Italy, together with Germany's political connections with Italy under the Salian and Hohenstaufen lines, were the main external influences favouring the growth of these larger towns in the south, while in the north-east the colonisation of Riga and Reval and the Land of the Teutonic Order,

Prussia, led to an active trade by sea with the northern ports that was extended before long to Poland, Russia, Scandinavia and England, and became almost a monopoly. The Hanseatic merchants overshadowed the trade of the north of Europe as the Italians did that of the south. In the twelfth century they were allowed by the English king, who still considered trade as a private, not a national, affair, to build the Steel-yard in London as a warehouse and inn for their members, and they had soon other centres in Novgorod, Bruges, Bergen, Wisby and elsewhere. This league of merchants grew into a league of towns, at least so far as the towns were represented by their merchants, and included in its prime eighty or ninety places scattered between the Lower Rhine and Livonia. As England gradually attained commercial independence, Cologne, the original leader, and centre of the English trade, gave place to Lübeck, that commanded communications between the North Sea and the Baltic. The sea-ports Hamburg, Bremen, Wismar, Rostock, Stralsund, Stettin, Danzig and the river-ports Frankfort-on-Oder and Breslau were the most important of the other members. These northern towns were engaged in the handling of goods, mostly natural products; wool from England, in return for wine, hardware, woollens, silk and later corn and wood; herrings from the Baltic, where they then abounded; and furs, leather, wood from Russia, for wine and beer, and later for linen, woollens and other manufactured goods.[1]

The prosperity of the southern towns, though originally founded on trade in goods, attained its later proportion chiefly through financial transactions. The first towns to gain importance were those on the Danube route to the east, particularly Vienna and Regensburg (Ratisbon), but as Italy grew in wealth and power, they had rivals in Nürnberg, Augsburg, Ulm and Basle. These southern towns, especially

[1] Monograph by D. Schäfer, in *Monographien zur Weltgeschichte*, 3rd ed. 1925. Selected documents with commentary in J. Bühler, *Bauern Bürger und Hansa*, Leipzig, 1929.

Nürnberg, were skilled in fine metal-work, both in iron and the precious metals, for which Germany, until the discovery of America, was the chief source for Europe. There were twenty-nine different varieties of iron-workers in Nürnberg in 1363. Their skill was no doubt influenced by their connections with the East and its exquisite workmanship. Augsburg and Ulm exported fustians, Basle woollen cloth, and Constance linen. All four towns were geographically well situated for trade and did not, like most towns in Europe, allow the Italian merchants to come to them with their oriental wares. They themselves went to Venice, Milan, Florence, Genoa and the Spanish coast towns and sold these goods in southern Germany, Austria and Hungary, where they predominated as the Hanse did in the north of Europe. Their Fondaco dei Tedeschi beside the Rialto, the counterpart in Venice to the London Steelyard of the Hanse, is still a monument to their importance. Giorgione and Titian painted its façade. But they could never obtain the same control as the Hanseatic merchants did in undeveloped northern lands, for the Italian towns were themselves too far advanced to allow it. In Venice they were not allowed to sail beyond the lagoon.

It was not till the second half of the fourteenth century and the fifteenth that Augsburg and Nürnberg reached the full tide of their prosperity. The merchants and patricians, having accumulated wealth by mining speculations, trade or ground rents, began, in spite of the Church's ban on usury, to lend money to princes and potentates on a large scale, with results at first very profitable to themselves. The most famous of these early financiers was Jakob Fugger, descended from a weaver of Augsburg who, by financing mining operations in South Germany, Hungary and Spain, and by loans to the Hapsburgs and others, increased his fortune ten-fold in twenty-five years and on his death in 1525 left nearly two million Gulden to his heirs.[1] The money of Augsburg is said

[1] For details see: R. Ehrenberg, *Das Zeitalter der Fugger*, 1896, and the same writer's *Grosse Vermögen*, 1. *Die Fugger*, 2nd ed. 1905.

to have played a decisive part in bringing Charles V to the imperial throne, and in the sixteenth century the financiers from southern Germany were amongst the leaders at the new money-market of Antwerp, especially when the Florentine bankers ceased to be rivals through the transference of the bulk of their business to Lyons, the other great financial centre of the time, after Austria's victory in Italy (1530). Their good fortune was unhappily short-lived. Owing to the growth of national feeling in England and France, the finances of these countries became more and more national, and Spain and Portugal were soon the only large borrowers from the South German bankers. Spain proved anything but a reliable debtor. Its first bankruptcy, together with that of Portugal and France, in 1557, is said to have cost Germany the equivalent of 200 million marks, and was felt throughout the South German towns.[1] It was followed by another in 1575, and this and subsequent losses completely ruined many of the financiers of Augsburg and Nürnberg. Even such large houses as the Welser were involved, while the Fugger and some other families of the purse only retained that part of their fortunes which they had invested in landed estates. From now onwards Germany was quite overshadowed as a financial power by the rising national states, who alone were able to keep and increase their wealth by trade and colonial ventures, developing new methods in finance, industry and trade to meet the new situation.

The financial losses of these, the wealthiest towns of sixteenth-century Germany, were no doubt partly responsible for Germany's failure during the next two centuries to maintain the eminence in trade and industry which had been hers at the time of the Reformation, and which is reflected in the thoroughly middle-class literature of that age, and above all in the buildings and art of the great towns mentioned above. But it is generally held that the root cause of her misfortunes

[1] Lamprecht, *Deutsche Geschichte*, VIII, 1. Teil.

was her inability to share in the advantages which accrued to Europe from the great geographical discoveries of that period, the discovery of the sea route to India and of the new world of America. By these discoveries new regions were opened up for European exploitation, and something resembling world trade came to be established for the first time. The old commercial routes and centres were not abandoned. Local trade, and trade between the countries of Europe, was only stimulated by the discoveries, and increased by leaps and bounds, but the old mainly overland route from northern Europe to the East was soon overshadowed in importance by the new ocean routes, which gave commerce an altogether new range and made possible the comparatively cheap and rapid transport of much greater quantities of goods. The leadership in this trade naturally passed from the Italians and the Hanse towns to the peoples of the Atlantic seaboard, the Portuguese, Spaniards, Dutch, French and English.

As the scope of trade was extended, it came to be an object of rivalry not between cities only but between the new national states. The new period is marked by a series of struggles for power between the European nations, struggles in which commercial motives played a very important part, for commerce and political power grew to be interdependent. The Conquistadores, Portugal and Spain, exploited their new discoveries to the utmost, but the less dramatic methods of Holland and England, both supported by well-developed home industries, proved to be more effective in the long run. The Dutch, with their colonial enterprise and their seamanship, were the great models and rivals of the English. England succeeded in asserting naval and commercial supremacy over Spain in the sixteenth century, over Holland in the seventeenth and over France in the eighteenth, and at the beginning of the reign of George III, to quote Mr G. M. Trevelyan's words, 'was held in higher esteem by the nations of the world than ever before or since'.

The position of Germany, or rather of the various states

of Germany, for Germany was not really one country, was very much less enviable. The Germans had had no direct share in the discoveries, or in the trade resulting from them. The Hanseatic merchants were too much occupied with their northern trade, no longer such an easy monopoly as in the past, for they had now to reckon with stronger forces in Scandinavia, England and Russia. They had neither the money nor the organisation necessary for fitting out large expeditions. Their prosperity was founded on the co-operation of a large number of comparatively small traders, with traditional markets and ports of call, and a truly medieval power of inertia to check any undue speculation. One can still trace survivals of this traditionalism in the early chapters of Thomas Mann's *Buddenbrooks*. The financiers of South Germany were, however, more enterprising. Some of them launched expeditions to exploit newly discovered countries (like that of the Welser to Venezuela), but they all came to nothing for lack of the requisite backing of technical knowledge and physical force. A more profitable and less risky line of business was the financing and fitting out of expeditions undertaken by other nations, notably Portugal and Spain. The important German houses soon had branches in Lisbon, and in Antwerp, when it took the place of Venice as centre of the spice trade. But though their Spanish connections brought the fortunes of the Fugger and other German houses to their zenith, about the middle of the sixteenth century, the value of the old trade with Venice was steadily declining, as that city lost her hold over the East. Her decline was indeed slow, for throughout the sixteenth century the transalpine trade was still considerable, but the smaller towns and the smaller merchants began to suffer before the end of the century, and were unable to recompense themselves by ventures further afield.

Though the immediate and direct effects of the colonial discoveries on Germany were small, their wider consequences were of the utmost importance, especially as regards Germany's relation to other countries and to the sources of world wealth. Her geographical position became a hindrance to her, and remained so until the nineteenth century, when the re-introduction of overland transport made her once more the clearing-house of a great part of Europe, and encouraged ideas of an independent 'Mitteleuropa'. Her lack of political unity, further, made it impossible for her to back up her merchants, as the great colonial powers all did, with force of arms. Schmoller sums up the general situation as follows:

Germany had a good start in processes, traffic, even foreign trade, but no authority able to take advantage of it. The Empire was kept busy in the sixteenth century with maintaining religious peace, and was subservient in the seventeenth to the Austrian and Catholic Hapsburgs....Everywhere economic bodies were becoming political except in Germany, where the advantages it had enjoyed before 1620 were being lost. It was not the loss of men or capital, nor the shifting of trade routes from the Mediterranean to the Atlantic, but the lack of politico-economic organisations, which caused Germany's decay.[1]

The chief factor we have not yet mentioned was the Thirty Years' War. Though it undoubtedly had very serious effects, it is no longer thought to have been so overwhelming in its consequences for German trade and industry as used to be imagined. All the leading powers except England had something corresponding to such a war of religion, yet only Germany was finally prostrated, for the main causes of her downfall were independent of the war and already effective before it. We must not, however, go to the other extreme and shut our eyes to the enormous loss of life, the reckless destruction of the fruits of long labours and the disastrous moral consequences of this most irregular of all modern wars. The peculiar brutality with which it was waged on both sides was due partly to the leaders, who, however ideal their motives at the outset, were in the end fighting for material and political gains, aims which were still more openly

[1] G. Schmoller, *The Mercantile System*, trans. Ashley, 1884.

pursued by their allies, and partly to the nature of the armies they commanded. That they should be made up of mercenaries was inevitable since the decay of the feudal system; they were given their peculiar stamp, however, by the way in which they were recruited. The task was entrusted to entrepreneurs, war-merchants, who were given a fixed sum to provide an agreed number of men in fighting trim. They were left complete freedom in their manner of obtaining them, and Falstaff's methods of recruiting were jests in comparison.

The pay of these rough troops was so difficult to raise that they were frequently given authority to shift for themselves, with the consequence that the direct losses of the inhabitants through their marauding were even greater than the heavy contributions demanded by their rulers for the upkeep of the armies. All armies in those days had a camp following two or three times as numerous as themselves, by whose combined demands the districts they visited were sucked dry of all existing supplies, while they were prevented from cultivating the land by the military operations. The atrocities and the wanton destruction for which these troops were responsible more than equalled even the worst achievements of the twentieth century. Many villages disappeared entirely. In Württemberg there were for instance in 1654 eight towns, forty-five villages and over 30,000 buildings in ashes. Great stretches of cultivated land were nothing but desolate moorland after the war; in Saxony in the years following the war the country was so wild that wolves would attack the villages.

The country population suffered more from direct violence than the townsmen behind their walls, but those who survived the war appear to have been better situated than the average town-dweller, for wheat was cheap for lack of purchasers and there was a great demand for their services to reclaim the damaged lands. The more complicated foundations of town life were very seriously undermined.

for the war had made regular communications impossible over the greater part of Germany, completely crippling trade and industry. Many towns had suffered in spite of their walls from direct visitations, and all had felt the still more terrible consequences of famine, and of the plague produced by hunger and unnatural foods. Comprehensive and reliable statistics are not available, but even allowing for great exaggerations in the local estimates, historians agree that the population of towns and villages was frequently reduced to a third, a quarter, sometimes even a tenth of its former number. That of Württemberg was reduced from 313,000 to 65,000 between 1634 and 1645, that of Bohemia from four millions to 800,000, that of Augsburg from 80,000 to 18,000, and so forth. It is generally agreed that Germany did not make good the population lost in the war till well into the eighteenth century.

The material damage that was done left traces till later still, for in nearly all towns there were large numbers of ruined or abandoned houses. The losses of the towns in direct contributions to the state were very heavy, often ruinous. Göttingen for instance had paid over 500,000 Thaler by 1629, and Lüneburg contributed a similar amount in the last ten years of the war. Only the northern ports and the great centres Frankfort and Leipzig retained their commercial importance.

The moral consequences of the war were extremely serious. A whole generation grew up without knowing what peace was like, living from hand to mouth and often driven to desperate remedies, while round about them they saw examples of every imaginable crime, not checked by any authority or any effective public opinion. A general relaxation of standards was inevitable. In their uncertainty of the future men lived for the present, and the most senseless luxury was displayed in a starving country by those who happened to have the means. The parallel with later crises, in 1806 and 1919, is most striking. When their money ran out, men took to the army while the war still lasted, and often to robbery when it was over. A great gulf was fixed between court circles and the rest of the people, for the rulers had for the most part lost all the sympathy of their subjects, while they were led by the foreign models, with which they became familiar through foreign alliances, to consider themselves as a different breed from the common folk. It seems to be a general effect of war to heighten contrasts. Certainly the German aristocracy became from this time on definitely estranged from the mass of the people. The effect of the foreign influences on literature and art in general is well known. They were also of importance in developing a taste for luxuries of every kind, and dissatisfaction with the badly finished work of the German craftsman. The war damaged home industries by hindering the further development of German technique and powers of production, and by leading to connections with foreign countries that opened up the way into Germany for their superior goods.

Throughout all these upheavals in the great world, the gild system of industry had persisted in Germany little changed, but it was already proving inadequate in the new circumstances. Despite all their efforts, the gilds could not escape the effects of the competition that was inevitable as intercourse increased between the various regions of Europe and between these and the world outside. The gild worker was best able to turn out a solid article in a traditional style. One has only to think of an old-fashioned shoemaker or carpenter in a small town to understand his idea of how things should be made. When the courts of even small princes were in touch with the great capitals of Europe there naturally arose a more discriminating demand than the old-fashioned craftsman could satisfy. A higher degree of specialisation, more elaborate tools and plant were required, for any master to keep the quality of his wares equal to that of his foreign competitors, and the old gild organisation was not elastic enough to admit of such developments. The work of the

German craftsman was generally looked upon with contempt by the fine ladies and gentlemen of the seventeenth and eighteenth centuries. Their almost slavish preference for anything made in France, though mostly a matter of fashion, had some real justification in the superior quality of the French goods with which the market was flooded. In the seventeenth century we read: 'No clothes will satisfy us Germans now that do not come from France. French scissors trim our German beards better than any others; our watches go better if the Germans in Paris have made them, for the air there is more favourable for their manufacture than at Augsburg', and so on for such varied articles as combs, ribbons, chains, stockings, boots, shirts, hats, sticks, powder, needles. Moscherosch's *Gesichte* are full of such complaints.[1]

A further disruptive tendency was the inability of the handicraft system to satisfy a mass demand. There were, it is true, no such large towns in Germany as in some other countries, calling for enormous quantities of similar goods, nor had it any colonies to swell the demand, but there were nevertheless articles in common use needed in great quantities, particularly articles of clothing, which the craftsmen could not produce as rapidly and consequently as cheaply as 'manufacturers' who co-ordinated the work of many employees, and used any labour-saving machinery that was available. Here again foreigners stepped in where Germany's organisation failed her. England, that had once exported raw wool to be dealt with in Flanders and Germany, had captured by the seventeenth century almost the whole of the German woollen industry, and supplied Germany with manufactured goods through the 'Merchant Adventurers'. This was a company, at first, in Elizabethan times, a regulated company or gild of independent merchants, that had established itself first in the Netherlands, and then in 1567 in Hamburg, where the city's private interest in the increase of its trade, even though it was under English initiative and

[1] See especially part II, 'A la mode Kehrauss'.

domination, prevailed against the general opposition of the Hanse to any trespassers in its domain. What the English and French did not bring was supplied by the Dutch, whose highly advanced industrialists found a ready market in the whole Rhine region, and established regular Dutch colonies in Krefeld, Mannheim, Hanau and other new towns, especially after their closing of the Scheldt had been legalised by the Peace of Westphalia. The consequences for Germany of the development of this 'passive' trade will be discussed in the next chapter.

Chapter II

GERMAN TRADE AND INDUSTRY IN THE EIGHTEENTH CENTURY AND ITS CHIEF CENTRES

The population figures for Germany in the eighteenth century are a sufficient indication that her economic state was nearer to that of the Middle Ages than to that of the late nineteenth century. The population had indeed begun to increase again, but at nothing like the rate at which it was to grow in the following century. For the preceding three centuries famine, plague and war had kept the population almost stationary. The Thirty Years' War had furnished the last and most effective 'check' on a large scale. Earlier in the Middle Ages, however, between the twelfth and fourteenth centuries, there must have been a steady increase in the population, to judge by the extensive colonisation of the country east of the Elbe. This progress was only resumed in the eighteenth century. Reliable data are difficult to obtain, but from estimates made on various evidence it would seem that the population of several Prussian provinces was doubled or even trebled during the century, though part of this increase was due of course to the vigorous efforts of the Prussian rulers to 'people' the kingdom. It is estimated that by 1740 the population of Prussia had increased owing to immigration by some 600,000, so that these immigrants constituted a quarter of the total number of inhabitants at that time.[1]

It seems improbable that this comparatively high rate of increase prevailed in those parts of the country where the growth of the population depended chiefly on the excess of births over deaths. In the eighteenth century almost every-

[1] *Handwörterbuch der Staatswissenschaften* ('Agrargeschichte').

thing had still to be learnt in hygiene; smallpox, typhus and children's diseases carried away large numbers of victims every year, and even the plague made one last onslaught on Germany early in the century before retreating to the East, reducing the population of the Duchy of Prussia by one-third. England, which was considerably in advance of the Continent in matters of hygiene, had only rid itself of the plague in 1666, and its normal death-rate in the eighteenth century was still 41 per thousand in a fairly good year, to be compared with a rate of about 13·7 before the Great War. In London it was over 50 in the first half of the century, though it fell to about 30 by its close. In all countries the death-rate was so high in the towns that many statisticians believed their numbers only to be maintained by a constant flow of newcomers from the country. In Berlin it was 40 or more per thousand at the beginning of the century, and it did not fall to below 35 at the end. The figures given by Nicolai in his *Reisen* for various German towns range from 50 per thousand for Vienna to half that rate for Coburg. In general, the bigger the town was, the higher was its death-rate. The birth-rate was still high in town and country alike, but infantile mortality was extremely heavy, between a fifth and a third of all children born dying in the first year. In almost all the individual families of which we hear at least four children were born, often six or more, but all but two or three usually died in childhood. The statisticians prove that this was generally the case, both in Germany and the neighbouring countries. Necker estimated that of the whole population of France, one-quarter died before attaining the age of three, another quarter between the ages of three and twenty-five, and a third quarter between twenty-five and fifty. Similar estimates were made for Germany.[1]

At the end of the century the number of the inhabitants of the territories forming the pre-war German Empire must have been round about twenty millions. The first official

[1] Kulischer, *op. cit.* II, 10.

figures are for 1816, and give a total of 24·8 millions. It gives us some idea of the growth of the population since then, and the enormous reduction in the death-rate that the nineteenth century has brought about, when we remember that in the matter of numbers the Germany of 1914 stood in about the same relation to Germany in 1800 as this did to the Empire of Barbarossa.[1] For comparisons it is interesting to note that in 1800 England and Wales had just under 10 million inhabitants (nearly twice as many as in 1700), Scotland 1·6 million, and Ireland over 4 million,[2] while France contained about 24 million people.

More important for the sociologist than the gross number of inhabitants is the density of the population, and its distribution between town and country, a sure index to the nature of its economic life. It is quite clear that the majority of the German people were dependent for their living on the soil even until the first half of the nineteenth century. 'Even in the middle of the nineteenth century Germany was an essentially agricultural land, sprinkled with a few unimportant small or medium-sized towns. The centre of gravity of its social life was still definitely in the country.'[3] In Prussia, even in 1849, only 28 per cent. of the inhabitants lived in towns, in Saxony rather more, about 34 per cent., in Württemberg 20 per cent., in Baden, Hesse-Darmstadt and Hanover 15 per cent., and in Bavaria just under 15 per cent. It should be remembered too that 'town' is here used in a legal sense, so that many of the places included would be extremely small. In Saxony, for instance, at this time only five 'towns' out of 140 possessed over 10,000 inhabitants, and most would be no larger than at the end of the Middle Ages. Statistics from occupations give us the same picture; in 1843 about 60 per cent. of the German population was still engaged in agricultural pursuits, in Austria 69 per cent.[4]

[1] Estimating the latter with Kötzschke at 7–8 millions.
[2] *Handwörterbuch der Staatswissenschaften*, art. 'Bevölkerungsstatistik'.
[3] Sombart, *op. cit.* II, 626.   [4] *Ibid.*

Contrast this with the figures for 1910, when out of a total population of 64·9 millions, 38·9 millions lived in towns of over 2000 inhabitants, and 13·8 in towns of over 100,000, while in 1907 only 28·6 per cent. of the population were engaged in agriculture or forestry, as against 42·8 per cent. in industry and 13·4 per cent. in trade.[1]

In spite of the increase in the population, Germany was far from being densely populated in 1800. On the rich soil of Württemberg there were 72 to the square kilometre, in Saxony with its manufactures 50, in Prussia only 30 (though this was at least twice as many as in 1700). Some of the more densely populated regions, beside Württemberg and Saxony, were (using the names of the modern Prussian provinces) Westphalia (55), Rheinprovinz (50), Silesia (45).[2] In England and the Netherlands the figure was 65.

It is clear then from these figures that no revolutionary changes in industry and commerce had taken place in Germany since the Middle Ages. The revolution came of course in the nineteenth century. In the eighteenth century, though the medieval pattern of economic areas each dominated by a market town had been disarranged, particularly by the activity of the territorial princes, something very like it still persisted. The main body of trade was still local. A glance at the communications then available convinces one that it could not have been otherwise except in a few specially favoured places, for although the amount of traffic by land and water had grown steadily since the Middle Ages, travel had become very little easier or safer since then. A longish journey was still something of an adventure even in the most civilised parts of Europe. Naturally the conveyance of goods and letters was also slow and expensive, in spite of the progress that had been made in the organisation of regular services.

[1] *Statistisches Jahrbuch des deutschen Reichs*, 1913, pp. 4, 5.
[2] Kulischer, II, 7. *Handwörterbuch der Staatswissenschaften*, art. 'Bevöl-kerungsstatistik'.

For land traffic, the difficulty still only very partially overcome was the provision of smooth hard roads, partly a
matter of deficient technique, partly of lack of capital and
co-ordination of effort. It seems that none of the European
countries had a really good system of roads before the nineteenth century. France was far ahead of the rest. In the
second half of the eighteenth century it had a good system of
metalled main roads, 'chaussées', radiating from Paris, but the
by-roads were still bad. In England the first turnpike trust had
been created in 1663, but in spite of dozens of turnpike acts
the roads, even the roads leading to London, remained very
indifferent, and the side roads often mere unmetalled tracks,
with ruts sometimes four feet deep. On a road of this kind
Young in 1770 found three broken-down carts between
Preston and Wigan. Pack-horses were in universal use till
the nineteenth century. When it had been necessary to make
good roads they had been made, by Wade, for instance, in
parts of Scotland, for military reasons, and near London, but
there was little co-ordination of effort, methods were bad
and the burden was too heavy for local authorities.

It can be readily imagined what the state of German roads
must have been, with a less insistent demand, a greater
multiplicity of authorities and even less possibility of co-
ordination for large areas. It is true that in autocratic states
with a fairly efficient bureaucracy it was easier to overcome
local indifference if the prince took it into his head to have
good roads. In this way some of the South German states
obtained improved metalled roads in the course of the
century. The first chaussées were made in Hesse in 1720,
in Baden in 1733, in Württemberg in 1772. Nicolai, who
travelled all over Germany in 1781, tells us that the roads
were infinitely better in the south than in the north, where
owing to the lack of stone the material difficulties were very
much greater. Even the main roads of Prussia were execrable;
sand in summer and mud in winter, in spite of all the efforts
of Frederick the Great. At the end of the century Reichard,

perhaps the chief forerunner of Baedeker, in his popular *Guide des Voyageurs*,[1] informed travellers that in the south they could go from Frankfort or Nürnberg to Vienna, from Vienna to Switzerland or Italy, and from Switzerland back to Italy without finding an unmetalled main road or a bad service of posts. Nicolai had said much the same in 1781, but had added that it had not long been so.[2] Reichard singles out the roads of Bavaria, Fulda and the Palatinate for special praise, then Würzburg and Württemberg, then Baden and Bayreuth. The pleasantest of all is the famous Bergstrasse from Darmstadt to beyond Heidelberg, highly praised by English travellers too.[3]

In the north, Reichard says, the roads are in general very bad. 'In certain seasons and in rainy weather, one is often obliged to leave the ordinary road.' Even in 1842 Howitt tells of 'ruts which swallowed the carriage up to the axle and piles of mud which stood, ground up by the action of the wheels, like walls' in the Harz.[4] The state of the roads was the ostensible reason (there were other obvious reasons) for the state regulations fixing the minimum number of horses to be hired by passengers travelling post. In Prussia for instance, even in the early nineteenth century, it was only a light carriage carrying one passenger and a single trunk that was allowed the minimum hire, two horses. For two people three horses were required, for three people four horses. For a heavier carriage with four passengers or more, the number of horses would be five, six, or even eight, if there was much luggage.[5] In Austria the regulations were less stringent, no doubt because of the better roads. Another indication regarding the state of the roads is the warning given by Nicolai, Reichard and others to strangers travelling

[1] *Guide des Voyageurs*, Weimar, 1793.
[2] *Reisen*, I, 117, 150.
[3] E.g. by Crabb Robinson in his letters (Edith Morley's edition, Oxford, 1929, p. 155).
[4] *Life in Germany*, p. 447.
[5] Reichard, 8th edition, 1817.

in their own carriage about the frequent changes in rut-gauge in the north. The ruts on the roads east of Hamburg for instance were wider than on those to the west. Either the track of the carriage wheels had to be adjustable, or one had to leave the road and drive over the fields. There were few stone bridges. In Bavaria and Austria bridges were usually of wood. On the Rhine below Basle, there were only floating bridges until the end of the eighteenth century. Small streams had usually still to be forded.

Though roads were poor, there were regular services of public conveyances, and post stations at intervals of two or three Meilen all over the country. The monopoly granted to the Thurn und Taxis family in 1615 had been greatly interfered with by the territorial princes since 1648. Many states now had their own services, but the Thurn und Taxis organisation still employed 20,000 people and, according to an estimate quoted by Reichard, made an annual profit of a million Thaler at the end of the eighteenth century. Until the end of the century few of the ordinary stage coaches were covered; they were great lumbering vehicles built to stand hard wear, much inferior, as Reichard admits, to the French and English coaches. Travelling post with one's own carriage, one could demand a speed of not less than a German Meile (about five miles) an hour on chaussées, but on roads classified as bad an hour and a half was allowed. Nicolai was very pleased when he did more than a Meile an hour on the good roads of the south. In the north of England twenty miles a day was a very good average, and that seems to have been about the usual distance covered in western Germany (5 Meilen or under). In the south, however, one could do three times that distance (15 or 18 Meilen, according to Reichard) in the latter part of the century.

The quickest way for younger men to travel was on horseback; the poorer travellers, wandering apprentices and most students had to be content to walk. Accommodation was primitive. There were good inns in the bigger towns, especially those with fairs (the Frankfort inns for instance are highly praised by English travellers), but in villages one had usually to be content with a 'Streu', a bed of clean straw spread on the floor of the public room. On the whole English inns seem to have been very much better in the eighteenth century than any but the best continental ones.

Travelling was not only slow and frequently dangerous, but expensive. Büsch reckoned in 1800 that it cost a business man travelling very modestly without a servant, and sharing a carriage with three companions, on the average about 1 Thaler 12 Groschen per Meile, roughly a shilling a mile, for all expenses (including tips and inn expenses). The post-chaise journey from Hamburg to Frankfort in 1800 cost Crabb Robinson £7. 8s., though he shared a carriage, first with three, then with four others.[1] After that experience he walked, although it was an almost unheard of thing for people of the better class to walk long distances for pleasure.

There had been a regular letter post all through the century, run by the Thurn und Taxis organisation or by individual states. To smaller places, if there was no 'fahrende Post' or mail there was a 'reitende Post' or messenger-service. Letters naturally travelled very slowly. They were usually sent by 'reitende Post' and paid for on delivery (though they could be prepaid). According to Reichard's tables it took a letter nine days to reach Frankfort-on-Main from Berlin (seven Meilen a day), four days to reach Munich or seven to reach Vienna from Frankfort (thirteen Meilen a day). This indicates incidentally the rates at which one could travel post. Small places made their own postal arrangements. The correspondence between Goethe in Weimar and Schiller in Jena was carried by Jungfer Wenzel, the Botenfrau, together with all kinds of parcels and garden produce.[2]

Waterways were in extensive use for the conveyance of

[1] *Crabb Robinson in Germany*, p. 178.
[2] See illustration in Könnecke's *Bilderatlas*.

goods and passengers. There were regular services of boats on the Rhine and Danube. One could sail from Ratisbon to Vienna for instance in three days, but the public boat was not well recommended. Wealthy travellers took a private boat for their party. David Hume, travelling with General St Clair in 1748, went from Ratisbon to Vienna 'in a large boat about eighty foot long, where we have three rooms, one for ourselves, a second for the servants and a third for our kitchen. 'Tis made entirely of fir boards and is pulled to pieces at Vienna. The wood is sold and the watermen return to Ratisbon on foot. We lie on shore every night'. Lady Montagu had travelled in a similar way in 1716. The journey up-stream on either river, pulled by horses, was intolerably slow for passengers. For heavy goods, water transport was the only available means. Big towns dependent on distant supplies or foreign trade were therefore only to be found on waterways or on the coast. All the navigable rivers were used, especially the Rhine, Danube, Elbe, Oder, Vistula and Main, and some canals had already been made. In Brandenburg, under the Great Elector, the upper Oder and the Spree, leading to the Havel and thus to the lower Elbe, had been connected by a canal. Under Frederick the Great the waterway from the Oder to the Elbe was greatly improved by the construction of the Plauer Canal and the Finow Canal, while the Vistula was linked to the Netze and Oder by the Bromberg Canal. Water transport was still greatly hampered by the existence of rapids and shallows, for the artificial 'regulation' of the rivers was hardly attempted before the nineteenth century, and, like the roads, the rivers were dotted with innumerable customs offices. Fourteen tolls had to be paid (many involving a long wait) between Magdeburg and Hamburg on the Elbe in 1800, thirty-three between Bamberg and Mainz on the Main, thirty-two on the Rhine between Strassburg and the Dutch frontier.

Poor as communications still were judged by nineteenth-century standards, they were good enough, especially by water, to make possible a great expansion of trade with distant towns and the export of a sufficient quantity of bulky goods to disturb the medieval 'town economy'. We have seen that in the Middle Ages there were a few towns standing out from the great mass of small market towns as centres of interregional or even international commerce, some of them owing their success mainly to trade brought by foreign merchants, others to pre-eminence in the production of some special kind of cloth or the like. This distinction was still maintained in eighteenth-century Germany, though it had grown less absolute than before, but the towns with wider relations were not always the same places which had been prominent in the Middle Ages. Through the shifting of trade routes, political changes, and variations in local enterprise over long periods, some of the old leaders had sunk to little more than local importance, and places insignificant or non-existent in the Middle Ages had taken their place. The leading towns of this later period may be further subdivided into those which were the capital of a small state, the place of residence of a prince and his court and administration, and those towns whose importance was not political but economic, the trading and industrial towns. The first class of towns has been described above, pp. 95 ff. Economically they were chiefly centres of consumption. They might have state-aided manufactures of some kind, but usually, as we have seen, these were on a small scale, concerned with luxuries and run at a loss, the products of a dilettante mercantilism. A second characteristic was that their fortunes, being dependent on the whims of a prince, were liable to sudden ups and downs. A state might be fused by inheritance with another state, or the prince might withdraw his court to another town in his state or found a new capital altogether (like Mannheim, Karlsruhe, Ludwigsburg). When that happened there would be a migration of craftsmen and servants from the old capital to the new. The old capital sometimes remained the centre of administration, but it might become simply a little market town again, as Durlach did when the capital of Baden was shifted to Karlsruhe.[1]

Of the older centres of trade, the northern towns steadily declined as the Hanse lost its monopoly of the Baltic and North Sea trade. The Hanse was officially dissolved in 1669, but it had lost all meaning long before this. England exported its own cloth and other products, through the Merchant Adventurers, from the time of Elizabeth, and the Dutch gained almost a monopoly of the Baltic trade during the seventeenth century, while the once profitable herring-fisheries of the Baltic passed to the North Sea. By the Peace of Westphalia the mouths of the great rivers (Rhine, Weser, Elbe and Oder) were left in foreign hands. The mouth of the Rhine was closed by the Dutch to German ships, and their closing of the Scheldt was legally confirmed. The main waterway of Germany, so important in the Middle Ages, came to be of merely local importance, except for the passive trade brought by the Dutch, for German shippers could not carry goods further than to Holland, and even on the Rhine itself were hampered by dozens of customs-stations.

The merchants of COLOGNE became agents of Dutch or English firms. Italian and Eastern goods no longer reached it through the south German towns, but through Amsterdam. Except for the commission trade and transport, it was of no importance in the eighteenth century. All visitors speak of its empty streets, its many beggars and monks. David Hume writes, for instance (in 1748): 'It is extremely decayed and is even falling to ruin. Nothing can strike one with more melancholy than its appearance, where there are marks of past opulence and grandeur, but such present waste and decay, as if it had lately escaped a pestilence or famine'. Like the southern towns it lost many opportunities by religious intolerance and narrow conservatism. Instead of welcoming Protestant refugees bringing new industries from Holland,

[1] For the effect on the population see Roller's admirable study *Die Einwohnerschaft der Stadt Durlach im achtzehnten Jahrhundert.*

as England and Prussia did, to their great gain, it put every difficulty in their way.

At the beginning of the century the mouths of the Weser and the Oder were under Swedish control. Although the Free Town of BREMEN remained independent, its trade was crippled by tolls, and its geographical situation was not favourable enough to attract foreigners, for the Weser tended to silt up and was not nearly such an important waterway as the Elbe. However, Bremen had survived the Thirty Years' War without serious loss, and continued in a state of quiet prosperity throughout the seventeenth and eighteenth centuries, though it was never a serious rival of Hamburg, the only Hanseatic town that made rapid progress in this period.

The Baltic ports, DANZIG, LÜBECK, KÖNIGSBERG and STETTIN, also could not compare with Hamburg during this period, but as ports they maintained a certain importance, though mostly through foreign initiative. Danzig was the great corn-exporting centre for Poland, on which it was politically dependent, and exchanged Polish natural products and those of the Vistula valley for English, Dutch and French industrial wares. Its main trade, with Holland, was carried on for the most part with the help of Dutch credit and enterprise. It had no important manufactures of its own, and its population was falling. With the rise of Prussia it lost a great deal of its trade to Königsberg and Stettin, thanks to the energetic mercantilist policy of the Prussian rulers. Both Königsberg and Stettin (when it became Prussian in 1720) grew steadily,[1] but were lacking in native capital and enterprise. In 1704 Königsberg had not a single sea-going ship of its own.[2] Lübeck, for many years the headquarters of the Hanse, had long lost its old pre-eminence, though it still contrived to maintain its independence in spite of the

---

[1] Königsberg 1688 c. 30,000, Stettin 1720 c. 6,000
        ,,   1780   60,000,   ,,   1800   23,000.
[2] Kulischer, II, 243.

successive attacks of Sweden, Denmark and Russia. As it could count on no support from the Hanse or the Empire, its position was one of continual uncertainty, and the Danes could practically blockade the port for years at a time. Lübeck served as centre for the exchange of raw material from the Russian Baltic coast with western European industrial goods. Attempts to start calico and silk factories proved fruitless against the resistance of the gild spirit, here unusually strong.

The old towns of the south were in a similar state by the eighteenth century. In the sixteenth, as we saw, they were still wealthy and influential. Though the oriental trade via Venice became less important every year, spices coming now from Antwerp to Frankfort, the old-established firms of Augsburg and Nürnberg transferred their depots to Antwerp and were very successful there, both in the spice trade and later, increasingly, in finance. Some of them (the Welser of Augsburg for instance) even owned plantations in the Canaries and Spanish concessions in America for a time, many (the Fugger and Welser leading) owned mines in Tirol and other parts, even as far afield as Spain and South America, the Germans being recognised at that time as the leading mining experts. But the causes outlined above, the wholesale loss of capital, the eclipse of Venice, the rise of Holland and the ravages of the Thirty Years' War brought about the decline of the south German towns from about 1600. Another factor was, as with Cologne, the short-sighted conservatism and intolerance of the old towns, which deprived them of the new industries they might have fostered, put every obstacle in the way of Italian and Dutch refugees and drove the Huguenots to smaller towns like Ansbach, Bayreuth and Erlangen, as the Nürnberg Jews had already been driven in 1499 to Fürth, outside the walls of Nürnberg and beyond the control of its gilds.

NÜRNBERG remained a centre of commission trade and continued to produce its hardware, objects of applied art and maps. Like most of the south German towns it manufactured linen and cotton goods, but it was outstripped in the more important industries by smaller towns like Erlangen with their foreign colonies, and its population was steadily declining.[1] Externally it still looked quite prosperous. David Hume speaks of its air of industry and contentment, without splendour, and finds its people handsome, well clothed and well fed, though the old houses which we now admire seemed to him 'old-fashioned and of a grotesque figure'. This was in 1748. Nicolai uses much the same language about it some thirty years later. The old houses look to him like prisons. Quoting the famous dictum of Aeneas Sylvius in the fifteenth century, to the effect that the average Nürnberg citizen was better housed than the kings of Scotland, his comment is that the kings of Scotland must have lived in a very wretched style. He particularly disapproves of the absence of pumps and street-lighting, and of the oligarchical government. He praises the workmanship and ingenuity of its craftsmen, but finds the style of their wares too old-fashioned and ornate, compared with the simpler and more practical products of Birmingham and Sheffield. ERLANGEN on the other hand delights him with its hard practicality. The monotonous new two-storied houses where everyone was busily at work, evidently in domestic industries, the 'manufacture' of hats, stockings and gloves, the occupied air and brisk gait of people in the street, the three plain courses of the inn 'ordinary' are all contrasted with corresponding features in Bamberg, the capital of an ecclesiastical state. Even orphan children in Erlangen could earn 100 Gulden a year, Nicolai admiringly adds, by cotton-spinning. Ulm[2] still retained some of its trade in south German linen with Italy. AUGSBURG[3] was the most prosperous of these old towns,

[1] 1602, c. 40,000; 1806, 25,000 (Schmoller, *Deutsches Städtewesen*).
[2] Population c. 10,000 (Schmoller).
[3] Population sixteenth century c. 50,000; after Thirty Years' War 19,000; 1818, 29,800 (Schmoller).

though it had suffered severely through the rise of Holland, and the Thirty Years' War. Nicolai ascribes its superiority over Nürnberg in part to its more liberal government. It was above all a financial centre for all the neighbouring lands, particularly Austria, Bavaria, and parts of Switzerland and Italy. Its textile manufactures were considerable, especially its printed cottons. There was one mill where 350 people were employed, including many women and children. Augsburg's goldsmiths had still a high reputation, but the use of porcelain had reduced the demand for fine plate, their chief product in earlier days.

The gild tradition being strong in the older towns, they did not as a rule welcome the new large-scale industries, which were at this period almost all 'domestic industries'. The actual processes were carried out by cottagers in the country, but their work was organised by an entrepreneur in a neighbouring town. In general it may be said that up to the end of the eighteenth century and even well into the nineteenth, capitalism had only very modest beginnings to show in Germany. There were, however, industries in which 'Verleger', entrepreneurs, played an indispensable part. A Verleger was a man of some means, usually a merchant, who advanced money to a craftsman (the verb 'verlegen' could mean 'to advance money' even in Middle High German) in order that the craftsman might exercise his skill and produce saleable wares. He might lend him tools in return for a rent, in which case the craftsman could still buy his raw materials and sell the product himself, or he might supply the worker with tools and materials, pay him a fixed wage for his work and market the product, generally a more profitable procedure, and the one which gradually prevailed. The craftsman's dependence was naturally greatest, and occurred earliest, where tools or raw materials were elaborate and expensive, as in the printing trade, in connection with which the word Verleger is still used (in the sense of 'publisher'), or where the markets available were distant or scarce. At first, it will be remembered, craftsman and merchant were one person. It was only in the thirteenth century apparently that the word 'mercator' acquired its modern sense, in Italy. With the growth of a separate and powerful class of merchants, it often became necessary for the craftsman to secure the help of the merchant in selling his goods, and from this to the next stage of working under his control was only a step.

The chief German industries in which this early form of capitalism was common were, in addition to printing, such things as mining, the iron industry, textile manufactures and paper-making. With unified control, the productivity of an industry was greatly increased, especially where by the domestic system every possible source of labour in a district could be made use of. So with the linen industry of Silesia, the watch-making of the Black Forest, the toy-making of Thuringia. Most of these industries were carried on out of reach of the regulations of the towns, especially in the uplands of Silesia, Saxony, the Thuringian Forest, Westphalia, Württemberg, and also in Switzerland. In such districts, where owing to the unproductive land wages were low, the villagers welcomed the opportunity of earning money by work in their homes. Conditions were similar in many parts of England in the early days of the woollen industry. The 'clothiers' of those days were typical 'Verleger'.[1] It is the life of the German domestic weaver, at its worst, which Hauptmann depicts in *Die Weber*. Sometimes the manufacturers were combined into a sort of trust, as in the much-quoted company of clothmakers and dyers at Calw in Württemberg, founded in 1626, which lasted till the end of the eighteenth century, and at its best period employed 6000 persons. This was quite exceptionally large. Generally capital was lacking, and all businesses, except in the large towns under foreign influence, mentioned below, were on a small scale, though the aggregate of these small industries

[1] See Lipson, II, chap. I.

might be considerable. South German and Silesian linen for instance was exported in large quantities.

It appears doubtful whether German enterprise would have effected the development to capitalistic methods until much later without the help of immigrants from already industrialised countries. Certainly the Protestant émigrés from France, Italy and Holland were the decisive factor in the spread of these methods, and helped to bring the Protestant parts of the country very much to the fore in economic matters. Brandenburg laid itself out to attract Protestant settlers from the time of the Great Elector, after the Revocation of the Edict of Nantes (1685). Through a number of edicts the country was thrown open to persecuted Protestants, and many privileges were conferred on them. Some were able to bring capital with them, others had to be helped by the state, which had great difficulty in raising the necessary funds and in finding markets for the goods produced. By 1740, as we saw, about one-quarter of the subjects of Frederick the Great are said to have consisted of immigrants or their descendants. In Berlin they were particularly to the fore. It would have been impossible to establish the new silk industry and the other minor industries, which the Prussian rulers fostered so assiduously, without their capital and technical skill, and these were the chief factors also in the rapid commercial advances made by Berlin in the seventeenth and eighteenth centuries.[1] They left a permanent trace on the intellectual and social life of the town, so that its clubs on the French model, the sociability, intelligence and political acuteness of the Berliner became a source of wonder to all visitors from other parts of Germany. It was no accident then that this capital became the focus of 'Aufklärung'. With Prussia one may contrast the south of Germany, where the Protestantism of the estates, and especially of the towns, was broken by the Catholic princes. First in Bavaria, then in Austria, the struggle

---

[1] For some details of the 'Industrial migration of peoples' which took place at this period see Kulischer, *op. cit.* II, 21 f.

led to a continual withdrawal of privileges from the towns, the emigration of many inhabitants and the gradual decay of their power in all domains, as compared with the more self-reliant and worldly-minded Protestant provinces. In the eighteenth century Bavaria had only thirty-nine towns, while Saxony had two hundred.[1] Beggars—and shrines— were the features that particularly struck the English traveller in south Germany, even in the early nineteenth century.[2]

The motives of the government in Prussia and other German states for encouraging manufactures were similar to those of the leading foreign powers in the mercantilist age, but in Prussia there was no power that could dispute the authority of the crown, and all measures were carried through more ruthlessly than in England, for example. The main problem of the government was how to support a large army in a country poor in natural resources. Frederick William I and Frederick the Great saw the solution in the fostering of industry and the taxation of its profits, encouraged in this by the example of Holland. Every method employed by the successful mercantilist nations was imitated. New industries were established, and it was sought to assure a safe demand for them by forbidding imports of the articles manufactured at home and exports of the raw materials needed for them. To encourage the cloth industry, Frederick William I not only clothed his army in Brandenburg cloth, but required the citizens of Berlin to wear it exclusively, with more success than had attended English regulations of the same kind, which had begun a hundred years before this under James I, or those of Weimar, where another English precedent was copied, and it was ordained that the dead should be buried in home-spun woollen cloth.[3] His efforts were in general not

[1] Lamprecht, VIII, 1.
[2] E.g. D. Hume, *Letters*, ed. Greig, I, 124, or W. Howitt, *Life in Germany*, 1842.
[3] Lipson, *Econ. Hist. of England*, III, 45; Hartung, *Das Grossherzogtum Sachsen*, 1775–1828, p. 93.

without effect; Russia in particular took large quantities of his cloth for her army. Silk spinning, dyeing, watch-making, and all the crafts practised by the immigrants were fostered in the same way.

One of the main advantages the newcomers enjoyed was that they were not made subject to the old gild regulations, becoming 'Freimeister' on the authority of the state. Repeated trouble with the Gesellen had, as we shall see, given the territories an excuse for attempts to suppress the gilds, and by an imperial law the Gesellen had been deprived of their right of association and handed over to the masters. The Empire did not, however, interfere with the masters, who also needed to be regulated in territorial interests. This reform was taken in hand by the individual states, led by Prussia from 1734. A great number of regulations were made settling the future of the gilds on the lines laid down in England under Elizabeth by the Statute of Apprentices (1563). The effect was to transfer the responsibilities of the gilds to the state and deprive them of their power, but to retain the gild forms to facilitate state control of industry. Local boundaries were broken down, and the restrictions concerning admission as a master, the 'Wanderjahre' of apprentices and other disputed points were much relaxed, to weaken the authority of the gilds. They were left little but the duty of supervising the quality of wares and workshop conditions. These regulations were imitated by most of the other German states in the course of the century.

Having broken what remained of the resistance of the gilds, the states proceeded to encourage the manufactures that suited their purposes, the chief of which was to raise revenue. They had not the capital necessary to take over the more important industries themselves, but gave concessions to manufacturers, bound up with regulations influenced by gild ideas. In general, each manufacture received a separate constitution, in which the interests of the workers too were considered. All the chief industries were in this way brought under state control. Efforts were made to adapt supply to demand, to ensure efficient technical working, to limit competition, and to set up organs for determining a fair rate of wages. It was only in Prussia that these measures could be carried through consistently and effectively, thanks to its elaborate civil service. The attempt was made everywhere, but not with Prussian energy, for in Prussia the official opinion was: 'Der Plebs geht von der alten Leier nicht ab, bis man ihn bei Nase und Armen zu seinem Vorteil schleppt'.

The manufacturer was not favoured at the expense of the country landowner and peasant, however, for if it was the duty of the town-dwellers to furnish revenue, particularly the excise levied at the town gates, the peasantry had to supply men for the army, and as the country squires were of the same class and tastes as the king himself, their interests could not be neglected. Accordingly, although the towns claimed the first call on the corn produced by the country, and would have had the Junkers only permitted to export what was over when their claims had been met, the Prussian kings in the eighteenth century allowed the nobles the right of freely exporting corn, as they desired, but in return restricted trade and industry to the towns. This latter concession to the towns was double-edged, for the excise, the chief source of revenue, could only be levied on town-made products, so that the concentration of all industry within the town walls was also in the interests of the government. It was possible, by keeping Poland economically a subject state, to combine the advantages of free export of corn with those of a stable and reasonable price for home consumers. The government, and only the government, could import Polish corn, and by doing so when it was cheap, it could lay in stores that were not only a reserve for the army, but could be released in years of bad harvests to bring down the price in the home market.

The smaller states too in many cases tried to make themselves economically self-sufficient, but their efforts were necessarily fruitless in view of their size and isolation. As we have seen (p. 38) many courts encouraged local industries, luxury trades for the most part, here a porcelain factory, there a silk or cloth factory, but they did so because of their French models, and many of their industries were as much of a caricature as their armies. They had to contend not only with foreign countries, but still more with other German states, especially Prussia and later Austria, which could take measures in the control of trade that did not remain mere paper threats. Prussia's policy for instance caused Leipzig and Hamburg very anxious times, however much it may have benefited them in the end. In general, though the subjects of these small states could not count on much direct assistance from their governments, they were comparatively free from interference, undisturbed in their 'Behaglichkeit' by a too rational and active ruler. Except for an occasional grand-motherly edict things were allowed to take their own course. The gilds retained greater freedom and power in these smaller states, and the whole view of life there was calmer, more philosophical, if more passive, than in the ambitious larger states. It was the view still typical of Germany taken as a whole, the view that is idealised in *Hermann und Dorothea*, traditional, modest, inclined to despise as upstarts the new manufacturers and merchants, though a little envious of their wealth.

Although the older towns were in decline and the new forms of domestic industry were cultivated above all in villages, there were a few towns which, owing mainly to their geographical position, had made considerable progress since the Middle Ages.

Dealings with foreign countries had to take place through certain centres, if only for the convenience of the foreigners themselves, and a number of towns on the borders of Germany or in other favoured positions were by these means able to avoid the fate of the great majority. Although this trade began by being almost entirely carried on by strangers, it provided many opportunities for the German inhabitants too. From these centres goods were carried all over the country by pedlars, whose part in distribution can hardly be appreciated by us now, with our immensely superior communications and shops in every village. They were looked upon by the old-fashioned Möser as an almost unmitigated evil. 'There are three times as many retailers (most of them pedlars) now', he says, 'as there were a hundred years ago, and only half as many craftsmen.' 'Not a year passes without at least ten Englishmen travelling in Germany for commercial purposes and canvassing for customers.' Ten sounds a small enough number, and indicates sufficiently how little the country depended on trade at all; but it was apparently large in comparison with the number of German traders. 'What is the Krämer (retailer)?' he asks. 'A man who only makes foreigners rich, whether they be friends or foes, and encourages luxury, tempting everyone with novelties, continually springing new fashions on us and making the craftsman's wares out of date. He is so proud too that honest handiwork is held to be contemptible, and every young man of parts must needs become a trader like himself.' Pedlars ought only to be permitted to sell goods from their country of origin, Möser says, and luxuries such as lace should not be allowed in at all. It is the same doctrine of self-sufficiency that we have met with in the medieval townsman and the later mercantilist alike.

Germany as a whole stood in the same relation of inferiority to countries like England and Holland as its own small towns did to the large centres, and the reasons for this relation were clearly perceived by contemporaries. We may sum them up with the invaluable Möser as follows:

(a) The successful masters in the large towns, having as many as thirty or forty Gesellen, had naturally introduced the principle of specialisation, with the result that in time their workmen, being only familiar with one subordinate process, could not become independent. The masters had the dvantage of the services of very highly skilled assistants at he wages they cared to fix.

(b) For first-class work the help of painters, gilders, culptors and so on was needed, and as they could not make living in small towns they were not to be found there.

(c) The general level of taste was higher in large towns han in small, which therefore turned out old-fashioned work.

(d) There was an economy in working expenses when a ingle master could have forty men busy in one building, nstead of twenty small masters having two men each.

(e) Many people could combine for the purchase of raw naterial in large towns.

(f) One particular kind of manufacture often needed the nelp of others, so that it was often impossible to start new ndustries in a small town because the supporting industries lid not exist there.

(g) Only large concerns could afford to instal machinery, nd use mechanical power.

(h) Talented men were attracted to the large towns, where they found a ready market for their inventions. It is worth noting that the use of machinery is not stressed by Möser. The fact that it comes so low down in his list is an nteresting confirmation of the opinion of those economic istorians who hold that centralised manufactures, carried on n factories by machinery, were rare, even at the end of the ighteenth century.[1] 'Fabrik' is used by Möser in the sense of 'manufacture', as the French word 'fabrique' was used n phrases like 'la fabrique des toiles'.

Of these newer centres of trade the most important was Germany's chief North Sea port, HAMBURG. Hamburg njoyed a great advantage in possessing the best natural harbour on the German North Sea coast, for along the reater part of this coast the water is shallow, only deepening ufficiently for large ships in the estuaries, especially in that

[1] E.g. Kulischer, II, 148 ff.

of the Elbe. Hamburg was therefore marked out as the port for bringing the North German plain into touch with England, France and Holland. As an internal avenue of trade the Elbe was second only to the Rhine. Hamburg was the seaport of Berlin. In the best times of the Hanse it had not been so flourishing as Lübeck, for the Baltic trade was then far more valuable than that of the North Sea, but it had later an advantage over Lübeck and all the other Hanseatic ports in being the depôt chosen as the most convenient by the English trading company that proved the Hanse's most serious rival. As we have seen, the Hamburger were false enough to the Hanse to welcome the English 'Merchant Adventurers' in 1567, and though forced later to eject them, it was not long before their city became the main depôt of this important company, which had the monopoly of English trade with Germany. It was already the most important port on this coast except Antwerp, and had built an exchange in 1558, only four years after Antwerp itself. The fall of Antwerp in the Spanish wars greatly increased its trade, though from now it had a serious rival in Amsterdam. Its participation in the colonial trade, combined with its English connections, made it a commercial centre of international importance, an importance that was not diminished even by the Thirty Years' War, in spite of the damage done to its hinterland. A Dutch bank was founded there in 1619, and the growth of the town's fortunes is reflected in the fact that the tax yield was doubled during the course of the war. The town was spared an occupation, and its population was swelled by numerous refugees. Through its neutrality in the various wars between the sea powers it was often able to play the part of *tertius gaudens*, acquiring at times almost a position of monopoly. As its capital increased, it was able to enter into competition with England and Holland in manufacture. Its local trade with Holland was enormously increased by Dutch immigration during the Dutch Wars of Independence. Its population soon became international, for like Amsterdam

nd unlike Nürnberg or Ulm it was a refuge for exiles of all
inds, Jews and Protestants. Even in the eighteenth century
nly about 160 of the 2000 ships that arrived and sailed each
ear were owned by residents, the rest coming from abroad.

was therefore naturally open to foreign influences in all
natters. It had the first coffee-house, the first 'Moralische
Wochenschriften' in imitation of the *Spectator*, the first
nasonic lodge, and it was the home of democracy in
Germany. Its importance for German civilisation was very
reat and its status among German towns from the end of
ne fifteenth until late in the eighteenth century was unique,
n view of its size, prosperity and activity in economic,
olitical and intellectual affairs.

Next in importance among the towns in German-
speaking lands was the group which acted as intermediary
etween Germany and Italy and southern France, namely
ne SWISS TOWNS and STRASSBURG. Although these towns
oo ultimately owed their prosperity mainly to their favour-
ble geographical situation on great ways of communication,
passive' trade no longer predominated in them to such an
xtent as in the northern ports. Thanks in great measure to
ne skill and initiative of Protestant refugees from Italy and
France they had developed by the eighteenth century im-
ortant export industries, notably silk and woollen weaving.
The prominent part played by Italian refugees in particular,
with their expert knowledge of the new industrial technique
nd organisation that were known in Italy long before their
doption in other parts of Europe, can still clearly be traced
y an examination of the names of Basle and Zürich patrician
amilies. Starting in the sixteenth century, they successfully
vercame Dutch competition in the seventeenth, being so
ttle affected by the Thirty Years' War that their land seemed
o 'Simplicissimus', for instance, an earthly paradise. 'The
ountry seemed so strange to me compared with other parts
f Germany that I felt I might have been in Brazil or China.
saw people going about their business in peace; the byres

were full of cattle, the farmyards full of hens, geese and ducks; the roads were used by travellers in safety, the inns were full of people making merry.'[1]

The hold of the gild system was shaken here even in the seventeenth century, and manufactures on a domestic basis, with workers in the country, began to grow up, depending on export trade for their existence. The Rhine was the great channel of communication with Germany, the route for a flourishing trade with Strassburg and Frankfort. Silk was exported too to the towns of Bavaria, Austria and Hungary. The export trade was directed by central organisations in Zürich, Basle, St Gallen and Strassburg from as early as 1670, and large-scale industrial interests soon acquired the lead in social and political matters. The effects of the decay of craftsmanship that ensued are perhaps still to be seen in the extent to which foreign craftsmen outnumber native Swiss. A more welcome feature was the attention paid to education by those in authority, and the intellectual and artistic activity of the leisured classes. Even in the seventeenth century nearly half the population of Zürich could read and write, and quite half the children went to school. Basle was a centre of learning as well as of trade, for it had the means to support the ancient university founded there by the Humanist Pope Pius II.

The comparative prosperity of the towns so far discussed was due to their favourable geographical position, which led to their becoming centres of trade. The same consideration determined the importance of certain central German towns too during this period, towns which were for the most part insignificant for their own production, but which formed convenient trade centres owing to their position on natural lines of communication. There was first LEIPZIG. Before any roads had been made in Germany it was divided into two main areas of trade, one in the north and one in the south, connected only by the Rhine in the west. Central German

---

[1] Grimmelshausen, *Simplicissimus*, Bk. v, chap. 1.

was a neutral area. It became necessary to find a route through this region too when the colonisation of the east began, to allow of the exchange of western manufactures with eastern raw materials. Towns already existed in these parts on the main rivers, mostly on what geographers call the 'fall-line', where the hills meet the plain and goods brought from the plains by road or river had to be unloaded and distributed by pack-horse. The new cross-connections joined the most conveniently situated of these towns. The main road was the one through Frankfort-on-Main (the western gate), Eisenach and Erfurt to Leipzig and Halle, an old route of the Halle salt trade, following a series of troughs running east and west. The other skirted the Teutoburger Wald, passed between the Harz and the Thüringer Wald and north of the Erzgebirge and Sudeten to the Silesian colonies, divided into three stages by Cologne, Leipzig and Breslau, each in a fertile, thickly populated district. Leipzig was the meeting point of these two roads, and this alone would have made it the chief town in Central Germany except Frankfort, which was also the junction of two main lines of communication, by road and river. It was further helped by the rise of Hamburg and the necessity under which southern Germany found itself of turning its face to the north instead of to Italy, after the great change of world trade routes. The southern towns had to find a road to a northern port; owing to Dutch control and the innumerable tolls on the Rhine, Hamburg was favoured, and Leipzig was the most convenient half-way house between the sea and the southern centre Nürnberg, besides being the natural centre of concentration for goods from Saxony, Silesia and Poland.

No wonder then that for contemporaries Leipzig was as great a wonder as Hamburg. In this 'Klein Paris', as Goethe tells us in *Dichtung und Wahrheit*, one met at fair-time foreigners from all quarters, Polish Jews, Russians, even Greeks in their strange garb, as well as Englishmen and Dutchmen, for by this time its fair, held three times a year, had quite outstripped that of Frankfort, its great rival. There might be anything up to 7000 visiting merchants at fair-times, and the turnover might be in the neighbourhood of a million pounds.[1] In the fifteenth and early sixteenth centuries the town had acquired extensive privileges, reducing Halle and Erfurt to dependence. Its 'staple rights' held good for fifteen Meilen around and it attracted traders by guile and by force in order to cripple the trade by rival routes, such as that between Hof and Dresden. A textile industry was started by Dutch refugees, but on the whole Leipzig was far more important as a centre of trade than for its own industries. It was the market for the products of Saxony, the chief industrial province, with its widespread domestic industries, its porcelain at Meissen (Dresden china) and cotton at Chemnitz, and its trade grew with that of the northern ports, especially from the second half of the seventeenth century. Even in 1765 it produced the impression of a commercial city of recent growth. 'Leipzig evokes in the observer no memories of bygone times; its monuments speak of a new and recent epoch; a period of commercial activity, ease and wealth', as Goethe says. It had already blocks of flats like 'great castles, or even whole quarters of towns', and was extremely open to foreign influences, especially French, for its culture was more recent than that of Frankfort, which had long been in touch with the civilising West.

In virtue of its position FRANKFORT had long been an important market for goods, where Eastern wares were exchanged with south and west German industrial products. The importance of its fairs was increased by the destruction of its rival Antwerp, Frankfort's central situation making it particularly famous as a money-market. During the Thirty Years' War its position in this respect was much weakened owing to difficulties of communication and general uncertainty, and it lost much of its business to Amsterdam, to which it now had to play second fiddle till the nineteenth

[1] Figures from Kulischer, II, 255.

century. It lost its leadership in the book trade to Leipzig early in the seventeenth century for a number of reasons—the falling-off of the Italian trade since the Index of Pius IV (*c.* 1570), the strict censorship of the Imperial Book Commission, the high-handed behaviour of the Frankfort booksellers against foreigners, the increase in the number of German publications as against Latin, which reduced the number of books printed abroad. It had been possible of course to print Latin books anywhere, but German could only be printed well in Germany, and in those days, when publishers went to the fair in person, Leipzig was a better centre for the home trade. The tendency of the southern trade to avoid Frankfort and the Rhine in favour of Leipzig and Hamburg, and the competition of Basle, Nürnberg, and later the new town Mannheim, the distributing centre of the English and Dutch, all contributed towards Frankfort's decline, but its geographical position and old connections enabled it to retain more of its old glory than most of the south German Reichsstädte. It was tolerant of Protestant refugees and Jews—the Jews expelled from Nürnberg, Augsburg, Ulm, etc. congregated in the Frankfort ghetto. Besides patricians and officials there were manufacturers following in the wake of Western developments—Goethe describes for instance an oil-cloth factory owned and directed by a painter, in which large numbers of people were employed, but many of the refugees were driven to settle in Höchst, Offenbach, or Hanau to escape gild regulations. There were also already merchants and financiers (the Bethmanns and later the Rothschilds) with large fortunes, but on the whole Frankfort had to be content to rest on its laurels during this period, contriving by timely compromises, of which its constitution might be taken as a type, to avoid the fate of the smaller towns, but never energetic and venturesome enough to make any rapid progress.[1]

---

[1] See *Die Stadt Goethes*, ed. Voelcker, 1932, for a full account of Frankfort at this period.

Such a vegetative existence was by no means the fate of BERLIN in the seventeenth and eighteenth centuries. From the time of the Great Elector, its development was due to conscious effort on the part of the Prussian rulers, whose vigorous mercantilist policy gradually succeeded in remedying the defects of its natural position and tapping some of Leipzig's stream of trade. By the construction of the Friedrich-Wilhelm canal the Oder was connected with the Spree, and Berlin became the half-way house between Breslau and Hamburg by the water route. The Breslau merchants were encouraged by preferential tariffs to use the new route instead of the roads, sending their Silesian yarn and linen down the Oder and Elbe, and receiving in return colonial goods, fruit, wine and textiles for Poland, Russia and Austria. This was to the advantage of Breslau, which grew to be a considerable town, and still more to that of Berlin, where these goods had all to be transshipped, so that Berlin now acquired some of the advantages that Leipzig had enjoyed. Its river connections were now excellent, and they were further improved under Frederick the Great; its competition had been felt by Leipzig even before the end of the seventeenth century. Its population grew continuously: 1661—6500; 1721—over 60,000; c. 1760—120,000; 1777—140,000; 1795—150,000. It has been pointed out that only part of this increase was due to the growth of trade and industry. A large proportion was accounted for by the influx of French and Dutch immigrants, who were encouraged to come because of their industrial skill, and a still larger one by the growth of the Prussian army and the increasing political importance of Berlin. We have seen above that in 1783, out of a total population of 141,000, the garrison with their families made up 33,000, officials and their families about 14,000 and personal attendants on these and the court another 10,000, a total of 57,000 persons directly dependent on the will of the king.

Chapter III

MUNICIPAL GOVERNMENT AND THE STRUCTURE OF TOWN SOCIETY

We have seen that the towns may be classified according to the range and nature of their economic activities. Their political relationships are a further ground of differentiation, and one hardly less important for the general life of the town dwellers. According to their legal status in relation to the Empire and its component states they had been divided since the Middle Ages into Imperial or Free Towns and 'Landstädte', or towns under the control of a Landesfürst, a territorial ruler. A brief historical retrospect is necessary to explain the situation as it was in the eighteenth century.

The effect of the rise of absolute territorial states in Germany had been particularly disastrous on the towns, for most of the gains of the princes were made at their expense. There was no longer any superior authority to regulate the relations of town to territory; the struggle was decided by the strength of the opponents. The lords had, however, allies in the lesser nobles and country squires who had seats in provincial assemblies, where the Landstädte were also represented. Being of similar tastes, habits and extraction to the princes, it was natural that these landowners, each of whom exercised on his estate the same kind of patriarchal authority as the princes themselves claimed over the whole land, should need little inducement to take the princes' side rather than that of the bourgeois, the upstart shopkeepers whose intelligence and *esprit de corps* made them so dangerous, and whose towns attracted the poor but indispensable lower members of the feudal hierarchy, threatening the security of the whole system. But perhaps the main cause of the triumph of the territories was the desertion of important town forces to the enemy. As the territories became closer and stronger units, the towns lost their old organising power and sense of self-help, for their most intelligent members entered some prince's service and helped him to establish his authority at the expense of the towns that had reared them.

It was more difficult for a society consisting, as town society did now, of widely differentiated elements to form an organic whole than it had been in a simpler age. When the giids demanded political authority in the towns proportionate to their numbers and importance, many of the wealthy old patrician families, which had always had much in common with the lesser nobility in their ways of life and general outlook, converted their fortunes into landed estates and deprived the towns of their capital and brains. They were often imitated in this by the most successful merchants, for they, like the craftsmen already spoken of, were not disposed to work any longer when they possessed a competence on which to retire and buy themselves a title and estate. Even where they did not do so, they generally no longer felt the interests of the town to be their own, and were ready to finance any prince, however hostile his intentions towards their fellow townsmen. Their loans and the great expansion of the currency due to the exploitation of the German, and later the American, mines brought about a revolution in prices, a fall in the value of money, which the masses attributed not merely to the Fugger and their kind, but to the bourgeoisie in general, so that they acquiesced in the policy of the princes, and looked upon robber knights as deliverers.

Thus even apart from the losses resulting from the Spanish bankruptcies and later from the ravages of the Thirty Years' War, there was not the same financial power at the disposal of the town authorities as in their prime. Many of those which had enjoyed the rights of toll and mintage lost them to the territorial lords, whose depreciation of the coinage impoverished them further. The princes exacted tolls of their own on roads, bridges and rivers, and prevented the towns from gaining any revenue from their own tolls by the provision that goods should pay duty only once within the territorial limits. The burden of taxation in the towns was, as we have seen, unevenly distributed, the rich and powerful paying least. The territorial finances, on the other hand, were rapidly improving, enabling the princes to buy the services of the mercenary troops that the towns had been the first to employ.

The old civic guards of volunteers had everywhere disappeared, for with money the towns had been able to pay for both men and material aids, strong walls and implements of war. They had thus been able for a time to maintain their rights against neighbouring nobles, but with the rise of the territories their own weapons were turned against them. The Lanzknechte went to the highest bidder, swelling the standing armies of the princes, while the invention of gunpowder and artillery made the old town walls almost useless. After the Thirty Years' War the trade of war became a territorial one, the princes alone having armies, which grew accordingly in size and efficiency, while the defences of the towns fell into decay. The difference between the Middle Ages and modern times in this respect may be seen by contrasting Machiavelli's description of the German Free Towns of his day, in the tenth chapter of the *Prince*, with Frederick the Great's comments on the passage in his *Anti-Machiavel*.

'The towns of Germany', says Machiavelli (he is referring to the larger 'free' towns), 'enjoy a high degree of freedom, although their territory is small; they obey the emperor when they so desire, and fear neither him nor any other powerful neighbour. For as they are all surrounded by strong walls and deep moats, possess an artillery suited to their needs and always keep their storehouses stocked with a year's provision of wood and foodstuffs, the investment of these towns is a long and difficult matter.... They keep themselves always in training in the arts of war, and have many usages besides to prevent themselves from falling into decay.'

To this Frederick remarks:

The picture presented to us by Machiavelli of the German Free Towns is quite different from their present state. One petard, or in default of that, one word of command from the emperor, would suffice to make him master of these towns. They are all badly fortified. Most of them have old walls with tall towers on them at intervals, and moats almost filled up with the earth that has fallen in. They have few soldiers and these badly disciplined; their officers are for the most part either obtained second-hand from German princes, or are old men no longer capable of service. A few Free Towns have fairly good artillery; but that would not be sufficient to enable them to oppose the emperor, and he takes every opportunity of making them conscious of their powerlessness.

Frederick is here alluding to those Reichsstädte which had at any rate maintained an outward show of independence, but even in these the same decay of the civic spirit had set in as in the other towns, a change clearly reflected in the oligarchical form of their government. The only towns that had changed their constitutions since the sixteenth century were Frankfort-on-Main and Hamburg. Although the Peace of Westphalia made them into sovereign states, the Free Towns had no real power in the Reichstag. Even in the middle of the sixteenth century they had only been heard after the other sections had come to an agreement. Their governments were thoroughly reactionary; the council consisted frequently of two bodies that relieved each other at intervals, and filled vacancies by co-option from the 'Ratsfähige Geschlechter'. There were in many towns hereditary posts, and even where this was not so, offices were chiefly valued for the pecuniary gain they involved, the reversion of some kind of office being a valuable form of legacy. The council had full power and no responsibilities. It would speak of 'its' citizens, and even assume a sort of divine right as sanction for its worst acts. The Hamburg[1]

[1] Hamburg, though it only became a Free Town in the eighteenth century, was relatively independent.

council for instance in 1602 addressed the assembly of citizens, supposed to share power with itself, in the following terms: 'Even if an authority is ungodly, tyrannical and avaricious, it does not become its subjects to rebel against it. They ought rather to recognise their fate as a punishment from the Almighty, which the subjects have brought upon themselves by their sins'.[1]

The paid officials who replaced the older voluntary ones, especially after the spread of Roman law, were often lawyers. Jurists assumed important functions in almost all towns, and were often members of the council as experts. In the Landstädte they, together with the council, were mere tools in the hands of the prince, who often appointed them and even nominated new members of the council when vacancies occurred. Independent town legislation was here a thing of the past, for every regulation had to be submitted to the central authority. Jurisdiction too had become a prerogative of the princes. There were no longer any town courts, with an appeal, if necessary, to their 'Oberhof', the court of the town that had served as model for their law. Roman law was everywhere recognised, and the only appeal was to the territorial supreme court.

That the management of the towns under these conditions was full of abuses was only to be expected. If the citizens appealed to the prince he had an excuse for sending commissaries to enquire into the matter, and really to replace the council entirely, so that democratic control was quite out of the question. There was no attraction in serving such a town for honour, when office-holders were responsible only in appearance and all real control was exercised from above. It became at last a common practice to pay the members of the council, which frequently consisted of superannuated state servants or invalided non-commissioned officers, for they were not even well paid. The mayor of Berlin for instance, who was in effect a minor state official, was paid 200 Thalers

---

[1] Preuss, *op. cit.* p. 147.

a year or less. Frederick William I said openly 'Mein Interesse ist, Bürgermeister zu setzen, die platt von mir dependieren'.[1]

The sovereign state had killed the spirit of autonomy, or at all events taken advantage of its decay, to substitute an authoritarian organisation, modelled on the disciplined armies of the time and receiving all orders from above, for the old decentralised self-government of independent groups. It is probable that this development was desirable in the interest of efficiency; a larger unit was necessary, and the towns were too much bound by tradition to recognise the fact. But that Prussia for instance went too far in the direction of centralisation, in the absence of any parliamentary corrective, is shown by the fact that Stein had to reverse the process in his 'Städteordnung' at the end of the eighteenth century.

The difference between Free and Territorial Towns was directly reflected in the structure of society in the towns, in municipal government and consequently in social life and ideals. It is a serious over-simplification to speak of a 'Bürger' without qualifying adjective, for citizens differed in different kinds of town and in the different social strata of any one town. Even in the medieval town, civic society was far from being a community of equals. There were harsh contrasts in plenty, with regard to social status and influence, wealth and manner of living. It is true that wealth was not the almost exclusive criterion of esteem that it has become to-day, but it was already a very important factor and was very unequally distributed. It has been calculated from tax-returns and so on that between one-fifth and two-fifths of the population in most medieval towns was quite without property. In Augsburg the proportion is said to have been two-thirds.[2] Usually more than half the total wealth was concentrated in the hands of some 4 or 5 per cent. of the

[1] Preuss, op. cit. p. 167.
[2] Kulischer, I, 176, where details are given.

population.[1] In every big town there were large numbers of crippled and blind beggars. Of course the ideal of individual equality was one that did not enter the heads of the citizens. 'Whereas the modern view is dynamic, and the struggle of whole classes to raise themselves not only in wealth and culture, but in political and social power, seems to us just as much a kind of moral duty as do the efforts of the individual to get on and if possible to rise into another class, the thought and feeling of the Middle Ages were static. Both the social orders in themselves and the bond between the individual and his order were looked upon as ordained by God.'[2] This instinctive acceptance of hereditary social orders was only slowly modified by the accumulation of wealth in the larger towns, and considerations of 'Stand' were, as we have seen, still very important in eighteenth-century Germany.

The sumptuary regulations which continued to be made (though no longer observed) well into the eighteenth century give us some idea of current opinion about the relative standing of various classes. In the last *Kleiderordnung* issued in Frankfort-on-Main, in 1731, five classes are distinguished. The first consists of the principal civic dignitaries (the Schultheiss, the Schöffen or Aldermen of the first bench, the town councillors of the second bench, the four syndics, etc.), the doctors (of law and medicine), and the members of noble families whose ancestors had taken part in the government of the town for at least a century. The second class consists of the councillors of the third bench (gild representatives), the most distinguished citizens, wholesale merchants and bankers with a capital of at least 20,000 Thalers. In the third class came notaries and advocates, artists and shopkeepers, and 'others of about the same standing'. In the fourth class we find 'die gemeinen schlechten Krämer'—small stall-holders and street-hawkers, shop assistants and craftsmen,

---

[1] J. Bühler, *Die Kultur des Mittelalters*, 1931, p. 124.
[2] *Ibid.*

and in the fifth class all the rest, labourers, coachmen, servants and the like.

This list reflects of course the reactionary town council's view of the social hierarchy, and would not have been accepted then by every one. It ranks the patricians of the town for instance higher than members of noble families from outside, of whom there were usually a number residing in the town. They are classed among the 'distinguished citizens' of class two, but would certainly consider themselves the superiors of any patrician. The wealthy merchants who were not in the council, again, would surely not hold themselves to be merely the equals of the gildsmen on the town council. But roughly speaking the list represents fairly enough the social order of precedence in a Free Town.

The patricians were amongst the wealthiest people in the town, but not all wealthy men were patricians. The patricians were 'the families with inherited wealth, organised as a caste' (v. Below). They liked to think that their ancestors had been the ruling class from time immemorial; they held themselves (as Goethe said to Eckermann) to be no whit inferior to the 'county families', the country nobility. Some few could trace their descent to the oldest town families, the early settlers who had fought for the town's rights with the town lord, or the lord's officials in the town, but though the governing class had tried from a very early date to close its ranks to newcomers, it had never succeeded in preventing the rise of new families to wealth and esteem, and had always gradually absorbed them. In Nürnberg itself the names in the various lists we have of patrician families at different dates are by no means always the same. 'A list of 1390 mentions 118 "ehrbare Familien", one of 1490, 112. Of these only 49 were named in the 1390 list. A list of 1511 mentions 92. Only 37 of the patrician families of 1390 are still amongst them.'[1] The patrician families usually formed

[1] v. Below, *Das ältere deutsche Städtewesen und Bürgertum*, p. 119.

themselves into a club or union to protect their rights, much as the craftsmen organised themselves in gilds. In eighteenth-century Frankfort for instance there were still two 'societies' of good families, the Limpurger and the Frauensteiner. The Limpurger claimed to be the older and more respectable, and looked upon the Frauensteiner as upstart traders, but it was a domestic quarrel and both alike held themselves to be equal to the nobility of the Reich. Their pride rested on a compound of inherited wealth, traditions of civic service, legal privileges and a high standard of living. As new members only sons of members were admitted, or full citizens who married into these families.[1]

In some towns old merchant families would predominate (in Hamburg and the ports), in others landowners and rentiers. In all towns, since the acceptance of Roman law, the class of university graduates in law had come, through their indispensability, to be considered amongst those of the first rank. Their right to this esteem was not undisputed. It was urged by the patricians that the status of a graduate was purely personal, confined to the man himself. He might be the son of a craftsman and his children might be 'Pöbel'.[2] There was not very much force in this last objection because it was only a man of considerable means who could afford to let his son study law. Poor boys usually had to be content with theology. The graduates (who had their own 'Kollegium' to defend their interests) were not lacking in arguments in their own defence. They appealed to old privileges, foreign example, and above all they urged that the claim of native ability was superior to that of inherited position. Legal training was a necessary qualification for most of the important civic offices and greatly increased a man's chances of being elected to the council. The 'doctors' enjoyed esteem accordingly as potential councillors. The university graduates,

---

[1] For details see article by Dr H. Voelcker in *Die Stadt Goethes*, p. 97 ff.
[2] *Id.* p. 210.

amongst whom the lawyers stood in highest esteem, were s
important in general in the development of German though
and literature, forming, as they came to do, virtually a nev
'Stand' between the landowning nobility and the merchant
and better craftsmen, that it will be necessary to devote
special chapter to them later.

The high standing enjoyed by the better merchants i
Frankfort is easily explained by their importance in the city'
economic life. We have seen earlier that though merchant
had come to the fore in the bigger medieval towns, it wa
only in modern times that they were to be found in larg
numbers in any but a few towns. We have seen also that th
distinction between merchant and shopkeeper was not rigi
in the Middle Ages, and it had not become so even in th
eighteenth century, any more than that between merchan
and banker. The social standing of a trader naturally de
pended on the scope of his undertakings and consequen
wealth. The social status of a master craftsman could still b
high, especially where, as in Frankfort, the gilds had success
fully claimed representation on the council. But generall
speaking, in consequence of the falling off in the demand fo
gild products and the growth of capitalistic forms of industr
in the country, it was not so high relatively as in the Middl
Ages. Though gild forms were still observed, there was no
the same proud spirit of independence among the master
as in earlier days. On the other hand, with the relaxation c
gild regulations which, in spite of protests, proved inevitabl
many craftsmen made considerable fortunes (one remember
Goethe's grandfather, the lady's tailor) and others becam
dealers and entrepreneurs. In the literature of the time,
master craftsman is usually represented as one of the lowe
middle class, a 'Kleinbürger', who works hard for a ver
modest living.

Below the master-craftsmen came, in addition to unskille
workers, the important class of those who were, at least i
theory, serving their time in the expectation of becomin

masters themselves, the apprentices and journeymen. A journeyman (Geselle) was an apprentice who had served his 'Lehrzeit', passed the journeyman's test and been solemnly promoted to the rank of 'Geselle' by his gild. He received a certificate to this effect, a 'Lehrbrief', which frequently contained good advice for his future conduct. Goethe made use of many of these details of course in his *Wilhelm Meister*. After his admission, the Geselle in the majority of gilds in Germany went on his wanderings for a period of years, as Wilhelm does. They might take him all over Germany and even into the neighbouring countries. The journeymen, then, were in the main a floating population of young unmarried men ('Junggesellen'), with few ties in the town. Many of them were naturally restless and irresponsible spirits, so that disputes between masters and journeymen were inevitable. Moreover, the rise of entrepreneurs and the growing exclusiveness of the masters within the gilds had led to an increasing disproportion in numbers between masters and journeymen. Many of the latter could no longer hope to attain independence; they might even suffer quite seriously from unemployment. The disproportion in numbers does not seem to have been very great in Germany in most trades until the nineteenth century, and the old patriarchal ways of life continued even in large towns, apprentices and journeymen still living and working in their master's house.[1] Yet it is clear from the unrest among them, which caused so much alarm in the seventeenth century and continued into the eighteenth, that the journeymen had become conscious of class interests of their own.

The separate organisations of journeymen deserve mention here, for they were hardly less important for their influence on life in the towns than the gilds of masters described in an earlier chapter. They combined some of the functions of a modern trade union with those of a labour exchange. From local fraternities with a function something like that

[1] Figures in Sombart, *op. cit.* II, 692.

of the Young Men's Christian Association, encouraged by town and Church, they had become unions for the defence of their members' rights as workers, joined in affiliations which covered the whole country. Each trade or group of trades had its 'Herberge' in every town, an inn where the members met for social intercourse and for the business of the association, which was conducted with many time-hallowed phrases and usages. The members enjoyed, in return for a fixed subscription, not only the privileges of local membership, but the certainty of a welcome from the allied organisations all over Germany. On coming to a town, the wandering journeyman would make his way to the Herberge of his craft, and here, if he had the necessary papers from his home-town and presented himself with the usual formula—at first a kind of shibboleth—he was received as a brother and helped to find employment by his fellow-craftsmen. If there were no vacancies, he received free quarters and was usually given a small sum of money from the common funds, to help him on his way to the next town. In any dispute with his master about wages or conditions of work the union would support him, if he seemed to them to be in the right, and to this end what we should now call the strike and the boycott were used by the journeymen with great determination.

It was a too class-conscious use of these weapons which evoked a series of measures passed by the Reichstag and culminating in an imperial law of 1731, by which the unions were deprived of their functions and every journeyman was compelled to carry a passport from his government on his wanderings. Led by Prussia, the territories very gradually proceeded to enforce these provisions, but many features of the old organisations survived, though under increasingly efficient state control. The journeymen continued to go on their wanderings, in some trades until late in the nineteenth century. The wandering handicraftsmen were still a prominent feature of German life for instance when Howitt

visited Germany in 1840. 'One of the first things on your
arrival in the country which strikes your eye', he says, 'is the
number of young men on the roads with knapsacks on their
backs, and stout sticks in their hands.' 'At each end of his
knapsack peep the soles of a pair of boots; and he has often,
moreover, attached to his knapsack, a pair of small wheels,
by which, when his back is weary of it, he can trail it after
him with his stick.' It was exactly in this way that Keller's
Drei gerechte Kammacher were equipped. The journeymen
were the first class of people, apparently, who were forced
to go through the procedure, which now seems to foreigners
so peculiarly German, of reporting to the police on arrival
in a town and again on departure. 'It is amazing in the large
cities the crowd of these Gesellen that you see at the police-
office, bringing their passports, or fetching them away again.'
This is not the only detail in Howitt's description of the
Handwerksburschen which reminds us how much of the old
way of life has survived into the present. The institution of
Wanderschaft, affecting as it did the lives of so large a proportion of the inhabitants of the towns, was bound to leave
its mark on German society even in the industrial age. The
ordinary working man saw more of his own country than
the same class in any other part of the world, as Howitt
points out, and it was probably not merely fanciful of this
writer to associate with the habit of Wanderschaft the
'nature-loving and poetic feeling which so universally
distinguishes the German, even to the commonest class'. It
is surely no accident that Germany, where wandering was
compulsory for craftsmen so much longer than elsewhere,
should have been the home of the Wandervögel and the
Youth Movement, of school-journeys and youth-hostels.
'Wanderlust' had become part of the social inheritance,
mainly through the century-old habits of the common
people of the towns. For the same reason the Wanderlieder
and the nature poetry, in which German literature is so rich,
cannot be looked upon as the creation of Romantic intel-

lectuals. They had their roots deep in popular habit and feeling.[1]

In every town the inhabitants formed nominally two, in reality in most towns three distinct groups in regard to their legal rights and duties as citizens. These legal survivals from the Middle Ages were still of some importance for purposes of taxation. In the Free Towns citizenship was still felt to be an honour, but in the other towns it seems to have been a privilege that was little esteemed. In towns like Frankfort and most of the Free Towns only the members of the 'Ratsfähige Familien' were really citizens in the fullest sense, enjoying an active share in the government. This seems to have been the normal state of things in the early days of the towns. In theory, however, the inhabitants of all towns were now either *Vollbürger*, citizens proper, or *Beisassen* (Hintersassen, Schutzbürger). The first were considered as full members of the city community, the second as 'associate members'. Only the citizens might own houses and land in the town area—though exceptions were made for noblemen and monasteries. Only citizens could be members of the council or civic officials. Only citizens could become master craftsmen or shopkeepers. The citizens still enjoyed privileges in the matter of tolls and dues and had rights in the city pastures and woods. It was not easy for strangers to become citizens, unless they married a citizen's daughter or widow, and they had to be men of some means. While sons of citizens became citizens themselves for a small fixed fee of a Gulden or so, a stranger paid 5 per cent. of his capital as entrance money, or $2\frac{1}{2}$ per cent. if marrying a citizeness, in Frankfort. In Nürnberg he mortgaged his property to the town. If he did not wish to declare his means, he had to pay 750 Gulden and be assessed in the highest grade for taxation. In Nürnberg he had to be a Protestant. It was cheaper to become a *Beisasse*,

[1] For the organisations and customs of the journeymen see, e.g., E. Otto, *Das deutsche Handwerk*, 5. Aufl. 1920; art. 'Gewerbe' in the *Handwörterbuch der Staatswissenschaften*, IV; Howitt, *op. cit.* chap. 10.

but one's rights were then correspondingly reduced, and one lived in the town only on sufferance. A Beisasse could exercise a craft or carry on trade under certain restrictions, but he could not acquire a house or land in the town, or keep cattle. His entrance-fee was a few Gulden, varying according to means, but he paid taxes at double the normal rate for citizens.

Strangers staying in the town for more than a month or two and wishing to live in a private house needed in eighteenth-century Nürnberg or Frankfort, and no doubt elsewhere, a 'permit' granted for a year at a time, and they had to take the oath and pay taxes like the citizens and Beisassen. They were not allowed to carry on trade except at the fair, or to own land—but exceptions were made for people of standing.

Special conditions were imposed everywhere on Jews.[1] In some towns (Nürnberg, Augsburg and several other German towns) they were not allowed at all. In Nürnberg Jews from Fürth entering the town on business had to pay a toll and the regulations prescribed that they should be accompanied by an old woman appointed for the purpose, but in Nicolai's day they merely tipped her.[2] In Ulm only one Jew was tolerated.[3] The Jews from these towns had all been received, at the emperor's request, in Frankfort. In its Judengasse, which could only be entered or left by gates at either end that were shut at night, a number limited to 500 householders (usually about 3000 individuals) were accommodated, subject to strict regulations and the normal taxes. A newcomer had to possess 1000 Gulden in capital, pay considerable fees (over 70 Gulden in all), and his permit had to be renewed for a fee ($12\frac{1}{2}$ Gulden) every three years. The restrictions were however relaxed in the course of the century. Jews were for instance not prevented from having shops outside the ghetto.[4]

The foregoing with unimportant variations applies to the

---

[1] Details in Bergius, *Policey- und Cameral-Magazin*, v.
[2] Nicolai, *Reisen*, I, 310.
[3] *Id.* IX, 47.　　　　[4] *Die Stadt Goethes*, pp. 63 f.

Free Towns in general. In the remaining towns, 'Landstädte' under the control of a territorial prince, there were Bürger and Schutzbürger, but a very large number of people were so-called 'gefreite Bürger'. In Durlach for instance these included all connected with the court, the nobility, all officials from the Bürgermeister down to the hangman, the purveyors by appointment to the court (Hofbäcker, etc.— this was the real value of the privilege), the personal servants of nobility and officials, all Lutheran ministers and their assistants even down to the organ-blower, school-teachers, doctors and apothecaries. Civic spirit had decayed so far that it was more honourable to be 'gefreit' than to be a full citizen. The wealthier and more esteemed inhabitants, the rich rentiers, artists, scholars, and later the factory owner and the chief men of his staff, were all Gefreite, and even the Bürgermeister, councillors and magistrates. The garrison were on the same footing. Officials, if natives and citizens, generally gave up their civic rights on appointment. In the Landstädte then, especially if they had any connection with a prince's court (Durlach as we have seen was originally a prince's seat), the medieval legal categories of citizens had lost much of their meaning. In Berlin, as was stated above, there were only 10,700 'Bürger' in 1755 out of a population of 150,000. Court, garrison, officials, and their dependents as well as the large foreign colony were all 'Gefreite'.

The second class, the 'citizens' proper, consisted therefore of shopkeepers, innkeepers, craftsmen and farmers. The great majority were craftsmen. They had much the same rights as the citizens of the Free Towns—the right to own land or exercise a craft in the town and to use the commons being the chief.

The third class, the 'Schutzbürger', included the agricultural labourers, small traders, pedlars, married journeymen, etc., all in fact who were not 'Gefreite' or 'Bürger', unless they escaped the notice of the authorities altogether, or like the new factory workers had been granted permission to live in the town on special terms.

There was not such a clear-cut distinction possible in any kind of eighteenth-century German town between municipal and state government as there is to-day, because the towns of the one class, the Free Towns, were states in themselves, while the territorial towns were controlled in all essentials by the central government of a territorial state. So Frankfort for instance had, as a republic, its 'Schultheiss' elected for life (originally an imperial official), whom one can look upon as a kind of president, and, as a municipality, it had its two Bürgermeister, elected for one year.

The council of a Free Town then was the government of a small republic. The town council enjoyed the same rights and prerogatives as a territorial prince, though under much stricter supervision by the imperial authority. Its delegates represented the town-republic in Reichstag and Kreistag, it directed 'foreign policy', made laws, levied tolls and taxes, and minted its own coinage like any sovereign prince. It was responsible for the administration of justice, and, since the Reformation, for the government of the established Church. As there was no strict separation of powers it was concerned both with legislation and in large measure with administration.

In such a town there was of course a regular system of Behörden, or departments of government, and a set of officials corresponding to the civil service of the states. No general description will serve for all towns, but taking Frankfort as a type of well-governed town the following departments may be distinguished.

The place of the *Regierung*, the superior judicial instance in a territorial state, was taken here by the senior bench of the council, the 'Schöffen', assisted by the four 'Syndics', trained jurists of distinction, under the 'Schultheiss'. In important matters an appeal was possible to one of the Reichsgerichte. The Bürgermeister, assisted by legal advisers, sat as a criminal court of first instance, and minor offences were investigated by the 'Oberstrichter', a kind of stipendiary magistrate. In serious suits, civil or criminal, recourse was often made to a university faculty of law for a final judgment.

For Church government and education Frankfort had its *Konsistorium*, with six lay and three ecclesiastical members. The *Treasury* was called *Rechneiamt*, and besides preparing a budget, taking charge of the town's income from every source and making all its payments, it administered all town property and exercised a considerable degree of control over industry and trade. It regulated weights and measures, fixed prices for bread, meat, cloth, issued licences to innkeepers and the numerous other persons who required them— barbers, brewers, smiths, bakers, café proprietors, etc., and farmed out the excise on meat, fish, salt, and several other dues to the highest bidder. As almost every function of the government had a financial aspect, the treasury tended to bring more and more affairs under its control every year. It absorbed the *Kriegszeugamt* and took over the recruiting and maintenance of the town's garrison of about 35 officers and 700 to 800 men. A special *Schatzungsamt* looked after the assessment of property and collection of direct taxes, and a *Rentenamt* the collection of the numerous indirect taxes, while five customs houses levied toll on goods coming into and passing out of the town.

In these various departments a large number of permanent officials were employed, in addition to the salaried Ratsherren who were delegated to supervise them. The number of officials was even greater in proportion in towns like Frankfort, where the ordinary citizen had asserted a measure of control, than in the territories, because there existed here a 'Bürgerkollegium' or citizens' committee, which besides deputing its members (at a small salary) to various departments for part-time service, maintained permanent 'Gegenschreiber' in all departments to keep a check on the official 'Schreiber' in all matters involving public expenditure. This meant a double system of accounts, but it put a stop to the

financial mismanagement that was common in these Free
Towns when the patricians had all their own way.[1]

In the Territorial Towns all essential affairs were controlled
by officials appointed by the central government. The
functions of the Steuerräte in the Prussian towns have
been described above (p. 27). Here and elsewhere, even
where the old forms of civic government were kept, they
had lost almost all their meaning. No vestige of democratic control was allowed to survive. Mayor and councillors
were as often as not nominees of the state, and any mismanagement of town affairs was used as the pretext for their
replacement by commissioners. The gilds were brought under
territorial control. The law of the territory was substituted
for the old customary law of the town. Finance was managed
in the interest of the territorial treasury, trade and industry
being fostered mainly for the sake of the excise duties that
could be levied on them.

[1] For Frankfort's Behörden see article by Dr O. Ruppersberg in *Die
Stadt Goethes.*

Chapter IV

ARCHITECTURE OF THE TOWNS. PRIVATE LIFE, OUTLOOK AND EDUCATION OF THE TOWNSMAN

The function and history of the towns, as well as the social differences amongst their inhabitants, were more clearly expressed in their architecture in the eighteenth century than they are to-day. A town was, for instance, still clearly distinguishable from a village by the wall, with turrets and gates, which appeared to defend it, and at least made it impossible for anyone to enter or leave unobserved. Few old towns had spread beyond their medieval walls yet, though in some of course an outer ring had grown round the oldest city and had been walled in in its turn before gunpowder made walls useless. In or near the town there was often still to be seen the castle of the original lords of the town, or a monastery or cathedral might point to its origin, but even where its early history was not to be read in stone, there was a central market place flanked by civic buildings that told of the town's chief functions. The new towns on the other hand, built since the Middle Ages, were all creations of princes, and in their architecture they expressed, as we have seen, the aim of the prince to submit everything to his rational control. The town was architecturally an extension of the palace.

This baroque ideal, both of town planning and of architecture, was, as Dehio says, an aristocratic one. Comparatively few features of it could be adopted by the citizens of the older towns. The streets of these still continued to be narrow and crooked, even though houses were being continually altered or rebuilt as they decayed, for the life of the usual type of house, the 'Fachwerk' or half-timbered house, was at most about 250 years. The new capitals, and the 'new towns' built on to various older ones by a prince, usually for a colony of Dutch or French immigrants, could be and were carefully planned from the start. A street map of Berlin still reveals at a glance, in spite of many changes, how the new geometrical Friedrichstadt was added to the old walled town clustering round the Altmarkt. Similar 'new towns' were built in Dresden, Kassel, Bayreuth, Erlangen.

In all such places two types of house were to be found, the old-town and the new-town type. 'The old-town house has to adapt itself to a traditional site, or at best two old sites might be combined. The growing lack of ground space can only be met by increasing the number of storeys, in a direction therefore that runs counter to the artistic ideal of baroque architecture. The new towns on the other hand are given broad airy streets and the houses have a tendency to breadth rather than to height.'[1] In the old town, houses were much improved inside, but in external appearance the changes that were gradually made were not striking. From the sixteenth century the direction of the main roof ridge came to be parallel with the street, as in a palace, instead of being at right angles to it, but the gothic tradition was so strong that the 'Zwerchhäuser' or large projecting top storeys came to present a very similar appearance to the old triangular gable-end facing the street, and the horizontal line which was the aim of the change was again broken. Other fashionable improvements of the façade, all borrowed from palace architecture, were the substitution of symmetrically grouped and higher windows with flat frames for the many-mullioned small windows with leaded lights of bottle glass, and perhaps one more transparent 'peep-frame', the abolition of the oriel windows called 'Erker', and the introduction of pilasters, horizontal strips and an elaborate moulding round the windows to break up the flat surface into definite fields.[2]

[1] Dehio, *Geschichte der deutschen Kunst*, III, 315.
[2] *Ibid.* pp. 315 f. For examples from Frankfort see *Die Stadt Goethes*, pp. 22 ff., 318 ff.

The town authorities had for long issued and enforced building regulations, less from aesthetic considerations than out of regard for public safety (from fire), health and convenience. From 1719, for instance, the lower storey in new Frankfort houses had to be built of stone, only three storeys were allowed and not more than one storey was allowed to project, but we know from Goethe's description of the rebuilding of his father's house that regulations could be circumvented. The changes made by the Herr Rat were of the nature outlined above. The main aim was naturally increased convenience, light and space inside.

An old town like Frankfort, as we saw from Goethe's description quoted above, though it might have nothing 'architektonisch erhebend', had an unmistakable character of its own. That it was neither a prince's court nor a village, but the settlement of an independent community of craftsmen and merchants, was clear from the buildings this community had erected, the town hall and administrative offices, arsenal, mint, gildhalls, clothhall and so on, though civic pride was not so much in evidence now as earlier, and many indifferent old buildings still had to serve. In some towns the ravages of war were still evident, and in all of them there were tumbledown quarters hard by the modernised houses of the rich. It is evident from the statistics we possess that only a minority of houses were tenanted by one family. In Frankfort for instance the average number of occupants to the house was fifteen or sixteen. In Durlach there were often six to ten persons or even more living in a three-roomed flat.[1]

Though there were considerable differences between houses—in Frankfort for instance there were houses with four and houses with sixteen or more rooms—they were all roughly of the same type in the old town, poorer people living usually not in smaller houses but in sublet portions of large houses. Even in a small town like Durlach (in 1716) only about a quarter of the total number of houses had one

[1] See tables in Roller, *Durlach*, pp. 122 ff.

storey, and were meant for a single family. Most had two or three, with perhaps a shop or workshop and one little flat (consisting of kitchen, 'Stube' or living-room, and perhaps a bedroom) on the ground floor, and two similar flats on each of the other floors. A flat of the kind described was the general unit. If a family needed more space, it had to take two.[1] The commonest type of house had three storeys. The ground floor was built round a big *Flur* or hall, entered from the street by a wide door and leading to a courtyard behind, with outbuildings round it. The merchant would have his counting-house on the ground floor, and use cellars and outbuildings for storage of goods. The craftsman's workshop would also be on the ground level. If the houses were arcaded, as they often were, he would perhaps work under the arcade for light. One can still see such houses in Berne. The shop window of the craftsman and small shopkeeper had shutters folding horizontally, one from below forming a counter and one from above a 'pent-house' for shelter. Sometimes, as in the Hanseatic houses described in *Buddenbrooks*, vehicles could drive right through the *Flur* to the courtyard. The first storey in such a large house contained the reception rooms, and a bedroom or two round an upper hall, where the great chests stood with the family linen (enough to last for months without a washing day), and the top storey the remaining bedrooms. But the possible modifications were innumerable, because every house was built to suit its first owner's taste, often with rooms of differing heights, necessitating many dark stairs and corridors. There was an individual note about the meanest house for this reason, as it was all craftsman's work, but the elaborately carved and painted façades, the wrought-iron grilles, which we admire in pictures of old towns or in museums, were of course confined to the houses of the well-to-do.

Stone houses were by no means common even for the rich. The usual type was the Fachwerk or timber-framed house,

[1] Roller, *Durlach*, pp. 9 ff.

in which the spaces between the timber beams were filled in with brick or with wattle and daub. Thatched and often shingled roofs had been prohibited in the bigger towns for a long time, in Frankfort since the fifteenth century, but even so fires easily broke out and it was the chief duty of the watchman on the church tower and those patrolling the streets to give notice of any outbreak immediately. They had had tolerably efficient pumps since the seventeenth century, capable of throwing a jet eighty feet high.[1] Some towns had their fire station, in others the 'fire barrels' and so on were kept in the arcades of the Rathaus.

The most striking improvement that has been made since the eighteenth century, one that benefits all classes alike, i in public sanitation and water supply. Even the best houses were then lacking in what now seem elementary conveniences, particularly of a sanitary kind. It was only a palace that had a bath. There was sometimes a very rough and ready drainage system for certain houses, in Frankfort for instance for those that happened to lie over the 'Antauche', the tenth-century ditch of the oldest and now central part of the town, or one of a number of channels that had been cut to join it. It was, however, a doubtful privilege to own a 'Sitzgerechtigkeit' and have a sewer under one's kitchen. The alternative was a privy in the back court or in the top storey (the 'Stankgemach'!). Water had usually to be fetched from the public fountain, the 'Brunnen', in the street. All towns of any size had had to provide a water supply from outside, besides using any springs there might be in the town. Nicolai says that water was brought to Augsburg from springs at least one and a quarter Meilen away, stored in four reservoirs dating from the sixteenth and seventeenth centuries, and supplied in houses for a special payment. A somewhat similar system, he says, was to be found at Leipzig, Dresden, Nürnberg, Nymphenburg, Herrenhausen.[2] That

[1] Schultz, *Häusliches Leben der europäischen Völker*, p. 108.
[2] *Reisen*, VII, 80.

the quality of the water was often poor was inevitable from the dirty state of the streets. In towns the main streets were by now all paved, but it was often left to the citizens to dispose of their own refuse (in Frankfort for example till 1775). In Berlin criminals were employed as street cleansers, says Dr Moore. Nicolai speaks with admiration of the streets of Jena, where a brook had been diverted to flow through the middle of the streets and sweep all the rubbish into the Saale. In small towns the cattle and pigs still kept by citizens befouled the streets. It was not until 1681 that the citizens of Berlin had been prohibited from keeping pigs.

Another great inconvenience suffered by even the richest was the absence of good lighting at night, both in streets and houses, and the darkness of the houses by day. This latter defect was being remedied in the new houses, but all had still to be content with candles, usually home-made ones of tallow, oil lamps being useless except as night-lights until the flat wick and later the glass chimney were invented in the second half of the eighteenth century. There were no matches till 1820; flint and steel had to serve. In their public rooms the rich had of course great 'lustres' or candelabra with wax candles, for tallow candles were malodorous and required constant snuffing.

A good first impression of a German town is given by Howitt in his book published in 1842, when conditions had not altered very much since the eighteenth century:

As you proceed through the streets, you find around you gabled and picturesque white buildings, old squares and markets, with avenues of limes, or of dwarf acacias; people, many of them in the garb of centuries ago; and dreadful pavements. Coleridge has celebrated the six-and-thirty stenches of Cologne, and the invention of Cologne water to cover them; but a wide acquaintance with German towns leaves me the conviction that Cologne can boast no more queer odours than any other of the towns of the nation; for in most of them, as we shall have to show, every street, almost every house, and every hour, has its own appropriate, peculiar, and by no means enviable smell. The pavements,

14-2

with a few exceptions, are of the most hobbly and excruciating kind. There appears no evidence of any special attention to them, or management of them. To pass through a German town or village in a carriage is one of the most rib-trying events in this life. But to walk through one is not much less hazardous. Russell, in his day, tells us, that to avoid being run over on the pavé by a barrow, you often step into the peril of getting your head split with an axe, or your arm torn off by a saw, from the people who are cutting up piles of firewood before the doors. This is pretty much the case yet. The pavés, where there are any, seem appropriated to every purpose but that of walking. There is a bit of pavement here, a bit there, or rather not a bit there. It looks as if the causeway were left entirely to the care, or want of care of the householders. Here is a bit of good pavement; in a few yards is a piece of the worst and most uneven pitching, evidently done ages ago. Here you go up a step, and there you go down one. If an Englishman, accustomed to his well-paved and well-regulated towns, were suddenly set down in a German town at night, he would speedily break his neck or his bones, put out an eye, or tear off a cheek. The towns, and that only on dark and moonless nights, are badly lit by lamps, hung, as in France, from a rope across the street. Here one twinkles, and at a vast and solitary distance glimmers another....All manner of trap-doors leading down into cellars are in the pavés, and none of them very carefully levelled with the flagging or pebbles. Their covers often cock up their corners, faced with iron in such a way that you strike your toes most cruelly against them. All manner of flights of steps, from shops and houses, are set upon the pave-ment, are pushed out one-third of the width across them, and sometimes wholly across them, so that a man whom daylight and a few trips over them had not made aware of them would blunder headlong....Then, every hundred yards, you are stopped by a great wood-heap, and its busy sawers and cleavers, or by a waggon or a carriage which is set on the trottoir to be out of the way![1]

The decoration and furnishings of the houses ranged from the most primitive to what seemed to the conservatives of those days a depraved degree of luxury. The walls of the

[1] W. Howitt, *The Rural and Domestic Life of Germany*, London, 1842.

better rooms in good houses had been panelled with wood in the Middle Ages, but panelling was no longer popular now because, though it made the rooms warm, it harboured vermin. Loose hangings hung on hooks were preferred, of woven stuff or preferably of leather and later of waxed cloth. People liked things that would last a lifetime, as Goethe says when describing the Wachstuchfabrik where these hangings were made in Frankfort,[1] and washable oilcloth hangings were preferred to wall-papers, though these were in common use, and had been obtainable since the seventeenth century, printed with patterns imitated from Chinese models. Poorer people had to be content with whitewashing their bare walls. Rugs and carpets were too expensive to be common even in good houses, but a kind of parquet floor laid with large square blocks was usual in the best rooms.[2] Ordinary folk were content (like Gretchen) with plain deal, well scrubbed and sanded.

Furniture was solid and plain; in the ordinary craftsman's house the furniture would be for the most part made of pine, painted green or nut-brown. There would be little beyond cupboards or chests for linen and clothes, a table, perhaps of oak, chairs and a box-bench, and a wooden bedstead or perhaps a simple form of four-poster. In better houses the old chests were being superseded by chests of drawers, a new invention, and deal by walnut. Canopied beds were carried to every degree of elaboration, and their curtains were still used.[3] Imported woods like mahogany, so fashionable in Georgian England, took a long time to reach the German middle class. The aristocracy had rococo and Chippendale furniture and German imitations of it, but in the ordinary 'Wohnstube' native oak, ash or alder were the rule. In pictures

[1] *Dichtung und Wahrheit*, 1, bk. 4.
[2] See e.g. the illustrations in Chodowiecki's diary of his journey to Danzig (*D. Chodowieckis Künstlerfahrt nach Danzig im Jahre* 1773, edited by W. Franke, Leipzig and Berlin, n.d.).
[3] A full inventory of typical Frankfort houses, both of a craftsman and a merchant, is given in *Die Stadt Goethes*, pp. 338 ff.

and drawings the rooms in middle-class houses appear rather severe, furnished only with the bare essentials.

The typical middle-class house, unlike those of the nobility, indicated in general a desire for comfort, rather than display. Well-to-do citizens made use of their wealth for lavish hospitality, and often for collections of pictures, books and natural curiosities. The poor man would be content with prints from an itinerant print seller. In every town there were well-known private art collections which the well-informed traveller did not fail to visit. The ladies for their part collected fine linen and displayed their polished copper and pewter vessels and their glass in the kitchen and even in the living-room. Later in the century a new luxury, porcelain, tempted the collector. It came in with coffee and tea, those unhealthy luxuries that Möser and others never tired of condemning. Coarse earthenware had been available for a long time for dinner services and so on, but it had not displaced pewter.

In the matter of food and drink, too, the demands of the bourgeoisie were naturally simpler than those of the nobility. They kept to the traditional dishes, little influenced by French fashions. Crabb Robinson gives an Englishman's impressions of German cooking in 1800 at some length in his letters home.[1] He is particularly struck with the excellence of German soups, but deplores the absence of puddings, for which England of course had been famous since 'George in pudding-time came round'. He quotes as a typical good meal the 'ordinary' at his inn in Frankfort, at which for less than half-a-crown he was given soup, boiled meat, a dish of vegetables ('in which the Germans infinitely surpass us') with an entremets, and lastly roast beef and no doubt dessert, the whole washed down with a pint of Rhine wine.

The Germans had long had the reputation of being great trenchermen and heavy drinkers. The worst period, by all accounts, was round about the sixteenth century, but the eighteenth-century Bürger cannot have been more refined

[1] *Crabb Robinson in Germany.*

than the nobility, whose reputation was still, as we have seen, rather low. The regulations limiting expenditure at weddings and so forth indicate that the most was made of such occasions. How far the Augsburg citizen from whose diary the following extract is taken was typical it is no longer possible to say, but he seems to have had many companions of the same mind as himself. In the month of May 1715 he mentions eleven days on which he had extraordinary expenses for beer, wine and meals away from home. On 1st May he writes: 'To-day I was bled together with my wife, because the weather was so extraordinarily fine. After dinner we went to the "Froschlache" for a glass of wine and stayed till four. Then we took a walk round by the gate and supped. It was still light, and my wife complained of indigestion, so we drank another measure of wine at the "Weberhaus". Total for the day 1 g. 30 kr.' On 2nd May a visit to a coffee-house while his wife was entertaining her neighbours at home, was followed by a call at the 'Prince' inn, where he met several friends. After dinner his brother-in-law called for them in a coach and took them to the 'Jägerhaus'. Here there was a very different menu from the sausage or cut from the roast of the ordinary 'beer-house': fish, crayfish, capons, pike's liver, peacock's tongues (!), etc., and to drink there was Alsatian, Würzburg, Rhine, Mosel, Neckar and red Schaffhausen wine, and even Sherry and Madeira. After a modest beginning, he ended by spending nearly fourteen florins. Many fellow guests, he says, with more appetite than money, had to pawn a watch, a snuff-box, a silver-cornered prayer book, or even small articles of furniture which they had purposely brought with them, to the host. 'So Crispin said to his wife: Well Kate, if the pillow tastes so nice, what will the bolster taste like!' The excuse that is pleaded for this extravagance, and for other lesser ones on following days, is that when a man has been bled he must take care of himself. No wonder that on 10th May he had to borrow thirty-six florins from his gossip to pay the house rent. The landlord made a fuss about the late payment 'but people like him may well talk. They live on their interest and do not know how hard an honest man has to work to scrape a living together in these bad times'. However, in the afternoon he took his gossip a walk that led them to the Jägerhaus again. Naturally he had to treat such a good friend well, but this time he got off with an expense of four Gulden. In this way the short and simple annals continue. The climax came on Whit Monday, when after a walk followed by a game of skittles —and beer, in the morning, he went out again in the afternoon in spite of the pricks of his conscience, half persuading himself that a man needed a 'Bürgerlust' to refresh a body tired out with the week's work. He walked out to a neighbouring village, found friends there, played cards and when his wife and family followed him they supped lavishly and ended up with a dance. By this time they were all so merry that the only fit end was to smash the glasses on the wall, and this they did. Of course they had to pay for them, and all in all it cost him over twelve Gulden, half of which he had to borrow from friends.[1]

At the other end of the scale we have men like the bookseller to whom Fr. Perthes was apprenticed in 1787 in Leipzig, who worked from seven in the morning till eight at night, never played cards, never went to an inn, invited no guests and drank only water. On Sundays after church he would read the *Jena Literaturzeitung* and then take a walk round the town. Apart from this his only relaxation was an occasional trip in summer with his family to Entritzsch, where they drank a bottle of 'Gose', and an annual ten-mile drive with his apprentices.[2] His wife, however, drank. There must have been citizens very different from this Herr Böhme in 'Little

[1] Printed in E. Buchner, *Anno Dazumal*, I, 257. Source not stated. If it is an invention it is a contemporary one (perhaps from a 'moral weekly'?) and its details are such as would seem probable to the readers of the time.

[2] C. T. Perthes, *Friedrich Perthes Leben*, Hamburg and Gotha, 1848, p. 12.

Paris', but it was men like him who were building up the book trade. From the literature and letters of the time we see in fact that there were men of every type, then as at all times. They were no doubt more easy-going on the whole in the south and west than in the north, where we already find the ancestors of the severely rational business men of the nineteenth century. Among the craftsmen there was the same variety. We read of the sanctimonious hatmaker in Brunswick to whom young Moritz was apprenticed, who would preach sermons for hours about the wickedness of mankind, and warn his men that unless they worked faithfully in his service they would burn for ever in hell fire. His men could never work hard enough for him—at least once a week they worked all night—and he made a cross over the bread and butter when he went out.[1] Or we read again in *Dichtung und Wahrheit*[2] of the philosophical shoemaker with whom Goethe stayed in Dresden, a man after Goethe's own heart, 'whose endowment was sound common-sense, founded on a cheerful temperament and contentment with uniform traditional work'. What we hear of the simpler Bürger of Treves was probably true of most men of this class: 'They were modest, pious and quiet in their behaviour; both men and women were fond of their homes and took particular delight in their gardens, which they looked after themselves. They lived very simply and economically and dressed plainly. It was only a councillor or citizen of means whom you would see in a suit of fine cloth of self colour, with heavy silver buttons, carrying a stick with a heavy silver knob. Powdered hair was seldom worn by the citizen class. A silver watch or snuff-box was a great rarity, so were silver buckles; copper and steel ones were the usual wear for rich and poor.'[3]

In the matter of dress we have seen that the town authorities

---

[1] *Anton Reiser*, Erster Teil.
[2] II, 8.
[3] Graf Boos von Waldeck, describing Treves in the middle of the eighteenth century, quoted in Buchner, *Anno Dazumal*, I, 365.

attempted in vain to keep clear the distinctions between classes. It became more and more difficult to do so as the hold of tradition over men's minds grew weaker and the old methods of home or local production were modified by the increase of trade and production for export. The development had already begun which has continued ever since and has resulted in a levelling out of all differences in costume, so that what conservatives were then afraid of, that you would not be able to tell a lady from her maid, is now literally true. Until the eighteenth century the rate of change in fashions was very slow, especially for the middle class and peasantry. In the course of the century it became very rapid for the aristocracy, and hardly less so for the better-placed middle class. Only the craftsmen and still more the peasantry were left behind in pursuit of fashion, and it is in this way, as we saw earlier, that what we now know as 'peasant costumes' arose. They represent the fashion of long-past ages. A Frenchman who lived seven years in a small German town in the time of the Revolution said that the women there followed the fashions as well and as quickly as they could, but their best attempts were unsuccessful and slow. They resulted in a heterogeneous mixture of styles of different periods.[1] It was in some such way that the fashions of the nobility spread in time to other social classes. Individual towns still had their own style of dress—one hears of Strassburg, Augsburg, Nürnberg dresses. These differences persisted longest, of course, in the country, in some parts down to the present day. The higher social classes in the towns, however, soon lost their individual character, and were, as the phrase went, 'französisch gekleidet', though the Ratsherren usually had an official costume of black trimmed with lace in the old Spanish fashion, like the merchants painted by Vandyck, the details varying from town to town in accordance with old traditions. Thus certain marks of difference between the classes persisted all through the century, and one could

[1] Quoted in Spiess, *Die deutschen Bauerntrachten*, p. 30.

usually tell at a glance to what 'Stand' a man or woman belonged. There were still traditional differences of costume for special occasions too, for weddings and funerals, for instance. Married women always wore a bonnet out of doors, only unmarried girls going bareheaded.

The best clothes of the Frankfort craftsman, a cooper, mentioned above, and of his wife, were black or brown and of serviceable materials, made like everything else in the house to last for many years. The wife had a black dress of English cloth and a brown cloth skirt, a black camel-hair bodice, a black cotton cape and a crepe bonnet; the husband a black coat and cloak. But he possessed twenty-six linen shirts and his wife eighteen chemises, because the 'grosse Wäsche' came so seldom. So even the craftsmen and their wives were no longer content with homespun. People with more to spend chose more expensive foreign materials, silks and velvets and brocades. As the lower orders could not usually afford these stuffs, they came to be regarded as a badge of rank. A difficulty arose when the much cheaper printed cottons were produced. In many places they were at first prohibited altogether, both because of their levelling effect and because they did harm to the wool trade.

From illustrations such as those of Chodowiecki in his 'diary' and in contemporary plays and novels, as well as from documents such as the inventory quoted above, it seems that almost all people who worked in their houses, and even merchants in their counting-houses, usually wore some kind of dressing-gown while at work. Good clothes were expensive, much more expensive relatively than now because there was no mass production. Fathers of families, even if they were in easy circumstances like Goethe's father, liked to save expense by taking a man servant who understood tailoring. In country ministers' houses linen, spun and woven in the village, might be taken to a town to be printed with a pattern, after which the ladies made their own clothes from it. For men's clothes the cloth was bought in the town and a tailor came for a fortnight a year to do all the tailoring required.[1] Facts such as these explain why even the better middle class did not usually succeed in imitating at all closely the latest French fashions, the product of wealth and idleness. Yet even in the island of Rügen in the 70's, as Arndt tells us in his memoirs, just the same attempts at French ceremony and elegance were made in the house of a comfortable farmer or country parson as in that of a baron or an army major of good family, with results that were often grotesque. 'Slowly and solemnly, with ungraceful twists and curtseys the plump Frau Pastorin and Pächterin and their daughters approached each other, with swelling "Poches" round their hips, their hair, often false, piled three storeys high and thickly powdered, their feet forced in Chinese fashion into the tightest of high-heeled shoes, in which they tripped about most uncertainly.' The men were like a parody of Frederick the Great and his heroes.[2] For the first five or ten minutes everyone always attempted to speak High German instead of their homely dialect, and even to lard it with scraps of scarcely recognisable French.

It was easier for men to imitate English fashions than for ladies to dress in the French style. In practical England, as we saw, a more serviceable type of costume, made of good cloth and leather, had become usual for travelling and for the everyday wear of all but beaux, and this and military fashions (particularly the Prussian pig-tail) were the chief models for the dress of the more active classes. A long cloth coat (the ancestor of the modern tail-coat for evening wear) in a brighter colour than is now usual, short cloth vest and knee-breeches of stout cloth like corduroy, or leather, with high boots, or woollen stockings and shoes, were its chief features. The 'Werther' costume (blue coat, buff vest and breeches and brown high boots) was just a form of this dress, a

[1] A. Schmitthenner, *Das Tagebuch meines Urgrossvaters*, p. 47.
[2] E. M. Arndt, *Erinnerungen aus dem äusseren Leben* (1840); Reclam edition, p. 251.

common one even before Goethe's novel in northern Germany.[1] It would strike contemporaries not as picturesque, it should be noted, but as practical, the dress of a man who paid no heed to the fashions of polite society, and liked to walk out to his favourite village without fear of the weather.

Until the Revolution, wigs proved difficult to displace. They too were subject to the dictates of fashion. Round wigs went out of fashion in the 70's and bag-wigs were worn instead. Among other minor features it may be noted that it had become usual for the nobility alone to wear swords. Until the eighteenth century even craftsmen had frequently carried them when they were out of the apprenticeship stage, but in this more peaceful age the ordinary burgher was content with a walking-stick. In the second half of the century the umbrella, at first an object of ridicule, became more popular. It had been invented late in the seventeenth century. In cold and rainy weather women usually wore a long cloak with a hood that covered them from head to foot, while men put on a long 'highwayman's' cape, or a 'surtout', which had sleeves. The well-to-do made use of sedan chairs or, very rarely, of carriages, like the aristocracy.

It was the same with new ideas and habits of mind as with fashions in dress. Every class had traditions of its own, and the lower a class stood in the social scale, the more impervious it was to outside influences, because its contacts with other classes were fewer and its system of education and training more bound by convention. But the great body of townsmen had probably a good deal more in common with each other in outlook than at any subsequent period, and in discussing the psychology of the Bürger class these common features will be mentioned first.

As he was so seldom called upon to adapt himself to new situations, the average citizen was in the first place intensely

---

[1] Cf. *Dichtung und Wahrheit*, 3ter Teil, 12tes Buch. Jerusalem, from Brunswick, one of the 'models' for Werther, used to dress in this way.

conservative. There was something almost sacred for him in the established order of things, both in the practice of his particular craft or calling, and even in quite trivial matters of everyday life, so that his life was governed by petty rules and conventions to an extent which is now scarcely credible. A pedantic orderliness is an outstanding characteristic of almost all the good Bürger of that age. Goethe's father is in this respect entirely typical. His grandfather too, Goethe tells us, was as regular and punctilious in his gardening as in his official business. Every day for him was like its predecessor, so that Goethe associated with his way of life the idea of 'inviolable peace and endless duration'. Moritz tells us of lower middle-class families in which the same unchanging order was observed for scores of years, and many more instances could be quoted. No wonder that to Madame de Staël it seemed that 'Le plus vif désir des habitants de cette contrée paisible et féconde, c'est de continuer à exister comme ils existent'. In forms of address, compliments, congratulations, few variations were allowed on accepted models. There were days set apart at regular intervals for formal calls, even for family purgings and blood-lettings. Family celebrations, weddings, christenings, funerals, birthdays, and the recurring festivals of the year, Christmas, Mayday, Midsummerday, Martinmas, all had their established ritual, much of the poetic charm of which has survived to our own day. The many places that were half town, half village, would have their harvest or vintage festivals, 'Schützenfeste' were still common, and everywhere the gilds kept up much of their old ceremonial and pageantry. The old customs are frequently described in the writings of the time, they were illustrated by Ludwig Richter and others in the Romantic period, and they have now been systematically studied by the experts in Volkskunde.

Another characteristic commonly to be found in all classes of the towns and closely connected with this traditionalism was the love of slow painstaking work, the attitude of the old-fashioned craftsman. It was to be seen not only in those who worked with their hands, but in the learned men whose systematic collections of material in dictionaries and encyclo-paedic works were already looked upon as a specifically German product. Goethe even finds in the Sisyphean labours of the jurists at Wetzlar 'that laudable industry of the Germans, which aims rather at the collection and arrange-ment of details than at results'.

Besides these historic traits of the middle class there were others, almost equally universal, which are less easily related to each other. There were survivals of the forthrightness and even coarseness of the peasant in many customs and many forms of speech. The old people ate and drank and said their say, and the young people made love, in a way which to sophisticated foreigners seemed at least naïve, and justified Goethe's line: 'Im Deutschen lügt man, wenn man höflich ist'. But there was also a strong sentimental strain in evidence, not peculiar of course to Germany at this time, but particularly pronounced there. This was perhaps most marked in the classes influenced by literature, though pietism had made it very widespread among the uneducated too. Occasions for emotional display were not avoided, as usually by the courtier, but sought after, tears were shed not only for sorrow, but for joy or gratitude, and the expression of friendship and admiration took extravagant forms. Yet, as often happens, these men of feeling were by no means unmoved by self-interest when it was a matter of arranging a marriage or gaining the favour of the influential. Marriages, as we see from almost any autobiography, were usually, in real life, affairs of good sense rather than of romantic love, certainly in the middle of the century and probably still at the end, and the court habits of dissimulation and flattery had spread to many sections of the middle class in their dealings with superiors.

The increasing refinement of the age had therefore its dark sides. The average citizen grew accustomed to taking his family to the 'coffee-gardens' that were now popular (the first cafés had been started in towns like Hamburg, Leipzig, Vienna very early in the century), instead of carousing with his fellows like the Augsburg citizen quoted above, but the feeling was widespread, especially after the Storm and Stress movement of the 70's, that the age was lacking in vigour and character. It is true that similar complaints had been made generations earlier by Moscherosch, Leibniz and Thomasius, who, like Lessing, had blamed French influence, with its emphasis on 'das Zärtliche und das Verliebte'. But Justus Möser and Goethe both ascribed this lethargy and ennui rather to the disproportion which they felt to exist between capacity and opportunity, in a Germany economically backward and politically in leading-strings. 'In such an atmosphere,' says Goethe, explaining the popularity of his *Werther*, 'tortured by unsatisfied passions, with no outward inducement to significant activities, with the sole prospect of persisting in a dull, spiritless, commonplace life, we became attached to the idea that we could at all events quit life at pleasure when we could no longer bear it.' The efforts of the great writers in the classical age were directed towards finding a new ideal for the middle class of their time, who were so lacking, as it seemed to them, in harmonious development of mind and body, in grace of bearing and personal dignity, and it is a strange comment on the period to discover that at one time Goethe, and not only Goethe, could imagine that the calling of an actor, in a world of make-believe, could afford an idealist like his *Wilhelm Meister* the opportunities of the good life which were denied to him as a merchant.[1]

In the middle-class home, to judge by the tone of letters and the frequency of the 'Haustyrann' in literature, the father was inclined to exact from his family the same deference that

[1] See 'Goethe's *Wilhelm Meister* as a picture and a criticism of society', by the present writer, in *Publications of the English Goethe Society*, IX, 1933.

he had to pay outside to his superiors. The discipline of the home seems to have been strict in all classes in the towns. 'Early to bed and early to rise', 'There is a place for everything', 'Speak when you're spoken to' and similar maxims were followed to the letter. Family prayers in the morning, in which servants or apprentices often joined, were usual even in families not ostentatiously pious. Personal relations between intimates were more formal, less spontaneous, than seems natural to us. It is hardly conceivable that the feelings of parents and children, brothers and sisters were really very different at bottom from what they are now, but they were certainly expressed in different forms, at least in the upper middle class. 'Sie' was used from child to parent, often between the parents themselves, and servants and apprentices might be addressed as 'Er'.

It hardly needs to be said that in such a society the place of woman was the kitchen and the nursery. The variety of tasks that fell to the lady of the house has been touched on above. All through the following century English visitors continue to express their astonishment at the contentment of the German Hausfrau with what seems to them such a restricted life. Howitt in 1842 speaks of their absorption in cooking and domestic management, their ceaseless sewing and knitting, their hoarding of linen and stockings. To a woman writer in *Fraser's Magazine* in 1875 the German married woman 'is simply an upper servant'. 'Of domesticities', she writes, 'there is enough and to spare, but of domestic life as we understand it, little or nothing. Beyond eating, drinking and sleeping under the same roof the sexes have little in common. The woman is a slave of the ring.' She speaks too of the devoted manner in which the young ladies of the house wait upon male visitors, and fetch and carry for their brothers. And Mrs Sidgwick in 1908 still has the impression that Germans think 'that woman was made for man, and that if she has board, lodging and raiment, according to the means of her menfolk, she has all she can possibly ask of life'. German women, she says, 'do not actually fall on their knees before their lords, but the tone of voice in which a woman of the old school speaks of *Die Herren* is enough to make a French, American or English-woman think there is something to be said for the modern revolt against men'. We may be sure that the lot of German women was no easier in the eighteenth century, though it probably never occurred to them, any more than to most of their sex later, to revolt against it, for individualism was a doctrine for men, but not for women. 'The husband who was willing to share a respected position and a sure income with the lady of his choice', says Freytag, 'was offering her in the view of that time a great deal; her gratitude had to take the form of ministering to the comfort of his hard, laborious days by unremitting faithful service.' The training of girls was naturally adapted to this end. In the classical words of Goethe in *Hermann und Dorothea*, it was for woman to learn in her early years to *serve* as nature meant her to do, to serve her brother and parents so that her life was a constant coming and going, a lifting and carrying, preparing and working for others. In such a school she would learn the unselfishness of which she would have so much need in married life, but she would also qualify herself for her future place of authority as mistress of a household. For a Martha of this type a literary education was of little use. It was enough if she could read and write and knew her catechism, and very few women, even wives of professional men, could write a good German letter or even spell correctly. But with the growth of circulating libraries the new novels found many readers among young ladies, too many for Goethe's taste, who, according to the second *Epistel*, would have had them all kept so busy in house and garden that they would want to read nothing but a cookery book. It is not surprising to learn that even in Howitt's day, household and social accomplishments were the sum of their instruction. There were exceptions, of course, but they were rare. The average middle-class girl was lucky if she received primary education. There were indeed few who shared the higher tuition received by their brothers, and girls' secondary schools were things of the future.

The bourgeoisie as a class prided itself on its virtue, its modesty, honesty and industry, as opposed to the loose living, the arrogance and the lack of principles of the aristocracy. These ideas must have been supported by age-old social tradition, by the discipline imposed for centuries by Church and gild, reinforced by the increased moral earnestness of Protestantism. The influence of the Pietist movement was very strong among all classes, and in many towns a little colony of Huguenots set a high standard of probity and moral zeal. The traditional virtues of the gildsman were, as we have seen, contentment and neighbourliness; their motto was 'Live, and let live'. These virtues would probably be most prominent now among the lower middle class. The more successful of the business community were more self-conscious in their industry. They did not merely work for their daily bread. Industry was for them a virtue in itself, like frugality and purity. Religion had become for the Aufklärung, in Goethe's words, 'trockene Moral'. It was concerned with the affairs of this world only and had allied itself half unconsciously with business ethics. The God-fearing man must know how to bear adversity, but he might legitimately hope for success in his enterprises because of his virtue. Not only might he aim at wealth, and not merely a sufficiency (as Luther and even seventeenth-century orthodoxy had enjoined); it was his duty, even when in possession of wealth, to work to maintain it. Sombart has made good use of Benjamin Franklin's famous autobiography as a document revealing the mind of the business man at this stage in economic development. Franklin's notions of an 'art of virtue', his belief that 'nothing was so likely to make a man's fortune as virtue', this marriage of virtue and worldly prosperity, was no doubt thoroughly characteristic of his time. It had come to believe, with the help of the English Deists, that virtue did not need a supernatural sanction but was justified of its fruits, even in a single lifetime. It even found a substitute for the confessional in self-examination, such as that which Franklin's autobiography made famous in his story of the little notebook with its thirteen columns of virtues, 'temperance, silence, order, resolution, frugality, industry, sincerity, justice, moderation, cleanliness, tranquility, chastity, humility'. There must have been many thousands of aspiring young men in Germany who made similar resolutions to attain moral perfection, and worldly success as its reward. F. Perthes was one.[1] And there were German writers, such as Thomasius and his pupil C. A. Heumann, who propounded very similar rules to Franklin's long before his time.

But in justice to Franklin it should be added that he possessed qualities of mind and feeling that are recorded not in this famous passage but between the lines of his autobiography and in his great public achievements. The natural wisdom of his mind enabled him to make good use of even the dry scraps of traditional morality, and the generosity of his temperament and his abounding public spirit made him a 'citizen' in a sense in which perhaps no German of that age deserved the name. Compared with him even the highest embodiments of German ideals, such as Lessing's *Nathan the Wise*, have something provincial and theoretical about them, while the citizen of reality displayed a submissiveness to authority very different from Franklin's 'humility', a late addition to his list, and a virtue which he was content with observing merely in appearance, by the avoidance of dogmatic statements of opinion. The average German business man was more like Werner in Goethe's *Wilhelm Meister*, who is eloquent in praise of order, frugality and industry but whose horizon does not extend beyond his own family. Of duties to town or state he has no conception. Freytag describes the

[1] *F. P.'s Leben*, pp. 28 ff.

middle-class Germans of the second half of the century admirably when he says:

They had become men of honour and strict principle, they tried with a touching conscientiousness to hold things ignoble at a distance; but they were still too much lacking in the manly energy that grows by co-operation with many of like mind in handling great practical questions. The noblest of them ran the danger of becoming victims rather than heroes in political and social struggles. This trait is very noticeable even in literary creations. Almost all the characters freely invented by the greatest poets in their best works suffer from a lack of energy, of virile courage and political acumen; there is an elegiac trait even in the heroes of the drama, where it is least pardonable, from Galotti, Götz and Egmont to Wallenstein and Faust.

In the beau monde, as we have seen, a cynical disregard for the moral values was far from being uncommon. It might sometimes be necessary to present the appearance of virtue, but this was a means to an end. It was usually taken as axiomatic that all men are moved by self-interest. Beyond this, regard was paid to aesthetic rather than moral considerations. The last thing to be desired was self-conscious virtue. Of course there were many exceptions, and what has been said refers chiefly to the nobility of the larger courts, but it is certainly true to say that the average respectable citizen looked upon personal integrity and the domestic virtues as the nobleman looked upon honour and 'reputation'. In the domestic tragedies and the family novels of the last third of the century the contrast between the cynical aristocrat and the virtuous middle-class father of a family is a constant theme. Even if these works do not represent the whole truth, they evidently express what the middle-class public liked to believe.

In one of the most famous of these early 'problem plays', Grossmann's *Nicht mehr als sechs Schüsseln*, it is a high legal official who is the protagonist of the bourgeois party. The rising class of officials, although in many respects assimilated by the aristocracy, retained its middle-class outlook in matters of morality and gradually came to influence the standards of the aristocracy itself. In Durlach for instance, Roller tells us, it was only the new class of officials who took sexual aberrations seriously and insisted on the highest standards of conduct, especially for its daughters. Even in the first half of the century, there is little evidence of any moral lapses on their part in Durlach, still less in the second. The various mistresses of princes, who are mentioned there, all belonged either to the nobility or to the artisan class. But girls of the artisan class who had disgraced themselves easily found husbands of their own class. It was only in the nineteenth century, according to this informant, that the artisan class came to be as strict in this respect as the higher middle class. It seems clear from the gild regulations that even in the Middle Ages the gilds in their corporate capacity displayed an almost exaggerated moral sensitiveness (in their exclusion from the gilds of illegitimate children and so on). But when their best days were over the economic was perhaps stronger than the moral motive for the retention of these regulations, and the artisan class as a whole had fallen behind the educated middle class in ethical feeling as in general culture.

The several classes of Bürger naturally differed from each other as much in education as in outlook. After his home training, the son of a craftsman did not usually receive anything that can be called education until he was apprenticed to a trade. Very often he would be working from an early age, helping his parents perhaps in some 'domestic industry', winding yarn, carding wool, even spinning and weaving, knitting, lace-making and so on, or doing similar work in one of the new factories, if there happened to be one near. This was usually regarded as an excellent training in habits of industry. It was particularly good for orphans, so orphanage, prison, poor-house, if there was one, and mad-house were usually grouped together, perhaps in the same building, and as many of the inmates as possible were employed in spinning and weaving, stocking-making and the like. J. Kerner tells us[1] of a partly philanthropic cloth factory of this kind at Ludwigsburg, started by the duke of Württemberg, about the same time as his model academy 'Solitude', no doubt with equally good intentions. There are many parallels elsewhere in Germany and Switzerland (Nürnberg, Ratisbon, Frankfort, Pforzheim, Basle) as well as in England, Holland and France.[2] The example of Germany (Nürnberg), where every child, though but seven or eight years old, was put to work and enabled to earn its own livelihood, was held up in England as early as 1638.[3] At twelve or fourteen a boy was if possible apprenticed to a trade, and apprenticeship was still a form of social training, the apprentice living with his master. The master was expected not only to give technical training but to bring a boy up in the fear of God, and to look after his manners.[4] Anton Reiser was constantly being corrected by Herr Lobenstein the hat-maker, who not only edified him with long religious discourses but watched his table manners. The journeymen's unions too concerned themselves with the general behaviour of their members.

It is true that since the Protestant states had taken over the control of education from the Church, as they began to do in the sixteenth century, attendance had gradually been made compulsory in theory for all children in almost all states. Every parish had to provide a school, and the ministers of the church were made responsible by the Konsistorium for its inspection. Some small states (Weimar and Gotha for instance), in their desire for the purity of doctrine, were even more active in this matter than Prussia.[5] But the decrees

---

[1] *Das Bilderbuch aus meiner Knabenzeit.*
[2] See Kulischer, II, 149 ff., 188 ff.
[3] Lipson, II, 61.
[4] This was often expressly mentioned in the articles of apprenticeship, e.g. in 1787 for F. Perthes (*Leben*, pp. 8 ff.).
[5] See F. Paulsen, *Das deutsche Bildungswesen in seiner geschichtlichen Entwicklung*, I, 85 ff.

could not be enforced. Many children were put to work both in the towns, as we have seen, and of course in the country, helping in the fields and even in mining. The ministers who acted as inspectors could not improve matters, even if they took their duties seriously, while attendance was still so irregular, and while teachers received nothing but their small fees. Teachers were often men who were unfit for other work, or they combined teaching (as Jung Stilling did in his early days) with tailoring or some such sedentary occupation. In the towns one hears more of licensed private schools than of public schools, and they were as bad or worse. There were at some periods thirty or more of them in existence in Frankfort, some with 200 to 300 pupils. The teaching in all of them consisted of the catechism, reading and writing, and perhaps a little arithmetic and geography. There were no good school books and above all no training colleges for teachers. In town after town visited by Nicolai he speaks of the 'German' schools as bad.

The period of Aufklärung was deeply interested in education, but such of its energies as were not absorbed in theoretical discussion only influenced the better placed middle class. Goethe's father was typical, indefatigable as he was in his care for the education of his own children by himself and by private tutors according to a well-considered plan. Children of the better families were, as Goethe tells us, all privately educated. It was the golden age of the private tutor. There could be no uniformity when parents were the sole directors of their children's education, and tutors varied so enormously, but it is clear that class distinctions were intensified by this system. The end in view was usually a compromise between the educational ideals of the nobility outlined above, with their stress on preparation for the fashionable world, and the more solid but often pedantic teaching of the Latin schools. Modern as well as ancient languages were taught and dancing, fencing and so on were not neglected.

The town grammar schools ('Latin schools'), the product of the Reformation age and humanism, occupied themselves with the propagation of classical learning and sound religion, the chief stress being laid on accurate and if possible elegant latinity. Form was placed above content, at least until the reform of classical teaching in the universities, with which the name of Gesner is chiefly associated, spread to the schools. They were 'Gelehrtenschulen', intended for boys proceeding to the universities to be trained in the liberal professions, but they were used also by the sons of merchants, and even of some craftsmen, who intended to enter their fathers' business and left school half way through the course. There were usually scholarships for clever poor boys, and these 'Pauperes' were often distinguished by some external mark from the fee-paying 'Divites'—in Ulm for instance they wore black, while the rest wore blue. The majority of the pupils would be sons of officials, shopkeepers and successful craftsmen. For quite half of them some kind of Realschule would have been more suitable, but although a Realschule had been started in Berlin in 1747 and had been imitated in some other towns, this form of modern school did not become common until the business men of the towns became more vocal. Basedow, though a poor organiser and rather a crank, did much to awaken interest in a more realistic education through his short-lived *Philanthropinum* at Dessau (1774) and its textbook, the *Elementarwerk*. He laid more stress on modern languages, taught by a direct method, general knowledge and physical exercises than on gerund-grinding.

Education, it will be seen, would not be likely to modify seriously the general view of life current in the class from which the pupil came. It was intended of course to conserve it. The very great differences that existed between the various forms of education available for boys reflect differences just as great between the habits of mind of the various classes of citizens, even though at first glance they might seem to have so much in common. A large proportion of the population even in the towns was illiterate, and of the rest only a comparatively small number would be interested in the same works as a 'denkender Kopf von klassischem Geschmack'. It was only as literature became more realistic and less learned, in the second half of the century and particularly from the 70's, that a wide circle of readers could be counted on, and even then it still made its chief appeal to the academically trained professional men.

Chapter V

THE PROFESSIONAL CLASS

'Professional men' are a product of modern times. In the Middle Ages of course the Church had for centuries a monopoly of education and book-learning. Priests and monks exercised the chief functions that were later to fall to the professional man. They were the lawyers, public officials, doctors, professors and schoolmasters, and it was only within the Church that trained intelligence, unsupported by advantages of birth or worldly possessions, could find scope. We have seen in earlier chapters how, with the revival of Roman law in the Italian universities and the decline of the temporal power of the Church, laymen came to replace clerics in the councils of princes. The Renaissance and Reformation, and the strengthening of state authority that accompanied them, increased the demand for trained laymen beyond all precedent. The old universities ceased to be semi-monastic institutions almost wholly controlled by the Church. Secular learning became more and more important even in Catholic universities, and the intellectual element in the education both of clergy and laymen came to predominate more than ever in the many new Protestant foundations.

It was only with the development of humanistic studies that intellectual training became a source of social distinction. In Germany in the fifteenth century doctors of theology and of canon law were recognised as the equals of the lesser nobility in cathedral chapters, to which only men of good birth had hitherto been admitted. In England the doctorate of a university conferred a higher social status on laymen too. In France a regular 'noblesse de robe' grew up on this professional and cultural basis. In Germany, as elsewhere, the status of the educated layman rose as individuals distinguished themselves as scholars, doctors and servants of the state. With the continuous spread of absolutism, the university-trained Jurists became the leaders in this social rise of the educated middle-class, for although as we have seen the highest state offices were usually reserved for men of rank, the services of trained lawyers were indispensable in subordinate offices and particularly in the local Ämter, where the important function of jurisdiction was generally exercised by the Amtmann, so that his authority approached that of a local magnate. At a much slower rate medical graduates began to rise in social esteem. The Protestant clergy did not usually enjoy anything resembling the social consideration due to the officials of a prince, not at any rate until, in the second half of the eighteenth century, they came to be something very like state servants themselves. They were as a rule poorer in the goods of this world, but learning, intelligence and piety, as well as their important administrative functions in country districts, secured for many of them a high degree of respect.

As to the graduates of the Arts or Philosophical Faculty, one can hardly speak of them as an independent group in the eighteenth century at all. Students were matriculated as soon as they entered the university in one of the senior faculties of law, theology or medicine, and looked upon their course in arts merely as a preparation for their serious studies, a completion of their schooling. Men who had studied only arts and perhaps taken a master's degree might be compelled by circumstances to accept a post as teacher or tutor, but such a post was seldom considered to be more than a means of keeping body and soul together while the 'candidate' was waiting for a living in the Church. Of course a very large number of 'Kandidaten' never got beyond this stage, and there were some teaching posts, in the universities and the better schools, that satisfied normal ambitions at least as well as a Church living, but arts graduates as such had no obvious social function until the great expansion of secondary education took place in the nineteenth century. As 'scholars', however, possessing a knowledge of Latin, they felt themselves and were generally acknowledged to be socially superior to the ordinary shopkeeper or craftsman, though the court class might despise them as pedants. It is characteristic that in places where, as in Frankfort-on-Main, university graduates were organised and met to protect their common interests, the so-called 'Graduiertenkollegium' (founded in Frankfort in 1613 and still functioning in the eighteenth century) only included graduates of the legal and medical faculties. The Protestant ministers had an organisation of their own, but there was no society of graduates in arts.[1]

To understand the social position of the professional class we must take a glance at the state of higher education in eighteenth-century Germany.[2] Schools and universities had gone through many changes since the Middle Ages, but none of them had been so catastrophic as to eradicate entirely older traditions. After the attempted fusion of Renaissance and Reformation ideas of education by Melanchthon, the creator of Protestant higher education in Germany, the chief turning points had been the foundation of the university of Halle in 1694 and that of Göttingen in 1737. The general tendency had been to secularise education more and more, and to provide more and more fully for the needs of the social classes that successively took the lead in the world of affairs.

It was at the Renaissance that the interest in the things of this world, never suppressed of course even when the Church was most powerful, began to displace the scheme of values of scholasticism. Emancipation from the bonds of traditions that seemed outworn came to be men's ideal, an ideal encouraged by a more direct acquaintance with Greek civilisation, its spirit of free enquiry and its love of beauty. Study

[1] *Die Stadt Goethes*, p. 103.
[2] The standard work is F. Paulsen's excellent *Geschichte des gelehrten Unterrichts*, 2 vols. (1st ed. 1885, 2nd enlarged ed. 1896–7). A much briefer outline is the same author's *Das deutsche Bildungswesen in seiner geschichtlichen Entwicklung*, 4th ed. 1912.

of antiquity opened men's eyes again to the concrete world about them, to the practical problems of everyday life and the opportunities it offered to the individual of satisfying his natural desire for power and knowledge and happiness. These ideas, at first confined to an élite, had quietly permeated the German universities by about the year 1520 and brought about many changes in the curriculum. But in the next ten years their progress was abruptly arrested by the essentially popular and anti-intellectual movement initiated by Luther. Even the consciousness of having a common enemy, the old Church, could not keep such different natures as Erasmus and Luther in the same camp for long. Free enquiry and the love of beauty were incompatible with the insistence on faith and grace and a new orthodoxy. The first effects of the Reformation on education were entirely negative. In 1530 university studies in Germany were at their lowest ebb. But Luther was by no means blind to the necessity of secular learning and to the responsibilities of those who had swept away the educational system of the old Church. In vigorous pamphlets he reminded the new authorities in things spiritual, the princes and magistrates, of the crying necessity for good schools and universities, both for the needs of the Protestant Church and of civil society, and his humanist ally Melanchthon, 'preceptor Germaniae', organised a new educational system for him, wrote new textbooks, and as the trusted adviser of the Protestant princes devised regulations and provided teachers for innumerable new institutions.

It was essential to remind ourselves of the beginnings of Protestant higher education, because the Latin schools of Germany remained until nearly the end of the eighteenth century very much what Melanchthon had made them. Their curriculum still showed in the main the desire for a compromise that would satisfy both humanists and reformers, for its two poles were Latin and the Catechism. The aim was still that of J. Sturm, 'sapiens atque eloquens pietas'. That religion should be one of the chief subjects of instruction was a consequence of the new insistence on purity of doctrine. The need for Latin was equally obvious to that age, for Latin only slowly lost its position as the *lingua franca* of the learned. Until nearly the beginning of the eighteenth century there were more Latin books published in Germany every year than German ones, and Latin was still commonly used for university lectures even in the second half of the century. Every educated man had to understand Latin to acquaint himself with contemporary thought, and it was chiefly as a living language that Latin was taught, with the emphasis on 'Eloquence', the power to use Latin in speech and writing, not on the study of classical literature for its aesthetic and intellectual value.

Schools then as now became what their teachers made them, and this depended largely on the teacher's own training at the university. Reforms begun in the universities gradually made their influence felt in the schools. In the period under review, between Luther and Goethe, several such waves of reform can be traced by the historian of education, all of which left their traces on the practice of the eighteenth century. In the universities reformed by Melanchthon the Philosophical or Arts Faculty prepared the young student (not usually much older than fifteen when he came to the university) for study in the senior faculties of theology and law, in much the same way as the higher classes of a gymnasium now prepare boys for the university. The students followed a prescribed course of instruction in such subjects as Latin and Greek grammar, dialectics and rhetoric, the elements of mathematics, and prescribed Latin and Greek texts. Aristotelian philosophy was still an important feature in the later part of the course. After two or three semesters an intermediate examination (for the bachelor's degree) had to be passed, before the student could proceed to the two-year course for the master's degree. Written and oral practice in Latin (and to a much smaller extent in Greek) was given by means of 'imitations' of classical models, declamations and public disputations. It was not by any means every student who took the whole course and the master's degree before proceeding to the study of law or theology. 'Magister' still meant one qualified to teach arts subjects in a university and few would seek this qualification. Specialised training in the appropriate higher faculty gradually came to be so indispensable for future Beamte and Pfarrer that a minimum of attendance on arts lectures was the rule. We hear in fact of many Protestant ministers who had only attended a university for a year or two in all.

Universities of this Reformation type were the new foundations Marburg (Hessen, 1527), Königsberg (Preussen, 1544) Jena (for Weimar, Jena, Eisenach, 1558), Helmstedt (Braunschweig-Wolfenbüttel, 1576), and the reformed older foundations Wittenberg (Sachsen), Tübingen (Württemberg), Leipzig (Sachsen), Frankfort-on-the-Oder (Brandenburg), Greifswald (Pommern), Rostock (Mecklenburg), Heidelberg (Pfalz). Every Protestant state of any importance had at least one university of its own, and universities now drew their students for the most part from the state in which they were situated and by which they were endowed.

The universities were fed by the town grammar schools and by the many new state schools (Fürstenschulen or Klosterschulen). The Fürstenschulen of Saxony (Pforta, Meissen and Grimma), founded by Moritz von Sachsen in 1543, sent a succession of able boys to the state universities Leipzig and Wittenberg. The Klosterschulen of Württemberg (founded 1559), feeding the Tübinger Stift with theologians, were no less famous. Brandenburg had its school at Joachimsthal (1607), Pommern at Stettin (1543) and even smaller states like Ansbach and Koburg followed suit. The aim of the founders of these schools was to provide future servants for the state in its Church and civil service. In many cases the whole training could be had free of cost in return for a promise to enter the state service. The state schools continued to lead until the nineteenth century. Those of Saxony turned out in the eighteenth century Lessing and Klopstock, those of Württemberg produced Hölderlin and Hegel, and they would have been able to claim Schiller if he had not been compelled by the prince to attend the newest state school of Württemberg, the 'Karlsschule', where everything but theology was taught. In the state schools, as in the grammar schools, founded and controlled by the town council, which existed in every town of any note, Latin was the main subject of instruction all through the period. Until late in the eighteenth century the entire stress was as we have seen on the practical command of the language. It was used as early as possible as the medium of instruction. Greek if taught at all was given far less attention. The only other important subject was religious instruction. The elements of rhetoric and dialectics, arithmetic and geometry, physics and cosmogony were thrown in, all taught in the medieval way. It will be seen that there was a very great deal in the school curriculum that had remained unchanged since the Middle Ages.

One can distinguish at least two subsequent waves of reform, each affecting the universities first and ebbing away in the Latin schools, that had left their mark on education by Goethe's day. The first was the modernism propagated by court circles, the demand for a realistic knowledge of the world of the day, for modern languages, geography and history, and above all for mathematics and the new sciences founded on it, all at the expense of Latin and religion in the timetable. We have seen above what was considered necessary for a gentleman in the age following the Thirty Years' War, and how these needs were met by the new Ritterakademien. These ideas first reached university circles through the foundation of the Prussian university of Halle in 1694.

It is significant that the new university was founded in a town in which the court of an archbishopric (Magdeburg) had resided, until the small state had fallen by inheritance to Brandenburg. In the buildings formerly used by the court

there was housed first a Ritterakademie and then the university
that grew out of it, and Thomasius, one of the two outstanding men among the professoriate, congratulated the
students on having before them as models of good breeding
the councillors of the old court. The French aristocratic
culture of the day was what he wished his German students
to emulate, that they might be men of the world and not dry
pedants. He discarded academic dress and gave university
lectures, for the first time in Germany, in the German
language. His aim was to break down the barriers that
existed between the learned and the ordinary society of their
day, to make useful knowledge available to the widest
possible circle. He appealed for complete freedom of
research, freedom from the gild tradition in scholarship
'which permitted no one to exercise the scholar's craft
without paying dearly for a master's rights, unless he were
a master's son or had married into a master's family', and
freedom from persecution for unpopular opinions. He was
supported in his opposition to medievalism by the theologian
A. H. Francke, who was with Spener the leader of the Pietist
movement. Francke too was of a practical turn of mind.
He was not interested in niceties of dogma so much as in the
raising of moral standards and the improvement of social
institutions. With his missionary zeal and his talent for
organisation he succeeded in making some of the dreams of
Comenius a reality in the great complex of institutions that
he built up in Halle, the Orphanage with its two schools,
a Latin and a German one, the Paedagogium, a secondary
school for paying pupils, and several appendages, such as a
printing-press and a bookshop. In the long run, however,
the rationalist and the sanctimonious elements in Halle were
bound to separate out. They did so soon after Thomasius had
been joined by Christian Wolff, the father of the Aufklärung
in Germany, whose textbooks, based on the work of the
seventeenth century, particularly that of Leibniz, soon entirely
displaced those in the tradition of Melanchthon, and sub-

stituted their 'Vernünftige Gedanken' in every sphere for the appeal to authority. The persecution of Wolff and his disciples only served to advertise his views, with the result that in 1740, when Wolff returned in triumph to Halle, they prevailed in almost all the German universities and had given rise to a critical school of theology (under J. S. Baumgarten, followed by J. S. Semler) in Halle itself.

Halle stimulated the Prussian spirit of efficient practical organisation. 'All the important Prussian civil servants of the eighteenth century were trained at Halle, and that characteristic tendency towards the rational, useful and practical, which everywhere is revealed in Prussian legislation and administration, is only the application of doctrines imbibed at Halle.'[1] But this is only one current in the thought of the time, though the strongest. It is obvious that the influence of Halle was not likely to be good on humane letters. Thomasius and his successors were of course enthusiastic moderns. They did much to encourage the use of the German language. But they were little interested in either the ancients or the moderns as literature. They were practical men with no literary taste. Humanistic studies were badly neglected at Halle, the whole arts faculty being a mere appendage to the faculties of law and theology. If Halle's example was contagious, as we are told it was, it is difficult to see how the humanistic spirit could become so strong as it clearly was in the second half of the century. The explanation is to be sought in the conservatism of the schools and in the revival of humane letters initiated by the second new foundation, the university of Göttingen.

The schools continued to teach Latin and sound religion, little affected by any changes in the universities. The only change noticeable was that modern subjects began to creep into the curriculum, chiefly as extras, to attract, if possible, pupils from the higher classes of society. Progressive schools

---

[1] An anonymous historian quoted by Hettner, *Geschichte der deutschen Literatur im achtzehnten Jahrhundert*, I, i, chap. 2.

began in the first half of the eighteenth century to engage a mathematics master and sometimes a teacher of French. Latin continued to be the central subject, but time had to be found gradually for a little mathematics, history and geography, French and even German. Greek usually lost ground to French. But change was very slow. In the gymnasium at Frankfort-on-Main, for instance, room was not found for French until 1784.[1]

In the meantime the teaching of the classics was slowly being adapted in the universities to the needs of the age. The progress of modern science and philosophy had undermined their position. Men had come to look less and less to the ancient world, to what Thomasius for instance called 'Das Geschmiere des heidnischen Aristoteles', for information and guidance, and to use French or their mother tongue more and more in place of Latin. It seemed possible that the study of the classics would gradually die out altogether. That this did not happen was due partly to the schools and partly to the influence of a few university teachers, formerly school-masters themselves, who discovered reasons convincing even to the enlightened for studying the classics, but for studying them in a different way. The aim of the old school was, as we have seen, to teach their pupils to use Latin as they sup-posed a Roman used it, to produce the best possible imitations of surviving Latin models. The aim of the new humanism of J. M. Gesner of Göttingen and his pupils was to train the taste, judgment and intellect of their pupils by a study of classical masterpieces. They aimed at some such cultivation of the mind as is so persuasively advocated by Newman in his *Idea of a University*. The controversy between the defenders of Oxford and the utilitarian Edinburgh Reviewers, who, as Newman points out, were reviving old ideas of Locke,[2] reminds one strongly of the contrast between

---

[1] For a brief history of the Frankfort curriculum see *Die Stadt Goethes*, pp. 154 ff.
[2] *Idea of a University*, Discourse VII.

Göttingen and Halle. Newman was like Gesner in believing that 'a cultivated intellect, because it is a good in itself, brings with it a power and a grace to every work and occupation which it undertakes, and enables us to be more useful, and to a greater number'.

This change of aim necessitated a change of methods, the shifting of the stress from speaking and writing to reading and appreciating. Through his philological 'Seminar' (the first Seminar in a German university) and his immense influence with school authorities Gesner's views were disseminated far and wide. At the same time his former colleague at the Thomasschule in Leipzig, Ernesti, was working in the same direction there, first in the school and then in the university. Gesner was followed up in Göttingen by the great scholar Heyne (in Göttingen 1763–1812), the founder of classical archaeology. These teachers gave humane letters a new prestige. The literary study of the classics came to be looked upon as necessary for any cultivated man. At the same time advanced study and research in history and law, as well as in the mathematical sciences and medicine, were actively encouraged in Göttingen by the endowment of the only really satisfactory university library in Germany, together with scientific and medical laboratories and museums. Göttingen completed the process begun at Halle of bringing the universities into touch again with life and attracting the best minds of the day to their service. The success of these efforts is best measured by a comparison with France or England. In the second half of the eighteenth century the universities of Germany had taken the lead, not only in scholarship, philosophy and science but to some extent in public affairs, a lead they maintained in the nineteenth century, while the English and French universities only gradually approximated themselves to the German model.

It should not be supposed, however, that the German universities had retained the independence of free corporations. Their progress had been made possible by state support and involved a large measure of dependence on the state. The professors had become civil servants, appointed and liable to be dismissed in the same way as other officials. The government kept an eye on their various activities, regulating their salaries and dealing out praise and blame accordingly. The system of benevolent despotism made no exceptions in favour of the university. The government view of their function was almost purely utilitarian. They existed to train men for the civil service, the Church and the schools. The law faculty, drawing its students from the higher middle class and even from the nobility, and preparing them for the most influential and lucrative public posts, enjoyed much higher prestige than any other and set the tone for the whole university. Here court traditions were strong. The students wore swords and imitated as best they could the dress and manners of the courts until, after the Seven Years' War, the middle-class influence gradually asserted itself.

The further reforms initiated at Göttingen gradually penetrated to the Latin schools. The effect was to encourage the study of Greek for its cultural value, and of German, for self-expression, at the cost of Latin 'eloquence'. French continued to make progress, history, geography, mathematics and physics were given more attention. At the same time religious instruction was modified in the direction of 'natural' theology, with its stress on the moral aim of religion, the point of view of Lessing's *Nathan der Weise*. But these changes failed to attract to the schools the sons of the nobility or even those of the patricians of the towns and the richer merchants. These boys were still taught at home by private tutors, usually young theologians who were waiting for a call, men ranging in ability and cultivation from the standard of Kant, Fichte, Hölderlin, Hegel (all of whom, as well as many other intellectual leaders of Germany in the eighteenth and early nineteenth centuries, were private tutors in their day) to that of poor theologians who had left the university after a few months for lack of means.

In considering the professions opened up to young Germans in the eighteenth century by a higher education, the question of social origins cannot be neglected. Equality of opportunity was very far from being a reality. It was hardly even thought of as an ideal. The prospects of even an able boy depended very much on his father's position in life. For a poor boy there were almost insuperable obstacles to advancement in the higher professions.

At the universities (Paulsen says) we find two groups of students. There are young men who are preparing themselves by the study of law and 'political science' for office under the state. They are all drawn from the better classes of society. And there are others from families living in straitened circumstances or actual poverty, who are preparing themselves through the study of theology and school subjects for the Protestant Church and its appendage, school teaching and tutoring. When his academic studies are over the law student learns the practical details of his future work by assisting some Justiz- or Regierungskollegium. The theologian on the other hand looks out for a post as private tutor or as teacher at a Latin school, to maintain himself until the church living that is his ambition turns up. Apart from a few posts in large town and state schools no one remained a schoolmaster any longer than he was obliged to. Towards the end of the century however there are signs of a change, the change that has been completed in the nineteenth century: the teachers begin to separate off from the clergy as a special profession, and at the same time they gain in status and recognition.

Of the students in the clerical and scholastic group the great majority came from the lower middle class and peasantry. Hardly any came from the nobility or the families of higher civil servants, but an increasing proportion were the sons of Pfarrer themselves. Regular provision was made by some Protestant states, as we have seen, for the free education of candidates for the ministry in state schools and special theological colleges at the state university, but only the ablest boys could hope for such scholarships. At all universities there were many other theological students, most of them poor, enjoying no regular assistance. They struggled along on a small allowance from home, eked out by occasional free meals from charitable citizens and by what they could earn by coaching, school-teaching, proof-reading, clerical work and the like. They were particularly numerous at Leipzig, because, as a big town and the centre of the publishing trade, it offered more opportunities than most universities of part-time employment. Here many lived like Jean Paul's *Quintus Fixlein* and his three room-mates, whose principal material necessities, such as bed and overcoat, 'resembled so many Phoenixes, each being the sole one of its kind', though their good humour remained indestructible.

It was a lucky theologian who was able to find a post even as temporary assistant to a Pfarrer immediately on leaving the university. Almost all had to resign themselves to a period of private tutoring or schoolmastering before they could hope for a living. For 'Hofmeister' or private tutors conditions depended almost entirely on the kind of family with which they found employment. Their position was necessarily insecure. In general they were apparently treated as superior domestics. 'People who treat their children's tutor like a domestic servant should be ashamed of themselves', says Knigge, and he speaks of tutors in good families not daring to say a word at table and being made to feel their social inferiority to the children under their charge by friends and servants.[1] They were usually paid about fifty Thalers a year in addition to their board. Families desiring a tutor often asked a university professor to recommend one. In the first half of the eighteenth century Francke in Halle was the most popular adviser. Later it was Gellert in Leipzig, and after him C. F. Weisse, of the same university, and J. J. Engel of Berlin.[2] A long list of famous men might be

[1] Knigge, *Umgang mit Menschen*, II, 10.

[2] See for this and further details Gustav Stephan, 'Hofmeister und Gouvernanten im achtzehnten Jahrhundert', *Zeitschrift für deutsche Kulturgeschichte*, N.F. I, 1891, and G. Steinhausen, 'Der Hofmeister', in his *Kulturstudien*, Berlin, 1893.

compiled who were tutors at least for a period. It would include Gellert, C. F. Weisse, Gleim, Götz, C. G. Heyne, Musäus, Hamann, Winckelmann, Boie, Voss, Lenz, L. Wagner, Jean Paul, Kant, Hölderlin, Fichte, Hegel and Schleiermacher. A tutor who was lucky might win the favour of a patron by good service in his family and be presented to a living, or he might be advanced to the post of secretary. Goethe's friend Behrisch for instance, who began as a tutor, displayed so much *savoir-vivre* that he ended by becoming a Hofrat.

The profession of schoolmaster in a Latin school was, as Paulsen states, not usually looked upon as an occupation for life, any more than tutoring. The status and conditions of life it afforded were such that it could only attract men from the lower middle class of the towns or from the peasantry. It was in the first place very badly paid. At the end of the century in Prussia a teacher's income ranged between 200 and 400 Thalers a year, little if any more than the average student required for his maintenance.[1] The greater part of it came from fees that he had to collect himself, and part often consisted of contributions in kind. For purposes of comparison it may be noted that village school teachers rarely received more than 100 Thalers, usually less than 40, while at the other end of the scale a university professor might receive up to 1200 Thalers, though the average salary would be well under half that sum. Almost every schoolmaster had to supplement his income by other work. Some (especially headmasters) were able to secure a few boarders, some might combine the office of schoolmaster with that of organist, some would earn a little by their pen. Their chief resource was the giving of private lessons. As we have seen, all the modern subjects were at first extras, but they were taught by the regular staff for special fees. The schools imitated here the practice of the universities, where it had become usual for a professor to treat the public lectures which he gave for his fixed salary

[1] Paulsen, II, 158 f.

rather perfunctorily, and to reserve his best teaching for private lectures, for which he received the fees himself. Even in the eighteenth century schoolmasters had often to join their pupils in the traditional 'Kurrende', hymn and carol-singing round the town at traditional times for alms, as well as to attend with them innumerable weddings and funerals. Schools were small, but they were nevertheless understaffed. A school rarely had more than three masters, called, in order of seniority, Rector, Conrector and Cantor. Schools were seldom if ever housed in specially constructed buildings. The accommodation ranged from the most primitive makeshift quarters to the gloomy old monastic building occupied by most state and town schools. No wonder that bitter complaints by schoolmasters were frequent. According to J. H. Voss, himself a schoolmaster, the schoolmaster ranked between the lowest of country ministers and the verger. In a prince's funeral procession Voss was asked to walk beside the valet.

The hardness of the schoolmaster's lot is less surprising when one remembers that university professors, especially those of the philosophical faculty, only slowly attained to the degree of social esteem that they enjoyed in the nineteenth century. The arts professors in particular usually came from the lower classes of society, for men with brains in other classes sought more highly respected and more lucrative callings. As study in the philosophical faculty had a preparatory character, the arts professors did not enjoy the same standing as the rest. They were glorified schoolmasters, who taught the elements of a fairly wide range of subjects for about as many hours a week as a schoolmaster teaches to-day. Being overworked and poor, and having had few opportunities of mixing in society, scholars usually lived the life of recluses. Amongst men of the world their vanity and pedantry were proverbial, and to judge by the fulsome dedications of their books, by the exaggerated value laid even by distinguished men like Gellert or Pütter on acquaintanceship with the great, and by the pictures of the typical professor drawn by Knigge and others, there were good grounds for the charge. The other side of the picture is to be seen in the heroic devotion to learning of a Heyne or a Winckelmann, and in the charming pictures of a scholar's happiness in his work and his family that we find in Semler's autobiography or the letters of Voss. Their world was admittedly not that of the 'man of the world', but it was just their willingness to devote their whole life to intellectual tasks, even at the cost of stunting themselves as men, that enabled the greatest of them to make the peculiar contribution of Germany to European culture. 'Amour de la retraite', to use Mme de Staël's phrase, was the characteristic feature of the life of Germany's scholars, philosophers and poets, as opposed to the 'esprit de conversation' of the French, and it was everywhere reflected in their work.[1]

It was only a few exceptionally able men who became university professors. The mass of the poorer students in the universities looked to the Protestant ministry as the goal of their ambition. By the eighteenth century a Pfarrer who had not studied for at least a year or two at a university was a rarity. In the early days of Lutheranism the reformers had had to improvise a ministry out of the available resources. Besides teachers and vergers, many printers, clothmakers and other craftsmen had been pressed into service, but in two hundred years of evolution the standard of culture of the average clergyman had risen to a fairly high level, and completely unsuitable appointments were not common. There was still, however, no satisfactory machinery to prevent mistakes. The power of nomination still remained in most parishes in the hands of an aristocratic and by no means always cultivated patron, who might be moved by one of

[1] The two books by Emil Reicke, *Der Lehrer in der deutschen Vergangenheit* and *Der Gelehrte in der deutschen Vergangenheit* (Monographien zur deutschen Kulturgeschichte) are popular and deal chiefly with the Middle Ages. They are largely dependent on Paulsen, *op. cit.*

a number of motives in making his selection, and who seldom consulted the congregation first. There was a theological examination, conducted by the consistory, which all candidates for orders had to pass. Sometimes, as in Prussia in the second half of the century, there were two, one to be taken after university study to qualify for the title of 'Kandidat' (which had previously been assumed by any who chose to use it), and one immediately preceding ordination to a particular parish. But no one was ever known to fail in these examinations. A candidate selected by a patron might be asked to present himself a second time if he proved utterly ignorant at the first attempt, but he was always successful in the end. A large proportion of the candidates were themselves sons of ministers. Not a few others, it seems, qualified for a vacancy by marrying the widow or a daughter of the previous incumbent, much as craftsmen married into a gild. Other strange conditions of appointment were sometimes imposed by patrons, while 'gifts' of money and discreditable intrigues were by no means unknown. A reference to them is admitted even into such an idyllic picture as Voss's *Luise*,[1] and Laukhard's autobiography is full of them.[2]

If the method of appointment did not tend to keep moral and intellectual standards high, the development of public opinion, under the influence of Pietism and rationalism successively, had done something to correct this defect, though neither movement had done much to earn for the clergy greater social esteem. The Pietist movement had shifted the stress from dogmatic teaching to care of souls, from preaching to pastoral visitations and prayer meetings, which brought the minister into closer touch with his parishioners. Rationalism had still further weakened the

[1]   'Ein ländlicher Pfarrer verbauert,
Haftet am Kloss und vergeht in Nichtigkeit oder Erwerbsucht,
Wenn nicht griechischer Geist ihn emporhebt aus der Entartung
Neueres Barbartums, *wo Verdienst ist käuflich und erblich.*'
                                                    Luise, 2te Idylle.
[2] Laukhard, *Leben und Schicksale*, I, chaps. 9 and 10.

hold of dogmatic religion. It had alienated the great mass of the educated laity from religion altogether, and made religion even for the nominally orthodox the handmaid of morality. As a class, therefore, the Protestant clergy, though their personal integrity was greater than ever, were not very highly respected in the latter part of the century. In spite of the vogue of Pietism in many courts, they were regarded by the majority of the court class with indifference or scorn, and by the cultivated as something of an anachronism.

Their standard of living was usually necessarily low, except in the towns, and here it was considerably below that of the official class. The average income of a country Pfarrer was only about fifty to seventy Thalers a year, his material comforts often fewer than those of a middling craftsman or peasant. He had always to eke out his income by gardening, bee-keeping, the cultivation of silkworms or regular farming. Part of his income was in the form of tithes. The Pfarrer's share of a crop might be laid out on the fieldpath and the whole of his family would have to help to carry it home. Most country Pfarrer would keep a cow or two and hens, so that though a minister's wife would buy very little in the way of food, she was always ready to entertain visitors, with the salt or smoked meat, poultry, eggs, vegetables and flour that she had at hand. She would make a thousand and one things at home that are now bought in shops, from preserved meats to soap and candles. Clothes too were nearly all made at home. The lady of the house and her daughters would spin their flax, weave it or have it woven in the village and perhaps send it to the nearest town to be printed with a pattern. There cloth could also be bought for the menfolk, and a tailor would be engaged for a week or a fortnight to help to make or repair the clothes of the family for the coming year. The few things that had to be bought would be provided by the annual fair in a neighbouring market-town.

In the Protestant states that followed the lead of Frederician Prussia the ministers of the Church came to be looked upon during the second half of the century as functionaries of the state. The absolute state had freed itself from every trace of theocracy and made a tool of the Church for its own secular purposes. This change gave Protestant ministers an assured place in society, but only with the sacrifice of much of their spiritual freedom. For the Aufklärung they were teachers of religion and instruments of social service. As religion was a useful prop for morality, it was in the interests of the state, even if it professed to concern itself solely with the temporal welfare of its subjects, to encourage it. At the same time the Pfarrer proved a very useful channel of communication between the government and the mass of the people. When newspapers were still rare and illiteracy widespread, to have a decree read from the pulpit was the most effective way of ensuring universal knowledge of it, and great use was made of this method of 'broadcasting' for purely secular affairs. Further, the Pfarrer, as perhaps the only educated man in the village, was called upon to perform all sorts of duties that now fall to state officials.

From the diary of a country minister in Baden, at the end of the eighteenth century,[1] we learn that he superintended the election of the village 'Vogt' and the appointment of midwives. With the 'Vogt' or village mayor he shared responsibility in all questions of administration. Not even the cleaning out of a brook or the repairing of a field-path happened without his knowledge. He was the confidential agent of the government in all sorts of matters. He was asked for reports about people in the village and about proposed changes involving government assistance or consent. The Pfarrer gave notice, for instance, as we learn from other sources, of epidemics, and of the death of persons on whose estate duties might be levied. He was the village registrar and statistician, who kept records not only of births, marriages and deaths but of the number of blind, halt, deaf and

[1] A. Schmitthenner, *Das Tagebuch meines Urgrossvaters*, Freiburg i. B. 1922 (3rd ed.).

dumb, of orphans, illegitimate children and homeless families. He conducted the census, drew up the list of recruits and had to be present when young men from his parish were called up for medical examination. In Prussia, we learn from other sources, the Pfarrer had to take care, if he valued his living, not to put any obstacles in the way of the king's recruiting officers. Our Baden informant was jointly responsible with the Vogt for poor relief. He was superintendent of the schools in the four villages in his parish and examined them all every quarter. He presided over the 'censura' or ecclesiastical court of the district, consisting of two elected representatives from each village and the mayors, the competence of which was very wide. It dealt with almost all offences except those against property and the person, and could not only reprimand offenders but sentence them to imprisonment in the village gaol. It was especially concerned of course with offences against morality. It will be evident that Herder sums up the position of the Pfarrer in his day truly when he says: 'A minister is only entitled to exist now, under state control and by authority of the prince, as a moral teacher, a farmer, a list-maker, a secret agent of police'.

With these secular duties in addition to his pastoral work, and perhaps the education of some of his children, even a country Pfarrer did not find that time hung heavy on his hands. In the towns there would no doubt be less administrative work and more visiting and preaching. That not all ministers were equally conscientious or well fitted for their task has already been noted. But if there were black sheep, especially in the country, who were almost as rude and ignorant as their peasant neighbours, and others who, like a familiar type in the Church of England, were more gentlemen-farmers than clergymen, there were hundreds of devout and learned men in Protestant parsonages and not a few of high literary cultivation. The part played by the clergy in literature was not, on the whole, very considerable in the eighteenth century. Herder is the only clergyman-author of the first rank; among authors of the second and third rank are Götz, Hermes, Miller, Lavater. It is interesting, however, as a partial index to the literary atmosphere of the Protestant parsonages, to note what a big part was played in the creation of an independent German literature by sons of Pfarrer, men like Lessing, Wieland, Claudius, Hölty, Miller, Boie, Bürger, Heinse, Lenz, Schubart. For all that it should be remembered that the pictures of Pfarrer painted by Voss in *Luise*, by Goethe in *Hermann und Dorothea*, or Jean Paul in *Jubelsenior* are much idealised.

Among professional men, doctors with a university qualification ranked high. They had usually had a good grounding in the classics, at any rate in Latin, at a grammar school, perhaps supplemented by a year or two in the philosophical faculty of a university, before entering on their professional training. Then three years of study in the medical faculty were necessary before they could obtain the medical doctorate of their university, the qualification usually required before a doctor could set up in practice in Germany. The doctor, or 'medicus purus', was still carefully distinguished from the surgeon, who till the end of the century, with few exceptions, was a man of little education who ranked no higher than a skilled artisan, trained as he was like a craftsman by apprenticeship in a gild. In Durlach, for instance, doctors and even apothecaries belonged to the 'exempted' class, but surgeons did not, any more than barbers, from whom they were often indistinguishable.[1] The two branches of the medical art were beginning to approach each other, but it was not until the second half of the nineteenth century that doctors in Germany were required to be competent in medicine, surgery and midwifery alike. In the eighteenth century they usually had at most a theoretical acquaintance with the last two branches and left the practice of them to the socially inferior barber-surgeon and midwife.

[1] Roller, *op. cit.* p. 407.

Medical teaching in the German universities varied very greatly in quality and quantity from place to place. At the beginning of the century few universities had more than two or three professors in their medical faculty. Each taught two or more subjects, usually in a purely theoretical way, with little or no practical anatomy or clinical work. By the end of the century, however, things had improved so much that the leading universities at least had medical faculties of specialists, provided with anatomy theatres, laboratories and clinical institutes. Vienna had nine medical chairs by 1780, Göttingen six by 1784. But figures are sometimes misleading. Würzburg for instance had five chairs according to the ordinances of 1749, but a student who went there in 1761 found that the professors received salaries of 200 to 300 Gulden and had had no pupils for several years. The number of students was small even at the bigger universities. At Göttingen it averaged 50 to 80 in all in the 'sixties and 'seventies, so that about a score would graduate each year. Jena in 1768 had 17, while Altdorf turned out an average of only two or three doctors a year throughout the century.[1] Comparing these numbers with those of the more famous medical schools abroad, we gain some idea of the relative standing of the German universities in medicine. Leyden, in the early years of the century, had about 300 medical students, and Edinburgh's average number in the second half of the century was 400.

The truth is that Germany had not yet attained the eminence in medicine which was to be hers in the nineteenth century. Holland led the way in medical science in the seventeenth and early eighteenth centuries, when Boerhaave (1668–1738), building on foundations well laid by his predecessors, attracted students from all Europe by his clinical skill, and though his pupils van Swieten (1700–72) and de Haën (1704–76) established a good medical school at Vienna, and Albrecht Haller, the poet-scientist, another pupil

---

[1] Puschmann, *Geschichte des medicinischen Unterrichts*, Leipzig, 1889, p. 325.

of his, as professor in Göttingen put physiology for the first time on a sound scientific basis and displayed immense learning in many fields, the German record of achievements during the century is inferior to that of France or England. Many Germans therefore studied medicine abroad, at Leyden, Utrecht, Paris or Strassburg. Surgery was particularly backward, the empirical skill of the surgeons being seldom backed by any theoretical knowledge. Academically trained surgeons like Heister of Altdorf (1683–1758) and A. G. Richter of Göttingen (1742–1812) were rare exceptions, and both had been trained abroad, whereas in France, largely through the foundation of the Académie de Chirurgie in Paris in 1743, the status of the best surgeons had been raised as high as that of good doctors and an equally thorough theoretical training had come to be demanded of them.

The opportunities for medical education being so unequal, and the reputation for honesty of some university faculties not being above reproach (they were often accused of selling degrees without examination), it was inevitable that the state authorities should insist on some form of supervision of doctors and surgeons. It was of course in Prussia that control was most effectively exercised, but most states made some attempt at it. By the Prussian 'Medizinaledikt' of 1725 medical graduates were submitted to a state test and obliged to attend lectures at the Royal Anatomical Theatre in Berlin before they could be recognised. Surgeons had to serve seven years' apprenticeship, gain experience in the field as 'Feldscher' or regimental surgeon, attend a 'course of operations' in the anatomical theatre and pass certain tests. They were not allowed to treat ordinary illnesses (which were the physician's province) except in small towns or in the country. There were so few large towns, however, that in practice the great majority of people had to be content with the services of a barber-surgeon.[1] Similar edicts were in

[1] For vivid pictures of a barber-surgeon's life and work see Meister Johann Dietz, *Lebensbeschreibung*, Munich, 1915.

force in most states and Free Towns. In Frankfort-on-Main for example control was exercised by the four 'Physicians' appointed and paid by the town council.

After their theoretical training young doctors might be called upon then to do some practical anatomy, the opportunity for which might not have been provided in the university—for it was only gradually that even the leading universities obtained proper dissecting rooms and a supply of material—but they were not yet compelled to seek clinical experience in a hospital or with an older doctor. Clinical teaching was usually scanty or non-existent in the universities, and only a few of them had satisfactory clinics by the end of the century. They were usually of course in small towns. Jung-Stilling, speaking from his own experience in the 'seventies, urges young doctors both to study surgery and to obtain experience under skilled guidance before setting up in practice. 'Where is there still more to be done', he says, 'than in the organisation of medical teaching and practice and state regulation of these matters?'[1]

The medical profession was by no means overcrowded in the eighteenth century. A well-qualified doctor, after the first difficult years, was assured of a comfortable living. In many states doctors were given a small official salary and their fees were often fixed, at any rate for certain poorer classes of patients. They generally settled in fair-sized towns or near some court, in a place, that is, where patients of the better middle class and the aristocracy were available. The barber-surgeon had usually to suffice for craftsmen and country folk. Even in the towns doctors proper kept strictly to their own sphere and assisted the surgeon or the midwife only with their not always highly respected theoretical advice. Though they were not numerous, most of the doctors one hears of seem to have led a very regular and unhurried existence. In Weimar, for instance, each doctor (there were four in this small town) had time enough to visit all the

[1] J. H. Jung-Stilling, *Lebensgeschichte* (Häusliches Leben).

families who had entrusted themselves to his care at least
once a week, whether anyone was ill or not, and it was
thought necessary for him solemnly to purge the whole
family with rhubarb once a quarter.[1] In the bigger towns
the medical men had their professional organisations, which
often played an important part in civic affairs. There were
many progressive and public-spirited men among them who
took the lead in pressing for the provision of more hospitals
(many towns had still only the hospitals originally founded
by the Church), better opportunities for medical and surgical
education, improvements in town drainage and water supply
and the systematic training of midwives, a very urgent
necessity. In all these things much progress was made in the
course of the century, and this is of course one of the reasons
for the unprecedented growth of the population in the
following century.[2] In *Dichtung und Wahrheit* Goethe draws
attention to the important influence they had in cultural
affairs. 'Following the example of a foreigner, Tissot,' he
says, 'the doctors too (like certain theologians) began eagerly
to make their influence felt in general culture. Haller, Unzer,
Zimmermann were great forces.' Many doctors began to
write not merely for other members of the profession but
for the general public, and helped in this way to raise the
level of German prose writing, more perhaps than the
lawyers and philosophers. As cultivated men they naturally
played their part too as patrons of the new poetic literature,
though in spite of Haller's example few were creative
writers.

We come now to the professional men who as students
had belonged to the most highly considered class, the Jurists.
They came almost always from what were considered the
higher ranks of society, the nobility and patricians and above
all the better placed bourgeoisie, prosperous merchants and

[1] Karl von Lyncker, *Am Weimarischen Hofe*, Berlin, 1912, p. 35.
[2] For details about these improvements see e.g. Puschmann's *Handbuch der Geschichte der Medizin* (ed. Neuburger and Pagel), Jena, 1905, vol. III.

successful state and civic servants. Nearly all law students aimed at entering the service of some prince or Free Town. The growth of a professional civil service has been traced in earlier chapters. We have seen that the benevolent despotism which was the political ideal of those in authority in Germany necessitated an expansion of the bureaucracy far in excess of English developments. The multiplicity of authorities in itself made necessary a much larger number of officials in proportion to the total population than is required to-day under a more highly centralised system. Apart from three hundred independent 'territories' there were five times that number of semi-independent Grafschaften, Ritterschaften and so forth, each of which needed its staff of officials, although it might have taken a score of these units to make up a modern Prussian Regierungsbezirk. The Reichsritter needed a few officials to collect revenues, dispense justice and maintain order, the Reichsgraf, a stage higher, required a 'Privy Council', a Free Town had to have its Senate and a whole series of committees served by permanent officials, and a ruling Prince, finally, had the Council, Treasury, Department of Justice, Consistory and so forth described in earlier pages. According to figures given by Biedermann[1] there seem to have been about twice as many officials in proportion to the population in most German states in the later eighteenth century as there were a hundred years later, when there was still certainly no lack of them. It did not escape the notice of independent-minded contemporaries that there were often too many cooks. K. F. von Moser[2] tells of occasions when five treasury decrees were needed before a few slates could be repaired on a palace roof, and he draws a similar contrast in 1758 between the treasury methods in small German states and those in Sweden as modern critics of officialdom do between the procedure necessary before permission to build may be obtained in

[1] *Deutschland im 18ten Jahrhundert*, I, 100 ff.
[2] *Vom Herrn und Diener*, 1758, quoted by Biedermann, *loc. cit.*

Berlin (involving a delay of from two to twelve months and the authorisation of some twenty-six departments) and that in London (where it is usually only necessary to consult the District Surveyor).[1]

The official class was of course chiefly concentrated in the towns, but scattered over the country a very large number of trained jurists were to be found in the Ämter, the smallest administrative units of the states of that day. We have seen above what paid officials were usual in little capitals and in town-republics like Frankfort-on-Main. Many of the higher posts were reserved in the courts, as we have seen, for noblemen, though trained lawyers could never be dispensed with. In the Free Towns, though patricians by birth were favoured for paid offices, they had usually received a university education and spent some time in travel before accepting office, and the highest posts were often occupied by men who owed their rise to personal merit and knowledge rather than to any advantages of birth. Everywhere there were large numbers of minor officials of every degree of cultivation, from brilliant young men from the universities awaiting promotion, to copying clerks and men of no literary education at all in the town watch, the cleansing department and so forth.

Conditions of appointment varied very considerably. In the more progressive states and the larger towns officials were by the second half of the century almost all appointed for long periods or for life (of course with safeguards) at a fixed salary, but in many smaller states and towns their appointments were still for short periods and terminable at any time, and they depended for their living almost entirely on the fees they were allowed to demand from the public. It is obvious that such a system was open to grave abuse. Abuses were still frequent, both in the manner of appointment of officials (nepotism and the sale of offices), and in their conduct in office (corruption, laziness and inefficiency). It was only very gradually, first in Prussia then elsewhere,

[1] W. Hegemann, article in *Neue Rundschau* of Aug. 1931.

that a tradition of honourable service was established. That it grew so slowly was not the fault of the employed only, but also that of the employers. What could be expected for instance from officials who were treated as they were by the 'extravagant and impecunious petty lords' of the first half of the century, who according to K. H. von Lang 'always did their utmost to induce wealthy men to take charge of their affairs, in order that they might make use of them for their personal credit like court Jews, and when they were squeezed dry dismiss them'?[1] In such small states the officials were, as Biedermann says, little more than members of the prince's court and household staff. Their only hope of advancement for themselves and their sons was to ingratiate themselves personally with their master. Schiller's picture of this relationship in *Kabale und Liebe*, where the son of the Präsident (the Minister of Justice, and in this court the leading influence) is asked, in view of the approaching official marriage of the prince, to become the legal husband of the prince's mistress, is historically justified.

K. H. von Lang in his memoirs gives many instances of the entire lack of consideration with which petty rulers treated their officials, and we gain the same impression from the memoirs of J. C. Mannlich, from Knigge's chapter on 'Intercourse with the Great',[2] and from innumerable memoirs and biographies of the period. The private life of civil servants was constantly being interfered with by their ruler. They might have to build themselves houses in a particular quarter (as in the Friedrichsstadt in Berlin), to hunt with the prince whether they wished to or not, to attend court ceremonies at considerable expense, to send their children, against their will, to a state school (Schiller!). It was only in the town-republics and towards the end of the century in the larger states that officials, apart from their

[1] K. H. v. Lang, *op. cit.* p. 15.
[2] *Ibid.* pp. 15, 66, 131, etc.; J. C. Mannlich, *op. cit.* pp. 310, 356, etc.; Knigge, *Umgang mit Menschen*, Teil III, chap. I.

definite duties, were allowed in their private life as much freedom as other citizens.

It goes without saying that security of tenure of office was an ideal seldom attained in practice. It was only under Frederick II in Prussia and Frederick Augustus III in Saxony that officials were given security of tenure provided that they duly performed their duties. In Prussia a spirit of military efficiency pervaded the civil service under Frederick William I. Centralised control was motivated, as we saw above, mainly by the desire to increase the military power of the state, and it was Frederick William I and not Frederick II who, according to his lights, was the first Prussian ruler to consider himself 'the first servant of the state'. But it was only under Frederick II that the spirit of service to an ideally conceived state permeated the general mass of officials, encouraged by Frederick's stern efficiency, his hardness with himself and others, and his strict control of his subordinates, together with the keen personal interest he took in their activities. In Austria even Joseph II compelled 2000 civil servants to retire with little or no pension, in the first two years of his reign, and in Bavaria, the civil service had no legal security even at the end of the century.[1]

If the status of the official class was somewhat indefinite, it is still less easy to make general statements about the payment they received for their services. Salaries varied over a wide range for different appointments and for different states, and even when nominally fixed they were subject to great fluctuations owing to the financial instability of the states. It was not uncommon for officials to receive no salary for years at a time.[2] This was one reason why the abolition of the old feudal practice, by which the prince's bailiffs were responsible for the administration of his estates and the collection of dues, as well as for dispensing justice, was resisted by the officials themselves; they had a first claim on

[1] Biedermann, *op. cit.* 1, 88 f.
[2] Examples in Biedermann, *op. cit.* 1, 83 ff.

the dues, fees and fines they collected. Their offices were sometimes so lucrative that great sums were paid into the exchequer by aspirants to them and the reversion was looked upon as a kind of pension for the holder's widow or children. This state of things continued in most parts of Germany till the second half of the century, in some until after the French Revolution.

A few examples of salaries may be given. A young man fresh from the university would usually, unless he had powerful connections, serve for a year or two for little or no salary, as Lang did in the Regierungskanzlei at Oettingen. After a year Lang was appointed Protokollist at a salary that amounted with extras to 200 Gulden a year (nominally £16. 13s. 4d.). A year and half later he became secretary with 240 Gulden (£20) and free firing. Ten years after leaving the university he was earning 1000 Gulden (£83) as Keeper of the Archives at Bayreuth. His highest salary was 4000 Gulden (£333), when after twenty-seven years service he became Archive Director and departmental chief in the Foreign Office at Munich. But this was in 1812, and Lang's was an unusually brilliant career. Körner, Schiller's Dresden friend, as a young man only earned 200 Thalers (£30) a year for the combined offices of Oberkonsistorialrat and Assessor on another board. Goethe in Weimar was given an allowance of 1200 Gulden (£100) on his appointment as Legationsrat. Later his salary rose to 1800 Gulden. Of the civil officials in Frankfort-on-Main we are told that only the Schultheiss (with 1800 Gulden) and the Syndics (1600 Gulden) received over 1000 Gulden a year. The Ratsherren, however, who were not civic servants but members of the governing body, received high salaries (the Schöffen or Aldermen 1800 Gulden, the Second Benchers 1200, the Third Benchers 500). Only very responsible officials (Town Clerk, Council Clerk, Treasury Clerks, etc.) received over 400 Gulden. Officials of the second rank received 200 Gulden or less, and the rest mostly under 100 Gulden, though many had houses rent-free or received other perquisites. Towards the end of the century salaries were rising:[1] To find the equivalent purchasing value of these sums one should multiply by at least three. A useful standard of comparison is furnished by Schiller's estimate of the income required about 1790 by a single man to live decently in Jena or Rudolstadt. It was 400 Gulden. In Dresden 600 Gulden would have been required, he said, and in Weimar, though it was such a tiny capital, nearly as much. From Goethe's letters to his protégé Krafft[2] we see that it was possible to live very modestly on about half the sum Schiller mentions.

It is clear from the foregoing that the standard of living of state and civic servants as a class was by no means uniform. There were many at least as poor as an average artisan and there were others enjoying an income and social consideration resembling those of a nobleman. It was only very gradually that the brain workers were differentiated socially from manual workers. It has been proved for instance for the town of Durlach in the eighteenth century that at least half of the members of the official class or their children married, according to present-day ideas, beneath themselves. Daughters of officers and officials frequently married artisans, footmen, ostlers, factory workers and common soldiers. Young ministers, doctors, officers and officials often married ladies' maids, who might however themselves, especially in aristocratic households, be daughters of professional men of high standing. As the century advanced fewer 'misalliances' of this kind occurred. The officials and professional men were slowly cutting themselves off from the rest of the middle class. This happened partly as a consequence of their growing economic security, which allowed them to follow the accepted social models, the aristocracy, as regards the material comfort and the external forms of their life. The conflicts that might result in families drawn between the

---

[1] *Die Stadt Goethes*, p. 69.
[2] Goethe allowed him 100 Thalers (£15) a year.

traditional ideals of the bourgeoisie and those of the nobility are well depicted in the literature of the time, in works like Grossmann's *Nicht mehr als sechs Schüsseln* for instance. In this play we have the theme of Molière's *George Dandin* (the rich peasant marrying into the nobility) translated into terms of German life in Grossmann's time. Instead of a rich peasant we find a Hofrat of middle-class origin, and instead of his humiliation at the hands of his aristocratic in-laws we witness his triumph. Further causes contributing to the separation of this new class from the bourgeoisie were the legal privileges conferred on it in many instances, its sense of solidarity, through its particular responsibility, with the ruling class rather than with the mass of the ruled, and its growing taste for and need of literary culture and that social refinement to which a young man was introduced by a university education, and which he was encouraged to maintain by the nature of his duties in later life.

There is a certain resemblance between the rise of some elements of the middle class, through the possession of knowledge and skill, to higher social rank, and the rise of the 'ministeriales' for similar reasons in medieval times. But whereas the successful ministeriales made their offices, and the fiefs by which they were rewarded for their services, hereditary in their families, and converted themselves into a new Estate of Knights, the boundaries of the official and professional class of modern times have remained fluid. They were rewarded by money payment, enjoyed therefore far less security than their medieval counterparts, and additions were constantly being made to their number from the class to which they belonged. The result was that they retained many more of their inherited habits of living than the Knights. They were not simply absorbed by the existing upper class but formed a group which, though not very clearly delimited, still had a character of its own.

The older middle class had comparatively little artistic or literary culture, while its ideas of physical well-being were at best unsophisticated. It liked plain solid furniture, clothes that would wear for ever, an abundance of simple whole-some food and drink and its traditional homely customs and amusements. The influence of the courts and of rationalism had produced only superficial effects on its way of life. As was to be expected in a compact and hard-working society, it took questions of conduct far more seriously than intel-lectual or artistic matters. It was conservative and provincial in thought and taste, strict and a little pharisaical in its ethical views, as we have seen from certain gild regulations. The court classes on the other hand were far less moved by considerations of principle. They had a certain code of honour, but they were more self-seeking and opportunist than the middle class. Their consideration for others seldom extended beyond their own ranks. They had however more external polish and elegance, more feeling for style both in art and in the details of ordinary life, though in Germany, as we have seen, their forms were usually rather slavishly copied from France. In their wealth and leisure they had at least the prerequisites for a predominantly aesthetic approach to life, and speaking generally the beautiful did even in Germany mean more to them than the good or the true.

The new class of brain workers owed its position to its knowledge and intelligence. It tended necessarily to put the intellectual values first. But through its origin it retained much of the ethical rigour of the middle class, especially in regard to the relations of the sexes. It has been mentioned above that its views in this matter were in marked contrast with those of the average courtier, and that from the solid bourgeoisie and the educated middle class a stricter sexual morality, at least for women, gradually spread in the late eighteenth and early nineteenth century to the class above and the class below, the nobility and the working class. It was much the same with the other virtues which we still think of as typically 'middle class', honesty, industry, and sweet reasonableness. The educated middle class did not quickly lose its virtue then in its new life. It could not, however, resist the contagion of aristocratic ways of living. It felt the attraction of new luxuries, it imitated the nobility, at a certain remove, in dress, manners, food and drink and all kinds of externals. Many also acquired a taste now for forms of art that had come to be in Germany the preserve of the courts, painting for instance, the opera and literary drama. It is not surprising that the educated middle class responded more readily than any other section of society to the writers of the great age of German literature, such as Herder, Goethe and Schiller, with their ideal of 'Humanität', in which an attempt was made to reconcile the respective claims of morality, religion, art and philosophy to be the supreme value, and if any class can be said to have evoked this philosophy of life by its need of it, it was this educated section of the middle class.

PART IV

REACTIONS ON LITERATURE

Chapter I

THE PROFESSION OF LETTERS

It was only in the second half of the eighteenth century that it became possible for a German writer to take up literature as a whole-time profession, and even at the end of the century Germany had probably fewer professional authors than England. The number of authors of the first rank who were entirely dependent on the public was of course small in both countries. Nearly all the considerable writers either possessed private means or exercised some lucrative profession. In England there had been a period during which writers who devoted their whole time to letters and possessed few or no other resources could count on the support of aristocratic patrons. Patronage had not been unknown in the Elizabethan age. When the appreciation of literature had become fashionable again after the Restoration, patronage again occurred, but it was not until the reign of Queen Anne that it became widespread. It was to ministers of state like Somers and Montagu, Harley and St John that men like Locke, Congreve, Addison, Newton, Steele, Swift, Prior and others owed their advancement, and the fashion of patronage set by these ministers was followed by many great aristocrats. In England's Augustan Age, the patronage of literature, either as literature or as a political weapon, was a well-established custom.

Under George I the sinecures and pensions previously granted to literary men were needed for the management of

Parliament, but the practice of private patronage was kept up for some time longer. In the second quarter of the century, however, patrons began to play a smaller and smaller part because the reading public was growing, and by 1760 Goldsmith could write: 'At present, the few poets of England no longer depend on the great for subsistence; they have now no other patrons but the public, and the public, collectively considered, is a good and generous master'. Long before this Pope had been able to dispense with patrons. His first imitators in the profession of letters, in Johnson's early days, had often a hard struggle, but with the rise of the magazines in the 'thirties, the vogue of the novel and circulating library in the 'forties, there came to be such a sustained demand for the written word that writers able to hit the public taste could make good terms with publishers, and live in comfort, while some publishers and booksellers made fortunes. Goldsmith is said to have earned as much as £1800 in one year, Arthur Young to have made over £1100 in 1770 by journalism. By the beginning of the next century popular poets were receiving offers of thousands of pounds for verse tales. Scott held the record with £4000 for *The Lady of the Lake*. Byron received £2000 for the third canto of *Childe Harold* and comparable sums for other works. These were men of genius, but even authors like Southey and Galt were able to earn a very comfortable competence by steady work.[1]

The history of the profession of letters in eighteenth-century Germany is not such a record of worldly success. Patrons were few and far between, there was as yet a much smaller reading public and, most important of all, there were no effective copyright laws. Moreover, the idea that it was beneath the dignity of an author, especially of a poet, to take money for his writings, died hard. Before Klopstock's time,

[1] For an admirable study of conditions in England see the two books by A. S. Collins, *Authorship in the days of Johnson*, 1927, and *The Profession of Letters*, 1928, or the briefer account in F. A. Mumby's *Publishing and Bookselling*, 1930.

as Goethe tells us in *Dichtung und Wahrheit*, 'the book trade was chiefly concerned with important learned works, books in steady demand, for which a modest honorarium was paid. The production of poetical works was looked upon as something sacred, and it was considered almost simony to accept or bargain for payment for them'.[1] Goethe takes the relations between Gottsched and his publisher Breitkopf as typical for that age. They lived in the same house, on the friendliest terms, and what the one gained in fame the other made up for in profits. In the circumstances of those days, a young author could consider himself lucky if he found a publisher to print his work, as success, especially in 'belles lettres',was so difficult to prophesy. If he made a name for himself, he was usually by that time in some official position and independent of literary earnings.

The authors of the sixteenth and seventeenth centuries had been men of academic training, and all of them, even Philipp von Zesen, or such a rolling stone as Grimmelshausen, had aimed at a post in the service of some state or municipality. It was their writing in many cases that enabled them to attract the attention of those high personages who had the gift of such posts or sinecures and who became in this sense their patrons, much as the ministers of state did in England. It was customary for authors, or publishers, for example, of reprints and translations, to reward the services of patrons by fulsome dedications, though the services might not necessarily be of a financial nature. It was desirable to enjoy the protection of some authority in publishing any work that might cause its author or printer difficulties. But owing to the intellectual deficiencies of the German aristocracy, the high prestige of French literature in court circles, and the lack of a capital where the habit of patronage might spread by emulation, nothing resembling the patronage of native poetry so extensively practised by the English aristocracy occurred in Germany.

[1] *Dichtung und Wahrheit*, Teil III, 12. Buch.

There was accordingly no profession of letters worthy of the name in Germany in the first half of the eighteenth century. Goethe has given us the classical description of the social position of literary men at that time.

German poets, being no longer members of a gild that could act as one man, enjoyed no advantages whatever in civil society. They had neither protection, social position nor esteem unless some other circumstance than their writing favoured them, and it was simply a matter of chance whether talent brought its owner honour or disgrace. A poor mortal, fully conscious of his mental powers, had to make his way in life as best he could and squander the gifts he had received from the muses in the struggle with the needs of the moment. The occasional poem, the first and most genuine of all *genres,* fell into such disrepute that the nation has not even yet attained to a conception of its high value, and a poet, even if he did not go the way of poor Günther, played a most melancholy rôle in the world, as a mere jester and parasite, so that both in the theatre and on the stage of life he was a personage whom anyone could treat just as he wished.

If on the other hand the Muse visited men of standing, she conferred on them a glory that was reflected back on to its source. Urbane aristocrats like Hagedorn, worthy city fathers like Brockes, distinguished scholars like Haller were accounted among the first men of the nation, the peers of those highest in birth and social esteem. And those men were particularly admired who besides possessing this agreeable talent had proved their worth as active and reliable men of affairs. Uz, Rabener, Weisse accordingly enjoyed a quite peculiar esteem, because they combined qualities of such an opposing character that they are seldom found together.[1]

The first German poet who looked upon his writing as a serious and all-absorbing calling, and who compelled respect from his countrymen solely on his literary merits, was Klopstock. In a certain sense he was, like Pope in England, the first professional writer of his country. But he was not able, as Pope was, to make himself independent of private patrons because of the ready sale of his works among an

[1] *Dichtung und Wahrheit,* Teil II, 10. Buch.

admiring public. He required a Maecenas, and found one in the king of Denmark. The first author of any standing who maintained himself for a lengthy period by writing for the open market was Lessing, and he needed all his spirit and Spartan endurance to make a bare living.

The possibility of earning money by writing depended on three factors, the existence of a public willing and able to buy books, of publishers willing to accept and pay for them and of effective legal protection against literary piracy. The political disunity of Germany made it impossible in the eighteenth century for publishers to secure a copyright law that would apply to the whole Empire. The first work for which legal copyright in the whole of Germany was sanctioned by the Diet was the definitive edition of Goethe's works, begun in 1828. There was no uniform law for the whole of Germany before the foundation of the German Empire. The state censorship that existed in all the leading states after the Reformation, with the system of 'privileges', granted by individual states for particular books for a short period, afforded a certain amount of protection to publishers, as long as the demand for books was still slight. Moreover, the states and towns controlled all those printing establishments that were not subject to gild regulations, and in general only permitted the establishment of presses in the larger towns. But as soon as piracy became profitable these measures of control proved quite ineffective. From the biography of G. J. Göschen, who published the works of so many leading writers of the classical age, it is clear that pirates were the bane of a publisher's life. In many small states in the eighteenth century the pirating by local printers of editions protected in some other state was even officially tolerated, for the encouragement of home industries. Baden was a very bad offender in this respect. Göschen had infinite trouble with Schmieder of Karlsruhe, in spite of many protests to the Margrave of Baden. But Schmieder was only one of many. There were others in Vienna, Berlin, Hamburg and every large town, and 'privileges' obtained at considerable expense were almost useless. It was not until 1794 that the first step towards the suppression of literary piracy was taken by Prussia, by a provision in the 'Preussisches Landrecht', and it was over forty years before the provision was made effective and imitated by other leading states. The result was that unauthorised editions of any book that seemed likely to prove popular followed hard on the heels of the first impression. The only remedy open to the legitimate publisher was the issue of special cheap editions to undersell the pirates, a step that was often taken by Göschen, Cotta and others.

In this respect then conditions were infinitely less favourable to the professional writer in Germany than in England, where a copyright act had been passed by Parliament on the petition of the booksellers in 1710. The only grievances of the English booksellers were that the penalties were not severe enough and that they had not been granted rights in perpetuity, but only for a limited period. Copyright was secured for fourteen years, and was renewable if the author was still alive for a further period of fourteen years. The Act did not apply to Ireland and was not imitated by the Irish Parliament, so English writers of popular works had practically no sale in Ireland, where they were pirated immediately. A publisher was still liable to be undersold in England itself by Irish or foreign pirate printers, but on the whole he was sufficiently protected.

In view of the danger of piracy and the risk that is always involved in publishing 'belles lettres', the terms offered by German publishers, at any rate in the second half of the century, do not seem to have been unreasonable. Of course they varied considerably, according to the power and desire of both sides to make a bargain, and other special circumstances. First novels or plays naturally did not earn high fees, but authors with a name were able to command quite considerable sums for their copyright. A few examples may be given from the records of the more important publishing firms, and particularly from those of G. J. Göschen, who was more generous than most publishers and was treated by many of his most distinguished clients as a personal friend.

At the beginning of the century, authors seldom received more than a trifling sum in money from their publishers, partly, as explained in Goethe's words above, because they disdained and did not need such earnings, and partly because their writings were by no means popular in character. The relations between Gottsched and Breitkopf have been mentioned. Those between Gellert and his publisher Wendler are an even better example for the transition period, when publishers, but not writers, had realised the commercial possibilities of more popular writings. Wendler bought the complete rights of the *Fables*, 'perhaps the most popular book of the eighteenth century', for a ducat (less than three Thalers) a sheet, and made a fortune out of them. In 1787, twenty years after his retirement, the stock and copyright of Gellert's works were sold for 10,000 Thalers, and Wendler had long had the reputation of a philanthropist for the gifts he had been able to make to charitable causes. When Klopstock and Wieland published their first works, their honoraria were still very low. For the first books of the *Messias* (1749) Klopstock received three Thalers a sheet. For the very different *Komische Erzählungen* (1765) Wieland was remunerated at about the same rate. But by 1773 Klopstock was receiving twelve Thalers a sheet for his still unfinished epic, while Wieland, at the height of the literary boom, asked and received up to fifteen or sixteen Thalers a sheet from Reich for his extremely longwinded later works. From this publisher alone Wieland drew 6700 Thalers, enough to keep him and his family for ten years,[1] while the *Collected Works* published later by Göschen brought him in at least 7000

[1] Figures from Goldfriedrich, *Geschichte des deutschen Buchhandels*, Leipzig, 1909, III, 118 ff.

Thalers.[1] Even authors of the middling sort were being paid five to six and a half Thalers a sheet by Reich in the 70's, and translators two Thalers.

In the classical period proper, we may note that Schiller's total gain from the book edition of his second play *Fiesco*, published by Schwan of Mannheim, was ten Karolin (about ten guineas), as he complained in 1788, when a third edition was being brought out. For the first instalment of his *Thirty Years' War* for Göschen's *Damenkalender*, on the other hand, he was paid a year in advance 400 Thalers (over £60). At this rate Schiller hoped to make 1000 Thalers a year from his writings. Goethe received 15 Thalers a sheet for the *Collected Works* brought out by Göschen in the late 'eighties. For the eight volumes he received a lump sum of 2000 Thalers (£300). Much of this work had of course appeared already. For new work he received far higher payment. For his contributions to Schiller's *Horen* for instance he received from Cotta 40 Thalers (£6) a sheet. A. W. Schlegel received half that amount. The highest honorarium paid by Göschen seems to have been the 30 Thalers (£4. 10s) a sheet paid to F. A. Wolf for his edition of Homer, more than was paid to A. Müllner for the second edition of his very popular play *Die Schuld* (for which the honorarium was 26 Thalers a sheet, but the first edition had already brought the author 200 Thalers). Among the more popular novels of the time, Thümmel's *Reiseroman*, in ten slim volumes, earned for the author 5000 Thalers (£750) from Göschen, more than Goethe and Klopstock together received from him for his editions of their collected works.[2]

Compared with what could be earned in England by writers of no greater merit, these sums were very small. There too, of course, new writers or those who did not press their claims received little, but the established writer could make high demands. So though Goldsmith only made £60

---

[1] K. Buchner, *Wieland und G. J. Göschen*, Stuttgart, 1874.
[2] See Viscount Goschen, *Life of G. J. Goschen*, London, 1903.

out of the *Vicar of Wakefield*, Fielding's *Tom Jones* brought him £700, and *Amelia* £1000, while *Rasselas* had earned Johnson £125 even in 1749. A really successful play was worth about £150 by 1780. Works of learning were very well paid for. The sums received by Schiller tor his historical writings seem modest beside Robertson's £600 for *The History of Scotland*, and £4500 for *Charles V*, or Hume's £3400 earned from *The History of England* between 1754 and 1760, or Smollett's £2000 in 1758, and Henry's £3300 in the 'seventies, for similar works. Percy gained £300 from his *Reliques* in 1765, and Adam Smith £500 for the first edition alone of *The Wealth of Nations* in 1776. As to periodicals, the £6 a sheet paid by Cotta to Goethe for *Die Horen* may be compared with Constable's ten to twenty guineas for reviews in *The Edinburgh Review* a few years later. The Jena *Litteratur-Zeitung* paid only 15 Thalers a sheet (£2. 5s.) for reviews. The enormous sums earned by Byron, and above all by Scott, in the literary boom of the early nineteenth century, were beyond the wildest dreams of any German author. Scott could make over £10,000 a year on his novels alone. Goethe received about £22,500 in the course of his lifetime from Cotta. This sum, together with the £300 which Göschen had paid him for the first collected edition of his works, represented almost the whole of his literary earnings. So Scott earned more from literature in three years than Goethe in all his long life.

The chief cause for the disparity between the two countries in the matter of literary earnings was no doubt, as has already been suggested, the more effective monopoly conferred by the possession of copyright in England, combined with the greater public demand for books there. As to the size of the reading public in Germany, the following figures will give some idea. In Germany as in England there was a wider and steadier market for the 'household stuff of literature', Isaac D'Israeli's term for cookery books, 'useful knowledge for the million', and so forth, than for the higher flights of literature. One of the most profitable publications of the leading Leipzig bookseller, P. E. Reich, was Peplier's *French Grammar*, of which editions of 5000 copies continued to be printed until the nineteenth century.[1] Much the best seller that Göschen ever acquired was R. Z. Becker's *Noth- und Hülfsbuch*, a kind of 'Outline of Knowledge' for the countryman in 800 pages, sold for eightpence. Of this 30,000 copies were printed for the first edition in 1787—it took two years to print them. Eleven authorised and four unauthorised editions had appeared by 1791. By 1811, according to its author, a million copies of this work had been issued.[2] The public for whom works such as this were published was of course not interested in literature proper, but the figure gives some idea of the numbers of buyers who might be attracted by the popular 'Calendars' that the pedlars carried in their packs. In the country round about Zürich 2500 copies of a Calendar could be sold in a year by such pedlars.[3] Next in order of popularity came the Calendars for better educated people, like Göschen's *Historischer Kalender für Damen*, of the first issue of which 7000 copies were sold in 1789, a record sale. It was for this calendar that Schiller wrote his *Thirty Years' War*. Of books properly so called, it was very rarely that more than three or four thousand copies were sold. Of Goethe's *Works* (1787–90) Göschen printed an ordinary edition of 2000 and a cheap edition of 3000, but they sold very slowly. There were only 602 subscribers to the whole series, and after two years only 536 other copies of the first four volumes had been sold, together with two or three hundred copies each of single plays, etc.[4] Even a popular play like *Die Schuld* was only bought by some five thousand people.[5]

[1] Goldfriedrich, *op. cit.* III, 41.

[2] *Life of G. J. Göschen*, I, 94. This works out at 40,000 a year, a figure difficult to accept. Murray in England considered 5–10,000 a year for Mrs Rundell's *Domestic Cookery* a very high figure.

[3] Goldfriedrich, *op. cit.* II, 279.

[4] *Life of G. J. Goschen*, I, 165.

[5] *Ibid.* II, 420 (1st edition 2000, 2nd 3000).

This figure was however exceeded by Schiller's *Tell*, of which 7000 copies were sold in a few weeks. A second edition of 3000 was exhausted by the end of the year. Of *Wallenstein* 3500 copies had been sold in two months.[1]

Perhaps a better indication of the size of the reading public for good literature is the circulation of the literary magazines and reviews. The best established of the reviews was the Jena *Litteratur-Zeitung*, which, as Göschen wrote to Wieland,[2] was 'read by all classes in every city, in every little town, almost in every village' of Germany. Yet 2000 copies were sufficient. Göschen's explanation is that ten or twenty people read a borrowed copy of this and other periodicals and books to one who bought them. *Die Horen*, with its staff of all the talents, only approached this circulation with its first number, of which nearly 1800 copies were sold, twelve or more copies being ordered even in small towns. Wieland's *Teutscher Merkur*, a private venture, cannot have had a circulation of much more than a thousand.[3] In addition to these there were at any time from 1775 onwards usually some half-dozen reviews and up to a dozen literary magazines in existence, most of them short-lived and with a small circulation, often restricted to the neighbourhood of the place of production. There were *Gelehrte Anzeigen* for instance in most universities and many capitals and Free Towns. The best known were those of Leipzig, Göttingen and Frankfort, in addition to the review already mentioned. Two other reviews of importance were Nicolai's *Bibliothek der schönen Wissenschaften und freien Künste* (mostly concerned with art) and his *Allgemeine deutsche Bibliothek*. Among the more famous magazines of the last quarter of the century may be mentioned, in addition to the *Teutscher Merkur* (1773–1810) and Schiller's *Horen* (1795–7), the *Teutsche Chronik* of Schubart (1774–81), the

---

[1] J. H. Eckardt, *Schillers Verleger*, Börsenblatt, 1905.
[2] *Life of G. J. Goschen*, I, 305.
[3] *Ibid.* I, 98. About 800 copies were to be sold through Göschen, and 'a certain number' of subscribers were supplied by post.

Deutsches Museum of Boie (1776–91), the *Berliner Literarisches Wochenblatt* (1776–97), the *Berlinische Monatsschrift* (1783–1811), Schiller's *Thalia* (1785–91), Bertuch's *Journal des Luxus und der Moden* (1786–1826), Archenholtz's *Litteratur- und Völkerkunde* and *Minerva* (1782–1809), A. W. Schlegel's *Athenäum* (1798–1800), Goethe's *Propyläen* (1798–1800).[1] Few of these would have a circulation of more than a few hundred copies. Of the *Völkerkunde* for instance, Göschen says in 1785 that it is read everywhere, yet his sale is only 400 copies.

Apart from the learned and the literary periodicals there were further, from early in the eighteenth century, a large number of so-called 'Journals' modelled on the English *Tatler* and *Spectator*, containing essays of general interest on a wide range of subjects, usually rather didactic in tone. The avowed aim of their editors was to raise the moral and intellectual standards of the middle class by the dissemination of useful knowledge and the philosophy of 'Aufklärung'. They flourished wherever a large middle-class public could be reached. Of the 182 Moral Weeklies that appeared in Germany between 1713 and 1761, almost all short-lived and appealing only to a local public, more than one-third were published in either Hamburg or Leipzig, the chief commercial centres. The first appeared in Hamburg in 1713, and the most influential were the Hamburg *Patriot* (1724–6), edited by Brockes and his friends, which had 5000 subscribers, and Gottsched's two weeklies in Leipzig (1725–7). The interest taken in these productions was so great that they were frequently reprinted in collected form and of course often pirated. Their successors in the last third of the century were publications like Möser's *Patriotische Phantasien*, Claudius' *Wandsbecker Bote* and the Almanachs and Journals already mentioned. It was mainly for the supply of such ephemeral literature and of newspapers that the Reading

---

[1] For complete lists see R. F. Arnold, *Bücherkunde*, section I, 3 *b* and III, 10, and for a full historical account Goldfriedrich, *op. cit.* II, 55 ff.

Clubs, so popular from the 'eighties onwards, were started. With the circulating libraries that began to flourish at about the same date the habit of reading spread with ever-increasing rapidity, so that the old-fashioned began to complain of the 'reading madness' of the young generation and even Goethe deplored the effects of so much indiscriminate light reading:

> Zwar sind sie an das Beste nicht gewöhnt
> Allein, sie haben schrecklich viel gelesen.

or

> Und was das Allerschlimmste bleibt,
> Gar mancher kommt vom Lesen der Journale.
>
> (*Faust*, Vorspiel.)

'Formerly', says a provincial journalist in 1806, 'reading was the affair of the scholar and the truly cultivated man. Now it is a general habit, even of the lower classes, not only in the towns but in the country too.' Even soldiers of the town guard take out books from the circulating library, says another already in 1780. The well-read craftsmen mentioned by Goethe, Moritz and others do not seem to have been very rare exceptions, and one master-tailor in Hanau had a library of 3600 volumes.[1]

For comparison we may take again a few figures from England, where according to the successful bookseller Lackington, writing at the end of the eighteenth century, more than four times as many books were then being sold as were sold twenty years earlier. 'The poorer sort of farmers, and even the poor country people in general', he says, got their children to read novels to them now in the winter evenings instead of telling ghost stories.[2] Lackington sometimes stocked 6000 copies of one book. Of a poem like Roger's *Pleasures of Memory* 8000 copies were printed and sold between 1792 and 1800, and by 1816 a further 10,000. Long before this over 1200 copies of Gray's *Odes* had been sold

---

[1] Goldfriedrich, *op. cit.* III, 256.
[2] Collins, *Profession of Letters*, p. 83.

in a month (in 1757), and a really popular play like Cumberland's *West Indian* (1771) could be sold at the rate of 12,000 in a season.[1] As to periodicals, the circulation of the *Gentleman's Magazine* had reached 10,000 by 1739, and a few years later 15,000, though it had many rivals, for between 1731 and 1780 sixty magazines were started in London, ten in Scotland and eleven in Ireland.[2] The later reviews on a higher intellectual level also sold freely. The sale of the *Edinburgh* in its best days (about 1808) was 11,000 copies, and that of its rival the *Quarterly* had reached 12,000 by 1817. At the height of the Romantic movement record sales were achieved by Byron's and Scott's poems and Scott's novels. Of *The Lady of the Lake* 44,000 copies were sold before 1830; 10,000 copies of *The Corsair* were sold on the day of issue. When eight volumes of the 1829 collected edition of Scott's novels had appeared, the monthly sale had reached 35,000.

It will be clear that there were good reasons for the unremunerative nature of the profession of letters in Germany, apart from the publisher's desire for profit, but it was natural that at the time this last factor should be most stressed by writers. Several attempts were made by writers for whom literary earnings were important to secure a greater material return for their labours by cutting out the publisher. Ideas of this kind went back as far as Leibniz. In the eighteenth century it was Bode, soon joined for a time by Lessing, who first attempted to realise them in his *Buchhandlung der Gelehrten* in Hamburg (1767). This was to be a press and publishing house run in the interests of first-rate authors. It was hoped that copies of books published would be ordered direct from Hamburg and paid for in cash, instead of being sent to Leipzig and sold through the agency of the 'Kommissionäre' there, or exchanged for the products of some other publishing firm, still a common practice.

There might have been some hope for Bode's undertaking

[1] Collins, *Authorship in the Days of Johnson*, p. 255.
[2] *Ibid.* p. 240.

if there had been a sufficient number of retail booksellers in Germany for the distribution of his publications, but book production and distribution were still closely linked. A bookseller was usually a publisher and *vice versa*. The old system had been for the bookseller-publisher to go to the book-fair at Leipzig or Frankfort with a stock of his own publications and exchange them for the books of other firms. He would then have a varied stock of books to sell at home. The system was adapted to the chaotic state of the currency in Germany after the Thirty Years' War, but it naturally brought with it many disadvantages, and had to be modified to suit changing conditions in the eighteenth century. But although books were no longer exchanged unbound, regardless of quality, and booksellers were often allowed to stock books on the 'condition' that they should be returnable if unsold before the following fair ('Konditionsgeschäft'), Leipzig retained its hold on the book trade through its 'Kommissionäre' or wholesale booksellers, who acted as middlemen between the big publishers and the country booksellers. The country booksellers, having little capital, would not pay Bode cash when they could have books from Leipzig 'for sale or return'. This difficulty, combined with piracy, proved fatal to the Hamburg experiment and to a rather similar but better organised one begun at Dessau in 1781, with which Wieland and Bertuch were closely associated.

The idea had meanwhile been given much publicity by Klopstock, the most respected author of the day. He suggested the formation of a German Academy, which should undertake the publication of the best new books and provide for the material needs of the leading authors and scholars of the day. Klopstock's ideas were very much in the air, but his preliminary notice, evoked a reply from the publishers and aroused great interest, so that his *Gelehrtenrepublik*, the book about the proposed academy for which he invited subscriptions, was sold without the help of the booksellers in large numbers all over the country. Two hundred and fifty admirers came forward to collect subscribers, and in all 3600 subscriptions were sent in. 6600 copies of the first part of the book were printed, an enormous edition for those days, but the second part never appeared because the first proved almost unreadable, with its description of the proposed hierarchy of the cultured, ranging from creative authors and scholars and their various 'gilds' down to the 'Volk' willing to buy their works, its tables of laws, expressed in language borrowed partly from the gilds and partly from the ancient 'bards', and its imaginary account of proceedings at the Diet of the Republic. But the astonishing success of Klopstock's appeal for subscriptions, the nearest German parallel to the success of Pope with his *Homer* (for which 6000 subscribed), encouraged other authors to imitate him. Bürger published his poems in this way, and Lessing his *Nathan*, of which the first edition of 2000 was fully subscribed. And many who did not appeal publicly for subscribers printed their first works at their own expense. In this case they usually lost heavily. Goethe, advised by Merck, brought out his *Götz* in this way and Schiller his *Räuber*, with 150 Gulden borrowed from friends, and both lost their money.[1]

Apart from the men of letters proper there were journalists and publicists, some of whom made a precarious living by writing. It is usual to make a distinction between periodicals and newspapers, but at this early date the distinction was not so clear as it is to-day, for newspapers did not necessarily appear daily or contain very much in the way of current news. The most influential publicist of the century, one might almost say the only man who deserved the name, was the Göttingen historian A. L. von Schlözer, whose *Briefwechsel meist historischen und politischen Inhalts* (1776–82) and *Staatsanzeigen* (1783–94), periodicals appearing about six

---

[1] For the history and organisation of the book trade and the relations between authors and publishers see, in addition to works cited, *Das Buchgewerbe und die Kultur*, Leipzig, 1907.

times a year, were read even by monarchs and exercised a considerable influence in minor political affairs. Even Maria Theresa is said to have urged her privy council to think twice about matters that Schlözer was likely to criticise. His organs were particularly effective in directing public attention to acts of petty tyranny on the part of minor rulers or their officials. Sometimes as many as 4000 copies of his *Staatsanzeigen* were sold. Schlözer was not however a professional journalist, or his influence would have been negligible, but a public-spirited and highly respected professor of history in the leading university of Germany. A further advantage he enjoyed was that as Göttingen was in the state of Hanover his writings were not nearly so strictly censored as they would have been in any other state. Most of his material was sent in by correspondents, often people of high standing, who desired to bring something before the public in this forum and received no material reward except perhaps a free copy or two.[1] The editors of the other leading periodicals were also almost all scholars, active or retired officials, or authors who had made a name with weightier writings. Justus Möser, Häberlin, L. von Göckingk, S. von Bibra, K. F. von Moser, Büsching, Wieland, Boie may be mentioned among the editors of this kind who at least occasionally commented on current affairs. In the south, however, there were two men, Schubart (*Deutsche Chronik*) and Weckherlin (*Das graue Ungeheuer* and two other periodicals), who lived dangerously as professional political journalists.

There were regular newspapers of a kind, it seems, in almost every considerable German town by the end of the seventeenth century. They had developed gradually here as elsewhere out of the written newsletters of the late Middle Ages, *pari passu* with the growth of trade and the improvement of communications. Weekly printed newspapers are proved to have existed from as early as 1609 in Germany. Then papers began to appear two or three times a week. The

---

[1] Biedermann, I, 120.

ancestor of the *Leipziger Zeitung* was the first daily (from 1660). The news in these papers was mainly political, and, because of the censor, fuller about foreign affairs than about events nearer home. About this time too there were opened in many German towns, following Paris and London, the first 'Offices of Intelligence' ('Adress-Comptoire') where local announcements of many kinds were to be read, corresponding roughly to the small advertisements of the modern newspaper (lost and found, sale and exchange, property for sale or to let, coach times, etc.), and these offices began to publish their own advertisers (*Anzeigen, Intelligenzblätter*). When these took in notices of town appointments, marriages, births and deaths and other items of local news they were beginning to resemble local newspapers. In the eighteenth century there were a score or so of local 'Advertisers', one or two newssheets in almost every little capital and a few better ones in Free Towns and the capitals of the larger states. In Berlin for instance there was the *Vossische Zeitung* (so styled from 1785, but with a history going back to the middle of the seventeenth century), and the *Haude-Spenersche Zeitung*, founded in 1740, as well as the official *Advertiser*. It was for the *Vossische* that Lessing was engaged to write reviews, as editor of the 'learned' section, soon after his arrival in Berlin. His cousin Mylius, who initiated him into journalism, may be taken as a type of the numerous second-rate literati of that day. For years he led a hand-to-mouth existence by editing a series of short-lived 'Moral Weeklies' and by writing odd articles for the papers of others.[1] The German newspapers produced by writers of this stamp cannot be said to have attained a high level. The best were to be found in the centres of commerce, Hamburg, Frankfort-on-Main and Leipzig. Readers interested in politics used the foreign papers, especially the Dutch ones, to supplement them, and in spite of prohibitions, written bulletins continued to circulate more intimate items of news

[1] See E. Schmidt, *Lessing*, I, 60 ff.

and gossip until late in the century. Even the printed papers consisted for the most part of a mass of ill-sifted 'faits divers'.[1]

The number of pens that were kept busy to produce this abundance of printed matter was of course large. Old-fashioned authors like Möser were constantly complaining about the excessive number of 'Gelehrten' and 'Schriftsteller' —'scholar' and 'writer' were then almost synonymous expressions. Knigge said that the title of scholar was as common in Germany as that of gentleman in England, and was applied to every wretched versifier, compiler, journalist, anecdote-hunter, translator, plagiarist and in fact to anyone who abused the incomprehensible indulgence of the public to publish whole volumes of nonsense or of things far better said before. Goethe and Schiller castigated such writers singly and in groups in their *Xenien*, in couplets such as the following:

> *Sachen, so gesucht werden.*
> Einen Bedienten wünscht man zu haben, der leserlich schreibet
>   Und orthographisch, jedoch nichts in Bell-Lettres getan.[2]

Various attempts were made by contemporaries to estimate the number of living German 'writers'. On the basis of these, Goldfriedrich states that in 1773 Germany had 3000 writers, and in 1787 already 6000, so that the number had doubled in the fourteen years between *Götz von Berlichingen* and *Egmont*. About the year 1780 it is said that there were 133 writers living in Leipzig, 77 in Dresden, 33 in Wittenberg, 21 in Budissin, and nearly 400 more scattered over some 200 towns and villages in Saxony alone.[3] Most of these must have been very small fry. Besides the authors who

---

[1] For a large number of representative extracts see the volumes of *Das Neueste von gestern*, edited by E. Buchner.

For a brief history of the newspaper see Goldfriedrich, *op. cit.* II, 39 ff.; K. Bücher in *Kultur der Gegenwart*, I, 1, Leipzig, 1906; H. Diez, *Das Zeitungswesen*, 2nd ed. 1919; Biedermann, *op. cit.* vol. I.

[2] *Wanted.* Man-servant required who writes legibly and spells well, but has done nothing in belles lettres.

[3] Weiz, *Das gelehrte Sachsen*, 1780, quoted Goldfriedrich, III, 249.

figure in histories of literature, they would include dozens of forgotten novelists, dramatists and scholars and a much larger number of occasional contributors to newspapers and journals, translators, editors of school texts, reviewers, proof-readers and the like. But the figures indicate at least a very high degree of intellectual activity in a great variety of places. According to another estimate quoted by Goldfriedrich, this activity was most intense in Göttingen (with one writer to every hundred inhabitants) and Leipzig (with 1 to 170). Berlin (with 1 to 675) and Vienna (with 1 to 800), in spite of their political importance, are far behind the centres of learning and the book trade. Taking the most conservative estimates, the numbers of writers and of writings must at least have doubled in the last three decades of the century. In the early 'nineties, says the Bernese bookseller Heinzmann, there were some 300 novels, original or translated, appearing in German every year,[1] while Herr von Göckingk even in 1784 knew of some 217 newspapers and advertisers appearing in Germany and thought that if the smallest and most primitive were included, the number could be doubled.[2] Between 1740 (the year selected by contemporaries as the turning-point) and 1800, Germany had changed from a country so unproductive of native literature that every educated man had depended on foreign writings for his culture to a land of 'poets and thinkers', amongst whom the few known to history were the apex of a pyramid firmly based on a countless mass of pedants and scribblers. It had developed a classical literature, and also something very like an intellectual proletariat.

[1] Goldfriedrich, III, 274.
[2] Quoted in P. Kampffmeyer, *Geschichte der modernen Gesellschaftsklassen in Deutschland*, 3rd ed. Berlin, 1921, p. 338.

Chapter II

THE INFLUENCE OF POLITICAL, ECONOMIC AND SOCIAL FACTORS ON LITERATURE

In the earlier chapters an attempt has been made to analyse the political and economic structure of German society in the eighteenth century, and to describe the social inheritance, the habitual point of view and the standard of living of each of the great social classes. In this final chapter some indication will be offered of the importance of this material for the student of classical German literature and the German national character.

Social and political factors exercise at all times a pervasive influence on culture in general, an influence which is none the less important for being difficult to trace with any final certainty. The study of them is an unsatisfactory pursuit for the precise scholar, because the result can hardly be more than an essay, but this is unfortunately the case with many other branches of literary study and criticism. Their interest is usually in inverse proportion to the degree of accuracy that can be attained in the result. Social influences are no more intangible than the personality of an author or the literary value of a work, and perhaps no less worthy of study.

In this brief study we will focus our attention first on the political and then on the economic and social influences, remembering always that to isolate any one influence completely from all others is impossible. Let us enquire in the first place what features in German literature and intellectual life can best be understood as a consequence of 'Klein-staaterei' and absolutism.

It is obvious that an association of jealous small states could not possess a single metropolis like London or Paris, where, in Goethe's words to Eckermann, 'the best minds of a great nation are assembled in one place, teaching and stimulating each other in daily intercourse, contention and rivalry, where the best products of nature and art from every corner of the earth are always there for them to see with their own eyes, where they are reminded whenever they cross a bridge or a square of a great past and where every street corner has seen history in the making'.[1] In his later years Goethe was for ever drawing unfavourable contrasts between his own country and France in this respect, and, though not blind to the dangers of over-centralisation, envying the French that high degree of general culture that gave even young writers, and men of no social standing like Béranger, the support of an intellectual and artistic tradition.

It is clear of course that in order to enjoy similar benefits it would have been necessary for Germany not only to have a capital, but also to have developed, like France, in a way that had made a capital a necessity, for the possession of a capital and of a unified tradition are to be regarded as different manifestations of one process rather than as cause and effect. It is true further that when a country once has a metropolis, a further concentration of intellectual life is bound to follow. This effect will be considered later, when French literature, as eminently 'social', will be contrasted with German. But the first and most general consequence of separatism, which in a sense includes all the others, is one which can hardly be denied. It is the lack of general culture, of a national style, that German weakness lamented by Goethe, Nietzsche and so many others down to the present day. It is remarkable, as has often been pointed out, that Germany succeeded, in the absence of such a national tradition and of political institutions to support it, in producing a literature that came to be looked upon as classical, though it was, in Freytag's phrase, 'the almost miraculous creation of a soul without a body'. But it seems probable that the writers of any 'classical age' have

[1] Eckermann, *Gespräche*, under May 3rd, 1827.

been leaders as well as led—for even in formulating views commonly held but necessarily vague a writer takes the lead, like the chairman of a committee—and that the German classics only differed from the French or the Greek in being rather further ahead of their age, though not so far removed from the ways of thinking of any of their countrymen that a later generation could not accept them as classics in the primary sense, namely as the best authors to be read in the classes of their schools. Whether on a large view of world literature they are to be considered classical in the more ambiguous sense that depends on the opposition of classical and romantic is a further question to which we shall return.

We must remember that in denying Germany 'general culture' Goethe was contrasting it with France. The Germans had in reality already a great deal in common, though less than their western neighbours. They were descended, if not from one race, at least from a small number of races fused by long generations of intermarriage. They had lived together for centuries on the same land. It is true that these geographical and blood ties fostered provincial rather than national loyalties at this stage, but the boundaries of these provinces were the result of dynastic, not of racial history, and a kind of clan feeling extended even then beyond them. On the other hand the geographical factors making for national unity were rather weaker than they would have been if the boundaries of the German-speaking lands as a whole had not been so vague and shifting. It was possible, though difficult in that stay-at-home age, to form a mental image of one's small state as a unit, but 'Germany' was far too amorphous to evoke in the minds of German patriots images such as those which the thought of 'England' called up in the mind of Shakespeare's John of Gaunt—

> This precious stone set in the silver sea,
> Which serves it in the office of a wall,
> Or as a moat defensive to a house,
> Against the envy of less happier lands.

Mr McDougall has pointed out how important such images are for the formation of what he calls a 'group mind'; for confirmation we have only to think of the use made of the magic word 'island' in English patriotic literature.

If common racial origins and geographical propinquity were important at least potentially, language was already a strong and steadily increasing force making for unity. It had been so at times in the Middle Ages, but if we compare the beginning of the seventeenth century with the middle of the eighteenth as regards the literary use of German, we find a remarkable development. In a graph showing the number of German books and the number of Latin books published each year during that period, the line for Latin is at first more than twice as high as that for German. Both lines drop suddenly for the period of the Thirty Years' War (1618–48), the Latin one much more steeply than the German, though it rises again about 1650, when there are again twice as many Latin books published as German. But from that point the lines gradually converge, they cross each other just after 1680, and then, though both have their ups and downs, the general tendency of the German line is steeply upwards, that of the Latin line slowly down, so that by the end of the 1760's, when Goethe's first book appeared, the relative position of 1610 was reversed, German standing now four times as high as Latin, though the total number of books published, Latin, German and French, was about the same as in 1610 (over 1500 volumes). The quantitative increase in the use of German for the communication of thought coincided naturally with the gradual unification and purification of the language, the emergence of a literary language which Germans were proud to own. Luther's bible and catechism, in daily use in home, church and school, gradually made the mass of the people acquainted with a standard book German distinct from their dialect, a standard that here as in other countries had been made both more necessary and more easily attainable by the invention of printing in the preceding century. Luther's work was continued by Opitz and his school, with the example of the Pléiade before their eyes, and through the efforts of the various 'Language Societies' their influence slowly began to permeate educated circles. It was a conscious attempt to improve the German language, and there was certainly national pride behind it, but it was a long time before scholars and courtiers could be persuaded that German could be made into as fit a vehicle of communication as Latin or French. Leibniz had still to confess that though a German boy spoke his own language at twelve, he had forgotten it by the time he was a student, to become a Frenchified courtier or a pedantic Latinist. But the vernacular was used more and more for serious purposes, and 'Meissner Deutsch' recognised as the best German by wider and wider circles.

Before the middle of the eighteenth century there was also already a fairly widespread desire for national originality in literary matters in Germany, even though patriotic feeling in the political sense hardly existed. This desire does not seem to have been common in the Middle Ages, when the originality of individual authors too was much less stressed than now, and one is tempted to assume that it arose in Germany mainly through the contagious influence of France. Certainly French taunts had a marked effect in stimulating it. When le père Bouhours had asserted that it was impossible for a German to be a *bel esprit*, Thomasius, the most progressive professor of his day (we have seen that he was the first to lecture in German, in 1687), had retorted that at least they were better scholars, because they had more patience. He admitted that the French had a livelier temperament, but thought that freedom from religious, social and political restrictions would soon do much to foster German originality. For fifty years after this the general opinion seemed to be that it did not much matter whether the works published in German were original or translations provided that they were

good, though the ultimate aim in view was an original
German literature. Gottsched's work for instance and that
of his circle consisted mainly of translations and adaptations.
But in 1740 Mauvillon, a French teacher in Brunswick,
roused German writers from their complacency by challenging them in his *Lettres françaises et germaniques* to name
a single German author who had any reputation abroad, or
whose work did not consist almost entirely of translations.
The effect of this and similar taunts was to make Germany
conscious of its language and literature as a national possession, and eager for literary prestige, long before it was a
nation in any other respect, and the fact that the word
'German' had a definite meaning and one charged with
emotion, at least as applied to language and literature, was
to prove very important for the political unification of
Germany later. It would hardly be too much to say that the
liberals of 1848 were still fighting for a Germany worthy of
Goethe, Schiller and Kant.

It cannot therefore be said that there was nothing in the
daily life of a German to remind him of kinship with a
community that extended beyond the boundaries of his small
state, but we easily realise how vague and inadequate these
reminders were if we contrast them with the symbols of
national unity consciously made use of in recent times. It is
undeniable that, as even the cosmopolitan Goethe who wrote
Dichtung und Wahrheit complained, German literature in the
eighteenth century was sadly lacking in 'national subjects'.
'If we look closely, what German literature lacked was a
subject, and a national one; there was never any lack of
talents.' 'It was Frederick the Great and the Seven Years'
War that first gave German literature a subject with a real
greatness and living interest.'[1] Not that a 'national subject'
is the only or even the most important factor required for
great literature. Goethe was probably inclined to stress
subject-matter too much at the period when he wrote

[1] *Dichtung und Wahrheit*, Bk. 7.

Dichtung und Wahrheit, and a study of some of the later German work on 'national' themes almost drives one to the view that they are the worst possible ones for poetry. But it does seem true that the greatest writing requires a subject of intrinsic dignity and human importance, and that patriotic subjects amongst others often have these qualities. Goethe's own *Faust*, *Paradise Lost*, *The Divine Comedy*, the *De rerum natura*—these all remind us that religious, moral, metaphysical ideas have also served as the foundation of masterpieces, but they indicate too that the lasting works of literature have been rooted in great systems of beliefs and emotions that far transcend the individual. One of these great complexes, piety, in the Roman sense of the affection and awe that men feel for the things that have made them, a watchful pride in the part still played by their country and a sense of responsibility shared with compatriots, was almost entirely lacking in Germany as a result of the conditions that had produced separatism, for the individual states were too small to inspire it except in a very limited degree.

It is well known that the word 'national' was almost meaningless for the average German citizen of those days. 'Vaterland' almost invariably meant one's own particular state; other parts of Germany were referred to as 'foreign parts' (Ausland). Woldemar Wenck[1] has collected a series of remarks by leading writers of that time which prove that hardly anyone thought of the German-speaking lands as one unit. The famous historian Schlözer of Göttingen, a man of exceptional public spirit, says that when, as a young man in St Petersburg, he looked at the boats going down the Neva to Germany, for the first and perhaps the last time in his life he thought of Germany as a single whole, even as a Fatherland. Wieland says that as a boy he had been told of his duty towards God and his neighbour, and, occasionally, to those set in authority over him, but never anything of the duty of being a patriotic German. 'German in the political sense was

[1] *Deutschland vor hundert Jahren*, Leipzig, 1887, vol. I, chap. IV.

then an unknown word.'[1] Lessing looked upon patriotism as a 'heroic failing from which he was glad to be free'. Goethe cried in his youth: 'Roman patriotism! Heaven preserve us from anything so monstrous'.[2] The young Schiller considered that patriotism was only for immature peoples. Later, when reading Müller's *History of Switzerland* with his wife, he could not agree that Winkelried was to be admired. It was only under the stress of the Napoleonic wars that he was moved to celebrate the patriotism of the Swiss in *Tell*, while Goethe, as is well known, held himself aloof from the national movement longer still.

It is possible indeed to point to a few writings like Klopstock's 'Bardic' poems and the imitations of them by the Göttingen poets, Thomas Abbt's *Vom Tode fürs Vaterland*, J. G. von Zimmermann's *Vom Nationalstolz*, Herder's youthful essays and his ode *An den Kaiser*, Goethe's essay on Strassburg Cathedral and his *Götz*, all of which show traces of national feeling, but these works were decidedly exceptional and in most of them the treatment of the theme is rather abstract and second-hand. It is not so much patriotism that they express as a longing for it. In Nicolai's *Sebaldus Nothanker*, the hero, when called upon to write an essay on 'Death for the Fatherland', is at a loss to know which fatherland to think of. Many more distinguished German writers seem to have been in rather a similar predicament. When writers do take up the theme of Germany as a whole, it is a cultural community they usually have in view rather than a political unit. A typical example is Herder's ode, *An den Kaiser* (Joseph II), written in 1778:

> O Kaiser! du von neunundneunzig Fürsten
> Und Ständen wie des Meeres Sand
> Das Oberhaupt, gib uns, wornach wir dürsten,
> Ein deutsches Vaterland,

[1] *Neuer Teutscher Merkur*, 1793.
[2] 'Über die Liebe des Vaterlandes' in *Frankfurter Gelehrte Anzeigen*, 1772.

Und Ein Gesetz und Eine schöne Sprache
Und redliche Religion:
Vollende deines Stammes schönste Sache
Auf deines Rudolfs Thron,

Dass Deutschlands Söhne sich wie Brüder lieben
Und deutsche Sitt' und Wissenschaft,
Von Thronen, ach, so lange schon vertrieben,
Mit unsrer Väter Kraft

Zurückekehren, dass die holden Zeiten,
Die Friederich von ferne sieht
Und nicht beförderte, sich um dich breiten
Und sei'n dein ewig Lied.

It was partly because literature was not deeply rooted in
the national life that it drew so much of its matter from
foreign sources, until as we have seen a desire for national
originality began to arise, in advance of political patriotism.
It is obvious that the free use of the intellectual and artistic
capital of her neighbours was an advantage, even a necessity
for Germany in her backward condition; these countries
themselves had freely plundered superior civilisations in their
own day as every 'young' literature must. Goethe in
particular made no secret of his immense debt to France and
England.[1] That the results of these borrowings were not
always fortunate goes without saying; *Insel Felsenburg* and
Die schwedische Gräfin have few of the merits of the work of
Defoe and Richardson. But what is perhaps peculiar to
Germany in this matter of imitation is that the habit became
so deeply rooted that even national pride could not affect it
much, and came in fact, by a natural compensation, to claim
this very receptivity as a national virtue.

The difficulties that its political condition put in the way
of the creation of a classical literature may be summed up in
Goethe's words in the essay *Literarischer Sansculottismus* (1795).
A classical 'national author' may be expected to appear, he

---

[1] See for details H. Loiseau, *Goethe et la France*, Paris, 1930, and J. Boyd,
Goethe's Knowledge of English Literature, Oxford, 1932.

says, 'if the history of his nation furnishes him with a happy
and significant system of great events and their consequences;
if his fellow-countrymen show him examples of high
thinking, deep feeling and bold and sustained action; if he
himself, filled with the spirit of his nation, feels he has genius
enough within him to share sympathetically both its past and
present life'. To be truly impressive a book, like a speech,
must have living experience behind it, and a national author
of the first rank can only be thrown up by a nation. The
German nation, narrowly confined geographically and
politically disunited, cannot be expected to produce one, and,
speaking just after the French Revolution, Goethe hesitates
to wish for the upheaval that would be required in Germany
to prepare the way for classical works. But his words indicate
that it is by no means certain that he would have disapproved
of the Nationalism of modern Germany if he could have
lived to see it. He might have looked upon it as a necessary
stage in the evolution of a truly classical German literature.

Continuing our survey of those characteristics of German
literature, so far mainly negative, which we must associate
with separatism, we note that besides being unnational, it
was unsocial, and this almost inevitably because of the lack
of big centres. Other factors of course in addition to the
political one entered in here, the condition of trade and
industry, communications, class distinctions and perhaps
deep-seated racial traits. Literature was the work either of
isolated ministers and officials in the country or of members
of small groups in provincial towns. Mme de Staël, with
great penetration and wit, drew a contrast in De l'Allemagne[1]
(elaborating after her tour in Germany ideas she had sketched
in De la littérature considérée dans ses rapports avec les institutions
sociales),[2] between the 'esprit de conversation' which,
spreading from the salons of Paris, had pervaded the whole
of France, and the individualism which resulted from the
solitary habits and the lack of lively social intercourse among

[1] London, 1810.   [2] Paris, 1800.

the Germans. Her explanation of the difference may be too simple, but her description of the two types is admirable. A Frenchman tends, she thinks, to sacrifice the matter of his thought to the form, and the German the form to the matter. The French feel a social need to think like everyone else, much of their conversation consists of ready-made phrases, in short they draw on a reservoir common to all. The Germans value only bold independence of thought resulting from long solitary brooding. In France they study men and society, and their writings have a practical end in view. In Germany they study books, for life around them is too uneventful to occupy their attention, and the nature of the government prevents the thinkers from having any influence on the course of events. They are strong therefore in abstract speculation and lyrical poetry. But while admiring the solid merits of the Germans, she cannot help desiring for them some of the Frenchman's feeling for form, which she explains as the result of natural vivacity combined with the desire to please. A French thinker or writer feels that he is usurping the attention of his audience, for everyone else is eager to talk too. He must do everything to avoid boring them, he must be brief, clear, pointed, ingratiating, gay. A German on the other hand feels that he has a rightful claim to the hearer's time, for he does not speak unless he has something to say. But what he says must express his deepest thought, exhaustively and not necessarily with good humour. The Frenchman, in short, is too fully conscious of belonging to a society, and the German too little.

These ideas became a commonplace of French criticism. They were developed further by Taine, who traced the origin of classical French literature to the salons, and by Brunetière. Brunetière[1] emphasises strongly the essentially social character of French literature, the 'civilité', which seems to him to account for the excellence of French

[1] *Etudes critiques*, vol. 5, 'Sur le caractère essentiel de la litt. française', and elsewhere.

dramatists, letter-writers, 'moralistes' and orators, for their *genres* depend on the co-operation of a public. Lyricism is not a strong point, and to foreigners at least French writers often seem lacking in profundity, because they prefer subjects that interest men in general, and give themselves so much trouble to be clear. The German writer, on the other hand, is satisfied if he understands himself; if others have difficulty in understanding him he is all the more convinced of the depth of his thought.

In his conversations with Eckermann and others Goethe often discussed this question of the differences between French and German national character and its determining conditions, and on the whole he would have agreed with the French views quoted, but with a difference in emphasis. He too missed in the Germans the sociability and vivacity of the French, and he gave to Eckermann exactly the same explanation of the merits of French style as Mme de Staël's, that they never lost sight of their public. German style, he added, was spoiled by too much philosophic speculation.[1] But he saw too that conventions and traditions can have a deadening effect and must be constantly revised if they are not to produce in literature works like those French writings of the age of Voltaire which had repelled him in his youth as 'bejahrt und vornehm'. French writers seemed to him on the whole less serious, less idealistic and less open to new ideas than the German. German writers of his age, he says in effect, had both the strength and the weakness resulting from not writing for a clearly defined public in the hope of influencing its views. They lacked the tug from reality that even the most unworldly of French or English authors constantly experienced.

Literature then was unnational and unsocial, but it had positive qualities too. It was in the first place highly individualistic. If Germany had few literary traditions, it was at the same time comparatively free from the clogging effect

[1] Eckermann, 14th April, 1824.

of conventions. Originality was at a premium, and if taste was not critical, it was all the easier for young writers to find a hearing. The result was sometimes eccentricity, paradox, even nonsense, at other times profound and novel ideas and bold literary experiments. The natural fertility of the mind was given full scope in a society where men wrote to express themselves, revelled in hard work and were in no hurry for results. The pace of life was slow, 'time fell drop by drop' as Mme de Staël discovered, and there was one tradition at least well established by the learnèd compilers of preceding centuries, that of thoroughness. Schiller was speaking for all when he praised 'Beschäftigung, die nie ermattet'.

The strange opinions that sometimes resulted from their solitary brooding could generally be expressed with more freedom than in most countries, in spite of censors, partly because autocratic authority was so firmly established that writers rarely even imagined that their work could have any immediate effect in practice, and partly because an educated man who made himself unpopular in one state could nearly always find some small official or professional appointment in another. As Mirabeau pointed out, discussing the advantages and disadvantages of separatism in his *De la monarchie prussienne*, each state needed good professional men, and there were still so few of them that the services of the best were eagerly sought after. Fichte, speaking from experience, makes the same point that there were many refuges for outspoken writers in Germany: 'A truth that could not be uttered at one place, could at another...and so in spite of much one-sidedness and narrowness, a higher degree of freedom of enquiry and expression was possible in (eighteenth-century) Germany as a whole than in any other state before'.[1] The variety of conditions stimulated political and social criticism of a general kind, and so long as it was ostensibly directed against rival states, it could easily and safely be uttered. As for new views in theology, the

[1] *Reden an die deutsche Nation.*

other dangerous subject, so many shades of opinion were represented in high places that it went hard with a man who could not find some prince or other to lend him support.

Speculative freedom in the literature of thought was matched by lyrical sincerity in the literature of feeling when poets were no longer overawed by foreign models and had mastered their medium. That other influences counted here beside the lack of social interests is obvious. The most important, no doubt, was Protestantism, and especially Pietism. It cannot be an accident too that Germany had for so long excelled in music. But it remains true that the 'Gemüt' is best cultivated in solitude, not in a courtly or urban society where 'the proper study of mankind is man'. Nature poetry of the modern romantic type is one form of expression for this kind of feeling. Hence the contrast mentioned by Brunetière between French literature, strong in 'moralistes', and German, strong in purely lyrical and nature poets. The contrast is not unlike that which we find in English literature, here too associated with contrasting habits of life, between the school of Pope and the school of Wordsworth.

For the lonely spirits we have been describing life would have been intolerable without books. Their education had been bookish and their tastes continued to be so. It was a bookishness necessarily little modified by experience of the world of men. These omnivorous readers were moreover, as we have seen, very much the reverse of insular. The Germany of Goethe's age was open to every foreign idea, new or old, and interested itself in every accessible literature. The number and excellence of the translations it produced is a sufficient indication of the interest taken in foreign masterpieces, especially if we remember that the translators included Lessing, Wieland, Herder, Goethe, Schiller, Voss, the Schlegels and many others of the best minds of the day. This open-mindedness was the obverse of the lack of a national style. It is not surprising that catholicity, inclusiveness, became an ideal and that the outstanding characteristic of Goethe himself is, to use a phrase of an English critic, quoted by Goethe with approval in his maxims, his 'panoramic ability'. One of the merits of modern German literature is its atmosphere of 'Bildung', or broad intellectual culture. From Wieland to Thomas Mann, the German novelists, for instance, have owed much of their charm for the cultivated reader to the allusiveness and the aroma of learning of their style. It goes without saying that fine tact is necessary to prevent such culture from degenerating into pedantry.

The leading German classics were not only cosmopolitan in their culture; they were perhaps the nearest approach to the type of the 'good European' that we know of. Goethe's words to Eckermann, explaining why it had been impossible for him to write patriotic poetry during the War of Liberation, are the classical expression of his cosmopolitanism.

How could I have written songs of hate without hating? And, between ourselves, I did not hate the French, although I thanked God when we were rid of them. And how could I, for whom the only thing that matters is whether people are civilised or barbarous, hate a nation which is amongst the most cultivated on earth and to which I owe so large a part of my own culture! National hatred is anyhow a peculiar thing. You will always find it strongest and most violent in the lowest stages of civilisation. But there is a stage at which it entirely disappears and at which one stands in a sense above the nations, and feels the good or evil fortune of a neighbouring nation as if it had happened to one's own. This stage was congenial to my nature, and I had been long confirmed in these views before I reached my sixtieth year.[1]

It is in a similar spirit that Kant sketched his plan for a League of Nations,[2] that Herder traced the development of 'Humanität', or that Schiller cried, in the song which Beethoven used as the text for his choral symphony,

Seid umschlungen, Millionen !
Diesen Kuss der ganzen Welt !

[1] Eckermann, 10th March 1830.
[2] In his *Universal History from a Cosmopolitan Point of View*.

For all these, as for Lessing, Klopstock and Hölderlin, it is the word 'humanity', not 'nation', that is invested with the fullest meaning. Yet they were certainly not 'intellectuals without roots anywhere', as writers expressing similar views in Germany would be styled to-day. They expressed universal values in a definitely German idiom. While still striving to acquire this idiom, some of them had passed through a stage when to be German had been their highest aim, the stage at which Goethe wrote *Götz* or the essay on Strassburg Cathedral. It was not through lack of understanding for their own nation, but through the increased sympathy with other nations gained through a full knowledge of their own, that they were able to rise without self-deception to the conception of serving humanity. If opinions such as these are suspect in Germany to-day, it is because the development that Goethe half desired and half feared in 1795[1] has now taken place and Germany has become, or is in process of becoming, a nation, but one too anxious as yet about the maintenance of her individuality to be able to rise to Goethe's impartial appreciation of the eternal values, whatever national dress they might wear. It was easier for Goethe to hold such a view, the modern German writer might with justice urge, because he lived in a disunited Germany that was not tempted to take herself seriously as a political force in Europe, in an age moreover when, largely owing to the political circumstances, the ablest Germans were accustomed to devote their best energies to the creation or appreciation of literature and philosophy rather than to the pursuit of wealth or power.

Cosmopolitanism, it is clear, was attractive partly as an escape from the pettiness of political conditions at home. It was a Utopian ideal natural to men who had been allowed no political schooling and found little in 'fatherlands' like Württemberg or Weimar to satisfy their political idealism. The atmosphere of absolutism and rationalism in which they

---

[1] *Literarischer Sansculottismus*, quoted above, p. 299 f.

had grown to maturity, as well as their natural bent as poets towards contemplation rather than towards action, tended to make them more concerned with formulating distant ideals than with practical suggestions for immediate improvements. Goethe, it is true, had some experience of practical administration, but after the disappointment of his first hopes he came to look upon it chiefly as a means of self-discipline. Though he believed that every one should perform cheerfully the tasks that lay to his hand, he was far less interested in political and economic problems than in personal culture and the things of the mind, so that in the *Xenien* of Goethe and Schiller we find dicta such as these:

Das deutsche Reich

Deutschland? aber wo liegt es? Ich weiss das Land nicht zu finden.
Wo das gelehrte beginnt, hört das politische auf.

Deutscher Nationalcharakter

Zur Nation euch zu bilden, ihr hoffet es, Deutsche, vergebens;
Bildet, ihr könnt es, dafür freier zu Menschen euch aus.

The anti-naturalistic and essentially unpopular character of the two poets' work during the period of their friendship, their preference for Greek forms and non-German subjects, is also to be explained in part as a reaction against the narrowness and meanness of ordinary life in their own country. Compared with the God-like heroes whom Winckelmann had taught them to see in Greek art, or the passionate natures drawn 'on a colossal scale' by Shakespeare, how foolish the foppish courtiers and the timid philistines of their own 'ink-splashing century' looked to them! Believing that it was a poet's business, in Dilthey's words, 'to create a new world of art, in which the meaning of the real world is revealed', they could not be content, like Iffland and Kotzebue, to draw

Pfarrer, Kommerzienräte,
Fähndriche, Sekretärs oder Husarenmajors.

They preferred symbolic figures like Iphigenie, Tasso, Faust or Wallenstein, who might serve as the subject of a religious or philosophical art, which interpreted not merely the life of their own time, but the deepest problems of humanity at all times. Even apparently realistic works like *Wilhelm Meisters Lehrjahre* or *Hermann und Dorothea* were partly shaped in accordance with theories, whether of conduct or of art, which restricted their appeal. It was reserved for later writers to reveal the poetic qualities of that very narrowness against which Goethe revolted, and to prove that provincial life in its picturesque variety makes a more direct appeal to the imagination than the intellectually more satisfying abstractions of classicism. The infinite richness and diversity of German culture, exploited in the 'village story' and 'Heimatkunst', and evident centuries before this in folk tales and poetry, is of course even more clearly a product of separatism than the features of classical art discussed above, but it was only appreciated in the eighteenth century by a few exceptional spirits like Möser and Pestalozzi. The Romantic movement was soon to make good this omission.

It would be a great mistake to imagine that the whole German people in Goethe's age shared the views of their intellectual leaders. They were on the whole very tolerant of foreigners, but more from the incapacity to rise to the conception of anything larger than their small town or state than from a laudable large-mindedness. While the élite were cosmopolitan, the masses were frankly provincial. Their intellectual horizon is well indicated in the popular novels and drama of the day. Engel's *Lorenz Stark* and Iffland's plays give a far more faithful picture of the average middle-class German than the best works of the classics. We learn from them how seldom the thoughts of the inhabitants of Germany's many small towns strayed beyond the confines of their homes and their immediate surroundings. The political condition of the country was not the least of the factors that tended to restrict the interests of the citizen in this way to domestic or at most provincial affairs. He was intentionally kept in blinkers by the ruling class, and even the classical writers reacted to the French Revolution with a perhaps excessive cultural conservatism, as we see from Goethe's *Hermann und Dorothea* and *Episteln*, or from Schiller's *Lied von der Glocke*. Faust as one of the élite might cry, 'Wie ich beharre, bin ich Knecht', but the average man, Goethe seemed to say, would find true wisdom expressed in such lines as these:

> Aber wer fest auf dem Sinne beharrt, der bildet die Welt sich,
> Nicht dem Deutschen geziemt es, die fürchterliche Bewegung
> Fortzuleiten, und auch zu wanken hierhin und dorthin.
> Dies ist unser! so lass uns sagen und so es behaupten!

The average woman, needless to say, was to find her sphere of activity in the home:

> Dienen lerne das Weib beizeiten nach seiner Bestimmung.

If a girl is given suitable tasks in the household, in the manner suggested in the second *Epistel* (1794), then

> Wünscht sie dann endlich zu lesen, so wählt sie gewisslich ein
> Kochbuch.

Though the early Romantic writers and their wives might find this view of society too complacently 'behaglich' and 'heiter', and parody it in such poems as A. W. Schlegel's

> Ehret die Frauen, sie stricken und weben
> Wollene Strümpfe fürs irdische Leben,

their views in this matter were probably shared only by a small group of intellectuals, centred mainly in Berlin, and we may take the popularity of just those works of the classics that are in the narrowest sense 'bürgerlich' as a reliable index to general opinion.

The adjective 'bürgerlich' reminds us that it is not enough to consider the culture of the age of Goethe from the political point of view. Much light is thrown on its peculiarities by a study of the social structure of the country and its economic basis. Here our first question is: what was the relative share of the various social classes in the shaping of the new literature and the general philosophy of life expressed in it? Was any single class its main creator and supporter, as the Clerics were in the Old High German and the Knights in the Middle High German period? It has been seen above how the system of absolutism tended to preserve something like the medieval division of society into 'Stände', broad social groups whose individual members were linked by the performance of a similar function in the general life, a function to which they had usually been predestined by the social standing of their parents. It should therefore be easier to trace any particular influence each class may have had on culture than it would be for contemporary England, where class barriers had begun to break down much earlier than in Germany.

In the seventeenth century, to go no farther back, the dominating influence in literature had been, as in contemporary France, that of the aristocracy. Not that the nobility were usually themselves creators, as they had been in the age of chivalry. The Dukes of Brunswick (Heinrich Julius and Anton Ulrich) wrote themselves, Friedrich von Spee (a count) and Friedrich von Logau (a baron) were notable poets, and a few minor writers of good birth might be mentioned. But for the most part court circles were content to set the tone and encourage literary work by their patronage. The courts of Brunswick, Cassel, Stuttgart, Heidelberg, Vienna, Munich, Dresden were at one time or another literary centres, the Polish court, as Nadler has pointed out, exercised an important influence on the Silesian poets, the duke of Anhalt founded the 'Fruchtbringende Gesellschaft', the emperor himself frequently rewarded literary merit with a title (Opitz, Zesen, Rist, Birken).

At the courts of the rising territorial states literature, like the other arts, was forced to reflect the absolutist court ideal. The *genres* cultivated were the political novel, the 'roman à clef', the heroic novel, the pastoral, and characteristically aristocratic forms of stage performance like the opera, ballet, masquerade and the drama of the Silesians and the Jesuits. In the main the actual writers of these works were university-trained court officials and high civil servants, usually of good middle-class origins. This class was as yet too weak numerically and too dependent on the favour of the great to have interests and ideals of its own. It was usually content to trick out those of its patrons in forms that displayed its own bookish culture. The middle class had lost the naïve self-confidence of the age of the Reformation and was content to follow the lead of court circles in everything. The councillors and high officials of the towns, and the patricians generally, had no desire but to express the same tastes as the nobility of which they considered themselves a part. The majority of the leading authors were civic or state officials (like Opitz, Logau, Moscherosch, Gryphius, Lohenstein, Hofmannswaldau, Harsdörffer and even Grimmelshausen in his later years); the rest were also university men in other professions, clergy-men, doctors or teachers in university or gymnasium. Zesen alone failed to find an anchorage. Among the actual creators of literature the middle class was just as strongly represented as at any time in the following century. The difference between the content and tone of their serious work, from which a realistic treatment of middle-class types was strictly excluded, and that of the later periods, would seem to have been very largely due to causes of a social and political nature, to that gradual social rise of the middle class described in earlier chapters.

The fact that it was the greater commercial centres like Hamburg and Zürich which first emancipated themselves from the influence of the courts is significant. In Hamburg, in the seventeenth century, as in Nürnberg and other big towns, the courts set the fashions in literature and the arts. It was the ambition of the patricians and rich merchants of Hamburg to equal the court towns in their own forms. They exchanged actors and operas with Brunswick, for instance, and their first theatre of note was an opera house, opened in 1678. It was only with the growth of English influence, resulting from the close commercial connection described above, that a literature more truly expressive of the middle class was able to arise. The example of the English middle class, already so fully aware of their own strength and importance, gradually roused the merchant class to a realisation of its own deepest needs and proved a stronger force than the prestige of the patricians with their aristocratic tastes. Opera, a court product, was from the first adapted to the requirements of a city audience, and given in German, not, as in the courts, in Italian. The only kind of opera that survived for long was a realistic comic opera; moreover many new forms of literature soon proved immeasurably more important. One of the chief aims of the writers in the 'moral weeklies', which now obtained such a vogue, was to encourage the self-respect of the middle class and to guide them to a culture of their own. Their establishment is the first clear sign of the coming age of 'Humanität'.

Leipzig was too much under the political and social influence of Dresden to follow this lead immediately, but Zürich, a strong city-republic, not overshadowed, like so many older German towns, by the power of any territorial prince, was free to go its own way. It was because the structure of their society was similar, as Nadler points out, that the Swiss towns and Hamburg repeatedly established cultural contacts with each other, and, one may add, with England. The famous quarrel of the Swiss and the Leipzig schools, on the other hand, was probably due in part to political and social differences, though of course many other factors entered in. Gottsched, in his laudable attempt to establish a literary German drama, could find no other model than the French plays performed for the delight of court circles in Dresden, a form of drama which was essentially the expression of an aristocratic minority, though at the same

time he followed Hamburg's example with his moral weeklies for the bourgeoisie. There was an inconsistency in his
position which paralleled that of the cultivated Leipziger in
general, half citizen, half courtier, and in his attempt to make
all Germany speak 'sächsisch' there was a despotic note
which was naturally resented by the republican Bodmer. In
Hamburg and Zürich, on the other hand, most of the best
writers were public-spirited citizens with some sense of their
dignity and responsibilities as such. It is noteworthy that
they did not separate the pursuit of literature from that of the
good life in the widest sense. Their chief literary societies (the
'Patriotische Gesellschaft' in Hamburg and, later, the
'Helvetische Gesellschaft' in Zürich) were also societies for
the promotion of every kind of public-spirited effort. Not
that these towns too did not produce authors like Hagedorn
who were uncomfortably astride between the court and the
middle-class ideal, but this was in the transition period at the
beginning of the eighteenth century. Their more characteristic writers were whole-hearted 'Aufklärer' who, though
their taste may not always have been impeccable, had usually
the merit of sincerity.

In the first sixty or seventy years of the eighteenth century
German literature gradually withdrew itself more and more
from the courts, first, as we have seen, in the great centres of
trade, and later almost everywhere. The few 'court poets' who
survived, in places like Dresden, enjoyed no esteem outside
their own circle, and patronage of German writers by German
princes became rare. The Prussian court under Frederick
William I had no use for poets at all, and, under Frederick
the Great no use for German poets. The only considerable
writer who enjoyed the patronage of a prince was Klopstock,
and it was the king of Denmark who was his patron.

We have seen in the preceding chapter how the reading
public gradually expanded and how with the absorption of
new elements its tastes changed, becoming more and more
markedly middle-class. The increased sale of books and

periodicals transformed the book trade and made literature into a possible though not yet a lucrative profession. It was still for most writers a pursuit for leisure hours, but even when economically independent of their public, writers could not if they wished resist the influence of their ways of thinking. The drama and the novel, under pressure from the middle class, inevitably became didactic and realistic. With the advance of science based on experience and reason the attitude of the instructed classes towards revealed religion and established institutions became more and more critical, and it was no longer possible to prevent this scepticism from trickling slowly down to the general reading public. Very timidly at first, especially in Germany, the middle class began to claim the right to order its life for itself in the light of reason, at least in those activities which concerned it most closely, its manner of making a living and its family life.

More than one generation's work was necessary in Germany to persuade the mass of the public which could read to turn to other books than the Bible and catechism, and the chap-books and calendars sold at fairs or by pedlars, as well as to enable the writers to discover by experiment a way of writing which would appeal to this new public. Between 1700 and 1750 much of this preparatory work had been accomplished, and a large number of writers, the 'niedere Aufklärer' as they are now ungraciously called, who filled the columns of the moral weeklies and newspapers, had learnt to write not for a gild of fellow scholars but for people who had no further equipment than common sense and the ability to read printed everyday German. This literature was hardly what is usually called literature at all. It was written for use rather than for delight, it provided enlightenment in a palatable form.

The new *genres* most favoured by the middle-class public were the domestic drama and the family novel, both distinguished from the older drama and romance not so much by their themes as by the general philosophy, the system of values which they implied. The serious drama of the French classical writers and their imitators had treated of princes and heroes whose will knew no restrictions except those imposed by fate, men without obligations to any society, for whom their lands and subjects were material that they might fashion according to their personal desires. In these figures, though they might be taken from classical history or myth, the feelings of a ruling caste could be fittingly expressed. In the domestic drama on the other hand, even when its figures (as in Lessing's *Miss Sara Sampson*) were not strictly of the middle class, the point of view was always that of this class, especially in questions of morality. It was not at all surprising that the Hamburg public listened to the enlightened merchant Mr Thoroughgood, in *George Barnwell*, with delighted approbation, whereas the Viennese nobility found him intolerably prosy.

Naturally the new forms had to be considerably adapted to suit the peculiar conditions that prevailed in German society. There was a rising middle class in Germany as in England, so that the fundamental social condition for the acceptance of these *genres* was present, but the German middle class differed, as we have seen, from the English in many particulars. It is characteristic, for instance, that in *Miss Sara Sampson*, the first German imitation of *George Barnwell*, the conflict is one between private individuals, not between society, or a particular class, and an errant member of it, and that even this family tragedy had to be displayed against an English background if it was to have sufficient dignity to be taken seriously. Lessing evidently felt that a German family in its natural setting was still only a fit subject for comedy. It is interesting again to note that the first German domestic tragedies in a purely German setting realistically treated were those of F. L. Schröder, produced for a Hamburg public. Here too, though the Hamburg citizen takes himself seriously, he is not shown in any conflicts that affect more than the immediate interests of his family; he has no public spirit or patriotism, and no sense of independence and of pride in his calling like Thoroughgood. The first figure in the domestic drama who really stands on his own feet is Major von Tellheim in *Minna von Barnhelm*, and to explain his manliness Lessing has to make him a Prussian officer and a nobleman, though, as Eloesser rightly says, he is not really a Prussian and at bottom not a soldier either. 'Military service is for him a passing phase, an education to manliness, such as the author perhaps desired for the peace-loving, mean-spirited bourgeoisie in general.'[1]

An interesting confirmation of this interpretation may be found in a very sensible essay by Christian Garve, the 'Popularphilosoph', entitled: *Über die Maxime Rochefoucaults: Das bürgerliche Air verliert sich zuweilen bei der Armee, niemals am Hofe*.[2] In this essay Garve analyses the character of the middle class in a way which frequently reminds one of certain late passages in *Wilhelm Meister*, passages perhaps influenced by this book. 'Embarrassment in intercourse with people of higher rank' seems to him the most characteristic feature of middle-class manners, and he considers that it is in the army that an easy self-confidence and personal dignity can best be acquired by one whose birth gives him no standing at court. Much of the so-called militarism of Germany in more recent times, in the sense of the belief in the moral benefits resulting from military training, probably proceeds from considerations not unlike those of Garve. But in its passivity and externality Garve's ideal falls far short of Goethe's. Wilhelm Meister progresses in the end beyond the stage at which the easy bearing of a gentleman (and of a good actor!) excites his admiration, and is turned into a good and active citizen,[3] whereas even Tellheim's ultimate aim was 'cultiver son jardin', to lead an idyllic life in some little haven

[1] A. Eloesser, *Das bürgerliche Drama*, Berlin, 1898, p. 93.

[2] C. Garve, *Versuche*, 1. Teil, Breslau, 1792.

[3] See the present writer's essay: 'Goethe's *Wilhelm Meister* as a picture and a criticism of society', in *Publications of the English Goethe Society*, 1933.

apart. This was in fact the ideal of the average good citizen in Lessing's time. *Emilia Galotti* gives us a similar impression of the age. It is, in Lessing's phrase, 'eine von allem Staatsinteresse befreite Virginia', true to its time in its presentation of a despotic but good-natured and charming prince and his unambitious subjects, whose one desire is, not to reform the world, but to be left in peace.

The second-rate writers of Lessing's time display the sentimental optimism characteristic of the Age of Enlightenment even more plainly. They shut their eyes to the evils of society and see only 'Wie wir's denn zuletzt so herrlich weit gebracht'. They treat social problems, such as that of the relation of the nobility to the other classes, much as Lessing treats the problem of religious differences in *Nathan der Weise*. Here the real difficulty of toleration is obscured because the representatives of the conflicting religions are made to appear so conciliatory and so like each other. So in the sentimental plays of the Aufklärung nobleman and bourgeois are represented as brother-classes, equally dear to the 'Landesvater' whom they both revere.

The young writers of the Storm and Stress period in the 'seventies were usually products of the same social stratum as their older colleagues, but they were, to use a modern phrase, much more class-conscious and consequently sound much more revolutionary. Steeped as they all were in the writings of the French critics of society, particularly Rousseau, they frequently present the conflict between classes, and almost always take sides for the middle class. They are far from objective in their pictures of contemporary society, painting their own class as unhappy but virtuous and the nobility as corrupt and arrogant favourites of fortune. They see defects in the middle class, narrowness of outlook, servility to superiors in some, boorish incivility in others, but they explain them as due to unfavourable social conditions.[1]

[1] See the well-documented study by Clara Stockmeyer, *Soziale Probleme im Drama des Sturmes und Dranges*, Frankfort, 1922.

The general tendency of their writings might be described as liberal. It is not the economic situation of the middle class —still less that of the peasant or the poorer town worker— which arouses their indignation, but their lack of equality with the nobility in social standing and legal privileges. The prince himself is never directly criticised, even in the boldest of Sturm und Drang plays, Schiller's *Kabale und Liebe*. It is always his advisers and agents who are to blame. There is never any incitement to political revolt. These writers hope rather by an appeal to the heart to secure recognition for the solid merit of their class, an extension of its rights and the outward respect due to its inner worth. They are interested chiefly in the section of the middle class to which they themselves belong, more or less cultivated and prosperous circles in the towns, and are usually indifferent to and ignorant of the life of the countryman and of the poorer townsman.

The passionate interest which the theatre at that time evoked cannot be explained as purely aesthetic in origin. The stage had come to be looked upon, in that age of waning faith, as a kind of substitute for the pulpit. In the earlier domestic dramas questions of private morality had been the subject of stage homilies. In this later phase a wider circle of interests was discussed and the topics ranged beyond those treated in moral weeklies to those of the so-called political journals. Being the work of young men, full of foreign theories but very ignorant of the world, the new plays made little appeal to court circles or to the more settled bourgeoisie, but the ordinary citizen found pleasure in them, says a contemporary, because, being excluded from court circles, he had no taste, and no sense for intimate relationships.[1] It was the contempt these writers felt for the Frenchified culture of the German aristocracy, rather than political nationalism, that lay behind their hostility to French forms of art, and particularly of the drama. In their criticism of the 'decorum', the 'squeamishness', the 'pursuit of external form' of the

[1] K. Risbeck, *Briefe eines reisenden Franzosen*, I, 71.

French dramatists they were repeating with more emphasis objections already raised by consciously middle-class French writers like Diderot and Mercier. It was class-feeling, far more than national feeling, that was expressed in these outbursts, so that it was not altogether unfitting that Schiller should be made a French 'citoyen' for his early revolutionary plays.

It is not surprising either that there was an open feud between several of the younger writers and Wieland, who had become more and more of a courtier in his outlook ever since his return from Switzerland and his friendship with the Stadion circle. Nothing could have been less revolutionary than his epicurean philosophy. Not that Wieland was without readers among the middle class. He was, on the contrary, almost a best seller. He appealed to people of taste through his wit and grace of style, to court circles through his urbanity and refined sensuality, to the cultivated middle class through his learning and sweet reasonableness, and perhaps not least through the aroma of social distinction that his books carried with them. But he was naturally anathema to the sworn enemies of the rococo. What could the author of *Luise* have in common with the author of *Musarion*? The young puritans of the 'Hain' solemnly burnt Wieland's works as those of a corrupter of youth, and the young Goethe wrote a skit against him.

But these generous young revolutionaries soon found that without more backing in society than they possessed they could only point to social evils and not do anything effective to remedy them. Theirs was from the first a theoretical protest, expressed with the exaggeration common in men whose words do not need to be followed by action. Their best works, like *Götz*, begin on a note of protest and end on one of resignation, and in their weaker works, as in the popular plays of Iffland made later on the same recipe, they are careful to lay the blame for the abuses of the time not on the princes but on their heartless ministers, not on the squires but on their bailiffs.

Most of the Stürmer und Dränger therefore soon made their peace with the courts. Before Schiller, the youngest of them, produced his *Räuber* and *Kabale und Liebe* in the early 'eighties, Goethe and Herder were established in high office at Weimar, Lenz had attempted to follow Goethe's example, and Klinger had begun the career at the Russian court which was to prove so brilliant. Just as Goethe and Schiller returned to verse and a form closely resembling the analytic construction of the French classical dramatists in most of the plays of their maturity, so also they came to perceive the value of many of the social conventions they had dismissed so impatiently in their youth. In *Tasso* Goethe praises just those qualities of reverence for tradition, restraint of impulse and respect for external forms which the companions of his youth, and he himself in some degree, had rejected as unnatural. The naïve individualism of the young middle-class 'geniuses' has given way to the considerateness and tact of the courtier. 'Erlaubt ist, was sich ziemt', not 'Erlaubt ist, was gefällt', is to be the motto even for an acknowledged genius. The ethical ideal put forward here and in all the great works of the 'nineties is 'Humanität', an ideal not discoverable by any man from his inner consciousness, or from the traditions of his class alone, but through intercourse with those by whom the culture gradually achieved by the best in each succeeding age had been inherited.

German classical literature then was the work of authors who were not restricted by circumstances to a narrow range of subjects, but could expatiate freely over the whole of nature and history, in an eclectic style influenced by innumerable foreign models. This literature was neither national in sentiment nor expressive of the outlook of any particular class of society. Cosmopolitanism and 'Humanität' were its ideals. Considered from the point of view of economic and social history, it was essentially the work of free artists, such as could only arise when the possibility existed of writing for a heterogeneous public, without much need of patronage or much fear of persecution. In earlier ages, a writer had not easily secured a hearing for himself as such. It has been pointed out how frequently writers in the *Spectator*, the *Tatler*, and their German counterparts, assumed some mask, such as that of a lady or gentleman of quality, instead of writing under their own names. It was not until late in the eighteenth century that the custom of making the hero of a novel an artist established itself. The first example was the half-merchant, half-artist Wilhelm Meister. Then with the Romantics the artist became almost the rule as hero, not only because of the technical advantage the author so gained, of being able to introduce his own verses and reflections and to draw more freely on his own experience, but because the artist embodied now the personal ideal of the educated middle class in Germany, the ideal of culture.[1]

In this culture of Weimar the broad stream of the humanist literary tradition was united with German currents from both the middle class and the courts. If, on the one hand, the great middle-class writers were influenced by the ideas of court circles, upholding as they did the accepted code of ethics and manners, the prevailing monarchical system of government and the division of society into 'estates' with relatively constant duties and privileges, the court itself was increasingly affected by ideas and habits which had their origin in the middle class. The irresponsible extravagant despots of the type of Augustus the Strong of Saxony were succeeded by princes more and more dominated by the ideas of duty, order and economy. In small courts like Weimar, owing to their modest resources, the forms of social intercourse, too, came increasingly to resemble those of the better middle class. There was nothing unique in this development. A similar fusion of middle-class and courtly ideals had already taken place, for instance, in French classical literature, to which

[1] See L. L. Schücking, *Die Soziologie der literarischen Geschmacksbildung*, 2nd ed. Leipzig and Berlin, 1931, p. 28.

German classicism owed so much. The really new feature about French classicism, as M. Berthelot[1] has pointed out, was the part played in it by bourgeois common sense. This is where it differed from the Italian and Spanish cultural tradition in which it was grounded.

C'est la formation de cette bourgeoisie organisatrice qui a le plus contribué à donner sa physionomie propre au siècle de Louis XIV. La bourgeoisie à ce moment s'appuie sur un ordre politique pré-existant, c'est à dire sur la monarchie militaire et administrative qui, seule, lui à permis de se constituer: son bon sens s'applique à la conservation et à la justification d'un certain ordre social et d'un ordre moral qui lui paraît lié avec la stabilité de cet ordre social.

The weakness of Weimar classicism, when compared with that of the age of Louis XIV, was that it did not proceed from so complete a synthesis. It was much less firmly rooted in the life of its time, more purely literary and derivative. This German classicism did not leave firmly established a cultural ideal fit to serve as the starting-point for the efforts of many succeeding generations, as French classicism had done. It owed its survival in the nineteenth century rather to the fact that it was made the basis of higher education than to its real fitness to express the deepest aspirations of the German people. Several phases of German life which were already in evidence and have since proved extremely important are scarcely to be traced in German classical literature. There is first all that is connoted by the phrase 'the Prussian spirit'. There is the spirit of capitalistic enterprise in commerce and industry. And there is that complex of tradition and sentiment proceeding from the old-time village which is now summed up in the vague conception of 'Volkstum'. The Germany of poets and thinkers was only one of several co-existing Germanies. There is therefore nothing surprising in the fact that large sections of the German people have often found themselves unable to accept the ideals of the Weimar classics,

[1] R. Berthelot, *La Sagesse de Shakespeare et de Goethe*, chap. III.

or if they remained unconscious of this essential incompatibility, paid Weimar only lip-service, neglecting in practice the humanistic teaching they had received at school.

The peculiar feature about German classicism is that it is not, like the earlier classical movements in other literatures, 'the product of a nation and a generation which has consciously achieved a definite advance, moral, political, intellectual, and is filled with the belief that its view of life is more natural, human, universal and wise than that from which it has escaped'. It is only in a very limited measure the expression of 'a body of common sentiments and thoughts which the artist shares with his audience, thoughts and views which have for his generation the validity of universal truths'.[1] Only a very small élite shared the view of life taken by the German classics. The figures in the last chapter show how limited the demand for their writings was in their own time. On the stage their plays aroused even less interest. The theatre at Mannheim, for instance, the first 'national' or repertory theatre of real importance, in the 27 years from 1781 to 1808 produced 37 plays of Iffland on 476 evenings, and 115 plays of Kotzebue on 1728 evenings. In the same period Schiller's *Räuber*, which had made the fame of Mannheim, was acted only 15 times, *Kabale und Liebe* only seven times, *Fiesko* and *Don Karlos* only three times each. Similarly at Dresden, between 1789 and 1813, out of a total of 1471 performances, Iffland and Kotzebue took up 477, about one-third, while Lessing, Goethe and Schiller together were acted only on 58 evenings.[2] Even in Weimar itself, under Goethe's management, the repertoire in the first seven years hardly differed at all from what was usual elsewhere. The opening performance in 1791 was of Iffland's *Jäger*, and the taste of the public continued to be met, with very few

[1] Quotations from H. J. C. Grierson's masterly essay on 'Classical and Romantic' in *The Background of English Literature*, London, 1925.
[2] M. Martersteig, *Das deutsche Theater im 19. Jahrhundert*, 2nd ed. Leipzig, 1924, p. 132.

experiments, until Schiller returned to the theatre in 1798 (*Wallensteins Lager*). From now till his death, Schiller provided the theatre with a good play every year, and the French classics and Shakespeare were occasionally attempted in his adaptations. Even Goethe's completed *Iphigenie* was at last staged (1802). *Tasso* was not acted till 1807, however, and *Faust*, part I, till 1829, in both cases rather against the author's wishes. In between the few literary plays, the only ones which are now remembered, the usual concessions were still made to middle-class taste. It is clear then, as Georg Brandes pointed out long ago, that Goethe and Schiller 'did not find a public in existence that understood them, still less a nation that could provide them with subjects and, as it were, commission work from them'. Their classicism was rather in the main a means of escape from their narrow world to that ancient Greece which they imagined as so free, so full of a noble simplicity and serene grandeur. For Mr Santayana, therefore, 'Goethe was never so romantic as when he was classical. His distichs are like theatrical gestures; he feels the sweep of his toga as he rounds them off'.[1]

But German classicism did not merely look backwards to the past. It was not always content to hold the world at a distance. It hoped to save the world through art. This is the sense of Schiller's *Briefe über aesthetische Erziehung* and of his philosophical poems, and probably a similar idea underlies the second part of *Faust*. Faust's vision of ideal beauty in Helen is a necessary step towards his realisation of the true aim of life, active co-operation with others for the good of the community as a whole. 'Classicism', says Strich, 'has usually been the product of corporate feeling, but German classicism looked upon it as its mission to call this corporate feeling into existence through art.'

This is not the place for us to consider how much Weimar contributed in actual fact to the creation of a unified Germany. On a superficial view the poets might seem through

[1] *Three Philosophical Poets*, Harvard, 1910, p. 176.

their horror of any state interference with the liberty of the
individual to have been partly responsible for the failure of
the German states to offer any effective resistance to Napoleon.
Goethe's remarks about internationalism, quoted above,
were his reply to the often expressed reproach that he had
not put his pen at the service of his country. Wilhelm von
Humboldt, the friend of Schiller, voiced the ideas of the
classical age in that essay on the *Sphere and Duties of Government*[1] which was the chief inspiration of Mill's *Essay on
Liberty*. 'The grand, leading principle, towards which every
argument unfolded in these pages directly converges, is the
absolute and essential importance of human development in
its richest diversity'—it is this sentence from Humboldt
which Mill quotes as a motto for his own essay, and he agrees
that it is the state's business simply to guard the lives and
property of its subjects. As Heinrich von Treitschke sees the
matter, however, this meant that 'the admirers of classical
antiquity preached flight from the state, the very antithesis
of Greek virtue'.

Yet Treitschke himself defends the poets' attitude.

They guarded the most individual possession of our people,
the holy flame of idealism, and we owe it to them, above all, that
there was still a Germany, when the German Empire had vanished,
that the Germans in the hour of suffering and humiliation were
still able to believe in themselves, in the abiding value of the
German spirit. It was from the complete development of free
personality that our political freedom and the independence of
the German state proceeded.... This active humanism was not
really either effeminate or hostile to the state. It had simply not
yet understood the nature of the state, and only needed the
schooling of experience to develop all the virtues of the good
citizen and the hero

—as is seen by the example of Humboldt himself. Hegel's
gloomy saying, therefore, that it is only in the dusk that the

[1] *Ideen zu einem Versuch, die Grenzen der Wirksamkeit des Staats zu
bestimmen*, 1792.

owl of Minerva begins her flight, was true of Greece, according to Treitschke, but not of Germany. 'Our classical literature was not the dying note of an old culture but the promising first phase of something new.'[1]

Though there is much truth in this, it is clear that the abundant new growth in the nineteenth century in both the political and the economic spheres was rooted in other soils than that of Weimar. Potsdam and Berlin on the one hand and the rising commercial towns like Hamburg and Leipzig on the other were the real growing points of Germany's power and wealth, while the innumerable small courts became less and less important even culturally, as first philosophy and then natural science celebrated their triumphs in the universities. Here, as at the beginning of our study, the essential ambiguity of the word Germany must be insisted upon. For some it means Goethe, Schiller, Kant, for others Haydn, Mozart, Beethoven, but their Germany, the Germany of poets and thinkers and musicians, was only one of several co-existing Germanies, in fact it did not exist at all as we know it from their work, for what we know is a world constructed by these artists, a 'world of aesthetic semblance'. They never ceased to complain of the harshness of the reality that surrounded them. It will not do, therefore, when modern Germany offends her neighbours in the field of politics or trade, to appeal against her to that older, better Germany that we imagine. What we conjure up is in the main a poet's dream; so far as it corresponded to any features of reality, these were but a fraction of the whole.

It is, however, true that whereas in Goethe's age the best minds of the nation were absorbed in poetry and philosophy, and a new poem was an event to be interpreted and admired in long letters and criticisms, the energies of the nineteenth and twentieth centuries have been directed far more towards the acquisition and control of material things. In this swing towards materialism Germany was following her western

[1] *Deutsche Geschichte*, Teil I.

neighbours, influenced like them by the needs of a rapidly expanding population and the corresponding development of technique and organisation. The realists (in Schiller's sense) triumphed over the idealists, but there was nothing unprecedented in this struggle between the spiritual and the material, and there is no reason to believe that it will ever end. How familiar Schiller was with the realist even in his idealistic age may be seen from his *Wallenstein*. Some words he puts into the mouth of his hero, anticipating as they do so much of the mind of nineteenth-century Germany, may serve as an epilogue to this study:

> Was die Göttlichen uns senden
> Von oben, sind nur allgemeine Güter;
> Ihr Licht erfreut, doch macht es keinen reich,
> In ihrem Staat erringt sich kein Besitz.
> Den Edelstein, das allgeschätzte Gold
> Muss man den falschen Mächten abgewinnen,
> Die unterm Tage schlimmgeartet hausen.
> Nicht ohne Opfer macht man sie geneigt,
> Und keiner lebet, der aus ihrem Dienst
> Die Seele hätte rein zurückgezogen.

Appendix I

GERMAN MONEY AND ITS VALUE
WEIGHTS AND MEASURES

(*The following notes are intended as a brief practical guide for the English reader. Fuller information will be found in Muret-Sanders' German-English Dictionary, second half, and in many older works of reference, such as those by Bergius and Reichard given in the bibliography.*)

COINAGE

The commonest terms used for the expression of money values are: Thaler, Gulden, Groschen, Kreuzer. Thaler and Groschen were commonest in the north, Gulden and Kreuzer in the south, but in all states the four values stood in the following fixed relation to each other:

16 (Gute) Groschen or 60 Kreuzer made one Gulden.

| 24 | ,, | ,, | 90 | ,, | ,, | Reichsthaler. |
| 32 | ,, | ,, | 120 | ,, | ,, | Speziesthaler (Konventionsthaler). |

A Gulden was therefore half a Speziesthaler, or two-thirds of a Reichsthaler. The Guter Groschen was divided into 12 Pfennige (while the Mariengroschen, less commonly used, was worth only 8 Pfennige), the Kreuzer into 4 Pfennige. Of the one kind of Pfennig there were therefore 192 to the Gulden, of the other 240.

Owing to the multiplicity of mints, the value of the Gulden and Thaler could and did vary considerably from state to state and at different times. There were five standards in common use for the minting of silver coins in the later eighteenth century, as well as some half dozen minor ones.

(1) In Braunschweig-Lüneburg the "Leipziger Münzfuss" of 1690 was still followed, giving 18 Gulden to the Cologne mark of fine silver. (This "mark" is of course a weight, not a coin.) The value of this Gulden in pre-war Reichsmark would be 2.338.

(2) In Lübeck, Hamburg, Bremen and Mecklenburg they observed the "Lübecker Kurantfuss", of 34 Kurantmark to the

Cologne mark of silver, established in 1726. A Thaler was equivalent to 3 Kurantmark, but values were more commonly expressed in marks. The value of a Gulden (two such marks) on this basis would be 1.857 Reichsmark.

(3) In Brandenburg-Prussia from 1750 the Prussian Kurantfuss of 21 Gulden (or 14 Thaler) to the Cologne mark was observed. A Gulden on this standard would be worth 2 Reichsmark.

(4) In Austria, Saxony, Braunschweig-Wolfenbüttel and most of Lower Germany the "Konventionsfuss" of 20 Gulden to the Cologne mark was the standard. The convention had been arrived at in 1753, in one of the numerous efforts to reduce the chaos of the German coinage. A Gulden of this type would be worth 2.105 Reichsmark.

(5) In 1754 Bavaria, one of the parties to the original convention, withdrew and depreciated its Gulden to 24 to the Cologne mark. It was followed by the Swabian and Franconian circles, the Palatinate, Frankfort-on-Main, and the territories on the Rhine and Main generally. This "South German" or "Rhenish" Gulden would be worth 1.754 Reichsmark.

The principal gold coins in circulation were:

Souverain d'or (Austrian), worth	9	Reichsthaler, or	13½	Gulden[*]
Carolin (Bavaria and else-where)	,,	6	,,	,,	9	,,
Pistole (also called *Louis d'or*, or named after the ruler, as *Friedrich d'or*, *August d'or*)	,,	5	,,	,,	7½	,,
Max d'or (Bavarian)	,,	4⅛	,,	,,	6¼	,,
Ducat (general)	,,	3	,,	,,	4½	,,

[*] 20-Gulden standard, No. 4 above.

Coins representing multiples and fractions of these, especially of the Ducat, were also issued, and some French and Dutch gold coins were in circulation, at recognised values.

For rough conversion into English money, the Speziesthaler, Reichsthaler and Gulden (except the Rhenish Gulden, No. 5 above) may usually be taken as equivalent to four, three and two shillings respectively. No simple rule can be given for arriving at the equivalent in purchasing power in present-day money, because some things were relatively cheaper than now, and some as dear or dearer. The factor for foodstuffs might be something like three, four or five, while for clothes and imported luxuries it might be one or even a fraction of one. The following specimen prices, etc. will give some idea of the purchasing power of money in the second half of the eighteenth century:

Typical commodity prices (taking the Gulden as equivalent to two shillings).

The price of beef, veal, lamb, pork in Frankfort-on-Main in February 1801 was 3¾d. to 4¾d. a pound. It had changed little since 1750, when an average price had been 3d.

Common ("black") bread at the same time and place cost 1d. a pound. (The price of bread was of course subject to variations according to the harvest and the price of grain.) Eggs were 1d. each at their dearest, and nearly 3 a penny at their cheapest. Fresh butter cost about 4d. a pound in summer, but up to 1s. in winter. (Careful householders laid in a supply in summer for salting.)

Luxuries like coffee, tea and sugar were dear, and their prices varied considerably according to trade conditions. In mid-century, coffee cost 1s. 6d. a pound and sugar 1s. In 1779 Herr Rat Goethe paid only 1s. a pound for coffee, and 1s. for sugar. For tea (usually bought by the quarter pound) he paid anything from 4s. to 8s. a pound.

Clothing was also expensive. A good scarlet dress for Goethe's mother in 1758 cost nearly £10, one for his sister in 1770 £3. 17s., a suit for himself £3. 10s. to £5. An ell of English cloth cost about 10s. in Silesia in 1756, and the best silk stockings for men over 10s. a pair.

Wages and salaries.

An unskilled labourer earned 6d. or 7d. a day or less, a master mason or carpenter round about 1s. a day (less in winter). A spinner made about 2s. to 2s. 6d. a week on piece-work, but a factory worker in a favoured industry, or a skilled workman in particular demand, could earn up to 16s. a week.

A good cook or man-servant could be had even in the second half of the century for 30s. a year, wages varying according to experience from 24s. to 60s. Goethe's father paid his cook £2. 8s. a year, his man-servant a little more, his house-maids £2 and 30s. respectively. A private tutor was paid anything from £3 to £8 a year. All these had of course board in addition. For a servant like a coachman who did not live in, the board allowance was about 3s. a week.

An average annual allowance for a student was £50 (though many had far less). A teacher in a Prussian Latin school received between £30 and £60, a university professor £60 to £180 and fees. A young jurist as a subordinate official earned £20 or £30 a year. He was considered to have attained a good position if he eventually earned over £100. Goethe as minister received at first £120, later £180 a year.

Living expenses.

Two modest furnished rooms could be had for from 8s. to 12s. a month. Schiller could dine in Jena for 3d. a day, and Crabb Robinson paid 5s. a week for dinner at the best inn there. To board with a private family cost him (in 1801) from 36 to 50 guineas a year. Schiller estimated that a single man of his class could live in Jena on £40 a year, in Dresden or Weimar on £60.★

WEIGHTS AND MEASURES

These varied as much from place to place as the coinage. A few examples may be given.

The pound (Pfund), of 32 Loth, was in the north 3 to 5 per cent., in the south (Munich and Vienna), 22 per cent. heavier than the English pound.

The chief measure of length for cloth was the ell (Elle), made up of two feet (Fuss) or 24 inches (Zoll). A Berlin foot was roughly an English foot, but a Viennese one was longer, a Hamburg one shorter. Some places had even different ells for different materials.

A German mile (Meile) varied between something over 9 kilometres and something under 7. The "common mile" was a geographical mile, one-fifteenth of a degree, about 4·6 English statute miles. A "Quadratmeile" was therefore about $21\frac{1}{4}$ English square miles.★

★ Chief sources: *Crabb Robinson in Germany*; *Die Stadt Goethes*; Schiller, *Briefe*; J. H. L. Bergius, *Policey- und Cameralmagazin* and *Neues Policey- und Cameralmagazin*, Frankfort-on-Main, 1767–1780; Reichard, *Guide des Voyageurs en Europe*; Biedermann, *op. cit.* 1.

Appendix II

STATISTICAL SURVEY OF GERMANY BEFORE THE NAPOLEONIC WARS*

A. ELECTORAL STATES

1. AUSTRIA within the Reich (Austrian Circle and Swabian possessions, Bohemia, and Burgundian Circle), 3534 Q.M.; 9,126,404 inhabitants.

   AUSTRIAN TERRITORY outside the Reich (Hungary, Illyria, Transylvania, Bukovina, East and West Galicia, Lombardy), 8105 Q.M.; 14,051,000 inhabitants.

   Towns with 20,000 inhabitants and over: Vienna (226,000), Milan (119,000), Brussels (80,000), Prague (75,000), Antwerp (60,000), Ofen and Pest (35,000), Graz, Trieste (30,000), Dobreczyn (25,000), Laibach, Lemberg (20,000).

2. PRUSSIA within the Reich, 1646 Q.M.; 2,756,600 inhabitants.

   PRUSSIAN TERRITORY outside the Reich (Kingdom of Prussia, Polish acquisitions, Silesia, Neufchâtel), 3685 Q.M.; 4,890,000 inhabitants.

   Towns with 20,000 and over: Berlin (143,000), Warsaw (67,000), Königsberg (60,000), Breslau (57,600), Danzig (36,000), Potsdam (26,700), Magdeburg (26,300), Halle (20,000).

3. BAVARIA with the PALATINATE (KURPFALZ), 1028 Q.M., 2,204,700 inhabitants.

   Towns: Munich (50,000), Mannheim (23,000). Of the rest, only Düsseldorf (18,000), Elberfeld (14,000) and Heidelberg (11,000) had a population of over 10,000.

4. SAXONY, 708 Q.M.; 2,104,320 inhabitants.

   Towns: Dresden (50,000), Leipzig (33,000). Four more towns had a population of 10,000 or slightly over, Naumburg, Zittau, Chemnitz, Freiberg.

* Summarised and rearranged from Reichard, *Der Passagier auf der Reise in Deutschland*, 2nd ed. Weimar, 1803.

5. BRUNSWICK with LÜNEBURG, 514 Q.M.; 787,200 inhabitants.
   Town: Hanover (15,500). No other town had 10,000 inhabitants.

6. MAINZ (KUR-MAINZ), 171 Q.M.; 224,734 inhabitants.
   Town: Mainz (30,000).

7. TREVES (KUR-TRIER), 110 Q.M.; 280,000 inhabitants.

8. COLOGNE (KUR-KÖLN), 130 Q.M.; 198,000 inhabitants.

B. SPIRITUAL MEMBERS OF THE COLLEGE OF PRINCES

(Area in Q.M. in brackets.)

Archbishopric of Salzburg (180), *Bishoprics* of Münster (230), Liège (105), Würzburg (90), Trient (70), Bamberg (65), Osnabrück (56), Paderborn (55), Augsburg (54), Hildesheim (54), Fulda (37), Speyer (28), Eichstädt (22), Basel (20), Brixen (17), Passau (15), Strassburg (13), Freisingen (13), Regensburg (6), Constance (5), Worms (5), Lübeck (1). *Order* of Hoch- und Deutschmeister (6). *Prince-abbots' lands* of Kempten (16), Berchtesgaden (10), Corvey (6), Ellwangen (5). Estimated total population of these spiritual lands: over two and a quarter millions.

C. LAY PRINCES

1. OLD DYNASTIES.

MECKLENBURG-SCHWERIN, 240 Q.M.; 240,000 inhabitants. (Schwerin, 10,000.)
MECKLENBURG-STRELITZ, 60 Q.M.; 60,000 inhabitants.
HESSEN-CASSEL, 156 Q.M.; 434,499 inhabitants. (Cassel, 18,560; Hanau, 11,000.)
HESSEN-DARMSTADT, 104 Q.M.; 655,685 inhabitants. (Darmstadt, 9500; Pirmasens, 9000.)
HESSEN-HOMBURG, 2 Q.M.; 7000 inhabitants.
HOLSTEIN, 175 Q.M.; 320,000 inhabitants. (Altona, 20,000.)
WÜRTTEMBERG, 150 Q.M.; 608,667 inhabitants. (Stuttgart, 18,000.)

SACHSEN-WEIMAR und EISENACH, 36 Q.M.; 106,400 inhabitants. (Weimar, 7500.)

SACHSEN-GOTHA und ALTENBURG, 55 Q.M.; 165,000 inhabitants. (Gotha, 11,430.)

SACHSEN-COBURG-SAALFELD, 18 Q.M.; 56,953 inhabitants.

SACHSEN-MEININGEN, 16 Q.M.; 51,000 inhabitants.

SACHSEN-HILDBURGHAUSEN, 11 Q.M.; 31,800 inhabitants.

BRAUNSCHWEIG-WOLFENBÜTTEL, 94 Q.M.; 166,340 inhabitants. (Brunswick, 26,000.)

SCHWEDISCH- oder VORPOMMERN, 70 Q.M.; 104,748 inhabitants. (Stralsund, 11,000.)

BADEN, 64 Q.M.; 194,118 inhabitants. (Carlsruhe, 9000.)

ANHALT-DESSAU, 20 Q.M.; 37,700 inhabitants.

ANHALT-BERNBURG, 16 Q.M.; 30,000 inhabitants.

ANHALT-CÖTHEN, 16 Q.M.; 30,000 inhabitants.

OLDENBURG, 45 Q.M.; 95,000 inhabitants.

ARENBERG, $55\frac{1}{2}$ Q.M.; 42,000 inhabitants.

2. NEW DYNASTIES.

Seventeen are mentioned, ranging from Nassau-Oranien-Diez, with 48 Q.M. and 97,000 inhabitants, to Lichtenstein, with 3 Q.M. and 6000 inhabitants. Total area of these principalities, about 200 Q.M.; population about 560,000.

D. IMPERIAL COUNTS (REICHSGRAFEN)

1. Wetterauisches Grafencollegium; thirty-one members, with about 125 Q.M. of land in all.

2. Schwäbisches Grafencollegium; thirteen members, with about 95 Q.M.

3. Fränkisches Grafencollegium; twenty-one members, with about 90 Q.M.

4. Westphälisches Grafencollegium; thirty members. (Total area unascertainable.)

E. REICHSSTIFTER

1. Twenty-seven Swabian Prelates.

2. Fifteen Prelates of the Rhine, with territory ranging from 6 Q.M. to $\frac{3}{4}$ Q.M.

F. FREE TOWNS (REICHSSTÄDTE)

1. RHEINISCHE BANK (fourteen towns). (*Population, in thousands, in brackets.*)

   Hamburg (150), Cologne, Frankfort-on-Main (50), Lübeck (42), Bremen (40), Aix-la-Chapelle (27), Mühlhausen (13), Nordhausen (10), Goslar (9), Wetzlar (8), Dortmund, Worms (6), Speyer (5), Friedberg (3).

2. SCHWÄBISCHE BANK (thirty-six towns). (*Population, in thousands, in brackets.*)

   Nürnberg (70 in republic, 30 in town), Ulm (37), Augsburg (36), Rothenburg (26), Ratisbon (Regensburg) (21), Schwäbisch-Hall (16), Rottweil, Schwäbisch-Gmünd (14), Esslingen, Memmingen (11), Heilbronn, Reutlingen (10), Biberach (9), Nördlingen (7), Kaufbeuren (6·8), Dinkelsbühl (6·5), Überlingen (6·3), Lindau, Weissenburg (6); and the following, in order of size, with less than 5000: Windsheim, Ravensburg, Schweinfurt, Kempten, Zell-am-Hammersbach, Wangen, Gengenbach, Offenburg, Giengen, Pfullendorf, Weil, Wimpfen, Leutkirchen, Bopfingen, Buchhorn, Isny, Buchau (1).

BIBLIOGRAPHY

A. CONTEMPORARY WRITERS

(NOTE: The imaginative works and letters of the classical writers have not been included in the bibliography.)

(Anon.) *Introduction to the knowledge of Germany.* London, 1789.

E. M. ARNDT, *Erinnerungen aus dem äusseren Leben*, 1st ed. 1840. (Reprint Reclam.)

Dr C. F. BAHRDT, *Geschichte seines Lebens*, 1st ed. Berlin, 1790–1. (Selection edited F. Hasselberg, Berlin, 1922.)

J. B. BASEDOW, *Elementarwerk*, 3 vols., Kupferstiche von Chodowiecki, 1774. (Reprint Leipzig, 1909.)

J. H. L. BERGIUS, *Policey- und Cameralmagazin.* Frankfort, 1767–74.

J. H. L. BERGIUS, *Neues Policey- und Cameralmagazin.* Leipzig, 1775–80.

ULRICH BRÄKER, *Der arme Mann in Tockenburg*, 1st ed. Zürich, 1789. (Reprint Reclam.)

A. F. BÜSCHING, *Beyträge zur Lebensgeschichte denkwürdiger Personen, insonderheit gelehrter Männer.* Halle, 1783–6.

A. F. BÜSCHING, *A new system of geography* (trans. by P. Murdoch). London, 1762.

D. Chodowieckis Künstlerfahrt nach Danzig 1773, ed. W. Franke. Leipzig and Berlin, n.d., Verlag Grethlein.

HENRY CRABB ROBINSON, *Diary, reminiscences and correspondence*, ed. T. Sadler, 3 vols. London, 1869.

Crabb Robinson in Germany, ed. E. Morley. Oxford, 1929.

Meister JOHANN DIETZ, *Lebensbeschreibung* (printed Munich, 1915, 'Schicksal und Abenteuer', XI).

C. W. v. DOHM, *Denkwürdigkeiten meiner Zeit.* Lemgo and Hamburg, 1819.

C. ESTE, *A journey in the year 1793 through Flanders, Brabant, and Germany to Switzerland.* London, 1795.

J. G. FICHTE, *Reden an die deutsche Nation.* 1808. (Reprint in 'Deutsche Bibliothek'.)

G. FORSTER, *Ansichten vom Niederrhein.* 1791–4. (Reprint Reclam.)

FRIEDRICH II, *Anti-Machiavel.* London and The Hague, 1740. (Reprint in 'Deutsche Bibliothek'.)

CHR. GARVE, *Versuche*, 5 Teile. Breslau, 1792.

CHR. GARVE, *Vermischte Aufsätze*, 2 vols. Breslau, 1796.

J. W. v. GOETHE, *Dichtung und Wahrheit*. 1811–33.

A. B. GRANVILLE, *St Petersburgh, a journal of travels to and from that capital*, 2 vols. London, 1828.

W. H. v. HOHBERG, *Georgica curiosa oder adeliches Landleben*, 2 vols. Nürnberg, 1687.

W. HOWITT, *The rural and domestic life of Germany*. London, 1842.

DAVID HUME, *Letters*, ed. J. Y. T. Greig. Vol. I. Oxford, 1932.

W. JACOB, F.R.S., *A view of the agriculture, manufactures, statistics, and state of society, of Germany, and parts of Holland and France*. London, 1820.

KAROLINE JAGEMANN, *Erinnerungen*, ed. E. v. Bamberg. Dresden, 1926.

J. H. JUNG(-STILLING), *Lebensgeschichte*. 1777. (Reprint in 'Deutsche Bibliothek'.)

. KERNER, *Das Bilderbuch aus meiner Knabenzeit* (1849). (Reprint Vienna, 1921.)

J. G. KEYSLER, *Travels*, 2nd English ed. 4 vols. London, 1756–7.

A. v. KNIGGE, *Über den Umgang mit Menschen*. 1788. (3rd ed. 1790, reprinted in 'Deutsche Bibliothek'.)

A. v. KNIGGE, *Der Roman meines Lebens*, 2nd ed. Frankfort-on-Main, 1805.

K. H. v. LANG, *Aus der bösen alten Zeit*. 1842. (Reprint Stuttgart, 1910, 'Memoirenbibliothek'.)

F. C. LAUKHARD, *Leben und Schicksale, von ihm selbst beschrieben*, ed. V. Petersen. Stuttgart, n.d. (? 1908).

J. M. v. LOEN, *Der Adel*. Ulm, 1752.

J. M. v. LOEN, *Freie Gedanken vom Hof*, 3rd ed. Frankfort and Leipzig, 1768.

J. M. v. LOEN, *Der redliche Mann am Hofe*. Ulm, 1771.

K. v. LYNCKER, *Am Weimarischen Hofe unter Amalien und Karl August* (written *c.* 1840). Berlin, 1912.

J. C. v. MANNLICH, *Histoire de ma vie* (written 1813–18, selection printed under title *Rokoko und Revolution*, 3rd ed. Berlin, 1923).

J. MARSHALL, *Travels . . . in the years* 1768, 1769 *and* 1770, 3 vols. London, 1772.

Lady M. W. MONTAGU, *Letters*. London, 1763–7. (Reprint in Everyman's Library.)

(Dr JOHN MOORE), *A view of society and manners in France, Switzerland and Germany*, 2 vols. London, 1779.

K. P. Moritz, *Anton Reiser, ein autobiographischer Roman*, 4 Teile, 1785–90; 5. Teil, 1794.

J. Möser, *Patriotische Phantasien*. Berlin, 1774. (Partial reprint, Reclam.)

J. J. Moser, *Von der Teutschen Unterthanen Rechten und Pflichten* (*Neues deutsches Staatsrecht* 18). Frankfort and Leipzig, 1774.

J. Nettelbeck, *Lebensbeschreibung von ihm selbst aufgezeichnet*. 1821. (Reprint Munich, 1921.)

F. Nicolai, *Beschreibung einer Reise durch Deutschland und die Schweiz*, 12 vols. Berlin, 1783–97.

J. Owen, *Travels* (in 1791 and 1792), 2 vols. London, 1796.

C. L. Baron de Pöllnitz, *Mémoires*. Nouv. éd. corr. Liège, 1734.

(C. L. Baron de Pöllnitz), *La Saxe galante*. Amsterdam, 1734.

C. L. Baron de Pöllnitz, *Mémoires pour servir à l'histoire des quatre derniers souverains de la maison de Brandebourg*, 2 vols. Berlin, 1791.

Peter Prosch, *Leben und Ereignisse*. Munich, 1789. (Reprint Munich, 1919.)

(A. Rebmann), 'Rabiosus der Jüngere', *Wanderungen und Kreuzzüge durch...Deutschland*. Altona, 1795.

H. A. O. Reichard, *Guide des voyageurs en Europe*, 2 vols. Weimar, 1793. (Many new editions.)

H. A. O. Reichard, *Der Passagier auf der Reise in Deutschland*, 2nd ed. Weimar, 1803.

H. G. Riquetti, comte de Mirabeau, *De la Monarchie prussienne*, 4 vols. 4th ed. London, 1788.

(K. Risbeck), *Briefe eines reisenden Franzosen über Deutschland*, 2 vols. 2nd ed. Zürich, 1784.

Angelika Rosa, *Lebensschicksale einer deutschen Frau im 18. Jh. in eigenhändigen Briefen*. Magdeburg, 1908.

J. Russell, *A Tour in Germany in 1820–22*. Edinburgh, 1828.

J. C. Sachse, *Der deutsche Gil Blas*. Stuttgart, 1822.

A. Schmitthenner, *Das Tagebuch meines Urgrossvaters*. Freiburg, 1922.

Johanna Schopenhauer, *Jugendleben und Wanderbilder*. 1839.

Dr J. S. Semler, *Lebensbeschreibung*, 2 vols. Halle, 1781.

J. G. Seume, *Mein Leben*. 1813.

Mme de Staël, *De l'Allemagne*. (1st ed. Paris, 1810—destroyed. 2nd ed. 1814.)

F. Freiherr v. d. Trenck, *Merkwürdige Lebensgeschichte*. (Written 1786. Printed in Collection Spemann, Stuttgart, n.d.)

ERNESTINE VOSS, *Erinnerungen*. (Reprinted in Kürschners *D.N.L.* vol. 49.)

N. W. WRAXALL, *Memoirs of the Courts of Berlin, Dresden, Warsaw and Vienna in the years 1777, 1778 and 1779*, 2 vols. London, 1799.

E. A. W. ZIMMERMANN, *A political survey... of Europe*. London, 1787.

COLLECTIONS OF EXTRACTS

M. BEYER-FRÖHLICH, *Deutsche Selbstzeugnisse*, vols. VII (*Pietismus und Rationalismus*), Leipzig, 1933, and VIII (*Höhe und Krise der Aufklärung*), Leipzig, 1934.

E. BUCHNER, *Das Neueste von Gestern*, vols. II, III (1700–87). Munich, 1912.

E. BUCHNER, *Anno Dazumal*, 2 vols. Berlin, n.d. (1926).

J. BÜHLER, *Deutsche Vergangenheit*, 7 vols. Leipzig, 1923–9.

REICHMANN, SCHNEIDER, HOFSTAETTER, *Ein Jahrtausend deutscher Kultur*, 2nd ed. Leipzig, 1922–4.

B. LATER WRITERS

(i) GENERAL

The Cambridge Modern History, vol. VI. Cambridge, 1909.

Deutscher Kulturatlas, herausgegeben von G. Lüdtke und L. Mackensen. Berlin and Leipzig, 1931– .

Handwörterbuch der Staatswissenschaften, ed. J. Conrad, 3rd ed. Jena, 1909–11.

Propyläen-Weltgeschichte, 6. Band, 'Das Zeitalter des Absolutismus'. Berlin, 1931.

K. BIEDERMANN, *Deutschland im 18. Jahrhundert*. Leipzig, 1854–80.

MAX V. BOEHN, *Die Mode... im 18. Jahrhundert*, 2nd ed. Munich, 1919.

MAX V. BOEHN, *Deutschland im 18. Jahrhundert*, 2 vols. Berlin, 1921.

W. H. DAWSON, *The evolution of modern Germany*. London, 1911.

W. H. DAWSON, *The Germany of the 18th century* (in Harmsworth's Universal History). London, 1929.

W. FRÄNZEL, *Deutschland im Jahrhundert Friedrichs des Grossen*. Gotha, 1921.

G. FREYTAG, *Bilder aus der deutschen Vergangenheit*. Leipzig, 1859–62 (ill. edition Leipzig, n.d. c. 1925).

B. GEBHARDT, *Handbuch der deutschen Geschichte*, 2 vols. 7th ed. Stuttgart, 1930–1.

P. KAMPFMEYER, *Geschichte der modernen Gesellschaftsklassen in Deutschland*. Berlin, 1910.

J. KUTZEN-V. STEINECKE, *Das deutsche Land*, 5th ed. Breslau, 1908.

K. LAMPRECHT, *Deutsche Geschichte*. Berlin, 1891–1909 (esp. vols. VII and VIII, i, and for bibliography XII).

H. LICHTENBERGER, *L'Allemagne Moderne, son évolution*. Paris, 1916.

O. HENNE AM RHYN, *Kulturgeschichte des deutschen Volkes*, 2 vols. Berlin, 1886.

W. H. RIEHL, *Naturgeschichte des Volkes*. Stuttgart, 1853.

F. C. SCHLOSSER, *Geschichte des 18ten Jahrhunderts*, 5th ed. Berlin, 1879.

G. STEINHAUSEN, *Geschichte der deutschen Kultur*, 3rd ed. Leipzig, 1929.

G. STEINHAUSEN, *Kulturgeschichte der Deutschen in der Neuzeit*, 2nd ed. Leipzig, 1918.

G. STEINHAUSEN, *Kulturstudien*. Berlin, 1893.

(ii) 'KLEINSTAATEREI' (Part I, Chap. I)

C. T. ATKINSON, *A history of Germany, 1715–1815*. London, 1908.

J. BRYCE, *The Holy Roman Empire*. London, 1864. (Many later editions.)

G. P. GOOCH, *Germany and the French Revolution*. London, 1920.

J. HALLER, *Epochen der deutschen Geschichte*. Stuttgart and Berlin, 1922.

L. HÄUSSER, *Deutsche Geschichte*, I. Berlin, 1854 (and later).

J. A. R. MARRIOTT and C. G. ROBERTSON, *The Evolution of Prussia*. Oxford, 1915.

C. T. PERTHES, *Das deutsche Staatsleben vor der Revolution*. Hamburg and Gotha, 1845.

Sir A. W. WARD, *Germany, 1815–1890*, vol. I. Cambridge, 1916.

W. WENCK, *Deutschland vor hundert Jahren*, 2 vols. Leipzig, 1887–90.

(iii) BENEVOLENT DESPOTISM (Part I, Chap. II)

A. LUSCHIN V. EBENGREUTH, *Die Verfassung und Verwaltung der Germanen und des deutschen Reiches bis zum Jahre 1806* (Kultur der Gegenwart, Teil II, Abt. II, I). Leipzig and Berlin, 1911.

F. Hartung, *Deutsche Verfassungsgeschichte vom 15. Jahrhundert bis zur Gegenwart*, 2nd ed. Leipzig and Berlin, 1922.

F. Hartung, *Das erste Jahrzehnt der Regierung Karl Augusts* (Jb. d. Goethe-Gesellschaft, II). 1915.

F. Hartung, *Das Grossherzogtum Sachsen unter der Regierung Karl Augusts*. Weimar, 1923.

R. Koser, *Staat und Gesellschaft zur Höhezeit des Absolutismus* (Kultur der Gegenwart, Teil II, Abt. v, 1). Berlin and Leipzig, 1908.

F. Kugler, *Geschichte Friedrichs des Grossen* (ill. by A. Menzel), new ed. Leipzig, 1860.

W. Oncken, *Das Zeitalter Friedrichs des Grossen* (Allgemeine Geschichte in Einzeldarstellungen, III, 8). Berlin, 1880–2.

H. Prutz, *Preussische Geschichte*, 4 vols. Stuttgart, 1901.

L. v. Ranke, *Zwölf Bücher Preussischer Geschichte*, vol. v, 2nd ed. Leipzig, 1879.

G. Schmoller, *Umrisse und Untersuchungen*. Leipzig, 1898.

(iv) The old order of society (Part II)

H. Brunner, *Grundzüge der Rechtsgeschichte*. Leipzig, 1901.

G. Dehio, *Geschichte der deutschen Kunst*, III, 2nd ed. Berlin, 1931.

W. Fleming, *Die Oper* (Barockdrama, Band 5). Leipzig, 1933.

A. v. Gleichen-Russwurm, *Das galante Europa*. Stuttgart, 1921.

J. v. Jordan-Rozwadowski, *Die Bauern des 18. Jahrhunderts und ihre Herren* (Conrads Jahrbücher für Nationalökonomie und Statistik, 3. Folge, vol. xx, 1900).

P. Kühn, *Weimar*, 4th ed. Leipzig, 1925.

Chr. Rank, *Kulturgeschichte des deutschen Bauernhauses* (A.N.G. 121), 3rd ed. Leipzig and Berlin, 1921.

K. Spiess, *Die deutschen Volkstrachten* (A.N.G. 342). Leipzig, 1911.

E. Vehse, *Geschichte der deutschen Höfe*. Hamburg, 1851–60.

(v) Economic history—general

A. Beer, *Allgemeine Geschichte des Welthandels*. Vienna, 1860.

J. H. Clapham, *The economic development of France and Germany 1815–1914*. Cambridge, 1921.

W. Cunningham, *An essay on western civilisation in its economic aspects* (medieval and modern times). Cambridge, 1900.

J. Falke, *Geschichte des deutschen Handels*. 1860.

R. Kötzschke, *Grundzüge der deutschen Wirtschaftsgeschichte bis zum siebzehnten Jahrhundert*, 2nd ed. Leipzig and Berlin, 1923.

J. Kulischer, *Allgemeine Wirtschaftsgeschichte*, 2 vols. Munich and Berlin, 1928–9.

W. Langenbeck, *Geschichte des deutschen Handels seit dem Ausgange des Mittelalters* (A.N.G. 237), 2nd ed. Leipzig and Berlin, 1918.

E. Lipson, *The economic history of England*, 3 vols. London, 1915–31.

M. G. Schmidt, *Geschichte des Welthandels* (A.N.G. 118), 4th ed. Leipzig and Berlin, 1922.

G. Schmoller, *The mercantile system*. 1884 (translated Ashley).

H. Sieveking, *Grundzüge der neueren Wirtschaftsgeschichte*, 2nd ed. Leipzig and Berlin, 1915.

H. Sieveking, *Wirtschaftsgeschichte*, II (A.N.G. 577). Leipzig and Berlin, 1921.

W. Sombart, *Der moderne Kapitalismus*, 3rd ed. Munich and Leipzig, 1919.

W. Sombart, *Die deutsche Volkswirtschaft im 19. Jahrhundert*, 5th ed. Berlin, 1921.

W. Sombart, *Der Bourgeois*. Munich and Leipzig, 1913.

R. H. Tawney, *Religion and the Rise of Capitalism*. London, 1926.

G. Unwin, *Studies in Economic History*. London, 1927.

M. Weber, *Wirtschaftsgeschichte*, ed. Hellmann and Palyi. Munich and Leipzig, 1923.

(vi) The German towns (Part III, Chaps. I–III)

G. v. Below, *Das ältere deutsche Städtewesen und Bürgertum*. Bielefeld and Leipzig, 1898.

B. Heil, *Die deutschen Städte und Bürger im Mittelalter* (A.N.G. 43), 4th ed. Leipzig and Berlin, 1921.

G. L. Kriegk, *Deutsches Bürgertum im Mittelalter*. Frankfort, 1868–71.

W. Lotz, *Verkehrsentwicklung in Deutschland seit 1800 bis zur Gegenwart* (A.N.G. 15), 4th ed. Leipzig and Berlin, 1920.

E. Otto, *Das deutsche Handwerk* (A.N.G. 14), 5th ed. Leipzig and Berlin, 1920.

H. Preuss, *Die Entwicklung des deutschen Städtewesens*. Leipzig, 1906.

O. K. Roller, *Die Einwohnerschaft der Stadt Durlach im 18. Jahrhundert*. Karlsruhe, 1907.

P. Sander, *Geschichte des deutschen Städtewesens*. Bonn and Leipzig, 1922.

D. Schäfer, *Die deutsche Hanse*, 3rd ed. Bielefeld and Leipzig, 1925.

G. Schmoller, *Deutsches Städtewesen in älterer Zeit*. Bonn and Leipzig, 1922.

H. Voelker (ed.), *Die Stadt Goethes, Frankfurt-am-Main im 18. Jahrhundert*. Frankfort, 1932.

(vii) Middle-class life (Part III, Chap. IV)

J. W. Appell, *Werther und seine Zeit*, 4th ed. Oldenburg, 1896.

W. Kawerau, *Kulturbilder aus der Zeit der Aufklärung*. Halle, 1886–8.

G. L. Kriegk, *Deutsche Kulturbilder aus dem 18. Jahrhundert*. Frankfort, 1874.

A. Schultz, *Deutsches Leben im 14. und 15. Jahrhundert*. Leipzig, 1892.

A. Schultz, *Das häusliche Leben der europäischen Kulturvölker vom Mittelalter bis zur 2. Hälfte des 18. Jahrhunderts*. Munich, 1903.

(viii) The professional class (Part III, Chap. V)

'Monographien zur deutschen Kulturgeschichte', ed. G. Steinhausen:

    E. Reicke, *Der Lehrer*, 1901.
    P. Drews, *Der Geistliche*, 1905.
    E. Reicke, *Der Gelehrte*, 1900.
    H. Peters, *Arzt und Heilkunst*, 1900.

J. Pagel, *Geschichte der Medizin*. Berlin, 1898.

F. Paulsen, *Geschichte des gelehrten Unterrichts*, 2nd ed. 2 vols. Leipzig, 1896–7.

F. Paulsen, *Das deutsche Bildungswesen in seiner geschichtlichen Entwicklung* (A.N.G. 99–100). Leipzig and Berlin, 1920.

Th. Puschmann, *Geschichte des medizinischen Unterrichts*. Leipzig, 1889.

Th. Puschmann, M. Neuburger, J. Pagel, *Handbuch der Geschichte der Medizin*, 3 vols. Jena, 1905.

(ix) The profession of letters (Part IV, Chap. I)

Das Buchgewerbe und die Kultur (A.N.G. 182). Leipzig, 1907.

K. Buchner, *Beiträge zur Geschichte des deutschen Buchhandels*, 2 vols. Giessen, 1873–4.

K. Buchner, *Wieland und G. J. Göschen*. Stuttgart, 1874.

K. Buchner, *Wieland und die Weidmannsche Buchhandlung*. Berlin, 1871.

A. S. Collins, *Authorship in the Days of Johnson*. London, 1927.

A. S. Collins, *The Profession of Letters*. London, 1928.

H. Diez, *Das Zeitungswesen* (A.N.G. 328), 2nd ed. Leipzig and Berlin, 1919.

Joh. Goldfriedrich, *Geschichte des deutschen Buchhandels*, ii, iii. Leipzig, 1908–9.

Viscount Goschen, *Life and times of G. J. Goschen*, 2 vols. London, 1903.

C. Th. Perthes, *Friedrich Perthes' Leben*. 1848–55.

E. Vollert, *Die Weidmannsche Buchhandlung in Berlin*, 1680–1930. Berlin, 1930.

(x) The influence of political, economic and social factors on literature (Part iv, Chap. ii)

In addition to the Histories of German Literature (especially those of Hettner, Nadler, K. Francke) the following are of service:

K. Brombacher, *Der deutsche Bürger im Literaturspiegel von Lessing bis Sternheim*. Munich, 1920.

F. Brüggemann, *Der Kampf um die bürgerliche Welt- und Lebensanschauung in der deutschen Literatur des 18. Jahrhunderts* (Deutsche Vierteljahrsschrift für Literaturwissenschaft und Geistesgeschichte, 3). 1925.

F. Brüggemann, *Die bürgerliche Gemeinschaftskultur der vierziger Jahre* ('Deutsche Literatur', Reihe Aufklärung, vols. v and vi). Leipzig, 1933.

F. Brüggemann, *Lessings Bürgerdramen* (Jahrbuch des Freien Deutschen Hochstifts, 1926).

A. Eloesser, *Das bürgerliche Drama*. Berlin, 1898.

P. Ernst, *Der Zusammenbruch des deutschen Idealismus*, 3rd ed. Munich, 1931.

P. Ernst, *Der Weg zur Form*, 3rd ed. Munich, 1928.

A. Hirsch, *Bürgertum und Barock im deutschen Roman*. Frankfort, 1934.

A. Kleinberg, *Die deutsche Dichtung in ihren sozialen, zeit- und geistesgeschichtlichen Bedingungen*. Berlin, 1927.

H. A. Korff, *Geist der Goethezeit*, 2 vols. Leipzig, 1923–30.

A. Köster, *Die deutsche Literatur der Aufklärungszeit*. Heidelberg, 1925.

346 BIBLIOGRAPHY

M. MARTERSTEIG, *Das deutsche Theater im* 19. *Jahrhundert*, 2nd ed. Leipzig, 1924.

G. MÜLLER, *Höfische Kultur der Barockzeit* (in Naumann-Müller, Höfische Kultur). Halle, 1929.

J. PETERSEN, *Die Wesensbestimmung der deutschen Romantik*. Leipzig, 1926.

L. E. SCHÜCKING, *Die Soziologie der literarischen Geschmacksbildung*. Leipzig and Berlin, 1931.

Mme DE STAËL, *De la littérature considérée dans ses rapports avec les institutions sociales*. Paris, 1800.

Mme DE STAËL, *De l'Allemagne*. 1814.

CLARA STOCKMEYER, *Soziale Probleme im Drama des Sturmes und Dranges*. Frankfort-on-Main, 1922.

F. STRICH, *Deutsche Klassik und Romantik*, 3rd ed. Munich, 1928.

F. STRICH, *Dichtung und Zivilisation*. Munich, 1928.

H. V. TREITSCHKE, *Deutsche Geschichte*, I and II. Leipzig, 1879–82.

O. WALZEL, *Deutsche Dichtung von Gottsched bis zur Gegenwart*, vol. I (Handbuch der Literaturwissenschaft). Wildpark-Potsdam, 1927–9.

W. WENCK, *Deutschland vor hundert Jahren*, vol. I. Leipzig, 1887.

INDEX